A History of Japanese Theatre

Japan boasts one of the world's oldest, most vibrant, and influential performance traditions. This accessible and complete history provides a comprehensive overview of Japanese theatre and its continuing global influence. Written by eminent international scholars, it spans the full range of dance-theatre genres over the past fifteen hundred years, including noh theatre, bunraku puppet theatre, kabuki theatre, shingeki modern theatre, rakugo storytelling, vanguard butoh dance, and media experimentation. The first part addresses traditional genres, their historical trajectories and performance conventions. Part II covers the spectrum of new genres since Meiji (1868–), and Parts III to VI provide discussions of playwriting, architecture, Shakespeare, and interculturalism, situating Japanese elements within their global theatrical context. Beautifully illustrated with photographs and prints, this history features interviews with key modern directors, an overview of historical scholarship in English and Japanese, and a timeline. A further reading list covers a range of multimedia resources to encourage further explorations.

JONAH SALZ is Professor of Comparative Theatre in the Department of International Studies at Ryukoku University, Kyoto, Japan. As director of the Noho Theatre Group (established 1981) he works with noh and kyogen actors to interpret texts by Shakespeare, Yeats, and Beckett, successfully touring the Edinburgh Fringe Festival and the Avignon Theatre Festival, and throughout the USA and Japan. As program director for Traditional Theatre Training from 1984 to 2014, he organized an intensive program to teach noh, kyogen, and nihonbuyo dance to Japanese and foreign artists and scholars. He has published numerous articles and translations as a leading scholar of kyogen comedy and Japanese interculturalism and has reviewed theatre and dance performances over three decades for English newspapers and monthly magazines in Japan.

A History of Japanese Theatre

Edited by
JONAH SALZ

CAMBRIDGE
UNIVERSITY PRESS

University Printing House, Cambridge CB2 8BS, United Kingdom

Cambridge University Press is part of the University of Cambridge.

It furthers the University's mission by disseminating knowledge in the pursuit of education, learning and research at the highest international levels of excellence.

www.cambridge.org
Information on this title: www.cambridge.org/9781107034242

© Cambridge University Press 2016

First published 2016

Printed in the United Kingdom by T J International Ltd. Padstow Cornwall

A catalogue record for this publication is available from the British Library

Library of Congress Cataloguing in Publication data
A history of Japanese theatre / edited by Jonah Salz.
    pages   cm
Includes bibliographical references and index.
ISBN 978-1-107-03424-2 (hardback)
1. Theater – Japan – History.   I. Salz, Jonah, editor.
PN2921.H5525   2015
792.0952 – dc23   2015014538

ISBN 978-1-107-03424-2 Hardback

CONTENTS

EXPANDED TABLE OF CONTENTS

FIGURES

TABLES

CONTRIBUTORS

Editor

Jonah SALZ, Ryukoku University

Contributing editors

David Jortner, Baylor University
Shinko Kagaya, Williams College
Laurence Kominz, Portland State University
Samuel L. Leiter, Emeritus, Brooklyn College/CUNY
M. Cody Poulton, Victoria University, Canada
Brian Powell, Emeritus, Oxford University
Minami Ryuta, Shirayuri College
Yoshihara Yukari, Tsukuba University

Assistant editor

Rachel Payne, Canterbury University, NZ

Contributors

Bruce Baird
Monica Bethe
James R. Brandon
Alan Cummings
Daniel Gallimore
C. Andrew Gerstle
Gotō Shizuo
Paul Griffith
Hong Seun-yong
Ikeuchi Yasuko
David Jortner
Kan Takayuki
William Lee
Minami Ryuta
Nagai Satoko
Christina Nygren
Mark Oshima
Rachel Payne
M. Cody Poulton

Eugenio Barba
Mari Boyd
Matthew Isaac Cohen
Mika Eglinton
Barbara Geilhorn
Gondō Yoshikazu
Yukihiro Goto
Eike Grossmann
Julie A. Iezzi
Iwaki Kyoko
Shinko Kagaya
Laurence Kominz
Samuel L. Leiter
Miura Hiroko
Nakano Masaaki
Okada Mariko
Otsuki Atsushi
Diego Pellecchia
Brian Powell

Shelley Fenno Quinn
J. Thomas Rimer
Jonah Salz
Sekiya Toshihiko
Matthew W. Shores
Joel Stocker
Terauchi Naoko
Alison Tokita
Kevin J. Wetmore, Jr.
Yoshihara Yukari

Eric C. Rath
Katherine Saltzman-Li
Minae Yamamoto Savas
Shimizu Hiroyuki
Carol Fisher Sorgenfrei
Suzuki Masae
Barbara E. Thornbury
Washitani Hana
Yamanashi Makiko
Guohe Zheng

Illustration assistants

Ikuta Yoshiho

Matsui Ikuko

CONTRIBUTORS' BIOGRAPHIES

BRUCE BAIRD is Associate Professor in Asian Languages and Literatures, University of Massachusetts Amherst, researching Japanese theatre, philosophy, and new media studies. He has written widely on butoh, including *Hijikata Tatsumi and Butoh: Dancing in a Pool of Gray Grits*.

EUGENIO BARBA has directed seventy-one productions with Odin Teatret (Nordic Theatre Laboratory), founded in 1964. His ISTA (the International School of Theatre Anthropology), has convened fourteen sessions with scholars, artists, and international masters since 1979. Publications include *The Paper Canoe: A Guide to Theatre Anthropology* and *Burning the House: On Dramaturgy and Directing*, and with Nicola Savarese the pioneering *The Secret Art of the Performer: A Dictionary of Theatre Anthropology*.

MONICA BETHE is retired Professor at Otani University, Kyoto. Her experiences with all aspects of noh performance and noh mask carving led to collaboration with Karen Brazell on *Noh as Performance*, *Dance in the Noh Theater*, and the GloPac website. She has written, translated, and edited books, articles, and exhibition catalogues on historical textiles.

MARI BOYD is Emerita Professor of Theatre at Sophia University, Tokyo, and author of *The Aesthetics of Quietude: Ōta Shōgo and the Theatre of Divestiture*. Her research interests include modern Japanese drama, intercultural theatre, and actor-puppet theatre. She is also translation editor of the ten-volume anthology *Half a Century of Japanese Theater* (1999–2008).

JAMES R. BRANDON was Emeritus Professor of Asian Theater at the University of Hawaiʻi. Founding editor of *Asian Theatre Journal*, he directed numerous kabuki, noh, and kyogen plays in English. His many publications include *The Cambridge Guide to Asian Theatre*; *Kabuki: Five Classic Plays*; *Kabuki Plays on Stage* (4 vols., ed. with Samuel L. Leiter); and *Kabuki's Forgotten War: 1931–1945*.

MATTHEW ISAAC COHEN is Professor of International Theatre at Royal Holloway, University of London. His research concerns Southeast Asian performing arts, cross-cultural theatre and performance, and world puppetry, with attention to tradition in modernity and emergence of new forms under conditions of cultural complexity. He performs puppetry internationally as Kanda Buwana.

ALAN CUMMINGS is Senior Teaching Fellow, Department of Languages and Cultures of Japan and Korea, School of Oriental and African Studies (SOAS), University of London. Research interests include kabuki playwriting and theatrical conceptions of time, criminality, and modernity. His most recent book is *Haiku: Love*.

MIKA EGLINTON is Associate Professor of English Theatre and Cultural Studies at Kobe City University of Foreign Studies. She holds a Ph.D. in English Literature (University of Tokyo) and a Ph.D. in Drama (University of London). She is actively involved in new theatre creation as translator, dramaturg, and critic.

DANIEL GALLIMORE is Professor of English Literature at Kwansei Gakuin University. He researches reception, particularly translation, of Shakespeare's plays in Japan, including early twentieth-century Shakespeare translations of Tsubouchi Shōyō. He has translated contemporary Japanese plays and Shakespeare adaptations.

BARBARA GEILHORN is a Japan Society for the Promotion of Science visiting research fellow based at Waseda University, Tokyo. Her current project examines Japanese theatre after the Fukushima catastrophe. Research interests include classical and contemporary Japanese theatre, cultural sociology, gender, and postcolonial studies. She co-edited *Enacting Culture: Japanese Theater in Historical and Modern Contexts.*

C. ANDREW GERSTLE is Professor of Japanese Studies at the School of Oriental and African Studies (SOAS), University of London. He has authored numerous publications on Edo period popular theatre, literature, and art. He was guest curator at the British Museum in 2005 for *Kabuki Heroes on the Osaka Stage*, and again in 2013 for *Shunga: Sex and Pleasure in Japanese Art.*

GONDŌ YOSHIKAZU is a freelance theatre critic with extensive publications on noh, kabuki, and bunraku. He studied under Takechi Tetsuji, editing *Engeki hyōron* (theatre criticism) and serving as his assistant director, then spent thirty years as Secretary-General of the Kyoto Kanze Noh Theatre. He retired as professor of traditional performing arts, International Studies Division, Osaka Gakuin University.

GOTŌ SHIZUO retired as Head of the Kyoto City University of Arts Research Center for Japanese Traditional Music in 2014. From 1970 to 2004 he worked in various production, education, and management positions at the Bunraku Association and National Bunraku Theatre. He researches the aesthetics and history of art, Japanese literature, and cultural anthropology.

YUKIHIRO GOTO is Professor of Theatre Arts at San Francisco State University. He is an actor

and director specializing in staging Western plays with Asian techniques. Publications include "Theatrical fusion of Suzuki Tadashi" (*Asian Theatre Journal*) and "Butō" (*Encyclopedia of Asian Theatre*).

PAUL GRIFFITH was Associate Professor in the Education Faculty, Saitama University, now a D.Phil. candidate at Oxford University focusing on early kabuki "lion" dances. He works as translator/commentator for English "Earphone Guides," and for DVDs and subtitles for the Cinema Kabuki series. Seven translations of kabuki plays and dances were published in *Kabuki Plays on Stage*, vols. I–IV.

EIKE GROSSMANN is Assistant Professor at the Department of Japanese Culture and Language, Hamburg University, Germany. Her research interests are in literature and culture of medieval Japan and Japanese performance traditions, in particular noh theatre and folk performing arts, and conceptions of childhood in medieval Japan.

HONG SEUNYOUNG obtained her Ph.D. at University of Tsukuba, and is a Research Professor at the Institute of Japanese Studies at Hallym University. She researches Japanese modern literature and the history of Korea-Japanese drama. Her publications include "Kikuchi Kan and Chosen's Art Award" (*Journal of Japanese Culture*).

JULIE A. IEZZI is Professor in the Department of Theatre and Dance, University of Hawai'i, teaching Asian theatre history, dramatic literature, movement, and voice. She translates for and directs English-language kabuki and kyogen productions and continues her artistic pursuit of *tokiwazu* singing, *nagauta shamisen*, and kyogen. Her translations appear in *Asian Theatre Journal* and *Kabuki Plays on Stage.*

IKEUCHI YASUKO is Professor Emerita of Theatre Arts and Gender Studies at Ritsumeikan University. She is author of *Feminizumu to gendai engeki* (Feminism and contemporary theatre) and *Jōyu no tanjō to shuen – pafomansu to jenda* (The birth and the demise of the "actress" – performance and gender).

IWAKI KYOKO is a performing arts journalist contributing to media such as the Asahi Shimbun. She is currently a Ph.D. candidate at Goldsmiths College, University of London, focusing on post-catastrophic theatre, especially the post-Fukushima disaster. She published bilingual *Tokyo Theatre Today: Conversations with Eight Emerging Theatre Artists* and *Des rivages d'enfance au būto de Sankai Juku*, a biography of choreographer Ushio Amagatsu.

DAVID JORTNER is Associate Professor of Theatre at Baylor University. His research interests include modern and contemporary Japanese theatre, postmodern American theatre, Occupation theatre, and intercultural theatrical exchange. He co-edited *Modern Japanese Theatre and Performance* and has published articles in *Asian Theatre Journal*, *Text and Presentation*, and *Theatre History Studies*.

SHINKO KAGAYA is Professor of Japanese at Williams College, teaching Japanese literature, culture, and language. She researches Japanese traditional performance, particularly noh theatre, in contemporary contexts.

KAN TAKAYUKI is a theatre critic who began his career as a playwright-director-critic in the underground movement of the 1960s. He has written extensively on Japanese postwar theatre and social issues, including *Tatakau engekijin* (Dramatists in the struggle) and *Nihon sengo engeki* (Postwar theatre in Japan).

LAURENCE KOMINZ, Professor of Japanese Literature and Drama at Portland State University, holds a Ph.D. from Columbia University. Publications include *Mishima on Stage: The Black Lizard and Other Plays*, and *The Stars who Created Kabuki*. He researches and translates kabuki, kyogen, and Mishima's drama and directs student productions of kabuki and kyogen.

WILLIAM LEE is Associate Professor and Director of the Asian Studies Centre at the University of Manitoba, Winnipeg. His principal areas of research are kabuki and the folk performing art of kagura. He has performed kyogen and kagura as well as directing a documentary on the latter.

SAMUEL L. LEITER is Distinguished Professor Emeritus, Brooklyn College and the Graduate Center, CUNY. He has published twenty-six books on New York theatre, Shakespeare, stage directors, and Japanese theatre. His latest books are *Rising from the Flames: The Rebirth of Theatre in Occupied Japan, 1945–1952* and *Kabuki at the Crossroads: Years of Crisis, 1952–1965*.

MINAMI RYUTA is Professor of English at Shirayuri College, Japan. He co-edited *Re-playing Shakespeare in Asia, Performing Shakespeare in Japan* and *English Studies in Asia*. He also authored chapters for *Shakespeare in Asia, Shakespeares after Shakespeare, Shakespeare and the Japanese Stage*, and *Shakespeare and the Second World War*.

MIURA HIROKO is Director of the Noh Research Archives, Musashino University, where she is a specially appointed professor. Research interests include the music and early modern history of noh. Author of seven books on noh's Meiji history, music, and masks, and introductory texts, she is also a long-term practitioner.

NAGAI SATOKO is Associate Professor, Cultural Policy and Management, Shizuoka University of Art and Culture. She researches Meiji and contemporary history and theory of the theatre and stage. She produces drama and advises the Shizuoka City Shimizu Culture Hall Theatre. Publications include *Gekijō no kindaika* (Theatre modenization).

NAKANO MASAAKI is Adjunct Researcher, Tsubouchi Memorial Theatre Museum, Waseda University, Tokyo. Research interests are twentieth-century Japanese popular theatre, including the history of Taishō and Shōwa comedy, musical revue, and Asakusa Opera.

CHRISTINA NYGREN is Professor of Theatre Studies and visiting Professor at the Department of Asian, Middle East and Turkish Studies at Stockholm University. During the last thirty years she has studied, researched and worked in Asia, mainly in China, Japan, India and Bangladesh, but also in Vietnam and Laos. Main interests are performing arts and popular culture. Publications include writings on traditional and modern theatre and dance, festival culture, folk performances and popular entertainments in Asia.

OKADA MARIKO is Associate Professor of Japanese Literature at the Faculty of Humanities, J. F. Oberlin University, Tokyo. Publications include an anthology of poetry for Japanese traditional dance and *Kyōmai Inoue-ryū no tanjō* (The birth of *kyōmai*: Inoue-school dance) which received the 2013 Suntory Prize for Social Sciences and Humanities in "Literary and Art Criticism."

MARK OSHIMA studied Japanese history and culture at Harvard and Waseda University. He is a performer, translator, scholar, and teacher in Tokyo with professional names as a singer in Kiyomoto school narrative music and classical Japanese dance. Translations include *Kabuki Backstage, Onstage: An Actor's Life* by Matazo Nakamura, numerous kabuki plays, and "The Black Lizard" by Yukio Mishima.

OTSUKI ATSUSHI is Associate Professor of Architecture at the Graduate School of Engineering, Mie University. Research interests cover a wide range of theatre-related fields, including its conceptualization. He has consulted on theatre construction projects including Kani Public Arts Center, Taketoyo Community Arts Center, and Gero Synergy Center.

RACHEL PAYNE received her D.Phil. from the Oriental Institute, Oxford University, and now lectures in the Japanese Programme at Canterbury University, New Zealand. She researches traditional Japanese theatre and its contact with the West.

DIEGO PELLECCHIA received his Ph.D. from Royal Holloway, University of London, and has been a Visiting Lecturer at Royal Holloway and East 15, University of Essex. He practices chant and dance with noh master Udaka Michishige (Kongō School), performing both in Japan and abroad. His research looks at interactions between aesthetics and ethics in noh.

M. CODY POULTON is Professor of Japanese Literature and Theatre at the University of Victoria, Canada. He has translated Japanese fiction and drama including contributions to *Kabuki Plays on Stage*, and *Half a Century of Modern Japanese Theater*. Most recently, he co-edited *The Columbia Anthology of Modern Japanese Drama*.

BRIAN POWELL is Emeritus Fellow at two colleges of Oxford University, where he taught Japanese theatre and literature. He has published books and articles on many aspects of modern Japanese theatre, and translated numerous plays by *shin-kabuki* playwright Mayama Seika and *shingeki* playwright Kinoshita Junji.

SHELLEY FENNO QUINN is Associate Professor at The Ohio State University where she teaches premodern Japanese literature and theatre. Her special research interest is the performance traditions and drama theory of noh plays, as both a medieval and a modern art. She is author of *Developing Zeami: The Noh Actor's Attunement in Practice*.

ERIC C. RATH is Professor of Premodern Japanese History, University of Kansas. His research broadly examines cultural history, especially the performing arts and dietary culture. Publications include *The Ethos of Noh: Actors and their Art* and *Food and Fantasy in Early Modern Japan*.

J. THOMAS RIMER is Emeritus Professor of Japanese Literature and Theatre at the University of Pittsburgh and author of numerous books on Japanese theatre of all periods, as well as on modern Japanese literature and visual arts.

KATHERINE SALTZMAN-LI is Associate Professor, East Asian Languages and Cultural Studies and Comparative Literature, University of California, Santa Barbara. She researches kabuki plays and playwriting, Edo period kabuki treatises, and theatre prints, and is author of *Creating Kabuki Plays: Context for Kezairoku, Valuable Notes on Playwriting.*

JONAH SALZ is Professor of Comparative Theatre, Intercultural Studies, Ryukoku University, Kyoto. He researches intercultural theatre, Beckett in Japan, actor training, and translation. Co-translated plays include contemporary comedy, "Super-kyogen," and Mishima Yukio. He co-directs the Noho Theatre Group (1981–) and was program director of Traditional Theatre Training (1984–2014), a summer intensive workshop.

MINAE YAMAMOTO SAVAS is Associate Professor of Japanese Studies, Bridgewater State University, Massachusetts, researching noh's dynamic negotiations among many forces. Publications include "Familiar story, *Macbeth* – new context, noh and Kurosawa's *Throne of Blood*," in *Education about Asia*, and "The complexities of translating Japanese traditional theatre kyogen libretti," in *Geinōshi kenkyū.*

SEKIYA TOSHIHIKO is Professor of Medieval Japanese, Kansai University. He studied under Itō Masayoshi and Nomura Man. He sits as Advisory Board Member for the Japan Society for the History of Performing Arts Research and is a founding member of the Association for Noh and Kyogen Studies. Recent publications include *Nō kyogen to Nihon no warai* (Noh kyogen and Japanese laughter).

SHIMIZU HIROYUKI is Professor of Architecture and Urban Planning at the School of Environmental Studies, Nagoya University. He is an expert on theatre planning, design, and management. He has planned over forty municipal theatres including the New National Theatre, Tokyo Metropolitan Theatre, Aichi Arts Center, and Kani Public Arts Center. He

was President of the Japan Association for Cultural Economics (2012–14).

MATTHEW W. SHORES has M.A. degrees from Tezukayama University and Portland State University and a Ph.D. from the University of Hawai'i. He was informally apprenticed with *rakugo* masters Katsura Bunshi V and Hayashiya Somemaru IV. He researches comic modes of expression, both performed and literary. Shores currently serves as lecturer of Japanese in the Faculty of Asian and Middle Eastern Studies, University of Cambridge.

CAROL FISHER SORGENFREI is Emerita Professor of Theatre, UCLA. She researches postwar Japanese performance and is a translator, director, and award-winning playwright. She is the author of *Unspeakable Acts: The Avant-Garde Theatre of Terayama Shūji* and *Postwar Japan* and co-author of *Theatre Histories: An Introduction* (3rd edn.).

JOEL STOCKER teaches communication skills and anthropology as an Associate Professor at National Yang Ming University, Taiwan. He holds a Ph.D. in cultural anthropology from the University of Wisconsin-Madison and has conducted ethnographic research on Japanese *manzai* comedy training and the significance of localism in corporate promotion of *manzai* performers.

SUZUKI MASAE is Professor of English at Kyoto Sangyo University. She has translated *Shinsaku-noh* (Newly written) *Macbeth* as well as plays by Noda Hideki. Her publications include "Shakespeare and class: the reception of *Othello* in mainland Japan and Okinawa" (*Shakespeare Yearbook*) and she is also a Ph.D. candidate at Royal Holloway, University of London.

TERAUCHI NAOKO is Professor of Japanology at the Graduate School of Intercultural Studies, Kobe University, where she teaches Japanese performing arts. Publications include *Japanese Traditional Music: Gagaku, Buddhist Chant* (CD, notes) and *Gagaku o kiku: hibiki no niwa e no izanai* (An invitation to *gagaku*: the topos of ancient and new reverberations).

BARBARA E. THORNBURY teaches in the Department of Asian and Middle Eastern Languages and Studies, Temple University, Philadelphia. She researches and writes on Japanese performing arts and cultural exchange, and Japanese literature and film. Her most recent book is *America's Japan and Japan's Performing Arts: Cultural Mobility and Exchange in New York, 1952–2011*.

ALISON TOKITA is Director of the Research Center for Japanese Traditional Music at Kyoto City University of Arts, and adjunct Associate Professor in Japanese Studies at Monash University. She has published widely on Japanese narrative music, currently working on *naniwa-bushi*, and the role of the art song in East Asian musical modernity.

WASHITANI HANA is Adjunct Researcher, Waseda University Tsubouchi Memorial Theatre. Her research interests are the history of Japanese visual culture including cinema, *gento* (magic lantern), *kamishibai*, manga, and animation. She is author of "*The Opium War* and the cinema wars: a Hollywood in the Greater East Asian co-prosperity sphere" (*Inter-Asia Cultural Studies*).

KEVIN J. WETMORE, JR. is Professor and Chair of Theatre, Loyola Marymount University, and secretary/treasurer for the Association for Asian Performance. Research interests include contemporary Japanese theatre, Christianity in Japan, and postmodern kabuki. He has edited numerous books on modern and comparative Japanese theatre.

YAMANASHI MAKIKO lectured at Waseda University and Tokiwa University. Currently based at Trier University (Germany), she researches urban studies and theatre interculturally. She studied at University College London and the University of Edinburgh. She authored *A History of the Takarazuka Revue since 1914: Modernity, Girls' Culture, Japan Pop*.

YOSHIHARA YUKARI is Associate Professor, University of Tsukuba. Publications include "Popular Shakespeare in Japan" (*Shakespeare Survey* 60), "Kawakami Otojiro's trip to the West and Taiwan at the turn of the twentieth century" (*Asian Crossings*), and "Is this Shakespeare? Inoue Hidenori's adaptations of Shakespeare," in *Re-Playing Shakespeare in Asia*.

GUOHE ZHENG is Professor of Japanese and Chair of Modern Languages and Classics, Ball State University. He researches politics in canon formation and Sino-Japanese literary/theatrical exchanges. Recent publications include "Chūshingura and beyond: a study of the Japanese ideal of loyalty," in *Text & Presentation*, and "The politics of canon formation and writing style," in *The Linguistic Turn in Contemporary Japanese Literary Studies*.

FOREWORD

JAMES R. BRANDON

I saw my first bunraku performance in Japan in 1951 and my first ever kabuki performance at the Shimbashi Embujō theatre in Tokyo in 1952. It was the height of the Korean War and I was a soldier passing through Japan. In addition to soldiering, I was a theatre-crazy young man. Having lived in New York City the previous year, with endless opportunities to see straight shows, musicals, ballet, and opera, I was confident that I knew what theatrical performance was all about. The two performances that I saw, and heard, in Japan shattered this misguided assurance. The vocal power of the kabuki actor and puppet narrator was beyond anything I could imagine. Nor could I take my eyes off the performers' expressive bodies, frozen into dynamic poses or moving with a powerful physical presence. The whole performance was imbedded within a web of music and sound effects, strange sounding but hypnotic. From those two experiences I set myself a goal of learning more and more about bunraku and, especially, kabuki.

Not only myself, but many others in the United States and Europe, have turned to Japanese theatre to learn new dimensions of theatrical art. As I've written elsewhere about the training in Asian forms:

> [P]articipation in theatre provides the potential for a direct experience in alternative human, cultural, and artistic forms. No and kyogen show us alternatives to our often harried and fragmented lives. They show the possibility of beauty that derives from order, of quietude that comes from an appreciation of poetry, of peace that derives from submersion of the ego (of the actor) into the flow of life shaped by forces outside of ourselves, and finally of self-worth achieved through self-discipline of body and spirit.[1]

I have had the privilege to study with, and later invite, great masters to visit to teach at the University of Hawai'i.

Although not all are fortunate enough to study under great masters in Japan or overseas, we can see live performances; and today we all can enjoy kabuki or noh or butoh performance via DVD, film, or video documentaries. Numerous books devoted to a single genre of Japanese theatre have

---

1 James R. Brandon, "Performance training in Japanese nō and kyōgen at the University of Hawai'i," *Theatre Topics* 3:2 (1993), 101–20.

been published. And in this electronic era, not a few actors maintain their presence on the web. However, it still remains difficult to gain a good understanding of the broad development of Japanese theatre through 1,300 years of history. How does *kagura* of the Heian court relate to noh or kyogen of the Muromachi period? How is plebeian kabuki of the Edo period a precursor of bourgeois modern theatre, *shingeki*, in the succeeding twentieth century? One of the most fascinating aspects of Japanese theatre is that all these genres are performed today, jumbled together, making the twenty-first century a kind of living museum of theatrical culture. How to make sense of it all? This is the right book.

It is extremely difficult for one author to properly cover the totality of theatrical creativity. Happily, this is not an issue with this publication: the text has been written by more than fifty theatre scholars, each a specialist is some aspect of Japanese theatre. In addition, each historical period or genre is examined and discussed by several specialists, often half-a-dozen or more. Each author thus is contributing to the creation of a fully rounded picture of the subject beyond what any one specialist could accomplish. The one (and only) previous history of Japanese theatre in English was published more than two decades ago. This is the right book at the right time.

ACKNOWLEDGMENTS

I am indebted to a team of associate editors that helped conceive the project from the beginning, translating, adapting, and rewriting where necessary, to help see the project through to its conclusion. Ian Carruthers provided early vision and introductions. Editorial assistant Rachel Payne uncomplainingly kept the project on course beyond her initial duties. Authors Daniel Gallimore, Mari Boyd, and Julie A. Iezzi shared their expertise as advisers, and assisted with translations. Authors took the time to make multiple revisions with biblical patience. Many photos were generously supplied by the Waseda University Theatre Library, and advice on how to get others from Tankosha's Takii Michiko was invaluable. All errors or sins of omission are my own. The Japan Research Centre, SOAS was a welcome and stimulating retreat. Cambridge senior editor Vicki Cooper has nurtured the project from well before I was aboard, while midwives Fleur Jones and Emma Collison have pushed and pulled throughout the long gestation period. I was fortunate to receive continuous support from my Ryukoku University Faculty of International Studies colleagues and its Socio-cultural Research Institute. My family in Kyoto and the USA has served as both my harbor and my sail.

The editor and Cambridge University Press gratefully acknowledge the Great British Sasakawa Foundation for their grant toward the permissions and production costs for this book.

This book is dedicated to James R. Brandon (1929–2015), mentor and inspiration to so many of us.

NOTE ON JAPANESE TERMS

Japanese personal names are written in the Japanese order, with family name first, unless the individual has chosen to reverse this according to Western name order. Macrons (ō) in Japanese words indicate long vowel sounds, but these have been omitted from capital letters, common placenames (Kyoto, Tokyo), and Japanese terms now accepted into the English language (noh, kyogen, butoh). Japanese terms are italicized only the first time they appear in each chapter, Interlude, Focus or Spotlight.

ABBREVIATIONS

ATJ   *Asian Theatre Journal*
CTJ   *Concerned Theatre Japan*
MN   *Monumenta Nipponica*
TDR   *The Drama Review*

TIMELINE BY RACHEL PAYNE

This Timeline is an attempt to show linearly the convoluted, inter-related trajectories of Japanese traditional arts through time. Some caveats concerning Japanese traditional arts deserve mentioning.

New genres evolve from older ones, but rarely is the older form completely abandoned. Instead, new genres distinguish themselves from previous ones often by borrowing from, or absorbing, a number of prior styles of music, song, costume, dance, or text, in an innovative manner. Establishing a popular new genre does not necessarily mean the diminishment of older forms. They may, in fact, benefit from a surge in popularity from new attention that newer genres focus on them.

Traditions, even after rigid codification, have expanded their repertoire by incorporating new pieces or accompanying music; expanded their audiences by performing at new venues or touring to new regions; or expanded their performers by admitting females into previously all-male traditions. Contrarily, some have condensed to narrow specialties when forced to compete with new genres or schools for ensuring niche market share. Shogunal restrictions on repertoire also resulted in much rationalization and reduction. Yet traditional performance in Japan is a braided strand of rope that rarely breaks despite the twists and frays that occasionally occur. In lean times, some genres are maintained by just a single family (or person) until their popularity revives, bolstered by branch families or even amateurs who broaden the art through their idiosyncratic variant interpretations.

Inevitably the Timeline's description of creative development may seem to some as mere competent continuation. A wave of new pieces and popularity may not necessarily demonstrate development: it could be a desperate attempt to regain popularity before fading from the scene. On the other hand, brilliant actors breathe new life into stale repertoire; even a few extant troupes can bring legions of fans to minor genres. While eliding such exceptions, the following schematic may provide some sense of the transmission and transformation trajectories of Japanese traditional dance and theatre through time, and the rich feast available to contemporary audiences of any time period.

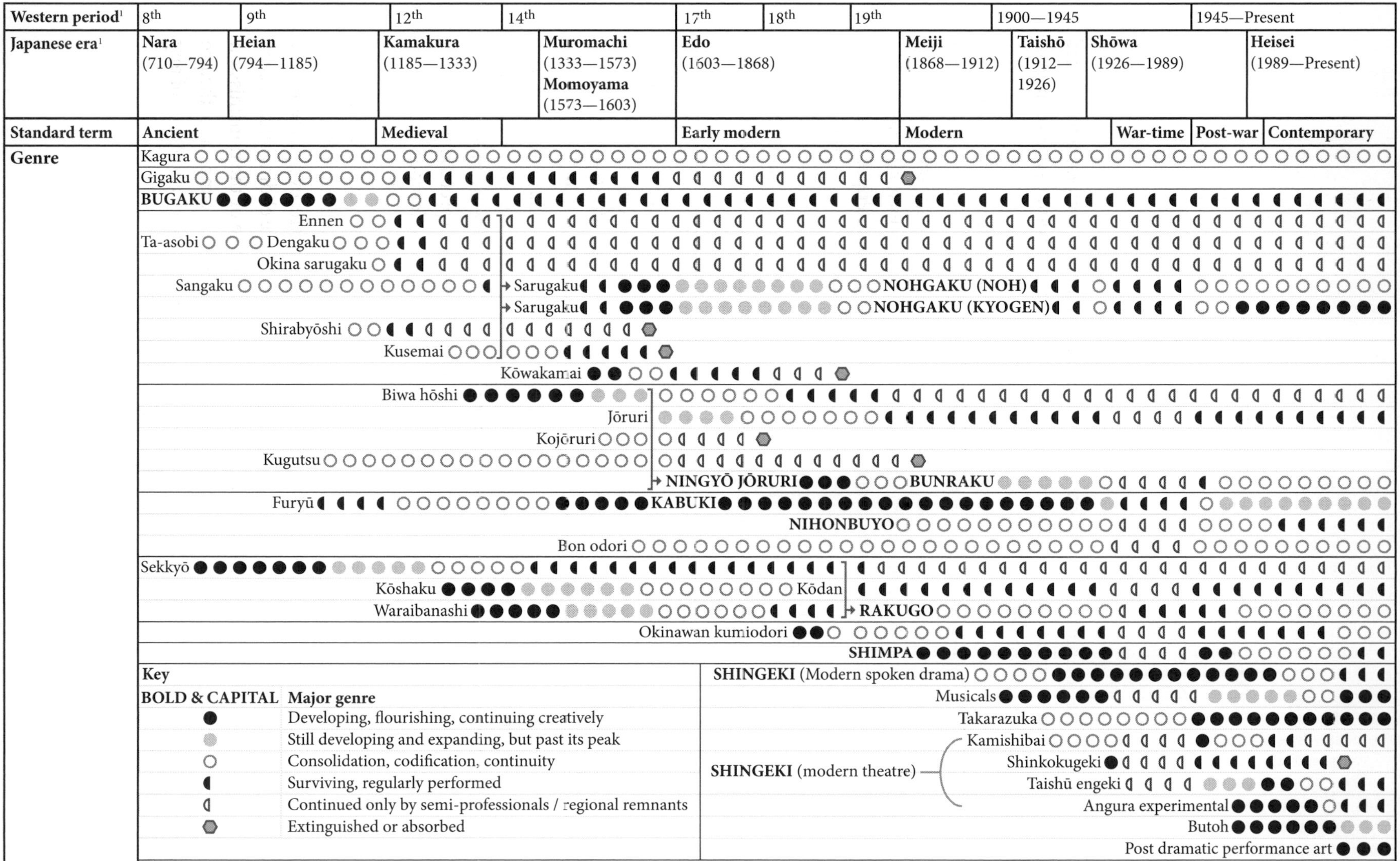

Western period[1]
8th
9th
12th
14th
17th
18th
19th
1900—1945
1945—Present
Japanese era[1]
Nara (710—794)
Heian (794—1185)
Kamakura (1185—1333)
Muromachi (1333—1573)
Momoyama (1573—1603)
Edo (1603—1868)
Meiji (1868—1912)
Taishō (1912—1926)
Shōwa (1926—1989)
Heisei (1989—Present)
Standard term
Ancient
Medieval
Early modern
Modern
War-time
Post-war
Contemporary
Genre
Kagura
Gigaku
BUGAKU
Ennen
Ta-asobi
Dengaku
Okina sarugaku
Sangaku
Sarugaku
NOHGAKU (NOH)
Sarugaku
NOHGAKU (KYOGEN)
Shirabyōshi
Kusemai
Kōwakamai
Biwa hōshi
Jōruri
Kojōruri
Kugutsu
NINGYŌ JŌRURI
BUNRAKU
Furyū
KABUKI
NIHONBUYO
Bon odori
Sekkyō
Kōshaku
Kōdan
Waraibanashi
RAKUGO
Okinawan kumiodori
SHIMPA
SHINGEKI (Modern spoken drama)
Musicals
Takarazuka
Kamishibai
Shinkokugeki
Taishū engeki
SHINGEKI (modern theatre)
Angura experimental
Butoh
Post dramatic performance art
Key
BOLD & CAPITAL
Major genre
Developing, flourishing, continuing creatively
Still developing and expanding, but past its peak
Consolidation, codification, continuity
Surviving, regularly performed
Continued only by semi-professionals / regional remnants
Extinguished or absorbed

Notes

[1] Time periods spans are not to scale.

EDITOR'S INTRODUCTION

JONAH SALZ

Japanese theatre is a remarkably vital contemporary art and living museum, comprising performance genres spanning a millennium. The classical forms of noh, kyogen, kabuki, and bunraku are dynamic traditions developed centuries ago, yet still performed to devoted audiences. Plays often use the same costumes, properties, and scripts, and are performed by the same acting families as in their earliest establishment as genres. Moreover, temple worshipers, amateur hobbyists, and aristocratic and samurai patrons nurtured grassroots support and connoisseurship that continues today.

Alongside these continued popular classical forms, a rich and varied modern theatre has developed. Kabuki continues to draw daily packed houses even as the boom in Takarazuka girls' opera and Western-style musicals continues unabated. Pioneers of succeeding generations mine the "strata" of Japanese traditional performance for treasures.[1] Western artists and scholars seeking alternatives to their own dialogue-driven theatre have long been fascinated by Japan's theatrical arts that combine ritual with entertainment, dance with drama, and poetry with spectacle. Japan's early adaptation of Western stage techniques, training, and playwrights has served as a model for many developing Asian theatrical cultures. This volume covers the vast range of this eclectic and original performance culture.

Waves of continuous tradition

Japan is a narrow island nation, isolated by dangerous seas. With nowhere else to export the artifacts and wisdom imported from the continent, Japan became the refiner, combiner, and conservator of a wide range of ancient culture, from India via China and Korea, and along the Silk Road. Itinerant and marginal entertainers learned to cater to rustic and urban, commoner,

---

1 Donald Richie, "The strata of Japanese drama," in his *A Lateral View: Essays on Culture and Style in Contemporary Japan* (Berkeley, CA: Stone Bridge Press, 1992), 133–8.

aristocrat, and warrior patrons. Artistic creation was codified by authoritative guilds appealing to spectators that often defied class distinctions. The *iemoto* headmaster system was the organizational instrument for maintaining such traditions and integrating innovation – or spurring competitive sectarianism.

However, for a supposedly conservative island once referred to as Wa ("harmony"), Japan has regularly suffered devastating cultural jolts. There were frequent, sudden ruptures in the slowly shifting tectonic plates of religion, politics, and Asian diplomatic relations, which caused unpredictable shudders, after-tremors, and occasional fissures and tsunami that altered the sociocultural landscape irrevocably. These shocks and waves were religious (Buddhist, Confucian, and Christian), political (power shifting from aristocrats to warriors to bureaucrats), and economic (agriculture to industry). Rural and urban artistic culture developed as relatively stable and familiar touchstones through such upheavals.

The last 150 years have been especially contentious. There was a sudden shift from shogunal bureaucracy to constitutional monarchy. Early war victories (China, Russia) allowed colonial expansion (East Asia, Southeast Asia, and Oceania), followed by devastating atomic attacks and humiliating defeat in the Pacific War. The American occupation swerved from support of democratic, liberal institutions to encouragement of a conservative, staunchly anti-communist Pacific ally. Student unrest of the 1960s was dampened by the miracle of economic recovery, lasting until the bubble burst in the 1990s. The lull that followed was interrupted by the triple disasters of March 2011, when an earthquake, a tidal wave, and a nuclear meltdown permanently scarred the country. Apathy, mistrust in government and media, and fear for the future pervade the atmosphere of an elderly nation stumbling about in the financial doldrums. There is both anxiety and hope today, leaning toward potential rejuvenation in anticipation of the 2020 Tokyo Olympics. Ironically, this instability may have given new impetus to the desire for the communion and communication possible in live theatre.

Sturdy but pliant diversity

Theatrical cultures have bent but not broken in these shifting winds, then seeded new distinctive genres. Chinese court entertainments were taught at the music school in Nara, then "nipponized" as *gagaku*, outlasting China's original. Pyramids of power in the *iemoto* (headmaster) system codified and maintained traditional artistic forms through prescribed patterns (*kata*), setting high standards and maintaining familial authority. Yet the towering strength of classical (and often calcified) forms nearly toppled with the collapse of shogunal patronage in 1867. With their popular entertainment monopolized by the samurai from the 1600s, townspeople turned to the melodramatic spectacle of bunraku puppet theatre and kabuki. The latter continued as popular art for centuries but found rivals at the turn of the twentieth century in *shimpa*'s political thrillers and melodramas, then the serious Western-style *shingeki* modern spoken theatre. Shingeki matured within this tortured political crucible of nationalistic suppression of dissent, proletarian social realism, and Westernized aesthetic lyricism. From the 1910s, light comedies, musical revues, and vaudeville banter appealed to the newly ascendant middle class seeking a (modern) night on the town. Co-existing genres helped define each art's particular identity, as well as offering ready plots and techniques for strategic appropriation.

The postwar economic boom escalated the pace of artistic change in modern theatre, now unfettered by nationalist censorship policies. European and American theatrical traditions continued their influence on Japan's modern theatre, which joined the anti-authoritarian spirit of the 1960s. The sixties' anti-shingeki "return to the gods" of *angura* underground theatre and later vanguard "little theatre" movement gave way to super-real, multimedia, and postdramatic turns. Semi-professional troupes cultivated cult-like followings, while a handful of directors and playwrights sought an international presence. Suzuki Method actor training and butoh contemporary dance are homegrown forms more influential overseas.

A common historical trajectory of genres examined here shows the synthesis of originally disparate musical, spoken, ritual, and dance dramas into a distinct form by an artist of genius, supported by discerning patrons. After attracting favor, the new composite genre establishes its own performance codes, and fixes its repertoire. Once hybrid popular arts calcify into a new form, this may in turn be cannibalized by the next new genre, eventually retrenching to a fixed, classical repertoire with tight restrictive conventions. Unlike in many other cultures, in Japan the source genre may continue indefinitely, preserving distinctive expression even as it diminishes in creative force and popularity. Practitioners claim authoritative but often spurious histories, and propagate minute distinctions with rival stylistic schools, often echoed by sympathetic scholars. One challenge of this comprehensive survey was to explore these tensions of preservation and innovation, and to untangle and describe its expression among diverse and interrelated forms.

Our approach: performative and encompassing

Comprehensive studies of Japanese theatre, whether by natives or not, often concentrate on major genres of "theatre," displaying a Eurocentric, logocentric bias. In this book we have covered the full range of musical, dance, and dramatic genres referred to as *geinō* (芸能, performing arts, a tenth-century term), including *koten* (古典, classical) and *minzoku* (民俗, folk), respectively, both considered *dentō* (伝統, traditional); *shibai* (芝居, "grass-seat"), theatrical performance, but not including Western plays in translation; and *engeki* (演劇, theatre, the most recent term).[2] The latter includes shingeki (新劇, "new theatre," as opposed to "old theatre," kabuki), vanguard *shōgekijō* (小劇場, "Little Theatre") movement, also called *angura* (underground), and commercial theatre (*shōgyō engeki*).

Such an inclusive perspective on *butai geijutsu* (stage arts) encompasses performance genres that may appear to the Western observer closer to folk ritual (*kagura*, Kurokawa noh), circus sideshow (*misemono*), storytelling (*katari*, *kamishibai*), dance (nihonbuyo and butoh), and revue (Takarazuka). Yet historically these religious, musical, and narrative genres have been intimately interwoven with stage performance. We have also tried to escape the normal boundaries of Japanese theatre to explore the margins. Geographically we include Okinawa, the only native genre where a postcolonial perspective is appropriate, as well as Japan's own colonial and wartime theatre in China, Korea, and Indonesia, and its influence. We also examine what Japanese actors, directors, and producers learned when touring or studying abroad, and what their Euro-American counterparts absorbed from books or tours. Actresses are introduced not just in terms of their contribution to modern theatre, but also as they have entered traditional forms in the past century. In this spirit of inclusiveness, female and Japanese authors are well represented here.

Syncretic and synchronic

This book sets out to trace independent genres processually, from eclectic roots to maturation as codified genres, then frequently dividing into new ones. And we try here to describe the playful intertextual borrowing, parodying, and adoption of novelty and technology that have created so many new strata. Each new layer adds to the existing rich firmament, without

---

2 After valiantly attempting to distinguish theatrical terminology, comparative theatre expert Mōri Mitsuya confesses that the task is "almost meaningless." Mōri Mitsuya, "The structure of theatre: a Japanese view of theatricality," *SubStance* 31, nos. 2&3 (2002), 73–74.

destroying what came before, for Japanese theatre is constantly drawing upon its past even while attempting to integrate new fashions and tastes. Noh is a syncretic mix of dances for ritual and entertainment; kyogen developed from folktales, mimicry, acrobats, and rustic drinking songs; kabuki integrated freelance kyogen actors and adapted noh plots, which were in turn 'dolled up' by bunraku puppeteers. Here we cover the genres that survived, but there are others, well documented and apparently once popular, that disappeared completely from the scene, having leaned too far to the vulgar tastes, or been protected too much behind the closed screens of the elite, unwilling or unable to change with the times. Yet even rare genres with a few practitioners struggle on, maintaining costumes and masks, discovering a few patrons (perhaps governmental) who recognize the beauty of the art (or tourist value in tradition), who are willing to sponsor a vanishing form.

As the terminology suggests, Japanese traditional and modern theatre scholarship is quite distinct, so that there are few single volumes (even in Japanese) covering theatre's full trajectory from historical origins to contemporary diversity. This book aims to give full weight to this rich range of performance, tipping the normal scholarly balance toward the neglected modern, and from literary analyses to performance. And we have tried to remain current: waves of Western influence (and resistance) created a resilient, self-critical, and hyper-active theatre community that continues to spawn novel, massively popular troupes and genres. Many major genres produced in the past 1,200 years are still performed today, although perhaps absorbed into newer genres, whether flourishing as popular entertainment (kabuki) or struggling in obscure regions (*kusemai*). This varied, vibrant theatrical scene seems to be one constant amid enormous change.

If the pleasures and potency of Japanese theatre are not reason enough to study it, its enormous influence on Western directors (Brecht, Brook, Barba), choreographers (Martha Graham, Maurice Béjart), playwrights (Yeats and Tennessee Williams), composers (Puccini, Britten), and actors deserves attention from students of Western modern cultural history. Yet rather than persist in the model of one-way Japanese influence in the West, chapters exploring the two-way exchange by theatre practitioners are prominent. Japanese theatre directors and producers traveled to the West at the beginning of the twentieth century, returning with texts, technologies, and theories that midwifed a modern theatre. Tours by Japanese artists influenced developments abroad, as well as in Japan upon their return, sometimes in ways complex and difficult to predict. Examining both the domestic and the foreign contemporary artists who were inspired by

Japanese traditional theatre will be one more way of explaining its endur-ing fascination.

Navigating this book

The book is divided into three parts. Part I charts the earliest ritual and fes-tival performances that developed into the austere masked theatre noh and comic cousin kyogen, and the baroque entertainments – bunraku and ka-buki. Their historic accommodations to modernity are traced to the present. Part II examines genres begun in the modern era (conceived of in Japan as beginning with the reign of the Meiji Emperor [1868–1912]), from shimpa melodramas to contemporary multimedia theatre. Parts III–VI are a trans-historical account of topics describing complicated trajectories and cross-genre perspectives to preceding chapters: playwriting, architecture, criti-cism, Shakespeare, and interculturalism.

Chapters in the first two parts covering specific mainstream genres are leavened with short Spotlight or shorter Focus pieces, or chapter-ending Interludes. These introduce especially significant individuals (Chikamatsu Monzaemon, Noda Hideki), relatively minor genres (*mis-emono* sideshows, *kamishibai* storytelling), epoch-making productions (Kawakami Otojirō's *Othello*), genre-crossing arts (*katari* narrative sing-ing), and related arts (costumes, shamisen music, actor prints). Each part culminates with an interview with a prominent theatre practitioner or scholar, providing an authoritative native perspective on how Japan got to this particular contemporary moment, and where Japanese theatre may be heading.

Often historical accounts, caught up in the hurtling trajectories of cul-tural developments, do not include the purely aesthetic pleasures of text and spectacle that ultimately made these theatrical forms so popular over the centuries. Here we provide an "Elements of performance" for tradi-tional genres of Part I, a concise sketch of present-day performance con-ventions and production circumstances. Plots and special challenges of iconic plays, glossed over as titles within the historical section, are given in "Representative plays" of Parts I and II. We hope that discussion of these plays, along with references to their translations in English, and audiovis-ual resources, will enable readers to pursue further research and spectator pleasures.

We have provided some tools to facilitate readers. The Timeline shows the origins and development of many genres, when their popular appeal peaked, and their continuing conservation and codification. References, including suggested further readings, are provided at the end of chapters, including a few key, Japanese references.[3] A list of more general suggested readings is found at the end of the book.

Expertise and a beginner's mind

The scholars assembled here range from recent graduate students to esteemed authorities in their respective fields, with a corpus of books and articles displaying their continuing devotion, erudition, and passion. They share the fruits of decades of research, but most have also been involved in practical aspects of theatrical production as disciples, translators, and producers. This practical experience and knowledge of performance from inside-out makes their chapters particularly instructive. We are especially pleased to introduce many Japanese experts in their first English-language work. If our multinational, multidiscipline (theatre, history, literature, architecture, music) approaches make for some occasional disjunctures, we are confident that this is compensated for by our authors' sure if idiosyncratic voices. My job as editor was shaping their expertise in ways newcomers to Japanese theatre might appreciate and be inspired by, recalling Zeami's dictum to always retain "a Beginner's Mind."

For me, personally, this was not difficult, considering my late and humble entry into Japanese theatre. I was drawn to Japan even before I knew anything about it: seeing John Dexter's noh-inspired staging of *Equus* on Broadway (1975) and *An Actor's Revenge* (1979, a contemporary opera employing kabuki-style staging), as well as reading Leonard Pronko's clarion call to the feast of Asian theatre, *Theatre East and West* (1974). When I finally saw kabuki in 1977, I knew I had discovered a total theatre totally distinct from Western psychological realism, one that I could learn much from as an aspiring director. This eventually led me to Kyoto in 1980, aged 23 and without a word of Japanese. There I absorbed as much performance as I could, inspired by the rigor of the noh training and performance, vigor of religious festivals and ritual dances, and eagerness of professionals to share their family lore as well as expand their own horizons. I co-founded the Noho Theatre Group then returned to the USA to attend graduate school in Performance Studies at New York University. I did not realize that my Ph.D. dissertation – on "roles of passage" kyogen comedians portray during a lifetime career trajectory – would be the first stage of my own career of theatregoing, creating, and teaching Japanese theatre.

---

3 We have concentrated wherever possible on English-language resources; Benito Ortolani, *The Japanese Theatre: From Shamanistic Ritual to Contemporary Pluralism* (Princeton: Princeton University Press, 1991) introduces many other European language sources.

Fig 1 Noho Theatre Group's *At the Hawk's Well* (1981), dir. Jonah Salz, composed by Richard Emmert (flute), Oe Noh Theatre, Kyoto.

Many contributors to this volume authored the books providing the literary, cultural, and performative contexts that served as beacons for me to deepen my own scholarship. I have edited this book as the volume I wish I had read when first embarking on my studies. Hopefully this work reflects our continuing fascination, and becomes a vessel for others to navigate their own journey on the wide, deep sea of Japanese theatrical performance.

PART I
Traditional theatres

PREFACE TO PART I
JAPANESE CIVILIZATION ARISES
LAURENCE KOMINZ

Japan's society and culture have been determined largely by its geographical location: a series of islands on the fringe of China, one of the most enduring civilizations of the world. Japan is just far enough away from China to make it safe from military invasion (most of the time) yet accessible for trade and religious/cultural exchange. This distance meant that civilization came later to Japan than to China's contiguous neighbors in East and Southeast Asia, but also that Japan was able to maintain cultural and political autonomy throughout its history (the only exception being the brief US occupation, 1946–53). Japan–China relations took the form of continuous and varied connections, ongoing debates about what aspects of continental civilization should be adopted by Japan, and, conversely, what was and should remain "Japanese."

Hybrid beliefs and language

While Japan's native language (in the Ural-Altaic family) and religion are very different from China's, Chinese civilization was perceived as so powerful and useful that Japan absorbed it while developing its own hybrid language and religion. Shinto (神道, the way of the gods), a pantheistic animist religion, has thrived from prehistory until today. Japan evolved into an agricultural society and Shinto believers prayed to, gave offerings to, and entertained their gods to ensure good weather and bountiful harvests, beseeching them to exorcise evil spirits that caused illness, crop disease, and infestation.

Buddhism came to Japan in the sixth century from India via China and Korea, embraced by the elite for its moral teachings and guarantee of an afterlife. Initially Buddhism helped the fledgling Japanese state solidify its political power, working in tandem with institutions and the political culture of Confucianism. Buddhism and Shinto have coexisted until today, enjoying a primarily harmonious and symbiotic relationship – most Japanese participate in rituals of both religions. The shrines and temples not only nourished ritual performances by priests and *miko* shrine maidens, but also became safe refuges and tax havens for secular entertainers at festivals.

By the seventh century, an imperial family emerged in Japan, head of a relatively small aristocracy that supported the emperor, while competing to wield power behind the throne. The Chinese model of a grand, long-lasting imperial capital inspired the Japanese to establish two great capitals in the classical age, Nara (710–84) then Kyoto (also called Heian-kyō, Miyako, or Kyō, 794–1868). Literature and performing arts in the Nara and Heian periods (794–1185) were centered in these capitals, from which sophisticated urban culture diffused to the rural provinces. Throughout the premodern era, vibrant traditions of travel literature celebrated Japan's natural beauty while depicting the pleasure and pain of life in the countryside.

Japanese was apparently a spoken language without written characters until these were imported from China and Korea in the sixth century. Japan's tiny, educated elite could write both Japanese and Chinese using the same script, much as our educated British forebears wrote in English or Latin. Despite heavy cultural borrowings of Chinese architecture, political organization, pictorial arts, and poetry, literary Japanese was also generally prized and preserved, perceived as different in purpose and feeling from Chinese. By 850, Japan had developed its own phonological script, used in tandem with, rather than replacing, Chinese logographs – demonstrating the hybridity so prevalent in the development of performative expressions.

Early arts: poetry and fiction

The earliest important literary genre was poetry, begun as Shinto religious rites, then popularized for secular uses. Japanese poetry from the beginning was affective and dialogic. The earliest recorded myths of the *Kojiki* (712) abound with exchanges of love poetry, and elegies to console the dead and their surviving kin. Vivid natural images were appropriated from mountains and seacoast descriptions to express human form, apparel, actions, and emotions. The first great anthology of Japanese poetry was the *Man'yōshū* (759). Compared to Chinese antecedents, Japanese poetry was considered private and personal. Japanese poetry was rarely used to express political or social concerns – Japanese wrote Chinese poetry for this purpose. A preferred literary meter emerged for Japanese poetry: the 5–7–5 syllable count, capturing the stressed, atonal, non-symmetrical rhythmic dynamic of the spoken language:

> Oki mo sede [5] Without arising –
> Ne mo sede yoru o [7] but also without sleeping
> Akashite wa [5] I passed the night till dawn.
> (first verse of anonymous *Kokinshū* poem, 905, author translation)

For a brief period in the late 700s and early 800s, Chinese poetry threatened to overwhelm Japanese, but love kept Japanese poetry alive. Women did not learn Chinese, which was felt to be too scholarly, so all courtship poetry and personal correspondence poetry had to be written in Japanese. Love and travel tales about the great poets of the first imperial anthology of Japanese poetry (*Kokinshū*, 905) would provide Japanese drama with stories and heroes for the next millennium. Criticism and standards were established, with poetry deemed the purest and most beautiful vocal expression of the human heart. When drama emerged, naturally it quickly took the form of poetic drama, often borrowing verbatim from the imperial anthologies or contemporary popular songs.

In the 900s–1100s courtly culture flourished among the ruling elite. A relatively genteel game of power politics required leaders to educate daughters for use in strategic marriages. Women writers came to dominate Japanese literature. They created poetic diaries and magnificent works of poetic fiction, epitomized by Lady Murasaki's *The Tale of Genji* (*c.* 1001–14). Romantic tales such as *Genji* and *The Tales of Ise*, and folktales and adventure tales (*setsuwa*) such as *Konjaku Monogatari* (Tales of times now past) from popular oral and written traditions, were adapted to the noh theatre, centuries later.

This golden age of courtly literature and relative peace ended with the rise of the samurai military elite, who ruled and fought over Japan from the 1160s until the dawn of the modern era in 1868. In 1192 the Shogun, a dominant military ruler, created a new government in Kamakura, his own alternative administrative capital, thus rendering the emperor and his surrounding aristocracy subservient. The bloody struggles for supremacy by rival clans Genji and Heike were recited by blind minstrels in the epic *Tales of the Heike* (*c.* 1200) then reimagined and reconstructed in myriad forms on stage for the next 800 years.

1 ∾ Ancient and early medieval performing arts

TERAUCHI NAOKO

A number of important Japanese performing arts (*geinō*, 芸能)[1] flourished before the appearance of the first dramatic forms, noh-kyogen, in the mid-fourteenth century. Some ancient geinō even offer complex stories using words, music, and dance.[2] Performances or rituals played at court, Buddhist temples, and Shinto shrines influenced later theatrical spectacle. Some survived, but others are traceable only through historical records, literature, or picture-scrolls.

Ancient performing arts show diversity in origin, patronage, and style. Some were imported directly from the Asian continent under the Yamato government's (fourth to seventh centuries AD) policy of progress through assimilation, while others are native to the Japanese archipelago. Some arts supported by the nobility were highly refined; others, enjoyed by the lower classes, were wild and dynamic. These arts were neither perfected nor isolated, but rather continuously mutually influenced each other. Some arts descended from and replaced older ones, while others intertwined to bring about new hybrids. This continuous recombination of court, folk, and religious genres is a defining feature of the fluid premedieval performing arts.

Continental imports: *gigaku, sangaku, bugaku*

Japan's interaction with the Asian continent was especially active during the seventh and eighth centuries, with the systematic introduction of Korean and Chinese arts that then became established in Japan via continuous transmission within permanent institutions.

---

1 "Gei" originally meant "to plant" or "sow," eventually indicating "skill" or "art", while "nō" means "ability" or "skill." Before the twentieth century, "geinō" included arts such as music, poetry, dance, calligraphy, medicine, horse riding, and scholarship. Today it refers to "performing arts" or "popular entertainment" generally, unless preceded by a qualifier: *minzoku geinō* (folk performance), *dentō geinō* (traditional performance), or *koten geinō* (classical performance).
2 "Ancient" in a Japanese context refers to the period from mythological times to the end of the Heian period (1185); "medieval" from Kamakura to the end of Azuchi-Momoyama (1185–1603).

Gigaku (伎楽)

Masked pantomime gigaku, also known as *kuregaku* 呉楽 (lit., 'music of China's Wu dynasty [222–80 AD]'), is one of Japan's earliest foreign performing arts. According to *The Chronicles of Japan* (*Nihonshoki* a.k.a. *Nihongi*), gigaku was introduced in 612 AD by Mimashi from the ancient Korean kingdom Paekche, who taught it in Nara. Gigaku was staged for the "eye-opening ceremony" of the Great Buddha in the Tōdaiji Temple in 752 AD and other annual, religious events.

Gigaku masks cover the entire head, unlike the smaller ones used in noh, and some are quite realistic and grotesque. According to the musical treatise *Kyōkunshō* (Anthology of lessons, 1223), gigaku was accompanied by flute, hip-drum, and cymbals. Plots described include:

- *Chidō* and *shishi* (herald and lion): A herald (chidō) and a lion (shishi) led by two boys (*shishiko*) purify the stage before a ceremony. A lion-like creature (shishi, 獅子) led by two boys walks around a stage. The gigaku shishi, believed to be a sacred beast capable of destroying invisible demons, inspired many types of lion dances (*shishimai*) in later folk festivals.
- Gokō (Lord of Wu): A Wu lord dances as if playing a flute (accompanied by an actual flute player).
- Karura (Garuda-bird): This character dances wearing a mask derived from the Indian sacred bird that eats snakes.
- Baramon (Brahman priest): Although this noble priest is from a Hindu high caste, his comic actions, such as washing diapers, satirize the earthy reality of high status.
- Konron, Gojo, Kongō, and Rikishi (the Villain, Lady, and Deva Kings): The villain Konron stalks and rapes the beautiful Gojo (a lady of Wu), before two Deva kings chase him away, pulling his symbolic phallus.
- Suikoō and Suikojū (Drunken Barbarian King and Servants): Details about these characters are not clear.

Thus gigaku pieces contain satiric, erotic, or comic flavors seemingly contradictory to Buddhist morality. However, these simple, easily understood gigaku were employed as a practical device for attracting people to temples, where they assimilated Buddhist ideology.

Gigaku declined after the thirteenth century, although there are records of its performances at Kasuga Shrine in Nara through the nineteenth century.[3] Its long-lost tradition has been revived by a former court musician, Shiba Sukeyasu (1935–), with masks reconstructed at Tenri University. It was

---

3 Kasagi Kon'ichi, *Gagaku to Nara* (Gagaku and Nara) (Nara: Nara City, 1980), 14.

performed during celebrations surrounding the renovation of the main hall of the Great Buddha at Tōdaiji in 1980.[4]

Variety entertainments: *sangaku* (散楽)

Sangaku, also known as *hyakugi* (one hundred entertainments) or *zatsugi* (miscellaneous entertainments), was also brought from the Asian continent, mainly for performance at Buddhist ceremonies. Sangaku comprises acrobats, conjuring, juggling, and comic skits. The picture-scroll *Shinzei kogaku-zu*, depicting performing arts of the early ninth century, includes sangaku arts: entering a small jar; a monkey passing through a metal hoop; sword swallowing; an acrobat riding atop four others' shoulders; three child acrobats riding on one man's shoulder; a tightrope walker; and the juggling of balls and swords.

The Japanese court provided a position for sangaku players in governmental institutions until the late eighth century. After its abolishment, performers were rehired as palace guards to perform sangaku at imperial ceremonies. Others became affiliated with temples where they served in Buddhist rituals or as freelance players in folk agricultural rites or street entertainments, later absorbed into *dengaku* or *sarugaku* (noh) troupes.

Sarugaku (猿楽, monkey entertainments) possibly derives from sangaku. According to the *Shin-sarugakuki* (Records of new sarugaku), written by aristocrat Fujiwara no Akihira (989?–1066), sarugaku at the beginning of the eleventh century included various acts, such as *noronji* (*shushi* wizardry), a performance deriving from an exorcism rite; dengaku dances and plays; *kugutsu* (puppetry); *shinadama* (juggling balls) and other forms of juggling; various comical mimicries or parodies; and narrative accompanied by a *biwa* (lute).[5]

Cosmic court dance and music: *bugaku* (舞楽)

Bugaku is a dignified dance repertoire accompanied by *gagaku* (雅楽, elegant music), consisting of instruments introduced from the continent, and adopted into rituals at court, temples, and shrines. By the seventh century, music and dance of Korea's three kingdoms, Kudara (Paekche), Shiragi (Silla), and Kōkuri (Koguryo) had been imported. Together with later music from Bokkai (Balhae, present-day Manchuria/North Korea), these were reorganized into *komagaku* (Korean music). Chinese and Vietnamese music and dance,

---

4 Kyogen actor Nomura Mannojō (later Manzō VI) attempted to revitalize the tradition with "new gigaku" in 2001, using masks and dance styles from Asia. Yoshiko Fukushima, "Masks, interface of past and future – Nomura Mannojo's Shingigaku," *ATJ* 22:1 (2005), 249–68.

5 Fujiwara Akihira, *Shin-sarugaku-ki*, reprinted in *Nihon shisō taikei*, vol. VIII: *Kodai seiji shakai shisō* (Tokyo: Iwanami shoten, 1979), 133–52.

Fig 2 Six-panel painted screen by Kanō Yasunobu (1613–85), illustrating bugaku.

called *tōgaku* (Chinese music), and *rin'yūgaku* (Vietnamese music), later categorized simply as tōgaku.

A bugaku piece is constructed of several parts comprised of choreographed foot-patterns and gestures; introduction, body, and exit. Some pieces have multiple sections for the main body; the typical three-section structure is called "jo-ha-kyū," which became an important concept in noh. *Jo* 序 (prelude) is usually in free rhythm with a slow tempo, *ha* 破 (breach) a metrical rhythm with moderate tempo, and *kyū* 急 (quick) a metrical rhythm with rapid tempo. Thus jo-ha-kyū originally was a notion of gagaku composition focusing on rhythmic traits, later enhanced into a more philo sophical concept.

Each dance consists of short choreographic patterns. For example, leg patterns include *hiraku* (open), *suru* (patter), *ochiiri* (sink down), *tateru* (stand), *fumu* (stamp), and *tobu* (jump), while those for arms include *hiraku* (open), *tojiru* (close), and *awasu* (join hands). Group patterns for four to six dancers are performed in a soft and elegant manner called "calm dance" (*hira-mai*), while solo or paired dancers perform a more active "running dance" (*hashiri-mai*).

Dancers wear ornate costumes and, for some dances, large, decorative masks. Bugaku dance is categorized either as "left dance," accompanied by Chinese music, or "right dance," accompanied by Korean music. Left and right dances are played alternately. Although there is neither a dramatic story nor even concrete meaning behind each choreographic motion, some pieces have a specific motif or background. The popular piece *Ryōō* employs a fierce, grotesque mask, portraying a king of ancient north

Qi (present Henan Province) who was so handsome that he wore an ugly mask when he fought. *Ryōō* was performed during sporting competitions featuring archery, wrestling, and horse riding, and on other noble, festive celebrations. In contrast, *Karyōbin* (迦陵頻; Kalavinka in Sanskrit, bird of paradise) and *Bosatsu* (Bodhisattva) are often staged during a temple service where dancers also participate in a food offering to the Buddha or saints.

In addition to each piece's character, the structure and dramaturgy of the whole bugaku ceremony deserves attention. Ceremonies at court, temples, or shrines utilize a large outdoor space in front of a main hall where personnel, instruments, and ornamental settings are placed in a symmetric position. The city plans of ancient Nara and Kyoto were themselves based on such a bilateral system. However, the principle indicates not just a pair of same or similar things but also a dichotomy of bright/dark, strong/weak, or male/female, derived from the yin/yang ordering principle. The left *dadaiko* (huge drum for outdoor performance) displays a golden disc above the drum skin, representing a sun, with dragon carving in the frame attached to the body, while the right one displays a silver moon above the drumhead and phoenix carving on the frame. Dancers' costumes also show contrasting colors signifying the dual forces of the cosmos: warm reds and oranges for left-dance costumes, cool blues and greens for the right.

During a ceremony, a host, guests, and other high-ranking nobles sitting inside the main hall gaze down into the south front yard where a pageant is performed. A Chinese-music dancer appears from the left (east) side, dances in the center of the yard, and exits, followed by a Korean-music dancer who mirrors the actions from the right (west). This series of alternate dances continues for hours, interpreted as symbolizing the rotation of sun and moon, or day and night. While the two opposites never merge into one, their circulation brings balance to the universe.

Bugaku boasts a continuous history of over 1,300 years. It has received governmental support since being instituted as the Gagakuryō in 701. However, in the ninth century, inner guards replaced the Gagakuryō musicians and since then have performed in various court rituals. These hereditary families then handed down the tradition over generations. Three large troupes established, respectively, in Kyoto, Nara, and Osaka, were active until the musicians moved to Tokyo in 1869, following Emperor Meiji. The forerunner of the current governmental institution, the Kunaichō Gakubu (宮内庁楽部, Music Department of the Imperial Household Agency), was established in 1870 in Tokyo, inviting musicians from Kyoto, Nara, and Osaka. They primarily serve in traditional court rituals, but sometimes offer public concerts. Large temples and shrines such as Shitennōji in Osaka and Kasuga

Shrine in Nara have maintained annual events showing a number of bugaku dances, performed today by amateurs.

Nowadays, tōgaku employs the *shō* (mouth organ), *hichiriki* (double reed pipe), *ryūteki* (transverse flute), *biwa* (lute), *koto* (zither), *kakko* (barrel-shaped drum), *taiko* (big drum), and *shōko* (small gong), while komagaku uses *komabue* (transverse flute shorter than ryūteki), hichiriki, *san-no-tsuzumi* (hourglass shaped drum), taiko, and shōko. Some gagaku instruments became popular with the public, bringing about other musical genres, such as noh. The ryūteki was transformed into the *nōkan* flute: the san-no-tsuzumi is the precursor of the *ōtsuzumi* (large drum), while *ikko*, a smaller sized san-no-tsuzumi, became the *kotsuzumi* small drum. The biwa lute became an accompaniment to narratives; the koto zither also became an accompanying instrument in the Edo period. Thus the gagaku ensemble can be seen as the progenitor of many later musical instruments and traditions.

Court and folk arts

Japan's native performing arts percolated up from lively folk entertainments and filtered down from court rituals, displaying a dynamic energy contained within strict forms and patterns.

Mikagura

Native music and dances have also been performed at courts, temples, and shrines, and on various secular occasions. *Kagura* (神楽; literally, "gods' entertainment") can be found throughout Japan in many styles, roughly classified into two types:

1 rites to purify a place for making prayer offerings for a peaceful world and healthy harvest
2 theatrical to embody the mythical worlds of Japanese gods.

Mikagura is the most noble and refined among various ritual forms performed exclusively at court and certain shrines, Iwashimisu-hachiman Shrine (Kyoto), Tsurugaoka-Hachiman Shrine (Kanagawa), and Hikawa Shrine (Saitama). Consisting of fifteen songs and two dances accompanied by a *kagura-bue* (flute), hichiriki (reed pipe), *wagon* (six-stringed zither), and *shakubyōshi* (clappers), the plotless pieces follow a precise structure:

1 introduction (purification of site)
2 welcoming the gods
3 entertaining the gods
4 conclusion and sending off the gods.

Fig 3 Miko channel gods and purify the stage at the Wakamiya Festival, Kasuga Shrine, Nara.

In the introduction, a sacred fire is lit and "Niwabi" (Sacred fire) and "Ajime" (meaning unknown) are sung to purify the venue. The lyrics of "Ajime" employ a few unintelligible syllables, reflecting a traditional belief that a word or even the voice itself retains magico-religious efficacy. To invoke the gods, "Sakaki" (Sacred branch) and "Mitegura" (Strips of paper) are sung to praise the god's symbols, danced by a trance-possessed leader with *torimono*, sacred implements acting as temporary abodes of the god. Then, a summoning of a god of Korean origin, "Karakami" (韓神), is sung and danced. The entertainment part includes several songs depicting sacred gods and local landscapes. The last song, "Sonokoma" (The horse) praises the sacred vehicle of the god.

The original forms, established at the beginning of the eleventh century, contained twice as many songs as now. Today, the Mikagura Rite is held annually on a mid-December evening at the Imperial Palace, requiring over five hours.

Miko-kagura shamaness rituals

While only men are permitted to perform mikagura, another type of kagura welcomes exclusively female performance: *miko-kagura* (巫女神楽) (shamaness kagura). The episode of the goddess Amenōzume found in the *Kojiki* and *Nihon Shoki* suggests that female priests have conducted important services from very early eras. In the Nara period and earlier, the Sarume-gimi family, claiming to be descendants of Amenōzume, contributed exclusively

∽ FOCUS 1.1   *Kagura* and the heavenly rock-cave

The myth of the "heavenly rock-cave" (*ama no iwato*), recorded in the eighth-century *Kojiki* and *Nihon Shoki*, tells of how the Sun Goddess Amaterasu hides herself in a cave, thereby plunging heaven and earth into darkness. Other deities devise a plan to entice her out:

> Ame-no-Uzume-no-Mikoto bound up her sleeves with a cord of heavenly pi-kage vine, tied around her head a head-band of the heavenly ma-saki vine, bound together bundles of sasa leaves to hold in her hands, and overturning a bucket before the heavenly rock-cave door, stamped resoundingly upon it. Then she became divinely possessed, exposed her breasts, and pushed her skirt down to her genitals. Then Takama-no-para shook as the eight hundred myriad deities laughed at once.[6]

Curious, Amaterasu emerges from the cave, thus restoring light to the world. The episode suggests an actual ritual performance, taken as the archetype of the Japanese performing arts. The tradition with the most legitimate claim to this mythic beginning, however, is the ritual art of *kagura*.

The word "kagura" may be a corruption of *kamukura*, meaning "god seat" or abode of the gods (*kami*), but it has long been written with the characters 神楽 ("god music" or "entertainment for the gods"). The earliest evidence of kagura is found in court documents of the ninth century. *Mikagura*, as the court variety is called, was performed in the eleventh month in connection with *chinkon*, a court ritual. This eventually became mi-kagura, a formal ceremony of music and dance, completely lacking the raucous character suggested by the rock-cave myth.

Outside the court other forms of kagura thrived; many local varieties are still performed. It is difficult to establish to what degree this folk or "village kagura" (*sato kagura*) represents a continuation of ancient ritual traditions. Nonetheless, most examples reflect the basic ritual structure of kagura,

Fig 4 Kagura: the god Susanoo and the bride he wins as a reward for defeating the eight-headed serpent in *Orochi*, performed by Nishimura Kagura Shachū in Hamada City, Shimane prefecture.

6 Donald Philippi (trans.), *Kojiki* (Tokyo: University of Tokyo Press, 1968), 84.

including the summoning, entertainment, and dispatching of kami. Although rare today, divine possession (*kamigakari*) and receiving of oracles have also been a part of the tradition.

Folk performing arts scholar Honda Yasuji devised a classification scheme for folk kagura based on ritual implements used to attract the kami or serve as their temporary resting place:

1 *miko kagura* (female priestess)
2 *torimono kagura* (*Izumo kagura*) (hand properties; Izumo-type)
3 *yudate kagura* (*Ise kagura*) (boiling water; Ise-type)
4 *shishi kagura* (lion head).[7]

Kagura typically consists of a series of masked and unmasked dances (*mai*) performed to instrumental music (flute, drum, and hand cymbals) and songs (*kamiuta*). Dances range from the solemn and ritualistic to the highly energetic and theatrical, and also the comic.

Today kagura is most often performed as part of Shinto shrine festivals, usually by the shrine association or "preservation society" of local community members. In the past, however, many kagura traditions were transmitted by itinerant religious practitioners, especially the *yamabushi* of the syncretic Shugendō cult. Thus, while many pieces are based on ancient myths, they are imbued with a religious outlook that also includes elements of esoteric and Pure Land Buddhism and even Chinese "five phases" cosmology.

The yamabushi also drew upon other medieval performance genres. Kagura dances can be traced to plays in the noh repertoire. That they lack noh's more consistent dramatic structure is usually attributed to their reflecting the state of *sarugaku* before Zeami gave the art its classical form.

WILLIAM LEE

to the *chinkon-sai*[8] or *daijōsai*[9] purification ceremonies at court.[10] Later, during the Heian period, sources such as *Records of New Sarugaku* and a picture-scroll of annual events completed in the late twelfth century portray and describe folk miko-kagura.[11] According to *Records of New Sarugaku*, miko specialized in fortune telling, making entertainments for the gods, plucking bows for exorcisms, and channeling spirits of the deceased. The miko was said to dance like an unworldly being, sing like a heavenly bird, and play zither and drum so beautifully that everyone was attracted. Scrolls depict festival scenes at Kyoto's Imamiya Shrine in which a single miko is dancing, bell in hand, accompanied by singing and drumming. Another invaluable medieval source, *Shokunin uta-awase* (Craftsperson song competition),[12] also depicts a miko plucking a bow, with a nearby drum.

7 Honda Yasuji, *Nihon no dentō geinō I* (1993), 3.
8 A ritual held at winter solstice. As the spirit of the sun, identified with the spirit of the emperor, is weakest in the winter solstice season, ancient people thought that it must be revitalized through rites.
9 At this imperial accession, an emperor partakes of new rice and *sake* wine with the god.
10 In part of the ceremony, a female performed seated on a small platform.
11 Komatsu Shigemi (ed.), *Nenchū gyōji emaki* (Picture-scroll of annual events) (Tokyo: Chūō kōronsha, 1987).
12 A variety of song and dance genres were recorded in noblemen's diaries in the eleventh to thirteenth centuries. Scrolls describe various professions in parody of an *uta-awase*, or *waka* poem competition. Although the competition is fictitious, the detailed costumes and properties provide invaluable knowledge of medieval performers.

Popular traveling entertainments: *shirabyōshi, kusemai-mai, kugutsu*

The miko, although affiliated with shrines, also influenced popular entertainment and ritual traditions nationwide as some became itinerant prostitutes or professional entertainers.

The *Shokunin uta-awase* scroll also introduced female entertainers called *shirabyōshi* (白拍子) and *kusemai-mai* (曲舞々). They both use tsuzumi drums and hold fans. Female entertainers, including miko, belonged to a low social class and often were also prostitutes. Shirabyōshi, "white beat" or "simple beat," appeared in the late twelfth century. They sang rhythmic *imayō* (今様, "trendy") songs and sometimes danced wearing a man's tall *eboshi* hat and carrying a sword. According to the *Ryōjinhishō* anthology,[13] most imayō lyrics were composed of seven and five syllables, making dances cadenced. Shirabyōshi performance was so popular that some performers gained the favor of extremely high-ranking nobles, similar to the marriage of leading politicians with geisha in the modern era. In *Heike monogatari* (Tales of the Heike, *c.* thirteenth century), one finds the names of Giō and Hotoke Gozen, favored by Taira no Kiyomori (1118–81), and Shizuka Gozen, loved by Minamoto no Yoshitsune (1159–89) (see representative plays, p. 35). Kusemai, possibly derived from shirabyōshi, popular in the medieval period, consisted of recitation and dance accompanied also by the tsuzumi drum. Unlike shirabyōshi, both men and women performed. Today, the tradition can be found in folk *kōwakamai*, in Ōe, Fukuoka prefecture.

Kugutsu (傀儡子, also pronounced *kairaishi*) puppeteers were entertainers similar to miko and shirabyōshi. According to *The Book on Kugutsu*,[14] written by aristocrat-scholar Ōe no Masafusa (1041–1111), they were traveling troupes of entertainers. Female kugutsu wore beautiful makeup and showy costumes, sang imayō, and sometimes practiced prostitution, while males performed juggling, alchemical conjuring, and puppetry. Remarkably, one finds sangaku juggling and conjuring surviving in kugutsu. The main attraction of kugutsu was its puppetry, the inanimate dolls deemed not merely playthings but sacred objects in which a god's spirit dwelled. This tradition survived through medieval times until developing into *ningyō jōruri* in the early Edo period. Today, a variety of folk puppetries can be found all over Japan.

---

13 Compiled by retired emperor Goshirakawa hōō (1127–92), who invited female singers of low class to stay at his residence, where he learned and recorded many imayō.
14 Ōe Masafusa, *Rakuyō dengaku-ki*, reprinted in *Nihon shisō taikei*, vol. XXIII: *Kodai chūsei geijutsuron* (Tokyo: Iwanami shoten, 1973), 217–22.

Rice-planting performance: *hayashi-da, ta-asobi, dengaku*

Performing arts related to rice-making rituals have flourished in Japan since at least the Nara period (710–85). The historic development of these folk performing arts is unclear. However, from the seventh or eighth century, the imperial court already held rituals associated with rice-making in which *tamai* (田舞, rice field dance) was performed.

Hayashi-da (囃子田) is a rice-planting ceremony (*taue*, 田植) accompanied by lively music, held in early summer. Female planters transplant rice seedlings while singing, accompanied by large and small drums, bamboo whisks, small cymbals, and flutes. The songs sung in call-and-response style between a male leader and female sowers include occasional erotic or comic lyrics to entertain the rice god and human participants:

> Could it be my lover coming? The rear door's creaking
> Kiriri kitto, it goes. The rear door
> Maybe my beloved. Maybe a puppy howling, can't get the door ajar
> The short sword put by the pillow. The long sword against the screen
>   where it folds
> I want to find you. Which room are you sleeping in?[15]

Ta-asobi (田遊, rice field play) mimics rice farming to pray for bounteous crops, held in early spring, prior to actual rice sowing. Farmers imitate procedures for rice farming (plowing a field with an ox, sowing seeds, weeding, scaring away birds, harvesting, and pounding rice-cakes) through mime, dialogue, song, and dance. Erotic dialogue or gestures are believed to bring procreation and prosperity both to rice fields and to humans. In one of the most famous of these fertility rites, the Asuka Onda Matsuri, a long-nosed goblin (*tengu*) chases and copulates with a farm-girl wearing a plump-cheeked mask (*otafuku*).

Another type of rice-making performing art is *dengaku* (田楽), comprising highly sophisticated singing, dancing, dialogue, and acrobatics. Today's folk dengaku is a local, amateur, traditional art, rather unsophisticated when compared to the popular and fashionable dengaku of the Heian period, performed by professionals called *dengaku-hōshi* (dengaku priests). The eleventh-century *Eiga monogatari* (A tale of flowering fortunes) describes a strange-looking ten-man group parading through the street, beating unusual drums attached to their bellies, playing flutes, clapping *binzasara* (bamboo whisks or plates), dancing, and singing merrily. *The Calendar of Annual Events Scroll* also reveals groups playing large and small drums, binzasara clappers, and flutes in procession to Kyoto's Gion Shrine and Jōnangū Shrine; at the latter, juggling is also depicted.

---

15 Frank Hoff (trans.), *The Genial Seed: A Japanese Song Cycle* (New York: Grossman, 1971), 144, no. 122.

Another important historical source is a record by Ōe no Masafusa, reporting that a 1096 dengaku includes performers of *takaashi* (stilts), *issoku* (single stilt), *yōko* (waist drum), *furitsuzumi* (shaking drum), *dobyōshi* (cymbals), clappers, *ueme* (planting girls), and *tsukime* (threshing girls). They drew the attention of passers-by with their extraordinary costumes of gold and silver brocade, but also through their eccentric behavior, quarreling and startling people. Dengaku seemed to gain an overwhelming contemporary popularity with no regard for status and rank, but the author commented presciently that this social "frenzy" was a sign of coming turbulent times. Such unusually showy performances given by a group wearing strange costumes and makeup were called *furyū* (風流).[16]

Religious performance as entertainment

It should now be clear that temple and shrine grounds offered sites for secular performances, drawing audiences through music, laughter, and outlandish behavior to religious ceremonies and rites. Actual Buddhist ceremonies have also been a cradle for many performing arts.

Shushi wizard spectacles

A spectacular performance of *shushi* (呪師), also pronounced *zushi, sushi,* or *noronji*, appeared in eleventh-century noblemen's diaries or records of annual events.[17] The performance included "running" (*hashiri*) or showy body movements offered by a gorgeously costumed performer. The genre is said to derive from a temple service executed by a shushi (literally, master of magic, wizard) priest. Shushi played an important role in *shushō-e* (or *shujō-e*) and *shuni-e*[18] at Nara's Tōdaiji, Yakushiji, and many other temples from the eighth century onward. Shuni-e consists of three parts, *keka-sahō* (a rite to repent one's sins), *daidōshi-sahō* (a rite to pray for peace), and *shushi-sahō* (a rite to purify the hall and welcome the gods). This shushi-sahō contains esoteric elements such as utterance of magic words or use of symbolic hand gestures, but sometimes employs movements like bell-ringing and racing around the altar combined with sliding feet and hands holding swords to create spectacular effects.

There are several interpretations for the emergence of *shushi-sarugaku* (sarugaku played by shushi), an early form of sarugaku noh. Some claim that

---

16 The term is applied not only to a human performance but also to physical constructions like gorgeously ornamented floats (*mikoshi, dashi, danjiri, yama, hoko*) and umbrellas (*kasa*).

17 See *Sakeiki* (a diary by Minamoto no Tsuneyori), *Gōkeshidai* (by Ōe no Masafusa), and *Chūyūki* (a diary by Fujiwara no Munetada).

18 In big temples like Tōdaiji and Yakushiji, shuni-e is now performed in the third month of the solar calendar, a grand spectacle that attracts a large audience.

shushi priests gradually developed their ritualistic performances into entertainment forms in the medieval period; others explain that sangaku players affiliated with temples gradually took over the roles of shushi priests to perform theatrical pieces at the end of Buddhist services.

Descent of the Buddha: *raigō-e*

Another type of visually theatrical ritual, *raigō-e* (来迎会), also known as *neri-kuyō*, displays the descent of Amida (阿弥陀、the Buddha of infinite light). Based on the rise of Pure Land Buddhist belief in the eleventh century, a number of rich people, wishing to be reborn in paradise, rushed to do a "good deed" by making a huge donation to a temple, or constructing a building. They often ordered paintings of the scene in which Amida, with an entourage of twenty-five *bosatsu* (bodhisattvas), descended to take a good person's soul to heaven.

Japanese people in the medieval era realized this imagined world in human performance. In Taimadera Temple in the southern Nara basin, a temporary bridge is constructed between Shabadō Hall, likened to "this world," and Gokurakudō Hall, symbolizing Amida's paradise. Masked bodhisattvas enter from the Gokurakudō, parade along the bridge to the Shabadō, accept the soul of Princess Chūjō (associated with the temple), and finally return to the Gokurakudō. Local temple adherents take on the roles of the bodhisattvas, wearing gold masks and costumes, the procession accompanied by Buddhist chanting and gagaku music. The raigō-e ceremony is assumed to have developed by the thirteenth century, when the oldest bodhisattva mask can be dated.

Buddhist chant: *shōmyō*

Buddhist ceremonies have rich sonority. Buddhist chanting called *shōmyō* (声明) may include dialogue or storytelling. *Rongi* (論義, to debate) is a catechism for inquiring about Buddhist teachings. One priest asks questions and the other answers, not simply spoken but sung in specific musical pitches and rhythms. *Kōshiki* (講式) also employs syllabic recitation, interpreting Buddhist teachings or introducing achievements of the Buddha or saintly priests. The recitation style of rongi and kōshiki is a continuous narrative tradition shared with secular variants in *heikyoku* (recitation of the *Heike monogatari* to biwa accompaniment) and *utai* (recitation of noh and predecessor of rakugo storytelling).

Religious ceremonies as sites for sacred entertainments

In addition to their utilization of such Buddhist performing arts, temples provided access and space for a great variety of entertainments. Some were performed during services, others for amusement afterwards. *Hōraku* (法楽) are "sacred entertainments" for the gods, but also enjoyed by humans.

Shushi-sarugaku was often presented at the rear door of a hall after the main service ended. Behind the chief Buddha, facing the rear door, another Buddha or god is often enshrined, for example Matara-shin, a representative god, particularly in Tendai sect temples. Possessed of a somewhat violent character, he must be pacified, but is also regarded as a god of entertainment. Therefore, the rear area of temples has provided a significant space for entertainments since medieval times.

Ennen (延年)

Ennen (lit. "long-life") is an entertainment performed after the completion of temple rites, not a genre *per se* but a framing event displaying a variety of performances of different styles. It was so popular during medieval times that great temples such as Kōfukuji, Tōdaiji, and Tōnomine (or Tanzan Shrine) competed as sponsors. Only Mōtsūji in Iwate prefecture and a few other temples and shrines still maintain the tradition. Mōtsūji ennen is performed as hōraku following the *Jōgyōzanmai-ku* service, extolling the name of Amida Buddha. The ennen dance genres employ various formations such as lines, squares, and circles, often accompanied by music.

Among the variants of ennen-mai are *romai* (*kara-byōshi*), danced by two children representing two mysterious, legendary boys witnessed by the priest who founded the temple, Jikaku Daishi (794–864). Song and drums accompany the dance as the boys walk with toes sliding on the floor, holding wooden plates, stamp the floor, and turn quickly. There is also *notto*, a prayer for the Matara-shin god, inaudible but indispensable in terms of religious meaning. In *rōjo*, a stooping, grey-haired woman gestures as if combing her hair, then dances holding a fan and bell. As the dance includes neither words nor music, it looks like mime. In contrast, *jakujo* presents a young woman who dances elegantly while holding a bell and fan, also unaccompanied. In the latter half, a male priest character joins in the dance.

Chigo mai (Children's dance) features two boys reciting and dancing, sometimes accompanied by adults' recitation. *Hanaori* (Gathering flowers) and *Obogamukashi* (Reminiscing) are staged in alternate years. Both pieces celebrate the beauty of nature. In the *chokushi mai*, Kyōdono, an imperial messenger from Kyoto, and Ariyoshi, a servant, banter and dance together. *Ennen no mai* (Long life dance) is considered an archaic style of noh by folk-art scholar Honda Yasuji, although only *Todomedori* (Staying bird) is performed today, followed by one bugaku piece, *Karyōbin*, danced by four boys.

Thus ennen has accommodated performing arts of different styles and periods, including dance, mime, and dialogue. The dialogues found in chigo mai and chokushi mai are important theatrical features that developed later in the Middle Ages into full-fledged dramatic genres.

∾ FOCUS 1.2   Medieval variety show today: Nara's *Onmatsuri*

The Kasuga Wakamiya Onmatsuri (おん祭) in Nara is one of the oldest festivals in Japan, combining various ritual and secular entertainments, held annually in winter since 1136. Its basic structure is typical: welcoming the gods, entertaining them, then seeing them off.

The most important part of the festival is held noon to midnight on 17 December at Nara's Kasuga-taisha Shrine and Kōfukuji Temple. The god of Kasuga-wakamiya (a son of the Kasuga gods) moves from his usual residence (Wakamiya-sha) to the *otabisho* ("a place to stay during travel"). The god is carried at night by some twenty priests in white costumes holding sacred *sakaki* branches, accompanied by prayers of purification and *gagaku* music. At the otabisho, food, drinks, and a variety of performing arts are offered, including *miko kagura, azuma-asobi, yamato-mai, bugaku, dengaku, seino-o*, and *sarugaku* (noh).

The miko kagura of Kasuga-taisha is danced by eight virgins ringing bells, accompanied by song, *koto* zither, flute, and *shakubyōshi* clappers. Azuma-asobi (literally meaning "play of the eastern country") and Yamato-mai (literally "dance of Yamato") are considered a pair of dances, one from eastern Japan and the other from the Yamato (Nara) region, both thought of as indigenous repertoire in gagaku as opposed to foreign bugaku.

The dengaku at Kasuga-taisha is an invaluable living example of ancient tradition. Although it has lost its original powerful expression, it preserves elements of medieval dance, music, juggling, acrobatics, and dialogue-based skits. The gorgeous ornamentations on the flute-player's hat are also a remnant of the *furyū* costumes that once flourished.

Seino-o, also known as "Isora-no-mai," is the most mysterious rite of the festival. Several men in white costumes hiding their faces with white cloths, walk backward and forward while playing flutes and drums. The term "seino-o" possibly means "a man of talent" and Isora is a sea goddess. According to Japanese myth, Isora was so ugly that she hid her face when meeting someone, but was also fond of performances by talented men. The sarugaku (noh) ritual *Okina* is also performed here.

After the service is over, the god is returned to Wakamiya-sha.

TERAUCHI NAOKO

From ritual to art

Various religious rituals are also performing arts enjoyed as secular amusements, incorporating prayers and offerings to native Shinto gods or Buddhist deities. Spectators enjoying music, dance, and play at temples or shrines unconsciously bond with gods and buddhas, which eventually leads to personal enlightenment and happiness. Therefore, Japan's performing arts have not been consumed as temporary diversions only but have been handed down over more than a millennium with respectful care. In other words, these arts have transmitted not only aesthetic techniques but also the faith of ancient and medieval people in the benevolent and procreative potency of the gods.

References and further reading

Amino Yoshihiko *et al.* (ed.). *Taikei Nihon rekishi to geinō: oto to eizō to moji ni yoru* (History and performing arts in Japan [presented by] sound, image and text), 11 vols. with videotape (Tokyo: Heibonsha, 1991)

Geinōshi kenkyūkai (ed.). *Nihon no koten geinō* (Japanese classical performing arts) (Tokyo: Heibonsha, 1970)

Hayashiya Tatsusaburō. *Chūsei geinōshi no kenkyū* (Research in the history of medieval performing arts) (Tokyo: Iwanami shoten, 1960)

Hoff, Frank. *Song, Dance, Storytelling: Aspects of the Performing Arts in Japan,* Cornell University East Asia Papers 15 (Ithaca, NY: Cornell China-Japan Program, 1978)

Honda Yasuji. *Honda Yasuji chosaku-shū* (Honda Yasuji's collected works) (Tokyo: Kinseisha, 1996)

Kokuritsu gekijō (ed.). *Nihon no geinōkōza buyō, engeki* (Tokyo: Tankōsha, 2009)

Lancashire, Terence A. *An Introduction to Japanese Folk Performing Arts* (Aldershot: Ashgate, 2011)

Matsuo Kōichi. *Girei kara geinō e: kyōsō, hyōi, dōke* (From rituals to performing arts: frenzy, possession, buffoonery) (Tokyo: Kadokawa gakugei shuppan, 2011)

Thornbury, Barbara. *The Folk Performing Arts: Traditional Culture in Contemporary Japan* (New York: State University of New York Press, 1997)

Togi, Masatarō. *Gagaku: Court Music and Dance* (New York: Weatherhill, 1971)

FOCUS 1.1 *KAGURA* AND THE HEAVENLY ROCK-CAVE

Averbuch, Irit. *The Gods Come Dancing: A Study of the Japanese Ritual Dance of Yamabushi Kagura* (Ithaca, NY: Cornell University East Asian Program, 1995)

Iwata Masaru (ed.). *Kagura* (Tokyo: Meicho shuppan, 1990)

Lancashire, Terence. *Gods' Music: The Japanese Folk Theatre of Iwami Kagura* (Wilhelmshaven: Florian Noetzel Verlag, 2006)

FOCUS 1.2 MEDIEVAL VARIETY SHOW TODAY: NARA'S *ONMATSURI*

Ishii Tatsuro. "The Festival of the Kasuga Wakamiya Shrine," *Theatre Research International* 12 (1987), 134–47

Interlude: *Katari* narrative traditions: from storytelling to theatre

ALISON TOKITA

Sung, spoken, or chanted narrative (*katari*) has a central place in noh, bunraku, and kabuki. Why did these theatrical forms retain the narrative voice and a narratorial onstage presence? One factor is the religious origins of narrative. In Japan's ancient and strongly shamanistic religion, a medium (*miko*) goes into trance, receiving and then transmitting messages from gods to humans. She uses narrative, song, and dance (*mai*), perhaps beating a drum or twanging a catalpa bow or other stringed instrument, believed efficacious in contacting spiritual realms. The earliest miko were often blind women who worked for shrines, or formed independent itinerant associations. The legends, myths, and genealogies of clan rulers contained in the *Kojiki* (712) were memorized, ritually recited, and orally transmitted by professional blind male narrators (*kataribe*). Eventually, narrative developed rich musical resources, generating diverse genres of sung narrative.

With the spread of Buddhism from the continent (sixth century), preaching the new faith called upon and blended with local narrative practices. In temples, a musical preaching called *kōshiki* ("lecture service") developed (tenth century): the officiating priest read a text based on sutras to instruct and inspire devotion. Although written in literary Chinese, it was delivered musically in Japanese, employing similar musical structures to later storytelling genres.

Preaching in temples was complemented by itinerant purveyors of Buddhism in streets and market places: storytelling monks; holy men of Mount Kōya; nuns (*bikuni*) of Kumano; *e-toki* (lit. "painting explicators"), who pointed to religious paintings while preaching about heaven and hell or saints' lives.

Heroic tales into drama: *Heike, Soga,* and *Kōwaka*

Two enduring narratives of the medieval era were the *Heike* and *Soga* cycles. The battles between the Heike and Minamoto clans (1180–5) were recounted in oral tales and written records that gradually coalesced into *The Tales of the Heike*. While the textual tradition has dozens of versions, it also thrived for

Fig 5 *Uesugi Kenshin and the Blind Biwa Player* (Tsukioka Yoshitoshi, 1893).

centuries as a performance tradition under shogunal patronage, performed exclusively by blind male quasi-priests (*biwa hōshi*) who accompanied themselves on a pear-shaped four-stringed lute (*biwa*). Initially recited to placate the souls of those felled in battle so they would not wreak havoc on the living,[19] Heike uses melodic patterns ranging from syllabic chant to highly melismatic extended melodies.

Equally influential was the Soga narrative cycle, based on a late twelfth-century vendetta. Originally narrated by blind women (*goze*), it survives only in textual form. The *Chronicle of Yoshitsune* (*Gikeiki*) is a set of apocryphal stories about the Heike hero that circulated orally before being compiled in this cycle. Episodes such as *Funa Benkei* (Benkei in a boat) and *Ataka* (The Ataka barrier) were adapted and recast in noh, jōruri, and kabuki.[20]

Female *shirabyōshi* dancers danced like *miko* (shrine maidens) with drum accompaniment. Kan'nami (noh's founding father) introduced the narrative *kuse* section from the *kusemai*, successor art to shirabyōshi. Noh drama combines narrative, song, and dance as it summons gods, ghosts, and other supernatural beings via masked protagonists, the stage equivalent of a medium. Whereas noh features both mimetic and formal dance, *kōwakamai*, a popular male narrative genre (fifteenth–sixteenth century), is sung to purely formal dance movement, and lacks dramatic costuming. Most of the fifty extant texts derive from the Soga, Heike, and Yoshitsune cycles, which also provided libretti for early jōruri.

19 A typical recitation is found in Lafcadio Hearn's classic "The story of mimi-nashi Hoichi" (1904), hauntingly portrayed in the film *Kwaidan* (dir. Masaki Kobayashi, 1964); the sound track is, anachronistically, *Satsuma* not *heike biwa*.
20 Helen S. E. Parker, *Progressive Traditions: An Illustrated Study of Plot Repetition in Traditional Japanese Theatre* (Leiden: Brill, 2006) traces their "plot repetition" through successive genres.

Dramatic narration: *jōruri*

Jōruri was the major narrative genre of the Edo period. This shamisen-accompanied chanting derives its name from the tale of Lady Jōruri, fictitious lover of youthful Yoshitsune. An assemblage of tales told by itinerant women entertainers, its popularity by the 1500s brought it to Kyoto, where biwa players adopted it. Like heike, jōruri narrative is structured in a series of short, unified sections, each marked with clear musical cadential patterns.

From around 1600, puppet jōruri proliferated: shamisen replaced biwa, and the repertoire expanded to encompass miraculous Buddhist salvation narratives, direct adaptations of kōwaka and noh, and original superhero stories. Takemoto Gidayū (1651–1714) brought jōruri to a new level of dramatization with *gidayū-bushi*. In addition to describing scenery and action, and impersonating characters, the onstage narrator provided interpretation, giving a perspective of social judgment or divine commentary. A contemporary of Gidayū, Miyakodayū Itchū (1650–1724) had a more refined style of narrative, popular in private salons of the entertainment quarters.

As kabuki matured, it welcomed jōruri musicians of various styles to accompany dance scenes, in addition to the gidayū-bushi (called Takemoto in kabuki) used in plays adapted from bunraku. The love suicide (*shinjū*) plot typical of Chikamatsu's *sewamono* (contemporary) plays developed the convention of poetic scenes of the lovers' last journey (*michiyuki*). Even historical plays also featured a colorful journey scene. When puppet plays were transposed to kabuki, michiyuki were narrated by more lyrical jōruri styles. Itchū's disciple, Miyakoji Bungo-no-jō (d. 1740), specialized in suicide journey scenes. After his "licentious" music was banned in 1736, his disciples continued to develop distinctive styles: Tokiwazu in 1747, Tomimoto in 1748, and Kiyomoto in 1814.

Kabuki dance-scene narrative

Kabuki dance (*shosagoto*; see nihonbuyo, Interlude, p. 141) today is accompanied by *nagauta*, tokiwazu, and kiyomoto music. Their common form continues the same basic narrative structure as heike, kōwaka, and gidayū, but with more clearly prescribed sections, reminiscent of noh. Typically, after a lyrical scene-setting section (*oki*), the actor-dancer enters along the *hanamichi* walkway; the character is dramatically depicted in a lively entrance narrative. After the actor reaches the stage, narrative and lyric music may follow. The highlight is the plaintive *kudoki* lament about unhappy love, followed by a lively song-dance (*odoriji*), then an urgent rhythmic dénouement (*chirashi*). Nagauta developed from popular songs, but acquired the same narrative form as kabuki dance. It further incorporated the bombastic jōruri genre, *ōzatsuma-bushi*, suited to the bravado of *aragoto* acting, providing powerful narrative resources utilized in direct adaptations from noh, such as *Kanjinchō* (The subscription list).

Naniwa-bushi emerged in the late nineteenth century from humble ritual and storytelling origins, rising to prominence in Tokyo's variety halls in the 1930s and 1940s. Other new narrative genres emerging from modernizing Japan are *satsuma biwa* and *chikuzen biwa*.

The centrality of narrative in noh, bunraku, and kabuki attests to the vigor of Japan's katari traditions, many of which continue to attract amateur students and spectators independently from theatrical performance. Non-musical storytelling arts such as *rakugo, kōdan, katsudō benshi* (movie narrators), and *kamishibai* storytellers were popular during the nineteenth and early twentieth centuries. Narrative voices distinct from actors have even contributed to some contemporary theatre, demonstrating katari's sustained potency.

References and further reading

Araki, James T. *The Ballad-Drama of Medieval Japan* [kowakamai] (Berkeley: University of California Press, 1964)

Goodwin, Janet R. *Selling Songs and Smiles: The Sex Trade in Heian and Kamakura Japan* (Honolulu: University of Hawai'i Press, 2007)

Kaminishi, Ikumi. *Explaining Pictures: Buddhist Propaganda and Etoki Storytelling in Japan* (Honolulu: University of Hawai'i Press, 2006)

Kominz, Laurence. *Avatars of Vengeance: Japanese Drama and the Soga Literary Tradition* (Ann Arbor: Center for Japanese Studies, University of Michigan, 1995)

Tokita, Alison. *Japanese Singers of Tales: Ten Centuries of Performed Narrative* (Farnham: Ashgate, 2015)

2 ∾ Noh and Muromachi culture

SHINKO KAGAYA AND MIURA HIROKO

Noh is masked, lyric dance-drama which developed alongside kyogen comedy in the mid-fourteenth century. Scripts of great poetic force tell of the spirits of unrequited lovers, fallen warriors, mothers who have lost children to slave traders, and hunters paying for their sin of killing sentient beings. One "dances" (舞う, *mau*) the central role of a noh play, unlike other theatrical genres, where one "acts" (演じる, *enjiru*). An elegant costume, wig, and painted fan are often the only properties, framing a delicately carved mask – an indispensable tool that controls all aspects of performance. As musical dance-theatre, noh has been compared to Greek theatre and to opera. It is considered the world's oldest continuous theatre tradition, with scripts, theoretical writings, masks, and family lines dating back six centuries. In 2001, noh, including kyogen, was designated by UNESCO in its first ever Proclamation of Masterpieces of the Oral and Intangible Heritage of Humanity.

ELEMENTS OF PERFORMANCE

Noh (能, sometimes transcribed as *nō*, "skills or artistry") is a musical dance theatre that is fundamentally non-realistic. One or two masked characters act while the chorus sings (*utai*, 謡) poetic verses of five–seven syllabic meter, with instrumental musical accompaniment (*hayashi*, 囃子). Noh performance is usually translated as theatre, because of its dramatic plots. However, Zeami Motokiyo (1363?–1443?), who perfected the art of noh in the fourteenth century, wrote that noh performers needed to master *nikyoku-santai*: the two basic arts of dancing and singing of the three roles of old man, woman, and warrior.[1]

Restrictive forms and space

Noh's smallest units of movement are called *kata* (型, forms), beginning with the most basic: posture (*kamae*) and walk (*hakobi*). Kata range from

---

1 *Shikadō* (A mirror to the flower) in *Zeami Performance Notes*, trans. Thomas Hare (New York: Columbia University Press, 2008), 108–10.

Fig 6 Umewaka Rokurō portrays the spirit of an ancient pine, *Oimatsu*.

simple movements such as standing and sitting to purely abstract ones, such as circling or zig-zag floor patterns, to stylized movements with clear meanings such as *shiori*, bringing the cupped hand to eye-level, symbolizing crying. With various kata as building blocks, a sequence of movements

∾ SPOTLIGHT 2.1   Noh stage

The noh stage, like the mask, is a precisely constructed wooden tool for dramatic expression. The dimensions, nomenclature, and use of the noh stage achieved their current standard by the end of the sixteenth century. Previously, shrine and temple stages were used, or temporary structures built to similar dimensions.

In (A) the mirror room (*kagami no ma*), the fully costumed actor puts on his mask – prepared with pads and tape to conform to facial irregularities – to scrutinize his appearance just before going on stage. Stage assistants or teachers can observe performances and spectators from (B) the lookout window (*bugyō mado*), remaining invisible to the audience.

The raised curtain (C) (*agemaku*) separates the bridgeway from backstage. The silk brocade purple-red-orange-yellow-white stripes denote the five primary elements according to Chinese yin/yang philosophy: earth, wind, fire, water, metal. Two stage assistants (*kōken*) hold bamboo poles tied to the bottom corners, raising the curtain on cue. The curtain can be manipulated for dynamic expression, spectators teased by a quick flick or long-held canopy, or even a "false start" with curtain half-raised, then dropped, then raised again.

The bridgeway (D) (*hashigakari*) connects the main stage with the backstage. Originally a practical pathway from dressing room to stage, its position became fixed at audience left at an obtuse angle, between 10 and 16 meters long. An extension of the main playing area, it has great symbolic value, conveying separation both physical and spiritual, whether of the dead from the living, heaven or hell from earth, or past from present. Often the bridgeway slopes slightly upward from curtain to main stage, so characters seemingly struggle in and dash off easily.

The length and angle of the bridgeway provides scope for fully visible theatrical effects taking advantage of the perspective. Three pine trees (E) are placed in front of the bridgeway, usually in ascending height from

the curtain. Large properties are brought down it, while major characters enter through the bridgeway curtain, often stopping past the second pine to turn to spectators in a framed "close-up."

The main stage (F) (*hon butai*) is approximately 5.4 meters squared. The cypress (*hinoki*) wood is highly polished to facilitate dancers' smooth glides. The stage is empty at the beginning and end of a performance; all set pieces and properties are brought on before the action begins and cleared afterward. Some stages are imperceptibly raked, allowing for dynamic "zooms."

The mirror-board (G) (*kagami-ita*) "reflects" the drums' relatively soft sounds. The large painted pine tree is an ancient one depicted from midway up its wide trunk, elevating the stage in the imagination. It is not a particular dramatic locale, but a permanent and evergreen part of the stage itself, recalling the original ritual descent of the god at the Yōgō pine in Nara's Kasuga Shrine. Stage assistants and chorus members use the cut-door entrance (O) (*kirido guchi*) surreptitiously. The pine, bamboo painted next to it, and three pines are reminders that noh was once outdoor theatre, where such natural features marked entrances and exits.

Four pillars hold up the roof. No longer structurally necessary, they are still needed for guidance by actors seeing out of tiny mask eyeholes. At the *shite-bashira* (H) the main actor turns to enter the main stage from the bridgeway. The *metsuke-bashira* (I) (eye-fixing pillar) is a vital fixed point when the actor is dancing, preventing him from falling off the stage. The *waki-bashira* (J) is where the *waki* accompanying player stands or sits; the *fue-bashira* (K) is where the flute-player sits. Pillars and roof frame the actor viewed from either spectator position.

Two separate, roofed structures abut the main stage. The chorus area (L), and the back area (M) (*ato-za*), where musicians sit on *yokoita*,

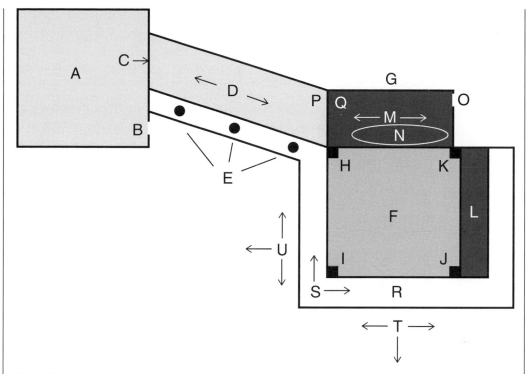

Fig 7 Noh stage.

floorboards running sideways in contrast to the vertical boards of the acting area; actors' sliding feet can feel this transition. Musicians' places (N) are fixed: flute, shoulder (small) drum (*kotsuzumi*), large drum (*ōkawa*), and stick drum (*taiko*). Chorus members and stage assistants enter and exit through an unobtrusive, meter-high, sliding door, the *kirido-guchi* (O) (cut-door, also called *okubyō guchi* [coward's door] and *wasure guchi* [forgetting door]), in the upstage left corner. The kyōgen actor and stage assistant sit upstage, respectively the *kyōgen-za* (P) and *kōken-za* (Q). Fully visible today, they would have been in shadows beneath temple eaves in pre-nineteenth-century outdoor theatres.

Noblemen once presented garments to favored performers from the now unused staircase (R) over the *shirasu* (S) (white pebble garden) bordering the stage. The narrow garden is a

remnant, separating the stage's potential pollution by once low-class actors from aristocratic spectators. When noh was performed outdoors, pebbles reflected light to actors in the shadows beneath the roof; they also reflected sound, enhancing acoustics. Beneath the stage are five to seven large clay pots (*kame*), tuned and angled to increase the resonance of demon and warrior stamps.

Spectators sit directly in front of the main stage (T) (*shōmen*), while musical connoisseurs may choose *waki shōmen* (U) (side seats) facing the chorus. Fluorescent lights and spotlights are generally used today, but natural daylight was the norm for half a millennium. The play of light and shadow can best be appreciated at occasional night-time torchlit (*takigi*) and indoor, candle-lit performances.

JONAH SALZ

is created. This limited number of kata is strictly choreographed; their size, speed, angle, or power is determined according to the character portrayed. Selection from multiple permissible kata allows some flexibility of interpretation. The appeal of kata lies in this paradox of restraint bringing forth infinite possibility.

There are also singing kata, adapted from contemporary medieval ritual chant and popular song. Noh verse skillfully employs various poetic wordplays: *kakekotoba* (pivot words), *jokotoba* (preface words), and *engo* (semantically related words). Buddhist chanting (*shōmyō*) and chanting in Japanese (*wasan*), as well as earlier performing arts *imayō* (contemporary Heian popular songs) and *waka* poetry influenced the singing style. Noh plays consist of compilations of small units (*shōdan*), often following characteristics of a Buddhist chant called *kōshiki* or *heikyoku* (musical narration of *The Tales of the Heike*). The rhythmic system of incorporating a five–seven syllabic meter into eight-beat phrases is shared with the Kamakura period song-style called *sōga*. There are two fundamental styles of singing, the dynamic *tsuyogin* "strong singing," and the more melodic *yowagin* "soft singing." As the play progresses, the chorus tends to sing more, and the *shite* (main actor) to dance more. Thus noh was formed from the corpus of techniques and characteristics of performing arts and literature of preceding eras, which have been synthesized into a dramatic expression of potent structural codes.

Such highly codified choreographies are possible because of the near identical dimensions of noh stages. There are approximately eighty active noh stages throughout Japan, approximately fifty used at least once annually by professionals: ten noh stages in Tokyo, six in Kyoto, three each in Kanagawa, Osaka, Hyogo, and Hiroshima, two in Aichi, and one each in Nara, Ishikawa, and other prefectures. There are also thirty-five noh stages on the small island of Sado, which once boasted 200 stages. Many stages impress due to their history and location: Kyoto's Nishi Honganji Temple's north stage is the oldest, built in 1581; the stage at Miyajima is famous for being submerged until low tide. At the other end of the scale, a teacher's home practice studio sometimes doubles as a small performance space.

Stages of training

Traditionally, a boy born into a noh performer's family is trained orally from infancy by his father or grandfather. In his teens, an actor becomes a live-in (or commuting) apprentice at the house of the *iemoto* (headmaster), learning all aspects of the art, including the importance of etiquette and relationships. Independence may be achieved around age 30, often announced widely to the noh world and public through commemorative performances. Students unaffiliated with traditional families hoping to become professional also train under the traditional apprentice system.

A shortage of successors has long been an issue for the so-called *sanyaku*, the three roles of *waki* (side-player) *hayashi* (drummers and flute), and kyogen. Considering cultivation of those performers an important mission, the Japan Arts Council, the administrative agency of the National Noh Theatre, has, since 1984, publicly advertised for applicants for the six-year training program for these three roles. Additionally, a *nōgaku* course established at the Tokyo Music School (since 1949 Tokyo University of the Arts) in 1931 and promoted to a major program in 1936, remains another training option for both noh family heirs and outsiders. Some students train both at university and as apprentices, following both new and traditional methods. Yet, even upon successful university graduation, a longer apprenticeship within a family is still necessary to be considered a full-fledged performer. Traditional training methods appear to be indispensable.

Performers and their roles

Professional noh performers are divided into *tachi-kata* (lit. standing roles) who act and sing – *shite-kata* (シテ方) perform leading roles, *waki-kata* (ワキ方) accompanying roles, and *kyōgen-kata* (狂言方) kyogen comedies or explanatory interludes – and *hayashi-kata*, musicians playing four instruments: shoulder, hip, and stick drums, and flute.

Each noh performance traditionally is held just once by an ensemble of around twenty-five performers from each of the seven roles – shite, waki, kyogen, and four instrumental musicians. Normally one masked protagonist speaks some *kotoba* in a recitative manner, but mostly sings (*utai*) accompanied by a chanting chorus (*ji-utai*). The chorus leader is responsible for pitch and rhythm. The chorus narrates the background to the unfolding events, describes actions as they occur, and also expresses the protagonist's emotions. Unlike the Greek chorus, the singers do not play a particular role, but adapt to exigencies of plot and dramatic necessity. Actors singing in the chorus are also performers of shite roles. Music is chanted to strict rhythms and melodies, without harmonies or separation of voices. Shite actors also serve as dresser, and *kōken* (後見, lit. "after watcher," stage assistant), ensuring the smooth progress of a performance by lifting the raised curtain (agemaku); on stage, they hand properties to dancers, and straighten their costumes. Actors thus participate in all aspects of a particular role before actually performing the lead.

Among noh professionals, the shite probably is the most versatile, needing to manage various jobs as performer, producer, and teacher. Usually shite actors produce the performance: deciding the program, date and venue, liaising with other performers, advertising and selling tickets, and performing the shite role. Other duties include training students – both professionals and amateurs – and producing and facilitating amateur students' recitals.

As children, shite actors play *kokata* (lit. "small roles"). These include children's characters, and some adult characters, all performed without a mask. Since children participating in ceremonies at temples and shrines were considered pure, possessed by the deity, the kokata was thought appropriate for roles of noble beings like the emperor. When kokata portray noble roles, it intensifies the tragedy and focuses attention on adult shite. Another reason for their prevalence was the adoration of beautiful young boys common during the medieval period. As an important process of training for future shite performers, kokata are encouraged to express their own youthful, innocent, natural energy and talent, rather than attempt imitative acting.

Staging

Noh does not require large stage scenery, and often only has a simple stage prop (*tsukurimono*). Properties are made anew for each performance, their construction also the responsibility of shite actors. Properties are roughly classified into four categories: natural landscapes such as mounds, mountains, and trees; buildings such as palaces, houses, huts, and bell towers; vehicles such as carriages and boats; other items such as musical instruments and wells. The shite also prepares other small props (*kodōgu*) that include treasures and spiritual objects such as fans; arms such as swords and pikes; ritual implements such as *juzu* Buddhist rosaries; musical instruments such as drums; everyday items such as *kazura-oke* (lit. "wig tubs," also called *shōgi*, stools); and living things such as falcons.

The accompanying players (waki) appear in all but nine of the regular repertoire of approximately 250 extant plays. Playing the role of traveling priest who offers prayers to the shite character's lost spirit to appease it, preventing it from returning to wander the earth, a waki often ushers the shite in and out, receiving and supporting him. The waki also plays antagonist to the shite protagonist, for example a *yamabushi* mountain priest who appeases demonic spirits through prayers. Waki can also play the role of a robust fisherman, boatman, warrior, or imperial subject. Historically, waki ("side") referred to the second leading performer who headed the chorus in a supporting role before the establishment of its current function. Waki characters are always living, adult men, performed maskless.

Noh's four instruments are a lacquered bamboo flute (*nōkan*); shoulder drum (kotsuzumi), "talking drum" squeezed and struck to produce various sounds; hip drum (ōtsuzumi or ōkawa) with a flatter, higher "clacking" sound; and, for approximately half the repertoire, especially plays depicting non-human roles, a tub-shaped stick drum (taiko) beaten in a steady, rhythmic pattern to produce a clear, powerful sound. The hayashi ensemble sits at the back of the stage, reacting to the lead actor's timing. Drummers' *kakegoe* calls provide cues to each other and the actors.

In 2014, the Nōgaku Kyōkai (the Nohgaku Performers' Association) boasted 1,230 professional members.[2] Most make their living teaching amateur students studying utai (singing) or *shimai* (dance). Often lessons take place at home studios, culture centers, and universities, with regular recitals on home or rented noh stages. Recital formats vary greatly, from simply singing a verse to performances in full costume, requiring professional supporting players.

Stylistic schools of noh professionals

The seven roles of noh professionals are currently further divided into twenty-four schools (*ryūgi*). There are five schools for shite divided according to similarities in artistic styles between *kamigakari* (upper group) and *shimogakari* (lower group). A noh performer is affiliated with a single school throughout his lifetime (see Table 2.1 p. 32).

Plays: plots and structure

Each school lists plays in the regular repertoire, publishing *utaibon* libretti complete with distinct musical notation. These contain the synopsis, text, descriptions of costumes, masks, singing, dancing, and rhythmic notation, so also function as convenient tools for training amateurs. Moreover, since copyright is held by the iemoto (head) of each school, it provides a regular source of income for the school. There are approximately 150 plays shared by all five schools, with a combined regular repertoire of about 250 plays.

Plays can be divided between *mugen* (phantasmal) noh and *genzai* (living) noh. In a typical mugen noh, a traveling priest encounters a spirit who tells the story of his or her past, then disappears as dawn arrives – as though the events occurred in a dream. Many mugen-noh have a two-act structure in which a disguised human in the first act reappears in the second act revealed as an unrequited spirit. In contrast, genzai noh follow a temporal progression, with a richer dramatic storyline.

---

2 The Nohgaku Performers' Association, www.nohgaku.or.jp/about/index.html.

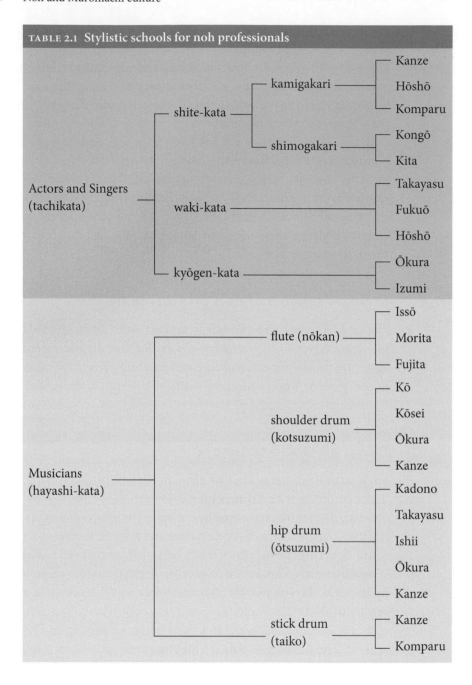

TABLE 2.1 Stylistic schools for noh professionals

Actors and Singers (tachikata)
- shite-kata
  - kamigakari
    - Kanze
    - Hōshō
    - Komparu
  - shimogakari
    - Kongō
    - Kita
- waki-kata
  - Takayasu
  - Fukuō
  - Hōshō
- kyōgen-kata
  - Ōkura
  - Izumi

Musicians (hayashi-kata)
- flute (nōkan)
  - Issō
  - Morita
  - Fujita
- shoulder drum (kotsuzumi)
  - Kō
  - Kōsei
  - Ōkura
  - Kanze
- hip drum (ōtsuzumi)
  - Kadono
  - Takayasu
  - Ishii
  - Ōkura
  - Kanze
- stick drum (taiko)
  - Kanze
  - Komparu

The rich variety of worlds depicted in extant noh plays is often classified into a five-play sequence based on the formal noh and kyogen performance program established during the Edo period (1603–1868). Following a performance of *Okina*, five noh plays are performed, interspersed with four kyogen plays. Since this type of program lasts an entire day, nowadays it is rarely held; more commonly, programs consist of two noh plays with one kyogen, interspersed with short dances.

First-category plays, *kami-nō* (god noh) or *waki-nō* (side noh), offer prayers for peace and abundance, conveying a celebratory or auspicious tone, often set at particular shrines and temples. The forty-odd waki-nō plays were once the prerogative of the troupe head, and have always been regarded with respect. Since full five-play programs are rarely performed nowadays, opportunities to see these plays are rare.

The second category is *shura-nō* (Asura noh, warrior noh), featuring plays depicting the perpetual suffering of warriors who, according to Buddhist teaching, are doomed to purgatory after death for their taking of human life. There are sixteen shura-nō plays in the regular repertoire, many based on *The Tales of the Heike*.[3]

Third-category *kazura-mono* (wig plays) or *onna-mono* (woman plays) – most with female protagonists and based on stories from *Ise monogatari* (The tales of Ise),[4] *Genji monogatari* (The tale of Genji),[5] *Kokinwakashū* (Collection of poetry of ancient and contemporary times),[6] and *Shin-kokinwakashū* (New collection of poetry of ancient and contemporary times)[7] – depict the wondrous beauty and complexity of the human heart as expressed in lyric court literature. The forty or so plays portray the spirit of an eminent female figure, nature spirits, celestial beings, handsome men, or old women.

The fourth category, *zatsu-nō* (miscellaneous noh), contains plays outside other categories. There are about ninety such plays in the regular repertoire, the largest among the five categories. 'Mad noh' is one sub-category that includes plays depicting a mother driven insane after the loss of a child. Possessed, obsessed, and vengeful spirits also appear. Other plays depict the confessional penitence of sinners, or spirits fallen into hell.

The fifth and final category is *kiri-nō* (finishing noh), also called *kichiku-nō* (demon and animal noh), performed with a brisk tempo, accompanied by the taiko drum. In plays such as *Tsuchigumo* (The earth spider) (see Figure 48) and *Nue* (Night bird), the shite appears as a powerful supernatural being. Also included in this category are celebratory plays marking a program's finale, such as *Shakkyō* (The stone bridge), in which the legendary *shishi* lion performs a magnificent dance.

---

3 A thirteenth-century compilation depicting the rise and fall of the Heike clan in the twelfth century.
4 The Heian period (794–1185) *Tales of Ise* is a collection of *waka* poetry and associated narratives.
5 A masterpiece of Japanese classic literature written by Murasaki Shikibu in the mid-Heian period, it is often considered the world's first novel or first psychological novel.
6 Early tenth-century imperial anthology of waka poetry.
7 Early thirteenth-century imperial anthology of waka poetry.

❧ FOCUS 2.1   Kurokawa noh

Fig 8 *Sambasō* is performed at Kurokawa's Kasuga Shrine.

Kurokawa noh is a seventeenth century noh-kyogen tradition organized by villagers in Kurokawa in Yamagata prefecture, northern Honshu, Japan's main island. It is profoundly embedded in the cultural life of the community, and the center of village sacred practice at their Kasuga Shrine. Kurokawa noh is not a mere regional variation of the elite genre, but an elaborate combination of festival, ritual, and performance.

A guild structure divides the village geographically in two, nurturing a competitive atmosphere. During the four annual shrine festivals, the two performance groups compete, including village youth. In 2012 there were approximately 240 parishioner households of the shrine; of these as many as 160 villagers were active as actors or musicians. Besides the shrine festivals, villagers also participate in secular events, sometimes up to twenty performances a year. The grandest is the *ōgisai* (fan festival), an all-night performance of five noh and four kyogen held in the cold and snow each February.

That a secluded village isolated by mountainous terrain should have developed and sustained an entertainment such as noh theatre and integrated it into Shinto shrine festivals has provoked considerable interest since the beginning of the twentieth century among folklore and theatre scholars, noh performers, and tourists. Advertised as "secret noh of the snow country," Kurokawa noh became one of the most well-known and long-studied traditions in Japan outside urban centers.

Despite such scrutiny, precisely how noh and kyogen came to be performed by these villagers is unknown. The Sakai clan, who governed the Shōnai domain (the area around Tsuruoka and Sakata), were powerful patrons of Kurokawa noh; from 1690 to 1865 the villagers were invited nine times to perform in Tsuruoka Castle. Eleven benefit or fundraising tours lasting up to twenty days were held, using revenues for shrine repairs or new costumes. Even after the shogunate was eliminated, the villagers discovered newfound interest in their tradition, performing for the Meiji Emperor (1881), and at Yasukuni Shrine in Tokyo (1910).

Declared an important intangible folk cultural property in 1976, the villagers are able to perform at least one hundred noh plays and claim a remarkable repertory of 540 noh and about forty kyogen originating in an expansion of the repertory in 1897. Libretti of the Kanze and Hōshō schools are used, but the repertory also contains extinct plays of the five schools. There are only male actors; interestingly, there is no division in training for main (*shite*) and side (*waki*) players as in professional noh; boys begin their careers in supporting roles, then progress to main roles. Perhaps Kurokawa noh preserved a noh closer to that of Zeami's, or that being part of a participatory community ceremony transformed noh into a rite of passage.

EIKE GROSSMANN

REPRESENTATIVE PLAYS

Takasago by Zeami

The best-known and most frequently performed waki-noh play is *Takasago*[8] by Zeami, in which a Shinto priest comes to Takasago Bay in Harima (Hyōgo prefecture). He encounters the shite and *tsure* (accompanying role) – an elderly couple raking leaves beneath a pine tree. They are the spirits of wedded old pine trees from Takasago and Sumiyoshi (Osaka); as their hearts are one, the distance between them is irrelevant. Celebrating the prosperity of waka poetry, longevity, and peace, the two depart saying they will meet again at Sumiyoshi. Accompanied by a local man on his newly made boat, the priest follows the two. In the second act, the Sumiyoshi Shrine deity performs an auspicious dance, offering a benediction for peaceful prosperity. The dignified old man in the first half is revealed as the virile god of Sumiyoshi, played by the same actor – a thrilling metamorphosis.

Matsukaze (Pine wind) by Kan'ami

The woman play *Matsukaze*[9] (Pine wind) (see Figure 9) was written by Kan'ami and adapted by his son Zeami. As a traveling priest (waki) visits Suma Bay on a beautiful moonlit autumn night, two young female divers appear, pulling a salt-gathering wagon. As the priest refers to Ariwara no Yukihira, an early Heian noble poet, the two reveal themselves as spirits of sisters Matsukaze and Murasame, his former lovers. Madly cherishing the memory, Matsukaze dances with Yukihira's memento robe and hat; asking the priest to offer prayers, she disappears at dawn. The complex weave of

8 Shelley Fenno Quinn, "An annotated translation of *Takasago*," in *Developing Zeami: The Noh Actor's Attunement in Practice* (Honolulu: University of Hawai'i Press, 2005), 303–19.
9 "Matzukaze – Pining wind," in Royall Tyler (ed. and trans.), *Japanese Nō Dramas* (London: Penguin, 1992), 183–204.

Fig 9 *Matsukaze* (Tomoeda Akio), the salt-water gatherer.

poetry (*matsu* = pine = waiting), and symbols of Buddhist salvation (salt-cart wheels of fate), and doubling (the two sisters; the moon reflected in the salt-bucket), and the dramatic trajectory of grief and joyful derangement make this one of the most cherished plays in the repertoire.

Sumidagawa (Sumida River) by Kanze Motomasa

Sumidagawa[10] (Sumida River), a popular "crazed woman" living play in the "miscellaneous" category, was written by Kanze Motomasa. A frenzied mother (shite) arrives at Sumida River from the distant capital in search of her son. As she crosses the river by ferry, the boatman tells her the story of an ill child who died, left there by human traffickers. On the other bank, his one-year memorial service is being held. Hearing the child's name, the mother realizes it is her son, and is led to his grave-mound. Amidst chanting prayers, the child's spirit appears; however, at dawn he disappears. Variant performances omit the child, so that the mother grasps at a phantom, invisible to the audience, providing another dramatic layer.

Funa Benkei (Benkei in a boat) by Kanze Nobumitsu

Funa Benkei[11] (Benkei in a boat) by Kanze Nobumitsu is one of the most popular fifth-category plays. After subduing the Heike clan, Minamoto no Yoshitsune is at odds with his elder brother Yoritomo. Accompanied by legendary warrior Musashibō Benkei, he prepares to flee. On their way, Yoshitsune makes his consort, the famous *shirabyōshi* dancer Shizuka-gozen, return to the capital. She dances a prayer for Yoshitsune's happiness then departs in sorrow (see Figure 14). The party embarks by sea but encounters a terrible storm, assailed by vengeful spirits of the defeated Heike clan. Taira no Tomomori's spirit wields a *naginata* spear, attempting to make Yoshitsune's boat founder. When Benkei offers prayers, the vengeful spirit is calmed by the power of Buddhist law, disappearing among the waves at dawn. The legendary dancer Shizuka and the enraged general Tomomori are tour-de-force roles played by the same actor.

Okina-sarugaku (翁猿楽) and *sarugaku* (猿楽)

It is not clear how early eleventh-century *sangaku, sarugaku,* and *shishi-sarugaku* developed into the dance and musical drama noh, but many have speculated over forces which made such transformations possible. Between the mid-fourteenth and the fifteenth century, sarugaku divided into kyogen, comical short drama that preserved more of the conventional nature of sarugaku, and noh, drama with song and dance. One of the earliest records of the term noh is in the *Fūshikaden* (1400) by Zeami and for kyogen in the

---

10 Tyler, "Sumida-gawa – The Sumida River," in *ibid.* 251–63.
11 Tyler, "Funa Benkei – Benkei aboard ship," in *ibid.* 82–95.

∾ SPOTLIGHT 2.2   Zeami: noh's founding genius

Zeami Motokiyo (1363?–1443?) was an actor, playwright, and theorist seminal in the development of noh theatre. A director and actor in his own troupe for almost four decades, he also produced twenty-one theoretical writings on noh informed by practice. As playwright, his legacy includes an attributed forty-plus works that continue to be performed.

Zeami trained under his father, Kan'ami Kiyotsugu (1333–84), star actor of a troupe from Nara, south of Kyoto. He considered his father a gifted performer, crediting him with greatly enhancing the rhythmic interest of *sarugaku* music by incorporating elements from contemporary, popular *kusemai*.

At age 12 Zeami accompanied his father to the capital Kyoto where Kan'ami performed in the presence of the third Ashikaga shogun, Yoshimitsu (1358–1408). Yoshimitsu promptly became their patron, allowing them access to many resources. Zeami composed linked verse with the most influential court poet of the day, Nijō Yoshimoto (1320–88). Such contact with Kyoto elites was unusual for a humble sarugaku performer, giving Zeami the opportunity for a classical education. Yet Zeami's attendance at the Gion Festival seated at Yoshimitsu's side prompted a courtier to remark in his diary that Zeami's was a profession for beggars – a chilling index of Zeami's social standing.[12]

Zeami was around 20 when his father died: he succeeded him as troupe leader. Yoshimitsu's patronage continued until his death in 1408. During that time, two sons were born to Zeami, Jūrō Motomasa (?–1432) and Shichirō Motoyoshi (dates unknown). Yoshimitsu's successor as

shogun, Yoshimochi (1386–1428), also supported Zeami but favored rival *dengaku*. When the sixth shogun Yoshinori (1394–1441) took power in 1428, Zeami's fortunes shifted. He and Motomasa were repeatedly passed over for prestigious venues in favor of Zeami's nephew (and possibly adopted son) On'ami (Saburō Motoshige, 1398–1467). In 1430 Motoyoshi left the sarugaku profession and took Buddhist vows. In 1432 Motomasa died mysteriously; Zeami was inconsolable. In a lament over the loss, *Museki isshi* (Remains of a dream – on one sheet, 1432), he wrote, "Though my own son, he was an incomparable master," and predicted the imminent demise of sarugaku.[13]

In 1433, On'ami succeeded Kan'ami and Zeami as head of the Kanze troupe. In 1434, when Zeami was around 71, Yoshinori exiled him to distant Sado Island for reasons still unknown. Also unknown is whether Zeami returned from exile, or when he died. If he was still alive after Yoshinori's assassination in 1441, it is likely he was allowed to return; he lived until around the age of 81.[14]

INTERTEXTUALITY AND DREAM-PLAYS

Such vicissitudes had their impact on Zeami's career and oeuvre. He addressed theoretical writings to his artistic heirs, treating such topics as actor training, playwriting, and audience reception to help them prevail in cutthroat competition to capture patrons. Zeami described playwriting as the life of the art and an important means of besting rivals.[15] The catalyst for his far-reaching innovations was probably very local. In his youth, the chief competition for Yoshimitsu's favor had been the Ōmi sarugaku player Inuō (?–1413). Zeami wrote that Inuō's style, which

---

12 Sanjō Kimitada in *Gogumaiki* (Clueless chronicle II), in Kobayashi Seki, Nishi Tetsuo, and Hata Hisashi (eds.), *Nōgaku daijiten* (Unabridged dictionary of noh and kyogen), s.v. "Zeami" (Tokyo: Tsukuma shobō, 2012), 498.

13 Omote Akira and Katō Shūichi (eds.), *Zeami, Zenchiku, gei no shisō, michi no shisō*, vol. I: *Nihon shisō taikei shinsōhan* (Theory on art, theory of the way I: Compendium of Japanese theory, new version) (Tokyo: Iwanami, 1995), 242.

14 Tanaka Makoto (ed.), *Kōhon yoza yakusha mokuroku* (Listings of performers in the four troupes [including variant texts]), *Nōgaku shiryō* VI (Tokyo: Wan'ya shoten, 1975), 29.

15 *Kaden dairoku, Kashu ni iwaku* (Transmitting the flower, part six: Training in the flower) in Omote Akira and Katō Shūichi (eds.), *Zeami, Zenduku*, 47.

excelled at singing and dancing, had "yūgen."[16] Yūgen seems to have referred here to a certain mood – a supple grace with a façade of serene beauty and aristocratic overtones, a style highly valued by Yoshimitsu. By contrast, the reputation of sarugaku troupes in the Nara area rested on forceful performances of demon roles. Zeami and Kan'ami must have realized that demons lacked the lyricism to keep Yoshimitsu's attention.

Unsurprisingly, then, Zeami worked to intensify the musical and choreographic interest. He developed a dramatic prototype in which chanted text and choreographed movement formed the primary media for staging mimetic scenes. Rather than plot development, a sequence of musical components determined the play's structure, acting as its soundtrack, and consequently determining its mood. Oftentimes the protagonist is the spirit of a long-dead person. The spirit lingers because of an all-consuming emotional attachment that is gradually revealed to a side actor (*waki*), typically a Buddhist priest, then relived through evocative dance.

Zeami favored spirits linked intertextually to history, legend, and literature. He composed many warrior plays inspired by the martial epic *Tales of the Heike*. In *Kiyotsune*, the spirit of the vanquished Taira warrior appears in his wife's dream to make her understand why he took his own life. Plays about women also tended to draw on familiar stories. The play *Izutsu* (Well cradle) builds on several episodes from the Heian classic *The Tales of Ise*; a young woman's spirit frequents her husband's grave and relives the memory of their relationship. As for demons, since realistic plot action was beside the point, in Zeami's spirit dramas their hearts too could be expressed through music without violating credibility.

Among the many influences of Zeami's work in modern times, his spirit play prototype especially has attracted actors, directors, playwrights, and other artists. Today such spirit noh form the heart of a classification of plays referred to as *mugen nō* in which a supernatural being appears to the waki. The scenario of a spirit returning to relive a deep-rooted emotional memory before a compassionate listener offers a vivid and frequently adopted alternative to realistic theatre.

SHELLEY FENNO QUINN

Suōnokuni-ninpeiji-kuyō-nikki (1352). Thus by the close of the fourteenth century, each genre had its own dramatic foundations.

Noh which is not noh: *Okina*

Performances held on formal ceremonial occasions, such as New Year or the opening of a new noh stage, often commence with the play *Okina* (lit. old man). Performers prepare for this play by observing several days of *bekka* ("separate fire" employed for cooking to avoid pollution) and purifying the body (adhering to a strictly vegetarian diet). On the day of the performance, they make offerings at the altar set up in the mirror-room with boxed masks and bells used in the performance, sacred sake, washed rice, and salt. Before going on stage, performers solemnly drink sacred sake, nibble at the rice, and purify their body with salt and sparks from a flint.

Okina itself has little dramatic development. Okina, Senzai (lit. one thousand years old), and Sambasō (lit. the third old man) appear in turn to offer prayers for peace and abundance, and perform dances of blessing and

---

16 Zeami, *Fūshikaden daisan, Mondō jōjō* (Transmitting the flower through effects and attitudes, part three: questions and answers on various matters), in *ibid.* 30.

benediction. First Okina offers blessing, then Senzai performs a celebratory dance. Okina then puts on Hakushikijō (the white mask of an old deity) to perform a dance of benediction. Sambasō – performed by a kyogen actor – then dances a dance of joy, followed by another congratulatory dance, this time wearing a Kokushikijō (black mask of an old deity) and shaking hand-held bells (see Figure 8).

Okina was also called *Shikisanban* (lit. ceremonial three) or *Okina-saru-gaku*, retaining ancient forms of pre-noh and kyogen religious rites, said to be "part of noh, but not noh." It is thought that *Okina* derives from *hashiri* performances executed by *shushi* priests during services in temples, like *Shushō-e* and *Shuni-e* devised by the end of the twelfth century.[17] The *Okina* performed at the beginning of the *takigi* (brazier-lit) noh at Nara's Kōfukuji Temple is to this day called *shushi-hashiri*. This shows that *Okina* has different artistic origins from noh, and also reveals the ritual and entertainment functions that noh has played over time. These services were held by temples to pray for the prosperity of the state. At that time, the state and Buddhism were supposed to govern the nation together, so these services were central to the state's offering of prayers and blessing.[18]

Throughout the Muromachi and Edo periods, the head of a noh troupe was expected to perform the role of Okina, as the requisite opening ritual of a noh performance. This in turn secured his position of authority.

Sarugaku had troupes organized to perform *Okina*. Among those that served influential temples and shrines in Yamato (current Nara prefecture) were the four troupes Yūzaki, Enman'i, Tobi, and Sakado, and also troupes specializing in the more entertaining aspects of sarugaku. These latter troupes gradually attained more popularity, surpassing the *Okina-sarugaku* specialists. As each group began to perform independently, they eventually grew distinct.

Muromachi (1392–1573) culture

Fourteenth-century Japan was in constant convulsion. After the fall of the Kamakura shogunate (1192–1333), Emperor Godaigo (1288–1339) established a new government in 1333, only to see its immediate collapse. During the Northern and Southern Courts Era (1336–92), the imperial court was split into two – the Northern Court established in Kyoto by Ashikaga Yoshimitsu (1358–1408) with Emperor Kōmyō, and the Southern Court, in Nara, established by Emperor Godaigo. Yoshimitsu became the third

---

17 Omote Akira and Amano Fumio, *Iwanami kōza nō kyōgen I: nōgaku no rekishi* (Iwanami courses on noh and kyogen I: History of *nōgaku*) (Tokyo: Iwanami shoten, 1987), 21.

18 Matsuoka Shinpei, "Nō-kyōgen no seiritsu no haikei" (Behind the formation of noh and kyogen), in *Nihon no dentō geinō kōza: buyō, engeki* (Series on Japanese traditional performing arts: classical dance, theatre) (2009), 117.

Ashikaga shogun in 1368. He succeeded in reintegrating the two courts, asserting control over powerful provincial lords, solidifying the nation's financial foundation, reestablishing diplomatic relations, and monopolizing trade with Ming China (1368–1644), as well as instituting the concept of absolute shogunal authority.

Unlike the previous era, when pursuit of profit and interest in money were considered evil, Emperor Godaigo and the Muromachi shogunate placed commerce and the financial market central to their policies.[19] Commerce was so important that merchants and craftsmen were even allowed inside the Imperial Palace.[20] After the dispute between the Northern and Southern Courts, people lost belief in the absolute imperial authority that was once sacred. Major temples connected with imperial courts also lost influence. With no overriding authority, and with the penetration of the money economy, self-governing cities and villages began to emerge,[21] ushering in the growth of new cosmopolitan audiences. This urban public could support the development of large-scale productions of noh, which required large audiences compared to earlier performing arts like *gagaku, imayō, shirabyōshi, kusemai,* or *heike,* noted in the previous chapter, which were more appropriate for smaller, salon-type spaces.

As with the Kamakura period, samurai continued to hold power in the Muromachi period, as distinct from the earlier Heian period, where the Emperor and court nobles were central to society. The central power of the earlier period was located in Kamakura in eastern Japan, but Yoshimitsu established his shogunate in Muromachi, Kyoto, near the imperial court, as a means to achieve supremacy. Yoshimitsu assumed the position of Dajōdaijin (Chancellor of the Realm) of the Dajōkan (Great Council of State), depriving the imperial court of the rights relating to holding rituals, made his wife Hino Yasuko mother figure to Emperor Gokomatsu, and was recognized by Ming China as king of the Japanese nation.

Yoshimitsu's influence continued until his death. The villa he built in 1397 in the northern hills of Kyoto, Kitayama (later Rokuon Temple, known as Kinkakuji, Temple of the Golden Pavilion), where he continued to deal with state affairs, is an excellent symbol of the culture of this early Muromachi era, the Kitayama era. The pavilion consists of three levels: *shinden-zukuri* (aristocratic mansions, the architectural style of the Heian nobility), *buke-zukuri* (samurai mansions, the architectural style of the Kamakura warlords), and

---

19 Amino Yoshihiko, *Chūsei no hinin to yūjo* (Non-human and courtesan in the medieval period), in *Kōdansha gakujutsu bunko* (Kodansha scholarly books), 1694 (Tokyo: Kōdansha, 2005), 274.
20 Amino Yoshihiko, *Igyō no ōken* (Deformed sovereignty), Heibonsha Library 10 (Tokyo: Heibonsha, 1993), 235.
21 *Ibid.* 43.

∾ SPOTLIGHT 2.3   Women in noh

Noh has been considered an exclusively male domain until now, although there have been women performing noh since the genre began. Noh performed by itinerant female troupes was first mentioned in the *Kanmon gyoki*, the diary of Prince Fushimi no Miya Sadafusa (1372–1456) in 1432, and became popular during the Muromachi period (1392–1573).[22] *Onna* (female) *sarugaku* participated in major events like fund-raisers for rebuilding temples and shrines. Documents attest to the high level of their art but also describe their beauty – apparently they performed without masks, alongside male accompanying musicians and kyogen actors. Wakita believes women acted in both female and male roles.[23] All-female kyogen troupes (*nyōbo kyōgen*) also performed throughout the medieval period. By the end of the Muromachi period, the precursors of modern noh stylistic schools had established themselves as the dominant guilds, receiving shogunal support. Not integrated into the medieval guild structure, female performers probably did not have the opportunity to join, their greatest obstacle to developing as professionals.

WOMEN ON THE MODERN NOH STAGE

As noh developed into a prominent classical performing art in the latter half of the Meiji period (1868–1912), both practicing noh and attending performances became increasingly popular among noblewomen and others of the upper strata of society. Eventually, middle-class women came to regard noh as a prestigious leisure activity. When leading critics and performers began discussing the role of women in noh in the early 1900s, the majority claimed that the comparatively high pitch of the female voice, as well as difference in physical strength and smaller body size, were not suitable for performing noh. They also feared the overt realism in female roles if performed by women (although, of course, the same could be said for men performing male roles). There was also a feeling that women "ritually defiled" (*kegare*) the performance space, especially in plays like *Okina*, considered sacred ceremony, not theatre.

Nevertheless, with the growing number of female amateurs,[24] there was a need for female instructors. The first generation of female noh players, mostly daughters of professional noh performers, began to receive formal training. Even though Tsumura Kimiko (1902–74) was not born into a noh family, she started dancing noh as a child, then studied with leading performers.[25] She debuted in an entire noh play in 1921. Although acting with a group of amateurs in Korea and not on a regular noh stage, her performance was considered taboo-breaking; she was expelled from the Kanze school. Nonetheless, Tsumura established her own noh troupe, Ryokusenkai, a pioneer of women professionals.

The attitude toward women in noh began changing in the 1930s. Activities of women like Tsumura and influential supporters like Kanze Sakon (1895–1939) contributed to this trend. Reviewers wrote positively on women performing noh, widely neglected before. Eventually, headmasters of the five schools of *shite* lead role players agreed on allowing women to perform.[26] This paved the way for the first two women to be admitted to train as shite at the precursor to Tokyo

22 Nose Asaji, *Nōgaku genryūkō* (On the origins of noh) (Tokyo: Iwanami shoten, 1938), 1156–67.
23 Wakita Haruko, *Josei geinō no genryū – kugutsu, kusemai, shirabyōshi* (The origins of women performing) (Tokyo: Kadokawa sensho, 2001), 209–10.
24 Katrina L. Moore, *The Joy of Noh: Embodied Learning and Discipline in Urban Japan* (Albany, NY: SUNY, 2014).
25 Kanamori Atsuko, *Joryū tanjō: nōgakushi Tsumura Kimiko no shōgai* (The birth of women's noh: the life of Tsumura Kimiko) (Tokyo: Hōsei daigaku shuppan kyōkai, 1994).
26 Itō Maki, "Nō to josei: Meiji-ki ni tsuite" (On women and noh in the Meiji period), *Taishō engeki kenkyū* 6 (1997), 71–80.

University of Arts in 1939.[27] Finally, the Nohgaku Performers' Association (Nōgaku Kyōkai) accepted the first three female members in 1948.[28] At present about 20 percent of the approximately 1,230 professional shite are female. In 2004, the first twenty-two women were appointed as "Important Intangible Cultural Property," thereby formally accepted as senior performers.

While all five schools of shite admit women professionals, not all schools of musicians do. Izumi Junko (1969–) and Miyake Tōkurō X (1972–), daughters of the former headmaster of the Izumi school, are the only two professional kyogen actresses. Moreover, women are not allowed to act as *waki* (deuteragonist) or *ai-kyōgen* interludes in noh, since these male roles are almost always performed without masks. Noh continues to be male-dominated. This refers to gender relations in the world of noh as a social community and performing style, deeply influenced by martial art principles.[29] In the aesthetics of noh, the male body is considered the standard, a fact that still represents a challenging obstacle for actresses.

Arguments against professional actresses have hardly changed since the Meiji period. Although women have performed noh since the fifteenth century, they are still considered as breaking with tradition. In fact, their situation largely depends on external factors such as affiliation with a certain school or troupe. Performances in which women and men act together are still exceptional. When an actress plays the lead role, a male chorus generally accompanies. Yet rather than evidencing the integration of women, this reflects the fact that few actresses are available to fill out an all-female chorus. Consequently, opportunities for women to perform are limited. Senior actresses are committed to providing training and performance spaces for women. But focusing on performances with a mainly female cast cannot be considered an ideal method, since that would only confirm existing notions of "women's noh" (*joryū-nō*), a minor deviant of the male norm. To overcome these problems, Uzawa Hisa (1949–), one of the most accomplished actresses in noh today, has trained a female chorus. It accompanies male colleagues in a new performance series that is groundbreaking in its attempt to bridge the gender gap.

BARBARA GEILHORN

above them a Chinese-style room. Thus this single building symbolized the amalgamation of court and samurai culture, and the extension of Yoshimitsu's interest to Chinese culture, as transmitted by Zen Buddhist priests.

These same characteristics can also be found in noh, which flowered during this period. There are many noh plays based on Heian literature depicting the lives of court nobles, richly elaborated with *waka* poetry. There are also plays based on the early Kamakura period depicting legendary battles of famous warriors. Even among the latter, many depict Heike nobles who, although samurai, were closer to nobles in their behavior. Thus Muromachi culture retained many elements of Heian court culture, and yearned for such a past. Interest in Chinese culture is also evidenced in the many plays with Chinese characters or settings.[30] This fascination increased rapidly when the

27 Aoki Ryōko, "Onna ga nō o enjiru to iu koto: Tanimura Kaneko to Yamashina Akiko no baai" (Women performing noh: the case of Tanimura Kaneko and Yamashina Akiko), *Gakugekigaku* 10 (2003), 1–18.
28 Kanamori, *Joryū tanjō*.
29 Omote Akira, "Nōgaku to budō," (Noh and the martial arts), *Gekkan budō* (1976), 110–15.
30 Zeami, *Fūshikaden* (Transmitting the flower through effects and attitudes), trans. Hare, 37.

official exchange between China and Japan, which had ceased in 894, was resumed in 1401.

The mid-Muromachi period plunged into even further political turmoil. The Ōnin War began in 1467, and lasted a decade; Kyoto was burned down. In strong contrast to the golden age of Yoshimitsu, the wavering power of the Ashikaga shogun was completely degraded, followed by the century-long Warring States (*Sengoku*) period. Finally, three powerful individuals emerged later in the sixteenth century to unite the state: Oda Nobunaga (1534–82), Toyotomi Hideyoshi (1537–98), and Tokugawa Ieyasu (1542–1616). Until then, military conflicts and social upheavals continued ceaselessly, as seen in numerous cases of *gekokujō*, "the low overcoming the high," and *ikki*, the local rebellions against the ruling warriors and daimyo by mobs of farmers, local nobles, Buddhist monks, and Shinto priests.

Despite such turmoil, the Muromachi culture continued to deepen, as represented in Higashiyama (eastern hills) culture. Its symbol is Jishō Temple (also known as Ginkakuji, Temple of the Silver Pavilion), which the eighth Ashikaga shogun, Yoshimasa (1436–90), built as his retirement villa in 1482. Compared to more aristocratic and glorious Kitayama culture, the Silver Pavilion, with its originally planned silver foil exterior overlay having never been realized, is said to illustrate the more subdued aesthetic quality that leads to *wabi-sabi* (impermanent, incomplete, flawed beauty), considered one of the quintessential Japanese aesthetic senses. During this era, various such Japanese arts known to this day – the way of tea, flower arrangement, the art of appreciating incense, Zen-style rock gardens, architecture, ink-painting, and linked verse (*renga*) – blossomed and flourished. Wider and deeper dissemination of cultural knowledge occurred, vertically to commoners and horizontally to the countryside, displacing the prior notion of the capital as cultural center. The chaos of the Warring States, collapse of central power, and ruin of Kyoto forced the relocated artists and intellectuals to rely on provincial lords for patronage.

This rich and progressive cultural atmosphere supported noh's amalgam of medieval themes. Symbolic of the reversals of traditional hierarchies, *tesarugaku*, noh performed by semi-professional performers – including those from other arts such as gagaku, which had declined after the fall of imperial and aristocratic power – also flourished in this era, even as sarugaku became firmly rooted among townsmen.[31] Tesarugaku performers were so highly skilled that they often played at performances with the four major Yamato troupes, in the Imperial Palace. Some local lords also patronized them. However, this vogue for tesarugaku came to an end after the Warring

---

31 Hayashiya Tatsusaburō, *Chōshū* (Townsmen) (Tokyo: Chūōkōronsha, 1964).

States period, when the new establishment began the reorganization of noh performers. Tesarugaku performers nevertheless continued to appear, maintaining sarugaku's popular constituency.[32]

Noh and Buddhism

Noh and Buddhism have profound connections on many levels, including sponsorship, philosophy, and plots. Sarugaku was performed at major temples such as the Kōfukuji in Nara. A major function of sarugaku was to collect donations for temples and shrines as *kanjin* subscription performances. Numerous noh plays refer to Buddhist thought, as much of its subject matter derives from various aspects of Buddhism. This is most clearly seen in plays in which a spirit appears to a traveling priest, and through his prayers attains salvation. Buddhism is also evident in plays depicting the suffering of sinners fallen into hell or the world of Asura (warrior purgatory); featuring the Boddhisattva of song and dance; illustrating the efficacy of chanting prayers to the Amitabha Buddha; or directly proselytizing religious doctrine.

Since Buddhism was introduced to Japan in the sixth century, syncretism with indigenous *kami* (the gods) persisted, in the belief that Shinto and Buddhist deities were manifestations of each other. Syncretism can be found in many kami-based noh plays, such as *Yōrō* (Nourishing longevity), where a mountain god sings, "whether kami or Buddha, it is like water and waves [the essence is the same]. To save all living beings, Buddha appears in the guise of the god." Such amalgamations continued until the Meiji Restoration in 1868, when the two were legally separated.

With the rise of warriors at the end of the twelfth century, the court's authority declined, as did imperial-related religious institutions like Buddhist temples established in each province. Consequently, those affiliated with such institutions, including ritual and artistic performers, faced a parallel decline. Noh as entertainment came to dominate over *Okina* performances.

Noh scholar Yokomichi Mario (1916–2012) observed characteristics of the performing arts of the medieval period, which he defined as from the early twelfth to the late sixteenth century:

> Both nobility and public shared the same performing arts, and consequently those arts grew. In the ancient era, performing arts with high artistic quality, such as *gagaku*, were reserved exclusively for court nobles, and in the premodern era the main supporters of performing arts were, without question, the townsperson class. However, the medieval era was an age where it was

---

32 Miyamoto Keizō, *Kamigata nōgakushi no kenkyū* (A study on the history of kamigata noh) (Tokyo: Izumi shoin, 2005).

∾ FOCUS 2.2   Noh's first tour to the West: Venice Biennale

Noh theatre was first performed in the West at the Venice International Theatre Festival "Biennale," August 1954. It featured members of both the Kanze and Kita schools, among them brothers Kanze Hisao and Hideo, who would later become key figures disseminating noh beyond the borders of tradition and abroad.

The Biennale events took place on San Giorgio Island at the Teatro Verde, a large, outdoor Greco-Roman amphitheatre, upon which a wooden structure similar to a noh stage was placed, specifically constructed for the occasion and shipped from Japan.[33] Since noh was frequently associated with classical European theatre, the location was thought to be particularly suitable. The plays performed were *Sagi* (The heron), *Hagoromo* (The robe of feathers), *Aoinoue* (Lady Aoi), *Shōjō* (The wine elf), and *Shakkyō* (The stone bridge), a program demonstrating the great diversity of the noh repertoire, but not including the usual kyogen comedies. Trilingual pamphlets (Italian, English, and French) with photographs and explanations were distributed, with surtitles projected on a small screen next to the stage. Capacity crowds of more than 1,100 spectators attended each day, thanks to generous newspaper coverage; part of the event was even broadcast live on the recently born national television.

Reviews and comments by Italian journalists reflected two types of reception. Newspapers affiliated with right and centre-right parties applauded noh performers for finally showing Western spectators the "authentic" Japanese tradition. Noh was praised for being deeply spiritual, following the common belief that the genre was high art reserved for a chosen audience. In contrast, newspapers associated with the Communist and Socialist parties harshly criticized it for being the product of an isolated and spiritually impoverished country whose only positive qualities were in fact imported from China. Noh was considered a feudal relic, one on which Japanese society was still based, associated with poet Ezra Pound, who had translated noh, and supported Mussolini's fascist regime. Frequent references to Buddhism and Shinto were considered evidence of a regressive civilization where church and state were still united, and actors' ritualistic gestures regarded as unnecessary, or even laughable.

A detailed account of the performance was left by Hideo, who remembered the tour as a success: the echo of the open-air stage and blue sky above reminded him of how noh might have looked at the time of Zeami.[34]

DIEGO PELLECCHIA

possible for the cloistered emperor Go-Shirakawa [1127–92], the highest authority in the land, to invite lowly female performers to the court to receive instruction on *imayō* [lit. contemporary style] songs, and shogun Yoshimitsu … could create a scandal by making a child of a humble noh performer [Zeami] a close attendant. Thus one can often observe in performing arts of the medieval period the refractions where art forms born in lower social strata rise in artistic quality and popularity through close proximity to the high, and then once again return to the public domain.[35]

33 Partial sponsorship came from the Venice municipality as part of the Marco Polo 700th anniversary, and from the Italian government.

34 Kanze Hideo, "Kaigai kōen de kanjita koto: 1954 nen no Benechia engeki matsuri hoka" (Impressions of performances abroad: the 1954 Venice Theatre Festival and others), in Nishino Haruo (ed.), *Gaikokujin no nōgaku kenkyū* (Foreign research on noh theatre) (Tokyo: Hōsei daigaku kokusai nihongaku kenkyū sentā, 2005), 141–53.

35 Yokomichi Mario, "Chūsei no ongaku" (Music of the medieval period), *Nihon no ongaku: rekishi to riron* (Japanese music: its history and theory) (Tokyo: Kokuritsu gekijō, 1974), 21.

This continual percolation and distillation of the culture – martial yet aristocratic, dynamic yet subdued, free yet austere – nurtured noh from infancy in the medieval period.

Early formation of noh: Kan'ami and Zeami

Kan'ami (original name, Kiyotsugu, 1333–84) was the first head of a troupe that performed an entertaining style of noh under the umbrella of Yūzaki, one of four troupes performing *Okina* in Yamato (Nara). From early in his career, Kan'ami made efforts to advance closer to Kyoto, the political center; in around 1375, he performed with his 12-year-old son at Kyoto's Imagumano Shrine in the presence of the third Ashikaga shogun, Yoshimitsu. Subsequently, with the shogun's patronage, Kan'ami climbed the ladder as prince of the entertainment world. This performance was epoch-making in the historical transformation of sarugaku troupes, for Kan'ami performed the role of *Okina*, thereby prompting independence of noh performing groups from the dominant *Okina* troupe.

Kan'ami was known for his broad range of artistic skills, but especially for imitation (*monomane*) and verbal amusement (*giri*), and the Yamato sarugaku specialty of demon (*oni*) roles. He was also known for his talent in more refined noh centering on song and dance. He authored *Sotoba Komachi* (Stupa Komachi), demonstrating his artistic technique of combining conversation-based dramatic development with elements of song and dance drawn from the rhythmic vitality of the then popular *kusemai*.

When Kan'ami brought young Zeami to perform in Kyoto, he received great favor from Yoshimitsu. A decade after that, Kan'ami passed away and Zeami succeeded as head of the Kanze troupe. Receiving Yoshimitsu's patronage meant that Kan'ami and Zeami were exploring support for their art from secular authorities.

In a secret transmission, *Fūshikaden*, Zeami evoked *two* origin myths for Noh – in Ame-no-Uzume's dance before the myriad deities to draw the Sun Goddess out of the heavenly rock-cave (see Focus 1.1), and also in the sixty-six entertainments devised by the Buddha as a skillful means to enlighten audiences at varying levels of knowledge.[36] In so doing he was not only recognizing his art's shamanic and religious origins, both in Japan and in India, but also elevating his own theatre company from its lowly position. Yoshimitsu's patronage helped legitimize samurai power within the minds of imperial Kyoto's aristocratic circles, for noh was at the epicenter of a political process of display. It demonstrated that newly arrived samurai culture could absorb the best elements of court and popular culture yet retain a distinctively martial art form.

36 Zeami, *Performance Notes*, trans. Hare, 47.

Zeami was an unsurpassed noh playwright, creating many plays rich in literary quality, original but referencing sources in literature and legend. By choosing a figure suitable for song and dance as protagonist, and structuring the story within the dream of a traveling priest, Zeami perfected mugen (phantasmal) noh. He also revised old plays, and left twenty-one practical and secret treatises (see pp. 366–8, 370–1 and Chapter 19). Zeami adopted concepts from other performing arts and literature in his playwriting, acting techniques, and theorizing about noh. He uses the term "jo-ha-kyū," a term derived from gagaku expressing the sense of tempo: introduction, development, conclusion. His concept also links to *renga* (linked verse) poetry, comparing the climactic *kyū* to *ageku* (the last verse). His term "yūgen" (mysterious elegance) comes from waka poetry; from gagaku and shōmyō chanting, he adopts the musical scale *ryo-ritsu* that applied to noh vocal methods: "*Ryo* is the voice of joy, the voice of breath exhaled. *Ritsu* is the voice of sadness, the voice of breath inhaled."[37]

After Zeami

After Zeami's passing, On'ami and Zenchiku were the two leading figures in the noh world. The Komparu (former Enman'i) troupe head, Zenchiku (1405–70?), married Zeami's daughter, and studied under Zeami, who held high hopes for him. Zeami transmitted his treatises on noh, the *Rikugi* (Six models) and *Shūgyokutokka* (Pick up a jewel and take the flower in hand) to Zenchiku, who also wrote his own theoretical treatises, including *Rokurin ichironoki* (A record of six rings and one dew-drop) and *Kabuzuinōki* (A record on the essence of song and dance). These develop far more philosophical concepts, compared with Zeami's practical advice. Many of his plays, such as *Nonomiya* (The shrine in the fields), combine song and dance with a tranquil atmosphere.

The next generation included Kanze Nobumitsu (1450–1516), Konparu Zenpō (1454–1517), and Kanze Nagatoshi (1488–1541). They wrote popular plays rich with spectacle, featuring many characters, employing dramatic scenes involving swordfights, boat-rides, or other exotic, foreign elements. Nobumitsu, the seventh son of On'ami, is credited with *Funa Benkei* (Benkei in a boat), *Momijigari* (Autumn foliage viewing); Zenpō, a grandson of Zenchiku, with *Ikkaku sennin* (One-horned hermit); and Nagatoshi, Nobumitsu's son, with *Ōyashiro* (The great shrine). These were all written during Kyoto's period of fiery tribulations noted above, suggesting that noh performers tried to survive by performing plays that could be enjoyed not only by sophisticated people in the capital, but also by provincials. Miyamasu, another contemporary noh performer, contributed popular plays including *Eboshiori* (Hat-maker) and *Kurama-tengu* (Long-nosed goblin of Kurama).

37 Zeami, *Ongyoku kuden* (Oral instruction on singing), trans. Hare, 85.

Although new plays were created after Nagatoshi's death in the mid-sixteenth century, few remain in the current regular repertoire; noh had already begun its transformation into a classic genre.

Samurai's ceremonial performance

Noh and kyogen's long continuous history can be attributed first to the genius of father and son Kan'ami and Zeami, and secondly to protection by statesmen. Through the patronage of Yoshimitsu, the third Muromachi shogun, Kan'ami and Zeami were able to establish themselves as top performers, and Zeami to further develop the complex, elegant poetry and music esteemed by the aspiring warrior class. Later shoguns protected and encouraged noh as evidence of their culture and power.

Toyotomi Hideyoshi (1537–98) is the general who brought an end to the Warring States period. Training in noh from the advanced age of 57, he became so enamored that he held performances in the Imperial Palace. Hideyoshi formulated policies to protect noh and kyogen, giving the four troupes of Yamato sarugaku (Kanze, Hōshō, Komparu, Kongō) their own dominions and rice allotments, and boosting their ranks by incorporating noh performers of other genealogies. Not shy about either his martial or his artistic abilities, he also ordered the creation of new noh plays depicting his own achievements, in which he starred.

The first shogun of the Edo period (1603–1868), Tokugawa Ieyasu (1543–1616), followed Hideyoshi's lead. Ieyasu had practiced noh since a young age. The second shogun Hidetada (1579–1632) also ensured that noh was officially protected, and from the time of the third shogun, Iemitsu (1604–51), strict regulations were put into place. During the reign of the fourth shogun, Ietsuna (1641–1680), noh was already transforming into the warrior-led government's *shikigaku* (式楽, ceremonial theatrical form).

Kita Shichidayū (1586–1653) was originally an amateur noh performer who later joined the Kongō troupe and even presided as its head. Hidetada favored Kita's fresh, heroic artistic style, so he was granted permission to found the Kita-za (troupe), joining the existing four troupes.

The reign of the fifth Tokugawa shogun, Tsunayoshi (1646–1709), coincided with the culturally prosperous Genroku era (1688–1707). As illustrated by his enforcement of the edict forbidding cruelty to living creatures, his reign was unpopular and financially unsuccessful. However, Tsunayoshi's influence on noh is significant. He made approximately a hundred noh performers resign from their positions and gave them the samurai rank of *rōkaban* (serving inside the shogunate), although their actual duties were to assist at his private noh performances. This is a significant number, even considering that some had previously served provincial lords in the capital, since the total number of noh performers retained by the shogunate in the mid-seventeenth century was around 350.[38]

In 1686, Kita Shichidayū and his son were banished, his costumes and household effects confiscated, his estate given to the head of Hōshō, and Kita performers were allotted to four other troupes.[39] Such heavy-handed control by the authorities placed artists in precarious positions, but also indicates noh's importance to the governmental bureaucracy as ceremonial entertainment.

Yet even as he was punishing players, Tsunayoshi also revived several rarely performed or earlier abolished plays, including *Utaura* (Divination by poetry), *Ōharagokō* (An imperial visit to Ohara), and *Semimaru*, plays included today in the regular repertoire. The sixth shogun, Ienobu (1663–1712), also indulged himself in noh, and he too reinstated approximately ninety plays that had been performed only rarely, including *Kinuta* (The fulling block), *Kochō* (Butterfly), and *Yoroboshi* (Tottering blind beggar), all still in the regular repertoire. Feudal lords who enjoyed noh also increased in number, as the art form spread through various clans, a natural extension of shogunal interest. Continuing their newfound hobbies in their home-lands, they also demonstrated their cultural awareness. As a result, from the late seventeenth to early eighteenth century noh flourished nationwide. Edo (Tokyo) was where the five troupes served, but Kyoto remained also a center of noh, having close to 300 noh performers in 1687, comparable to Edo.[40]

Partly as a reaction to the perceived excessive indulgence in noh by successive shoguns, the eighth shogun, Yoshimune (1684–1751), started a reform movement. In 1721, heads of all troupes and accompanying waki, musicians, and kyogen groups were ordered to submit detailed descriptions of the histories of their art, genealogy of each family line, authors of plays, received gifts, costumes and masks, and both their active and dormant repertoire. In all, thirty-eight families submitted these documents, the oldest record of collected genealogies. Record-keeping of noh performances at the Edo castle started the same year. Also in 1726, Yoshimune established the post of teaching noh to the shogun or his heir, with the head of Kanze ordered to hold the position.[41] It probably brought restraint and clarified the responsibilities of each party, shogun and tutor, since noh troupes were under the authority of a high shogunal official.

---

38 Omote Akira and Amano Fumio, "Meireki 3-nen nō yakusha-tsuke," (1657 list of noh performers) (1987), 100–5.
39 They were eventually forgiven, with the condition that the father serve as *rōkaban*, and the young son succeed as fourth head. *Ibid.* 113–14.
40 *Ibid.* 117–21.   41 *Ibid.* 125–6.

ꙮ FOCUS 2.3   Kanze Hisao: renaissance actor

Kanze Hisao (1925–78) was an acclaimed noh performer, essayist, and inter-genre collaborator. He was born in Tokyo, eldest son of Kanze Tetsunojō VII (Gasetsu, 1898–1988), hereditary head of an important collateral line of the Kanze school. Never content to rest on that pedigree, Hisao insisted that noh's future depended on "training and study rather than on system or lineage."[42]

As a young man, the tumultuous changes of the postwar years caused him much soul-searching. He realized that old institutional hierarchies could endanger noh from within. He was equally concerned about Japanese postwar audiences, who showed a growing penchant for dismissing traditional arts as irrelevant or outdated. He devoted his life to negotiating such obstacles in order to secure a place for noh as a viable form of contemporary theatre, primarily through his performances, but also through essays and interviews, which fill four volumes.

Hisao turned for inspiration to the critical writings of his ancestor, actor, theorist, and playwright Zeami Motokiyo (1363?–1443?). He saw Zeami's ideas as a way around the conservative orthodoxy of the modern *iemoto* "school" system, whose members mostly ignored Zeami's transmissions. Participating in the Society for Research on Zeami's Secret Transmissions in the 1950s, Hisao forged lasting affiliations with prominent noh scholars. He "was surprised at the vital energy of noh in its seminal period," wanting to recapture that "creative spirit."[43] As a performer, Hisao's technical skill and beauty of form were peerless. He also was known for the freshness of his interpretations, grounded in critical rethinking of libretti.

At the invitation of French stage director Jean-Louis Barrault (1910–94), in 1962 Hisao spent six months based at Théâtre de l'Odéon. While studying the Paris theatre scene, he observed the place noh occupied among global stage arts. Over the years, he had contact with other European theatre figures such as director Jerzy Grotowski (1933–99) and playwright Eugène Ionesco (1909–94).

Hisao's artistic contributions include an unparalleled level of commitment to both high-caliber and innovative noh productions staged with his troupe, Noh Laboratory Theatre Tessenkai, and to experimental productions with stage actors, dramatists, composers, musicians, and directors, including director Takechi Tetsuji (1912–88), composers Takemitsu Tohru (1930–96) and Yuasa Jōji (1929–), actress Shiraishi Kayoko (1941–), and director Suzuki Tadashi (1939–). Hisao collaborated broadly in mixed-genre, collaborative productions ranging from modern dramas to classical Greek tragedies, including Dionysus in Suzuki's acclaimed 1978 *The Bacchae*.

When Hisao died prematurely in 1978, his brothers Hideo (1927–2007) and Shizuo (Tetsunojō VIII; 1931–2000) maintained their shared commitment to promoting noh as contemporary theatre. Shizuo became head of Tessenkai in 1980 and continued its tradition of innovative performances. Active as a noh and avant-garde theatre performer, Hideo also had a distinguished career directing and performing in experimental noh and fusion productions.

SHELLEY FENNO QUINN

These new regulations ushered in equality and stability. Yet as noh and kyogen became the shogunate's official ceremonial theatrical forms, monitoring of their repertoire diminished the opportunity to create new plays.

---

42 Kanze Hisao, "Nō to watashi" (Noh and I), in *Kokoro yori kokoro ni tsutauru hana* (The flower passed from heart to heart) (Tokyo: Hakusuisha, 1979), 234.
43 *Ibid.* 238.

Thus repeated performance of established plays became the norm, thereby stimulating development of highly codified methods of executing performance and music. Yet demand for new and unusual performances and musical delivery produced variations, contrived within the traditional repertoire. Alternative versions (*kogaki*) included differences in selection of masks, costumes or stage props, inclusion of particular characters or dances, changes to the libretti, musical accompaniment, or even the play structure. Many became codified as sanctioned versions still used today.

In the rather calm noh world of the latter half of the Edo period, the fifteenth head of Kanze, Motoakira (1722–74), advanced some dynamic reforms, including revisions of texts, adoption of new stage directions, and changes in kyogen interludes. Although the changes were reversed after his death, many of the performance variations he incorporated were retained, leaving the Kanze troupe the most kogaki variations today.

By the end of the Edo period, the performance duration for a noh play was twice that of the Muromachi period,[44] the result of a gradual transformation of noh from an art participated in by a wide range of social strata to a ceremonial art exclusive to the samurai. During the Tokugawa peace of 250 years, commoners rarely had the chance to see it, except for *machiiri* (town entry) noh, held for the Edo townsmen once or twice per year. On these occasions, they were allowed inside the property of Edo castle to view the first day performance of the official noh at the outside stage from *shirasu*, the pebble garden between stage and samurai spectators. *Kanjin* (subscription) noh, used to collect donations for reconstruction of shrines and temples, in the Edo period mainly became charity events for troupe heads, and each town was allotted a mandatory share in the expenses. In Kyoto and Osaka often noh performers other than the head asked for permission to perform out of financial hardship. *Tsuji* (crossing) noh, held at open spaces such as shrine and temple precincts by tesarugaku amateur noh performers, were also frequent in major cities. Apparently their high skills threatened the performers of the five troupes, who asked iemoto headmasters in Edo to forbid their activities. Probably such pressures caused their eventual extinction in the early modern period.[45]

If performance itself was restricted to samurai, utai (singing) was certainly in vogue throughout the Edo populace. As publishing prospered from the beginning of the Edo period, various *utaibon* (songbooks) were sold; more than 300 kinds existed for the Kanze style alone.[46] Professional utai

44 *Ibid.* 136.   45 *Ibid.* 154–5.
46 "Utai kō" (Investigation of utai), in Omote Akira, *Nōgakushi shinkō* I (New insights into noh performers I) (Tokyo: Wanya shoten, 1979); Takemoto Mikio, "Edo jidai no shomin to nō" (Commoners of the Edo period and noh), in Yokohama Noh Theatre (ed.), *Nōgakushi jikenbo* (Anecdotes in noh history) (Tokyo: Iwanami, 2000), 139–61.

instructors formed utai training organizations in most urban areas. *Ko-utai* (singing passages from plays) were especially popular, included in children's textbooks used at *terakoya*, private schools that taught townsmen reading, writing, and abacus. As utai popularity increased, so did *shimai* dance. Noh was fortunate to attract such hobbyists, spread widely both generationally and geographically, who would later provide vital support and energy as noh groped to reorient itself after samurai patronage disappeared with the shogunate's fall.

The Meiji Restoration and beyond

With the Meiji Restoration in 1868, noh faced the worst of three historical crises (the other two being the Ōnin War with the subsequent Warring State period [1467–1572], and World War II). With the dissolution of the shogunate, noh professionals lost the remuneration they had received from the Tokugawa shogunate and daimyo for over 250 years, not only stripping them of an immediate source of income, but also threatening the very future of their art. No longer assured of artistic patronage, many were forced to abandon their profession altogether. By the middle of the first decade of the Meiji era (1868–1912), noh performers were struggling to survive. Masks and costumes were sold, many to overseas museums and collectors. Altogether nine schools of waki, music ensemble, and kyogen were extinguished, and eleven schools either interrupted their iemoto lineage or vanished altogether.[47]

A new age demanding new patrons

This dark period for noh professionals coincided with the start of Japan's modernization process, as the nation struggled to catch up with imperial Western powers and establish itself as an influential member of international society with a solid cultural heritage. Several great performers with support from prominent figures of Meiji society grappled with ways to reorient noh. Umewaka Minoru (1828–1909), fifty-second head of the Umewaka school, arguably made the foremost contribution toward stability at this most fragile juncture. His efforts created a whirlpool-like force that attracted interest and support from prominent members of the new Meiji society. The list of roughly 1,000 amateur disciples, including many of Meiji's most celebrated and powerful political, cultural, and economic elites, also testifies to his

---

47 Kobayashi Seki, "The Meiji Restoration and noh-kyogen," *Journal of the Noh Research Archives* 23 (2011), 19–20.

charisma.[48] Distinguished foreign students included Edward Morse (1838–1925) and Ernest Fenollosa (1853–1906), who would go on to make great contributions to Western understanding of Japanese arts and culture.

Iwakura Tomomi (1825–83), a court noble and influential politician, was another visionary who exerted considerable effort to restore noh. In 1871, he led the Iwakura Mission, a delegation of representatives of the new government, on a two-year grand tour of advanced Western countries. Kume Kunitake (1839–1931), who served as Iwakura's Assistant Secretary for the Study of Foreign History, recorded: "Seeing those grand opera houses in Europe, I felt acutely the need for a [Japanese] national entertainment … firmly rooted in the heart of our national identity."[49] After the delegation's return, Kume supported Iwakura in recognizing the value of noh, contributing greatly to its protection and promotion. They eventually succeeded in shifting noh's identity from a samurai ceremonial art to a national one, patronized by the new government and imperial family.

In 1876, Iwakura organized a *tenran-nō* (noh performance for the Emperor) at his residence in the current outer gardens of the Imperial Palace in Tokyo. Attended by members of the imperial court, aristocrats, and government figures, it featured performers still practicing in Tokyo. Significantly, it also included non-professional but high-ranking officials among the performers. Hōshō Kurō (1837–1917), sixteenth school head, was there persuaded by Minoru to return to the noh world. Minoru and Kurō, along with Sakurama Banma (1835–1917), a Komparu performer from the Kumamoto clan who moved to Tokyo in 1879, were known as the three Meiji noh masters.

Performances were arranged to mark visits by foreign dignitaries; over twenty were given during the Meiji period, including for the Duke of Edinburgh (1869), a Russian prince (1872), the King of Hawai'i (1881), opera singer Minnie Hauk (1894), Qing imperial family member Dai Zhen (1902), and Dr. Robert Koch of Germany (1908). One performance was held at Iwakura's residence in 1879 in honor of the recently retired President Ulysses S. Grant (1822–85), who reportedly urged the art's preservation.

The establishment of the Nōgakusha (Noh and Kyogen Society) for protection and promotion of nōgaku in 1881 culminated efforts of Meiji advocates. The term nōgaku henceforth became the generic term for both noh and kyogen, replacing the less-respectful sarugaku, written with characters 猿楽, meaning "monkey entertainments." The Shiba Nōgakudō (Shiba Noh

---

48 The first Umewaka Minoru Study Group, "An annotated directory of the first Umewaka Minoru's amateur disciples, 1–5," *Journal of the Noh Research Archives* 15–19 (2004–8).

49 Ikenouchi Nobuyoshi, *Nōgaku seisui ki: Tokyo no nō* (The rise and fall of the noh drama: noh in Tokyo) (Tokyo: Shunjūsha, 1926), 42. Trans. Kagaya.

Theatre) was completed in the same year within a public park, with the Nōgakusha as its main administrative body.[50] Prior to this, the major roofed noh stages were located outdoors within the grounds of shogunal or feudal lords' residences or shrine and temple precincts. The Shiba Noh Theatre was the first built with its own indoor auditorium (*kensho*).[51] Each school constructed its own indoor stage during the next decade. This combination of roofed stage and auditorium in one building became the established style.

A dispute involving the Umewaka family exemplifies tensions between hereditary iemoto headmasters and ambitious and popular branch families. In early Meiji the twenty-second head of Kanze, Kiyotaka (1837–88), moved with the Tokugawa head to Shizuoka. The lone fort of Kanze in Tokyo was held by the Umewaka family, which had originally played tsure accompanying roles in the Kanze shite school, and the fifth Tetsunojō, Kōsetsu (1843–1911), a Kanze branch family. Through marriages, both families' ties were strengthened. Although Kiyotaka eventually returned to Tokyo in 1875, Minoru, having amassed great influence in the Meiji noh world, began issuing licenses to disciples, violating the prerogative exclusive to the school head. However in 1921, as Kanze gradually regained prestige, the twenty-fourth head, Motoshige (1895–1939), excommunicated the Umewaka family. Although the Umewaka established its own school, this resulted in excommunication from the noh world, which strictly prohibited, on pain of blacklisting, waki, musicians, and kyogen players from performing for Umewaka. Umewaka was forced to use actors in its own school or amateurs to perform those roles. The situation was only resolved in 1954, when the Umewaka branch officially returned to Kanze school, yet with permission to continue to issue its own utaibon libretti.

In the twentieth century, nōgaku not only continued to prosper, but also became the focus of genuine academic study for the first time. Ikenouchi Nobuyoshi (1858–1934)[52] moved to Tokyo from Ehime prefecture, determined to promote nōgaku, and launched *Nōgaku* magazine. In 1904, together with Takata Sanae (1860–1938), later the first president of Waseda University, he started the noh literature research group, leading to the discovery and publication of Zeami's *Sarugaku dangi* (Talks on sarugaku) in 1907 by historian Yoshida Tōgo (1864–1918), followed the next year by *Zeami jūrokubushū* (Zeami's sixteen secret transmissions). The publication of these

---

50 Erected in Shiba Park, an entertainment area in Tokyo, it was moved to Yasukuni Shrine in 1903.
51 The stage and auditorium were under separate roofs until joined into one building in 1897. *Nōgaku daijiten* (2012), 682–3.
52 *Ibid.* 31–2.

texts, available previously only within families or through direct transmission to a single heir, marked a significant point of departure for noh research.

Other measures initiated by Ikenouchi included the movement to cultivate hayashi musicians and raise their performance fees, inaugurating the now common monthly evening performances, and even student discounts. Following his proposal for protection of traditional Japanese music to the House of Representatives, a noh music course was established in 1912 at the Tokyo Music School. Unlike conventional methods of individual training under one's master (still the mainstream approach today), such an institutional curriculum for traditional arts was revolutionary.

Post-World War II recovery and diversification

Following World War II, nōgaku faced its third historical crisis. Although the country was in ruins after Japan's defeat in August 1945, its reconstruction was swift. Symbolic of the noh world's resilience was the Somei Noh Theatre (one of three in Tokyo that had survived the fire bombings) (see Chapter 8). A "Martial Noh" was held there on 14 August, one day before the surrender, and then a "Peace and Reconstruction Noh" on 16 September, as the first performance of the Nōgaku Kyōkai (the Noh Performers' Association).

With the proclamation of the Law for Protection of Cultural Properties in 1950, the system to protect the nation's tangible and intangible cultural properties was put into effect. In 1955 three noh performers were among the first to be designated Preservers of Important Intangible Cultural Properties (Living National Treasures) by the Ministry of Education, Science and Culture (since 2001, Ministry of Education, Culture, Sports, Science, and Technology). In 1957, with the designation of the entire art form nōgaku as an Important Intangible Cultural Property, the Nihon Nōgakukai (Japan Noh Association) was formed from highly skilled performers with over twenty-five years' experience as designated by the Agency for Cultural Affairs.[53] In the immediate postwar era, efforts of performers to further develop their art, and increased audience support and students, as well as systemized state support, not only enabled recovery, but ushered in noh's most popular and solid period of modern history.

In 1983, the Kokuritsu Nōgakudō (National Noh Theatre, hereafter NNT) opened as a venue available to all schools. Conventionally, fans of noh consist of amateur disciples learning noh chant, dance, or music, but NNT offered increased opportunities for general audiences to attend performances. Tickets are reasonably priced compared to private noh theatres. Detailed

53 *Ibid.* 670.

∾ FOCUS 2.4　　New and revived plays

Most noh and kyogen plays performed today are extant from the repertoire established in the Edo period (1603–1868). On the other hand, *shinsaku* (newly created) noh refers to over 300 plays written after the Meiji Restoration (1868–) by various noh performers and researchers, playwrights, poets, and dilettantes. Some have only been published, while others have been performed, yet a few have entered the regular repertoire, including *Yumedono* (Hall of dreams, premiered in 1940) by the fifteenth Kita Minoru (1900–86) and Toki Zenmaro (1885–1980), a poet and scholar of Japanese literature. New plays reflect the social climate as represented in those plays of Meiji nationalism, celebration of the accession of the Taishō Emperor in 1912, or instigation of war in the early 1930s. More recently, contemporary issues – brain death and organ transplants, a Korean war-widow and her husband who died of forced labor in a coalmine in Japan, Einstein's theory of relativity and its relevance to humankind, or an atomic bomb memorial – have been dealt with by Tada Tomio (1934–2010), a doctor of immunology.[54]

In addition to new plays created within existing noh methods – language, musical composition, structure, and performance styles – experimental new works have appeared since the 1950s, including those based on foreign or modern Japanese literature and themes, or new renderings of existing themes, such as *Yume-no-ukihashi* (Floating bridge of dreams, 2002) by Buddhist nun and writer Setouchi Jakuchō (1922–), adapted from her novel based on *The Tale of Genji*. The 56th Umewaka Rokurō (1948–, now Gensho) created and performed numerous new noh including those on Hosokawa Garasha, a sixteenth-century female Christian convert;

Kūkai (774–835), founder of Shingon Buddhism; *Giselle*, after the ballet; *Gurasu no kamen* (Glass mask), a popular *shōjo* (young female) manga by Suzue Miuchi (1951–); and *Shiranui* (Phosphorescence) concerning industrial contamination of the ocean and Minamata Disease by novelist-poet Ishimure Michiko (1927–). English noh created within the boundaries of traditional noh music and performance has recently also explored possibilities of new plays, especially in cultivation of new themes and audiences.

Plays revived after a period of dormancy are called *fukkyoku* (revivals). Although a recurrent historic practice, revivals have particularly thrived since the 1950s, with over a hundred attempts. Often a school will revive a play lost from its own repertoire, but still performed by a rival school, easily supported by waki, musicians, and kyogen, familiar with other schools' versions. In general, revivals are done based on the contemporary skills of producer-performers, who devise their own stage choreography. However, revivals may also follow a classical style when the play was performed in the past, based on old performers' libretto notations, and through collaboration between the performer and scholars, especially in the postwar era when noh research has developed remarkably. The application of alternative classic stage directions on regular repertoire plays may result in significantly altered performances, which are also referred to as revivals. Like new plays, revivals are creative activities done with contemporary knowledge, exploring past, present, and future potential.

SHINKO KAGAYA AND MIURA HIROKO

54　Tada Tomio, *Nō no naka no nōbutai* (A noh stage in the brain) (Tokyo: Shinchōsha, 2001).

program notes are distributed. In addition to the training program for musicians, waki, and kyogen players, the NNT also contains a research library, including video documentation of programs, and sponsors performances for children and new audiences, as well as commissioning newly created noh and kyogen plays.

In 2006, the NNT installed a subtitling system, in both Japanese and English, for major performances. While contributing to the further promotion of noh, this also reflects an increase in the number of spectators without familiarity with Japanese classics, symbolizing the complicated issue of how to bridge the distance between historical texts and the contemporary world. An earphone guide system has also been used at many performances, including at outside *takigi* (torchlit fire) noh. Although popular with new audiences, some issues linger, as both audience and performers complain about the difficulty of drawing the audience's concentration solely to performance because of intrusive technological mediation.

The future of noh

Noh professionals and promoters attempt a diverse array of marketing and promotional schemes to lure newcomers and maintain regular theatregoers, including pre-show lectures, lecture-demonstrations, and experiential workshops. Annual takigi (torchlit) noh – over 150 performances per year at their peak in the 1990s – can often lure thousands to purpose-built stages in open-air spaces. Student discounts are substantial. Professionally designed leaflets attract spectators, and copious program notes encourage appreciation.

Even so, the future cannot be considered bright. The rapidly declining birth rate in Japan has affected the nōgaku world, too, bringing problems both internal (a shortage of successors) and external (a decrease in the number of spectators, with youth the minority). And among roughly 1,300 professional nōgaku performers, there are only about fifty in their twenties.[55] The most serious issue is the paucity of performers who can devote themselves exclusively to stage activities, since most performers must rely on teaching amateur disciples to earn their livelihood. Yet attaining supreme artistic skills and quality, including the understanding of fine and complicated literary pieces, requires lifetime devotion.

---

55 Nishino Haruo, "Gakugeki to gakugeki no genjō o kangaeru: nō kyōgen bunraku, kabuki" (Considering the current situation of musical theatre: noh, kyogen, bunraku, kabuki) *Gakugekigaku* (Musical Theatre Studies) 20 (March 2013), 49.

In the sustenance of the art of noh, this dilemma, between teaching and training, has long existed. However, because of rapid changes in Japanese society, the current situation seems to present the severest modern challenge. The nōgaku world, which has repeatedly survived by transforming itself, could be at yet another turning point. It has to grapple seriously with new methods and their potential to sustain and further develop artistic standards for the future, and to cultivate new generations of performers and audiences.

References and further reading

Bethe, Monica, and Karen Brazell. *Dance in the Nō Theater*, 3 vols., Cornell University East Asia Papers 29 (Ithaca, NY: Cornell China–Japan Program, 1982)

Brandon, James R. (ed.). *Nō and Kyōgen in the Contemporary World* (Honolulu: University of Hawai'i Press, 1997)

Brazell, Karen (ed.). *Twelve Plays of the Noh and Kyōgen Theaters* (Ithaca, NY: Cornell East Asia Series, 1988)

Goff, Janet. *Noh Drama and* The Tale of Genji: *The Art of Allusion in Fifteen Classical Plays* (Princeton, NJ: Princeton University Press, 1991)

Groemer, Gerald. "Nō at the crossroads: commoner performance during the Edo period," *ATJ* 15.1 (1998), 117–41

Hoff, Frank, and Willi Flindt (ed. and trans.). "The life structure of noh: an English version of Yokomichi Mario's analysis of the structure of noh," excerpt from *Concerned Theatre Japan* 2–4 (1973–4)

Keene, Donald. *Nō: The Classical Theatre of Japan* (rev. paperback edn.) (Tokyo: Kodansha International, 1973)

(ed.). *Twenty Plays of the Nō Theatre* (New York: Columbia University Press, 1970)

Kobayashi Seki, Nishi Tetsuo, and Hata Hisashi (eds.). *Nōgaku daijiten* (Great dictionary of *nōgaku*) (Tokyo: Chikuma shobo, 2012)

Komparu, Kunio. *The Noh Theater: Principles and Perspectives*, trans. rev. and exp. edn. Jane Corddry and Stephen Comee (New York: Weatherhill, 1983)

LaFleur, William R. *The Karma of Words: Buddhism and the Literary Arts in Medieval Japan* (Berkeley: University of California Press, 1986)

Lim Beng Choo. *Another Stage: Kanze Nobumitsu and the Late Muromachi Noh Theater* (Ithaca, NY: Cornell University East Asia Series, 2012)

Looser, Thomas D. *Visioning Eternity: Aesthetics Politics and History in the Early Modern Noh Theatre*, Cornell East Asia Series 138 (Ithaca, NY: Cornell University East Asia Program, 2008)

Nakamura, Yasuo. *Noh: The Classical Theatre*, Performing Arts of Japan IV (New York and Tokyo: Weatherhill, 1971)

O'Neill, Patrick G. *Early Nō Drama: Its Background, Character and Development 1300–1450* (London: Lund Humphries, 1958)

Scholz-Cionca, Stanca, and Christopher Balme (eds.). *Noh Theatre Transversal* (Munich: Ludicium, 2008)

Tyler, Royall (ed. and trans.). *Japanese Nō Dramas* (London: Penguin, 1992)

Yasuda, Kenneth K. *Masterworks of the Nō Theater* (Bloomington: Indiana University Press, 1989)

WEBSITES AND DVDS

Japan Arts Council, "An introduction to noh and kyogen," www2.ntj.jac.go.jp/unesco/noh/en

Nogami Memorial Noh Theatre Research Institute of Hosei University, www9.i.hosei.ac.jp/~nohken/

Premodern Japanese Studies (PMJS), "Noh translations: noh plays in alphabetical order of the Japanese titles," www.meijigakuin.ac.jp/~pmjs/biblio/noh-trans.html

The noh.com, ed. Akira Kinoshita, Caliber Cast Ltd., www.the-noh.com

The National Noh Theatre, www2.ntj.jac.go.jp/unesco/noh/en/

JAANUS (Japanese Art and Architecture Net Users System), "noumen," www.aisf.or.jp/~jaanus/deta/n/noumen.htm

This is Noh/Izutsu (DVD), Kyoto Noh Association (Insight Media), 2000

SPOTLIGHT 2.1 NOH STAGE

Amano Fumio. *Gendai nōgaku kōza* (Contemporary noh lectures) (Osaka: Osaka University Press, 1984)

FOCUS 2.1 KUROKAWA NOH

Baba Akiko, Masuda Shōzō, and Otani Jun, *Kurokawa nō no sekai* (The world of Kurokawa noh) (Tokyo: Heibonsha, 1985)

Grossmann, Eike. *Kurokawa Nō: Shaping the Image and Perception of Japan's Folk Traditions, Performing Arts and Rural Tourism* (Folkstone: Global Oriental, 2013)

Kelly, William K. "Japanese no-noh: the crosstalk of public culture in a rural festivity," *Public Culture* 2:2 (1990), 65–81

Martzel, Gérard. *La fête d'Ogi et le noh de Kurokawa* (Paris: Publications orientalistes de France, 1982)

Sakurai Akio. *Kurokawa nō to kōgyō* (Kurokawa noh and performances) (Tokyo: Dōseisha, 2003)

Yokomichi Mario (ed.). *Kurokawa nō* (Tokyo: Heibonsha, 1967)

SPOTLIGHT 2.2 ZEAMI: NOH'S FOUNDING GENIUS

De Poorter, Erika. *Zeami's Talks on Sarugaku: An Annotated Translation of the Sarugaku dangi* (Amsterdam: J. C. Gieben, 1986)

Omote Akira. *Nōgakushi shinkō* (New research on noh history), vol. I (Tokyo: Wan'ya shoten, 1979)

Omote Akira and Amano Fumio. *Nōgaku no rekishi* (History of noh-kyogen), *Iwanami kōza nō kyōgen* (Iwanami course on noh-kyogen), vol. I (Tokyo: Iwanami, 1987)

Omote Akira and Katō Shūichi (eds.). *Zeami, Zenchiku. Gei no shisō, michi no shisō*, vol. I: *Nihon shisō taikei shinsōhan* (Theory on art, theory of the way I: Compendium of Japanese theory, new version) (Tokyo: Iwanami, 1995)

Ortolani, Benito, and Samuel L. Leiter (eds.). *Zeami and the Nō Theatre in the World* (New York: CASTA, 1998)

Quinn, Shelley Fenno. *Developing Zeami: The Noh Actor's Attunement in Practice* (Honolulu: University of Hawai'i Press, 2005)

Yamazaki Masakazu (ed.) and J. Thomas Rimer (trans.). *On the Art of the No Drama: The Major Treatises of Zeami* (Princeton, NJ: Princeton University Press, 1984)

Zeami Performance Notes, trans. Thomas Hare (New York: Columbia University Press, 2008)

Zeami's Style: The Noh Plays of Zeami Motokiyo, trans. Thomas Hare (Stanford, CA: Stanford University Press, 1986)

SPOTLIGHT 2.3 WOMEN IN NOH

Geilhorn, Barbara. "Between self-empowerment and discrimination – women in noh today," in Stanca Scholz-Cionca and Christopher Balme (eds.), *Noh Theatre Transversal* (Munich: Ludicium, 2008), 106–22

Weibliche Spielräume – Frauen im japanischen Nō- und Kyōgen-Theater (Female spaces – women in Japanese noh and kyogen theatre) (Munich: Iudicium, 2011)

Rath, Eric C. "Challenging the old men: a brief history of women in noh theater," *Women and Performance* 12:1 (2001), 97–111

Teele, Rebecca. "Women in noh today," *Mime Journal* 17 (2002–3), 67–79

FOCUS 2.3 KANZE HISAO: RENAISSANCE ACTOR

Hoff, Frank. "Kanze Hisao (1925–1978): making nō into contemporary theatre," in Benito Ortolani and Samuel L. Leiter (eds.), *Zeami and the Nō Theatre in the World* (New York: CASTA, 1998), 77–99

Kanze Hideo. "Noh: business and art," *TDR* 15:2/3 (1971), 185–92

Kanze Hisao. *Kanze Hisao chosakushū* (Collected writings of Kanze Hisao), 4 vols. (Tokyo: Heibonsha, 1980–1)

Nagao Kazuo. "A return to essence through misconception: from Zeami to Hisao," in James R. Brandon (ed.), *Nō and Kyōgen in the Contemporary World* (Honolulu: University of Hawai'i Press, 1997), 111–24

Interlude: Noh and kyogen costumes and masks

MONICA BETHE

In the rule-laden, formalized performance traditions of noh and kyogen, costuming – including masks and fans – is one vital means for interpretation. Although on stage (as in life) the age, gender, profession, and status of a character determine the outfit to be worn, the color combinations, design patterns, and specific masks within a generic type are fundamentally the actor's choice.

Interpretation

On the bare noh stage, the ability of costume and mask to express season and scene, and to evoke emotional state, stature, and the non-human, was recognized by Zeami (1363?–1443?) already in the fifteenth century. In the *Fūshikaden* 風姿花伝 (Transmitting the flower through effects and attitudes), he goes so far as to define the portrayal of certain roles by their costume, particularly roles that cannot be played realistically by a male actor, such as women, deities, and Chinese. Zeami also comments on the effectiveness of other actors' costuming – an expressive element that adds a fresh touch to a well-known piece.[56]

The actor chooses a costume within codified rules. Today noh libretti (*utaibon*) stipulate mask and costume elements for each character, down to fans, small properties, headgear, and under-robes. The type of mask and style of broad-sleeved outer cloak (*ōsode*) and box-sleeved *kosode* robe were determined by the mid-Edo period (1603–1868) according to traditions of each noh or kyogen school.

In preparing for a performance, the *shite* actor often starts by selecting the specific mask within a name-type; there are over two hundred, about

---

56 Erika DePoorter (trans.), *Zeami's Talks on Sarugaku: An Annotated Translation of the Saru-gaku Dangi: with an Introduction on Zeami Motokiyo* (Leiden: Hotei, 2002 [1986]), 83, 84, 118.

eighty being standard stock for a family-based theatre troupe. The types, such as *beshimi* (clenched mouth) or *ko-omote* (small face, see Figure 9), define unique iconographies carved and painted to detailed specifications, such as curvature of silhouette, placement and thickness of eyebrows, and even number of loose strands of hair. Most types, however, are not play-specific, but can be used for any number of roles. Conversely, each mask of a type, however closely it follows an ideal model in measurement, modeling, and painting, contains a unique spirit – this is what the actor assesses in making selections.

When choosing his garments, the actor has the greatest freedom in selection of color and pattern. Outside the use of red (*iroari*) to indicate youth, color choice is informed by centuries of associations generated by plant dyes used for aristocratic dress. The motifs derive from traditional decorative designs, but their combinations, modifications, and interplay create endlessly new expression. The brocaded *karaori* robes (see Figure 48), are composed of repeated patterns, yet shifts in balance created by ever-different color arrangements mitigate that monotony. In selecting patterns, the actor seeks seasonal appropriateness (spring cherry blossoms, autumn grasses), balancing size and density of motif to suggest gentle femininity (smaller, delicate) or fearsome virility (large, bold, geometric).

The actor's interpretation of Tomonaga's youth and elegance in Figure 10 is reflected in his choice of the imawaka mask, rather than lieutenant general *chūjō*, divided skirts with (rather than without) pattern, box-sleeve kimono with embroidered (rather than woven) design, and chōken cloak (rather than *happi* jacket).

Origins and categories of masks

The noh-kyogen mask types developed out of masks used for demon (*oni*) exorcism and for the ritual *Shikisanban* (Figure 8). Historically, masks representing supernatural beings followed, such as the bulging-eye *tobide* and clenched-mouth beshimi, and masks of old men, such as *shiwajō* ("wrinkled old man," see Figure 6). Around the time of Zeami, ten master mask-carvers followed by six others created many new varieties, including women, like the angelic *zō-onna* and the middle-aged *fukai*; suffering ghosts, such as the gaunt *yaseotoko*; and beasts, like the kyogen monkey (*saru*) and fox (*kitsune*). Human males were originally portrayed maskless (see Figure 48); masks for adult males, like young warrior-courtiers (see Figure 10), came somewhat later, while the iconic horned mask for jealous women, *han'ya*, was probably not created until the late fifteenth century.

(d) warrior's cap
(*nashiuchi eboshi*)

(c) white sweatband
(*hachimaki*)

(a) mask of a young
warrior (*imawaka*)

(b) black wig
(*kurotare*)

(i) sword (*tachi*)

(f) green inner
box-sleeved
kimono (*nuihaku*)

(e) dark blue
cloak (*chōken*)

(h) waist sash
(*koshiobi*)

(g) divided skirt
(*mon ōkuchi*)

(j) white, split-toe
cotton tabi.

Fig 10 Izumi Yoshio in *Tomonaga*.

Shite (main character): The phantom of wounded warrior Minamoto no Tomonaga. In Act II, his ghost appears in warrior attire. He dons (a) the mask of a young warrior (*imawaka*) with (b) a black wig (*kurotare*), (c) white sweatband (*hachimaki*), and (d) warrior's cap (*nashiuchi eboshi*). He wears (e) a dark blue cloak (*chōken*) with woven gold pattern, bound at the waist with cords and the right sleeve slipped off and rolled up at the back. This exposes (f) a green inner box-sleeved kimono (*nuihaku*) with embroidered cherries (suggesting the spring setting) on stenciled gold water ripples. His (g) divided skirt (*mon ōkuchi*) features fans floating in swirling waves woven in gold. Three paulownia flower medallions decorate his (h) waist sash (*koshiobi*). He sports (i) a sword (*tachi*) and steps forward in (j) white, split-toe cotton *tabi*.

By the late sixteenth century, certain masks were designated "authentic models" (*honmen* 本面). Following the late sixteenth-century master carver Suminobō, noh mask carver families like the Deme of Ōmi (present-day Shiga prefecture) refined the art of recreating from these models.

Development of robes

The twenty-something styles of noh-kyogen robes reflect garments worn by the upper classes in the late sixteenth century. Already in Zeami's time, actors were often paid in bolts of cloth, or garments, sometimes straight off patrons' backs. This custom encouraged a correspondence between street-wear and stage costume. The matched suits, like the *suō*, were worn in both noh and kyogen by commoners and samurai, and used essentially as is.

For many costumes, however, records suggest a major shift in usage over time. Zeami instructs that, to represent a court lady, one must scrupulously copy her dress, the *kinu-hakama* that combines layers of wide, open-sleeved garments with trailing skirts. By the Edo period, the same roles were played with a brocaded box-sleeved karaori robe tucked up (*tsuboʾori*) over broad divided skirts (*ōkuchi*). Although the karaori robe, with its elegant embroidery-like woven designs, was a luxury garment at its peak of popularity in the late sixteenth century, the tsuboʾori draping style was devised for the stage. In the early Edo period (1603–1868) the karaori robe went out of fashion for street-wear, yet remained essentially unchanged in the noh theatre. It is this aristocratic aesthetic, frozen in time, that accounts for some of the most representative overall design systems, such as the checkerboard background (*dangawari*), split body (*katamigawari*) with different left–right patterns, and shoulder–hem (*katasuso*) patterning with empty midriff. By the seventeenth century, everyday wear was made from softer fabrics, of which plain-weave *noshime*, embroidered *nuihaku*, and gold-stenciled *surihaku* survive as noh-kyogen costumes (see Figure 8).

Portraying deities, ghosts, beasts, and spirits demanded an otherworldly, dynamic image expressed through combining rare and expensive materials with unusual techniques. Some garments, like demons' broad-sleeved *happi*, ghosts' diaphanous dancing robes (*chōken*), and kyogen vest-like *kataginu* (see Figure 14), were probably invented for the stage. As weaving and dyeing techniques developed during the Edo period, patterns grew more dynamic and complex. Today, in addition to learning dance and mask-expression techniques, a young shite performer must learn how to choose, drape, and store appropriate combinations of costumes from family or school storehouses.

Draping costumes and mask manipulation

Like most Japanese garments, noh and kyogen robes are constructed out of rectangular strips of cloth, folded flat for storage. They are draped on the actor in layers, pleats, ties, and stitches giving them full, sculpted form. The same garment may be draped differently for distinct roles. Sleeves may be tied up (by an onstage, "invisible" *kōken* stage assistant) to indicate activities like rowing or released during performance, and garments added (for a dance) or shed (to reveal a hidden identity). As the performer moves, the broad sleeves of the outer cloak catch the air, emphasizing even small gestures; dances are punctuated by flipping the sleeves over the arms (see Figure 10), or swirling them into a funnel-shape, or veiling the mask.

As the performer moves, the mask comes alive according to the play of shadows and light on their subtly carved features. Masks representing humans are slightly smaller than the face, with eyeholes restricting vision. Angling the mask downward through leaning slightly forward, or rotating it left and right (gently for humans or sharply for vengeful spirits) are conventional manipulations, but the delicate carving even makes a still figure appear to subtly change expression.

Unlike noh, where main (shite) roles generally use masks to express spirits who may transform between acts, most kyogen roles represent ordinary people, not requiring masks. The fewer kyogen masks exhibit freer sculpting and overt comic expression. Ugly women wear masks, but generally draping a long white sash (*binan*) around the head and belting the ends at the waist suffices to indicate most female roles (see Figure 13). Masks are primarily used to characterize gods, animals, and plants. However the demon mask *buaku* may also be openly used as a disguise, as when a servant fakes being a demon to scare his master, or to get himself some sake, or when the mask is donned by a phony sculptor to fool a gullible buyer.

References and further reading

Kanze Yoshimasa and Shoda Matsuko. *Enmoku betsu ni miru nō shōzoku* (Noh costumes as seen in character roles) (Kyoto: Tankōsha, 2004)

Kirihata Ken. *Nō shōzoku* (Noh costumes). *Nihon no senshoku* (Japanese textiles), vol. VIII (Kyoto: Kyoto shoin, 1993) [bilingual]

Miura Hiroko. *Men kara tadoru nōgaku hyakuichiban* (101 noh traced from their masks) (Kyoto: Tankōsha, 2005)

Nagasaki Iwao and Monica Bethe. *Patterns and Poetry: Nō Robes from the Lucy Truman Aldrich Collection* (Providence, RI: The Museum of Art, Rhode Island School of Design, 1982)

Nakanishi, Tōru. *Noh masks* (Osaka: Hoikusha, 1981)

Takeda, Sharon S., with Monica Bethe. *Miracles & Mischief: Noh and Kyōgen Theater in Japan* (Los Angeles, CA: Los Angeles County Museum of Art, 2002)

Tanabe Saburosuke. *Nōmen* (Noh masks) (Tokyo: Shogakkan, 1981)

Teele, Rebecca (ed.). *Noh-Kyōgen Masks and Performance, Mime Journal* (Claremont, CA: Pomona College, 1984)

3 ❧ Kyogen: classical comedy

JONAH SALZ

Kyogen (狂言) are short classical comic plays performed with stylized vo-calization and gestures. Developed from sketches in variety acts comprising *sangaku* entertainments (later called *sarugaku*), by the early fourteenth century they incorporated medieval Buddhist and secular folktales and an-ecdotes, proverbs, and popular songs. Plots range from auspicious dance to comedy of manners, slapstick to dark comedy, absurd fantasy to noh parody. Most plays feature two or three characters and no set, with only fans for properties. Kyogen became paired with noh by the mid-fifteenth century, serving three functions: in the role of the old man Sambasō in *Okina* (*Shiki-sanban*), "a person from the area" in *ai* narrative interludes between acts of noh plays, and in their own independent comedies.

Kyogen developed as freewheeling, popular, festive entertainment dur-ing the Muromachi period (1392–1573), its improvisatory verve comparable to that of Roman comedy, miracle plays, or commedia dell'arte traditions.[1] From the late Muromachi period and throughout the Edo period (1603–1868), aristocratic patronage was generous, but as samurai bureaucrats suc-ceeded to power they limited performers to authorized, guild-like schools attached exclusively to one of four official noh schools (Kanze, Hōshō, Kom-paru, Kongō [and Kita from 1619]). Shogunal authorities demanded titles, and later scripts, be submitted, and kyogen became accordingly codified, as befitting "ceremonial entertainment" (*shikigaku* 式楽). However, the fluctu-ating fortunes of the aristocracy, and regional daimyo sponsorship of noh, dispersed branch families widely throughout the country. Other families especially in the Kansai region (Kyoto, Osaka, Nara) continued as popular entertainers at temples, shrines, and the imperial household.

Following the dissolution of the shogunate in 1868 and consequent loss of patronage, kyogen actors sought new teaching and performance out-lets at shrines and temples, culture centers, civic halls, and schools. Since World War II, kyogen has experienced unprecedented waves of popular and

---

1 Takeo Fujii, *Humor and Satire in Early English Comedy and Japanese Kyōgen Drama: A Cross-Cultural Study in Dramatic Arts* (Hirakata: Kansai University of Foreign Studies, 1983).

scholarly attention, fueled by innovative young actors of the extant schools, Okura and Izumi. New audiences have discovered in kyogen's stylized classicism the dynamic earthiness of secular medieval satire and farce, and native techniques of vocalization and dramaturgy.

ELEMENTS OF PERFORMANCE: KYOGEN TODAY

Kyogen is traditional physical theatre *par excellence*. Actors announce their identities and motives in carefully enunciated declamations, creating an imaginative stage space through exaggerated physical expression and stylized yet detailed mime.

Performance context

Kyogen today are performed on noh stages in major cities throughout Japan. Typically, one kyogen is performed between two noh plays. Plots are independent of the noh, adjusting instead to the anticipated occasion: type of audience (initiates or connoisseurs), number of players, time, and season. Generally 20 to 40 minutes in length, plays are performed by two or three actors in an archaic and artificial, yet generally comprehensible, stage language. While sharing noh's emphasis on stylized gesture and movement patterns, and song and dance expression, kyogen plays are dialogue-based lighter fare: a respite from the high tension of noh's ritualistic dance-drama.

Plots sketch the foibles and contradictions of everyday life in medieval Japan in broad, forceful strokes. Characters reveal themselves as types: friendly gods, arrogant but stupid lords, lazy but clever servants, shrewish wives, browbeaten husbands, awkward bridegrooms, greedy priests, or fake *yamabushi* mountain wizards.

Kyogen actors also perform in 210 of the extant 250 noh plays as *ai* (アイ、間), referring both to the interludes and to the players themselves. In two-part noh plays, these interludes permit noh actors time to change mask and costume for Act II. The ai local villager helps clarify and further the plot. Often, he merely declaims a parallel tale or back-story, presaging the revelation of the noh *shite* in the second act as ghost, demon, or god. At times, he interacts with shite lead, *tsure* secondary lead, or *waki* accompanying players, carrying messages or properties. Although audiences for noh today often prepare through program summaries or even read complete scripts, the *ai-kyōgen* remains an important interlocutor.

There are 136 kyogen actors who are members of the Nohgaku Performers' Association as of 2014: about half are full-time professionals. In addition to primarily weekend performances in noh programs, there are over one hundred all-kyogen annual programs. A series of "kyogen booms" since the 1950s have led to kyogen-only recitals given regularly in major cities, focusing on a particular family or individual performer. Family-based troupes perform at annual shrine and temple festivals, tour schools and civic halls, or regularly produce New Year's or children's events. At a typical all-kyogen performance, three plays are presented. Short *komai* (小舞) dances, performed to *kouta* (小歌) songs, or *katari* narratives round out the program.

Kyogen actors since World War II have adapted folktales, Shakespeare, Grimm, and science fiction, collaborating with playwrights and performers from other genres. Recognized as a living repository of native vocal and movement skills, kyogen actors offer regular lessons for modern theatre groups, culture centers, university clubs, and home studios. Since the 1950s, actors teach foreign students in Japan and offer frequent overseas workshops.

Play repertoire and categories

There are approximately 250 plays in the combined repertories of the two extant schools, Okura and Izumi, most created anonymously by the seventeenth century. They serve as an invaluable reflection of the popular songs, fashions, language, and everyday life of the late Muromachi and early Edo periods. There are currently 180 plays in the Okura School (twenty plays eliminated during the Meiji period remain in the repertory of two major branch families, the Shigeyama and Yamamoto). There are approximately 250 plays in the Izumi school.

Plays are classified according to various systems. Categories were created to follow the order of a full program of noh plays in the early Edo period (typically divided into seven or nine plays), classified by role type of the major character, type of story, order on program, or difficulty of learning.

Okura school classification, number[2]
Waki (auspicious) 23
Daimyō (large landholder) 20
Shōmyō (small landholder) 28
Muko, onna (bridegroom and female) 28
Oni, yamabushi (demon, mountain wizard) 17
Shukke, zatō (priest, blind man) 33
Atsume (miscellaneous) 25
Omō Narai (advanced) 3
Goku omō narai (extremely advanced) 3

2 Kobayashi Seki, *Kyōgen handobukku* (Kyogen handbook) (Tokyo: Sanseido, 2008), 33.

Plots span a wide range. Festive and auspicious dance-plays hark back to kyogen's ritual roots, while bittersweet melodramas, situation comedies, absurd fantasies, and slapstick buffoonery are harbingers for later kabuki. Tarō Kaja, the lovable scamp, features as the wily, lazy, sake-loving servant in about one third of the plays. Drinking songs and popular ballads, accompanied by lively dance, are found in about a third of the repertoire. Plays parodying noh feature a full accompaniment of noh drums and flute.[3]

Dramaturgical patterns

Plays begin with a *nanori* name-saying opening sequence. The actor enters the main stage from the long bridgeway, turns to the audience and declares his status and purpose. He might then triangulate the stage (*michiyuki*), returning to the name-taking place, upstage center, then call his servant or neighbor (*yobidashi*), seek out a merchant, or summon a priest or drinking companion. Plots then follow various formulae: the master commands the servant, who banters awhile about a tiresome chore; couples, neighbors, or passers-by engage in an escalating argument; a ruse rapidly unravels; a god agrees to dance. Plays may end with a song, chase, scolding, laugh, or even sneeze.

Kyogen gestures are stylized, repeated variations on a theme; even first-time audiences easily grasp these conventions. A bow begins with knees bending while hands slide along the side of the thighs to the knees; "thinking" is shown similarly to a half-bow with a head-tilt for accent; laughing begins like a bow, then rising with a booming "haa-haa-haa"; crying leans forward, hands shielding the eyes, "hei-hei-hei." Perfected over the centuries, these mimetic expressions are readable even from a distance of hundreds of meters at outdoor theatres or temple stages.

Kyogen speech has been compared to the cutting of green bamboo: clean, clear, and direct, the natural voice children use when shouting, or a booming "Yahoo!" shouted across mountain ravines.[4] Dialogue, memorized according to strict intonation, is developed from childhood through oral transmission (*kuchi-utsushi*) – no written texts are permitted until teenage years – when the complete dialogue becomes second nature, firmly embedded as muscle memory. Once dialogue for a play is absorbed, the student shadows the teacher from back and side. Facial expression is eschewed in favor of mask-like neutrality to emphasize body expression. Gestures are almost

3 Carolyn Haynes, "Parody in the maikyōgen and the monogurui kyōgen," Ph.D. diss., Cornell University, 1988.
4 Shigeyama Sennojō, *Kyōgen yakusha: hinekure handaiki* (Kyogen actor: chronicle of a perverse half life) (Tokyo: Iwanami shinsho, 1987), 20.

always accompanied by onomatopoeic sounds which may imitate the sound of the object itself – "sara-sara" for a paper door opening, "gara-gara" for a heavy wooden one – or animal cries (dog = "byo-byo," roosters = "ko-kaaa," foxes = "kuwaii"). Through these vocal sound effects, stage actions can depict reality in clear and amusing ways with minimal properties and stage settings.

Professional training follows a strict progression of "roles of passage" designed to teach necessary skills at each stage of development "from monkey to fox."[5] *Shibiri* (Cramps) and *Iroha* (ABCs) are short, repetitive plays with few movements. The 4- or 5-year-old actor often performs with a grandparent for his stage debut in *Utsubozaru* (The monkey-skin quiver [Figure 11]; see p. 73) or *Iroha* (ABCs). After his voice has broken, he will perform *Nasu no Yoichi katari* (Tale of Nasu no Yoichi), a variant ai-kyogen interlude tale requiring great breath control and imitation of the three characters portrayed. *Sambasō*, debuted at around 15, is the young actor's first stage interaction with noh players, and first use of a non-animal mask. *Tsurigitsune* (Catching the fox), considered a "graduation piece," performed at around 20, is a grueling play taking over an hour about a fox disguised as a priest to dissuade his nephew, a hunter, from taking sentient life. At around 30, the full-fledged actor emerges after performing *Hanago*, an hour-long play portraying a lust-smitten husband, requiring a full spectrum of solo storytelling, singing, and acting (see representative plays, p. 75). An actor must achieve the proper *kurai* (dignity) with age to perform the three plays about elders which complete the training trajectory, including *Makura monogurui* (Pillow-crazy) concerning a love-struck 99-year-old. They are notable for their lack of complexity, providing an opportunity for actors to appeal to audiences through their personal artistic flavor (*geifū*, 芸風).

In contrast to noh's elaborate folds, ties, and wigs requiring dressers, kyogen costumes, originating in the everyday wear of the early Edo period, can easily be put on aided by a single dresser or even by actors themselves. The fan is the common, handy prop. When closed it becomes a saw for cutting wood, a pipe for smoking, a spoon for stirring sugar, or a stick for poking roasting chestnuts; when opened, a scoop for water, a bowl for pouring or drinking sake, rooster wings, or even a fan for blowing away poisonous fumes. More complex stage scenery is created through mime and sound: a boat being poled downriver is created solely by actors – one standing at the "stern," pushing a long pole, the other at the "prow" swaying with the motion. As short, small-cast fillers between noh plays, which might deploy raised platforms, large properties, and twenty performers, a typical kyogen's flexible minimalism is clearly an asset.

5 Jonah Salz, "Roles of passage in kyogen training," in John Singleton (ed), *Situated Learning in Japan* (Cambridge: Cambridge University Press, 1998), 233–45.

REPRESENTATIVE PLAYS*

Fig 11 Four generations of the Shigeyama Sengorō family perform the auspicious kyogen *Utsubozaru* (The monkey-skin quiver).

Utsubozaru (The monkey-skin quiver)

A Trainer (traditionally, as with actors, from the outcaste class) enters with a Monkey on his way to perform streetcorner and festival tricks, wearing a mask and fur costume. When a Daimyo, wearing an *eboshi* lacquered hat and holding a bow, demands the monkey's skin to make into a quiver, the Trainer refuses. The Lord threatens to kill them both, so the Trainer tearfully says farewell to his pet. Yet when he raises his stick to strike, the Monkey grabs it, performing the "rowing the boat" trick on cue. The amused Lord releases the Monkey to the Trainer, who gratefully performs several tricks and dances: "moon-viewing," "sleeping," and "rice-planting." The amused Lord imitates the monkey's antics, then bestows presents before joining in a felicitous harvest dance. Often the real-life grandfather or even great-grandfather plays Lord to the 4-year-old child debuting as the Monkey; bestowing gifts from the family head (and spectator applause) can be read as a welcome into the kyogen family.

---

* Translations, often multiple versions of the same play, can be found at www.meijigakuin.ac.jp/~pmjs/biblio/kyogen.html.

Bō shibari (Tied to a pole)

The Master feigns interest in servant Tarō Kaja's abilities at pole-fighting. He then ties up both servants to prevent them from stealing his liquor while he is away on business. The pinioned pair manage to open and drink the sake. The Master returns, and furiously chases the tipsy servants off. The brotherly banter between servants, and slapstick fun as they figure out how to drink while tied up, makes this one of the most popular plays in the repertoire.

Fusenaikyo (Forgotten payment)

A Priest offers a family service, but then must remind the Parishioner about his forgotten fee through a sermon filled with increasingly obvious double-entendre hints. There is little stage action, but laughs derived from the dignified Priest's ever more desperate attempts at puns and stories to jog the Parishioner's memory.

Hanago

A wealthy Husband begs permission from his suspicious Wife to go away on a zen retreat; he settles for an undisturbed night of meditation at home, then orders his Servant to impersonate him while he races to his mistress. The Wife discovers the conspiracy, replacing the Servant beneath a kimono. The Wife shudders with rage as the Husband returns from his tryst to relate the lustful details in song and dance. The second half of the play is a solo tour-de-force of drunken balladeering. *Hanago* was successfully adapted to kabuki as *Migawari zazen* (The zen substitute, 1910).

Mikazuki (The winnowing basket)

The Husband spends all his time and money attending and hosting linked-verse poetry parties, so his Wife threatens divorce. Agreeing, he offers her as traditional parting token a winnowing basket for rice. However, as she departs for her parents' home, the Husband is inspired to declaim the first link of a poem, her basket a crescent moon. When the wife completes it, saying she is "parting light, with heavy body," he is overjoyed: if she can compose poetry, there is no need for him to go out anymore. They exchange re-marital cups, and he sings and dances for her.

Funawatashi muko (Bridegroom on a boat)

A Bridegroom brings sake to a ceremonial visit to his Father-in-law. However the Boatman ferrying him across the river demands a drink, and they end up finishing the cask. The Bridegroom staggers to his Father-in-law's home, but runs off ashamed when the barrel is discovered empty. In the Izumi school

Fig 12 Boatman (Sengorō) poles Bridegroom (Akira) across the river in Shigeyama kyo-gen *Funawatashi muko* (Bridegroom on a boat).

version, the Father-in-law is the Boatman. When discovering he has guzzled his own Son-in-law's liquor, he shaves his beard. The Son-in-law soon recognizes the familiar face, and the Father-in-law runs off in shame. (See Figure 12.)

Kusabira (Mushrooms)

A Man whose land is infested with mushrooms asks a yamabushi wizard for help. But his prayers backfire when an army of mushrooms gives hopping chase. This is a spectacular play, with sometimes dozens of actors thronging the stage, leaping and yelping, in bright costumes, straw hats, and paper umbrellas.

Fig 13 Kyogen version of French farce *Le Cuvier* (*Susugigawa*, The washing river), performed bilingually (English and Japanese) by Noho Theatre Group.

Susugigawa (The washing river)

While washing clothes by the river, a cowardly Husband is overwhelmed with additional chores demanded by his Wife and Mother-in-law. As an adopted son, he has little authority in his Wife's family. He timidly suggests that they list up everything. When he drops a kimono in the river, the Wife falls in trying to retrieve it. But the Husband refuses to help: "It's not on the list." He thus renegotiates his position as family head. This adaptation of the medieval French farce *Le Cuvier* by comic playwright Iizawa Tadasu was successfully adapted to kyogen in 1953, becoming part of the standard Okura repertoire.

Early history

The historical neglect of scholarly study of performing arts in Japan is due both to their ephemeral nature and to the fact that early practitioners undoubtedly came from the outcaste class living confined to ghetto life.[6] Kyogen's status as vulgar comic interlude has further obscured its scholarly worth. Its early history must therefore be assembled from titles, omissions from official programs, passing mentions in diary entries on more esteemed

---

6　Benito Ortolani discusses modern reassessments of folk and elite performing arts in *The Japanese Theatre: From Shamanistic Ritual to Contemporary Pluralism* (revised edn.) (Princeton, NJ: Princeton University Press, 1990), 133–5.

arts, chronicle entries reprimanding certain players, and prescriptive treatises intended to curtail kyogen's vulgar slapstick and irreverent satire.

By the mid-fifteenth century, kyogen became embedded within a program
of noh plays in roughly the same form that has endured today. However, for
at least two centuries prior, largely improvised, small-cast, dialogue-based
comic skits were performed for both popular and elite audiences at shrines,
temples, and great houses. These plays mocked traditionally revered figures –
mountain wizards, priests, and nuns – and depicted city slicker pranks and
country bumpkin escapades. While traces of a coherent tradition cannot be
proven, regular signposts suggest that kyogen-like performances were given
for centuries prior to the birth of "kyogen" as a genre.

Mythical origins

The luring of the Sun Goddess from the Rock-Cave through an erotic dance
(see Focus 1.1) is an oft-mentioned forebear to kyogen's willful stretching
of the boundaries of taste and form. Taboo-breaking clowns who invited
laughter at solemn gatherings can be found in many early records of Japanese history. The *Kojiki* and *Nihongi* record the tale of two brothers who
quarrel over a lost fish-hook. To subdue Fire-subsiding's wrath, Fire-shining
hilariously imitates drowning, presumed to be the origin of *hayabito* "court
jesters."[7] When two brother musicians were asked by the Emperor Horikawa
(1079–1107) to perform a sarugaku skit, the older brother declared, "I'm going to get into the bright light of one of the bonfires, pull my skirts right up
and show my bony legs. Then I'll call out, 'It's v-v-very l-l-late, I'm f-f-frozen
stiff. I th-th-think I'll w-w-warm m-m-my b-b-balls,' and run around the
fire three times." However, he is dissuaded by the younger brother – who
promptly steals his idea. The "emperor and all present explode in laughter."[8]
Once again, scatological humor and childish antics are rewarded by felicitous laughter.

Another kyogen predecessor may be found in *modoki* parodies, whereby
solemn performances were followed by comic burlesques in an approved
transgression. An official record of court music describes *gigaku* (masked
mime plays) parodying important religious deities at the consecration ceremony for the Great Buddha at Tōdaiji (782). The formal *bugaku* dance-
drama *Ama* was followed by *Ninomai*: actors in masks of a leprous old man
and woman parody the movements of exiting dancers. Such solemn content

---

7 W. G. Aston (trans.), *Nihongi: Chronicles of Japan from the Earliest Times to A.D. 697* (London: George Allen & Unwin, 1956), 107.
8 *Uji shūi monogatari* (Gleanings from tales from Uji), trans. in Carolyn Anne Morley, *Transformation, Miracles, and Mischief: The Mountain Priest Plays of Kyogen* (Ithaca, NY: Cornell East Asia Series, 1993), 34.

lampooned immediately by complementary characters is a performance structure found from mythic times to the present.

Kyogen before noh

Humorous skits, under various rubrics, comprising slapstick, parody, and satire, were part of sarugaku, which also featured tumbling and acrobatics, magic tricks, singing, and dancing. While mimicry, sketch comedy, and parody continued throughout the centuries in kagura and sangaku as popular accompaniments to more serious performance genres, the first record of kyogen-like skits being performed comes from the *Shin sarugaku-ki* (Records of new sarugaku) of Fujiwara no Akihira (989–1066). At a sarugaku noh performance at the Inari festival on the outskirts of Kyoto including other entertainments,[9] several comic skits were given. Titles suggest plots similar to later kyogen plays: *A Country Man from the East Visits the Capital*; *A Prankster Comes to the Capital*; *A Priest Looks for Vestments*; *A Nun Begs for Diapers*. The plays managed "to twist the entrails and dislocate the jaws of its spectators with foolish nonsense."[10]

Formerly itinerant actors were given "lay priest" status, and began to form *za* (guilds) to maintain standards and protect territory. There were at least five guild-like associations of comic skit specialists, each protective of repertory and territory, affiliated with Nara's Kasuga Shrine and Kyoto's Gion Yasaka by the twelfth century. Shrines and temples, medieval cultural and trade centers, provided raised stages for rituals which could also be used to display performing arts. In exchange for protection, sarugaku performers played for free at festivals and ceremonies, given "lay priest" status. Sarugaku included magic, acrobatics, dance, and song, as well as comic skits; the earliest record of the independent genre of comedy known as *okashi* is a performance at Tango in 1333. The term "okashi" today means "humorous" or "strange," but then had a nuance of "violation of territory and norms." At the Kasuga Wakamiya Festival in 1349, not only was the term "sarugaku noh" first employed, but two actors of dengaku noh and *shirabyōshi* dance interludes were listed as "okashi hōshi" (comic lay priests). Their performance consisted of impromptu comic banter between plays, as well as within a danced section of a dengaku performance.

In a record of an *ennen* celebration in 1352, a "kyogen yamabushi sermon" is mentioned – the first time "kyogen" appears. The term *kyōgen* (狂言)

---

9 *Kokusho kankōkai* (1928), 991–1002, trans. in Dorothy Shibano, "Kyogen: the comic as drama," Ph.D. diss., University of Washington, 1973, 323.
10 Trans. in Sakanishi Shio, *The Ink-Smeared Lady and Other Japanese Folk-Plays* (Rutland, VT: Charles Tuttle, 1964), 5.

derives from "*kyō*," wild or crazy, and "*gen*," words. Wild words, first mentioned in the mid-eighth-century *Manyōshū*, were derived from Po Chui's "kyōgen kigo," irrational, decorative language that might lead one astray from the true path of Buddhist enlightenment by wild fictions.[11] The term had negative connotations throughout the Heian period, meaning "superfluous" or "ostentatious." Okashi skits, eventually known as kyogen, became an independent genre performed alongside other entertainment genres.[12]

Zeami and the uneasy marriage of kyogen and noh

After their epochal performance before the Ashikaga shogun in 1374, Kan'ami and son Zeami, competing with the more popular rustic dengaku tradition, raised sarugaku noh's status as an increasingly refined art patronized by the aristocracy and samurai. Yet sarugaku noh could not be performed alone; preparations of costumes, masks, and properties for long programs of multiple plays featuring the same lead actors demanded other entertainments to fill the gaps between plays. Sarugaku noh programs of the thirteenth and fourteenth centuries featured flute, shirabyōshi dancing, and dengaku singing alternating with okashi "fillers" between noh plays. According to Zeami's *Shūdōsho* (Learning the way, 1430), however, three noh plays with two comic plays had become the ideal.[13] Within the noh plays themselves, increasingly complex plots required colloquial speaking parts, originally by tsure accompanying actors or waki, but eventually ceded to versatile kyogen performers. Eventually, noh absorbed kyogen as indispensable if subsidiary performers within a troupe. Gradually kyogen specialists took over essential functions for the noh, establishing their place firmly within the troupe, performing: the character Sanbasō (三番叟 or 三番三) in the ritual opening piece *Shikisanban* (式三番), and also the mask-bearer Senzai (in two of the four schools); a local person, attendant, or minor deity explaining the background to the main characters within a noh play (ai); and humorous plays between noh plays on a program (*hon-kyōgen*).

Thus coincidental proximity of okashi entertainers with sarugaku noh performers on various stages during Zeami's lifetime developed quickly into a noh-kyogen performance system. Kyogen actors shifted from promiscuous performances alongside various popular genres, and popular all-kyogen programs, to exclusive attachment within noh programs to sarugaku noh troupes. Their accidental pairing became dramaturgic necessity, further expanding noh's theatrical potential.

---

11 Arthur Waley, *The Noh Plays of Japan* (New York: Grove Press, Evergreen, 1957), 18.
12 Sitasuwan Kanlayanee, "Language usage in kyōgen," Ph.D. diss., University of Washington, 1988, 4–5.
13 *Zeami Performance Notes*, trans. Thomas Hare (New York: Columbia University Press, 2008), 422.

Both noh and kyogen, begun among commoners, grew more stylized with elite patronage. Yet kyogen actors continued to tread a thin line between amusing audiences with inspired improvisations reflecting contemporary concerns, and offending patrons and authorities with vulgarity or inappropriate themes. Excesses are recorded in *Prince Sadafusa's Diary* (1424): actors were punished for performing a play mocking "hardships of the nobility" at his Fushimi Gokōnomiya residence, where impoverished aristocracy were in attendance, incurring the wrath of the Emperor, who reprimanded the troupe leader. Historian and poet Sadafusa took the opportunity to note similar recent incidents, including monks who chased kyogen actors from Enryakuji Temple on Mount Hiei in Kyoto for imitating monkeys, considered sacred messengers, and punishment for ridiculing pitiful Buddhist acolytes at Ninnaji Temple. The plays were not intrinsically problematic, but performing them for those particular spectators revealed an unforgiveable error of judgment.[14]

Maintaining the solemnity of the noh-kyogen program while playing for laughs also required careful calibration. Zeami constantly struggled to raise noh from rustic vulgarity to polished and elegant performance worthy of elite patronage, yet in his nineteen treatises he rarely mentions kyogen. This suggests both a lack of interest in the light form, as well as kyogen's relative independence within the troupe. He seems to regard it as a necessary evil, praising subtlety of acting and attunement to mood, and admonishing those actors whose crude antics gain laughter at the expense of the overall atmosphere. In *Shūdōsho* (1430) he describes "the kyogen actor's function," allowing for the need to be interesting in comic skits, but advising actors that as interlude explicators, "their function does not involve any need to amuse the audience."[15]

Since these interlude speeches were often left to the actor's discretion, Zeami warns in *Sarugaku dangi* (1430) that "supporting actors and Kyogen [actors] have to say everything as in the libretto. For in ignorance they deviate from it, which is bad."[16] Clearly Zeami had found kyogen actors' improvisations during serious noh plays distracting and disruptive of the refined *yūgen* (darkly elegant) mood constructed so carefully.

Yet even in independent hon-kyogen, Zeami rejects laughter at any cost:

Kyogen itself would merely be considered vulgar if its only aim were to make the audience laugh boisterously on all occasions. It is said that true gaiety lies within a delicate smile and such impressions are always effective and moving

---

14 Fushimi Sadafusa, later Emperor Go-Sukō (1372–1456), *Kanmongyoki* (Record of things seen and heard) (1424), in *Zoku Gunsho Ruijū*, vol. III (Tokyo: Naigai shoseki, 1933), 427.

15 *Zeami Performance Notes*, trans. Hare, 421.

16 Erika DePoorter (trans.), *Zeami's Talks on Sarugaku: An Annotated Translation of the Sarugaku Dangi: with an Introduction on Zeami Motokiyo* (Leiden: Hotei, 2002 [1986]), Section 146, 117.

for an audience … Whether in terms of words or gestures, a kyogen actor must, avoiding all vulgarity, allow his well-born audience to experience humor that is both clever and endearing.[17]

That such admonitions can be found centuries later (see Focus 3.1) demonstrates that experienced kyogen professionals, accustomed to earning laughter at shrines and temples, in city or country, alternating with other genres or on independent programs, frequently overstepped their place in the more refined settings of aristocrat patrons.

Acting organization

Yet Zeami saw the benefit of tying secular frivolous comedians to the art of noh, thereby raising the comedian's status while bringing entertaining skits to the fledgling noh. A noh troupe, including musicians, chorus, and subsidiary actors, would employ two or three actors from a small kyogen guild (*za*). The few large-cast plays are largely structured around a pair of lead characters, with extras for group scenes of singing and dancing at a drinking or flower-viewing party, roles easily assumed by other troupe members. And the existence of relatively long, large-cast plays requiring platforms and properties demonstrates kyogen's entertainment appeal independently, not merely as practical necessity as "interlude."

Kyogen actors' development as professionals within the noh system can be traced through Zeami's various remarks. He castigates a successful country *tesarugaku* (semi-professional) performer as unworthy of competing before the connoisseurs of the capital, a shallow player of "far-reaching but empty fame." Zeami instead praises a kyogen master, the elder Tsuchidayū, for his subtle portrayal of a son, wounded in battle, attempting to reach his captured father, and the younger Tsuchidayū for maintaining his comic persona in everyday life.[18] One particularly detailed record of a 1464 subscription performance in Kyoto provides rich materials from which to judge kyogen's artistic role and organization. Twenty-three plays were performed over three days in between noh plays.[19] This is the first time titles were actually listed in a program. On the basis of the estimated times of the rising and setting sun, the number of plays on each day's program, and allowances for some pauses, O'Neill estimates noh then to have lasted 40 minutes on average, and kyogen 20 – about half their present lengths; Komiya suggests kyogen were

---

17 Yamazaki Masakazu (ed.) and J. Thomas Rimer (trans.), *On the Art of the No Drama: The Major Treatises of Zeami* (Princeton, NJ: Princeton University Press, 1984), 133.

18 DePoorter (trans.), *Zeami's Talks on Sarugaku*, Sections 158, 159 (1986), 119–20.

19 *Tadasu-gawara kanjin sarugaku nikki* (Record of Tadasu riverbank subscription sarugaku), ed. Kokusho Kankō-kai, vol. XIX (1933), 717–21, 722–3; titles listed in Sakanishi, *Ink-smeared Lady*, 10–11.

only 10 minutes long to noh's 30 minutes.[20] These early records of performances, and a later documentary history (1653), indicate that these comic farces were often maintained within family lines: father to son (natural or adoptive) and brothers.[21] Early in the Edo period, shogunal authorities restricted kyogen actors to noh troupes performing exclusively in noh-kyogen programs, so popular and widespread all-kyogen programs ceased. As previously largely improvised kyogen came to share the stage with the noh, it underwent codification following patterns alongside those established within noh. Comedians, like noh actors, had become a respected hereditary art.

Codification and diversification: Edo period

Kyogen actors were thus embedded with noh as both interlude narrators and comic players, appearing together exclusively since Zeami's time. Their fortunes paralleled the noh's development through the Muromachi period, sponsored by aristocrats, then the urban population, eventually filtering out to the provincial capitals. Shogunal demands on pedigree and repertoire meant consolidation of formerly independent, even rival, families into *ryūgi* (stylistic schools). Kyogen actors affiliated to the four Yamato noh troupes served the Edo shogun, as well as regional daimyo seeking to study and perform these elegant ceremonial arts, receiving stipends.

Yet at the same time, tesarugaku semi-pros, especially strong in Kyoto and Osaka, performed at shrines and temples. They assisted the official troupes on their regular visits to Nara's *takigi* torchlit noh or Kyoto ceremonies. Certain families also had privileges to perform and teach within the Imperial Palace. Those unaffiliated kyogen actors who either were excluded from official guilds or chose to leave them joined kabuki, which had replaced it as popular theatre. Kyogen players affiliated with noh troupes began to codify and record their scripts and performance practice. This ensured stability of their families, but maintained crucial family distinctions of performance style and texts.

Schools and families

The three kyogen stylistic schools – Okura, Izumi, and Sagi – spuriously cite Priest Gen'ei (*c.* 1269–1350) as founding author. However, their common

---

20 Patrick G. O'Neill, *Early Nō Drama: Its Background, Character and Development 1300–1450* (London: Lund Humphries, 1958), 89–90; Koyama in Hashimoto Akio, Koyama Hiroshi, and Taguchi Kazuo (eds.), *Kyōgen no sekai* (The world of kyogen), *Iwanami kōza no-kyōgen* (Iwanami's Noh-kyogen course), vol. V (Tokyo: Iwanami, 1987), 433.

21 *Yoza yakusha mokuroku* (Catalogue of actors of the four noh troupes, 1653), in Hashimoto et al. (eds.), *Kyōgen no sekai*, 19–20.

origins and distinction are documented only from around the end of the Muromachi period. The *iemoto* headmaster system positioned household heads as authorities in kyogen as well as noh, but smaller, family-based teams attached to different noh schools permitted greater flexibility and status fluidity throughout history. During the Edo period, dispersal to feudal daimyo throughout the country, and exclusive affiliation with each noh school, further invited diversity. Professionals served the shogun in Edo or provincial lords, while regional semi-professionals were employed to fulfill ceremonial duties at the court in Kyoto, participate in festivals, and teach amateurs. These Kyoto tesarugaku or *machiiri* performers are thought to have fostered the generous and familiar style of today's Nomura and Shigeyama families, as opposed to the martial formality of the daimyo-patronized Yamamoto family.

Okura school kyogen

The Okura school is the oldest, comprising the Okura, Yamamoto, and Shigeyama families, strongest today in Tokyo and Kansai (Kyoto-Osaka). The school genealogy cites a Hiyoshi (outside Kyoto) noh troupe member as their founder, succeeded in the tenth generation by Komparu Shirōjirō (*c.* 1500), son of Zeami's son-in-law, the noh actor Zenchiku (1405–68), eighth generation head. Contemporary scholarship says instead that Komparu Mangorō, a disciple of Shirojirō (also listed in genealogies of the Sagi and Izumi schools), attached to Nara's Komparu noh school, was the founder. The ninth generation Yatarō, originally an Uji noh troupe actor, took the Okura family name from a branch family of the Komparu noh troupe.

Samurai embraced kyogen as they had noh. Warlord Toyotomi Hideyoshi (1536–98) favored Okura actors, performing *Ear-pulling* (*Mimi-hiki*, now called *Igui*) with fellow generals Tokugawa Ieyasu and Maeda Toshiie in 1593. Oda Nobunaga (1534–82) bequeathed costumes and the hereditary name "Tora" (tiger) to the eleventh headmaster, Toramasa Yaemon (1539–1614). Tora'akira (1597–1662), thirteenth headmaster, compiled the first extant book of scripts (1642), while the sixteenth generation headmaster Torabun submitted official texts and costume inventories to the shogunate. The main school moved from Nara to Edo in the early seventeenth century, serving the shogun throughout the Edo period. In the seventeenth century, there was a proliferation of semi-independent branch families, often established by younger brothers or sons, answering the need to provide kyogen players who could serve official noh troupes, exclusive to a particular school, in diverse regions.

Izumi school: regional players

The Izumi school is strongest today in Tokyo, Nagoya, and Kanazawa, comprising the Izumi, Nomura, and Miyake families. Under Tokugawa Iemitsu

(1604–51), the shogunate authorities demanded that smaller kyogen *za* (troupes) become official schools (*ryūgi*) affiliated with noh troupes, so the small Kyoto-based Izumi-Yamawaki family invited two other active Kyoto kyogen families, Nomura Matasaburō I (1641–1711) and Miyake Tōkurō I (b.?–d. 1708), to establish the Izumi school. Family texts would remain independent. Although the Izumi head in 1614 officially became vassal to the Owari (Aichi, including Nagoya) lord, the Izumis and other branch families remained in Kyoto, performing and teaching Kyoto's court and commoners throughout the Tokugawa era. While the shogunate made kyogen along with most traditional arts more centralized and codified, powerful lords sponsored favored performers and families in their own feudal domains. Izumi Motokazu, the tenth headmaster, moved to Nagoya, some of the Miyake family to Osaka and Kanazawa, and the Nomuras to Kumamoto. Known during Edo as "Kyoto kyogen," eventually, more so than with the other two schools, they became regional professionals.

Sagi school: flashy newcomers

Sagi school players were originally tesarugaku players of Chōmei noh in Sakai who in 1614 joined the Kanze school on shogunal command. Although deprecated in Okura Tora'akira's *Waranbegusa* for their loose and flashy style, the charismatic seventh headmaster Niemon Sōgen (1560–1650) was retained by Tokugawa Ieyasu and later shoguns as personal tutor. Texts, first published in 1724, well after and seemingly derivative of the other two schools, indicate a rival spirit toward them. Despite its being favored by the shogun, Sagi school's flavor betrayed its easygoing and flashy origins. Niemon was punished once for leaping off the stage into the audience; another Sagi actor playing Senzai in the play *Okina Sambasō* imitated puppet movements, forcing a repeat of the entire ritual play. Tora'akira seems to disparage them when writing: "The Kyogen popular today have no substance and are performed in haste and roughly. Rambling remarks are made, and the actor twists his face, opens wide his eyes and mouth, and makes meaningless gestures, and laughs. This pleases those of low station but embarrasses those with discernment."[22] He likens them to the comic pieces in the increasingly popular kabuki, although Morley assumes this is professional jealousy.[23]

The Okura school's long attachment to the shogunate led to a martial ceremonious, coupled with somewhat ambiguous and formal, dialogue. This contrasts with the Izumi school's larger repertoire and realistic dialogue

---

22 *Waranbegusa*, 682, in Steven Addiss, Gerald Groemer, and J. Thomas Rimer (trans.), *Traditional Japanese Arts and Culture: An Illustrated Source Book* (Honolulu: University of Hawai'i Press, 2006), 208.
23 *Waranbegusa*, trans. in Morley, *Transformation*, 32–3.

∾ FOCUS 3.1 Okura Tora'aki(ra): comic texts and theory

Okura Tora'aki (1597–1662),[24] thirteenth *iemoto* master of Okura school kyogen, compiled the first book of kyogen scripts and notes on acting (*Tora'aki-bon*), and the first treatise on kyogen history and acting, entitled *Waranbegusa* (Notes for children).

Son of Okura Torakiyo (1566–1646), and grandson of Kōgorōjirō Masayoshi, a shoulder-drum master, he began studying kyogen under his father's guidance in 1601. In 1609, along with noh performers staying at Osaka Castle, Tora'aki moved to Suruga (present-day Shizuoka prefecture) where retired shogun and de facto ruler Tokugawa Ieyasu (1542–1616) resided. Later, Ieyasu ordered resident troupes to perform for the shogunate at Edo Castle. In 1628, Tora'aki became a leading kyogen performer for Nara's Komparu school of noh.

Upending the custom of oral transmission, Tora'aki compiled 237 play texts in 1642, an invaluable resource. Unlike the *Tenshō-bon* (1576), which merely provided summaries, Tora'aki's scripts included dialogue and some stage directions for plays divided into role type categories. Subsequent scripts by his heirs and other schools reveal the accuracy of his transcriptions; over 180 plays remain in the current repertoire.

NOTES FOR CHILDREN: *WARANBEGUSA*
In 1660 Tora'aki completed the five-volume *Waranbegusa*, taking nearly a decade to polish it. The book covers the history and philosophy of kyogen, practical hints on performing, and methods of training and playwriting. It discusses the principles of kyogen comedies' complementary nature within a solemn noh program, warning, "It has been said that a noh presented by an unskilled performer will turn into a kyogen, and a kyogen presented by an unskilled performer will turn into a noh."[25]

Waranbegusa suggests drinking water for a better voice, cultivating a forward-leaning posture, distinguishing use of the mask and face, and analyzing varieties of tears and laughter. One must be diligent in practice, yet relaxed on stage. Sincerity and correctness are vital, as it is better to be clumsy than deceitful. Most kyogen are auspicious pieces. Its art is a tall, straight bamboo with few joints. If the stage is the body, then bridgeway entrances and exits are as vital as inhaling and exhaling. When kyogen is too serious it becomes noh, yet if too vulgarly entertaining it becomes kabuki. Being interesting is more important than being funny, peer respect more important than popular acclaim.

In spite of Tora'aki's endeavors, he ultimately failed to develop distinctive principles of kyogen independent from noh. His discussion was narrow, as noh and kyogen had already been established as the official ceremonial music (*shikigaku*) of the Tokugawa rulers. Nevertheless, his concept of *sōō* (相応, suitability) became a salient element in principles of kyogen training. "You should not look down upon young kyogen performers who cannot attain satisfactory results in their performance … because their skills do not match up to their expectations. As they get older and more mature, some of them will naturally produce better results." Tora'aki's insistence on suitability was indeed a precursor of the early modern performance theory known as *kyojitsu himaku ron*, a doctrine advocated by puppet playwright Chikamatsu Monzaemon (1653–1724), in which he contends that art lies in the interspace of the skin membranes, between the unreal and reality.[26]

Tora'aki's disparaging comments concerning rival Sagi school kyogen reflect the climate of the times. Okuni's kabuki was achieving sudden popularity and beginning to attract lesser kyogen

24 His registered name was Toratoki, later known as Tora'aki, aka Tora'akira.
25 Shibano, "Kyogen: the comic as drama," Section 49, 84.
26 Ohashi Ryosuke, "The hermeneutic approach to Japanese Modernity: 'art-way,' 'iki,' and 'cut-continuance,'" in Michael F. Marra (ed.), *Japanese Hermeneutics: Current Debates on Aesthetics and Interpretation* (Honolulu: University of Hawai'i Press, 2002), 28–9.

players, although such acting was criticized for being "kabuku," deviant. Tora'aki's critical comments thus reveal his efforts to distinguish the Okura school style from this new, popular drama. The *Waranbegusa*'s completion greatly contributed to this, and Tora'aki transferred patrimony to his son in 1661. Today *Waranbegusa* is highly valued. Many original treatises remain in the hands of the Okura Yauemon family.

MINAE YAMAMOTO SAVAS AND
SEKIYA TOSHIHIKO

that might appeal more to commoners. The Sagi school, developing somewhat later, borrowed from both while displaying a newcomer's novel appeal. However, individual families established their particular flavors within the larger guild, retaining rights to their own jealously guarded scripts, accommodating their particular circumstances of regional/urban and samurai/townsperson spectatorship.

From skeletal outlines to fully fleshed scripts

Kyogen written texts developed quite distinctly from noh; in fact no extant written texts predate 1642, 200 years later than noh's oldest. Kyogen are anonymous, as opposed to noh's wealth of performer-playwrights. In *Waranbegusa*, Okura Tora'akira attributes plays to the great priest Gen'ei of Mount Hiei and Komparu Shirojirō, a spurious bid for respectable authority to a murky past. Kyogen began as improvisations on familiar comic tales, proverbs, or contemporary anecdotes. They employed vernacular language, adapting to contemporary audiences.

Eventually, 102 were written only as summaries in the so-called *Tenshō-bon* (1578).[27] These were scenarios written without dialogue, nonetheless providing a solid basis for actors to improvise dialogue. *Suehirogari* (The felicitous fan), a typical auspicious play still performed, is translated here in its entirety:

> A Daimyo appears and calls his servant. He tells the servant to go [to] the capital and buy the most expensive fan (*suehiro*) he can find. [The servant goes to Kyoto, and begins calling about that he wants to buy a suehiro.] A Shyster appears and sells him an umbrella instead. The Shyster also tells him that if his master gets angry at him, he should sing this song. "On Umbrella Mountain, on Umbrella Mountain, if other people open their umbrellas, I'll open my umbrella too." The servant goes home. When the Master sees what the Servant has bought, he gets angry. He chases the Servant out of the house. Then the Servant begins singing and dancing. The Master listens and enjoys the song so much that he begins dancing too. Master and Servant dance together. The play ends with a sound from the flute.[28]

27 The table of contents contains 150 titles, yet inexplicably there are summaries of only 102.
28 Hisashi Hata, *Kyōgen*, trans. Don Kenny (Osaka: Hoikusha Color Books, 1982), 33.

While entrances and some blocking are thus carefully described, there is no dialogue. Song lyrics are given in their entirety; in other plays, important *katari* speeches are also recorded. Such skeletal texts allowed a team of professional players to mount performances with a minimum of rehearsal. The exact language used, including extemporaneous ad libs, was left to performers' discretion, allowing kyogen to be continually refreshed by inspired improvisations according to the day's audience.

The *Tenshō-bon* summaries clearly were meant for actors. Scholars are divided about whether this was indeed the first book of scenarios, or merely the only extant copy of what may have been a continuous tradition. The plays are well developed in structure and closely resemble scripts that would be published nearly a century later. Yet not until 1642 did the thirteenth head-master of the Okura school, Tora'akira, record 182 plays (see Focus 3.1), yet these diverged even from his father's texts (recorded later). Similar compilations by the Izumi school, *Rikugi* or *Tenri-bon* (1646), and Sagi school (1724) followed. Successive headmasters revised these scripts, while branch families employed their own sometimes strikingly variant versions. The nineteenth Okura headmaster compiled the *Torahiro-bon* (1792), containing 165 scripts in versions rationalizing much of the 1642 version; the sixth Izumi head, Yamawaki Mototada (1747–1816), compiled the *Kumogata-bon* (Cloud-pattern book) of 200 plays. These are close to those versions performed today. Distinctions of roles, plots, and dialogue demonstrate the fluid nature of early performance. Contemporary reference books and song collections show that kyogen texts comprised authentic vernacular locutions and popular ditties of several centuries, leavened with a stage language found only in the codified scripts.[29]

Okashi or kyogen with consistent titles and themes were performed continually for centuries since the thirteenth century by amateur and professional players, alternating officially with noh on programs since the early fifteenth century. Yet if complete summaries of a large repertoire were available by 1570, why were no scripts including dialogue recorded until 1642? Possibly there were written records guarded among families and troupes that disappeared. The aforementioned punishments suggest that it might have been dangerous to commit some of the sharper-edged satire to print. Furthermore, in a competitive business, when kyogen's simple banter and songs could be performed by talented tesarugaku players, committing memory to paper distributed to ambitious troupe members or amateurs, rather than teaching them orally, might risk oversaturating the market.

Koyama further argues that there was no need for texts to be written, since performers had set patterns of actions and verbal banter that required

---

29 Sitasuwan, "Language usage in kyogen," 33.

just the bare outlines of a premise. Only with the establishment of the four schools of noh (later five) by the shogunate in early Edo were titles required to be submitted for inspection, and approved prior to performances. Soon, the fluid language of the plays was set in print. Once vernacular spoken language was transcribed, it soon grew archaic compared with the rapidly changing spoken language of faddish Edo society. Actors needed to standardize speeches such as *nanori* name-taking and *yobidashi* calling of servant merely in order to memorize the unfamiliar language for hundreds of plays in the repertory.[30] For example, four names for the lead servant character in the 1662 *Tenri-bon* were reduced and rationalized to one in the 1792 *Torahiro-bon*: Tarō Kaja. By the early eighteenth century, each of the three kyogen stylistic schools had family-maintained texts with character names, dialogue, and stage directions, and with phonetic pronunciation guides for difficult terms in what had become a conventional stage language.

Numerous extant family scripts, diverging from the official standard canon, are evidence of the semi-independent nature of the family-based troupes. There are variant titles, inserted speeches, and even alternative endings (see representative plays, p. 74). A series of illustrated kyogen texts reprinted continuously from 1700 for two centuries demonstrate the popularity of the dialogue-based comedic art.[31] Yet despite the apparent authenticity of their illustrations and dialogue, they are regarded by scholars today as pirate editions of professional plays, published for the curious public, rather than authentic family texts.

The extant total of 264 plays performed today is the result of centuries of selection, for reasons both artistic and political, winnowing thousands of play-scripts or summaries found in variant family and school traditions. Some were eliminated from the official *nayose* (title list) submitted to the shogunate because of satiric or scatological dialogue, others because they were of inferior quality or too similar to better plays. Still other large-cast plays were taken off the menu, too challenging to serve up on command.

Reviving plays extinguished from the current repertoire is a time-honored way for actors to assert themselves. The skills of a contemporary playwright, dramaturge, director, and producer are employed while hedging against criticism for something entirely new by securely locating the site of experiment as archival revivals (*fukkyoku*: 復曲). Actors pay obeisance to their ancestors by combing through secret transmissions and texts, discovering plays that deserve recognition, then rewriting and restaging them. Sometimes a play from another school not in their own school menu is tweaked, adding to

---

30 Hashimoto et al., *Kyōgen no sekai*, 33.
31 Sekiya Toshihiko, *Kyōgen-shi no kisoteki kenkyū* (Fundamental research in kyogen history) (Osaka: Kenkyū sōsho, 1994).

their permanent school repertory. Shigeyama Sennojō (1923–2010) revived eight plays in the 1960s and 1970s, including the large-scale satire of samurai folly *Konomi arasoi* (Battle of fruit and nuts), self-dubbed "porno kyogen" *Negawari* (Sleep substitute), Izumi school *Rokujizō* (Six Jizō sculptures), and solo kyogen *Hitorimatsutake* (Mushroom hunting). Each time, he returned to prewar compilations or texts found in the 1648 *Toraʾakira-bon*, to discover some grains among the chaff. With no performance history, actors could direct innovatively: in *Mimeyoshi* (Handsome boy), Sennojō employed two *hashigakari* bridgeways flanking the stage as a revival of an occasional practice in noh theatres. Successful revivals bring novelty to the standard repertoire: the aforementioned plays are still performed by members of the Shigeyama family today.[32]

Explicators and facilitators: ai-kyogen

Solemn, straightforward, and practical, ai-kyogen have been often over-looked by spectators and scholars until recently. These once vital and en-tertaining explanations often serve as excuses for spectators to take a break or exchange greetings, or read their printed summaries. However kyogen actors have always provided necessary support to noh players as messen-gers, explicators of complex tales, or suspenseful harbingers of second-act climaxes. The importance of ai is evidenced by their pervasivenesss: of the 250 or so extant noh plays, 100 employ ai.

The ai-kyogen actor moves the story along, accomplishing small tasks for masked characters who might otherwise find such movements undignified, too realistic, or undramatic. Ai also clarify plot points or allusions to historic events that might otherwise be lost as noh came to feature longer and more complex song and dance, stylized recitative, and masks that made dialogue less comprehensible. As audiences expanded from aristocracy to lesser sam-urai and commoners after Zeami, and diffused from urban cultural centers to distant provinces, references to obscure Chinese poetry would also have been difficult to follow.

The ai also served the practical purpose of providing time for actors to change costumes. Noh plays are estimated to have taken only 40 minutes (less than half that taken today) yet costumes were simpler in Zeami's day, so a leading noh master might perform in the majority of plays in a program of seven or nine plays. These demanded kyogen interludes to the two-act structure as well as *hon-kyōgen* between plays.

---

32 Shigeyama Sennojō, *Kyōgen yakusha: hinekure handaiki* (Kyogen actor: chronicle of a perverse half life) (Tokyo: Iwanami shinsho Series 396, 1987), 166–80.

Fig 14 The *ai-kyogen* (Shigeyama Sennojō) comforts *shirabyōshi* dancer Shizuka (Matsui Akira) in *Funa Benkei* (Benkei in a boat).

Ashirai interludes, mostly found in fourth-category living persons category plays, feature kyogen actors playing an attendant or maid who engages the shite, tsure, or waki in conversation. The Boatman leading Yoshitsune and Benkei to safety in *Funa Benkei* (Benkei in a boat, see representative plays, p. 35 and

Figure 14) creates great tension while poling the boat through choppy waters. The Hanjō introductory ai features an inn proprietress explaining why she must fire a prostitute who has fallen in love with a passing nobleman. These dialogue ai may include unrelated characters and even self-contained plays (*geki-ai*), large-cast plays performed only occasionally as alternative ai. Many are performed today independently of the noh play to which they were originally attached, such as *Sarumuko* (Monkey bridegroom), a simian wedding ceremony entirely in gibberish that was once a variant ai in the noh *Arashiyama*.

Eventually, perhaps to prevent kyogen actors from stealing the show, the ai took on a more explicatory role, with simple declamation. Among *katari-ai* narrative interludes, the most common is the *igatari* seated narrative (found in sixty-five plays, with another ten mixed with other ai types). Normally, the local person waits until summoned by the waki to take center stage, then relates incidents relevant to the drama, local legends, or parallel tales, before retreating, as prologue to the shite's reappearance.

Tachishaberi (standing speech) interludes feature standing or kneeling declamation. The majority are *kuchiake* (opening) introductions that set the atmosphere and context in a solo narrative. Tachishaberi include *matsusha* (minor god) interludes usually performed in first-category noh plays, where a lesser god, or spirit of a dragon, *tengu* goblin, hermit priest, or even fruit or fish, reveals the miraculous powers of the featured deity. Even more active (*shikata*) interludes are formal narratives, with pantomimic gestures describing a historic tale. These dynamic narratives, such as one describing the great archer in *Yashima*, are rarely performed alternative interludes (*kae-ai*), dramatic self-contained tales displaying the actors' vocal and acting virtuosity. The most dramatic are *hayauchi* (quick drumbeat) interludes, where the attendant rushes in to warn of and confront an imminent threat, shouting "Hurry!"

The development of ai displays a clear trajectory from active banter to staid narration, with flashier, longer, and large-cast interludes relegated to alternatives, or independent plays. Why did ai grow increasingly important? Gorgeous costumes donated by noblemen and daimyo required longer changing times between acts. As noh flourished in both town and country, spectators of a widening spectrum of classes were unable to otherwise follow the stories, reliant as these were on allusions to old poetry and tales, chanted by chorus and sung behind masks, which had become standard by mid-Muromachi (late fifteenth century). Since ai were largely improvised in a vernacular language, they continued adapting long after noh language had been fixed as written texts. Denied movement, the kyogen actors' storytelling technique improved, so that spectators requiring the information they imparted could also enjoy their narrative artistry.

TABLE 3.1 Major kyogen families today				
Izumi (和泉)				
	Tokyo		Nagoya	
Yamawaki – Izumi	Miyake Tōkurō	Nomura Manzō	Nomura Matasaburō	Kyogen Cooperative Society
Okura (大蔵)				
	Tokyo	Kyoto		Osaka-Kobe
Okura Yaemon	Yamamoto Tōjirō	Shigeyama Sengorō	Shigeyama Chūzaburō	Zenchiku Yagorō

Kyogen decline and restoration in Meiji

With the fall of the shogunate in 1868, school headmasters' main lines, loyal to their foundering patrons, largely disappeared. However regional performers gathered in major cities to pursue their craft, seeking new patrons among the new political and economic elites, as obscure branch families often ended up leading the traditions' revival (Table 3.1).

The Okura headmasters' line was temporarily extinguished with twenty-second headmaster Toratoshi (1841–81), who had declared that, rather than invite confusion, it was "better to be destroyed through defending."[33] The Yaemon branch, established by a younger brother to the *iemoto* in 1634, died out during Meiji with the eighth generation. However Yamamoto Tōjirō (later Azuma, 1836–1902), who had been a favorite rehearsal partner of head Toratoshi, received thorough training and family texts. This Yamamoto family moved from service to Bungo samurai (Oita prefecture, Kyushu) to Tokyo in 1878, preserving there the Okura school's severe, formal style. Of entirely different complexion, the Shigeyama Sengorō family continued a line of actors serving the imperial family and townsmen of Kyoto since 1687. Revived by an adopted son Sengorō Masatora (1810–86), along with branch family Chūzaburō, they served the imperial court. There, ceremonial music was *gagaku*, while noh-kyogen was considered entertainment, one that also appealed to Kyoto commoners. Such grassroots support allowed the Shigeyamas to better withstand the winds of the Meiji change than the main school families in Tokyo.

In contradistinction, Izumi school branch families gradually moved with political and economic shifting tides to Tokyo. During the Meiji Restoration, top-down authority of all kinds was being questioned. When Motokiyo, the sixteenth Izumi headmaster, expelled three actors for performing an important school play without permission in 1907, he himself

---

33 Kobayashi Seki, "Kyogen in the postwar era," adapted and trans. Shinko Kagaya, *ATJ* 24:1 (2007), 164.

was excommunicated, leading to the headmaster's vacancy until 1940. In 1936, Miyake Tōkurō V, semi-professional disciple attached to the Maeda clan of Kaga (Kanazawa), revived his defunct teacher's line with his son as Miyake Tōkurō IX (1901–90). His eldest son was adopted as Izumi Motohide (1937–95), nineteenth Izumi school iemoto. Another son, Manzō VI (1898–1978, National Living Treasure 1968), headed the Nomura family. Nomura Matasaburō XII (1921–), historically attached to the Owari daimyo, moved to Tokyo but returned to Nagoya in 1959, alongside the Izumi style carried on by the Kyogen Collective, a group of seven unaffiliated actors established in 1949.

The Sagi school, historically more innovative and flashy, made the greatest attempt to adapt to the new Meiji circumstances, eventually leading to their demise. With the shogunal patronage gone, the nineteenth headmaster could not continue performing, or prevent dispersal of the few branch families. More so than other schools, there were few branch families, and most were affiliated with the Kanze school, whose dependence on the shogun proved costly. Some underemployed Sagi school actors participated in performances of Azuma noh-kyogen, a new musical entertainment genre of mixed-school and kabuki musicians. They also taught and sold costumes to actors of kabuki, the flourishing people's theatre, including one for *Hanago* (see representative plays, p. 74). The new genre did not catch on, however, while their mingling with vulgar kabuki brought excommunication by the Nohgaku Performers' Association. Thus lack of leadership, dependence on shogunate patronage, and loss of talented members through excommunication resulted in the school's extinction. Amateur traditions continue in Yamaguchi prefecture and Sado Island in Niigata prefecture.

Revival and boom

Renewed nationalism earned new respect and attention from scholars and patrons beginning in the 1930s. Largely ignored after the Meiji Restoration as frivolous, kyogen was viewed as a living treasure house of folk and literary traditions, medieval language, and life among everyday townspeople. Reflecting the anti-nationalist rhetoric at war's end, articles reassessed kyogen as festive and satiric critiques of shogunate taboos, expressing farmers', townspeople's, and lower-ranked samurai rebellion against feudal authorities. New scholarly and traditional arts support societies emerged, bringing kyogen actors together with noh actors and musicians on equal footing, unthinkable in prewar hierarchies.

Postwar meritocracy, ease of travel on bullet trains (the line connecting Osaka with Tokyo began in 1964), and a surge in all-kyogen performances led to the rise of ambitious and talented individuals, regardless of school or even family hierarchies.

∾ **SPOTLIGHT 3.1**   **Family rivalries: the Nomura and Shigeyama families**

Throughout kyogen's modern history, entrepreneurial branch troupes and second sons within them have frequently established, by necessity, new financial opportunities and creative turf. Brothers Shigeyama Sengorō and Sennojō in Kyoto, and Nomura Manzō VII (now Man, 1930–) and Mansaku (1931–) in Tokyo and their descendants lead the postwar kyogen world with accessible traditional interpretations and experimental collaborations and revivals.

As youths, Sensaku IV and brother Sennojō (1923–) engaged in performances outside the kyogen sphere. They kyogenized the medieval French farce *Le Cuvier* (The washing bucket), adapted Mishima Yukio's *Aya no tsuzumi* (The damask drum, 1955) with Western singers and noh musicians, appeared in kabuki in Kyoto (1955) and Tokyo (1964), and even choreographed a "nude noh" for a girls' revue in Osaka (1956). Nearly excommunicated from the Nohgaku Performers' Association, they were saved by their father's intervention, the Association's debt to producer Takechi Tetsuji for his support during the war, and mass media rallying against feudal authorities. They thus managed to gain relative independence, paving the way for other performers. Sengorō was considered a "once in a century performer," who merely steps on stage to embody the persona of Tarō Kaja, and also an inspired collaborator on kyogen-style Greek comedies, radio drama, and new kyogen. His grandchildren are well known through their energetic renditions of traditional kyogen, as well as appearances in television dramas, and collaborations with noh, kabuki, *rakugo*, and *buyō*, and modern theatre performers.

Apprenticing under Takechi, Sennojō's activities included acting, writing, reviving, and directing traditional kyogen, inter-genre experiments, and opera. He appeared as the farmer-husband in Kinoshita Junji's classic modern theatre play *Yūzuru* (Twilight crane, see representative plays, p. 283) over 500 times throughout Japan. His son Akira (1952–) directs opera and collaborates with rakugo storytellers and commedia dell'arte troupes. He co-founded the Noho Theatre Group in 1981, performing short plays by Samuel Beckett, Shakespeare adaptations, and bilingual kyogen in Kyoto and frequent tours abroad (see Figure 13).

If Kyoto's Shigeyamas represent the power of complementary teamwork, Tokyo's Nomuras display the creative friction of sibling rivalry. Nomura Manzō VI, Living National Treasure, was a superb performer, mask-carver, and author of numerous invaluable texts on kyogen practice and philosophy. His treatises stressed the lifetime training necessary for kyogen mastery, plotting the actor's growth in especially challenging roles from "monkey to fox."[34] Putting theory into practice, his sons Manzō VII and Mansaku both became National Living Treasures. The brothers have carved out niches for themselves in traditional theatre and beyond as disciplined yet creative masters who have a thorough technical mastery of vocalization, dance, and acting, and a keen sense of kyogen's dramatic potential. They appeared in Takechi's kabuki performances with the Shigeyamas, in adaptations of Mishima's modern noh, folk-plays by Kinoshita Junji, and other new noh experiments alongside Kanze Hideo and Hisao.

Manzō VII directed new kyogen and revivals, and many versions of Yeats' *Takahime* (Hawk Princess), a directorial vision inherited by his eldest son Mannojō (posthumously Manzō VIII [1959–2004]). He presented kyogen at Eugenio Barba's ISTA seminars and Ariane Mnouchkine's ARTA workshops, and directed adaptations of Japanese horror stories and imaginative children's

---

34 Nomura Manzō, *Manzō Nomura chōsaku* (Collected writings of Manzō Nomura), ed. Hisashi Furukawa and Seki Kobayashi (Tokyo: Satsuki shobo, 1982).

tales such as *Snow White* and *Little Red Riding Hood*. Drawing on Asian mask traditions from Tibet, Bali, and India, he revived the lost masked-drama *gigaku* as an exotic musical parade.[35]

Mansaku, younger by a year, became a tenacious rival. He teaches and tours abroad frequently, training early English kyogen exponents Yuriko Doi of Theatre of Yugen in San Francisco and Tokyo's Don Kenny. Mansaku's direction of a kyogen based on Falstaff tales, *Hōrai samurai* (The braggart samurai, 1991), was well received at home and abroad.

His son Mansai (1966–) has achieved unparalleled success off the noh stage. Receiving government support for two years to study theatre at the Royal Shakespeare Company and with Theatre de Complicité in London, he returned with a new perspective on kyogen's place in world theatre. He has shown an affinity for Shakespeare, playing Hamlet, and directing adaptations of *The Comedy of Errors* (2002)[36] and a much-revived *Macbeth*. He has directed-adapted *Rashōmon* (2001),[37] and starred in Ninagawa Yukio's *King Oedipus* (2002). As artistic director of Tokyo's Setagaya Public Theatre since 2002, Mansai has produced a Contemporary Noh series written by contemporary playwrights, including Noda Hideki's *The Bee*, Kawamura Takeshi's *Aoi/Komachi*, and Sakate Yōji's Ibsen adaptations. His tremendous popularity extends beyond the kyogen stage, appearing in Kurosawa Akira's *Ran* (1985) and as wizard Abe no Seimei in the historical fantasy *Onmyōji* (2001), on a children's public television program and on frequent outreach programs.

With the noh world's decline in popularity and young actors, the kyogen Shigeyama and Nomura families continue to prosper through their energetic interpretations of tradition, while opening the classic art to outside influences and collaborations.

JONAH SALZ

Regional distinctions consequently became less important. Director-producer Takechi Tetsuji (1912–88) promoted Kansai actors in Tokyo, and even mixed-school east–west kyogen recitals in 1948 and 1949 in Tokyo. A series of kyogen experiments in the 1950s led to the so-called "kyogen boom," a rise in awareness, popularity, and esteem theretofore unrealized. All-kyogen programs of experimental works were attempted: mixed-school performance of *Buaku* (1953), an adaptation of the French farce *Le Cuvier* (The washing bucket) as *Susugigawa* (The washing river, 1953) (see representative plays, p. 76), "Kyogen à la Mime," and noh-style adaptations of *shingeki* plays *Yūzuru* (Twilight crane), with music by Dan Ikuma, and kyogen-style *Higashi wa Higashi* (East is East, [Iwata Toyoo, 1893–1969]) depicting a Chinese–Japanese international marriage squabble, broke many precedents by pairing a Takarazuka actress with a kyogen actor, featuring gagaku music.

35 Yoshiko Fukushima, "Masks, interface of past and future: Nomura Mannojo's Shingigaku," *ATJ* 22:2 (2005), 249–68.
36 *The Kyogen of Errors* (DVD) English subtitles (Columbia, 2005).
37 *Yabu no naka* (In a thicket) DVD, English subtitles (Tokyo: M & O Productions, 1999).

Schools today

The Okura school today is comprised of seventy-six professionals (approximately half of them full-time) of the Yamamoto and Okura families in Tokyo, Shigeyama Sengorō and Chūzaburō in Kyoto, and Zenchiku in Osaka-Kobe. Since the Okura headmaster and Zenchiku branch families were both originally Shigeyamas, there are basically only two artistic branches, Yamamoto and Shigeyama. The Yamamotos, sole preservers of the conservative, austere ceremoniousness shared with noh as practiced under the shogunate, flourished under Tōjirō (1898–1964), an intellectual and precise performer.

Tōjirō disparaged the Sengorō family style and their mingling with kabuki actors in the 1950s, even refusing temporarily to perform with them. When a journalist criticized the Sengorō family's ubiquitous shrine and temple festival performances as cheap and plentiful as tofu, they appropriated it as their family slogan. They prided themselves on "tofuism," providing high-quality and enjoyable comedy accessible to the masses through a wide variety of events: commemorations, temple celebrations, regular civic programs, and school tours. The Sengorō family have enjoyed a remarkable run of exceptional performers, including Sensaku III (1896–1986, Living National Treasure 1976) and Sensaku IV (1919–2010, Living National Treasure 1989). The success of the current three generations of actors on television, in sci-fi and contemporary-themed kyogen, and adaptations of Grimm, Beckett, and Shakespeare, and as collaborators with a wide spectrum of writers, genres, and venues, demonstrates their continuing ability to ride the tides of popular entertainment.

Their branch family member Chūzaburō, having spent longer in Edo before returning to Kyoto, has a somewhat gentler but formal style. The second son of Chūzaburō III, Yagorō (1883–1965) achieved numerous accolades and awards, establishing the Zenchiku branch family (1963) and being declared a Living National Treasure in 1964, a first for a kyogen actor. His precise, realistic style won admirers, and under his five sons the family now flourishes in Osaka, Kobe, and Tokyo. His second son married the former Okura headmaster's great-granddaughter, reviving the dormant Okura headmastership in 1941 as the twenty-fourth head, Yatarō (later Yaemon, 1912–2004).

The performers in the Izumi family comprise the Nomura Matasaburō family and Kyogen Collective in Nagoya, and three families based in Tokyo – Izumi, Miyake, and Nomura – derived from the same Miyake family. The nineteenth iemoto Motohide caused significant strains within the school by promoting his daughters to the professional Nohgaku Performers'

Association, Junko (1969–) in 1989 and Miyake Tōkurō (1972–) in 1993. Yet after his untimely death at 52, the sisters had yet to be fully accepted into the conservative noh-kyogen world. This was further complicated by the fact that Motohide's eldest son Motoya (1974–), who attempted to don the headmaster mantle at 20, was expelled from the Nohgaku Performers' Association for failure to respect stage commitments. While, in a few generations, the iemoto's prestige and power thus disappeared, the Izumi school still flourishes due to talented and entrepreneurial sub-clans.

Kyogen's popularity is evident from postwar regular all-kyogen programs, school tours, and university club and culture center classes. These led and fed a rise in disciples and fans supporting individual actors, who enjoyed a golden age of talent, popularity, and performance opportunities. Their dynamic interpretations, often accompanied by explanatory lectures and detailed program notes, contribute to kyogen's continuing popularity as accessible traditional entertainment. To give just one example of the breadth of experiment, many kyogen actors have challenged Shakespeare. Performances have been well received in Japan and abroad of the Izumi family's *Twelfth Night* and *A Midsummer Night's Dream*; Nomura family's adaptation of Falstaff tales, *The Braggart Samurai*, and *The Comedy of Errors*; Shigeyama Akira as Gravedigger in Noho's *Hamlet* and Porter in *Macbeth*; the Zenchiku family adaptations of *Twelfth Night, Othello, Macbeth*, and *Romeo and Juliet*, by noh actor Sekine Masaru. Kyogen nurtures its young audiences, despite the recent economic downturn, through websites, workshops and lectures, fan club events, and photo opportunities, ensuring the continuation of this classical yet perennially popular entertainment.

References and further reading

ATJ, Kyogen issue, ed. Julie Iezzi and Jonah Salz, 24:1 (2007)

Furukawa Hisashi *et al. Kyōgen jiten* (Kyogen encyclopedia), 3 vols. (Tokyo: Tokyōdo, 1963–76)

Geinōshi Kenkyûsha. *Kyōgen: okashi no keifu* (Kyogen: geneaology of jesters) (Tokyo: Heibonsha, 1970)

Hashimoto Akio, Koyama Hiroshi, and Taguchi Kazuo (eds.). *Kyōgen no sekai* (The world of kyogen), *Iwanami kōza nō-kyōgen* (Iwanami's Noh-kyogen course), vol. V (Tokyo: Iwanami, 1987)

Hata Hisashi. *Kyōgen*, trans. Don Kenny (Osaka: Hoikusha Color Books, 1982)

Hayashi Kazutoshi. *Nō, kyōgen no seisei to tenkai ni kansuru kenkyū* (Birth and development of noh and kyogen) (Kyoto: Sekai shisōsha, 2003)

Kenny, Don. *A Guide to Kyogen* (Kyoto: Hinoki shoten, 1968)
    The Kyogen Book: An Anthology of Japanese Classical Comedies (Tokyo: The Japan
        Times, 1989)
Kobayashi Seki (trans. Shinko Kagaya). "Kyōgen in the postwar era," *ATJ* 24:1 (2007)
        144–77
McKinnon, Richard. *Selected Plays of Kyogen* (Seattle: Uniprint, 1968)
Morley, Carolyn Anne. *Transformation, Miracles, and Mischief: The Mountain Priest
        Plays of Kyogen* (Ithaca, NY: Cornell East Asia Series, 1993)
Sakanishi, Shio. *The Ink-Smeared Lady and Other Japanese Folk-Plays* (Rutland, VT:
        Charles Tuttle, 1964)
Salz, Jonah. "Roles of passage in kyogen training," in John Singleton (ed.), *Situated
        Learning in Japan* (Cambridge: Cambridge University Press, 1998), 233–45

WEBSITES AND DVDs
(Kenny, Don). Kyogen in English http://kyogen-in-english.com
Shigeyama Akira (dir.) Jonah Salz (adapt. and trans.). *This is Kyogen* (DVD) (Kyoto:
        Shigeyama International Projects, 1993)
Shigeyama Akira (dir.) Jonah Salz (adapt. and trans.). *Busu* (Poison sugar) (DVD)
        (Kyoto: Shigeyama International Projects, 1993)

FOCUS 3.1 OKURA TORA'AKI(RA): COMIC TEXTS AND THEORY
Okura Tora'akira. *Nō Kyōgen-shū: honkoku chūkai* (Collection of annotated Okura
        Tora'akira's kyogen plays) (Tokyo: Seibundo, 2006)
Sasano Ken (ed.). *Waranbegusa* (Tokyo: Iwanami shoten, 1962)
Shibano, Dorothy. "Kyogen: the comic as drama," Ph.D. diss., University of
        Washington, 1973
Ueda Makoto, *Literary and Art Theories in Japan* (Cleveland, OH: Press of Western
        Reserve University, 1967)

Interlude: *Iemoto*: the family head system

ERIC C. RATH

The development of the *iemoto* (family head, 家元) system shaped the history of many traditional Japanese performing arts and continues to have a weighty influence on training, repertoire, and staging in noh and kyogen, nihonbuyo (classical Japanese dance), and kabuki musicians. Additionally, the iemoto system offers a point of commonality between traditional drama and other arts, such as tea ceremony, flower arrangement, and martial arts' organizational structures. Conversely, the lack of an iemoto distinguishes kabuki from noh and kyogen, although several kabuki actors head schools of classical Japanese dance. As scholar Nishiyama Matsunosuke has explored, familiarity with iemoto and their institutional powers, which comprise an "iemoto system," sheds light on continuities across traditional arts.

Though translated as "family," *ie* also means "lineage and household," and usage, especially before World War II, "evokes the image of an absolute and often arbitrarily exercised patriarchal authority."[38] The authority of the iemoto (also referred to as the *sōke*, 宗家) derives from being the primary successor by birth, adoption, or marriage to a family controlling an artistic dynasty with a distinct style (school or *ryūgi,* 流儀) of performance established by the family's founder.

Noh provides an example of one of the most orthodox and powerful iemoto systems of all Japanese arts. Kanze Kiyokazu (1959–), current iemoto of the Kanze school, is the twenty-sixth hereditary leader, tracing his ancestry to Zeami (1363?–1443?) and his father Kan'ami (1333–84). Kiyokazu's position gives him power over professionals and amateurs in the Kanze school. Familial authority not only makes the iemoto synonymous with his artistic lineage, but also grants him a direct line to the highest and most complete expertise of his specialty, whether found in secret manuscripts transmitted in his family or received in specialized training from the best teachers, including the

---

38 Jordan Sand, "At home in the Meiji period: inventing Japanese domesticity," in Stephen Vlastos (ed.), *Mirror of Modernity: Invented Traditions of Modern Japan* (Berkeley: University of California Press, 1998), 191.

previous iemoto. The depth of iemoto expertise is exemplified by the expression "isshi sōden" (exclusively transmitted to one child), referring to knowledge so secret that only one person per generation is entitled to receive it.

Use of the word iemoto in relation to performing arts dates to the mid-eighteenth century but, from at least Zeami's era, leaders of noh troupes (*za*) jealously guarded secrets of their craft. They carefully transmitted knowledge to successors and select disciples just as aristocratic families in the Heian period (794–1185) restricted access to their expertise in areas of specialized training like poetry and astrology. The heads of medieval noh troupes ruled over a small company of performers, but from the late 1500s, with increased specialization in aspects of noh performance such as musical instruments, noh eventually gave rise to multiple iemoto. Today, the five schools of principal performers (*shite*) are headed by their own iemoto, who are descendants of leaders of medieval and early modern noh troupes, while different schools of musicians, side actors (*waki*), and kyogen actors have their own iemoto (Table 2.1). From the early modern period (1600–1868), noh iemoto published libretti (*utaibon*) and other pedagogical texts for professional and amateur use, facilitating stylistic uniformity and further extending the iemoto's authority. The iemoto sets standards for their style, including the most prosaic choreographed movements (*kata*), and his permission is required for any variations (*kogaki*) on standard staging.

Scholars Yokomichi Mario and Kobayashi Seki have described the extensive powers the five iemoto of the shite schools wield today:

1 control of the repertoire
2 final decision over contents of texts
3 discretion over staging, including right to allow or disavow performances, to ban actors from taking certain roles, and to approve actors' use and ownership of stages, masks, and costumes
4 right to determine an actor's professional status and membership within a school of noh and to decide which actors can perform together
5 power to establish and gain revenue from licenses
6 authority to publish plays and related media, enforce their use, and derive income from them.

Watching noh today, one might forget the extent to which a performance must follow the iemoto's guidelines, but his powers also extend into the training of amateur students. Noh actors earn most of their income from teaching non-professional students studying the art as a hobby.[39] Serious amateur students purchase licenses before being permitted to study certain dances

---

39 Katrina L. Moore, *The Joy of Noh: Embodied Learning and Discipline in Urban Japan* (Albany, NY: SUNY, 2014).

and plays, and then again to perform them at a recital. Sales of licenses and approved pedagogical materials, such as copyrighted libretti or DVDs, account for a major source of income for iemoto. In schools of classical dance, tea ceremony, and flower arrangement, the more exalted the license – which at the highest level includes taking an "artistic name" (*natori, geimei*), incorporating some of the Chinese characters of one's immediate teacher's name into one's own artistic name – the higher the cost.

The iemoto's steady hand ensures preservation of traditional performing arts at a very high standard, but innovation and individual artistic interpretation potentially suffer (see interview with Takemoto Mikio, p. 192). Iemoto may allow the staging of new noh plays, but usually permit only senior actors to appear, and few modern works are allowed into the repertoire. Noh and kyogen are traditional not only in the sense of their fixed canon of plays and classical performance style, but also in their patriarchal and feudal modes of organization that comprise their iemoto systems.

References and further reading

Keene, Donald. "The iemoto system (nō and kyōgen)," in John Rosenfeld (ed.), *Fenway Court 1992,* Isabella Gardner Museum papers (Boston, 1993), 30–6

Nishiyama Matsunosuke. *Iemoto no kenkyū* (Research on family heads) (Tokyo: Yoshikawa kōbunkan, 1982)

    Iemotosei no tenkai (The development of the family head system) (Tokyo: Yoshikawa kōbunkan, 1982)

    Edo Culture: Daily Life and Diversions in Urban Japan, 1600–1868 (Honolulu: University of Hawai'i Press, 1997)

Ortolani, Benito. "Iemoto," *Japan Quarterly* 16:3 (1969), 297–306

Rath, Eric C. *The Ethos of Noh: Actors and Their Art* (Cambridge, MA: Harvard University Asia Center, 2004)

Singleton, John (ed.). *Situated Learning in Japan* (Cambridge: Cambridge University Press, 1998)

Yokomichi Mario and Kobayashi Seki. *Nō, kyōgen* (Tokyo: Iwanami shoten, 1996)

4 ❧ Kabuki
Superheroes and *femmes fatales*

JULIE A. IEZZI

Kabuki is a vibrant traditional form, known worldwide for its colorful make-up, complex plots, beautiful dance, all-male performance tradition, intimate connection with the audience, broad, presentational, bravura acting, and integrated, cinematic use of music. Kabuki, which emerged alongside bunraku as the first commercial theatre forms in Japan, was largely nurtured by the commoner class, blossoming despite strict government regulation throughout the Tokugawa (Edo) period (1603–1868). When Japan was forcibly opened to the West in the Meiji era (1868–1912), kabuki responded to vast and rapid changes as leaders sought to remake this popular theatre form into one capable of representing a modern nation.

Rising nationalism with the spread of the Pacific War prompted renewed censorship and censure, but kabuki again adapted by creating new stage works to support the war effort. After World War II, kabuki reemerged with the more "classical" persona by which it is known today. Four centuries of accommodating public interests, artistic strengths, technological developments, and political changes have generated the living tradition of twenty-first-century kabuki, with markers of its evolution and eclectic origins still visible in the variety of plays staged today.

ELEMENTS OF PERFORMANCE

Performance context

Today, the Theatre Division of entertainment conglomerate Shōchiku Company controls all permanent kabuki venues, with the exception of the National Theatre, and manages all kabuki actor contracts. Monthly programs in Japan generally run for twenty-five days, with the remaining five or six for rehearsal of the following month's production. The Kabuki-za (Tokyo) runs monthly programs year-round. The Shōchiku-za (Osaka), Minami-za (Kyoto), Misono-za (Nagoya), Hakata-za (Fukuoka), Shinbashi Embujō (Tokyo), and Kanamaru-za (Shikoku) have kabuki programs one to three months each year, while summer touring productions bring single performances to civic halls in areas not served by major theatres. Kabuki can thus be seen throughout the country. There have been over sixty overseas tours of "Grand Kabuki" since World War II, giving 110 performances in ninety-six cities throughout Europe, North America, Asia, and Africa.

Programs at Shōchiku theatres consist of a late morning and an early evening show of about four hours each, offering a balance of dance pieces (*shosagoto*), excerpted highlight acts from popular traditional plays, and shorter one- or two-act *shin* (new) kabuki. By contrast, the National Theatre of Japan (Kokuritsu Gekijō, est. 1966) presents full-length (*tōshi kyōgen*) revivals, or several highlight acts from the same play. In the mid-1980s, the fast-paced "Super Kabuki" developed by Ichikawa Ennosuke III (1939–) brought in younger audiences while fueling dialogue about the genre's parameters. Beginning in the early 1990s, annual productions at Tokyo's Cocoon Theatre, and tent shows of Heisei Nakamura-za, both under Nakamura Kanzaburō XVIII (1955–2012), recreated the intimate and boisterous atmosphere of Edo era theatres, attracting younger audiences. A revival movement in the Kamigata area (Osaka and Kyoto), beginning in the 1990s, resulted in more productions, now available four or five months a year. Kabuki houses accommodate from 1,000 to 2,600 people, with tickets ranging from ¥2,000 to ¥20,000 (approximately US $20 to $200). Spectators in cheaper seats are rewarded with close proximity to connoisseurs who enliven the atmosphere with their calls of praise (*kakegoe*).

Staging and performance conventions

Although kabuki is often called an "actor's theatre," the elaborate costumes and highly specific wigs, conventionalized sets and props, and use of multiple musical genres require the teamwork of many specialized professionals.

As with many other traditional genres, kabuki is performed on a custom-built stage featuring several unique features. The *hanamichi* (lit. "flower path"), a passageway from the back of the auditorium to the stage, has been a regular part of kabuki architecture since the 1730s, creating an intimacy between actor and audience, whether used for the hero's grand entrances or high-ranking courtesan processions. The large revolving stage (*mawari butai*), first used in 1758, enables quick set changes or even continuous action on stage during scene changes. Numerous large and small trap doors (*seri*) enable everything from massive scenic units to musical ensembles or individual actors to emerge and disappear seamlessly.

∾ **SPOTLIGHT 4.1   Kabuki stage**

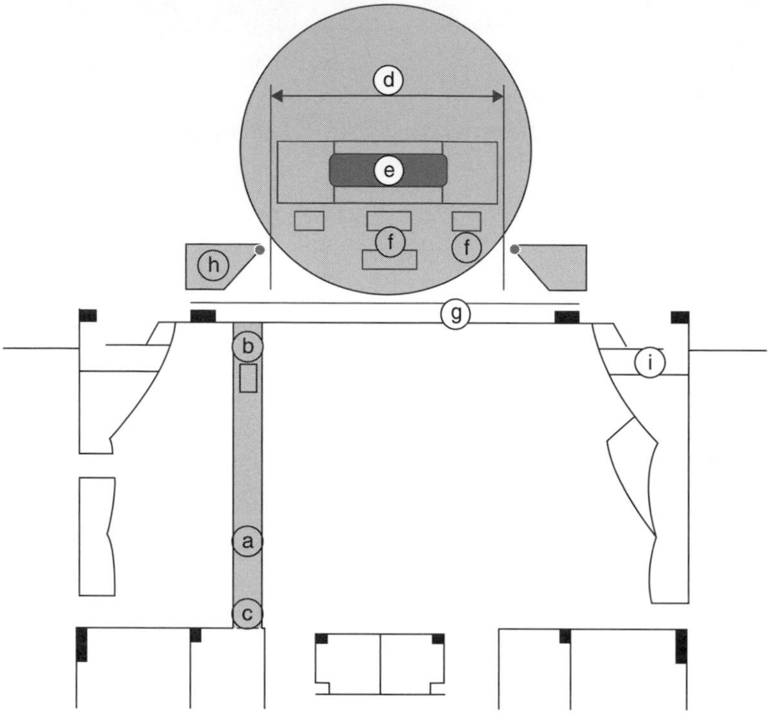

Fig 15 Kabuki stage.

It is difficult to see in today's kabuki stage the physical components of the noh stage, its original source. The first three centuries of kabuki history witnessed an evolutionary process as the kabuki stage shed the noh theatre's four pillars, bridgeway (*hashigakari*), and gabled stage roof, taking its present form in the late Meiji period (1868–1912).

(a) The **hanamichi** (walkway, lit.: flower-path) is inside the rectilinear auditorium, with one or two balconies, on the audience's left. This runway-like stage extension creates an intimate relationship between audience and actors. Five feet wide, extending from the forestage, it contains an elevator trap (**suppon**) (b) seven-tenths (*shichisan*) from the rear of the auditorium. Hanamichi acting highlights occur here, clearly visible to most spectators. Regardless of the auditorium rake, the runway remains level with the stage proper; a vital acting area, not merely an aisle. A dark blue curtain (**agemaku**) (c) is swished aside for entrances and exits of actors, who use the runway for processions and

important bits of acting, including supernatural characters rising from the trap. A twin hanamichi is sometimes set up audience right, but the consequent loss of income-generating seats has made its deployment infrequent, although it was a permanent feature of premodern theatres. Old-time theatres included an "empty well," a small, square space at the junction of the hanamichi and stage proper, filled with water and mud for special scenes.

The Stage Proper (**hon butai**) (d) was originally a playing area at one end of a temporary structure, without proscenium; it grew from eighteen feet wide during the Genroku era (1688–1703) to thirty-nine feet by 1889, when the first Kabuki-za opened. After the Meiji period, a proscenium was added and the stage dimensions grew wider. The current Kabuki-za stage is more than ninety feet wide but only twenty or so feet high. The flooring in first-class theatres, like that of noh, is cypress wood; to act on one is a high honor.

For scenes set on water, the stage and hanamichi are covered with blue ground cloths on which waves are painted; snow scenes use white cloths. For dance plays and certain highly stylized plays requiring reverberant stamping, special platforms are placed over both stage and hanamichi. Revolving either partially or completely allows for rapid shifting of scenes, prepared on the other side. More cinematic effects are also possible, as when the actor walks in the opposite direction to the revolve, passing through the changing scenery behind him.

Set within the revolving stage are a large elevator trap (**ōzeri**) (e) and one or two smaller ones (**kozeri**) (f). These permit actors, either alone or in tableaux, to rise and sink; they are also used for scenic units, one spectacular example being a huge temple gate.

Kabuki has multiple curtain (**maku**) (g) types; most notable is the standard curtain, an expansive draw curtain whose vertical colored stripes of black, green, and persimmon have become symbolic of kabuki itself. Premodern theatres each had their own color variations. The curtain opening and closing is dramatically accomplished by a black-garbed stage assistant who pulls it along to the rhythmic, accelerating and crescendo beating of wooden clappers (**hyōshigi** or **ki**). Non-classical and dance plays use a beautifully embroidered drop curtain typically bearing the sponsor's name. During the Edo era, the draw curtain was permitted in only a handful of licensed theatres; others used a drop curtain. Another useful device, the "**asagi maku**" (pale blue curtain), drops suddenly to reveal the scene behind it.

The offstage musicians who accompany plays occupy a music room (**geza or kuromisu**) (h) at stage right (stage left in the Edo period). The façade contains a rattan screen enabling musicians to observe the stage while being barely visible from the auditorium.

In plays requiring the bunraku-derived chanter and shamisen player combination, a chanter-shamisen player platform (**chobo yuka**) (i) is set up in front of an angled wall stage left. For minor scenes, the duo sits in a screened-in room on the second story.

Scenery (**ōdōgu**): Kabuki scenery ranges from realistic (mainly for dramas) to imagistic (primarily for dances). Some settings are spectacular, others darkly naturalistic, and still others abstract. Many take advantage of the revolving stage and elevator traps to shift from one locale to another or alter a scene's appearance, in full view of the audience.

Numerous specialized techniques are employed. The **gandō-gaeshi** flips a three-dimensional scenic unit backward ninety degrees on an axis so that a new set appears on the unit's underside. In **hikiwari**, a set separates at center to slide apart while a new one rises on an elevator trap. With **dengaku-gaeshi**, flats are rotated on an axis so that when one side is flipped, another comes into view.

Sets are constructed from standardized units, combining flats, pillars, steps, and platform units to depict many interior locales, including restaurants, homes, palaces, shops, and temples. These standardized units are combined with backdrops, three-dimensional, and cutout pieces to create exteriors such as valleys, forests, and riverbanks.

SAMUEL L. LEITER

Everything from character interpretation to choreography, costuming, and scenic design is governed by set patterns (*kata*). Kabuki acting is conventionalized, ranging from a slightly stylized "daily" presentational manner to *aragoto*: a bombastic, bravura acting. Acting and costuming kata, in particular, vary depending on the actor's artistic lineage. Regardless of play, character, or kata, kabuki acting is a frontal, presentational style that creates stage pictures reminiscent of historical woodblock prints (*shibai-e*).

∾ FOCUS 4.1   Actor prints

Fig 16 Diptych print by Utagawa Toyokuni III (1786–1865). *Koi moyō furisode meoto* (Narukami, the thunder god) performed at the Ichimura-za (1851).

The visual record of kabuki is by far the most extensive in world theatre. Woodblock print technology allowed for publication of tens of thousands of actor prints (*yakusha-e*) and illustrated books (*ehon*) from the late seventeenth century until the early twentieth century, in black and white (sometimes hand-colored), then from the 1760s in multiple colors. Actor prints and courtesan or beautiful women prints (*bijinga*) were staples of *ukiyo-e* throughout its history. Until the

Fig 16 (*cont.*)

1790s the common format was the *hosoban* (*c.* 33 ×
14 cm), after which the wider *ōban* (*c.* 37 × 26
cm) became standard. Prints often came in sets of
two, three, four, or more. Textual information on
each print varied over time, from just artist and
publisher, to including also actor and role, carver,
and sometimes poems by actors or patrons. Prints
tend to depict actors in dramatically charged
moments; in most cases these can be dated to a
particular year and performance.

Prints played an important role as both
promotion and souvenirs. They were an integral
part, along with semi-annually published actor
critique books (*yakusha hyōbanki*), of a flourishing
"kabuki fan culture," including privately produced
surimono: prints that contained images and
recorded poems from poetry gatherings. These
were often issued using sophisticated techniques
such as embossing, with even gold and silver leaf, to
produce luxury editions. Surimono including actors
(sometimes in the same character as the image)
were distributed to patrons by promoting actors

both as stage performers and as cultured literati.
Actor prints and surimono also recorded particular
events in an actor's career, especially the taking of a
new stage name (*shūmei*), and death prints (*shini-e*).

Until around the 1750s, actors tended to be
represented by indistinguishable generic faces, often
only identified by their name on the print and/or by
the crest on their costume. Torii Kiyonobu (1664–
1729) and the Torii school dominated production
until the 1760s. From the 1750s we begin to see
more realistic portrayals in paintings and prints,
and from the 1760s, with the advent of color
printing and new artists such as Katsukawa Shunshō
(1726–92) and his Katsukawa school, a recognizable
"brand" face (*nigao-e*, likeness) was created for
each actor. Female-role actors (*onnagata*), however,
tended to be represented with only slight variation
on ideal female beauties. The Katsukawa school
dominated actor print production in Edo from the
late 1760s until the early 1790s.

The city of Edo led actor print production, but
from the 1780s a separate actor print tradition
developed in Osaka, spearheaded by Ryūkōsai
Jokei (active 1777–1809), who developed a more
realistic likeness style, with female-role actors
depicted as men rather than as beautiful women.
Movements in general in the arts toward more
realism in the 1780s–90s saw a convergence of
different styles of actor prints in Edo, evident
in the prints of Katsukawa Shun'ei (1762–1819),
Tōshūsai Sharaku (active 1794–5), and Utagawa
Toyokuni (1769–1825). The 1790s was a vibrant,
innovative decade in which numerous artists tried
their hand at actor portraits. From 1800 onwards
the Utagawa school (particularly Utagawa
Kunisada/Toyokuni III, 1786–1865) dominated
actor print production.

The thousands of surviving actor prints are a
magnificent resource for theatre research. Today,
many actor prints can be accessed online from
collections around the world, including "A Guide
to Ukiyo-e sites on the Internet": www.ukiyo-e.
se/guide.html, and Waseda Theatre Museum
(the largest single collection of actor prints, with
over 40,000): www.enpaku.waseda.ac.jp/db/
enpakunishik/.

C. ANDREW GERSTLE

Costumes and makeup

The more realistic costumes used in *sewamono* ("contemporary" or "domestic" plays, featuring commoners) are subtly theatricalized versions of Edo period dress. Costumes in *jidaimono* ("historical" or "period" plays), featuring high-ranking samurai and aristocratic characters, range from exaggerated versions of Edo era daily dress to highly inventive robes. The latter are reserved for those of superior rank or from the distant past: the further a character from contemporary Edo reality, so too the costume. Grandiloquent aragoto hero costumes are striking and unforgettable, such as foothigh clogs (*geta*), sleeves so large they require a stage assistant (*kōken*) to hold them up, six-foot-long swords, or wigs with coifs so huge they border on the bizarre. Costumes can also incorporate symbolic meaning, such as the shape in which a footman's sash (*obi*) is tied to indicate the ideographs 大 入 (*ō iri*, "full house") in anticipation of a sell-out. Costumes can be single-layer, light cotton summer robes (*yukata*), or weigh over 40 pounds, such as a high-ranking courtesan's multi-layered cotton undergarments, silk kimono, satin-embroidered frontal obi sash, and brocade silk outer robe, topped by a highly ornamented wig.

Makeup begins with a white base (*oshiroi*), shades vary according to a character's gender, status, age, and nature. Women and high-ranking refined characters are whiter; older, coarse, or evil characters are darker hued. Details of lip shape and eyebrows also vary, with comic characters often sporting down-turned eyebrows. The bold red, blue, or brown lines of *kumadori* makeup used for aragoto characters are designed to accent the musculature, and were originally used on the body as well as the face; today patterned tights and body suits are used to indicate the bulging muscles of arms, legs, and torsos of these larger-than-life superheroes.

Acting and actors

Role types are identified by makeup, costume, and acting kata established as far back as the Genroku era (1688–1703), kabuki's first "golden age," or as recently as the twentieth century, such as those established by Onoe Kikugorō VI (1885–1949). Contemporary actors utilize this rich conventionalized system when creating characters for newly written plays or revivals of older ones that have fallen out of the active repertory. Most kabuki actors specialize in either male roles (*tachiyaku*) or female roles (*onnagata*), further subdivided according to age, occupation, and nature (positive, negative, comic etc.). The late eighteenth century saw a rise of virtuosic actors (*kaneru yakusha*) who could play a wide variety of both male and female roles.

There are approximately forty different acting lineages in kabuki today, with those originating in Edo (Tokyo) tending to have longer histories, since artistic heredity was more strongly emphasized in the shogun's capital than in Kamigata (Kyoto-Osaka). While family name connects an actor to his artistic lineage, an actor changes his given name (and occasionally family name as well) one or more times during his career, receiving the names of his forebears to mark achievements in skill and status.

Training

As in other traditional arts, those born into kabuki families begin training from an early age, studying nihonbuyo (Japanese dance) for movement foundation, and one or more narrative musical genres for vocalization. Budding actors observe their fathers and uncles on stage, and study an instrument such as shamisen or *taiko* (drum). Children generally debut between 4 and 7, in prominent child's roles such as the brave Senmatsu in *Meiboku Sendai hagi* (The precious incense and autumn flowers of Sendai), who eats a poisonous sweet, sacrificing himself for his lord's son. *Renjishi* (Two lions), depicting a rite of passage of a mythical young *shishi* (lion), is often danced by a father and son team. The spectacular twin swirling of long, trailing wigs at the finale makes for a popular debut piece.

Those born outside of kabuki families may apprentice directly with a kabuki actor, although almost all first complete a two-year basic training program at the National Theatre Kabuki Training Program (est. 1969), or the Kamigata Kabuki School (1997–2003) in Osaka. As of December 2014, 293 actors were listed with the Kabuki Actors Association.

Tokugawa cultural milieu

Toward the end of the sixteenth century, after more than a century of civil war, Japan was gradually unified under three consecutive warlords, who implemented policies that laid the groundwork for a long era of relative peace and self-imposed isolation. The consequent flourishing of commoner culture gave birth to and supported kabuki throughout the Tokugawa era. Oda Nobunaga (1534–82) implemented free market policies and improved roads, facilitating trade among neighboring castle towns. Successor Toyotomi Hideyoshi (1536–98) built on those policies, establishing free trade zones in Osaka that encouraged growth of this future mercantile center. Hideyoshi also implemented policies rigidly fixing the hierarchical Confucian four-class social structure of samurai-farmer-artisan-merchant, removing all weapons from farmers, and requiring samurai to move into castle towns under lords (*daimyō*), where they essentially became administrators paid a fixed rice stipend. In 1600, two years after Hideyoshi's death, senior general Tokugawa Ieyasu (1543–1616) seized control, and was given the title *shōgun* (supreme commander) in 1603. This marked the beginning of the Tokugawa era. In the subsequent 265 years, kabuki and bunraku developed in the midst of a thriving money-based economy that nourished a vibrant merchant class. Class conflicts and economic tribulations that emerged are at the heart of much of the drama created for these theatre forms.

Tokugawa Ieyasu established his administrative center in Edo, a small fishing village in his home domain that by 1720 boasted a population of over a million, the largest city in the world. One reason for the rapid growth was the system of alternate attendance (*sankin kōtai*), requiring all daimyo to reside in Edo every other year. Wives and children resided permanently there as hostages to ensure good behavior when daimyo were in their home provinces and away from the shogun's watchful eye. This resulted in a concentration of samurai, creating a demand for commoner labor to supply the necessary artistic as well as practical goods and services. Returning to their home provinces, samurai brought back goods, hobbies, and tastes acquired in the capital. Edo thus became central in the creation and dissemination of common culture throughout Japan. The newness of the city, its samurai-heavy populace, and close proximity to shogunate power are important factors in the style of kabuki acting and plays that developed there.

Kyoto, the imperial capital since 794, remained the home of the emperor, albeit one without any political power. As Kyoto had enjoyed over two decades of revival and prosperity prior to the establishment of the Tokugawa shogunate, it was the center of artisanal production, trade, and finance at the turn of the seventeenth century. It was also the largest of the three main cities at the beginning of the era, with nearly half a million people, followed by Osaka's approximate 400,000; the populations of both remained fairly steady throughout the era. Its status as capital and finance center at the start of the era gave birth to kabuki itself. Kyoto's preferred acting styles reflect the refinement of the historic imperial capital.

The port city of Osaka in western Japan stood at the confluence of rivers that connected it to Kyoto. Osaka was also the trade center, where daimyo from throughout the country sold their rice allotments for cash in order to purchase other goods and services. Strategically located for inland sea routes as well, Osaka quickly grew into a bustling merchant center, where money and ingenuity were more important than hereditary status or education in high culture. This, too, is reflected in the character types, plots, and theatre practices popular there.

Kabuki – Okuni and the early years

In the early seventeenth century, Kyoto was alive with energy, home to numerous rebellious masterless samurai (*rōnin*), labeled *kabukimono* ("deviant ones") for their tendency to stray from laws and conventions. Social – and sometimes political – outlaws, these unemployed youths were known as much for parading in outlandish and exotic dress and hairstyles as for their disruptive habits, ranging from smoking and unbridled sexual pursuit to rioting, killing, and kidnapping. Association with avant-garde fashions and irreverent attitudes led to the name "kabuki" for a new theatre form that arose. Originally written in the phonetic syllabary (*hiragana*), referencing the "deviant" or "leaning" kabukimono, the term was later written with three kanji characters, *ka* (歌 song), *bu* (舞 dance) and *ki* (妓 prostitute), later changed to *ki* (伎) [skill].

A woman known as Okuni first performed the popular, vigorous, and erotic dances and skits that came to be called kabuki. It is generally accepted that Okuni was a shrine priestess from Izumo Province on the Japan Sea. By 1600, a duo of Kuni and Kiku from Izumo Province are recorded dancing *yayako odori* (a popular folk dance) at the Imperial Palace. In the spring of 1603, Okuni is known to have performed in northern Kyoto at the Kitano Shrine, and later that year on the banks of the Kamo River near Gojō Bridge, both entertainment districts on the city's outskirts. Spring 1603 also coincided with Ieyasu's grand celebration of his newly bestowed title of shogun, to which he summoned daimyo from throughout the country. This confluence of patron and performer marks the birth of kabuki, and rapid proliferation throughout the country.

Okuni traveled to Edo in 1607 then toured the country for five years before returning to Kyoto in 1612. Other troupes, both male and female, emulated her performances. Troupes of prostitutes, sponsored by brothel owners, also sprang up in cities and towns throughout the country, sometimes sparking local bans against kabuki in an attempt to maintain social order. The few contemporary written records about Okuni mention yayako odori, *nembutsu odori* (a secularized Buddhist circle dance), and *kabuki odori* almost interchangeably, clearly indicating that dance was central. "Odori" refers to an energetic dance in which the feet lift high off the ground. Indeed the postures and positions of reveling dancers depicted in late sixteenth-century circular nembutsu dances, and depictions of Okuni and women's kabuki in the early seventeenth century, indicate an erotic body expression sharply contrasting with the grounded, gliding steps of *mai*, the dance of noh and kyogen.

Okuni adopted these popular dances for the stage, accessorizing with the latest fashions, such as the large crucifix commonly seen on the Portuguese

Fig 17 Screen painting of Kyoto circular dance (*furyū-odori*) (Kanō School,
c. 1596–1615).

missionaries who were still present in cities during the first decades of
Tokugawa rule. Her androgynous hairstyle – cropped short, tied high on
the head – popular among the "deviant" kabukimono, suited her portrayal
of young sword-carrying samurai going to teahouses (*chaya*) to hire prostitutes. *Kunijo kabuki ekotoba*, the earliest pictorial record of Okuni's performances, depicts a *chaya asobi* or "dallying at the teahouse" scene. On a
noh-like stage, Okuni in Buddhist robes holds a small gong and intones the
nembutsu, a prayer for a departed soul, who appears from the audience. He
reveals that he is the spirit of Nagoya Sanza, then relives his brothel-going
days, as prostitutes dance before him.

Okuni's play seems to parody the stately noh, while also being cutting-edge contemporary in style. The recently deceased kabukimono Nagoya Sanza, infamous in Kyoto as a handsome *bon vivant* with numerous love intrigues, is not, as might be found in noh, a soul seeking release from earthly attachment and lamenting the transitory nature of life. Rather, he laments the transience of his love affairs, reveling in leg-lifting, foot-stomping prostitutes' dances accompanied by popular songs. His spirit appears not from the stage, but from the audience, presaging by decades the intimate audience–actor connection created by the hanamichi passageway. Later scenes depict Okuni portraying a swaggering samurai.

The erotic dances, brothel scenes, noh parodies, references to contemporary events, and cross-gendered performances at the core of Okuni's kabuki remained central in prostitutes' kabuki. The essential morality of the Confucian Tokugawa government, with its emphasis on societal duty and class division, opposed both theatres and brothels, considered as *akusho* – places of vice – where craftsmen, merchants, farmers, and samurai rubbed elbows, and even fought over enticing young women or adolescent boys (*wakashu*). Such public unruliness, as well as challenges that unlicensed actor-prostitutes presented to a fledgling licensed prostitution industry in the 1620s, led to the shogunal ban of women from the public stage in 1629, thereby ending the era of female (*onna*) or prostitute (*yūjo*) kabuki. Yet the ban was repeated several times in the succeeding decade, indicating the difficulty of controlling this wildly appealing new genre.

Youth gives way to increasing artistry

Around this time, the shogunate began licensing noh and kyogen troupes as "ceremonial entertainment," designating those considered professionals. Many disenfranchised noh and kyogen actors joined kabuki troupes, likely improving the quality of the music and dance. For the next two decades, kabuki was performed by troupes of predominantly adolescent males (*wakashu kabuki*): lively drinking scenes and short dances (*komai*) of kyogen were common elements in their plays. Ukon Genzaemon (1622?–late 1670s?) performed the kyogen dance *Nanatsuko*, but accompanied by shamisen and using the stiff, round *uchiwa* fan of kabuki. Genzaemon is believed to have come from a kyogen family. He began his kabuki career as a wakashu, then shifted to female roles, and is known as the "originator of the *onnagata*" (female role specialist).

Saruwaka Kanzaburō I (1598–1658), who founded the Saruwaka-za (later Nakamura-za), Edo's first licensed theatre, in 1624, is another early kabuki performer with close kyogen ties. His elder brother was an actor from the Okura school of kyogen, and records show that Saruwaka Kanzaburō I (the line later took the family name Nakamura) performed plays such as *Itoyori* (Twisting thread), first summarized in the 1578 book of kyogen plots, *Tenshō kyōgen bon*. Additionally, the 1640 *Komai jūrokuban* (Sixteen short dances), the earliest extant kabuki dance lyrics, shows the clear influence of kyogen komai, though kabuki's poetic double entendres are much more erotic. The appeal of these attractive youths was a big factor in their frequent invitations to give command performances at daimyo residences; several high-profile disputes are partially responsible for the 1652 ban on wakashu kabuki.

While the government may have wanted to exterminate the "blight" of kabuki, it recognized its importance in entertaining and placating Japan's burgeoning urban center populaces. Consequently, the ban was lifted in 1653, but kabuki was restricted to adult males (*yarō kabuki*) doing "fully acted plays." Though adolescent boys shaved their pates (a sign of adulthood) to fulfill the rule of the law, the long-standing catamite tradition did not magically disappear, as patronage of these young men by samurai and commoner alike continued for decades. Many teahouse owners and older actors even kept a group of young boys, registered as "actors," for such purposes. Many of kabuki's onnagata, including the great Yoshizawa Ayame (1673–1729), came from such a background.

These governmental constraints prompted further developments in playwriting and cultivation of requisite performance skills, especially for onnagata, over the next four decades. This was accompanied by articulated criteria for judging artistic accomplishments of actors, as seen in the *yakusha hyōbanki*, or actor critiques, which, with actor prints and illustrated playbooks, grew with the blossoming publishing industry in the 1680s. By the beginning of the Genroku era, a period of great cultural and artistic flowering, many aspects of kabuki coalesced into clear dramatic and artistic lineages that continue today.

Theatre regulations and production conventions

Theatre licensing laws were similar throughout the country, yet local production practice, regional preference, and proximity to the shogun resulted in variant systems in each of the three main cities. In Edo, a license was granted to a hereditary *zamoto*, who owned the theatre building, held the license to produce, served as theatre manager, and often acted minor roles as well. The zamoto produced the season in conjunction with the theatre's leading actor, the *zagashira*. Following the aforementioned Saruwaka-za (1624), many licensed theatres operated throughout Edo until the great fire of 1657, which destroyed half the city's theatres. In 1670, only four large theatres, located in neighboring districts, were permitted licenses: the Nakamura-za, Ichimura-za, Morita-za, and Yamamura-za. After 1714, the Yamamura-za was closed permanently, and the manager's assets liquidated because of an illicit love affair between one of his actors and a shogunal lady-in-waiting, leaving only three Edo theatres. The drum tower symbolized a large licensed theatre. Situated on the roof in front of the theatre and surrounded by bunting bearing the crest of the zamoto, the drum's early morning beat signaled the opening of the theatre day. The financial burden of operating a theatre was great. Edo in particular was known for its conflagrations, and the theatres were rarely spared; in its first hundred years of operation the Nakamura-za burnt down twenty times, relocating three times.

Sumptuary laws were enacted several times during the Tokugawa era in an attempt to control the ostentatious consumption by merchants and actors. In late 1841, the Tempō Reforms forced the three licensed theatres of Edo to move from the city center to Saruwaka-chō near Asakusa, then a remote suburb near Yoshiwara, the licensed (prostitution) quarter. Despite incredible financial hardship, all three theatres managed to survive into the Meiji era, when new ordinances permitted their return to the city center.

In Kamigata (Kyoto-Osaka), duties and financial liabilities of operating theatres were divided among three or more individuals: the theatre owner, the licensee, and the company's lead actor (confusingly also called "zamoto," the same as the Edo owner-manager). The lead actor, who also served as artistic manager, would borrow the license from a licensee and the building from the owner, and have support from financial backers. Unlike in Edo, hereditary licensing here was not the norm, and the financial burden did not reside with one individual. Consequently there was more fluctuation, with between two and seven theatres operating at any given time in both Osaka and Kyoto. From the early days of women's kabuki, Kyoto's licensed theatres were located near Shijō (Fourth Street) by the Kamo River, on the edge of the city limits; while Osaka's lay in Dōtombori, a street along a major canal designated as a pleasure district in 1621. In all three cities, kabuki and puppet theatres were in close proximity, encouraging continuous artistic exchange throughout the Tokugawa period.

In addition to the permanent large theatres (*ōshibai*) described above, numerous small theatres (*koshibai*) were also granted licenses in cities throughout the country. These were referred to as "small theatres," "shrine theatres" because of their location, or "hundred-day theatres" reflecting their limited annual operation. Additionally, Kamigata had two further types: the medium theatre (*chūshibai*) and children's theatre (*kodomo shibai*), both often serving as stepping-stones along an actor's path to larger venues. An actor could begin acting in children's theatre, move up to a medium theatre

∾ SPOTLIGHT 4.2   *Onnagata*: kabuki female role specialists

Onnagata are male specialists in female roles employing elaborate conventions for expressing femininity in kabuki. At the beginning of the seventeenth century, dances and skits performed mostly by women were offered at Kyoto's riverside and other temporary performance venues as kabuki's earliest entertainment. The commotion and occasional brawls that resulted from male interest in these eroticized displays led to a ban on actresses in 1629. Young men (*wakashu*) replaced them; however from 1652, for similar reasons, youths could no longer appear on stage unless they shaved their forelocks to lessen their sexual attractiveness. Thus the mid-seventeenth century marks the beginning of adult male (*yarō*) kabuki with its important defining feature, the female role specialist. Ukon Genzaemon (mid-seventeenth century) is credited with pioneering onnagata acting during this transitional period.

The erotic focus of the early period remained central to the new genre's burst of popularity, while the advent of adult male onnagata performers led to the development of their physical, gestural, vocal, costuming, and role type traditions. These matured in the Genroku period (1688–1704), especially around the turn of the eighteenth century, beginning with two great contemporary onnagata, rivals Mizuki Tatsunosuke (1673–1745, retired 1704) and Yoshizawa Ayame (1673–1729). Onnagata were already expected to excel in two types of performing: "realistic" characterization and dance expression. Tatsunosuke was renowned for his dancing (especially *hengemono*, multiple-character dances). Ayame, particularly appreciated for his acting, was the first onnagata to promote living offstage as a woman in order to master onstage "femaleness." "It is difficult to become a great onnagata if you don't live like a woman in your everyday life. You may think it is only important to express yourself as a woman while on stage. But

the more you think this way, the more masculine you will appear. Consistency is crucial."[1]

Among highly lauded eighteenth-century onnagata were Segawa Kikunojō I (1693–1749) and Ayame's son, Nakamura Tomijūrō I (1719–86), who both initiated significant acting lines. Kikunojō's ideas on the art of the onnagata were recorded in *Onnagata hiden* (Secret teachings of the onnagata). Tomijūrō was equally famous for his dancing and ability to perform many female types.

The word onnagata (also *oyama*) refers to both female roles and the specialist actors. Female roles are categorized according to age, together with position and/or nature. Young women roles (*waka onnagata*) include princesses (*hime*), marriageable women, or *musume* (lit. "daughters"; commoners), and *keisei* (courtesans). Ayame considered such roles fundamental, since "if an *onnagata* made a success of a keisei role, all others were easy to perform. The reason for this is that, since he is basically a man, he possesses, by his nature, a faculty of strong action, and he must carefully bear in mind the softness of the keisei and her feminine charm."[2] There are also a variety of middle-aged and older women.

In order to portray a woman, an onnagata uses a high range of the natural voice, developed first by studying breath control of *gidayū* chanting, then adapting it for theatrical expression. Onnagata are said to "kill" the body to perfect techniques of stance and movement that allow them to appear female. Their relatively constricted and confined posture, walking, and emotional expression contrast distinctly with those of male roles. An onnagata narrows the shoulder blades, flattens the hands with fingers together and thumbs tucked under, and walks with knees touching and feet pointing inward (actors practice with paper held between the knees). Holding the arms at his side, or folding them in front of his chest or stomach signals respectively a young girl, chaste

---

1 From "The words of Ayame," in Charles J. Dunn and Torigoe Bunzō (trans. and eds.), *The Actors' Analects* (Tokyo: University of Tokyo Press, 1969). Includes Japanese text and English translation. This quote translated by the author from the Japanese, 288–287.
2 *Ibid.* 49–50.

wife, or older woman. Female types are further distinguished through costume: colors and relative extravagance, sleeve style, method of tying the *obi* sash, type of footwear, and complexity of the wig.

A strict separation between actors playing female and male roles (*tachiyaku*) has not always been observed. Audiences have often appreciated versatile actors, such as Onoe Kikugorō V (1844–1903), who appeared in both. The two leading mid-twentieth-century onnagata, Onoe Baikō VII (1915–95) and Nakamura Utaemon VI (1917–2001), like Ayame and Tatsunosuke, had their careers partially shaped through contrast. They were rivals whose interpretations and techniques offered audiences the continuing pleasure of appreciating distinctions and engaging critically in the onnagata art. Since the 1990s, Bandō Tamasaburō V (1950–) has been kabuki's leading onnagata, excelling in both dance and realistic acting.

KATHERINE SALTZMAN-LI

as age and skill increased, and, if successful, progress into the large theatre. In reality, there was a great deal of ambiguity and fluidity in these classifications. Records show "children" over the age of 20 and successful adult actors sometimes moving back to the medium theatres, either preferring to be stars in the smaller "pond," or unable to shoulder the financial burden of supplying their own costumes, expected at large venues.

Teahouses, abundant in the theatre districts, were commercially symbiotic with kabuki itself. Tickets for more expensive boxed seats (*sajiki*) were purchased through teahouses, where patrons could take a break from all-day performances to eat or change clothing. Following a show, they could continue merry-making, or even arrange to meet favored actors. Some teahouse private rooms led directly to the theatres, an ideal arrangement for discreet assignations. This interdependence between teahouses and theatres continued into the Meiji era.

Playwriting

Actors were the earliest kabuki playwrights. Kamigata actor Tominaga Heibei (dates unknown) was the first to be acknowledged on billboards as "kyōgen zukuri" (play-maker) in 1680. In Edo, Ichikawa Danjūrō I (1660–1704) is believed to have authored more than fifty plays. The actor-playwright was common into the early decades of the 1700s, and in small and medium-sized Kamigata theatres into the mid-1800s. Even Chikamatsu Monzaemon (1653–1725), one of the first to specialize as a playwright, collaborated closely with actor Kaneko Kichizaemon (d. 1728) when writing for kabuki.

Kabuki scripts have always been mutable. Plays could be slightly revised under new titles, or scenes borrowed and recontextualized in a new play. The play *Shibaraku* (Wait a Moment!) was included annually in the eleventh-month, season-opening *kaomise* ("face showing") production in Edo.

Details, dialogue, and characters' names changed from play to play, but the basic scenario and identifying acting "bits" (forerunners of kata) often remained constant. Although modern productions of classics follow more standardized scripts, still some degree of dialogue and scene editing occurs.

Like actors, playwrights in the Edo period were contracted to a theatre on an annual basis, and wrote to highlight the skills of their theatre's acting company. In the 1720s, a system of multiple authorship (*gassaku*) developed, becoming standard practice by the mid-1700s. Ranking from lead playwright down to apprentice determined the scenes each wrote, as well as duties such as creating play titles (usually consisting of five or seven allusion-laden ideograms), conducting rehearsals, copying sides (part booklets) for actors, and other menial tasks. This system, in which playwrights were nurtured alongside actors, remained intact until Meiji. Reform efforts seeking to raise playwrights' status resulted in a gradual shift away from scripts (*kyakuhon*) written by in-house dramatists – who now were seen as "pandering" to the actors – to scripts (*gikyoku*) written by novelists, journalists, and scholars who, greatly influenced by Western drama, focused on literary aspects of the text.

Development of plays

Until the 1660s, kabuki consisted of one-act plays organized around proven, largely improvised, scenarios. Many involved "prostitute-buying" scenes, until outlawed in 1664. In the same year, the invention of the pull curtain (*hikimaku*) led to the emergence of two-act plays in both Edo and Kamigata. By the end of the century, Edo theatres were offering five-act plays (*goban tsuzuki*), which combined a jidaimono in the first half with a sewamono in the second. These multi-act plays were constructed with a climactic scene (*miseba*) in each somewhat independent act, resulting in a rather tenuous overall relationship among scenes. Plots became more cohesive by the 1720s, building to a single climactic point rather than one in each of its individual acts. In Kamigata, more tightly structured two- or three-act jidaimono followed by a separately titled one- or two-act sewamono was standard.

Throughout the Edo period, the combination of preexisting with new material remained at the heart of play creation. By the mid-1700s, the terms *sekai* (world) and *shukō* (devices) came to define these core concepts, called the "warp and the woof" of plot creation in *Kezairoku*, the late eighteenth-century treatise. The world determined the play's parameters of time and characters, and provided a few well-known incidents. Into this a playwright wove innovative devices, which included incorporating current or topical

Fig 18 Hayano Kampei (center) with two suspicious samurai retainers in the vendetta league in *Kanadehon chūshingura* (The treasury of loyal retainers).

events, revising role types, adding new characters, or exploiting signature acting routines of popular actors.

Worlds could be historical or contemporary, based on historical events or figures, or published literary works including imperial poetry collections, war chronicles, or contemporary literature. Newly created worlds could also become established when a play based on a contemporary event was successfully dramatized, resulting in the creation of more plays on the same topic featuring the same characters. Incidents involving the samurai class, however, were barred from direct dramatization, leading to the practice of transposing recent events into an established historical world and altering the characters' names. *Kanadehon chūshingura* (The treasury of loyal retainers, 1748; see representative plays, p. 160 and Figure 18), transposed the 1701 Akō incident (and subsequent 1703 vendetta by forty-seven loyal retainers) to the fourteenth century.

House playwrights selected worlds for an upcoming season prior to the *kaomise*, which introduced the theatre's acting and playwriting lineup for the coming year. Subsequent productions generally opened in the first, third, fifth, and ninth months, with a seventh-month summer production left to younger artists. This flexible framework allowed for the run of a play from two weeks to several months, according to its staying power.

The close physical proximity of the kabuki and puppet theatres facilitated ongoing borrowing, most evident in the shared repertory today. *Maruhonmono* (lit. "full book play") refers to those plays adapted for kabuki from the puppet repertory. Begun in Kamigata in the first decade of the eighteenth century, this practice became more frequent in the 1730s as the development of three-person puppets brought greater complexity and popularity to the puppet theatre. This peaked mid-century during the "golden age" of the playwriting trio Namiki Sōsuke (1695–1751), Takeda Izumo II (1691–1756), and Miyoshi Shōraku (1696–1772). This remarkable but short-lived (1745–50) team produced a series of blockbusters, adapted to kabuki within months of their puppet premieres, retaining many puppet-theatre conventions such as an on-stage chanter who described scene openings and climactic actions, and occasionally even spoke dialogue for actors at moments of great physical or emotional intensity. Maruhonmono greatly influenced subsequent kabuki playwriting; writing of narrative passages was considered one of a playwright's "four important areas of cultivation."[3]

Play types

A popular entertainment continually incorporating new ideas and trends for over 300 years, kabuki has developed a plethora of play types and classification systems. One system categorizes the 250 to 300 plays in the active repertory by origin: *junsui* or "pure" plays originally written for kabuki; maruhonmono; and *shin* (new) *kabuki*, plays influenced by Western dramaturgy written from the late Meiji era to the end of the Pacific War. Identifying plays by subject matter or type of character featured – *chūshingura-mono* (plays about the forty-seven loyal retainers), *kaidan* (ghost plays), or *shiranami-mono* (bandit plays) – is another way of classification. More common is the division into sewamono (contemporary dramas), jidaimono (historical dramas), and *shosagoto* (dance plays), each of which contains several subcategories.

---

3 Katherine Saltzman-Li, *Creating Kabuki Plays: Context for Kezairoku, "Valuable Notes on Playwriting"* (Leiden: Brill, 2010), 71.

Sewamono

Sewamono (lit. "current gossip plays") are set in contemporary times, featuring commoners and low-ranking samurai who dress and speak in a familiar daily manner. The term, first used in Kamigata in 1700, referred to the one-act final play of the program. These often dramatized current scandals – murders, lovers' suicides (*shinjū*), or untimely deaths of courtesans – often worked into plays quickly, so-called *ichiyazukemono* ("overnight pickle plays").

In the last quarter of the eighteenth century, kabuki audiences included a broad range of commoners, from wealthy merchants to day laborers. Plays, too, began featuring more everyday characters. By the Bunka–Bunsei eras (1804–30), thieves, murderers, and usurers became the main characters of contemporary plays, dubbed *kizewamono* for their "raw" (*ki*) gritty depictions of contemporary life: peasant uprisings, currency debasement, and a poor samurai class living amidst an increasingly wealthy and flamboyant merchant class. Tsuruya Namboku IV (1755–1829) penned memorable kizewamono, such as *Sakurahime azuma bunshō* (The scarlet princess of Edo, 1817), featuring the rapist, thief, and murderer Tsurigane Gonsuke (see representative plays, p. 137). Namboku was also known for ghost plays such as *Yotsuya kaidan* (The ghost stories at Yotsuya), creating horrific, mistreated, and disfigured characters while utilizing the full range of stage tricks (*keren*) popular in the early nineteenth century.

By the middle of the century, Kawatake Mokuami (1816–93) had moved toward a more lyric, romanticized style of kizewamono. *Sannin Kichisa kuruwa no hatsugai* (The three Kichisas and the New Year's visit to the pleasure quarters, 1860), one of his bandit plays, depicts thieves in an inescapable cycle of karma, waxing poetic during focal scenes in the alternating seven and five syllable phrases (*shichi-go-chō*) of classical verse.

"Cropped hair" plays (*zangirimono*), named after the Westernized male hairstyles that replaced outlawed topknots in the Meiji era, reflected fresh ideas, popular trends, newsworthy events, and widespread societal transitions. Most were penned by Kawatake Mokuami for Onoe Kikugorō V (1844–1903), a popular and versatile actor skilled at both male and female roles. *Onna shosei Shigeru* (The female student, 1877), inspired by a newspaper story about a woman arrested for posing as a man, highlighted Kikugorō V's talents, though ultimately this and other zangirimono fell from the active kabuki repertory.

Thus sewamono in a variety of forms continuously reflected contemporary commoners' interests, helping kabuki maintain popularity for over three centuries.

Jidaimono

Jidaimono dramatize actual or fictionalized events set in the pre-Tokugawa era, a framework sometimes used to circumvent bans on depicting contemporary events concerning the samurai class. Featuring imperial courtiers and samurai, jidaimono were nevertheless written for, and from the perspective of, a predominantly commoner audience that reveled in the romanticized portrayals of honor and sacrifice. Sets, costumes, language, and customs also reflect the Edo period rather than attempting any medieval verisimilitude.

By the 1680s in Kamigata, the *oie sōdō* (succession dispute play) was highly developed. These typically focused on power struggles within an important family, where the search for a lost or stolen family heirloom inevitably included a scene set in the licensed quarter. This was one way to circumvent the 1664 ban on prostitute-buying scenes, but also served to insure that the distant historical samurai world retained a contemporary relevance for the audience – and to leaven martial bluster with romantic intrigue. These kinds of plays remained important throughout the eighteenth century, the inclusion of one contemporary scene (*sewaba*) within a jidaimono becoming standard practice

Under the influence of Kamigata, Edo also developed succession dispute plays. Being a city of samurai near the shogunal seat of power, Edo playwrights tended to use settings in the distant past of the Nara or Heian period (694–1185) and focus on intrigues of imperial society and courtiers. These *ochō-* or *ōdaimono* also remained popular throughout the Edo period. Most plays adapted to kabuki from puppet theatre in the mid-eighteenth century were jidaimono, increasing the number of worlds at the disposal of the kabuki playwright.

The Meiji era saw the development of a new type of jidaimono that experimented with historical accuracy in set, costume, and even language. Most *katsurekigeki* ("living history plays") were penned by Kawatake Mokuami for Ichikawa Danjūrō IX (1838–93), staged between 1871 and 1886. Danjūrō's attempts at realistic costuming, language, and acting were at odds with long-established and well-loved staging and musical conventions. When they were received poorly, he abandoned them to return to the classical repertory.

Shosagoto

The umbrella term shosagoto (lit. "movement piece") is used for all dance, whether independent plays or scenes forming part of longer plays (see p. 142). Dance is always accompanied by the lyrical *nagauta* ("long song"), which developed within kabuki, or other narrative musical genres: *gidayū* (from the puppet theatre), *tokiwazu,* or *kiyomoto.*

❧ FOCUS 4.2 *Aragoto* acting and the Ichikawa Danjūrō line

The Ichikawa Danjūrō kabuki actor lineage has continued for twelve generations, from the late 1600s until today. Dominating and symbolizing Edo (Tokyo) kabuki, it has created drama on and off the stage.

Danjūrō I (1660–1704), descended from samurai, debuted at 13 playing a rambunctious martial hero. He created trademark *aragoto* (bravura) acting, performing warriors who, empowered by deities, engage in superhuman feats of strength and valor: smashing down buildings, tearing wild animals to shreds, and throwing enemy soldiers around like stones. Acting techniques include dynamic kick outs (*fumi-dashi*), swaggers (*roppō*), and stop-action poses (*mie*). Danjūrō the playwright drew on a wide range of literary sources to craft history plays about superheroes. Inspiration for aragoto acting came from special effects in puppet theatre and from the wild dancing and dynamic statuary of Danjūrō's family's religion, tantric Shingon Buddhism, particularly the ferocious Fudō deity. Danjūrō I overcame alcoholism and sexual profligacy, but was also competitive and arrogant. He was murdered on stage by a rival actor.

Danjūrō II (1688–1758) developed new makeup for virtuous aragoto heroes – red stripes on a white base. He also devised a "gentle aragoto" hero, as much invested in romantic love as in martial victory. Danjūrō II was an avid writer of diaries, poetry, and humor – his best wordplay can be found in the plays *Ya no ne* (The arrow sharpener) and *Uirō uri* (The medicine peddler). Danjūrō III (1721–42), adopted son of Danjūrō II, died young. Danjūrō IV (1711–78), perhaps the illegitimate son of Danjūrō II, began his career specializing in villain roles. He was famous for playing conflicted aragoto heroes and opening his acting workshops to all, not just family disciples.

Danjūrō V (1741–1806), a very versatile actor, dominated the stage from the 1780s until 1800, and was also an avid poet and essayist. Known for performing *Shibaraku* (Wait a Moment!)

every year for his *kaomise* ("face-showing," annual opening) production, he rewrote a text portion each year. Danjūrō VI (1778–99) died suddenly after a highly acclaimed debut performance of *Sukeroku*, and was the first to be memorialized by commercially available death prints (*shini-e*).

Danjūrō VII (1791–1859), grandson of Danjūrō V, cemented the family's dominance of Edo kabuki for future generations by proclaiming the "Eighteen Great Plays" (*kabuki jūhachiban*), most created by and for Danjūrō II. Danjūrō VII played villains in several new "raw domestic plays" by Tsuruya Namboku. With *Kanjinchō* (The subscription list) in 1840, Danjūrō VII invented *matsubamemono*, dance-dramas based on noh plays. Danjūrō VIII (1823–54), eldest son of Danjūrō VII, was renowned as an actor of romantic male roles, not aragoto. Women adored him: look-alike dolls were sold to female fans, who also drank water from barrels in which Danjūrō had immersed himself on stage. He committed suicide and was memorialized in hundreds of death prints.

Danjūrō IX (1838–1903), younger brother of Danjūrō VIII, dominated the kabuki stage during Japan's transition to the modern era. He performed in traditional plays and participated in kabuki's first modern reform movement, acting in plays set in the Meiji period (*zangirimono* "cropped hair plays,") and more realistic "living history plays" (*katsureki geki*).

Danjūrō X (1882–1956) married the daughter of Danjūrō IX. Danjūrō XI (1909–65), adopted son of Danjūrō X, was one of the most popular actors on the stage in the 1950s–60s, excelling in varied male lead roles. Danjūrō XII (1946–2013) was among Japan's leading kabuki actors. A dedicated conservator of the family's acting heritage, he revived several "lost" plays from the aragoto repertory. His son, Ebizō (1977–), will likely become Danjūrō XIII.

LAURENCE KOMINZ

Lyrics to the earliest extant dances (1640s) reveal their erotic nature, appropriate for the prostitute-buying scenes in which they were performed. The courtesan remained a central figure in dance, domain of the onnagata. *Musume Dōjoji* (The maiden at Dōjō Temple, 1753), premiered by popular onnagata Nakamura Tomijūrō I (1719–86), typifies these early nagauta dances. Onnagata dominance of dance roles ended in the latter half of the eighteenth century, when development of narrative musical genres necessitated more character interaction, leading to actors of male roles (*tachiyaku*) with strong dance skills. Nakamura Nakazō I (1736–90), who learned dance from his mother before apprenticing as an actor, was central in developing male dances, such as the classic *Seki no tō* (The barrier gate, 1784). In the Tempō era (1830–43) a technique known as *ningyōburi*, moving like a puppet, was developed in Kamigata, primarily derived from dance scenes of puppet plays.

Outstanding dancers found a vehicle for their virtuosity in dance suites called *hengemono* (transformation pieces), named for the quick changes required of the star, who portrayed a different character in each section. Early transformation pieces, such as those danced by onnagata Mizuki Tatsunosuke I (1673–1745), were nagauta compositions on a theme that highlighted a variety of female characters. Hengemono blossomed in the first decades of the nineteenth century, fueled by an abundance of narrative and lyrical musical genres as well as the rise of the virtuosic actor, excelling at both tachiyaku and onnagata roles. Nakamura Utaemon III (1778–1838) performed twelve-part hengemono featuring a different genre of musical accompaniment for each section. Many of today's independent dance pieces, such as the popular *Fuji musume* (The wisteria maiden, 1826) and *Yasuna* (1818), were originally individual sections of a dance suite. Short and self-contained expressions of urban occupations, love, or the passing of the seasons, they made excellent teaching pieces for an increasing number of merchant-class amateur disciples.

Matsubamemono ("pineboard pieces") are dance plays adapted from noh and kyogen. Although many earlier dances and plays alluded to noh or even borrowed short sections of lyrics, the first direct adaptation utilizing the pineboard set was based on the noh play *Ataka* (The Ataka barrier), becoming *Kanjinchō* (The subscription list, 1840), starring Ichikawa Danjūrō VII (1791–1859). The next was not until 1881, when *Tsuchigumo* (The earth spider; see representative plays, p. 138) launched a trend of noh and kyogen adaptations that should be seen in light of Meiji Reform efforts to elevate the vulgar plebeian kabuki into a national drama, borrowing the prestige of older, elite forms.

Actors and acting: role models and role types

If kabuki theatre was at the center of commoner life in the Tokugawa period, actors were the beating heart, often holding cult status and admired far beyond what their official status as *hinin* (non-person) warranted. Forbidden to have family names, they instead adopted stage names, conferring hereditary status on both family and given names, which were then passed down to artistic progeny. Most actors resided by law within the theatre districts, though wealthy stars managed to build homes in other areas, and many operated side-businesses by lending their brand-name, selling everything from makeup and hair oil to sweet rice-cakes (*mochi*) and fans. Fashion trends also bore the mark of famous actors. Dye colors and patterns for kimono, styles of tying kimono sashes, umbrellas, and hair combs were named after kabuki icons who had popularized them on stage.[4] Actors could draw crowds to temples for special exhibits of Buddhist icons, or even be depicted in prints as Buddhist icons.

Sumptuary laws attempted to restrain actors' ostentation, holding them to a lifestyle suitable to their low status: capping their salaries, restricting fabrics worn, and periodic controls over actor prints. Infractions normally only received warnings, but occasionally high-profile individuals were held up as examples. In 1842, Danjūrō VII, known for his luxurious lifestyle, was banished from Edo for using genuine samurai armor and weapons, rather than stage props, and the city was deprived of one of its greatest actors for ten years. Government restrictions could also unwittingly nurture new trends. The Kansei Reforms, carried out between 1787 and 1793, banned actors from wearing brocades and silks. Unable to display sumptuously elegant costumes, actors used lighter-weight cotton, enabling quicker costume changes. This is at least partially responsible for the vogue in *hayagawari* (quick-changes) arising in the early 1800s.

The ingenuity of pioneering actors brought fame during one's lifetime, but more importantly lived on as the basis for acting and costume conventions (kata), as well as character types (*yakugara*) comprising kabuki today. Of course not everything survived, for natural selection was as vital to kabuki as a commercial venture as it is to the survival of biological species. Successful creations were emulated by other actors, resulting in cross-fertilization when actors worked in other theatres and cities.

Already by the 1670s, seven character types were clearly identified in kabuki – *tachiyaku* (righteous male roles), *katakiyaku* (villainous male

---

4 Taguchi Akiko, *Edo jidai no kabuki yakusha* (Edo era kabuki actors) (Tokyo: Oyamakaku, 1997), 203–6.

∾ FOCUS 4.3   Regional kabuki

Throughout the Tokugawa era (1603–1868), *shibai*, meaning "play" or "theatre," was the term for kabuki, presented in the large cities of Edo (Tokyo), Osaka, and Kyoto, as well as small towns and rural villages. Any kabuki outside cities was called *jishibai*, or "regional theatre," whether touring professional troupes (*tabi shibai*) from large or provincial cities, or amateur groups (jishibai, or more recently, *jikabuki*). As touring regional companies disappeared in the 1960s, amateur jishibai traditions were being resurrected, with many of the approximately 200 extant traditions now designated important cultural assets.

Development of amateur jishibai is intimately tied to professional regional troupes in the Tokugawa era. Many castle towns throughout the country had small theatres (*koshibai*), with licenses limiting them to a hundred days of operation annually. Nagoya, geographically central and blessed with more lenient policies toward kabuki, had its first theatre in 1644 and was a center of regional activity. Regional theatres were also common in "gate towns," near entrances to important pilgrimage sites, such as Furuichi near the Grand Shrine of Ise, which had two theatres. When not engaged near their home base, regional troupes – sometimes joined by *ōshibai* actors from major theatres in the big cities – toured castle towns, gate towns, and inn towns, particularly those along the Tōkaidō and Nakasendō (coastal and inland, respectively) highways. They even performed in rural mountain towns and coastal fishing villages at annual festivals or showings of Buddhist treasures, invited by villagers who pooled their resources. Actors stayed with village residents, and villagers filled minor roles when needed.

By the early 1700s, rather than hiring a troupe, more villages began renting costumes and inviting a single actor from a regional company to advise and choreograph locals to perform at their own annual festivals, thus giving rise to amateur jishibai. Approximately 200 rural stages, taking diverse forms, have been identified, ranging from permanent stages with a working revolve, like the Nakayama Nōsonbutai on Shōdo Island, to towering floats used in the Nagahama Hikiyama Festival in Shiga prefecture, to boat stages like the Sanjinmaru in Yanagawa in Fukuoka.

Professional regional troupes and theatres also thrived, reaching a peak around 1825, despite periodic edicts intended to limit their growth, with 150 licensed theatres throughout the country. Post-Tokugawa, from the 1890s to the 1930s was the apex for regional touring companies. Tokugawa restrictions were no longer enforced and local kabuki was the only entertainment in town. Troupes even toured to California and Hawaiʻi to entertain Japanese emigrants and advise local amateur troupes. Increasing popularity of motion pictures coupled with government restrictions during Japan's long war in Asia led to a severe decline by the late 1930s.

Some theatre buildings from this heyday have been restored and are again being used, such as the Uchiko-za (1916, Ehime prefecture, Shikoku), Yachiyo-za (1910, Kumamoto, Kyushu), and Kanamaru-za, near Kompira Shrine (1836, Shikoku), the oldest extant kabuki theatre, which hosts the Grand Kabuki every April.

JULIE A. IEZZI

roles), *dōkegata* (comic male roles), *wakashugata* (adolescent male roles), *kakagata* (older female roles), *waka onnagata* (young female roles), and *koyaku* (child roles). By the early 1700s, this had increased by at least half, with subdivisions of ever more narrowly defined character types appearing.

Tachiyaku, for example, came in many variations. While Ichikawa Danjūrō I was developing aragoto characters in Edo, in Kamigata the *yatsushigata* arose, a disgraced or fallen samurai character in disguise as a townsman or artisan. Actor Arashi San'emon I (1635–90), the purported originator, portrayed two different types – lovers in the licensed quarter, and townsmen such as blacksmiths and tobacco cutters.[5] Sakata Tōjūrō I (1647–1709) became famous for the lover type in the 1680s and 90s, associated with love scenes (*nuregoto*), a slight comic flair, and long semi-improvised monologues. His more "daily" acting style eventually came to be known as *wagoto* (lit. "gentle style").

Other tachiyaku excelled at *jitsugoto* characters. There were the "true" loyal, morally upright samurai central to jidaimono, epitomized by the main character of Yuranosuke in *Kanadehon chūshingura*. The *shimbōyaku* is a samurai character who endures great suffering yet remains loyal, while the *wajitsu* has a gentler demeanor.

Villain roles (katakiyaku) also came in many forms, proliferating particularly in the mid-eighteenth century. *Jitsuaku* are "true villains," usually of high rank, who conspire to usurp power. Ichikawa Danzō IV (1745–1808) created another approach to evil in 1781 with his interpretation of the robber Sadakurō in Act V of *Kanadehon chūshingura* as an *iroaku* (sexy villain). Such evil-erotic roles were popular in early nineteenth-century plays, such as *Sakurahime azuma bunshō*. Even comic characters had an "evil twin," the *handōgataki*, a blustering villain who verges on the ludicrous, exemplified by footman Sagisaka Bannai in *Kanadehon chūshingura*.

While male character types tended to be defined by their essential nature, the guiding principle for onnagata subtypes was age or occupation. This was a reflection of women's roles in society at large as well as in kabuki plays. Until the early nineteenth century, the male protagonist and antagonist were central, while female characters served supporting roles. Young female roles included *keisei* (high-ranking courtesan), *musumegata* (commoner daughter), and *akahime* (lit. "red princess"), while older ones included *nyōbō* (commoner wife), *kashagata* (teahouse maid and madam), and *katahazushi* (high-class lady-in-waiting). In the first half of the nineteenth century, Iwai Hanshirō V (1776–1847) perfected the counterpart to the evil-erotic role type – the *akuba*, or "evil woman" character. These strong, lower-class, mature female characters, like Dote no Oroku in *Osome Hisamatsu ukina no yomiuri* (The scandalous loves of Osome and Hisamatsu, 1813), may be extortionists or murderers but are often motivated by a strong sense of duty

---

5 Nao Yotsumoto, "Kamigata kabuki ni miru tachiyaku to jitsuaku no ichizuke" (Tachiyaku and jitsuaku as seen in Kamigata kabuki), in *Toshi bunka kenkyū* (Studies of Urban Culture) 9 (2007), 118–31, p. 9.

(*giri*). Such characters paved the way for the practice of writing plays featuring female protagonists.

The early nineteenth century also saw the rise of the virtuosic actor who could perform a whole spectrum of role types. In addition to Oroku, Hanshirō V played six other roles in *Osome Hisamatsu*, spawning the popular title of *Osome nanayaku* (Osome's seven roles). Nakamura Utaemon III, Onoe Kikugorō III (1784–1849), and Bandō Mitsugorō III (1773–1831) were known for acting multiple roles in the same play or in hengemono dance suites. Writing for Ichikawa Kodanji IV (1812–66) in the mid-nineteenth century, Mokuami drew on such versatility in creating gender-bending disguised cross-dressing characters such as Benten Kozō in the eponymously nicknamed play.

Restoration, reform, and beyond

The 1853 Treaty of Kanagawa forced an end to more than two centuries of Japan's relative isolation, marking the beginning of rapid social and political change. In 1868 the Emperor was officially restored to power, the capital moved from Kyoto to Edo (renamed Tōkyō, eastern capital), and a new "enlightened rule," the Meiji era, began. Diplomatic missions dispatched to Europe and the United States to learn about political, social, and cultural institutions also brought back firsthand experience of Western theatrical traditions, the esteem with which they were regarded, and ideas about theatre's importance as a national showcase. In 1871, kabuki actors' status changed from "non-person" to "new commoner" (*shin heimin*). A series of government policies over the next two decades shifted kabuki from the pariah status of over two and a half centuries into the mainstream of society, where some in the Meiji government hoped it could serve important educational and ceremonial functions.

In 1872, governance of entertainers came under the newly formed Ministry of Religious Affairs, which charged the theatre with educating rather than merely entertaining the populace. Theatre managers were warned against licentiousness, told to honor the Confucian ideal to "encourage virtue and chastise vice," and urged to produce plays faithful to historical fact. The period's realistic new "cropped-hair" and "living history" plays attempted to satisfy these demands.

In 1886, the Engeki Kairyō-kai (Society for Theatre Reform) was formed by dignitaries, politicians, and scholars who wished to hasten the pace of reform. While the society itself was short-lived, its hotly debated views were widely distributed in newspapers and pamphlets. Its three ambitious goals were: (1) to rid kabuki of its many alleged abuses, (2) to make playwriting a more honorable profession, and (3) to construct a modern theatre building that would accommodate theatre as well as music. Though largely

❧ FOCUS 4.4 Ichikawa Kumehachi: kabuki actress

The acting career of Ichikawa Kumehachi (1846?–1913) provides a three-way link between Edo period private kabuki performances by women, mainstream kabuki as it adjusted to social changes at the beginning of the modern era, and the return of actresses to the public stage after centuries of prohibition. Kumehachi's first important teacher was one of the last *o-kyōgenshi*, female kabuki performers in Edo daimyo mansions. With the shogunate's fall in 1868, o-kyōgenshi lost daimyo patronage, leading many to act in public. Kumehachi performed kabuki as well as newly evolving theatre forms. From 1895, she acted alongside actors and male *onnagata* (female-role specialists) in *shimpa* but was most suited to kabuki.

Kumehachi performed at Tokyo's minor theatres. She became a disciple of onnagata Iwai Hanshirō VIII (1829–82). She also studied other kabuki actors' methods, becoming well established by the late 1870s. When the Society for Theatre Reform (Engeki Kairyō-kai) was formed in 1886 to address the modernization of Japanese theatre, one concern was the reintroduction of women into kabuki. Danjūrō IX (1838–1903), the most influential actor of his day, began to train his two daughters, and in 1888 he adopted Kumehachi as a troupe member under the stage name Ichikawa Kumehachi.

Kumehachi played both male and female roles. For the former, she trained her voice to a lower register and padded her shoulders to suggest muscular strength. She considered it necessary to approach onnagata roles as though she had a male body and perspective. She thus practiced the same adaptive techniques that male actors had evolved for playing women, such as constricting the shoulder blades for a more feminine appearance.

Kumehachi was known as the "female Danjūrō." In 1891 she was expelled from Danjūrō's acting house for performing a major Danjūrō role, Benkei in *Kanjinchō* (The subscription list), without permission, although she was eventually reinstated. In spite of his initial excitement about women performing in kabuki, Danjūrō was unable to accept the idea in practice. He famously regretted the fact that Kumehachi had not been born a man, as her acting was so in accord with traditional methods like his own. Danjūrō – and a changing society that increasingly cast kabuki into a classical mold – kept Kumehachi from major stardom and performing opportunities expected in the new age of female actors.

Kumehachi was a devoted actor-manager of all-female troupes and a late-career teacher. She received much critical attention and positive reception, and left a legacy of artistic memoirs. While her remarkable career was the principal test case that ultimately led to an unbridgeable divide between male and female kabuki, she is equally remembered as the most acclaimed kabuki actress at the beginning of the modern period.

KATHERINE SALTZMAN-LI

unsuccessful, in April 1887 the Society arranged a command performance of kabuki for the emperor, empress, and dignitaries. Interestingly, many of the elements that theatre reformers sought to eliminate – the onnagata, the hanamichi, and use of narrative and offstage musical accompaniment (*chōbo* and *geza*) – were the very elements written about favorably by the first Westerners viewing kabuki.[6]

The biggest impact of Meiji Reforms was on playwriting, as house playwrights were joined and gradually replaced by outsiders. The prolific

---

6 Jean-Jacques Tschudin, "The French discovery of traditional Japanese theatre," in Stanca Scholz-Cionca and Samuel Leiter (eds.), *Japanese Theatre and the International Stage*, Brill's Japanese Studies Library 12 (Leiden: Brill, 2000), 50–2.

Mokuami, who penned in whole or part nearly 360 plays in his five-decade career, is considered the last "true kabuki playwright." Journalist turned playwright Fukuchi Ōchi (1841–1906) served as chief playwright for the newly opened Kabuki-za, from 1890 to 1903. Critic, translator, and English literature scholar Tsubouchi Shōyō (1859–1935) wrote plays with psychologically complex characters, such as *Kiri hitoha* (A single paulownia leaf, publ. 1894), while critic and dramatist Okamoto Kidō (1872–1939) wrote nearly 200 new kabuki plays. Many of these plays by outsiders, heavily influenced by modern Western drama and novels, are peopled with more psychologically motivated characters, and often eschew traditional musical and staging conventions.

Government regulation of theatres also changed drastically in Meiji. In 1872, theatres were allowed to move back to the city's center. New regulations permitted licenses to a total of ten (and later twenty-two) theatres in Tokyo, broadening potential clientele and revenue. Simultaneously the distinction between "major" and "minor" theatres was destroyed, the long-held privileged position of Edo's three main theatres dissolved. Disputes among actors ensued, especially in Tokyo where the distinction between major and minor actors was strong, but were put to rest in 1895 when laws barred divisions among actors based on the theatres in which they performed.

The Morita-za of Morita Kanya XII (1846–97) was the first to move back into the city center, changing its name to the Shintomi-za. When the theatre was rebuilt in 1878, Kanya installed gas lighting, enabling regular evening performances. For several years the Shintomi-za played host to visiting dignitaries, including Crown Prince Heinrich of Germany, former US President Ulysses S. Grant, and Hawaiian King David Kalākaua, although its anticipated status as national theatre never materialized.

Theatre management also underwent a gradual shift in Meiji. Entrepreneurial twin brothers Shirai Matsujirō (1877–1951) and Ōtani Takejirō (1877–1969) began taking control of theatres in the Kamigata region in 1895. They extended their reach to Tokyo with acquisition of the Shintomi-za in 1910, then emerged as the Shōchiku Corporation in the 1920s. They came to have a near monopoly on kabuki theatres and hold all kabuki actors under contract – a situation persisting today. The Tōhō Company, founded in 1932, made concerted, though ultimately unsuccessful, attempts to wrest some control of kabuki from Shōchiku between 1936 and 1939, and again between 1955 and 1982, when they established Tōhō Kabuki. The greatest effect was felt between 1961 and 1972 when thirty actors, led by Matsumoto Kōshirō VIII (1910–82), performed under the Tōhō banner. Ultimately all returned to Shōchiku, except Nakamura Matagorō (1914–2009), who became head teacher at the National Theatre training program. Although the shift from individual to corporate control probably enabled kabuki theatres to survive the downturn in theatre attendance beginning in the 1920s, it also led to unified production practices at the expense of regional variations. Repertory, too, determined by Shōchiku, was largely pared down after the Pacific War.

In contrast to the overhaul in production practices, the internal conservative hierarchy of kabuki acting families remained fairly constant, leaving little opportunity for those born to "minor" families, regardless of talent, to obtain starring roles. Encouraged by the growing proletarian movement of the 1920s, several groups of actors formed their own troupes, challenging Shōchiku's monopoly and the hierarchical acting system, only to be forced to return after financial disaster. In 1931, the Zenshin-za (Vanguard Troupe), a left-wing collective of mostly lower-ranked kabuki actors and a few *shingeki* (modern theatre) actors, led by Kawarazaki Chōjurō IV (1902–81) and Nakamura Kan'emon III (1901–89), created a successful alternative troupe. The company diverged from Shōchiku kabuki in its slightly faster, less codified presentations of classic kabuki plays, as well as its communist affiliation, collective decision-making process, and egalitarianism. They also performed *shimpa* and many new kabuki plays.

Meiji policies enabled and, indeed, expected kabuki to become a responsible institution playing its part in a new enlightened society, paving the way for the political voice previously denied. Yet the voice that emerged was not one of dissent. Beginning with the first Sino-Japanese War in 1894, through the 1904 Russo-Japanese War, and up to the end of World War II in 1945, numerous new kabuki plays supporting Japan's military actions were produced. Some were "overnight pickles" such as *Dai Nippon senshō* (Greater Japan's war victory, 1894), *Gunkoku bidan: meiyo no sekkō* (Scouts of glory: beautiful tales of a military nation, 1904), and *Nikutai sanyūshi* (Three heroic human bombs, 1932), dramatizing recent heroic acts by the Japanese Imperial Army. Other new history plays (*shin jidaigeki*), such as Mayama Seika's (1878–1948) ten-play cycle *Genroku chūshingura* (Loyal retainers of the Genroku era, 1934–41), retold historic events, infusing its feudal heroes "with the contemporary ideal of loyalty to the emperor."[7]

The kabuki that emerged immediately after the war was markedly different from that of pre-1945. In spite of the Allied Forces' Civil Censorship Detachment (CCD) directives that 30 percent of the kabuki produced be new plays promoting democratic ideals, with the exception of a very few

---

7 James R. Brandon, *Kabuki's Forgotten War: 1931–1945* (Honolulu: University of Hawai'i Press, 2009), 5.

"overnight pickles" in 1945, Shōchiku chose to produce traditional plays. While it could be argued that postwar rebuilding necessitated reliance on an established repertoire that would require much less effort than the creation of new plays, James R. Brandon suggests that this was a strategic effort on the part of Shōchiku to situate kabuki as a "classical genre," impervious to censorship.

While rare during the Occupation, newly written plays (*shinsakumono*) became a regular component of most major programs after the 1951 success of *Genji monogatari* (The tale of Genji) at the newly rebuilt Kabuki-za. Two sequels followed, sparking a trend in "great history plays" (*ōchōmono*), set in the Nara and Heian periods, written in contemporary language and using a blend of Western and Japanese music. Many were written by established playwrights composing for kabuki for the first time. Novelist Mishima Yukio (1925–70) wrote six plays, later dubbed "Mishima kabuki," produced between 1953 and 1969. Five were written for Nakamura Utaemon VI (1917–2001), whom he considered the ultimate onnagata. From 1952 to 1965, the Kabuki-za alone produced nearly 140 new plays, decreasing thereafter.

Producing innovations

In 1949 critic, director, and producer Takechi Tetsuji (1912–88) began offering brief runs of controversial kabuki stagings in Osaka. These "Takechi Kabuki" were instrumental in nurturing Kamigata traditions and young actors like Bandō Tsurunosuke IV (1929–2011; later Ichimura Takenojō VI and Nakamura Tomijūrō V) and Nakamura Senjaku II (1931–; later Nakamura Ganjirō III and Sakata Tōjūrō IV). In 1981, the future Tōjūrō created the Chikamatsu-za, a touring troupe aiming to revive Chikamatsu's plays, including two written for Tōjūrō I, whose lineage Ganjirō III restored when he took the name Tōjūrō IV in 2005. This Living National Treasure remains one of kabuki's leading actors.

Popular actors, international tours, and government support have all contributed to the resurgence of kabuki's popularity since the 1960s. The very first international kabuki tour was in 1928, when Ichikawa Sadanji II (1880–1940) and Kawarazaki Chōjūrō IV (founder of the Zenshin-za) led a troupe that performed in Moscow and Leningrad, meeting Konstantin Stanislavski and Sergei Eisenstein, who wrote enthusiastically about this encounter. Postwar international tours began in 1955, when Ichikawa Ennosuke II (1886–1963; later Ichikawa Enō I) led a troupe to China. By 1965, there had been tours to the USA, China (by the Zenshin-za), the USSR, Hawai'i, and Western Europe, making Grand Kabuki, as it was billed, one of the world's

∾ SPOTLIGHT 4.3   Modern stars: transforming traditions

At the end of World War II, kabuki faced an extensive rebuilding process. Mainstream kabuki continued the transformation begun in the Meiji period (1868–1912), bringing traditional kabuki into the modern world. At the same time, several influential actors deviated from the mainstream yet were nevertheless embraced by the public. Ichikawa Ennosuke III, Bandō Tamasaburō V, and Nakamura Kanzaburō XVIII have done the most important work in creating new plays and venues for kabuki today.

SPECTACLE AND SPEED

Ichikawa Ennosuke III (now En'o II, 1939–) comes from a minor Ichikawa family branch that for several generations had been considered upstart rivals to the dominant Danjūrō line. Beginning in the 1970s, Ennosuke revived full-length plays, trying to appeal to modern audiences through speed, spectacular stage tricks (keren), and quick costume changes. As kabuki had modernized and sought to present itself as highly refined drama in the Meiji era, it had distanced itself from vulgar, showy, and erotic elements of the Edo period (1603–1868). Chūnori, flying through the air, having fallen into disuse, was revived for the National Theatre performance of Yoshitsune senbon zakura (1968) with Ennosuke, playing the magical fox Tadanobu, rising above the stage to the third balcony, strapped to a harness on a hydraulic cable.

Chūnori eventually became indispensable to Ennosuke's theatrical technique, with variants such as Date no jūyaku (The ten roles of the Meiboku Sendai Hagi play, 1974) where, for the hanamichi walkway exit of sorcerer villain Nikki Danjō, he walked in the air, soaring higher and higher above the hanamichi. In the same play, Ennosuke performed ten major roles with over forty quick costume changes (hayagawari), one occurring in just a few seconds as two characters bump into each other.

Date no jūyaku is one of several Ennosuke-style tōshi kyōgen (full-length plays). Many are based on originals by Tsuruya Namboku IV (1755–1829), but Ennosuke reworked scripts to emphasize speed and spectacle, providing ample opportunities for keren as well as lengthy, stylishly choreographed tachimawari fight scenes. While a few major actors joined Ennosuke in these new plays, most supporting roles were performed by his own troupe of young actors, including many graduates of the National Theatre training program.

In addition to such refashioned revivals, Ennosuke also created a genre called Super Kabuki. These plays appeal to new audiences by using new scripts in contemporary Japanese language, combining modern stage technology with traditional acting and staging techniques. Yamato Takeru (1986) was the first Super Kabuki play, scripted by philosopher and historian Umehara Takeshi (1920–), about a legendary hero from Japan's prehistory. In death, Takeru is transformed into a great white bird, which flies over the audience, exiting near the roof of the theatre, wearing a glittering white costume with huge wings and feathers, dripping with jewels.

Ennosuke's efforts have been praised, but also criticized as cheapening kabuki. Yet their tremendous popularity earned him authority within the production structure of Shōchiku, which now supports frequent performances by his troupe and builds flying equipment in all new theatres. Ennosuke III had a stroke in 2003, appearing rarely after that; in June 2012, he passed on the name of Ennosuke IV to his nephew, Ichikawa Kamejirō (1975–).

Bandō Tamasaburō V (1950–) is not from a kabuki family, but studied classical Japanese dance as a child to strengthen his legs. He was adopted by Morita Kan'ya XIV (1907–75), giving him entrée into the kabuki world. Tamasaburō's charm and beauty as a youth afforded him several noteworthy performances. However, mainstream kabuki was dominated by giants like Nakamura Utaemon VI (1917–2001), so it was not easy for Tamasaburō to obtain the best roles. He appeared frequently with another young actor, Kataoka Nizaemon XV (1944–), playing powerful, sexy, dramatic, and comic women in plays such as Tsuruya Namboku's Sakurahime azuma bunshō (The Scarlet Princess of Edo, see p. 137) and shimpa melodrama Nihonbashi by Izumi Kyōka (1873–1939).

Fig 19 Bandō Tamasaburō performs the Sun Goddess in *Amaterasu,* accompanied by Kodō taiko drum.

Tamasaburō has emerged as kabuki's leading *onnagata*, female role specialist; after decades of estrangement, Utaemon personally taught many of his greatest roles to him. Tamasaburō has also collaborated with leading actors in other genres, and with artists and directors from around the world. He has been fond of the fantastic shimpa plays of Izumi Kyōka, carrying on acting traditions of *shingeki* (modern theatre) star Sugimura Haruko (1909–97) and great shimpa onnagata Hanayagi Shotarō (1894–1965). A dancer of exquisite taste in costumes and choreography, and a dignified actorly presence, Tamasaburō has been involved in various non-dramatic stage and film productions. He worked with renowned cellist Yo Yo Ma on filmed fusion dance-pieces,[8] and even attempted to revive the portrayal of females by males in classical Chinese Kunju opera *The Peony Pavilion* (1989), in Chinese, to great acclaim. More recently he has returned to the roots of Japanese performance as the shaman-dancer in *Amaterasu*, a collaboration with the Kodō taiko drummers. He was designated a Living National Treasure at the remarkably young age of 61.

Nakamura Kanzaburō XVIII (1955–2012) was the most talented and versatile actor of his generation. He expanded kabuki's boundaries with the first performances in the newly built Theatre Cocoon in Shibuya in 1994. *Tōkaidō Yotsuya kaidan* (The ghost stories of Yotsuya, 1824), created together with modern playwright and director Kushida Kazuyoshi, incorporated elements of modern and underground theatre while taking advantage of the theatre space to create a dynamic intimacy reminiscent of Edo period kabuki.

The mixing of kabuki and modern theatre grew into lively, hybrid productions by Kanzaburō, directed by Noda Hideki. Kanzaburō's devotion to traditional theatre spaces led him to create the Heisei Nakamura-za in 2000 – a temporary, movable theatre that attempted to partially recreate an intimate Edo period theatre. Heisei Nakamura-za has toured Japan and New York, and, while the Kabuki-za was closed for rebuilding (2011–13), opened in the traditional

8 Niv Fischman, dir., *Struggle for Hope*, DVD, Sony, 1997.

entertainment district of Asakusa in Tokyo for frequent performances. Kanzaburō's work focused on moving kabuki away from its elite status and closer to the common people. Both Kanzaburō and Tamasaburō have been active in restoring and using old kabuki playhouses located in the provinces. Kanzaburō died in 2012; the future of his innovations lies in the hands of his sons Kankurō (1981–) and Shichinosuke (1983–).

MARK OSHIMA

most recognizable theatre forms; consequently, it was utilized by the government for its "soft power" diplomatic value.

While financially supporting tours abroad, the Japanese government also invested in securing kabuki's future. The Kokuritsu Gekijō (National Theatre of Japan, 1966) initially consisted of a large theatre for kabuki and a small theatre for bunraku. One of its original missions was to restore and revive *tōshi kyōgen* ("full length" plays), the standard premodern practice that was gradually replaced in the nineteenth century by programs featuring excerpted highlight scenes. Given that there are no definitive scripts in kabuki, reviving a play involves kabuki scholars, rather than actors, in the revision process. Over the years the National Theatre has established a (not entirely uncontested) reputation as the authoritative voice on "authentic" kabuki, maintaining archives and publishing voluminous research in tandem with the restoration and revival of every production undertaken.

In response to a dearth of available low-ranking actors, the National Theatre also established a two-year training program in 1970, adding a program for kabuki percussionists in 1981. While this was successful in producing students trained in basics and ready to apprentice under senior actors and musicians, there remains little opportunity for those not born into kabuki families to perform major roles. Notable exceptions include Ichikawa Emiya II (1959–), one of many to apprentice with Ichikawa Ennosuke III (1939–; later Ichikawa En'o II) and gain some recognition in Ennosuke productions, though opportunities in the broader kabuki world remain limited.

Though kabuki cannot be identified with Japan's youth culture, there have been several movements in the past few decades that successfully broadened its appeal among younger audiences. Ennosuke III's revival of early nineteenth-century stage tricks (*keren*), like flying (*chūnori*) and quick changes, and his fast-paced Super Kabuki productions, brought pageantry and spectacle rivaling the largest musical theatre productions. To increase access to conventions of kabuki (and bunraku), Asahi Newspaper Company established an earphone guide company in 1975, offering simultaneous aural and digital commentary in English and Japanese.

Star kabuki actors also appear on shimpa and shingeki stages, or in historical television dramas. Mass media appearances in particular draw new, often younger, audiences to the kabuki theatre to see a favorite television drama star in his traditional context. Employing big-name contemporary stage directors like Ninagawa Yukio to direct young kabuki stars in non-traditional plays also entices younger as well as international audiences to explore more traditional fare. The 2005 *Ninagawa jūniya* (Ninagawa *Twelfth Night*) enjoyed more than 200 performances throughout Japan, touring London in 2009.

The passing of several of kabuki's veteran star actors in recent years (Kanzaburō XVIII [formerly Nakamura Kankurō V, 1955–2012], Ichikawa Danjūrō XII [1946–2013], and Nakamura Tomijūrō V [1929–2011] among others) has led some to predict a crisis in contemporary kabuki. But kabuki's repertory, acting families, and production system are strong, as evidenced by the fanfare accompanying the grand reopening following the rebuilding of Tokyo's iconic Kabuki-za in 2013. The next generation has taken up the reins and continues to do what kabuki has adeptly done for four centuries – adapt to financial, political, social, and artistic circumstances to survive as a vital artistic commercial enterprise for contemporary audiences.

REPRESENTATIVE PLAYS

Narukami fudō kitayama zakura (Narukami the thunder god, *cherry blossoms of Kitayama*), Tsu'uchi Hanjirō, Yasuda Abun, Nakada Mansuke, 1742) (see Figure 16)[9]

This *aragoto* tour-de-force weaves favorite characters of Ichikawa Danjūrō I (1660–1704) into a loose plot, framed as an imperial family succession play (*ōchōmono*). Evil Prince Hayakumo, passed up as heir to the throne, angers sage Narukami (thunder god), who imprisons the rain god and causes drought. Imperial official Ono no Harumichi also faces a succession dispute when his family heirloom poem card, which produces rain when submerged in water, is stolen. Envoy Kumedera Danjō solves Harumichi's problems in a series of delightful scenes. In *Kenuki* (The whisker tweezers), he attempts to seduce a page, then a lady in waiting; discovers magnet-wielding spies in the ceiling of Harumichi's mansion (the cause of the strange, floating hair affliction of Harumichi's daughter); and kills the villainous Genba, center of the conspiracy.

In another act, *Narukami*, the drought is remedied when Princess Taema seduces Narukami and releases the rain god. An angry Narukami transforms into the thunder god in a spectacular onstage *bukkaeri* (quick change) before battling an army of monks in a grand *tachimawari* (stylized fight). The god

9 Trans. Brandon, *Five Classical Plays*.

Fig 20 The Scarlet Princess (Sakurahime, Nakamura Jakuemon IV) tormented by her cruel robber-husband Gonsuke (Matsumoto Kōshirō).

Fudō appears in a literal *deus ex machina* ending, vanquishing Hayakumo and appeasing Narukami's spirit. Retaining the bold eroticism of early Edo kabuki, *Narukami* remains a perennial favorite.

Sakurahime azuma bunshō (Scarlet Princess of Edo, Tsuruya Namboku IV, 1817)[10]

Characters from lowest to highest social strata interact in this complex *kizewamono* that mixes historical and contemporary worlds, while twisting characters and conventions against all expectations. Priest Seigen lusts for Princess Sakura, the reincarnation of his acolyte lover of seventeen years prior, but Sakura falls in love with the thief Gonsuke, her rapist and unwitting father of her child. Marrying Gonsuke, she descends from princess to street whore, while pursued by Seigen – and later, Seigen's ghost. Accidentally discovering that Gonsuke is her father's murderer, Sakura kills him and their child, recovers the heirloom sword he stole from her father, and restores her family's honor.

Star actors are often paired, such as Kataoka Nizaemon XV (1944–; formerly Kataoka Takao) and Bandō Tamasaburō V (1950–), playing multiple types – respectively the thief/priest/ghost and the acolyte/princess/prostitute, keeping alive the spirit of the original, written at the height of the craze for virtuosic actors and quick changes.

10 Trans. Brandon, *Five Classical Plays.*

Tsuchigumo (The earth spider, Kawatake Mokuami, 1881; music by Kineya Shojirō III)[11]

This *matsubamemono*, based on a noh play (see Figure 48), deals with the legend of a shape-shifting earth spider, the demon-quelling tenth-century warrior Minamoto no Yorimitsu (or Raikō) and his four warrior guardians (*shitennō*). In the first half, the spirit of the earth spider in priestly disguise prays for the ill Yorimitsu. Noticing his spider-shaped shadow, Yorimitsu and attendants attack but the injured priest escapes. Following his blood trail, Yorimitsu's warriors arrive at the spider's lair. The spider's spirit reappears, costumed in long, shaggy, black wig, wearing bold black and brown *kumadori* makeup. The battle is notable for the spider and multiple streamers it tosses, its blood-red tongue stuck out in defiance. One of the *Shinko engeki jisshū* (Collection of ten new and old plays) of the Onoe Kikugorō line, *Tsuchigumo* was premiered by Kikugorō III, remaining a favorite of the line.

References and further reading

Brandon, James R. *Kabuki: Five Classic Plays* (Honolulu: University of Hawai'i Press, 1975)

   Kabuki's Forgotten War: 1931–1945 (Honolulu: University of Hawai'i Press, 2009)

Brandon, James R., and Samuel L. Leiter (eds.). *Kabuki Plays on Stage*, vols. I–IV (Honolulu: University of Hawai'i Press, 2001–2)

Brandon, James R, William P. Malm, and Donald Shively. *Studies in Kabuki: Its Acting, Music and Historical Context* (Honolulu: University of Hawai'i Press, 1978)

Ernst, Earle. *The Kabuki Theatre* (Honolulu: University of Hawai'i Press, 1974)

Kabuki Haiyū Kyōkai. *Kabuki Haiyū Meikan* (Listing of kabuki actors) www.kabuki.ne.jp/meikandb/meikan/

Kawatake Mokuami. *The Earth Spider,* in *Tsuchigumo, The Spider: A Kabuki Adapted in 1881 from the No Drama Written during 1449*, trans. Donald Richie (Tokyo, 1947)

Kawatake, Toshio. *Kabuki: Baroque Fusion of the Arts*, trans. Frank and Jean Connell Hoff (Tokyo: International House of Japan, 2004)

Kyoto University Library, Kunijo Kabuki Ekotoba (Okuni kabuki in picture and words). http://edb.kulib.kyoto-u.ac.jp/exhibit/okuni/eng/okutxte.html

Leiter, Samuel L. *Frozen Moments: Writings on Kabuki 1966–2001* (Ithaca, NY: Cornell University East Asia Series, 2002)

   Kabuki at the Crossroads: Years of Crisis, 1952–1965 (Leiden: Global Oriental, 2013)

   Kabuki Encyclopedia: An English Language Adaptation of Kabuki Jiten (Westport, CT: Greenwood Press, 1979)

   (ed.). *A Kabuki Reader: History and Performance* (Armonk, NY: M. E. Sharpe, 2002)

Scott, A. C. *The Kabuki Theatre of Japan* (London: George Allen and Unwin, 1955)

---

11 Trans. Donald Richie, *Tsuchigumo, the spider; a kabuki adapted in 1881 from the Nō drama written during 1449* (Lima, OH, 1949).

Shaver, Ruth M. *Kabuki Costume* (Tokyo: Charles Tuttle Company, 1990 [1966])

Takano Toshio. *Yūjo kabuki* (Prostitute kabuki) (Tokyo: Kawade shobō shinsha, 2005)

Takei Kyōzo. *Wakashu kabuki, yarō kabuki no kenkyū* (Studies in adolescent male and adult male kabuki) (Tokyo: Yagi shoten, 2000)

Tokita, Alison. *Kiyomoto-bushi: Narrative Music of the Kabuki Theatre* (Kassel: Bärenreiter, 1999)

Torigoe Bunzō, Uchiyama Mikiko, and Watanabe Tamotsu (eds.). *Iwanami kōza: kabuki, bunraku*, vol. II, 3: *Kabuki no rekishi* I, II (History of kabuki) (Tokyo: Iwanami shoten, 1997)

Tsuda Rui. *Edo no yakusha tachi* (Actors of Edo) (Tokyo: Pelican Books, 1987)

INTERNET AND DVD RESOURCES

Kabuki 21: www.kabuki21.com

Facts and Details: http://factsanddetails.com/japan/cat20/sub131/item715.html

Invitation to kabuki, Japan Arts Council: www2.ntj.jac.go.jp/unesco/kabuki/en/

Marty Gross Film Productions: "Masterpieces of Kabuki Theatre Series" www.martygrossfilms.com/films/masterpiece/masterpieces_kabuki.html

FOCUS 4.1 ACTOR PRINTS

Akama Ryō (ed.). *Zusetsu Edo no engekisho: kabuki-hen* (Theatre documents of kabuki in the Edo period) (Tokyo: Yagi shoten, 2003)

Clark, Timothy *et al. The Dawn of the Floating World 1650–1765: Early Ukiyo-e Treasures from the Museum of Fine Arts, Boston* (London: Royal Academy of Arts, 2001)

Clark, Timothy and Osamu Ueda. *The Actor's Image: Print Makers of the Katsukawa School* (Chicago, IL: Art Institute of Chicago and Princeton University Press, 1994)

Gerstle, C. Andrew, Timothy Clark, and Akiko Yano. *Kabuki Heroes on the Osaka Stage, 1780–1830* (London: British Museum Press and University of Hawai'i Press, 2005)

SPOTLIGHT 4.2 *ONNAGATA*: KABUKI FEMALE ROLE SPECIALISTS

Foley, Kathy (ed.). "*Onnagata*" (three articles) *ATJ* 29:1 (2012)

Fujita Minoru and Michael Shapiro (eds.). *Transvestism and the Onnagata Traditions in Shakespeare and Kabuki* (Folkstone: Global Oriental, 2006)

Isaka, Maki. *Onnagata: A Labyrinth of Gendering in Kabuki Theater* (Minneapolis: University of Minnesota Press, 2016)

Leiter, Samuel L., "From gay to *gei*: the onnagata and the creation of kabuki's female characters," in Samuel Leiter (ed.), *Frozen Moments: Writings on Kabuki, 1966–2001* (Ithaca, NY: Cornell East Asia Series, 2002), 211–29

Mezur, Katherine. *Beautiful Boys/Outlaw Bodies: Devising Kabuki Female-likeness* (New York: Palgrave Macmillan, 2005)

FOCUS 4.2 *ARAGOTO* ACTING AND THE ICHIKAWA DANJŪRŌ LINE

Kawatake Toshio. *Kabuki: Eighteen Traditional Dramas* (San Francisco, CA: Chronicle Books, 1984)

FOCUS 4.3 REGIONAL KABUKI

Gunji Masakatsu. *Jishibai to minzoku* (Regional theatre and folk traditions) (Tokyo: Iwasaki Bijutsusha, 1972)

Leiter, Samuel L. "The Kanamaru-za: Japan's oldest kabuki theatre" and "Gimme that old time kabuki," in Samuel Leiter (ed.), *Frozen Moments: Writings on Kabuki, 1966–2001* (Ithaca, NY: Cornell East Asia Series, 2002), 231–56; 257–94

Moriya Takeshi. *Mura shibai* (Village theatre) (Tokyo: Heibonsha, 1988)

Yasuda Bunkichi and Yasuka Tokuko. *Hida, Mino jishibai no miryoku* (Hida, the charm of Mino regional theatre) (Saga: Saga shimbunsha, 2009)

FOCUS 4.4 ICHIKAWA KUMEHACHI: KABUKI ACTRESS

Edelson, Loren. *Danjūrō's Girls: Women on the Kabuki Stage* (New York: Palgrave Macmillan, 2009)

"The female danjūrō: revisiting the acting career of Ichikawa Kumehachi," *Journal of Japanese Studies* 34:1 (2008), 69–98

Ihara Seiseien. *Meiji engekishi* (Meiji theatre history) (Tokyo: Kuresu shuppan, 1933)

Kamiyama, Akira. "Kumehachi no zanzō: onna yakusha to joyū no aida" (Looking back on Kumehachi: between female actor and actress), *Geinō* 34:9 (1992), 17–23

SPOTLIGHT 4.3 MODERN STARS: TRANSFORMING TRADITIONS

Kominz, Laurence. *The Stars Who Created Kabuki: Their Lives, Love, and Legacy* (Tokyo: Kodansha International, 1997)

Interlude: Nihonbuyo: classical dance

PAUL GRIFFITH AND OKADA MARIKO

The term *buyō* is a translation of the English "dance," combining characters for two common terms, *mai* (舞) and *odori* (踊り). After theatre scholar and playwright Tsubouchi Shōyō (1859–1935) employed the term in his *Shin gakugeki ron* (New musical theatre theory, 1904), "buyō" was universally adopted, but in order to distinguish the classical Japanese repertoire from other dance forms, and as part of his larger project to develop a national drama (*kokugeki*), *nihon* (Japan) was appended. Nihonbuyo comprises both kabuki buyō and non-kabuki dances, mostly from the *kamigata mai* tradition of Osaka-Kyoto. Nihonbuyo performers are organized into schools, some headed by kabuki actors who adhere quite strictly to kabuki choreography, others by unaffiliated dancers who perform replications as well as adaptations of kabuki dance, in addition to new choreographies exclusive to nihonbuyo repertoires.

While nihonbuyo shares kabuki's dance repertoire, it has nonetheless developed a distinct identity. The majority of nihonbuyo instructors work outside the kabuki world; both male and female professionals teach amateurs of both genders. Since the Edo period (1603–1868), it has been an essential outlet for aspiring female performers, considered a "polishing school" for the arts of deportment and kimono-dressing, and, more recently, valued as a connection to Japanese heritage.

Historical overview

Nihonbuyo inherits movement styles from older dance forms derived from shrine, court, and folk dance. These may be analyzed as mai (circular), odori (leaping), and *furi* (mime).

The word mai comes from the verb *mau* (舞う), a contraction of *mawaru* (to rotate), signifying slow and deliberate circling movements. The body is held stiffly, the center of gravity low, knees bent slightly, while the soles of the feet are in continuous contact with the floor (*suriashi*). This strong relationship between dancer and floor is further emphasized by occasional stamping. The origins of mai can be traced back to the earliest forms of *miko kagura* in which shrine priestesses circle around to reach a state of trance, as well as *bugaku*, the stately court dance imported from China. Mai became the principal movement style in the noh theatre, appropriating popular *kusemai* in Kan'ami's time, then subsequently exerted a major influence on popular kabuki dance.

Odori (踊り) refers to a much looser kind of leaping movement in which the body breaks away from such earthbound constrictions. The arms swing more freely, the body jumps, and the movements are faster and lighter than mai, more tightly linked with the melody and livelier rhythms of musical accompaniment. This style of movement may also stem from the practice of miko kagura performers who leapt, perhaps, as inducement to possession. Odori was later popularized with the stamping and rhythmic body movements of *nenbutsu odori* (Buddhist prayer dance), established by the priest Kūya (903–72), and later by colorful group *furyū odori* in the 1400s and 1500s (see Figure 17). These large, freewheeling festival dances took place both in cities and in villages, and could even evolve into riots. In one form of furyū odori, *bon odori* – dances to welcome the spirits of the deceased – groups of people dance as they circle around a large central scaffold (*yagura*) which also serves as platform for musicians and singers. Bon odori began around the sixteenth century, and is still performed annually in countless regional varieties in summer during the Obon Festival throughout the country, and among overseas communities.

These stately, shamanistic, festive, and dramatic dances braided with entertaining and comic kyogen dances in the Edo period to become fully developed stage arts within the kabuki repertoire. Themes expanded from seductive dances by females (or male female-role specialists) to powerful displays by *tachiyaku* (leading men roles), then to the varied everyday scenes of commoner craftsman and merchants. Dance has always been integral to kabuki. Today, at least one dance-scene is found in multi-act plays, and a dance-play is offered usually on a full program between two dramatic pieces. Even kabuki dialogue-based plays are rooted in dance training.

Dance and role varieties

Traditionally, many dances were created as integral parts of longer plays, featuring characters already familiar to spectators. When dances are performed independently today as 10–40 minute solos, they frequently contain strong dramatic elements, including lines of dialogue. Even when the dance does not originate from a longer drama, characterization is essential. Dances feature roles fictional or factual ranging from high-born princesses to lowly street peddlers, or dashing firemen – or a *tour de force* of several contrasting types within the same dance.

Many dances are variations on certain conventional themes. *Shūgimono* are auspicious pieces performed as part of a celebration or to commemorate an anniversary, wedding, or building opening rite, performed in formal kimono rather than stage costume. *Michiyukimono* (travel pieces) typically describe the thoughts and feelings of a couple on a journey. *Fūzoku buyō*, depicting the "ordinary customs" of contemporary townspeople, are further subdivided into works featuring city festivals, annual events, street vendors such as medicine peddlers, and street entertainers such as itinerant dancers. Even specific subjects, such as *Shakkyō* lion dances and *Dōjōji* have dozens of variants performed in numerous styles: solos and duets, kabuki dance and kamigata mai.

Kyoto-Osaka tradition: *kamigata mai*

Unlike the main tradition of kabuki dance, kamigata mai was nurtured in the pleasure quarters of the Osaka-Kyoto region; dancers were mainly women such as courtesans and geisha. In contrast to the musical styles developed for kabuki in Edo, salon music called *jiuta* was established by blind musicians in Kamigata. While kabuki music is performed by several shamisen players, singers, and percussionists, jiuta is usually performed by a single shamisen player who sings at the same time as he or she plays. Compared to other styles, jiuta is subdued, reflecting typical Japanese aesthetics of *wabi* and *sabi* (impermanence and melancholy).

Among the huge variety of jiuta songs written from mid-Edo through Meiji, some adopt noh themes. The accompanying movement is called *jiuta-mai*, or *zasshiki-mai*, indicating the traditional room where banquet customers were entertained. It is said that the dance can be performed within the space of a single tatami mat (approximately 1 × 2 m), demonstrating its minimalist movement vocabulary, and ability to express a cosmos within strict confines. Nowadays kamigata mai may take place in theatres as well, the original atmosphere evoked with elegant candle lighting and gilded folding screens.

During Japan's process of modernization, many pleasure quarters established a tradition of public dance performances by geisha; these can be seen even today in Tokyo and Kyoto. The *Miyako odori* in Kyoto's Gion district was inaugurated in 1872 to attract people to the Kyoto industrial exposition. Thirty-two dancers and twenty musicians in identical costumes performed a spectacular stage show featuring simpler choreography, mostly

Fig 21 Kamigata dancer Yoshimura Kōsen dances *Neyano ōgi* (Bedroom fan).

unison and group dances, a rare instance then of kamigata mai as stage performance.

Dance schools and the headmaster system

Many of today's most important dance schools (*ryūha*, 流派) are rooted in the professional theatre, having been founded either by kabuki actors or by related artists. The evolution of the dance choreographer (*furitsukeshi*, 振付師) as specialist occupation in the early eighteenth century was vital to bridging the gap between professional and amateur worlds. As kabuki dance grew in popularity, so too did demand among townspeople to be taught those dances. In response, many choreographers also became teachers. As pupils proliferated, dancers distinguished themselves from rivals and organized into stylistic schools, each school led by a headmaster, *iemoto* (家元). Especially significant was the fact that, as the system flourished, so too did participation of women. From as early as the eighteenth century, actors' female kin and disciples were able to take up dance professionally as instructors and entertainers (*o-kyōgenshi*, not to be confused with kyogen, comic counterpart to noh), who were permitted into the secluded women's quarters of daimyo mansions to teach serving ladies. Gradually this cachet increased their presence in society so that many new schools headed by women flourished. In Kamigata, new choreography was created for dances in the entertainment district performances, distinct from kabuki.

Tsubouchi's aforementioned coinage of nihonbuyo was employed in arguing for a new type of musical dance-drama, a national dance reflecting the modern Japanese state; his *Shinkyoku Urashima* (New Urashima, presented in fragments from 1904) was a model. Yet the "new dance" movement that he envisaged, of folk tales and legends dramatized through connected scenes of physical expression, and employing any number of Japanese and Western musical styles, never proved as successful as the traditional repertoire. Fujima Shizue (later Fujikage Seiju, 1880–1966) quit the geisha world in 1919 to devote herself to improving Japanese dance by creating original dances, becoming the first professional dancer outside the entertainment district. A few kabuki actors attempted modern choreographies, some influenced by Russian ballet. However the separation of dance from the stage, and new choreographies by non-iemoto performers, met with harsh criticism, making such innovations difficult. The Nihonbuyō Kyōkai (Japanese Dance Association, 1930) stressed its roots in ancient ritual and classical theatre; the Intangible Cultural Properties laws of 1949–51 sought to fix nihonbuyo's repertoire to the established kabuki dances. Tourists visiting for the 1964 Olympics and 1970 Expo were entertained by pure Japanese culture, not a hybrid with Western instruments or modern dance. The conservative iemoto system of schools and hierarchies, and their fans, succeeded in preserving traditions, yet at the high cost of losing out on much innovation.

Today, 5,200 dancers from 120 schools are registered with the Japanese Dance Association. Among the largest schools in Tokyo are Hanayagi and Fujima; in Nagoya, Nishikawa; while in the Osaka-Kyoto region, Yamamura, Yoshimura, and Inoue specialize in kamigata mai. Yet schools share repertoire and styles, as masters from one school switched to another throughout history, so techniques are less rigid and distinct than in other genres; the Inoue school even claims choreography influenced by both noh and bunraku puppetry.

Although open to all, studying the art today tends to be a middle-class pastime. Costs for hiring accompanying musicians, costumes, makeup, sets, and lighting can reach more than one million yen (over US $10,000) per performer, in addition to tuition or fees for receiving an artistic name (*natori*) or teaching license (*shihan natori*). Fees vary greatly: dance recitals may be done in plain kimono (*suodori*) or with full costume and wig, with recordings or live professional accompaniment.

Now in danger of losing its middle-class hobbyist base to Japan's financial crisis, and unable to attract young people to its calcified repertoire, nihonbuyo is facing a crisis of identity and self-preservation. After World War II, dancers both inside and outside the world of nihonbuyo began to dance to popular songs such as *min'yō* (folk songs), *enka* (popular ballads), and *kayōkyoku* (popular songs). These pieces, called *shinbuyō* (new dance), are free from traditional constraints; amateur dancers can even choose their favorite music upon which to base their choreography. Large-scale dance-dramas with spectacular costumes and sets, based on folktales or myths, are also attempted, such as Kyoto's Kamishichiken geisha district's *Snow White* (1997), or the Japanese Dance Association's *Faust* (1985) and *A Streetcar Named Desire* (2005). Western instruments and contemporary lighting are often employed. The traditional repertoire and choreography, however, remain the conservative core of the nihonbuyo tradition.

ELEMENTS OF PERFORMANCE

The majority of dances in the nihonbuyo repertoire derive from kabuki performance, adhering to the same aesthetic principles. Traditional kabuki is presentational, every effort being made to show actions outwardly to the audience in a conscious and beautiful manner. Regardless of the specific character or circumstance portrayed, every aspect of performance strives for visual beauty. This ranges from the overall set construction or large-scale tableaux (group poses), down to the smallest details of costume and properties, and each movement and gesture.

Performers must conform to set patterns of movement that vary according to specific role types and gender. In kabuki, female roles require *onnagata* (female role specialists) to appear smaller than their male role counterparts, as well as to display a delicate sensuality vital to kabuki's feminine ideal. This effect is produced by maintaining knees bent and pressed together, with toes pointing inwards. The line of the shoulders is slanted downwards by pressing the shoulder blades together at the back. This feminine ideal also determines how costumes are manipulated in order to create beautiful body lines. For male roles, the feet are positioned straight or pointed outwards, the entire body held in a more expansive manner.

For female roles in particular, the narrow, tube-like kimono is a physically constricting garment that creates elegant shapes yet limits movement. Dancers use props such as long cloths (*tenugui*), umbrellas, or ubiquitous fans (*ōgi*) to extend the line of the body. Fans are used for mimetic gestures, occasionally thrown in the air or spun for visual effect.

Movement with "meaning": *furi*

Furi refers to gesture and mime. Over centuries, gestural vocabulary has evolved to illustrate song lyrics; regular spectators come to recognize individual gestures for scattering petals, pouring sake, or writing letters. The mime conveys sequential images with fluid elegance: an open fan held aloft represents the moon at a moon-viewing banquet where a young courtier first spies his lover; holding it up, its ribs become a slatted fence through which he peeks at her; half-folded, it finally becomes a letter upon which to write her a message. He mimes grinding ink on an inkstone, then an extended finger becomes the brush that he dips before composing his epistle. Other gestures are extremely subtle, such as passing a hand above the head to indicate clearing clouds. Yet not all gestures have a literal meaning; far more important than "readability" of every action is the delicacy and flow of movements. Superb dancers can combine rhythmic and gestural precision with the dynamic stage presence of a particular role.

Through their wit and frequent quotations from, or allusions to, classical literature and poetry, dance lyrics attest to a highly refined literary sensibility. Choreography interprets both the melody and the literal meaning of the sung text, literally or obliquely. This interplay between lyric, music, and movement is one unique aspect of nihonbuyo.

Fuji musume (The wisteria maiden) demonstrates how choreography and lyrics interact. In the *kudoki* (entreaty) section, the maiden expresses her love for an imaginary man and also her bitterness at his inconstancy. Skillfully interwoven with the lyrics is a sequence of puns alluding to the eight most beautiful views of Ōmi Province (*Ōmi hakkei*). Long celebrated in woodblock prints and poetry, each view is associated with a particular situation and mood. The "autumn moon above Ishiyama" suggests a feeling of serenity, while "night rain at Karasaki" signifies tears. The emotional connotations of each placename reinforce the maiden's stage narrative, further accentuated by evocative mime.

Shortly after the kudoki begins, a single musician sings plaintively, "Their vows were firm as rock at Ishiyama." The maiden thinks back to the early stages of her romance as she ties together her hat ribbons to symbolize the couple's union; inclining her head, she poses. Yet when her lover is absent she is disconsolate, her life "empty as a cicada's discarded shell" ("empty" [*kara*] is a literary pun, the first half of the placename Karasaki). Standing, she revolves one hand over the other, a flowing movement expressing delicacy and femininity, as she steps backwards. The maiden turns round, shades her eyes to look at the view, then pauses. "Indifferent to the nights, I lie awake waiting, he is cold as the snows of Mount Hira." She pillows her cheek with her hand and closes her eyes, suggesting the anxious nights she spent, awaiting his return; seated, she holds her hat vertically as she inclines her head once more, as though imploring.

Visual imagery of the lyrics is complemented, not merely imitated, by physical actions. The total effect of melody, musical tempo, and expressive singing

Fig 22 Seki Sanjūrō II performs *Fuji musume* (Wisteria maiden) in this 1826 print by Utagawa Kunisada I (1786–1865).

is one of extraordinary emotional impact. Of course the "meanings" delineated here are only the simplest level of what may be a complex layering of competing feelings. The seeming narrative gaps and contradictions ironically contribute to the dance's dramatic potency when synthesized by a great artist.

References and further reading

Gunji Masakatsu. *Odori no bigaku* (Aesthetics of dance) (Tokyo: Engeki shuppansha, 1957)

    Buyo: The Classical Dance, trans. Don Kenny, intro. James R. Brandon (New York: Walker/Weatherhill, 1970)

Hahn, Tomie. *Sensational Knowledge: Embodying Culture through Japanese Dance* (Middletown, CN: Wesleyan University Press, 2007)

Hanayagi Chiyo. *Fundamentals of Japanese Dance,* trans. Leonard Pronko and Tomono Takao (Tokyo: Kōdansha, 2008)

Malm, William P. *Nagauta: The Heart of Kabuki Music* (Rutland, VT: C. E. Tuttle, 1963)

Matida Kasyo. *Odori* (Japanese Dance) (Tokyo: Board of Tourist Industry Japanese Government Railways, 1938)

Nishikata Setsuko. *Nihonbuyō no sekai* (The world of Japanese classical dance) (Tokyo: Kōdansha, 1962)

Sellers-Young, Barbara. *Teaching Personality with Gracefullness: The Transmission of Japanese Cultural Values through Japanese Dance Theatre* (Lanham, MD: University Press of America), 1993)

Tsubouchi Shōyō. *Shin gakugeki ron* (On a new music-theatre) (Tokyo: Waseda daigaku shuppanbu, 1904)

Watanabe Tamotsu. *Nihon no buyō* (Japanese dance) (Tokyo: Iwanami shoten, 1991)

Interlude: Okinawan theatre: boundary of Japanese theatre

SUZUKI MASAE

Okinawa developed a culture outside the framework of the Japanese state for much of her history. This was reflected in the dramatic form first created for court performances in the eighteenth century, during a period of "dual subordination" to Japan and China. *Kumiodori* (*kumiudui*, "ensemble dance") and *uchininā shibai*, performed in "Okinawan language" (*uchināguchi*), developed as distinct genres at the boundary of Japanese theatre, and still function to project and affirm the cultural memory and identity of Okinawans today.

Dual fealty: envoy entertainments

Okinawa is a series of islands lying midway astride the Ryūkyū archipelago, separating Kyūshū from Taiwan. In early Japanese historical records, it was only considered a shadowy primitive border region, referred to as Nantō (Southern Islands). After its period of warring provincial chieftains, Satto (1350–1405) of Chūzan ("Central Land") became the most influential, initiating a tribunal relationship with Ming China, which acknowledged it as the "Ryūkyū Kingdom," and eventually succeeded in uniting the archipelago. Between 1404 and 1866, Chinese envoys came twenty-two times on *ukwanshin* ("crowning ships") to officially install new Ryūkyūan kings, and stayed as guests of the Ryūkyū court for several months each time. Special performances of music and dance called *ukwanshin udui* ("dances for crowning ships") were prepared for welcoming feasts. The study of literature and performing arts was encouraged among the ruling class as a way to educate young Ryūkyūan aristocrats about Chinese learning and culture.

Meanwhile, mainland Japan's southernmost Satsuma domain (present-day Kagoshima prefecture) claimed rights to the Ryūkyū archipelago, sending an expeditionary force there in 1609. The kingdom thus technically came under Satsuma control. The Ryūkyūans began sending envoys to central Japan while remaining a Chinese tributary state. Since court entertainments played important roles for Ryūkyūan dual diplomacy, art and music, rather

Fig 23 Kumiodori variant of the Dōjōji story, *Shushin kani'iri* (The passion and the bell) (National Theatre Okinawa, 2004): Noho Miyagi as the Woman.

than swordsmanship, came to be regarded as important accomplishments for court officials. Each time emissaries from Okinawa were sent to Kyoto and Edo (present-day Tokyo) via Satsuma (eighteen times between 1634 and 1850), a prince was chosen as ambassador, assisted by bureaucrats including those in charge of court entertainments. Chinese plays and music,[12] possibly taught by Chinese immigrants to Ryūkyū, along with native Ryūkyūan dances, were included in these ambassadorial shows during the journey to display the expected "foreignness" to mainland Japanese. Such trips also provided opportunities for emissaries to see Japanese performing arts, which were then incorporated into their eclectic repertory.

Tamagusuku Chōkun (1684–1734), a Ryūkyūan aristocrat-bureaucrat, assisted five such missions before being appointed Odori (Udui) Bugyō, overseer of court entertainments for Chinese envoys. Chōkun created kumiodori: a musical drama based on Ryūkyūan history and legends, combined with both Confucian morals and elements borrowed from noh, kyogen, and *jōruri* that Chōkun had seen while visiting and studying in Satsuma. For example, *Mekarushii* is based on the legend of King Satto's mother, a celestial being, whose Okinawan husband stole her heavenly gown; the noh *Hagoromo* merged with legends of Okinawa's semi-divine king. Kumiodori

---

12 Itaya Toru, *Kōsaku suru Ryūkyū to Edo no bunka* (Crossing of cultures on Okinawa and Edo) (Ginowan: Yūju shorin, 2010), 7–8.

first appears in *Chūzan denshinroku* (The record of Chūzan), documenting feasts held at Shuri Castle for the coronation of King Shōkei in 1719. Plays were performed after the genuine *ryūbu* (Okinawan court dance) pieces on an outdoor stage. In addition to "the five great plays by Chōkun," influenced by noh,[13] the Ryūkyūan court created new kumiodori for each envoy visit; there are now over sixty kumiodori pieces by other authors, including *Manzai tichiuchi* (Revenge disguised as celebration) by Tasato Chōchoku (1703–73).

ELEMENTS OF PERFORMANCE

Currently kumiodori refers to classical Okinawan theatre based on the performance style inherited from those who witnessed the last court productions. The performers are traditionally male, consisting of *tachikata* (actor-dancers) and *jiutai* (chorus and music). The music consists of three *uta-sanshin* (singer musicians) who also play the three-stringed shamisen made from snakeskin, imported to the Ryūkyūs in the fourteenth century from China, accompanied by *kokyū* (bowed string instrument), flute, *koto*, and drums. Accompanying chorus and musicians provide atmosphere and narrative accompaniment throughout, while *uta-shanshin*, sometimes solo, express emotions in climactic scenes. Entrance music introduces dancer-actors as they appear on stage, with special pieces for male characters of high rank. The songs, combining local ballads and folk songs, are in classical Okinawan, employing the same 8–8–8–6 syllabic rhythm as *ryūka*, Okinawan lyric poetry. Dialogue (*tonae*) is also in 8–8–8–6 syllables, as opposed to the 5–7–5–7–7 syllabic rhythm of *waka* poems found in noh.

Movements are based on Ryūkyū dance patterns, suppressing realistic expressions. Role types include *aji* (lords), *ufu-nushi* (high-ranked officials), *nii-sei* (young men), *wakashu* (boys before coming-of-age), women, old men, and *marumun* (clowns representing ordinary local people). Some scholars see influence from other Asian countries, while others see that of ancient, indigenous female ritual dances.

Unlike noh, masks are not used when portraying female roles, apart from non-humans such as in *Shūshin kani'iri* (a *Dōjōji* variant), as female roles were traditionally performed by beautiful teenage boys. Colorful *bingata* kimono with long sleeves are used as costumes for both female characters and young male roles, distinguished by their hairstyles and robe length. High-ranked male characters usually wear thick robes embroidered in red and

---

13 Four of Chōkun's kumiodori, *Shūshin kani'iri*, *Nidō tichiuchi*, *Mekarushi*, and *Onna monogurui* parallel respectively *Dōjōji*, *Kosode soga*, *Hagoromo*, and *Sumidagawa*.

gold with ornamental hoods; secondary characters are less colorful, while tertiary characters dress in black.

Chōkun's plays, the most regularly performed, are relatively short, less than an hour as performed today, compared to later plays, which may take nearly three hours. Some scholars argue that kumiodori is still "unfinished" as performance art, leaving room for further creativity.

From court ceremony to stage show

After the Ryūkyū Kingdom's abolition following its annexation as a Japanese prefecture in 1879, some court performers survived by performing at the newly built commercial theatres in Naha. Introduced outside the court for the first time, kumiodori caught the attention of intellectuals, but did not succeed long among the general populace. Instead, with some influence from both kabuki and *shimpa*, a genre called *uchinā-shibai* ("Okinawan language drama") was created with kumiodori as its base, further developing into *shigeki* (history plays) and *kageki* (Ryūkyūan Opera). The court performers who turned to farming in local areas also introduced their arts to their new neighborhoods, and productions of popular variants of Ryūkyūan court dance and kumiodori developed as part of their village festivals. Thus, kumiodori and its variants, originally a high art written and performed by aristocrats to be shown to Chinese emissaries on special occasions, spread into Okinawan popular culture.

At the close of the Pacific War, in the spring of 1945, Okinawa was invaded in the deadliest engagement of the war, sustaining terrible damage. Since many male actors lost their lives or became prisoners, it was their female disciples who played active roles in passing on theatrical traditions. When the Okinawan Civil Administration under the American Occupation Army encouraged the revival of local theatres, new performance groups flourished, including some with actresses. When Okinawa reverted to Japanese control in 1972, kumiodori was proclaimed an Intangible Cultural Property. The Traditional Kumiodori Preservation Society moved their headquarters to the National Theatre Okinawa when it opened in 2004.

The opening season of the new national theatre premiered *Madamamichi* (The rainbow of Madama Bridge), a newly created kumiodori by Ōshiro Tatsuhiro (1925–), a prominent Okinawa-born Akutagawa Prize winning writer, along with several of Chōkun's classical pieces and other popular Okinawan-language plays. Students and graduates from the Department of Music of the Okinawa Prefectural University of Arts perform with distinguished actors, including Living National Treasure Miyagi Nōhō (1938–).

In 2009, Kōki Ryoshū (1938–), an Okinawan of Chinese ancestry with experience directing *shingeki* plays, was appointed artistic director of the Okinawan National Theatre. He explored creative fusions including productions of another Oshiro play, *Uminari no kanata* (Beyond the noise of the sea), depicting the tragedy of *Tsushima Maru*, a ship torpedoed in 1944 while evacuating Okinawan children.[14] In March 2013, Kōki invited Bandō Tamasaburō, prominent kabuki star, to collaborate with young kumiodori actors in *Chifijin tanjo* (The birth of the supreme priestess), another new Oshiro kumidori. As further demonstration of kumiodori's status as Japanese Intangible Cultural Asset, it was co-produced by the National Theatre in Tokyo, and the Emperor and Empress attended its premiere. Kōki was succeeded in 2013 by actor-writer-director Kakazu Michihiko (1979–), who created new Okinawan dance and plays for adults and children.

References and further reading

Ito, Sachiyo. "Origins of traditional Okinawan dance" (Ph.D. diss., New York University, 1988)

Ochner, Nobuko Miyama. "*Manzai Tichiuchi* (Vendetta of performers of "myriad-year" felicity): a kumi odori by Tasato Chōchoku, as staged by Kin Ryōshō in 1982," *ATJ* 32:1 (2015), 1–36

Ochner, Nobuko and Kathy Foley. "*Shushin kani'iri* (Possessed by love, thwarted by the bell): a kumi odori by Tamagusuku Chokun, as staged by Kin Ryosho," *ATJ* 22:1 (2005), 1–32

Thornbury, Barbara. "National Treasure/National Theatre: the interesting case of Okinawa's kumi odori musical dance-drama," *ATJ* 16:2 (1999), 230–47

Toma Ichirō. *Kumiodori kenkyū* (Studies of kumiodori) (Tokyo: Daiichi shobō, 1992)

Yano Teruo. *Kumiodori e no shōtai* (Introduction to kumiodori) (Okinawa: Shimpo shuppan, 2001)

Yonaha, Shoko. "Okinawan drama, its ethnicity and identity under assimilation to Japan," in Ravi Chatrurvedi and Brian Singleton (eds.), *Ethnicity and Identity: Global Performance* (Jaipur: Rawat Publications, 2005), 442–45

National Theatre Okinawa: www.nt-okinawa.or.jp

---

14 Oshiro Tatsuhiro, *Manishi ga fukeba: zoku Ryūkyū kumiodori jūban* (When the north wind blows – ten additional new works of kumiodori) (Tokyo: K and K Press, 2011).

5 ✑ Bunraku: puppet theatre

GOTŌ SHIZUO

Translated and adapted by **ALAN CUMMINGS**

Traditional three-man puppet-theatre bunraku (文楽) should properly be called *jōruri ayatsuri* (浄瑠璃操り) or *ningyō jōruri* (人形浄瑠璃). These terms stress the two major elements of the art: performed to the accompaniment of recited narrative music (*jōruri*) known as *gidayū bushi*, it involves the manipulation (*ayatsuri*) of puppets (*ningyō*). Texts of high literary quality and psychological nuance are expressed through delicate-featured puppets, intricately controlled by three-person teams. It provided urban audiences in Tokugawa Japan (1603–1868) with a serious, ethically and emotionally complex theatre form that has survived to the present day.

ELEMENTS OF PERFORMANCE

By Alan Cummings

Bunraku is a composite performance art in which stories are narrated to musical accompaniment while being enacted by puppets. The combination of the realistic, delicate movement of the large puppets with the intensely dynamic, virtuosic narration and shamisen playing creates a uniquely emotionally affective form of theatre.

Performance conventions

Puppets for major roles are large, between a half and two-thirds life-size, manipulated by three puppeteers moving in unison. The lead puppeteer (*omozukai*) is dressed formally with his face visible, while two hooded assistants are dressed in black. Puppets consist of a frame, head, hands, and feet, the last for male roles only – female feet are covered by kimono. Puppets are elaborately constructed, with movable eyes, eyebrows, mouths, wrists, and fingers, controlled by a hand-held toggle. Simpler, one-man puppets are used for minor roles and animals. Heads are categorized according to age, sex, marital status, class, and type of character, with seventy distinct heads in general use. Puppeteers dress their own puppets, padding the frame with cotton wadding to create the sense of the character's body before adding a wig and sewing the costume to the frame.

Fig 24 Three black-clad puppeteers demonstrate the manipulation of an unclothed puppet (in performance, the puppets are always dressed). They control respectively the head and right arm, left arm and props, and legs.

The movement of the puppets is fluid and remarkably lifelike, with puppeteers learning several dozen movement patterns (*furi*) to suggest everyday actions like sitting, running, and smoking, as well as more abstract patterns (*kata*) demonstrating intense emotion or to display a puppet's costume.

The chanter (*tayū*) provides narration as well as all dialogue. He must suggest the characters' mental state and emotions, as well as their words and actions. Voice projection is powerful and delivered from the diaphragm, supported by a cloth belly-band and a heavy sandbag placed in the kimono. The chanting during a single scene will move between relatively realistically delivered dialogue (*kotoba*) and melodic sung portions (*fushi*), with several intermediate styles of delivery (*ji*).[1]

Bunraku uses the thick-neck (*futozao*) shamisen. The shamisen's thick braided silk strings, high water-buffalo horn bridge, and large ivory plectrum in combination create a powerful, percussive sound. Set phrases punctuate and accent the narration, while more melodic passages underscore transitions or accompany dance sections. The shamisen player does much to set the scene's mood and tempo, forming close and long-lasting partnerships with chanters.

Performance context

While there are several provincial puppet troupes, Osaka's professional urban tradition is managed by a performers' association, the Bunraku Kyōkai, supported financially by national, prefectural, and city governments. Each year the Bunraku Kyōkai presents four regular runs of twenty-two days at the National Bunraku Theatre in Osaka (January, April, July/August, November), and four shorter runs at the National Theatre's small theatre in Tokyo (February, May, September, December). March and October are usually devoted to provincial tours of between fifty and sixty performances. The organization also mounts occasional overseas tours and regular introductory performances (*kanshō kyōshitsu*) that include a lecture-demonstration and play.

Regular programs are generally divided into afternoon and evening shows, lasting between three and four hours, comprising select scenes from different plays. Sometimes full multi-act plays are produced, lasting nearly ten hours. Earphone Guides (in Japanese or English), projected Japanese titles, and reasonably priced programs facilitate spectator appreciation.

The repertory largely consists of plays written during the theatre's heyday in the eighteenth century. History plays (*jidaimono*), ostensibly set in the past, treat struggles for power within great samurai families or imperial household, yet many actually comment covertly on contemporary political developments.[2] While epic in temporal and geographic scope,

---

1 Chieko Yamada, "*Gidayū-bushi*: music of the *bunraku* puppet theatre," in Alison Tokita and David Hughes (eds.), *The Ashgate Research Companion to Japanese Music* (Farnham: Ashgate, 2008), 197–227.
2 Uchiyama Mikiko, *Jōrurishi no jūhasseiki* (A jōruri history of the eighteenth century) (Tokyo: Benseisha, 1989).

◕ FOCUS 5.1   Bunraku stage

The bunraku stage today closely resembles the kabuki stage in general spatial arrangement (see Figure 15), though far less grand in scale and with several unique features supporting puppet use. In fact, bunraku theatres contain two performance

Curtains and hanamichi At the start of each act, a vertically-striped draw curtain (*jōshiki maku*) identical to those used in kabuki, is run open, always from stage left to stage right. Most entrances and exits are made through the short

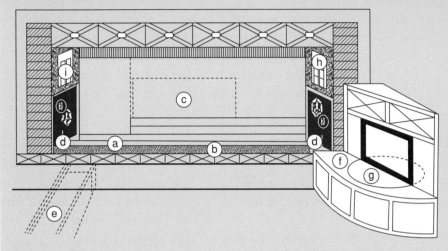

Fig 25 Bunraku stage.

spaces: one for puppeteers, the other for chanters and shamisen players.

The main stage is 17.5 meters wide, 18.5 meters deep, and 6 meters high. The downstage area is called the "ship's hold" (*funazoko*) (a), since its floor is sunk below the rear part of the stage. Divided from the audience by a meter-high railing (*tesuri*) (b) serving to conceal puppeteers' legs, it gives the effect that puppets are walking on the ground. The raised upstage acting area (*hon yatai*) (c) is separated from the ship's hold by another railing, and typically represents a house, palace, or other interior space. The fourth wall, facing the audience, is removed, making action taking place within visible. A separate area with sliding screens is often constructed upstage left to mark off an inner room. Painted backdrops and flats, similar to those in kabuki, are used to represent outdoor landscapes. Bunraku stages employ a full array of modern stage lighting, including footlights.

black curtains (*komaku*) (d) that flank the ship's hold at stage left and right, though occasionally puppets enter through an upstage doorway from a presumed interior room. The komaku are dyed with the crest of the Takemoto-za or Toyotake-za theatre. Rarely, a temporary walkway (*hanamichi*) (e) is erected, running from stage right through the audience. A slightly sunken hanamichi concealing the manipulators' feet was previously used, but since 1984 a regular kabuki-style hanamichi has become standard.

At far stage left, a small dais (*yuka*) (f) protrudes into the audience at an angle. Chanters and shamisen players sit on thick cushions here, in front of a gold-leaf screen. The chanter sits behind a small, elaborately carved lectern on which he ceremoniously places his text at the start of each scene, thus assuring his fidelity to the playwright. The dais contains a small revolving platform (*bunraku mawashi*) (g), allowing for rapid changes of narrators and shamisen players between scenes or during lengthy scenes.

Infrequently, the chanter and shamisen player perform from the misu no uchi ("behind the blinds") (h), a small latticed room above stage left, also used by inexperienced chanters and shamisen players. The stage right *hayashibeya* (i) conceals musicians, who provide sound effects on percussion instruments and flutes.

ALAN CUMMINGS

their most tragic scenes focus on ordinary people. Contemporary life plays (*sewamono*) were based on real-life incidents, depicting pressures affecting commoner classes during the Tokugawa period. Dance scenes (*shosagoto* or *keigoto*), their content more lyrical than narrative, make use of multiple chanters and shamisen players. New plays are occasionally written, drawing upon recent historical events and literary works in both Japanese and English, including adaptations of manga and anime aimed primarily at schoolchildren.[3]

Training

Like other Japanese traditional performing arts, bunraku stresses the ideals of artistic transmission and lifelong training, although father-to-son transmission is relatively uncommon. Most new performers are graduates of the two-year training program established in 1972 by the Bunraku Kyōkai and National Theatre. After eight months of general study, students specialize in chanting, puppetry, or shamisen. On graduation, students take one of eight traditional family stage names. By April 2013, there were seventy-one graduates of the program; forty-two remain active as professional performers, nearly half the troupe's eighty-six performer members.

REPRESENTATIVE PLAYS

Sonezaki shinjū (The love suicides at Sonezaki, 1703)[4]

Chikamatsu Monzaemon wrote this play, which opened just one month after the real-life suicides of two young lovers in Osaka. Tokubei, a clerk in his

---

3 Stanleigh H. Jones, "Experiment and tradition: new plays in the bunraku theatre," *MN* 36:2 (1981), 113–31.
4 Translated in Donald Keene, *Major Plays of Chikamatsu* (New York: Columbia University Press, 1961).

uncle's soy sauce business, and Ohatsu, a teenage prostitute, have fallen deeply in love, but their affair is complicated by circumstances. Tokubei's uncle is determined to have him wed his niece, paying a dowry to his step-mother to arrange the match. Tokubei manages to retrieve the money, but naively lends it to friend Kuheiji, who then publicly denies all knowledge of the loan, accusing Tokubei of forgery, and beating him. Penniless and hu-miliated, Tokubei visits the now unobtainable Ohatsu, and the two decide to die. But first he must endure Kuheiji's insults at Ohatsu's brothel, hiding beneath her kimono under the veranda (see Figure 27). Finally sneaking away, they travel to the woods around the Sonezaki Tenjin Shrine where they commit double suicide.

The focus on such lowly characters was groundbreaking for the puppet theatre. With its pure-hearted lovers, *The Love Suicides at Sonezaki* presents a simpler, more romantic story than Chikamatsu's later love suicide plays. With the outcome never in doubt, dramatic interest is located rather in the explication of an inexplicable act, the touchingly realized lovers, and the lyr-ical final journey (*michiyuki*). The play was revived in 1955 after a 250-year absence, and has since become a company staple.

Kanadehon chūshingura (The treasury of loyal retainers, 1748)[5]

Takeda Izumo, Miyoshi Shōraku, and Namiki Senryū wrote this sprawl-ing epic based on the 1703 Akō Incident in which forty-seven retainers took revenge on the man they held responsible for their lord's death. The play's eleven acts portray the attack that leads to the lord's suicide ordered by the Shogun, and the hardships faced by the avengers as they pretend dissolution while biding their time for two years, to the final at-tack on their enemy's mansion. Themes of loyalty and self-sacrifice are explored through the subplots of several major characters, male and fe-male, selling swords and their bodies, and sacrificing their lives to enable the revenge.

Written a decade after the development of the three-man puppet, *The Treasury of Loyal Retainers* provides a balance of tragic dramatic plot with spectacular action. In the nine hours of its full production, its panoramic lens moves sympathetically from the plights of younger characters to older ones, from great palaces to teahouses to peasant huts.

5 Donald Keene, *Chūshingura: The Treasury of Loyal Retainers* (New York: Columbia University Press, 1971).

GOTŌ SHIZUO
Translated and adapted by ALAN CUMMINGS (continued)

The beginning of jōruri ayatsuri puppetry

Recited narrative has a long tradition in Japan, with multiple genres. Jōruri developed at the start of the sixteenth century when blind priests began chanting the love story of Lady Jōruri and Ushiwakamaru to the accompaniment of *biwa* (lute) or rhythms simply rapped out, fan against palm. These performances, originating in Mikawa (near present-day Nagoya), soon spread to other areas. As performers used the same melodies to chant other stories, this new genre came to be referred to as "jōruri." The three-stringed shamisen, newly introduced from Okinawa, replaced the biwa for a louder, more sensuous sound palette, and rich expressive potential. Whereas the earliest performers sang and accompanied themselves, after the arrival of the shamisen, performance duties were eventually split between a dedicated chanter (*tayū*) and a shamisen player, permitting more nuanced musical and vocal expression.

Puppetry also had a long tradition in Japan. *Kugutsu mawashi* ("magic doll manipulators") descend from ancient immigrant performers from China. Early puppetry was often linked to popular religious belief, such as the *ebisu-kaki* proselytizing for Ebisu belief. An ebisu-kaki troupe from Nishinomiya shrine near Kobe and another from nearby Awaji Island, were particularly important, performing occasionally to much acclaim in the Kyoto capital.[6]

It is thought that synthesis of jōruri and puppetry began in Kyoto in the late sixteenth or early seventeenth century, approximately the same time that kabuki rose to prominence. Both jōruri ayatsuri and kabuki were new theatrical arts aimed at large, heterogeneous audiences of urban commoners, in contrast to earlier performance forms, such as court *gagaku* or samurai noh.

As jōruri spread from Kyoto to Edo and Osaka, chanters created their own styles and artistic lineages, competing by adopting texts from folktales, *kōwakamai*, and noh. In Edo, the new shogunal capital, Edo Izumidayū (dates unknown) enjoyed great success with his *kinpira jōruri*, dramatizing exploits of superhuman warrior characters, using an array of bombastic and spectacular effects. Earlier jōruri had relied heavily upon Buddhist ideals of karmic retribution and resignation to structure its plots, leading to very conventionalized heroes. But Izumidayū's characters felt larger than life in their expression of a wider range of emotional possibilities.

When the great fire of 1657 devastated much of Edo, Kyoto and Osaka again became centers of jōruri innovation. Two chanters were particularly important in its continuing evolution. Inoue Harimanojō (d. 1685?) combined

---

6 Jane Marie Law, "Religious authority and ritual puppetry. The case of *Dōkumbō Denki*," *MN* 47:1 (1992), 77–97.

∾ FOCUS 5.2   Shamisen minstrelsy

The single most important instrument in Edo period (1603–1867) music and theatre was the shamisen, a primarily solo instrument with strong percussive qualities that arrived in Japan via the Ryūkyū Islands (Okinawa) in the 1560s. This three-stringed banjo-like instrument was quickly adopted by wandering *biwa hōshi* (lute playing balladeers, see Figure 5), who not only developed new playing styles using the spatula-shaped biwa plectrum, but spread the new sound throughout the country. By mid-Edo, this versatile and evocative instrument was played in urban and rural settings, in solo and small ensemble settings, and by high- and (mostly) low-class men and women.

By the end of the sixteenth century, shamisen accompanied narrative chanting (jōruri) for the nascent puppet theatre. Competition among chanters yielded countless new narrative singing styles named after the originator, such as the deeply resonant *gidayū bushi* named for Takemoto Gidayū (1651–1724), which came to predominate in the bunraku puppet theatre. Prostitutes in the licensed quarters quickly adopted the shamisen as their instrument of choice, bringing it to kabuki as early as the 1610s to accompany erotic double-entendre *kouta* (short songs). By 1650, shamisen was central to kabuki dance accompaniment, and *geza* (offstage music) expanded dramatically throughout the following century. The genre that developed within kabuki, later called *nagauta* (long song), incorporated folk and popular songs, and was used cinematically in plays to evoke place, season, setting, and mood. Other narrative forms (*tokiwazu, kiyomoto, tomimoto, katobushi, shinnaibushi* etc.) also accompanied dance.

Regional styles of *min'yō* (folk song) also developed signature styles, like northern Japan's *tsugaru jamisen*, noted for its quick tempo, percussiveness, and improvisatory openness. It spread throughout the country in the early twentieth century, leading to annual contests today, drawing young musicians and producing international stars, such as the Yoshida Brothers. Bright and lively, Okinawan *sanshin* (the origin of mainland shamisen) became popular after the region's return to Japanese control in the 1970s.

Shamisen are distinguished by their necks: narrow- (*hosozao*), medium- (*chūzao*), and thick-necked (*futozao*) varieties, with progressively thicker strings and deeper pitch. Lyrical kouta (short songs) and *hauta* (popular songs) use a narrow; narrative tokiwazu, tomimoto, kiyomoto, and shinnaibushi utilize the medium; while gidayū and tsugaru utilize the thick-necked varieties. Each genre utilizes prescribed plectrum and bridges, a signature playing style dictating placement and attack of the plectrum, and particular melodic tendencies and cadences. Traditionally, music was transmitted aurally, with the *gidayū shu*, developed around 1780, as the first shamisen notation system. Rather than indicating pitch and duration, this acts as a memory aid relying on the shamisen player's experience. Since the Meiji era (1868–1912), other genres have each developed exclusive tablature notation systems.

Deep associations of the "sensuous" and "erotic" sound of shamisen with theatre and licensed quarters rendered it unsuitable for enlightened Meiji era Japan. Excluded from the national music education curriculum, it gradually faded from everyday life. Yet shamisen remains integral to traditional theatrical genres (kabuki, bunraku, *rakugo*), geisha entertainment, and numerous concert ensembles. In 2002, the Ministry of Education began requiring direct experience of traditional music for junior high students, which may eventually help balance the stress on Western music education and expand interest in traditional musical genres.

JULIE A. IEZZI

Fig 26 The jōruri chanter Takemoto Sumitayū VII (1924–) and shamisen player Nozawa Kinshi IV (1917–88).

heroic bluster with pathos, enjoying great popularity. Meanwhile in Kyoto, Uji Kaganojō (1635–1711) did much to raise the dignity of jōruri by developing his own heavily ornate style of chanting, modeled on noh. Indeed, his works are counted as the most accomplished of this early period, referred to as the *ko-jōruri* (old jōruri) period to distinguish it from that dominated by later gidayū bushi.[7] Chanters commonly wrote their own play texts.

Takemoto Gidayū

The most influential figure in the history of jōruri, however, was an unlikely outsider, Takemoto Gidayū (1651–1714). Born into a peasant family in Osaka, he became obsessed with the chanting of Harimanojō. He spent several years in intense study of the techniques of Kaganojō and other chanters, as well as related genres, including noh chant, the recitation of *Heike monogatari* (The Tales of the Heike), lay Buddhist storytelling (*sekkyō bushi*), popular songs (*hayariuta*), and folk songs (*min'yō*). Gidayū seems to have taken the best of each genre, expanding the musical and dramatic possibilities of his chanting, then melded them into a highly original, richly expressive new form. His long years of practice enabled him to hone a wide range of vocal techniques to convey the full emotional range of characters portrayed.

7 Charles J. Dunn, *The Early Japanese Puppet Drama* (London: Luzac, 1966); Janice Shizue Kanemitsu, "Guts and tears: kinpira jōruri and its textual transformations," in Keller Kimbrough and Satoko Shimazaki (eds.), *Publishing the Stage: Print and Performance in Early Modern Japan* (Boulder: Center for Asian Studies University of Colorado Boulder, 2011), 15–35.

In 1684 Gidayū opened a puppet theatre called the Takemoto-za in the Dōtombori area of central Osaka. Gidayū bushi, his eponymous style of jōruri, proved immensely popular with the burgeoning, economically powerful merchant class of Osaka. Word of Gidayū's success reached Kaganojō in Kyoto, who moved to Osaka to set up his own rival theatre, the Uji-za, near the Takemoto-za. The two chanters began a fierce competition, with Kaganojō engaging the *haikai* poet and popular novelist Ihara Saikaku (1642–93) to write two new plays for him, while Gidayū hired the Kyoto playwright Chikamatsu Monzaemon (1653–1725). In the middle of the competition, however, a fire destroyed Kaganojō's theatre; in despair he returned to Kyoto, never again attempting to compete with Gidayū in Osaka.

While the competition ended in stalemate, this first collaboration between Gidayū and Chikamatsu provided a turning point in the history of jōruri. The chanter and playwright began a long-term collaboration. Gidayū's performance style exploded in popularity, so appealing that people hummed favorite passages on the streets; many fans studied the art as amateur chanters. Nevertheless the Takemoto-za was never financially stable, forcing Gidayū to make fundraising provincial tours to Kyoto, Sakai, Nagoya, and even the pilgrimage tourist site of Ise. These tours had the side-effect of expanding the fame of his new style of jōruri to such an extent that he was eventually recognized with an imperial title.

Love Suicides and the Toyotake-za

Jōruri plays were constructed from preexisting historical or literary material, but in 1703 Chikamatsu composed *Sonezaki shinjū* (The love suicides at Sonezaki) for Gidayū, normally referred to as the theatre's first contemporary-life play (*sewa jōruri*). Chikamatsu's development of this genre was rooted in his experience of writing for kabuki, which used comparatively less historical material. Dramatizing the real-life suicides of an Osaka prostitute and her shop-clerk lover, the play was a huge hit. It resonated deeply with Osaka audiences as a familiar event, using contemporary language combined with an elevated literary style. With *Love Suicides*, Chikamatsu properly established jōruri as contemporary dramatic literature. Moreover, with its huge success, the Takemoto-za was able to pay off its debts. Success attracted rivals: that same year, one of Gidayū's former apprentices, Toyotake Wakatayū (1681–1764), opened his own rival theatre, the Toyotake-za, on the eastern side of Dōtombori.

Fig 27 At the Tenmaya teahouse, lover Tokubei (Yoshida Tamame, lead puppeteer) conceals himself beneath the veranda while courtesan Ohatsu (Kiritake Kanjūrō) banters with the villainous Kuheiji (Yoshida Minosuke).

The struggle for succession at the Takemoto-za

Gidayū's theatre often struggled financially, but he did manage to maintain its preeminent position in the performance of ningyō jōruri. However, in 1704 Gidayū suddenly announced his retirement. The Takemoto-za designated Takeda Izumo I (d. 1747), an influential theatrical producer, as the theatre's new manager, with Chikamatsu appointed as chief playwright. These measures persuaded Gidayū to return as chanter.

Takeda's family ran a mechanical puppet (*karakuri ningyō*) troupe that had enjoyed success in several provinces. These mechanical dolls, animated by whalebone springs and wooden cogwheels to dance, shoot arrows, or serve tea, were a popular draw as *misemono* (sideshow attractions), and were also used on festival floats. Takeda improved the Takemoto-za's scenery and puppet costumes. Chikamatsu moved from Kyoto to Osaka and began to concentrate on writing for the puppets alone. He created successive contemporary dramas of a high literary quality that presented the keenly observed emotions of larger-than-life characters.

Gidayū passed away in 1714, secure in the knowledge that he had created a new narrative genre. He designated Takemoto Masatayū (1691–1744) as his successor, but Masatayū's youth and inexperience triggered a struggle for succession. Finally, Chikamatsu lent his support to Masatayū and in 1715

❧ SPOTLIGHT 5.1   Chikamatsu Monzaemon: puppet playwright

Known posthumously as the "god of playwrights," Chikamatsu Monzaemon (1653–1725) composed more than a hundred plays over a forty-five-year career. Each work was written for particular performers in commercial theatres in Kyoto and Osaka. His thirty or so surviving kabuki plays were published not in complete editions but in illustrated abridged versions (*e-iri-kyōgenbon*), while his *jōruri* (bunraku puppet) works were published at the time of first performance, in authorized complete editions, including chanters' notations. Today his oeuvre, particularly the works written for the puppet theatre, holds an important place in Japanese literary and dramatic canons, performed in both kabuki and bunraku.

There are parallels with Shakespeare, in that Chikamatsu wrote many period plays (*jidaimono*) on all aspects of Japanese history, as well as works set in contemporary domestic life (*sewamono*) covering incidents from love suicide and adultery to murder and smuggling. His influence on later popular theatre and fiction was unparalleled. Because of the popular tradition of amateurs learning to chant jōruri plays (*gidayū*), many works remained available in woodblock print editions until the late nineteenth century, much longer than most literary works from this period.

INSIDER PERSPECTIVE

Born Sugimori Nobumori into a well-to-do and highly cultured samurai family in Echizen (Fukui), a Tokugawa fief north of Kyoto, he likely learned noh as a child and studied Chinese from his grandfather, the daimyo's doctor. Around his thirteenth year, the family gave up their samurai status and later moved to Kyoto. He served the nobility, and so had unparalleled access to samurai and courtier life. His subsequent experiences writing for jōruri chanters and kabuki actors, and even working backstage at the Mandayū-za theatre and as a street storyteller, took him into the opposite end of the social spectrum.

Until Chikamatsu's time, chanters and actors composed plays. Chikamatsu sought recognition as a professional playwright by having his name on playbills, published texts, and theatre marquees at a time when this was uncommon. He wrote puppet plays in Kyoto in the 1670s, under the guidance of and in collaboration with the chanter Uji Kaganojō (1635–1711), who did not allow Chikamatsu's name to appear as author, and then for Takemoto Gidayū (1651–1714) in Osaka from the mid-1680s. From the 1680s he also wrote kabuki plays. In 1695 he became staff playwright at the Mandayū-za, writing primarily for the kabuki actor Sakata Tōjūrō I (1647–1709), in collaboration with actor/writer Kaneko Kichizaemon (d. 1728). After success with his puppet play *Sonezaki shinjū* (The love suicides at Sonezaki, 1703) and retirement of Tōjūrō, Chikamatsu moved to Osaka in 1706, becoming staff playwright for the Takemoto-za puppet theatre, where he produced his final masterpieces. He was deeply involved with theatre and learned his craft working with performers over his entire career.

HISTORY OR PERIOD PLAYS

Chikamatsu's period plays are usually in five acts, performed from morning to dusk. They grandly depict historical moments at both public and private levels, and at both extremes of the social scale. Plays such as *Kokusen'ya gassen* (The battles of Coxinga, 1715) and *Futago Sumidagawa* (Twins at the Sumida River, 1720) have supernatural elements, spanning many years. They usually end with a resolution of the original crisis that earlier had cast the world into turmoil. Acts III and/or IV witness intense tragedies, usually in real time and realistically. Often, women or men who have lost their status sacrifice themselves for a higher cause and thereby help restore political order. These important tragedies usually focused on figures outside the realm of political or military power, and thereby brought the story closer to the social level of the contemporary audience.

Like Shakespeare's "history plays," jidaimono period plays, although set in the past, are not primarily about history; instead they use history as a vehicle to comment on or criticize contemporary society and government.[8] Audiences recognized performance codes referring to public and governmental affairs. This convention allowed playwrights to discuss contemporary events, even though any such open criticism was officially banned in Tokugawa government edicts from at least the seventeenth century.

KABUKI AND CONTEMPORARY-LIFE PUPPET PLAYS

Kabuki plays tended to be set in a contemporary context. Sakata Tōjūrō promoted a realistic acting style, later termed *wagoto* ("gentle style"), that would have been an interesting contrast for Chikamatsu, who learned initially to write for the more fantastical world of the puppet theatre. Writing narrative period plays set in the past, and at the same time writing for Tōjūrō's relatively realistic, dialogue-heavy contemporary kabuki drama, would inspire his twenty-four sewamono (contemporary-life) jōruri plays, beginning with *The Love Suicides at Sonezaki*, 1703 (see p. 159). These consisted of three scenes tightly framed in time and place, realistic in action, and focused on relatively low-status characters enmeshed in tragedy.

Contemporary-life plays include *Shinjū ten no Amijima* (The love suicides at Amijima, 1721) and *Onnagoroshi abura no jigoku* (The woman-killer and the hell of oil, 1721). They are performed regularly, even in translation outside Japan, and have been made into films. During the last five years of his career, Chikamatsu incorporated his experiences of probing individual psychologies

in his realistic contemporary-life works into his mature period plays such as *Kawa-nakajima kassen* (Battles at Kawa-nakajima, 1721) and *Kanhasshū tsunagi-uma* (Tethered steed and the eight provinces of Kantō, 1724).

TRAGIC CORE

One remarkable aspect of Chikamatsu's works and jōruri in general written by later playwrights is that almost every play has death and tragedy at its core. In period plays, which tend to end happily with a resolution of the play's crisis, this usually comes in the third act of five, and in contemporary-life plays in the final of three scenes. Another distinctive aspect of Chikamatsu's plays is that heroes and heroines who face tragedy and its consequences are not high-status figures as in Aristotelian tragedy or European classical drama. Usually, lead characters are men without significant political status, those who have lost their position after a crime or transgression, or women who do not have any power in the public sphere. Contemporary-life plays often feature orphans and prostitutes, at the bottom of the social scale. Yet these lowly characters achieve grand stature when facing tragedy, often accepting self-sacrifice for a greater cause – to save a loved one, to repay an obligation, or out of passion in a love suicide. Such explorations of the lives of ordinary commoners within the context of tragedy as a key and ongoing motif is distinctive in world drama.

C. ANDREW GERSTLE

wrote *Kokusenya kassen* (The battles of Coxinga) for him. The plot's dramatic scale and novelty, about a conflicted half-Japanese, half-Chinese warrior hero, created a hit that ran for three years.

The structure of jōruri – *jidaimono, sewamono, keigoto*

Jōruri plays were originally chanted in twelve acts (*dan*), but eventually this proved too long, and they were reduced to just six. Both Harimanojō and Kaganojō experimented with five-act plays, but the six-act structure

8 See Uchiyama Mikiko, *Jōrurishi no jūhasseiki* (A jōruri history of the eighteenth century) (Tokyo: Benseisha, 1989).

remained popular. From the start of his career, Gidayū chanted only five-act plays, but retained a custom from the previous age of placing entirely independent interludes (*aikyōgen*) performed by puppeteers alone between acts. *The Battles of Coxinga* did away with these interludes, an innovative step in establishing gidayū bushi as an independent dramatic form and raising its literary level, in terms of both content and structure.

Gidayū embraced the standard five-act play structure of noh (god, warrior, woman, miscellaneous, demon) as themes for his five acts in history or period plays (jidaimono):

> Act I: Love. From the opening lines to the end of the prelude is the *Sanbasō* section … One should chant vigorously as if handling loose and wild reins … The final scene of the first act is particularly crucial … Act II: Battles (*shura*). In the second act, the mood of the first act must be discarded. One must chant without any touch of heaviness and the mood should be light … Act III: Pathos … The third act is the heart of the play … When chanting scenes of pathos and grief, one must not disregard reality. They must be chanted as if holding the essence of the entire play within your heart … Act IV: *Michiyuki* Travel Song. One should extend the pauses and chant more gently than in the previous act … The melody is the most important aspect of the *michiyuki* [journey] scene … Act V: Conclusion. Since this act must conclude the whole play, it is a difficult section. The mood is auspicious.[9]

Gidayū's stipulations extend to composition and style of chanting, all of which must conform to content. In contrast to Kaganojō, who declared noh the sole "parent" of his jōruri, Gidayū argues that noh is more like a foster parent, whereas the true parents are the famous chanters of the past. In this statement, we can see both Gidayū's admission that the form of his art was borrowed from noh, and his pride in the fact that he has furthered the artistic lineage of recited narrative. Gidayū's five-act form remained central to subsequent jōruri.

Contemporary-life plays were originally considered as mere additions (*tsuke kyōgen*) to the main history play (jidaimono). The simple contents were presented in three (sometimes two) scenes, which parallel the *jo-ha-kyū* structural dynamic of noh plays. Themes were simple, characters few, and dialogue, performance, and tempo were all rapid and realistic. The third scene was sometimes composed as a lyrical travel scene (*michiyuki*). In later years, multi-act plays treated subjects like intrigues in samurai households, combining both contemporary and historical elements.[10]

---

9   Gidayū's preface to *Jōkyō yonen gidayū danmonoshū* (Collection of jōruri scenes, 1687), trans. in C. Andrew Gerstle, *Circles of Fantasy: Convention in Chikamatsu's Plays* (Cambridge, MA: Harvard University Press,1986), 189–96.

10 Donald H. Shively, "Tokugawa plays on forbidden topics," in James R. Brandon (ed.), *Chūshingura: Studies in Kabuki and the Puppet Theatre* (Honolulu: University of Hawai'i, 1982), 1–61.

The revival of the Toyotake-za

The Toyotake-za struggled to compete with the Takemoto-za, but eventually became financially unsustainable and, in 1703, was forced to close temporarily. Toyotake Wakatayū reopened it at the eastern end of Dōtombori with the help of popular puppeteer Tatsumatsu Hachirobei (d. 1734), appointing Ki no Kaion (1663–1742) as playwright. Ki no Kaion's *Kamakura sandaiki* (Kamakura trilogy, 1716) became a big hit, giving the Toyotake-za greater financial stability. Tatsumatsu later moved to Edo, where he opened the Tatsumatsu-za.

There was a clear contrast between the bold, dignified plays that Chikamatsu wrote at the Takemoto-za for Gidayū and Masatayū and those that Ki no Kaion wrote to take advantage of Wakatayū's beautiful voice and ornate phrasing. The intense competition between the two theatres became the talk of Osaka, boosting the popularity of ningyō jōruri, referred to with reference to their location on Dōtombori. The solid seriousness of Takemoto-za was known as the "western style" while the showier technical artistry of Toyotake-za became the "eastern style."

Masatayū took the name Gidayū II in 1734, symbolizing his rightful succession to his teacher's art. He brought a deep textual understanding to Chikamatsu's plays, grasping the psychological complexity of the characters coupled with an ability to display their emotional reality. Gidayū II's warmly humanistic delivery valorized Chikamatsu's contemporary plays, allowing the playwright to create a string of popular masterpieces including *Shinjū ten no Amijima* (The love suicides at Amijima, 1720), *Onnagoroshi abura jigoku* (The woman-killer and the hell of oil, 1721), and *Shinjū Yoigōshin* (The love suicides on the eve of the Kōshin Festival, 1722). Chikamatsu's love suicide plays in particular, based on real-life tragedies of frustrated lovers, proved popular in kabuki too, until banned by the shogunate in 1723 for inspiring too many copycat suicides by those wishing to achieve momentary fame. Through his collaboration with Takemoto Gidayū and his successors, Chikamatsu was able to transform jōruri into one of the outstanding art forms of the Tokugawa period, rivaling and often surpassing contemporaneous kabuki.

The era of multiple authorship

During Chikamatsu's lifetime, plays were generally composed by individual playwrights. During his last years, he consciously began to train potential successors at the Takemoto-za, including Takeda Izumo I (1691–1756) and Matsuda Bunkōdō (dates unknown). Several of their extant texts bear the annotation "corrected by Chikamatsu Monzaemon." Multiple authorship in puppet theatre, where several playwrights would work collaboratively on a single play, began in 1723, the year before Chikamatsu's death. Takemoto-za's chief playwright was Takeda Izumo I, while Toyotake-za's was Namiki Sōsuke (1695–1751), but both worked in collaboration with other playwrights. Their multiply authored plays (*gassaku*) are grand in scale with complex plots. Playwrights strived to outdo each other, often at the expense of plot unity.

Improvements in puppets and staging

Advances in puppetry paralleled developments in chanting and playwriting. From the theatre's earliest days, puppets were manipulated by a single puppeteer, who inserted both hands inside the back of the puppet's costume. These small (around 50 to 60 cm high), simple puppets were known as *tsukkomi* (thrust) *ningyō*. Manipulators held the puppets above their shoulders, concealed from spectators by a rail with a curtain suspended from it, boards, or standing screens. Because some puppeteers were said to rival kabuki actors with their skillful emotional expression, however, theatres began to place a temporary platform in front of the curtain, so that puppeteers could perform in full view of the audience (*dezukai*). This allowed spectators to view the puppeteers' art at closer quarters, and freed manipulators from straining behind screens. Chanters and shamisen players would also sometimes perform on this platform.

As noted earlier, the theatre had adopted elements from the popular tradition of mechanical dolls. As a result, a new method of manipulation developed in which puppets were held from the back, facilitating more varied and precise movements. Texts such as *Chikuhō koji* (History of the Takemoto and Toyotake theatres, 1756) describe improved mechanisms giving puppets legs, and allowing them to open and close their mouths and even to move their fingers.[11]

These advances culminated in the invention of the three-man puppet, first used in *Ashiya Dōman ōuchi kagami* (The courtly mirror of Ashiya Dōman) in 1734. Three-man manipulation necessitated larger puppets, doubling from 50–60 cm to 100–120 cm high. Yet such a major development could not have occurred out of the blue, so it is more reasonable to imagine a series of experiments finally coming to fruition in this performance.

While many puppeteers contributed to this innovation, particularly important was Takemoto-za puppeteer Yoshida Bunzaburō (d. 1760). The

---

11 Ichirakushi, *Chikuhō Koji* (The history of the Takemoto and Toyotake theatres, 1756), in Geinōshi Kenkyūkai (ed.), *Nihon shomin bunka shiryō shūsei* (Collection of sources on Japanese popular culture) (Tokyo: San'ichi shobō, 1975), vol. VII.

conventions for three-man manipulation he developed were essentially the same as those used today. It is uncertain when the current performance practice of leaving the faces of lead puppeteers visible to spectators first began, but visual sources suggest sometime between the late eighteenth and early nineteenth centuries.

Improvements in stage machinery continued alongside those in puppetry. In 1728, the chanter and shamisen player were moved from a concealed position at stage front to the side. Puppeteers had more stage space, while scenery grew larger and more complex. Thus new developments in the mechanics and techniques of puppetry, in combination with multiple authorship of plays, and ongoing rivalry between theatres, saw the art move from the literary toward the performative.

The golden age

Multiple authorship reaches its peak

In the 1730s, multiple authorship became the dominant mode of playwriting. Miyoshi Shōraku (1696?–1772?), Takeda Izumo I (d. 1747), and Takeda Izumo II (1691–1756) at the Takemoto-za and Namiki Sōsuke (1695–1751) and Asada Itchō (d. 1780) at the Toyotake-za competed to create works packed with action and variety. The system encouraged complex plays with multiple climactic scenes, spurring theatres to divide these among different chanters, instead of the prior practice of employing a single chanter for the whole play. The Takemoto-za and Toyotake-za came to employ many headlining chanters distinguished by unique styles.

The Takemoto-za enticed Namiki Sōsuke to join its playwriting team. Under his new name, Namiki Senryū, he, Miyoshi Shōraku, and Takeda Izumo II created in quick succession the three most popular puppet plays in history: *Sugawara denju tenarai kagami* (Sugawara and the secrets of calligraphy, 1746), *Yoshitsune senbon zakura* (Yoshitsune and the thousand cherry trees, 1747), and *Kanadehon chūshingura* (The treasury of loyal retainers, 1748). Both the Takemoto-za and the Toyotake-za used ever more spectacular and sophisticated sets and costumes, vying to create ever more expressive puppets. In Osaka it was said that "puppet theatre has become so popular, it is as though kabuki no longer existed."[12] This was the golden age of ningyō jōruri.

As theatricality became ascendant, concealed puppeteers came increasingly to audience attention. The drawing power of the Takemoto-za's Yoshida

---

12 *Jōrurifu* (Chronology of jōruri, *c.* late 1790s), in Shuzui Kenji (ed.), *Chikamatsu sewa jōrurishū* (Collection of Chikamatsu's domestic jōruri) (Tokyo: Hakubunkan, 1928), 707.

Bunzaburō rivaled that of leading kabuki actors. The theatre even backed him when he disagreed with a chanter concerning the pace and mood of a particular scene. Both refused to back down, causing an exchange of chanters between the Takemoto-za and Toyotake-za; this accident seemingly led to a blending of their previously distinct styles. However, it is unlikely that one incident could have had such a serious effect on such well-established styles. Rather, a gradual process in which each rival theatre borrowed the strengths of the other in a process of mutual influence seems more convincing. Ultimately, however, this incident ended the system of stylistic rivalry between the Takemoto-za and Toyotake-za.

As we have seen, theatrical aspects of puppets had become ever more important. Izumo's partner in instigating this shift, puppeteer Bunzaburō, had been acclaimed for his genius since his youth. Soon he became key puppeteer in the troupe, inventing many new techniques and mechanisms. In addition to his contribution to the development of the three-man puppet, he also invented mechanisms that made this leap possible, such as the long rod (*sashigane*) used by left-hand manipulators. Also credited to Bunzaburō are movable eyebrows, the movable ears used by the Fox Tadanobu puppet in *Yoshitsune and the Thousand Cherry Trees*, and its spectacular flying technique (*chūnori*). As a playwright, however, he primarily rewrote earlier works by Chikamatsu and others, creating more scenes where his puppetry could be displayed to best advantage.

Rise of kabuki and decline of ningyō jōruri

Resurgence of kabuki

The success of ningyō jōruri in the 1730s and 1740s needs to be seen in the wider context of official regulation of rival kabuki. Kabuki originated in the performance of songs, dances, and skits that showed off performers' bodies, faces, and voices, but by the late seventeenth and early eighteenth centuries it began producing many excellent actors with outstanding dramatic skills. As dedicated playwrights appeared, kabuki consolidated its position as popular theatre. However, the *bakufu* authorities felt that preservation of the feudal system was endangered by the increasing financial power held by urban, middle-class merchants, so enacted a raft of new regulations. Some were financial, but many targeted popular culture. Kabuki in particular was targeted by laws that established status discrimination against actors, prohibited many topics, and instituted controls on theatre numbers and locations. As a result, kabuki was unable to build upon momentum gained at the turn of the century, entering a period of temporary decline.

At the same time, ningyō jōruri was entering its golden age with matura-tion of the multiple-authorship system and collaboration between Takeda Izumo and Yoshida Bunzaburō producing radical advances in playwriting, stage construction, production, and performance technique. Kabuki began borrowing widely from the puppet theatre: popular plays (adaptations from puppet-plays, *maruhonmono*), styles of voice production from gidayū bushi, even puppet movement patterns (*ningyōburi*) and stage expression. In 1758 the playwright Namiki Shōzō moved from ningyō jōruri to kabuki, intro-ducing the revolving stage (which utilized similar technology to *karakuri* mechanisms), leading to new staging possibilities. These improvements fi-nally began to bear fruit: Osaka kabuki had eclipsed the city's puppet theatre in popularity by the 1760s.

Decline of the Toyotake-za and Takemoto-za theatres

Ningyō jōruri had been able to dominate kabuki by reducing its reliance on the literary and increasing its theatricality. One could also argue that puppet theatre had become more kabuki-like. Staging advances that kabuki had pio-neered were in turn frequently borrowed by the puppet theatre, as it began to use increasingly elaborate sets.

Around the middle of the eighteenth century, when Izumo I and Bunzaburō passed away in quick succession, ningyō jōruri seemed to lose its way. Audiences melted away and the theatre fell into financial decline. Toyotake Wakatayū, who had founded, managed, and composed for the Toyotake-za, died in 1764. The following year his theatre was sold, becoming a kabuki theatre. The ningyō jōruri performers split into two troupes that toured the provinces in hopes of raising funds to reopen the theatre.

The Takemoto-za struggled on, but decline was unavoidable; in 1768 it too was sold, becoming a kabuki theatre. Performers continued to play around Osaka, but their dreams of rebuilding the theatre remained unre-alized as puppet theatre fell further and further behind kabuki in popu-larity. Both troupes had lost their homes on Dōtombori, but continued to perform irregularly in Osaka and the provinces, even staging joint performances.

Playwrights from the period of decline

Just as the puppet theatre entered its period of decline, there was also a gen-eration change for the playwrights; the theatre ceased to produce as many masterworks. Even so, there were playwrights who struggled to revive the theatre's fortunes, namely Chikamatsu Hanji (1725–83), who was attached to the Takemoto-za troupe, and Suga Sensuke (dates unknown) for the Toyotake-za troupe.

Hanji was the son of Confucian scholar Hozumi Ikan (1692–1769), who had transcribed Chikamatsu's theories on art.[13] Hanji admired Chikamatsu and took his surname, but chose Hanji (半二, "half two") to indicate that he possessed not even half the great playwright's skill. But whether writing alone or in collaboration with other playwrights, Hanji's conceptions were grandiose, with complex, multiple plotlines featuring an unusually large amount of speech (*kotoba*) as opposed to dramatic or lyrical singing. His staging displayed a fondness for equilibrium between stage left and right, and for spectacular sets with multiple scene changes. These characteristics are similar to kabuki; in fact, many continued to be performed regularly on both kabuki and puppet theatre stages.[14]

Sensuke began as a chanter with Toyotake-za, but later became a dedicated playwright. He specialized in contemporary-life plays but showed a great understanding of the preferences of audiences and needs of performers. Many are adaptations of earlier plays by Chikamatsu or Kaion.

Classicization and codification

After Hanji and Sensuke, new plays ceased to be written; the theatre began to rely on older masterpieces. This had the effect of freezing innovation in the theatre as a whole, and spectator interest moved away from text to performances of chanters, shamisen players, and puppeteers. As the once distinct styles of the two theatres began to blend, chanters developed their own unique performance styles which became the focus for audience appreciation. An approach to a certain scene became linked to a particular chanter who had been the first to perform it or was especially adept; an individual chanter's style was called *fū*.

As this process of classicization and idiosyncratic interpretation continued within ningyō jōruri, questions of transmission grew in importance. In around 1780, shamisen player Tsuruzawa Seishichi I (1748–1826) devised a system known for representing the fingering points (*tsubo*) on each of the three strings using variants of the classical syllabary. Called *shu* (red) since written in red ink alongside the text, the system was easy to memorize and transcribe, and soon became widely used by performers. Shu began as an

13 Translated in Haruo Shirane (ed.), *Early Modern Japanese Literature: An Anthology 1600–1900* (New York: Columbia University Press, 2002), 347–51.
14 On Hanji, see C. Andrew Gerstle, Kiyoshi Inobe, and William P. Malm, *Theater as Music: The Bunraku Play "Mt. Imo and Mt. Se: An Exemplary Tale of Womanly Virtue"* (Ann Arbor: Center for Japanese Studies, University of Michigan, 1990).

aide-mémoire for shamisen players, but as it became more widely employed, it also became integral to codification of gidayū bushi.

Puppets in Edo

From the early seventeenth century, several Edo troupes staged puppet theatre performances using sekkyō bushi or kinpira bushi narrative styles. Gidayū bushi was probably first performed there when Osaka puppeteer Tatsumatsu Hachirobei opened his own theatre in Edo in 1720, or soon after, when chanter Toyotake Shintayū (1705–58) moved to the city, opening the Hizen-za. Gidayū bushi became more established in Edo in the mid-eighteenth century, after the conversion of Dōtombori theatres from puppets to kabuki.

As gidayū-accompanied puppet performances increased, more plays were written in Edo. Some were popular enough to be performed in Osaka, including the still popular Hiraga Gennai's (1728–79) *Shinrei Yaguchi no watashi* (Miracle at Yaguchi ferry, 1770).[15] Ningyō jōruri was hurt by restrictions instituted during the Tempō Reforms in the 1840s, noted below, never regaining its former popularity in Edo.

The last great premodern chanter: Uemura Bunrakuken

At the very beginning of the nineteenth century, gidayū bushi chanter Uemura Bunrakuken (1751–1811) moved to Osaka from the island of Awaji, which had its own indigenous puppetry tradition.[16] Bunrakuken opened a jōruri training school just south of the current National Bunraku Theatre. Bringing together a troupe of professional performers, he opened a new theatre in 1809. Bunrakuken's heir soon moved the business to the center of Osaka, opening the Inari no Shibai theatre within the Namba Shrine grounds. The theatre employed experienced chanters, shamisen players, and puppeteers, securing financial stability.

Tempō Reforms

This stability was threatened in the 1830s and 1840s by both religious and political pressure. Priests of Miidera Temple in Ōmi (present-day Shiga) demanded that performers become affiliated with their Osaka shrine; Bunrakuken III (1813–87) successfully fought off the challenge. Then, in 1841, the

---

15 Stanleigh H. Jones, Jr., "Miracle at Yaguchi Ferry: a Japanese puppet play and its metamorphosis to kabuki," *Harvard Journal of Asiatic Studies* 38:1 (1978), 171–224.

16 Jane Marie Law, *Puppets of Nostalgia: The Life, Death and Rebirth of the Japanese Awaji Ningyō Tradition* (Princeton, NJ: Princeton University Press, 1997).

shogunate's senior councilor, Mizuno Tadakuni (1794–1851), began a series of reforms aimed at shoring up the feudal order and restoring shogunal power. Since he viewed theatre as having a particularly pernicious effect on morality, many regulations targeted kabuki and the puppet theatre directly. Theatre numbers and locations were prescribed, and shrine performances banned. In Osaka, kabuki and ningyō jōruri performances were limited to just five; the following year, to just two Dōtombori theatres.

These measures had a huge impact. It became virtually impossible to stage ningyō jōruri within the city, so chanters and shamisen players eked out a living with puppet-less chanting performances (*sujōruri*) at variety theatres or in the provinces. Bunrakuken III continued to perform at small rented spaces or on parcels of reclaimed land, until finally, in 1856, he was permitted to rebuild his theatre at the Inari Shrine. Other troupes gradually returned to the city center.

Three modern masters

From the start of the nineteenth century to the Meiji Restoration (1868) many excellent performers laid the foundation for contemporary ningyō jōruri. The careers of three representative performers whose art transcended the challenges of this period are now examined.

Takemoto Nagatotayū (1800–64) was the leading chanter of gidayū bushi from the 1820s until the 1860s, often described as the father of the art's revival. In 1855 he became the *monshita* (lead chanter and artistic director) at the Bunrakuken Hama no Shibai. Nagatotayū trained under the notoriously strict shamisen player Tsuruzawa Seishichi III (d. 1856), then partnered with shamisen player Toyozawa Danpei II (1828–98). Danpei then transmitted Nagatotayū's chanting style to the next generation. Nagatotayū's art was peerless, wide ranging and possessed of great depth. He was also an accomplished teacher, training many chanters who would lead the theatre during the Meiji era.

Danpei II studied under Toyozawa Hirosuke III (d. 1846). Following the death of Nagatotayū, he played shamisen for several other lead chanters, as well as helping to hone the art of chanters like Takemoto Koshijidayū II (1836–1917) and Takemoto Ōsumitayū III (1854–1913) who would soon lead the Meiji period theatre. He became the first shamisen player to attain the honor of headliner. Danpei was single-handedly responsible for a systematic analysis of shamisen melodies and historic performance techniques. This reorganization of shamisen fundamentals created a modern, realistic foundation. Danpei applied his deep understanding to the composition of new plays, including *Sanjūsansho hananoyama* (*Thirty-three holy places*, 1887), two scenes still frequently performed. Danpei served as bridge between the premodern and modern eras.

Yoshida Tamazō I (1829–1905) first appeared as puppeteer with the Bunrakuken troupe from the 1850s, displaying an unusually wide range, manipulating lead male and female characters, wild younger men, and animals. His use of quick-change costume techniques and wire-work proved very popular. Almost all contemporary bunraku puppeteers trace their roots to him; he became the first puppeteer to occupy the position of headliner.

These three performers symbolize the artistic strength of Bunrakuken's troupe, considered to be the only one of many troupes active in Osaka that stood on a comparable artistic level to major Dōtombori kabuki theatres. Bunrakuken's troupe continued to mount performances right through the chaotic Restoration period of 1868; change in political power seems to have caused little disruption.

The modern period

Around the mid-1860s, Osaka authorities began offering incentives to licensed quarters and theatres to move to Matsushima, an area of reclaimed land. Bunrakuken accepted their offer in 1872, renaming his theatre the Bunraku-za. The popular headliners were chanter Takemoto Harutayū V (1808–77), shamisen player Danpei II, and puppeteer Tamazō I. In 1883, the accomplished young chanter Takemoto Koshijidayū II (1836–1917) was promoted to headliner alongside Tamazō and Danpei. These three performers dominated ningyō jōruri during the Meiji era.

Several smaller puppet theatres also continued to operate after the Meiji Restoration. The Hikoroku-za troupe was formed in 1883 at the Namba Shrine in central Osaka. Hikoroku-za headliners were all defectors from Bunraku-za: chanter Takemoto Sumitayū IV (1829–89), shamisen player Toyozawa Hirosuke V (1831–1904), and puppeteer Yoshida Saiji IV (dates unknown). Their theatre, near the Minami entertainment district, soon gained fans while the rival Bunraku-za, in western Osaka, struggled to attract audiences. In autumn 1884, its management reopened at a vaudeville theatre in the precincts of Goryō Shrine close to Hikoroku-za.

The Hikoroku-za managed to gain commercial advantage by modernizing their theatre and improving audience facilities. The health of the puppet theatre during these years was founded on cutthroat competition between the two theatres over chanters, plays, musical performance, technique, and audience facilities. Under the leadership of Danpei, a distinctly showy and populist Hikoroku-za performance style emerged. Contemporary performance traditions for several plays preserve both the more refined Bunraku-za style and the flashy Hikoroku-za style. Following an arson attack and the death of two headliners, the Hikoroku-za closed in 1893. By 1921, the Bunraku-za was the only troupe regularly performing puppet theatre.

Bunraku-za's affiliation to Shōchiku

In 1903, several promising younger performers were promoted, and Bunraku-za's audiences were record-breaking. During this period, "bunraku" began to become synonymous with ningyō jōruri.

However, this period also saw the introduction of new, modern forms of mass entertainment, particularly cinema. Traditional theatre, music, and sideshows (*misemono*) were all badly affected, and Bunraku-za audiences declined. Following internal disputes within the Uemura family, control of Bunraku-za passed in 1909 to the Matsutake Partnership, a newly influential entertainment company. This syndicate (later named Shōchiku) had been established in Kyoto in 1895, characterized by its modern management style and aggressive expansion. The Uemura family agreed to cede the theatre building itself, plus all puppet heads, costumes, properties, and scripts. Virtually all 113 performers joined the new company.

The Bunraku-za name was retained, but several important reforms were implemented. The custom of allowing the longest-established performers to pick their own scenes was abolished; roles would be decided on merit. However, studies of period programs (*banzuke*) indicate that these proposals were probably not carried out rigorously.

Koshijidayū III's (1865–1924) art was typical of the bunraku style, with a restrained mode of delivery and tone that allowed him to excel at both historical and contemporary plays. But there was little he could do in the face of the rising popularity of cinema. Then, in 1926, a fire broke out at the theatre, and the Bunraku-za burnt to the ground. It was the end of a glorious four-decade history.

The Yotsubashi Bunraku-za

To free themselves from the lingering influence of the Uemura family and to facilitate a modern theatre management style, Shōchiku set about building a new theatre in the Yotsubashi neighborhood of Osaka in 1930. The theatre was a pioneering piece of modern architecture, made of reinforced concrete with entirely Western-style seating, apart from box seats which retained traditional tatami mats and partitions. Innovations in program structure were also instituted: instead of a single, day-long play, the *midori* (pick-up) system of performing a combination of selected scenes from longer plays was instituted, having proved commercially successful in kabuki when Shōchiku introduced it at the turn of the century.

Shōchiku introduced midori programs in order to better showcase individual performers, yet while initially successful, the new system was not without problems. Traditionally, performers had been allocated to scenes not purely for commercial reasons, but rather for factors including the need for training, transmission, and evaluation. While bunraku may have gained some short-lived popularity, the theatre's economic position remained precarious, while the number of new apprentices fell.

The Yotsubashi Bunraku-za period was also notable for interest it generated from leading literary figures and intellectuals, including Tanizaki Jun'ichirō (1886–1965) and Satō Haruo (1892–1964).[17] Bunraku's image began to shift from popular performing art toward classical theatre.

Women's gidayū (*musume gidayū*)

Female performers were banned from appearing on the public stage during the Edo period, but female gidayū bushi performers eked out a precarious existence by performing mainly at smaller vaudeville halls and theatres. During the Tempō Reforms in the 1840s, even performances at these venues were banned, so performers were forced to set up in small temporary buildings in remote locations. Following the overturning of these regulations after the Meiji Restoration, female chanters once again returned to vaudeville halls. In the 1880s, several teenage performers from Nagoya and Osaka, referred to as *musume gidayū* (young girls' gidayū), began appearing on stage in Tokyo, causing a sensation.[18]

Fans of young female chanters were primarily students and young men who would flock to performances and call out at emotional climaxes. These fans had a strong tendency to value performers' physical beauty and gestures over talent. Such passion soon came to be viewed askance, attracting the opprobrium of the mass media.

However, among these performers Toyotake Roshō (1874–1930) became valued for the power and sonority of her voice. Eventually she left the vaudeville halls behind for larger theatres. Taking advantage of the new medium of the phonograph recording, she became well known nationwide. While the genre never developed a star draw comparable to Roshō, fans developed a different appreciation of the art that allowed them to support the best singers even after they lost their youthful good looks. Today the art, now known as *joryū* (women's) gidayū, is carried on by a small number of performers in Tokyo and Kansai (Osaka-Kyoto).

The postwar period

During the latter half of the 1930s, many of the most experienced performers retired or died. In September 1945 the first postwar performance was

---

17 Tanizaki's *Tade kū mushi* (Some prefer nettles, 1919) concerns the perverse infatuation of a Western-educated man for a puppet head he sees on Awaji, and the young mistress of his father-in-law who resembles it in doll-like compliancy.

18 A. Kimi Coaldrake, *Women's Gidayū and the Japanese Theatre Tradition* (London: Routledge, 1997).

mounted, and the rebuilt Bunraku-za opened in February 1946. As younger performers gradually returned from the war in Asia, the troupe soon regained full strength. However, in the chaotic, economically challenging conditions of the immediate postwar period, it proved virtually impossible to attract new apprentices. The most important performer in this period was Toyotake Yamashiro no shōjō (1878–1967), who based his understanding on rigorous readings of the original text, deploying masterful tonal control to accurately portray each character's emotional reality (*jō*). His Yamashiro style of chanting appealed to intellectuals and greatly influenced subsequent jōruri.

A schism

Contracts between bunraku performers and Shōchiku had always been oral, with performers only being paid for days they actually appeared on stage. But as labor unions became more common in postwar Japan, bunraku performers formed their own; almost all performers joined. Their union brokered negotiations over remuneration and conditions with Shōchiku. Among the Mitsuwa-kai's demands were status guarantees, an increase in fees, and a move toward fixed salaries; however, the company was unwilling to budge on any of these issues. While negotiations continued, performers wanted to continue performing, but Shōchiku announced that since performances were no longer profitable, they would be suspended. With no alternative, the union hired a venue and started mounting self-produced performances.[19]

Some of the performers announced their skepticism about the union and returned to Shōchiku. Attempts were made to reconcile the two sides but their respective positions were too deeply entrenched. Finally, in 1949, the two sides split completely into opposing camps, with the non-union side forming the Chinami-kai, and each troupe producing its own performances. This schism further weakened bunraku, already lacking in performers.

In 1956, Shōchiku opened a new Bunraku-za in Dōtombori. Audiences initially increased, but against flourishing new forms of entertainment, it was not enough to stem the long-term decline in numbers; the future of bunraku itself came into doubt. Shōchiku eventually concluded that there was no viable financial future for bunraku and that continuing support of the theatre was impossible. Faced with the very real possibility that the puppet theatre could cease to exist, the two factions began to consider seriously

---

19 Meaning "three rings," the union's name referred to the logo mark for the Mitsukoshi Group, where they held performances, and the three arts of puppetry, chanting, and shamisen. Patricia Pringle, "Mitsuwa Kai vs. Shōchiku: occupation reforms and the unionization of bunraku," in Samuel L. Leiter (ed.), *Rising from the Flames: The Rebirth of Theater in Occupied Japan, 1945–1952* (Lanham, MD: Lexington Books, 2009), 185–216.

the possibility of reconciliation. Intellectuals and opinion leaders threw their weight behind the idea. The Bunraku Kyōkai was finally established in 1963; all Chinami-kai and Mitsuwa-kai performers signed new contracts with it. Influential supporters secured financial support for the foundation from the national as well as Osaka prefectural and city governments, and national public broadcaster NHK. Bunraku remains today the only traditional art in Japan to be so subsidized.

Revivals and new works

Bunraku has had a mixed history of creating new works since the end of the nineteenth century. Bunrakuken III composed new plays during the Meiji era and morale-boosting pieces were presented during the war, but none remained in the repertoire.

In the postwar years, classicization and popularization both contributed to expand the repertoire through newly written plays or revivals. The period of the schism in the 1950s proved particularly fruitful in both respects. The Chinami-kai staged a critically and commercially successful revised version of Chikamatsu's *Love Suicides at Sonezaki* (1955), leading to the reevaluation of other Chikamatsu plays. There were also experiments with adaptations of opera (*Madame Butterfly*, 1956) and works by Shakespeare (*Hamlet*, 1956; *The Tempest*, 1992).[20] The most successful adaptations have been of popular literary works, including Oda Sakunosuke's *Meoto zenzai* (Stories of Osaka life, 1956), Tanizaki's *Shunkinshō* (Shunkin, 1957), Kinoshita Junji's *Urikohime to Amanjaku* (Princess Melon and the Demon, 1956), and *Saiyūki* (Journey to the West, 1981). However, the limitations of jōruri language and puppet techniques have meant that very few works based on contemporary life have entered the canon.

The National Theatre and National Bunraku Theatre

In 1966 Japan's first National Theatre (Kokuritsu Gekijō) opened in Tokyo. Bunraku began to be staged at the smaller of the venue's two theatres, the first time that there had been regular puppet theatre performances in the capital. In 1984 the National Bunraku Theatre opened in Osaka, presenting performances and training students, with a research library and exhibition space.

20 Stanleigh H. Jones, Jr., "Puccini among the puppets: *Madame Butterfly* on the Japanese puppet stage," *MN* 38:2 (1983), 163–74; Minoru Fujita, "Tradition and the bunraku adaptation of *The Tempest*," in Takashi Sasayama, J. R. Mulryne, and Margaret Shewring (eds.), *Shakespeare and the Japanese Stage* (Cambridge: Cambridge University Press, 1998), 186–96.

While bunraku's art has been recognized domestically and internationally, even designated by UNESCO as an Intangible Cultural Heritage of Humanity in 2003, its position remains uniquely perilous among Japanese traditional performing arts. Audiences can be sparse, in spite of innovative attempts to attract new fans with special performances targeting first-timers, students, and young children. The troupe is expensive to maintain, theatre sizes are limited by puppet visibility, and even the well-attended Tokyo performances invariably lose money. The danger of bunraku's reliance on external funding was highlighted in late 2012 when the populist mayor of Osaka threatened to slash the city's support. However, bunraku has always been a financially unstable art form, marked by theatre closures and bankruptcies. The political attacks against bunraku galvanized bitter opposition from the public and intellectuals. Somehow, the unique art of bunraku has always found a way to weather these artistic, political, and financial difficulties.

References and further reading

Adachi, Barbara. *Backstage at Bunraku: A Behind-the-scenes Look at Japan's Traditional Puppet Theatre* (New York: Weatherhill, 1985)

Dunn, Charles James. *The Early Japanese Puppet Drama* (London: Luzac, 1966)

Gerstle, C. Andrew. *Chikamatsu: Five Late Plays* (New York: Columbia University Press, 2002)

Gidayū Kenkyūkai (ed.). *Bunraku dangi: kataru, hajiku, tsukau* (Lectures on bunraku: chanting, shamisen playing, puppet manipulation) (Osaka: Sōgensha, 1993)

Jones, Stanleigh (trans.). *The Bunraku Puppet Theatre of Japan: Honor, Vengeance, and Love in Four Plays of the 18th and 19th Centuries* (Honolulu: University of Hawai'i Press, 2012)

  (trans.). *Sugawara and the Secrets of Calligraphy* (New York: Columbia University Press, 1985)

  (trans.) *Yoshitsune and the Thousand Cherry Trees: A Masterpiece of the Eighteenth Century Japanese Puppet Theater* (New York: Columbia University Press, 1993)

Keene, Donald. *Bunraku: The Art of the Japanese Puppet Theatre* (Tokyo: Tokyo News Service, 1964)

  (trans.). *Chūshingura: The Treasury of Loyal Retainers* (New York: Columbia University Press, 1971)

  (trans.). *Major Plays of Chikamatsu* (New York: Columbia University Press, 1961)

Kimbrough, R. Keller (trans.). *Wondrous Brutal Fictions: Eight Buddhist Tales from the Early Japanese Puppet Theater* (New York: Columbia University Press, 2013)

Kimbrough, Keller and Satoko Shimazaki (eds.). *Publishing the Stage: Print and Performance in Early Modern Japan* (Boulder: Center for Asian Studies University of Colorado Boulder, 2011)

Scott, A. C. *The Puppet Theatre of Japan* (Tokyo: Tuttle, 1963)

Torigoe Bunzō, Uchiyama Mikiko, and Watanabe Tamotsu (eds.). *Iwanami kōza kabuki bunraku* (Iwanami seminar series: kabuki and bunraku), vols. VII–X (Tokyo: Iwanami shoten, 1997)
Yūda Yoshio. *Jōrurishi ronkō* (Studies in the history of jōruri) (Tokyo: Chūō kōronsha, 1975)

INTERNET RESOURCES
The Barbara Curtis Adachi Bunraku Collection: www.columbia.edu/cu/lweb/digital/collections/eastasian/bunraku/
The Puppet Theatre of Japan Bunraku: Japan Arts Council: www2.ntj.jac.go.jp/unesco/bunraku/en/

FOCUS 5.1 BUNRAKU STAGE
Kokuritsu Bunraku Gekijō Kanrika (ed.). *Bunraku no butai bijutsu: bunraku no butai to haikei* (Bunraku stage design: sets and scenery) (Tokyo: Nihon Geijutsu Bunka Shinkōkai, 1991)

FOCUS 5.2 SHAMISEN: PLUCKY MINSTRELS
Johnson, Henry. *The Shamisen: Tradition and Diversity* (Leiden: Brill, 2010)
Malm, William P. *Nagauta: The Heart of Kabuki Music* (Rutland, VT: C. E. Tuttle Co., 1963)
Yamada Shōichi. *Kabuki ongaku nyūmon* (An introduction to kabuki music) (Tokyo: Ongaku-no-tomo sha, 1986)

SPOTLIGHT 5.1 CHIKAMATSU MONZAEMON: PROLIFIC PUPPET PLAYWRIGHT
Gerstle, C. Andrew. *Circles of Fantasy: Convention in Chikamatsu's Plays* (Cambridge, MA: Harvard University Press, 1986)
Keene, Donald. *The Battles of Coxinga: Chikamatsu's Puppet Play, Its Background and Importance* (London: Taylor's Foreign Press, 1951)

Interlude: *Misemono* and *rakugo*: sideshows and storytelling

MATTHEW W. SHORES

In the early modern era commoners could enjoy myriad forms of entertainment besides kabuki and bunraku, for a fraction of the price. Prior to the nineteenth century these tended to be outdoor spectacles, including non-theatrical attractions such as mechanized dolls (*karakuri ningyō*) that performed fascinating tricks, and booths featuring Dutch imports such as microscopes to examine things like fleas and lice, and "seven-faced mirrors" showing viewers' faces hilariously distorted. Storytelling employing properties and music also became especially popular in the course of the Edo period (1603–1868).

Misemono sideshow attractions

Religious or folk "street arts" (*daidō gei*) presented at temple festival grounds or crossroads since the medieval age gave birth to Edo period *misemono* (見世物, lit. "things for showing"). These innumerable inexpensive acts and attractions were presented by amateurs or professionals outdoors, or in small tents or shacks (*koya*) erected temporarily on temple and shrine grounds, or more permanently in the market areas of towns such as Ryōgoku in Edo (present-day Tokyo), or Osaka's Sen'nichi-mae.[21] While certain sideshows developed into sophisticated performance traditions, countless others were amateurish or hoaxes, short-lived and forgotten. A small admission fee gained one access to view an exotic person, creature, object, or act. Instead of a cover charge, sometimes tips were solicited; traveling peddlers used such attractions to lure customers to their wares.[22]

Misemono included magic tricks, acrobatics, top-spinning stunts, balancing acts, feats of strength, dance, martial arts, and other entertainments. There were also "freaks of nature," people with handicaps and deformities,

---

21 Morinishi Mayumi (ed.), *Kamigata geinō jiten* (Kamigata encyclopedia of performing arts) (Tokyo: Iwanami shoten, 2008), 107–8.
22 Ozaki Hotsuki notes that tooth powder salesmen employed *kowairo* (kabuki actor impressions; commonly called *monomane* in Kamigata). See Geinōshi kenkyū kai (ed.), *Nihon no koten geinō (dai kyūkan): yose* (Japan's traditional performing arts, vol. IX: Yose) (Tokyo: Heibonsha, 1971), 222–3.

Fig 28 Street performers and vendors, clockwise from bottom right: kabuki impersonator, storyteller, confectionery vendor, "Chinaman" hard candy vendor, (paper) scrap collector, traveling monk, scrap metal dealer, juggling bean slicer, amateur noh actors, water-balancing musician, *mochi* balloon artist, Daikoku dancer. *Edo shichū yowatari shū* 4: *Fūzoku gahō* 4:48 (December 1892), illustrated by Ōtake Masanao. Reprinted in Uchida Mitsufumi (ed.), *Edo Tokyo shokugyō zuten* (Edo occupation illustrations) (Tōkyō: Tōkyō-dō shuppan, 2003).

unusual beasts (camels, elephants), insects and fish, plants, trees, and stones. Exhibitions of sophisticated craftsmanship could also be found, such as papier mâché puppets, mechanical apparatus, glasswork, basketwork, shellwork, and chrysanthemum art (weaving).[23] Misemono were aimed at general audiences, but there were also misemono specifically for adults. Sexual misemono were officially banned in the early Meiji period (1868–1912), but could be found well into the 1920s.[24] Today misemono can still be seen at local festivals and street corners, some absorbed into variety hall (*yose*) sideshow acts (*iromono*).[25] Some flea market or door-to-door food vendors still perform entertaining lines of narrative or songs, or strike out rhythms with their hands or cooking utensils.

23 Furukawa Miki, *Zusetsu – shomin geinō: Edo no misemono* (Illustrated – commoner entertainment: Edo misemono) (Tokyo: Yūzankaku, 1982), 18.
24 *Ibid.* 271–2.
25 These include magic tricks, balancing acts, and female shamisen virtuoso-comics.

Sit-down comedy: *rakugo* storytelling

Rakugo (落語, telling stories with *ochi*, punchlines) is solo comic storytelling. Although rakugo developed throughout the nineteenth century, it can be connected to earlier narrative arts (*wagei*) traceable to the sixth century. Before "rakugo" came into regular use in the 1890s, comic storytelling was referred to as *waraibanashi, karukuchi*, and *otoshibanashi*, among other names. Rakugo developed parallel to *kōshaku* (modern *kōdan*), a storytelling art featuring serious themes such as medieval battle tales. Both derived in part from *sekkyō* (Buddhist sermons) and *dangi* (public lectures) traditions.

Three men are regarded as the founders of rakugo. Osaka-born Shikano Buzaemon (1649–99) moved to Edo (Tokyo), narrating funny tales mostly indoors (private party spaces and residences) in the Genroku period (1688–1704), inaugurating the Edo style. Around the same time, Kyoto-based Tsuyu no Gorōbei (1643?–1703) and Osakan Yonezawa Hikohachi (d. 1714) performed outdoors at shrines and marketplaces, initiating the Kamigata tradition. To lure passers-by, Osaka-based Kamigata rakugo quickly became more theatrical, frequently incorporating music (heavily influenced by kabuki, *nagauta* and *hauta* shamisen), and instrumental sound effects (temple bells, thunder, snow, wind, and water splashing). In contrast, Edo style rakugo is more subdued because it evolved in a city populated by a high percentage of samurai. Many artists and fans consider Edo storytelling to be a "purer" form.

Riding late eighteenth-century popularity, Sanshōtei Karaku (1777–1833, Edo) and Katsura Bunji (d. 1816, Osaka) almost simultaneously established Japan's first successful yose variety halls devoted to comic storytelling.[26] Rivals soon followed with affordable yose flourishing in major cities. Kōshaku, *naniwabushi* (later *rōkyoku*), folk songs, and dance numbers were performed at these small (generally 100–300 cushion) local venues, but rakugo became the most popular attraction by the turn of the twentieth century. Writers struggling to devise a new voice for Japan's modern literature, including novelists Futabatei Shimei, Natsume Sōseki, and Nagai Kafū, were inspired to experiment with the yose language.

ELEMENTS OF PERFORMANCE

In most rakugo today, after formally addressing the audience, the performer offers a topical, ad libbed *makura* (pillow), then narrates the story proper (called the *hondai, hanashi, neta*, or rakugo). The repertoire includes both

---

26 Depending on geographic area or genre, these were also called *ba, jōseki, mise*, or *seki*.

Fig 29 Katsura Kikumaru III (previously Someya) performs *Toki udon* (Time-noodles).

traditional and newly written pieces, normally lasting 30 minutes or less but sometimes up to an hour.

One storyteller plays all characters, distinguishing gender, age, and social position through voice, posture, and gaze. Typically, just two properties are employed. A paper folding fan (*sensu*) and hand towel (*tenugui*) become pipes, writing brushes, swords, umbrellas, abaci, tobacco pouches, books, ledgers, roasted sweet potatoes, microphones, and mobile phones (for newly composed tales). The Kamigata tradition usually employs a small table, miniature wooden clappers, and a short wood screen ("knee cover"). The *hanashika* storytellers present multiple characters by shifting their body or adjusting their gaze from left to right and near to far. Some mimic multiple voices, while others use a single voice for all characters.

Booming comedy

Despite the proliferation of modern entertainments, rakugo today enjoys a large following and can be a lucrative profession, passed down in family lines such as Katsura and San'yūtei, as with other traditional arts (see p. 99). Since the Taishō era (1912–26), rakugo – particularly in Osaka – has lost fans to *manzai* and other popular variety acts and shows. Some hanashika found new avenues to ply their verbal dexterity as silent film narrators (*benshi*). Notwithstanding, rakugo avoided complete marginalization with help from dedicated artists, scholars, fans, and broadcasting and publishing industries. Thanks to the construction of new yose, the appearance of various commemorative CD and DVD collections, and hanashika and their fans taking to Internet social media, another rakugo boom is under way in the 2000s. In 2014 there were over 600 professional hanashika based in Osaka and Tokyo, continuing two distinct traditions. Until 1974 this was an all-male art, but more than twenty women have since apprenticed and become professionals.

Hanashika continue to tell both traditional and new stories but, since rakugo remains a predominantly oral tradition, they do not adhere to formal scripts. They may deliver lines as they wish, so long as basic storylines are upheld. Some take great liberties and make major changes to stories; rakugo is by nature in a constant state of flux. Performers occasionally experiment by fusing rakugo with other arts such as kyogen and even Western classical music while maintaining the core traditional stories.[27] Yose are open every day in Tokyo and Osaka (tickets average ¥2,500, US $25). Hanashika appear constantly as emcees or glib guests on radio and TV, and there is no shortage of young men and women begging masters to take them on as new apprentices. Since 2000, there has been a steady stream of television shows and movies about the rakugo world. One can even stream rakugo live or same-day delay on the Internet.

The Kamigata rakugo story *Karuwaza* (The acrobat) provides a useful if exaggerated illustration of several *misemono-goya* (entertainment stalls).[28] These stalls had barkers outside luring in customers with dramatic pitches (*yobikomi kōjō*). The streets outside were loud and lively. Two men from Osaka who are on pilgrimage to Ise stop on their way in a village bustling with people visiting the local shrine and nearby rows of misemono-goya. They are duped at several shows; risking a few coins to try their luck at discerning genuine attractions from fake ones was simply part of the fun. An excerpt demonstrates the appeal of both rakugo and misemono.

> Barker: Step right up! … The best show in town, right here! … We've got a whopper of a weasel (*itachi*) right inside! Just trapped in the mountains, get too close and you'll be in some real danger!

27 Kabuki and bunraku themes were adapted early on and remain integral to the repertoire. Conversely, kabuki imported rakugo storylines and narrative techniques.
28 This story is named for its final scene, featuring a famous acrobat.

Kiroku: How 'bout it? Let's have a little look.

Seihachi: Nah, forget it. This place is a fake …

…. (they pay)

Barker: Thank you. Off you go, all the way to the front, to the front!

Kiroku: Okay, we're all the way at the front but there's nothing here. Hey, hey! Where's that big weasel of yours? …

Barker: It's standing right in front of you, isn't it?

Kiroku: Standing? Huh, what? There's nothing here but a board! …

Barker: Look, that's a 6-foot board (*ita*), right? And look, there's a red spot right in the middle of it, ain't there? Well, that's blood (*chi*), and that makes "weasel" (*itachi*).

Kiroku: Weasel? Hey, you said you just got it in the mountains!

Barker: Well, boards don't come from the sea, you know.

Kiroku: Wise guy! And you said it would be dangerous …

Barker: It is, if it falls on you! …

Interlude: *Kamigata geinō*: Kyoto-Osaka style

GONDŌ YOSHIKAZU
Translated by SHINKO KAGAYA

Kamigata (上方) refers to *Kyō*, or Kyoto, seat of the imperial court from 794 to 1868, and its surrounding areas. *Kamigata geinō* refers to the performing arts of the Kyoto-Osaka area, a millennium-old tradition displaying distinct characteristics compared to upstart Edo (Tokyo) forms. Kyoto, and then the commercial center Osaka, were cradle and constant contrast to artistic styles developed in the later capital of Edo.

Nations develop representative culture and performing arts at their political centers. In Japan's Yamato and Nara eras (300–784), the capital Nara was its center; when the capital transferred to Kyoto in 794, the cultural center also shifted. Yet even after Edo became the political center in 1603, Kyoto's centrality to culture and performing arts continued for another century. When Edo developed as a political and cultural capital, it first borrowed Kyoto culture, then gradually created its own performing arts style. After 1700, the performing arts of each of Japan's great cities – the political capital of Edo, the old capital of Kyoto, and the merchant hub of Osaka – began to develop its own distinctive characteristics.

Three competing cities

During the Edo period (1603–1868), the three cities of Kyoto, Osaka, and Edo enjoyed special status, and the discourse concerning these three cities (*santo-ron*), comparing their unique characteristics, was in vogue. The system to deal with the three cities as distinct entities was also employed in *kabuki-hyōbanki* (commentaries on kabuki) published annually, beginning in the middle of the Edo period. Even after the abolition of feudal domains with the Meiji Restoration, the three cities had their status changed to *fu* (regions) not *ken* (prefectures), as in the rest of the country, as they had never been feudal domains originally.

As Kyoto's power declined with the shogunate's transfer to Edo, Osaka's economic power grew, and "Kamigata" came to include both places as antipode to Edo. As Osaka's power increased further, Kamigata culture and performing arts became dominated by those of Osaka. However, in nihonbuyo, at least, Kyoto retains its distinct culture even today.

Even before the city of Edo was formed, numerous branches of literature, fine arts, and performing arts developed and flourished in Kyoto. Music and dance genres introduced from abroad such as *gagaku* and *bugaku*, appropriated to forge a national culture, had by the eleventh century already become distinctively Japanese performing arts. In the fourteenth century, noh and kyogen developed syncretically from local folk performing arts, and were then refined as quintessentially Japanese. Significantly, such forms were nurtured by educated and refined populations, both as spectators and as hobbyists. Kabuki also originated in Kyoto at the turn of the seventeenth century, and was centered in Kamigata for a century. Only after the turn of the eighteenth century did Edo kabuki reach its first stage of perfection, with a style independent of Kyoto influence.

Generally speaking, performing arts developed in the newly populated districts of the shogun's capital of Edo with a comparatively shallow history. They are considered rough yet lively, simple but clear, and then developed into emotionally rich and elaborated stylized forms. On the other hand, those of Kamigata, especially Kyoto, have long been characterized by distilled simplicity, both realistic and rational, revealing the contrasts of over eight centuries of subtle distinctions in the accumulation of culture.

Although each genre of music, dance, and theatre traditionally makes distinctions between Edo and Kamigata styles, some general characteristics can be observed. In contrast to Edo's youthful liveliness and dynamic energy, Kamigata performing arts are said to contain not only *miyabi* (refinement/ elegance), a gentle and subdued characteristic of Kyoto, but also a mature serenity and optimism reflecting Osaka's economic dynamism. Recently, some Kamigata performing arts have been characterized as vulgar and extravagant, but this tendency started only after World War II, especially since the 1960s. Despite stylistic mixtures and homogenization brought about by mass media and ease of transportation between Tokyo and Osaka-Kyoto, performers and spectators alike continue to enjoy distinguishing and appreciating the special Kamigata flavor.

References and further reading

Morinishi Mayumi. *Kamigata geinō jiten* (Kyoto-Osaka performing arts encyclopedia) (Tokyo: Iwanami shoten, 2008)

Kamigata geinō (Kamigata performing arts) quarterly covers contemporary Kyoto-Osaka arts.

Interlude: Traditional theatre tomorrow: interview with Takemoto Mikio

SHINKO KAGAYA

Takemoto Mikio is Professor, Faculty of Letters, Arts and Sciences, Waseda University. He was Director of the Tsubouchi Memorial Theatre Museum (2004–13). Awardee of the Kanze Hisao Noh Award of Hōsei University, his publications include *Edo jidai no nōgaku ni kansuru kisoteki kenkyū* (Studies on noh during the Edo period, 1993), *Kan'ami Zeami jidai no nōgaku* (Noh in the times of Kan'ami and Zeami, 1999), and *Muromachi chūkōki no nō no keisei katei ni kansuru kisoteki kenkyū* (On the development of noh in the Muromachi period, 2002). This October 2012 interview surveyed Professor Takemoto's long experience as archivist, fan, and critic of traditional performance.

*

The particular position of Japanese theatre in the world can be summarized in two points:

1 that it has a rich tradition – noh has been performed continuously for over 600 years, and kabuki and bunraku for over 300 years;
2 that Japan was one of the first Asian nations to be strongly influenced by European theatre, intensifying after the Meiji Restoration (1868).

Japanese traditional drama has struggled until now to find ways to assimilate and co-exist with Western theatre, striking a balance between preservation and adaptation. On the other hand, Japan was fortunate to have been recognized early in the West for its theatrical traditions. At the same time as Japan was importing Western techniques and texts, the early introduction of noh to the West by Ernest Fenollosa through Ezra Pound's skilled translations began the fascination with noh in Europe. These texts were soon followed by translations of such fine works as *The Tale of Genji*, further revealing the high level of classical Japanese literature overseas. These dual unique aspects – simultaneously assimilating from, while promulgating to, the West – are not found in other Asian countries.

National policy inadequacies

Despite these felicitous beginnings for noh's interaction with modernity, in order for traditional performing arts in Japan today to build new audiences to sustain themselves, outreach to youth is vital. Encountering fine things at a young age is especially important. Yet in the Japanese school system, theatrical education consists of student performances of skits and pageants, but does not introduce pupils to fine-quality professional theatre. Cultivation of new audiences and sustenance of traditional arts are not supported by national cultural policy. In an era when information is overabundant, students tend to just reach for the most easily accessible entertainments. Redirecting school education to introduce and present fine performing arts could be an important step in traditional arts' survival.

Efforts by the government to sustain creation of new works and train new generations of performers compare unfavorably with most industrialized countries. This is because theatre education in Japan started from the wrong direction. For example, unlike other countries, Japanese national theatres' support is only supplementary, its role considered merely complementary to the *iemoto* (family head) system or traditional training system of each school or family. To prevent claims of bias, national theatres must invite players of many families to perform in subsidized programs, regardless of their talent.

Again, unlike other countries where many universities have their own theatre departments, in Japan there is no movement to create higher educational institutions that teach theatre, nor is theatre established as part of liberal arts studies. Traditional theatre is something that the nation must treasure, but there seems to be no such deep understanding on the side of cultural administrators, probably reflecting conscious discrimination against the status of theatre that has lasted since the Meiji period (1868–1912).

Training future professionals

Especially for noh, the current style of training is becoming increasingly difficult. Though the National Theatre has a training program, there is no shared foundation or liberal arts education; instead, the curriculum is an arbitrary program of individual arts, such as drum, flute, or dance. Such pedagogies may have worked in the past, but they cannot be effective in training modern students who have been educated at higher educational institutions like universities. The Tokyo University of Arts has a Department of

Traditional Japanese Music that offers a degree for traditional art specialists, but its educational content is so vague that even graduates are insufficiently competent to become professional performers, and must further apprentice themselves with master performers to become full-fledged professionals. Bunraku's situation is even direr. Much more governmental support for systematic training of future generations is necessary.

This lack of governmental support and failure to establish a proper theatre educational system also applies to modern theatre companies. Each troupe is administered like a private school with its own bureaucratic regulations. Training is sectionalized, dictated by authoritarian administrators. How many Japanese actors are flourishing on the world stages or in films? Not many. In most cases, under severe financial duress, without an educational foundation in subjects such as foreign language learning, actors are bred in a private hothouse-like environment. This has already continued for more than a century, but I consider such a situation to be the shame of Japanese theatre.

In this sense, kabuki is an exception, as it has maintained its own world that excludes outsiders, yet has been successful as show business for over 300 years. Thus there is no need for the government to intervene. Rather, if anyone tried to manage its existence, there could even be the possibility of ruining it entirely. Actors have thrived and audiences have been happily entertained without reliance on national support. They can and should maintain the status quo. Additional opportunities to perform at the National Theatre and government support for overseas performance are sufficient for kabuki's continuing prosperity.

Thus, considering all forms of traditional theatre, I must conclude that Japanese theatre has a rich history and fine resources, but is in a state of underdevelopment and impoverishment as far as educational systems and infrastructure go, receiving only supplementary governmental support incommensurate with national wealth.

The potential of technology

Technology offers a certain potential for support, but has not yet been used to full advantage. It should be used to create archives, information that could lead to the reconstruction of theatre methods. Digital data could record theatre groups' training, organization, acting methods, and stagings. I believe that individual actors are utilizing such recordings on a private basis, for private viewing or analysis, such as in classrooms. It is useful to have visual images. However, such documentation has yet to be compiled as a comprehensive resource.

Devices such as subtitling and earphone guide systems, such as those employed at the National Theatres and Kabuki theatres, are useful for spectators but are clearly only aimed at beginners. It is as if you stop at the entrance to admire one or two performances, and that is enough. This reflects the government's fundamental attitude toward classical arts. Connoisseurs would not use such devices. They do not contribute to the promotion of the traditional performing arts or cultivation of high-level audiences and performers.

The single constant in these traditional arts is the text, even while the performance expression has continuously transformed and continues to adapt. Kabuki changes dialogue to a certain degree, but bunraku and noh cannot, thus the language of the text becomes further removed from the contemporary idiom, and will soon become something like a foreign language. Then the need for explanatory and translation devices will definitely increase, eventually becoming indispensable. Thus the development of high-technology devices that do not interfere with or disrupt performances is vital.

Cross-cultural experimentation

If traditional Japanese theatre existed independently in Japan alone, one would not need to be conscious about experimental new work and cross-fertilization. However, if it strives for World Cultural Heritage status, or recognition as an Intangible Cultural Property, it is not right just to preserve the old ways. Traditional theatre genres must continue to adapt and transform. This is their destiny. Without such efforts, their appeal will definitely disappear, so exchanges with different cultures must take place. Through such cross-cultural or cross-genre exchanges, traditional Japanese theatre can evolve and gain new perspectives. However, when there is too much difference among the theatrical methods, training, and acting styles, such collaborations may end up as merely strange. The lack of clear expectations, and how to achieve them, makes directing these hybrid productions challenging.

On the other hand, it seems absurd that new noh plays have not been created for a long time. Even when they are written, they remain at the experimental level. The reason is that there are no noh playwrights – those who understand noh and can also write noh plays. Often new noh pieces are written by literary authors lacking a thorough understanding of noh as a performing art, including its metrics and musicality. For instance, those by Tada Tomio contain important messages, but such didactic statements to me feel somewhat out of place in noh.

The future of traditions

As for the future of traditional Japanese performing arts, I see different prospects for kabuki, noh, and bunraku. Kabuki will continue to be vigorous. In the future it may come to be considered completely contemporary, rather than a classical theatre. Whether it remains a traditional performing art will depend on how often and how well classical works are performed. Specific styles of kabuki could be easily adapted and contemporized and plays with classical performance style but contemporary content are possible.

Bunraku remains active even today, with subsidies from national and local governments. However, with just this support and its self-help efforts, I doubt that puppet theatre can develop. Bunraku fans must strenuously search for ways to support it. We cannot be optimistic that in a decade or three bunraku will be able to sustain itself at the current level, or that it will even exist at all.

Nohgaku is the most unpredictable. The clearly apparent fact is that without amateur practitioners,[29] actors cannot secure their livelihood. Such a support system from amateurs is gradually falling into crisis, and may be unsustainable. The number of spectators is in decline; currently this audience is comprised mostly of those who view only noh, not other genres. With the decline of the connoisseur audience, artistic standards may become vague and begin to erode. The only way for noh to survive is for professionals to polish their art, although it is very difficult to imagine how they will be able to balance such efforts. Noh professionals need to commit themselves to developing elite performers, and cultivate avenues by which they may continue to support themselves financially. I am more optimistic about kyogen, considering how its current talented successors are thriving, enjoying robust attendance.

There are some negative issues from efforts of noh actors to make money from teaching amateurs. Amateur students tend to take the most popular dates for recitals (Fall weekends), requiring numerous rehearsals, with professional accompaniment. This leaves professional players with less time to spend on their own rehearsals, and they cannot always count on the busiest and best performers to accompany them. The quality of noh naturally suffers, since the most talented teams of performers cannot be gathered.

---

29 Amateur practitioners pay for lessons and recitals, and buy tickets to their teachers' performances.

PART II

Modern theatres

PREFACE TO PART II
BRIAN POWELL

Modernity comes to a country in many ways, but for Japan and many countries in East Asia in the nineteenth century, contact with cultures of Western imperialist powers was a major formative element. Japan had seen off its uninvited Western guests in the seventeenth century, but by the mid-nineteenth century these returning visitors represented enormous military power. Beginning with the "black ships" of American Commodore Perry, which in 1853 showed they could anchor in Edo Bay with impunity, Western powers forced Japan to open itself to trade, imposing economically unfavorable and legally humiliating treaties. Between 1853 and 1868, debate raged among the most powerful military houses over how to deal with this very present external threat, and a series of political and military struggles resulted in a transfer of power.

The Tokugawa family, which had ruled Japan from Edo (present-day Tokyo) for more than two and a half centuries, was replaced by a tense oligarchic coalition of samurai from western clans long inimical to the Tokugawa. Mindful of the precarious nature of their power and of the weakness of a divided Japan in a predatory world, they sought legitimization for themselves and a unifying force for the whole country in the imperial institution. Emperor Meiji (the name chosen to designate his reign, 1868–1912) was symbolically "restored" to his rightful place in the state. Political events of 1868 are referred to as the Meiji Restoration; when Japanese mention "modern," the writer usually indicates the historical process set in train at this time.

As Japan entered her modern era (1868–), her sovereignty as a country was severely compromised by "unequal treaties" and legal extraterritoriality imposed by the Western powers. However, less than forty years later, Japan had vanquished Russia in the Russo-Japanese War of 1904–5, thus defeating one of those very Western powers she had so feared. It was clear to Meiji leaders that strong military forces, which could only be achieved with a strong economy, were key to achieving some sort of parity with Western nations, but what they could not know in advance was how much of Western culture apart from the economy had contributed to their internationally dominant position.

The victory over Russia seemed to confirm that the mix they had adopted had been about right; in the 1900s Japan was still recognizably Japan, with continuance of her traditional theatre very much part of that. Much had changed since the Tokugawa period, however, and this began to be reflected in literature and theatre with the development of radically new genres.

Keeping control

Throughout the Meiji period, a continuing theme in government policy was to promote or permit reform only to the extent thought necessary to achieve parity with the West, but otherwise to keep strict control. Some government reform was far-reaching on the surface – within ten years after the Restoration, the feudal society that the Tokugawa shogunate had painstakingly constructed was completely dismantled. Samurai lost all their privileges – their stipends, right to wear swords, monopoly of going into battle, and distinctive hairstyles. Thus the stock character of kabuki *jidaimono* (history plays) did not exist any more; samurai could only be depicted as historical personages. A conscript army, trained and armed in Western martial techniques, put down a samurai rebellion in 1877.

The ethics by which Edo period samurai lived their lives, however, remained largely unchanged. The government officially reinforced Confucian values of hierarchy and respect through the Rescript on Education of 1890, in spite of having pushed through a comprehensive and highly successful reform of the education system which raised literacy to near European levels and introduced Western ideas to all children. Technical knowledge from abroad was welcomed, but the spread of philosophical and political thought deemed subversive was tightly controlled through a harsh censorship system designed to inflict heavy financial damage on publishers and theatre managers alike.

Political reform followed along much the same lines. Early disagreement among the ruling oligarchs resulted in defections and vigorous debate among political activists and intellectuals known as the Freedom and Popular Rights movement. A constitution and some kind of legislative body were essential for Japan's recognition as a civilized country, but during the years before these were realized, in 1889 and 1890, the remaining oligarchs made clear they would control the whole process. There was no freedom to express opposition to the government and no freedom of assembly, thus preventing public discussion of political issues. The constitution eventually laid most stress on citizens' duties rather than rights, and the Diet was based on a very limited franchise with little real power.

Meiji rulers were also very suspicious of any religion that they could not manipulate. While forced to guarantee freedom of religion in the 1889 constitution (thus allowing the practice of Christianity, which had been banned for over two centuries), they carefully fostered a national form of Shinto centered on the emperor, while removing all official support from Buddhism, the religion of the now discredited feudal system. Thus another traditional theatre genre – noh – saw its ideological foundations removed from under it, as Buddhism permeated many aspects of noh creation and presentation.

Economic change also proceeded apace during the Meiji period, with new rural taxation helping to foster industrialization. By the 1900s Japan possessed a wide range of light and heavy industries, some started with government money and then sold to private interests. Here was the beginning of the cosy relationship that successive Japanese governments have enjoyed with the business community.

Most industry was concentrated in the towns and cities, with rapid urbanization also one consequence of economic change. This trend, together with deliberate centralization of power and authority as the hallmark of government policy, made Tokyo into a metropolis as dominant as Paris or London. Aspiring novelists, poets, and playwrights were drawn to Tokyo; by the end of the Meiji period in 1912, Tokyo was the center of modern culture. Developments in Japanese theatre since then have taken place predominantly in Tokyo.

6 ❧ Birth of modern theatre: *shimpa* and *shingeki*

BRIAN POWELL

Achieving a viable theatre alternative to the venerable traditional genres in the modern period, a theatre that could resonate easily with Japan's changing society, was no easy task. This chapter charts the various steps in this quest up to the late 1920s.

Continuity, reform, and radical change

Theatre had been directly caught up in another facet of the Meiji modernizing process. An urgent preoccupation of Japan's political leaders in the 1880s had been how to convince Westerners that Tokyo really was modern. After 1883, visiting dignitaries and diplomats were treated to receptions, banquets, and balls at the Rokumeikan, a grand Western-style building constructed specifically for that purpose. Entertaining foreign visitors in a manner to which they were accustomed was bound to include the theatre, because Japanese visitors to the West had been taken to the theatre and opera in New York, London, and Paris, initially much to their amazement. To take Western visitors to kabuki – bawdy, boisterous, and officially despised – could not be contemplated, so kabuki would have to be reformed.

Reformers duly appeared from inside the kabuki world. Ichikawa Danjūrō IX (1838–1903) and Morita Kan'ya XII (1846–97) willingly and Kawatake Mokuami (1816–93) somewhat less so responded to government encouragement during the 1870s in their respective fields of acting, theatre management, and playwriting. Already in 1874 the influential intellectual journal *Meiroku Zasshi* (Journal of the Meiji 6 Society) had carried an article urging theatre reform, followed by vigorous intellectual debate in a number of publications in the early 1880s. This decade saw the buzzword *kairyō* (reform) prefixed to just about everything, but only the theatre acquired, in 1886, a "reform society" to which some of the most powerful politicians affixed their signatures.

From the present viewpoint, Japanese theatre in the modern period has had an abundance of genres. In Tokyo in the mid-1880s it seemed that it might only have one – kabuki, which the government-backed Engeki Kairyō-kai (Theatre Reform Society) was trying to refashion into a national theatre. Noh and bunraku, for their parts, were verging on the moribund. Kabuki changed in several ways after the theatre reform movement, but acting families, the core of the genre, stayed intact. A new theatre would have to emerge from outside the kabuki establishment.

Students playing politics: *sōshi shibai*

Informal alternatives to the highly structured, insular, family-based art of kabuki had flourished earlier in the nineteenth century, especially in the Kansai region. Small bands of entertainers, some of them actors who had failed on the kabuki stage, roamed the countryside performing to village audiences, often including in their shows pastiche reenactments of well-known kabuki plots. In the 1880s a catalyst appeared that converted this informal theatre into what became *shimpa* (new sect), one of the major genres of Japan's modern theatre, namely the aforementioned Freedom and Popular Rights movement.

Unfortunately for Freedom and Popular Rights campaigners, the difference between opposition and dissidence had not been assimilated by the authorities, so activists often found themselves in conflict with the forces of law and order. Banning of political meetings and short-term imprisonment were common experiences; occasionally, an entire city could be deemed out-of-bounds for someone regarded as a troublemaker.

Among those exiled from Tokyo were the liberal thinker Nakae Chōmin (1847–1901) and political activist (*sōshi*) Kawakami Otojirō (1864–1911). Nakae chose journalism to expound his political views. In 1887, in Osaka he founded an opposition newspaper, employing as a journalist Sudō Sadanori (1867–1907), a young political activist. At a time when getting a political message across either in print or through a speech was frequently interfered with, Sudō watched the relatively realistic acting of the kabuki actor Nakamura Sōjūrō (1835–89) and concluded that theatre held the key to propagandizing. When Sudō started performing plays with a political message, Sōjūrō sent one of his assistants to help the untrained actors with bits of kabuki business. Kawakami was also impressed by theatre as a potential political platform after watching Sōjūrō perform. He in turn formed his own theatre company, which opened in Sakai, a port city near Osaka, in 1891.

Sudō and Kawakami performed what has come to be known generically as *sōshi shibai* (theatre by political activists). For a few years they and others like them utilized the theatre to awaken a political consciousness in their audiences. Even from the stage this could only be done indirectly, but

Kawakami's first program included a piece entitled *Itagaki-kun sōnan jikki* (Disaster strikes Itagaki: the true account). It reenacted the attempted assassination of an opposition leader at a political meeting, so the message must have been clear enough. Sudō used the term "reformed theatre" (*kairyō engeki*), aligning himself with his mentor Sōjūrō's kabuki reform movement, while Kawakami preferred "students' theatre" (*shosei shibai*). Kawakami, by contrast, was inviting his audiences to remember that they would be seeing a new form of theatre: "shosei" referenced contemporary shosei novels, focused on the new phenomenon of the student with his social, political, and amatory preoccupations

Despite its ideological roots, the new theatre had to be commercial for its very survival; these early productions suggested it could be very profitable. Of the two pioneers, Kawakami was by far the more ambitious and commercially minded. He set his sights on Tokyo and was immediately successful there in 1891. He even achieved an appearance at the new and very grand Kabuki-za in May 1895 – after which "pollution" the proud kabuki actors demanded the floor be sanded.

Kawakami Otojirō: showman extraordinary

Kawakami possessed just the right mix of showman, opportunist, networker, and adventurer to succeed in the fluid world of theatre in 1890s Japan. He had discovered success a few years earlier when working in *yose* (small-scale variety shows) with his satirical skit *Oppekepe*, poking fun at establishment figures:

> In these days when the price of rice is rising,
> You completely ignore the plight of the poor …
> You bow to men of influence and position
> And spend your money on geisha and entertainers,
> And piling up rice in your storehouses at home,
> Will you let your fellow countrymen perish? …
> But if you think you can get to Paradise
> … by using a bribe when you encounter The King of Hades in hell
> You'll never get there! Oppekepe, oppekepeppo, peppopppo.[1]

In Tokyo he played it as an interlude between conventionally structured plays; it became his trademark.

Kawakami assiduously fostered contacts with politicians at the highest level, and married their favorite, the period's most popular geisha, later

---

1 William Malm (trans.), "The modern music of Meiji Japan," in Donald Shiveley (ed.), *Tradition and Modernization in Japanese Culture* (Princeton, NY: Princeton University Press, 1971), 283–4.

❧ FOCUS 6.1 Sadayakko: first modern actress

Fig 30 Sadayakko (center, beneath umbrella) in *The Geisha and the Samurai*, 1900.

Kawakami Sadayakko (1871–1946) was one of Meiji Japan's first, most famous, and influential actresses, and also its first international stage star. Through tours abroad with her husband Kawakami Otojirō (1864–1911) from 1900 to 1902, she helped him discover the melodrama and kabuki blend known as *shimpa*. Female roles in Meiji Japan were typically played by *onnagata* – male actors specializing in depicting women on stage – but Sadayakko's career marked the beginning of the end of the onnagata outside kabuki.

Sadayakko was born in Tokyo, where her parents sent her for adoption as a geisha. This training prepared her for an illustrious career; she boasted clients among the political and industrial elite. Her patron, Prime Minister Itō Hirobumi, took Sadayakko to see a performance by the dashing young star Kawakami. Despite their celebrity marriage, the new-style theatre troupe could not sustain themselves. So in 1899 Kawakami's troupe left Japan (and debts) with Sadayakko to tour the USA and Europe. They struggled in San Francisco, but eventually succeeded in expanding their repertoire and

discovering Western tastes with performances up the West Coast and in Chicago, Boston, and New York, and at dancer Loie Fuller's pavilion at the Paris Expo in 1900. Fuller produced the second tour, which visited most European capitals, and included dancer Isadora Duncan during Russian performances. While Kawakami relied on onnagata on stage in Japan, on tour "Madame Yacco" made her stage debut immediately, and, as with many contemporary headlining actresses like Ellen Terry, Duse, and Modjeska, quickly became the troupe's primary draw.

One of their most popular plays was *The Geisha and the Samurai*. This combined multiple plots from kabuki, with dialogue reduced to a minimum, and heavy reliance on Sadayakko's training in traditional dance. With a bewitching courtesan, romantic banter, swashbuckling, and hara-kiri disemboweling for a finish, the show was both exotic and accessible to Western audiences. The astute Edward Gordon Craig acclaimed Sadayakko as equal to even such celebrated contemporaries as Sarah Bernhardt.

Upon returning from Europe, her international success gave her unique credibility and theatrical opportunities in Japan. In roles including Ophelia, Portia, and Salome, she leveraged Western exoticism in a mirror image of her European public persona as an exotic oriental, then used the success to pursue pioneering projects such as establishing a children's theatre and a school for actresses. The latter helped to bestow respectability upon the profession, which in turn was instrumental in changing theatrical norms governing gender performance.

Partly through these efforts, the discussion over the use of actresses was largely settled by the 1910s. For decades after this, actresses appeared opposite male onnagata, an increasingly vestigial and declining role limited primarily to traditional theatre.

JONAH SALZ

known as Sadayakko. He kept the stage action fast, especially fight scenes, as these contrasted so clearly with the symbolic, acrobatic, but essentially unexciting kabuki set-piece fights. Also in character was Kawakami's retreat from any confrontational political stance. With the outbreak of the Sino-Japanese War in 1894, he realized the potential for patriotic war drama. His capacity for self-publicity reached its apogee in a sensational visit to the front in China. Immediately on his return, his highly successful productions of "war reports," complete with battlefield sound effects and mechanical contrivances, created a trend – one that kabuki tried, rather unsuccessfully, to join, before returning to its traditional repertoire.

Kabuki is old, shimpa is new

The term "shimpa" was coined to distinguish what was a new (*shin*) genre from kabuki, which rapidly came to be seen as classical theatre (referred to as *kyūha*, "old school"). "New" was a catchword of the time and even kabuki used it for original, commissioned plays.

So what was shimpa at this time? Inspired by Sudō's and Kawakami's activities, a number of shimpa troupes were operating, particularly in the Kansai area, in the mid-1890s. They were staffed mainly by amateur – that is, non-kabuki-trained – actors and, increasingly, actresses. The ban on women appearing on stage with men was relaxed in 1888; shimpa took selective advantage of this new freedom, whereas kabuki ignored it. This did not mean that in shimpa all female roles were played by women. Female parts had been exclusively played by male actors for two and a half centuries and audiences were long since conditioned to expect this convention. Sudō himself played a female character in his first production. The kabuki *onnagata* female role specialist occupied so central a part in Japanese popular theatre that shimpa would hardly have been credible as a genre without its own counterpart. Already by the late 1890s two superb shimpa onnagata were emerging; the genre has continued to mix actors and actresses in female roles to this day.

Meiji shimpa has often been defined derogatorily by its repertoire of adaptations of novels serialized in newspapers. Playwriting for the new age, however, was still in its infancy, whereas fiction writing in the new genre of novels was well under way by the 1890s. There quickly developed a circular form of mutual commercialization, in which a shimpa company would perform an adaptation of a newspaper serial, which the newspaper would publicize or even sponsor, with the expectation that the newspaper would enjoy an increased circulation if the play succeeded.

The serialized novels were not all trash, although some of the adaptations were. Serious novelists were first publishing their work in newspapers in nineteenth-century Europe and the same was true in Japan. Both Ozaki Kōyō (1868–1903) and his disciple Izumi Kyōka (1873–1939), whose fictional works caused sensations in the literary world of the 1890s, were dramatized by shimpa. Kawakami appropriated Kyōka's "tightly paced and dramatic tale" with its "considerable command of language and a sure sense of plot and scenic structure" entitled *Giketsu kyōketsu* (Loyal blood, valiant blood) a few months after its publication as a serial in the *Asahi Shimbun* in 1894.[2] The stage version, under the title *Taki no Shiraito* (the name of the heroine), became one of the most frequently performed shimpa plays. After 1900, there was a rush of Kyōka adaptations by shimpa. In 1898 a shimpa company, a rival to Kawakami's, staged an adaptation of Ozaki's novel *Konjiki yasha* (Gold demon), an instant hit. Shimpa may have resensationalized what was already sensational, but this forged a significant link between the theatre and the emerging modern literature.

After kabuki's three great stars died in quick succession in 1903–4, shimpa dominated the Tokyo theatre world, but by the early 1910s it began to decline as audiences lost interest in its increasingly formulaic presentations of geisha love affairs, where social norms require love to be sacrificed. Its fortunes revived later in the decade, thanks to the plays of Mayama Seika (1878–1948), who breathed new life into shimpa by reworking classic adaptations that were becoming stale and by offering many original plays. His own adaptations of literary works were not always popular, but he stoutly defended his artistic aspirations. With him as their playwright, shimpa stars were forced for the first time to recognize that well-written plays were in their interest.

---

2 M. Cody Poulton, *Spirits of Another Sort: The Plays of Izumi Kyoka* (Michigan: Center for Japanese Studies, University of Michigan, 2001), 31–2.

Shimpa received a further boost in the 1920s with the emergence of two stars who were to carry the genre through into the postwar period: Mizutani Yaeko (1905–79), an actress of extraordinary stage presence, and Hanayagi Shōtarō (1894–1965), an onnagata of great beauty who often played opposite her. By the end of the 1930s, shimpa had reached its pinnacle of success, with four companies competing against each other. Although it survived the postwar disappearance of the world of the geisha, its mainstay plot locus, shimpa lost ground from the 1960s onwards until by the end of the century it was represented only by periodic productions.

Shimpa's problem was always how to position itself between kabuki, some of whose conventions it successfully imitated, and more modern forms such as *shingeki* (new theatre), the genre inspired by Western theatre. This tension is well illustrated by the career of Inoue Masao (1881–1950), who, in spite of his great success as a shimpa actor, wanted the genre to be more ambitious. He was active in shimpa's involvement with the early Japanese film industry in the 1910s. He played in many *rensageki*, a theatre/silent-film hybrid in which certain scenes were filmed on location and then projected onto onstage screens, with dialogue spoken by actors behind or beside the screen, while other scenes were played live. In the 1930s he advocated what he termed *chūkan engeki* (middle-of-the-road theatre), by which he meant a distinct move of shimpa toward shingeki. To this end he commissioned shingeki directors such as Murayama Tomoyoshi (1901–77) for his productions. In the end, however, shimpa stayed with what was familiar to it and its patrons.

When Kawakami resumed his theatre career in Japan in 1903 after his various foreign tours, he had a leading lady in his wife Sadayakko, while shimpa's leading players of female roles were still male. He also created an unfamiliar atmosphere in the auditorium. He avoided using the *hanamichi* walkway, still a standard feature of theatre architecture, and his scenery, and especially lighting with its revolutionary use of coloured gels, suggested more a foreign theatre experience than a Japanese one. He called this *seigeki* ("correct theatre," meaning, in the eminent writer Mori Ōgai's formulation, a theatre based on text rather than spectacle, a straight play). The first seigeki production (in 1903) was of Shakespeare's *Othello* in a free adaptation set in Japan and its new colony Taiwan, with Washirō (Othello) rumored to be a member of Japan's outcaste community. A huge success, it was followed later in the year by the trial scene of *The Merchant of Venice* and *Hamlet*.

Kawakami's legacy to theatre lay in his willingness to experiment with new forms of lighting, scenery, and stage business generally, and his attitude toward actresses. He cast Sadayakko as Desdemona, Portia, and Ophelia and established in practice the idea that women should play female leading roles, if possible. Yet there were few actresses around at the time and the early modern theatre groups sometimes relied on audiences' continuing acceptance of male-to-female cross-dressing to fill gaps in availability. Kawakami raised money in 1908 to found an actor training school for women with Sadayakko as its first head.

New drama

Tsubouchi Shōyō (1859–1935) was not impressed by Kawakami's seigeki Shakespeare. Tsubouchi was at the time a lecturer at prestigious Waseda University. He and Osanai Kaoru (1881–1928), then still a Tokyo Imperial University student, later became leaders of the two theatre organizations credited with launching shingeki. Both had witnessed the practical show-man Kawakami's attempt to move beyond shimpa toward a modern theatre. Both were highly educated, and their activities in the theatre signaled that shingeki would be the thinking person's theatre. As like-minded people be-came involved, theatre in Japan developed two streams: shimpa and kabuki, where audiences were entertained, excited by the brilliance of certain actors, and moved to tears of sympathy, relief, or joy, and shingeki, where audiences went to learn, to be made to think, and to watch – through translated drama – foreign characters interacting on a personal level in ways not at all common yet in Japanese society.

In the early 1900s the gulf between these two was enormous. With the accelerating import of Western literature, especially the plays of Henrik Ibsen, intellectuals were realizing that the whole basis of modern Western theatre was quite different from traditional native theatre. Every facet of theatre practice, including playwriting, stage language, acting, set design, and lighting, was being reconsidered. No wonder, therefore, that theatre his-torian Matsumoto Shinko was able to fill more than a thousand pages in her survey of drama theory in the Meiji period alone.[3]

From the point of view of contemporary intellectuals, the central issue was the art of the playwright. As we have seen in Chapter 4, one of the aims of the Drama Reform movement was to establish the playwright as an in-dependent artist in his own right. Those who were writing for kabuki and shimpa were still writing perishable plays with particular actors in mind – thus they were writing plays that they hoped would be theatrically effective with a certain cast, but whether or not those plays might be actable by other actors or have something to say to future generations of theatregoers was hardly a consideration. To Tsubouchi must go the credit for trying to change

---

3 Matsumoto Shinko, *Meiji engekironshi* (History of drama theory in the Meiji period) (Tokyo: Engeki shuppansha, 1980).

∾ FOCUS 6.2   Tsubouchi Shōyō: romantic visionary

Tsubouchi Shōyō (1859–1935) was a central figure in the early development of modern Japanese drama. As an academic, dramatist, and pioneering Shakespeare translator, Tsubouchi provided much of the theoretical basis for the emergence of *shingeki* in the twentieth century. His Shakespeare translations (completed between 1909 and 1927), mixing kabuki and contemporary styles, remained integral to the shingeki repertoire through the 1960s.

Tsubouchi's ideas on drama originated in his initial career as a novelist in the 1880s and, as professor at Waseda University, in rejection of aesthetic idealism in favor of social and psychological realism. In 1885 he produced *Shōsetsu shinzui* (The essence of the novel), an influential treatise criticizing didacticism and frivolity of lowlife fiction (*gesaku*) of the Edo era (1603–1868), paving the way for a modern Japanese fiction capable of reflecting new subjectivities. Unable to write the kind of novel he was advocating, he turned in the late 1880s to the study and eventual translation of the complete works of Shakespeare, whose genius he believed lay in the ability to conceal important ideas and ideals within a broad representation of reality.

At the same time, Tsubouchi remained indebted to traditional Japanese theatre, especially kabuki, of which he was a connoisseur, while calling for a more realistic historical drama than the often fantastic *jidaimono* (period pieces) of classical kabuki. In the 1890s and 1900s, he wrote a series of such plays focusing especially on the fall of Osaka Castle in 1615, of which *Hototogisu kojō no rakugetsu* (A sinking moon over the lonely castle where the cuckoo cries, 1897) is still performed.[4] Tsubouchi also wrote kabuki dance-dramas,

whose relatively simple plots allowed for clearer exposition of his brand of realism than his history plays; *Onatsu kyōran* (The madness of Onatsu, 1908) has been popularized recently by leading *onnagata* Bandō Tamasaburō V. A 1909 essay comparing Shakespeare with kabuki and bunraku playwright Chikamatsu Monzaemon and Ibsen offered a provocative account of how idioms like realism may transcend historical and genre differences. Tsubouchi's *En no gyōja* (En the ascetic, various versions, 1914–21) was selected as the first native drama presented by the Tsukiji Shōgekijō, "Japan's first modern theatre," its stylized realism considered an actorly challenge.

Influenced by his mentor, kabuki playwright Kawatake Mokuami (1816–93), Tsubouchi believed that dramatic meaning was communicated primarily through the voice, and so in 1891 started a Waseda group for recitation of Western and Japanese plays. Some participants later acted with the Bungei Kyōkai (Literary Arts Association, 1905–13), Japan's first modern drama school, which admitted female actors and innovated production of Shakespeare in faithful translation, rather than adaptation, as had theretofore been done by kabuki and *shimpa* troupes.

Waseda University honored Tsubouchi's achievements with the Tsubouchi Memorial Theatre Museum, 1928; the building imitates the façade of the Elizabethan Fortune Theatre, and above the entrance is inscribed the motto of Shakespeare's original Globe Theatre, *Totus mundus agit histrionem* (All the world's a stage).

DANIEL GALLIMORE

that authorial stance. In the mid-1880s and early 1890s he argued for characterization based on believable motivations.

Language was understandably something that much concerned all literary artists – novelists, poets, and playwrights – in the 1890s. The traditional

---

4 Trans. J. Thomas Rimer, in James R. Brandon and Samuel L. Leiter (eds.), *Kabuki Plays on Stage*, 4 vols. (Honolulu: University of Hawai'i Press, 2001–2), vol. IV, 364–93.

Japanese literary language, especially in drama, fiction, and essays, was highly embellished, priding itself on mediating its subject matter in a distinctive way. In Europe, however, as young Japanese intellectuals were fast learning, both the Romantic and the Naturalist movements wanted literary works to have a direct impact on readers or audiences through a strong link with emotional and social reality. In Japanese theatre, an abrupt shift into contemporary colloquial speech was problematic, as the elaborate language of kabuki was an intrinsic part of the art. So intellectuals like Tsubouchi and Ōgai had the contradictory tasks of elevating drama to the status of literature while removing the elaborate, lyrical dialogue. They succeeded against the odds, and writers began experimenting with drama just as they were with other literary forms. Not all of this was in the colloquial language and much of it was not intended for actual stage production. The turning point was a poetic play written by a young poet, Kitamura Tōkoku (1868–94), *Hōraikyoku* (Ballad of Mount Paradise, 1891). It was irrelevant that the theatre world of the day took no interest in it. Here was a literary man, strongly influenced by the poetry of Byron, writing a play as a conscious literary exercise. He was the first, and others soon followed.

Japanese playwriting of the early decades of the twentieth century is often categorized in Western literary terms: Naturalism, Symbolism, and so on. Nagata Hideo (1885–1949) and Nakamura Kichizō (1877–1941) probed social problems using Naturalist methodology in their plays: Nagata in *Kanraku no oni* (A fiend for pleasure, 1909), heavily influenced by Ibsen's *Ghosts*, and Nakamura with *Kamisori* (Razor, 1916), exposing the extreme inequalities of opportunity in Japanese society. Kinoshita Mokutarō (1885–1945) with *Nanbanji monzen* (Before the gate of the Nanban Temple, 1909), a play professedly without a hero or a plot, conveyed multiple meaning through image and mood in the Symbolist style. Akita Ujaku (1883–1962) chose an Expressionist mode for his hard-hitting play about the scapegoating of Koreans after the Great Kantō Earthquake of 1923 (*Gaikotsu no buchō* [The skeletons' dance], 1924).[5]

In the decade between the mid-1910s and mid-1920s drama came into its own as a literary genre, when people began to enjoy reading plays in literary and general interest magazines. Most plays catching the attention of the theatregoing public were written not by specialist playwrights, who were often too beholden to certain actors or companies, but by novelists not professionally connected to the theatre world who had begun to regard drama as an alternative vehicle for their ideas. Kikuchi Kan (1888–1948) scored a singular success with *Chichi kaeru* (Father returns, 1917), when it was premiered

---

5 Trans. with an extended preface in M. Cody Poulton, *A Beggar's Art: Scripting Modernity in Japanese Drama, 1900–1930* (Honolulu: University of Hawai'i Press, 2010), 134–52.

in 1920 (see pp. 223–4). Mushanokōji Saneatsu (1885–1976), leader of the Shirakaba (White Birch) humanist literary group, also found success with his plays, particularly *Aiyoku* (Passion, 1925), a dark, terrifyingly realistic study of passion, jealousy, and terror.

As the 1920s progressed, playwriting became dominated by "proletarian" drama, when a new realism came to the fore. While in proletarian drama authors were exhorted to observe and appreciate the greater reality of societal and historical change as defined by Marxist theory, audiences empathized with Kikuchi's and Mushanokōji's characters because they recognized them as real human beings.

The director arrives: Jiyū Gekijō

At the beginning of the twentieth century, theatre celebrities were still all actors. As the shingeki movement got going, directors' names came to the fore. The idea of the director as someone in overall control of all aspects of a production had only recently been established in Europe; in Japan it was unknown. Kabuki actors directed themselves, with seniority endowing authority, and early shimpa as an artistic enterprise was similarly actor-centered. By the early 1900s a functionary whose job was *butai kantoku* (stage supervision) had appeared, in most cases doing little more than stage management. Osanai Kaoru became Japan's first director in the Western sense. Pursuing a career halfway between the stage and the literary world, he was the prime mover in launching a new literary journal in 1907 dedicated to introducing Ibsen to Japan at the same time as preparing play scripts for a shimpa company. Later that same year he was engrossed by descriptions of Western theatre given to him by the young kabuki actor Ichikawa Sadanji II (1880–1940), who had just spent nine months energetically trying to get to the core of European theatre. Then reading Edward Gordon Craig, Osanai determined to become a director.

Osanai and Sadanji founded the Jiyū Gekijō (Free Theatre). The idea for the company came from Sadanji, and actors in all plays that the company performed, both Western and Japanese, were from kabuki. Could having a director (Osanai) qualify it as a pioneer of modern theatre? Kabuki actors performing Western plays under Osanai's direction were also performing kabuki classics and even similar Western plays at Sadanji's theatre, the Meiji-za. Again we are talking about atmosphere. The ambience of the Meiji-za's Western productions would have been quite different from that of Jiyū Gekijō presentations. Osanai could be quite free in directing his actors to move realistically or in achieving special lighting or sound effects, whereas Sadanji had to be careful, as the Meiji-za was a theatre with a resident kabuki company and its audiences would only tolerate so much innovation. The Jiyū Gekijō, to achieve freedom from commercial pressures, attempted to finance itself by a membership system, like contemporary theatre clubs in Europe.

The Jiyū Gekijō's first production was Ibsen's *John Gabriel Borkman* (1909), and of the fourteen plays performed subsequently, eight were foreign (by playwrights as diverse as Wedekind, Maeterlinck, Gorki, Andreyev, Brieux, and Hauptmann). Osanai wanted to usher in an era of true translations, as opposed to adaptations then the norm in kabuki and shimpa. If he wanted to work with professionally trained actors, however, he had no choice but to use kabuki actors. Various attempts to set up actor-training facilities for the modern theatre had not yet resulted in a pool of actors and actresses who could take on Ibsen, Gorky, and Wedekind.

Kabuki actors were rigorously trained from an early age within their acting families, but the formidable stage presence that resulted from this training was not usually suitable for these contemporary Western plays. Osanai had to persuade these actors to become "amateurs," although when the company started, he himself had no experience of Western actor training. Ironically the only Japanese actor who had actually attended a Western acting school was Sadanji, who had spent three weeks at a school associated with Ellen Terry in London. There were many problems for the Jiyū Gekijō actors, not least because the majority of the Western plays required natural interaction between characters on the stage. The breath control and timing that they had perfected for kabuki over so many years simply would not work for the verbose expression characteristic of Japanese translations of Western plays. Moreover, female roles were played by males, as in kabuki. So by 1910 the Japanese theatre world had three types of onnagata – for kabuki, shimpa, and now shingeki – and the demands made on each were quite different. Whereas female parts in kabuki and much shimpa were written for men, Ibsen had never imagined that the dialogue between two female characters that begins *John Gabriel Borkman* would ever be played by males. It was therefore incumbent on men who were to play female roles in shingeki productions to move more in the direction of impersonation unfiltered by accustomed stylistic conventions.

The Jiyū Gekijō's repertory introduced its audiences, as per Osanai's intention, to a range of contemporary European drama, mainly Naturalist or Symbolist. Many spectators went to see these plays just for the content, and this concept of going to the theatre to be taught something continued well into the 1920s. There were no sensational intersections with Japanese social mores; Osanai must have been chagrined that this kind of useful notoriety was reserved for one of Jiyū Gekijō's principal rivals, noted below. Although the legacy of the venture was limited, in that none of the next generation of shingeki leaders was particularly influenced by it, it was a brave experiment to enlist the full array of traditional artistic resources to a project of creating a modern theatre for Japan.

Amateurs to the rescue: Bungei Kyōkai

The Bungei Kyōkai (Literary Arts Association) started in 1906 as a university-based student literary and play-reading society under the leadership of two teachers at Waseda University: Tsubouchi Shōyō and a younger colleague and ex-student, Shimamura Hōgetsu (1871–1918). Their approaches to theatre modernization were quite different. Shimamura had returned to Japan from two years and about 150 theatre visits in Europe in 1904, and was now convinced that Naturalism was the future in both literature and theatre. In 1906 he was instrumental in relaunching the journal *Waseda Bungaku* (Waseda Literature), arguing there for the realization of a Naturalist drama. Tsubouchi, by contrast, was a gradualist who believed that kabuki was the type of theatre best suited to communicating with Japanese audiences; while a new theatre must of necessity develop new conventions, these would not be based on the reality of everyday life. As a translator of Shakespeare, his intimate acquaintance with the sonorities of Shakespeare's dialogue encouraged his interest in declamation; from there he began to develop a style of elevated stage diction that he thought key to the performance of modern drama.

Bungei Kyōkai meetings consisted of play readings at which Tsubouchi would instruct in his declamatory style. This was not at all to the liking of many of the students, most being inclined toward Shimamura's ideas. They wanted to perform and Tsubouchi was persuaded to let this happen, although certain they were not ready. *Hamlet* (1907) aroused considerable intellectual interest, being the first in Japanese faithful to the text. Casting, however, had been highly problematic and much of the acting attracted harsh criticism. Pressure was put on Tsubouchi by Shimamura and others to reorganize Bungei Kyōkai as a more comprehensive institution within the theatre and literary worlds. Tsubouchi eventually complied, even providing land in the grounds of his house for a study center. A new Bungei Kyōkai came into existence in 1909, and in 1911 issued a mission statement: "[The Association] will have as one of its objectives the raising of levels of taste in society at large."[6]

Unlike the Jiyū Gekijō, with its highly professional, if struggling, kabuki actors, Bungei Kyōkai's actors were mainly amateurs. It needed trained modern actors and its training program was to be a serious enterprise. The

---

6 Ōzasa Yoshio, *Nihon gendai engeki-shi, Meiji Taishō-hen* (History of modern theatre in Japan, Meiji and Taishō) (Tokyo: Hakusuisha, 1985), 82.

entrance examination consisted of four parts, testing (1) strength of the applicant's motivation through an interview; (2) applicant's knowledge of English; (3) how well the applicant could read aloud; (4) a written exam on a subject in theatre history. Those who passed the examination would attend evening classes for three hours. The weekly schedule consisted of sixteen units, with a mix of practical and theoretical instruction. The latter was particularly prominent, with six sessions being lectures (including Tsubouchi translating Shakespeare line by line) and one an English lesson.

As the company approached their opening production of *Hamlet*, Tsubouchi told his cast that what they were facing was more difficult than an Antarctic expedition.[7] He rehearsed them hard for three months. In the end, *Hamlet* was a popular success, filling a large, very modern theatre to over 90 percent capacity, but not all critics liked it. Tsubouchi had mixed colloquial and literary language, difficult to understand; the cast was so well drilled that acting and diction seemed stiff. Anyway, why was the Bungei Kyōkai spending time on Shakespeare when there was so much exciting contemporary European drama to perform? This *Hamlet*, however, had achieved something important in Japanese theatre history. The text had been treated with great respect and overall artistic control was in a director's hands. This created an unprecedented unity of approach.

Consummate actress: Matsui Sumako

Rightly or wrongly, perhaps, most attention in contemporary reports was reserved for Matsui Sumako (1886–1919), who played Ophelia; consensus was that Japan had acquired a real actress. She had proved herself a dedicated student in the acting course, more ambitious than her classmates. She seems to have communicated well with her audiences, reportedly making them think it natural she should go mad with grief over Hamlet's callousness and her father's death. Her rendering of Ophelia's song was certainly beyond anything a male actor could have done.

Shakespeare soon gave way to contemporary European drama, as the company's younger members came to the fore. Ibsen's *A Doll's House* was produced in November 1911 with Sumako playing Nora, directed jointly by Shimamura and Naturalist playwright Nakamura Kichizō (1877–1941). Shimamura's directing was still prescriptive, but much more thoroughgoing than Tsubouchi's. He wanted perfect memorization of all lines, moves, and

---

7 Brian Powell, "One man's Hamlet in 1911 Japan: the Bungei Kyōkai production in the Imperial Theatre," in Takashi Sasayama, J. R. Mulryne, and Margaret Shewring (eds.), *Shakespeare and the Japanese Stage* (Cambridge: Cambridge University Press, 1998), 38–52.

Fig 31 Nora (Matsui Sumako) dances the tarantella in Bungei Kyōkai's *A Doll's House* by Henrik Ibsen, 1911.

gestures. Sumako responded well to this. She was still feeling her way in a world dominated by better-educated males. The production was a triumph; the critic of one newspaper was moved to write: "It is no exaggeration to say that the Nora of this actress will long be remembered as having solved for the first time Japan's actress problem."[8]

A Doll's House was important in another way. It was the first stage production to have had a tangible impact on social thinking. Ibsen's plays spoke in a graphic way of the problems facing the independent individual in a conservative traditional society, exactly the kind of problem then exercising the minds of young Japanese intellectuals. Sumako's powerful acting drew attention to Nora, a privileged woman who breaks free to realize who she is. This excited general interest in the press, among intellectuals, and especially among members of the incipient feminist movement. The Bungei Kyōkai's next production, Hermann Sudermann's *Die Heimat* (1912), starring Sumako as Magda, a woman who defies her father in the cause of her own self-identity, provoked more than just comment. The censoring authority rejected the script when submitted for prior approval. Shimamura was required to rewrite the last scene, to make Magda seem less unfilial. Yet with these two plays the shingeki movement found a voice, and this intersection with what authorities considered social norms gave shingeki a firm place in modern Japanese culture.

8 *Yomiuri Shimbun*, in Toita Yasuji, *Joyū no ai to shi* (Love and death of an actress) (Tokyo: Kawade shobō shinsha, 1963), 84.

❧ FOCUS 6.3　*Tabi-shibai*: barnstorming troupes

Taishū engeki (theatre for the masses) is an itinerant variety theatre mixing kabuki plots with popular song, attracting avid fans for regular tours to small theatres throughout Japan. Known as *dosa-mawari* (rural touring troupes, barnstormers) and pejoratively as "third-rate kabuki," troupes perform both in modern, well-equipped theatres in entertainment districts of major cities such as Tokyo and Osaka, and at *onsen* hotspring recreation establishments, offered alongside bathing, amusement arcades, and karaoke. Shows at shabby theatres tucked away in urban backstreets and bathhouses are performed almost exclusively by *tabi-shibai* (travelling theatre troupes), who may perform twice a day for a month before moving on.

Restrictions on *chambara* (swordfighting) and *shinkokugeki* (patriotic samurai dramas) under the American Occupation created a boom in tabi-shibai, whose unscripted and fleeting appearances at country fairs and festivals slipped by the censors. Over 700 troupes toured the country in the genre's heyday from 1945 to 1953. Television and dwindling audiences nearly killed the form, but media interest and the rise of Umezawa Tomio (1950–), the "*shitamachi* (downtown) Tamasaburō," fueled a mid-1980s revival for the neo-nostalgic form. Traveling groups were often associated with the shady *yakuza* world. Performances included rough expressions and pornographic elements, such as striptease. This gradually changed, thanks in part to Kataoka Chōjirō (1929–2008), who organized the first meeting for leaders of the traveling groups in 1979, aiming to restore their reputation. A decade later, many shows had changed into more decent, family-friendly entertainment. Since the early 1990s, more than a hundred traveling troupes belonging to regional organizations have survived, and an unknown number of unaffiliated troupes.

Shows consist of either comedies or sentimental melodramas followed by musical entertainment and dances; *onnagata* (males portraying female roles), often performed by troupe heads, draw the most attention. Dialogue is improvised within a set storyline. Slang, strong dialects, and gangster language are common. Heavy makeup, gaudy kimono, and exaggerated acting are hallmarks of the taishū engeki style. The company master (*zachō*) selects a play from the group's repertoire of more than 300 plays, which sometimes rotate twice daily to attract repeat visitors. The second-act "grand show" consists of songs, music, and dance with emphasis on pop music (sometimes played live) and well-known *enka* (sentimental ballads).

Stories, dances, and songs have uncomplicated themes, bringing to mind romantic stories printed in weekly magazines, entertaining feature films, and soap operas. Performances last a few hours, instead of kabuki's half-day programs that appeal to more leisured spectators. Historical plays (*jidaigeki*) set in the Edo period (1603–1868) describe moral issues and codes of honor, problems relating to conflicts between *giri* and *ninjō* (social obligations and natural human emotions), and struggles to repay debts both of honor and money. Tragic endings in kabuki originals may be changed to happy ones. Conflicts within yakuza groups are set in an idealized, unspecified period. The yakuza hero, consistently portrayed in films and popular stories as a criminal outlaw, gambler, or petty thief from the Edo period, here becomes a Robin Hood figure who comes to the aid of the weak and poor.

Whether in well-equipped commercial theatres or in small, dilapidated ones, performers display professionalism and a keen awareness of their audience's tastes. Aspects of the garish, erotic, and transient outlaw nature of taishū engeki were appropriated by such sixties rebels as Terayama Shūji and Kara Jūrō.

CHRISTINA NYGREN

Moneymaking to support art: Geijutsu-za

In the space of a single year the Bungei Kyōkai had achieved more than any other contemporary theatrical enterprise in pulling theatre away from its roots in kabuki and engaging with various facets of the contemporary modernization process. The company was not destined to last long, but it was not the authorities that closed it down. While unconventional moral attitudes were just barely permitted on the stage, there was still a limit to personal freedom within the organization. Tsubouchi, conscious that mixed educational establishments were still rare, had imposed Draconian rules governing personal behavior. Unfortunately, his most talented actress and most brilliant pupil, Sumako and Shimamura, fell in love. As Shimamura was married with a family, Tsubouchi could only tolerate this public love affair for so long; Shimamura finally resigned and the group disbanded in 1913.

Shimamura is often described as somewhat languid and unworldly, but this stereotype is belied by the energy with which he launched a new company with Sumako. Within six months of leaving the Bungei Kyōkai, their Geijutsu-za (Art Theatre) opened with a ten-day run of two plays by Belgian Symbolist Maurice Maeterlinck. The production had been sold out well before the first night, establishing the Geijutsu-za's position as the day's leading shingeki group. Financially, however, in spite of full houses, this enterprise only confirmed what was already accepted as inevitable, that shingeki was a loss-making concern.

Shimamura realised that, artistically, he had a strong company. Apart from Sumako, several of the Bungei Kyōkai's more gifted actors had joined. He wanted to use their combined talents to hone the group's ability to take on challenging European plays and to encourage young playwrights. Nakamura Kichizō, after being supported by the Geijutsu-za, went on to be one of Japan's leading dramatists. To subsidize this unprofitable work, Shimamura decided to commercialize Sumako's singing talent, so evident in her performance of Ophelia. Some of the troupe's most serious work would be in adaptations of Tolstoy novels, but for the first, *Resurrection*, Shimamura engaged the services of a gifted song-writing team.

Given the reading public's interest in Tolstoyan humanism, the Geijutsu-za's *Resurrection* at the 1,700-seat Imperial Theatre, Tokyo's largest commercial theatre, would probably have been an ordinary success in 1914, but with "Katyusha's Song" sung by Sumako it was a show that everyone wanted to see. Moreover, the merchandizing that followed brought handsome profits. The recorded version became Japan's first hit record (making Sumako Japan's first pop star) and Katyusha trinkets sold everywhere. Shimamura was able to pay his actors' salaries with enough left over to build an Arts Club, with facilities for rehearsals and small-scale performances, and accommodation for himself and Sumako.

At a stroke a star system had been created, something still foreign to shingeki. Assessments of the success of this twin-track policy vary. It caused tensions within the company. Purists thought such commercialization too high a price to pay. The company came to be dominated by two personalities, a problem in a new artistic venture when all members consider themselves to be creating something new together. On the other hand, the list of serious productions enabled by this policy was impressive. A 1916 adaptation of Tolstoy's *Power of Darkness* was lauded, including by Osanai, as the best shingeki production yet, high praise indeed considering that around thirty organizations were then engaged in mounting productions of new plays. Perhaps the best indication of the Geijutsu-za's importance in shingeki history is the debt openly owed to it by many of the next generation of shingeki leaders.

The Geijutsu-za had a sad end. Shimamura died in the influenza pandemic of 1918 and, a few months later, Sumako hanged herself. The troupe disbanded soon after.

Art subsidised by swordfights: Shinkokugeki

Financing was to remain a shingeki problem throughout the twentieth century. In the 1950s and 1960s shingeki groups depended on their most popular actors donating part of their film, TV, and radio earnings. In Japan, drama that made its audiences think was never able to attract sufficient spectators to be financially viable. With kabuki, at least in the way Shōchiku organized it, you could either just sample the acting of the biggest stars or, if you felt so inclined and had the experience, you could seriously compare current players with others you had seen before. Kabuki could be enjoyed either way. Shimpa guaranteed that your emotions would be engaged in familiar ways. Shingeki, of course, tried to do this as well, but essentially in unfamiliar ways. Aspiring actors were given the message that they needed to have brains to be able to act modern plays and early presentations of contemporary European drama were mostly cerebral affairs (sometimes even preceded by lectures). Shimamura hoped that those who came to see Sumako as Katyusha or Salomé would also come to studio productions.

Another member of the Geijutsu-za, who left to form his own company, was forced to compromise in yet another way to create the kind of theatre he wanted. Sawada Shōjirō (1892–1929) had become one of the troupe's leading actors, playing opposite Sumako (and frequently clashing with her in rehearsals, both being strong-willed and artistically uncompromising). He resigned in disgust at the company's commercial operations, briefly rejoined, then left for good in 1917 to set up a new company named Shinkokugeki (New National Theatre). When its opening program of four new Japanese plays failed, the company repaired to the Kansai area, where artists struggling in Tokyo conventionally went to reinvigorate their art.

To secure his company's continuation, Sawada was forced by his sponsors to include swordfights – not kabuki's balletic stylizations but realistic, even dangerous, duels – in all productions. This made Shinkokugeki instantly famous and highly profitable. With fame and fortune Sawada was able to return to his original intention of fostering good new drama. Shinkokugeki mounted highly acclaimed productions of such plays as Kikuchi Kan's *Chichi kaeru* (Father returns, 1917; see pp. 223–4) and Nakamura Kichizō's *Ii Tairō no shi* (Death of Ii, the Regent, 1920). The latter was for Nakamura a new venture into historical playwriting, examining the issues surrounding the assassination of Regent Ii Naosuke in 1860. Shinkokugeki's repertory of serious plays contained many like this which could naturally incorporate swordfighting, including a wildly successful *Cyrano de Bergerac* (1926). Sawada rationalized his policy by the term *hanpo-shugi* or "half-a-step-ism." "Always extend a kindly hand to the people, but always advance with one foot half a step ahead of the people. It must be half a step. If you advance by a full step, your and the people's hands will part. You cannot hope for progress if you forget to advance half a step at a time. Half a step, half a step. One pace following the tastes of the people, making possible one pace toward better art."[9] Sawada died an untimely death in 1929. Although Shinkokugeki lasted as a company (and as a genre) until 1987, it never quite achieved the edge it had with Sawada.

From 1926 Sawada teamed up with Mayama Seika, a versatile playwright, who wrote complex psychological dramas for him. Shinkokugeki's production of *Sakamoto Ryōma* (1928), a play charting the eponymous hero's powerlessness in the face of his own changing political ideas that seemed to have a life of their own, filled the Imperial Theatre for thirty days. Mayama, however, went on to become a famous *shin kabuki* (new kabuki) playwright and during the 1930s Shinkokugeki was associated with Hasegawa Shin (1884–1963), a playwright (and novelist) specializing in stories of the easily romanticized lone traveling yakuza, who would kill when asked to but who also protected the weak and vulnerable. Shinkokugeki's popular productions of Hasegawa plays resulted in their legacy to Japan's modern theatre lying

---

9 Quoted in Akiba Tarō, *Nihon shingekishi* (History of Japan's shingeki) (Tokyo: Risō-sha, 1955), vol. I, 443.

more in what became known as *taishū engeki* (popular theatre) than in the serious drama that Sawada would have liked (see Focus 6.3). The new genre of *kengeki* (sword plays, usually historical) that emerged at the end of the 1930s has been attributed to Shinkokugeki's influence.

Famous and not-so-famous in 1910s theatre

The companies mentioned here – Jiyū Gekijō, Bungei Kyōkai, Geijutsu-za, and (initially at least) Shinkokugeki – are ones history has credited with taking the lead in bringing Japanese theatre into the modern age. With their fame helped by celebrities associated with them, these companies and personalities certainly set the pace and tone for modern theatre development, yet they were not alone. A bewildering array of nearly a hundred theatre groups came and went during the 1910s and early 1920s.

Many were short-lived; a few survived but with long periods of inactivity, and from time to time one of them achieved singular success. Although mention of them in general histories of Japanese theatre is often brief and sometimes non-existent, they were part of the rich fabric of theatre at the time.[10] Just the lists of names associated with their productions give clues to their importance: there was some movement of personnel between the major companies and these smaller groups, and among the credits can be found names of those already well known for their involvement in modern theatre (such as Ōgai) and those who would later become stars (such as Mizutani). The conspicuous involvement of kabuki and shimpa actors suggests that in the cause of modernization genre boundaries were less defined than they subsequently became.

The ideals these groups embraced, issues such as censorship they faced, and financial problems they shared, mirrored much of what was happening at the top of this theatrical pyramid. Some espoused Japanese playwriting (such as the Shin Nihon Gekidan [New Japan Company] and Bungei-za [Literary Arts Company]), while others committed themselves to mixed repertories of Western translated drama and Japanese originals (such as Butai Kyōkai [Stage Society]). One would emphasize realistic acting, another place most importance on the artistic level of the *mise-en-scène*. Actors would be either kabuki trained (Ennosuke's Shunjū-za [Spring and Autumn Society] and Kan'ya's Kuroneko-za [Black Cat Society]) or shimpa trained (Shingeki-za) or have no traditional training (although unkindly referred to

---

10 The exception is Akiba, *Nihon shingekishi*, vol. II, 289–388: Tanaka Eizō, *Meiji Taishō shingekishi shiryō* (Materials relating to shingeki history in the Meiji and Taishō periods) (Tokyo: Engeki shuppansha, 1964) lists production details for many more.

as "amateurs" in the parlance of the day, some of them already had considerable experience in productions of modern plays). All these groups found it impossible to make modern drama pay, even when productions were critical successes, so some tried membership systems (like Jiyū Gekijō), while others were tempted to move toward a more commercial formula (as had Geijutsuza and Shikokugeki).

There was both a fragility and solidity about such earnest activities. Organizational continuity was difficult to achieve and artistic consistency was elusive. However, the large numbers involved and the sustained enthusiasm they demonstrated indicated an astonishing hunger for an alternative theatre that could take its place alongside shimpa, kabuki, and the other traditional forms.

Little theatre with large impact: Tsukiji Shōgekijō

The pioneers of modern Japanese theatre in the major groups mentioned here were all aware of the possibilities opened up by embracing new European drama, but were also acutely conscious that actor training, theatre buildings, and, above all, audience reception could not yet permit a full-scale modernizing project. In 1924 this situation changed radically with the founding of Japan's first comprehensively modern company.

In the early 1920s, kabuki and shimpa were artistically much as they had been twenty years previously. Both had had fluctuations in popularity, kabuki after the deaths of its three most famous actors in 1903–4, and shimpa during the mid-1910s through the illness or absence abroad of several leading actors. Organizationally there had been great changes with the growth of the entertainment conglomerate Shōchiku, which by the early 1920s (only some twenty years after its founding in Kyoto in 1901) had achieved a near monopoly on Tokyo's commercial theatre. Despite these changes, kabuki and shimpa retained a clear sense of identity and artistic self-confidence. They knew what they were doing and, to a large extent, where they were going. This was an enviable luxury to the many groups who were trying to establish modern theatre during the same period. We have seen how difficult it was for pioneering groups to pursue their ideals, not only because circumstances forced compromises, but also because of the very nature of the project. Osanai had ruefully observed at a New Year's Eve party in Stanislavski's house in 1912 that the interaction between the guests, the way they talked, danced, and so on, was exactly the same as he had just seen on the stage of the Moscow Art Theatre. Chekhov on stage in Moscow was real Russian life, but this identification of life and theatre was still only a dream for Japanese theatre modernizers.

The problem was constantly in Osanai's thoughts, and in 1924 he finally had an opportunity to put his own solution into practice. Some years previously he had met Hijikata Yoshi (1898–1959), a young aristocrat with a passionate interest in theatre. In time-honored fashion Hijikata became a disciple of the greatly more experienced Osanai; they studied various aspects of modern Western theatre together and planned to open an acting school. In 1922 Hijikata left Japan for a ten-year fact-finding tour of Western theatre capitals, starting in Berlin with its vibrant avant-garde theatre culture. After an exciting year there he had to return home because of the devastating Great Kantō Earthquake of 1 September 1923, which destroyed Tokyo, including most of its theatres. En route in Moscow he met Meyerhold, supremely confident in his Biomechanics actor-training system, and watched two of his productions. Those few days were a revelation to him.

Hijikata decided to use his own funds to build Japan's first dedicated shingeki theatre. The Tsukiji Shōgekijō (Tsukiji Little Theatre) featured stage equipment (including a magnificent *Kuppelhorizont*) rivaling any contemporary European theatre. Osanai and Hijikata were the resident company's leaders, but brought a difficult mix of qualities to this new enterprise. They were master and disciple, Osanai much older and more experienced, Hijikata the possessor of new ideas and money. Osanai was convinced that stage realism must be internalized first; Hijikata was excited by the prospect of experimental productions.

The theatre opened in June 1924. Publicity in the months before and after was dominated by Osanai. He insisted that there was initially to be a complete break with kabuki and shimpa, but also with contemporary Japanese playwriting.

> Let kabuki tradition go on being kabuki tradition.
> Let shimpa tradition go on being shimpa tradition …
> The mission of Tsukiji Shōgekijō lies completely apart from these traditions.[11]

During a rehearsal he is reputed to have uttered the legendary lines: "Get away from *kabuki*. Ignore tradition. Don't dance, move. Don't sing, speak."[12]

In May, Osanai infuriated the burgeoning number of Japanese playwrights by rejecting all their plays. They did not excite his interest as a director, he declared. For the first two years the Tsukiji Shōgekijō would only produce foreign plays in translation. His point was reasonable: the company needed

---

11　This August 1924 mission statement is fully translated in Brian Powell, "Japan's first modern theatre: the Tsukiji Shōgekijō and its company, 1924–26," *MN* 30:1 (1975), 75–7.
12　Mizushina Haruki, *Osanai Kaoru to Tsukiji Shōgekijō* (Osanai Kaoru and Tsukiji Little Theatre) (Tokyo: Machida shoten, 1954), 138.

time to consolidate its style, which would be based on Western acting techniques exercised in a purely Western-style theatre building. The playwrights' anger was also reasonable: they had never had the opportunity to write for a Western-style theatre, with its possibilities for closer emotional focus. They now found themselves shut out of the only one in Japan.

As Osanai had promised, only foreign plays were performed until July 1926, a veritable cornucopia unprecedented in scope and longevity. Twenty-eight different playwrights, representing all major schools of literature, were performed. Osanai's hope that their actors would mature through a concentrated exposure to Western realism was largely fulfilled: many of postwar shingeki's leading actors had been part of the Tsukiji venture. It was clear from the start, however, that Osanai would not have everything his own way. He directed Chekhov for the theatre's opening, but Hijikata directed an Expressionist play by Reinhart Goering in the same program. Hijikata pursued his interest in German Expressionist drama alongside Osanai's more conservative approach. In the Tsukiji Shōgekijō's first year it was an Expressionist play with a Constructivist set that excited most critical attention (Kaiser's *From Morn to Midnight*, designed by a radical young artist, Murayama Tomoyoshi, 1901–77).

In July 1926 the Tsukiji Shōgekijō premiered Tsubouchi Shōyō's *En no gyōja* (En the ascetic, 1916), a mystical play about the founder of Buddhism's Shugendō sect; it was the theatre's first Japanese drama. Afterwards, it varied its repertory between Western and Japanese plays. The times were overtaking the company, however. Osanai directed a number of Japanese plays such as Kubota Mantarō's *Ōdera gakkō* (Ōdera school) that he believed furthered the work being achieved by Western realist dramas, but it was plays on subversive subjects that caught the public's attention. In 1927 the Tsukiji Shōgekijō's house magazine included calls for plays with a defined worldview, suggesting that this year's influx of young trainee actors was changing the company's ideological composition. Literature and drama that were politically left wing were gaining ground in literary circles and the Tsukiji Shōgekijō, Tokyo's only modern theatre, could not escape their influence.

The tensions among company members for and against politically oriented drama intensified through 1928; two of the former, including Senda Koreya (1904–96), later a dominant figure in postwar shingeki, resigned. Osanai was still able to marshal enough authority to be a unifying force, but he had returned exhausted from a trip to Moscow in 1927, and in December 1928 he died, and the Tsukiji project as he had conceived it died too. In March 1929 the company split into two, roughly along the line between the politically committed and the artistically dedicated, although the former included many for whom political commitment was secondary to improving their acting skills.

More genres, more problems

By the late 1920s shimpa and shinkokugeki had become mature genres, joining the three traditional genres (noh-kyogen, bunraku, and kabuki) as part of the wide choice available to Japanese theatregoers. Assessing shingeki's achievement is problematic.

One senses that the Tsukiji Shōgekijō actors and directors were still pioneers, even though they were operating almost half a century after the first tentative steps to find an alternative to kabuki. This may just reaffirm how complex the theatrical enterprise is. When a culture has as consummate a traditional theatre culture as Japan's, challenging it in search of a deeply different expressive paradigm is bound to require enormous resources. Energy and enthusiasm the modern movement certainly had in abundance, but these were often tempered by financial anxieties. Osanai wanted to create a laboratory for drama, but shingeki could never have isolated itself from its environment. Censorship was always a problem, aggravated in 1925 with the passing of the Peace Preservation Law, which prescribed harsh penalties for anything deemed subversive by the authorities. Tsukiji Shōgekijō depended on the support of intellectuals and an educated public, but at a time of intellectual volatility, such expectations were sometimes difficult to meet. And finally the emergence of a radical political opposition movement, which, as in the 1880s, needed the stage to give expression to its views, ensured that shingeki would be in almost constant conflict with the authorities, a massive drain on its energy, detailed in the following chapter.

REPRESENTATIVE MODERN PLAYS

Chichi kaeru (Father returns, 1917) by Kikuchi Kan[13]

Members of the Kuroda family – mother and three grown-up children – are discussing everyday family matters, such as marriages and careers, except that for this family these are complicated because the family was abandoned by the father when the children were very young. The father returns, penniless and broken, but elder son Ken'ichirō, who has supported the family, rejects him and he leaves the house. Appealed to by his mother and sister, Ken'ichirō suddenly relents, but the father is nowhere to be found. This tightly written one-act play's theme of intergenerational conflict at a time of changing family values appealed to audiences then and later. It has been frequently performed across genres.

---

13 Trans. in Glenn W. Shaw, *Tōjūrō's Love and Four Other Plays by Kikuchi Kwan* (Tokyo: Hokuseidō, 1925).

Fig 32 *Chichi kaeru* (Father returns, 1917) by Kikuchi Kan. The father appeals to his long-abandoned family. (Shimpa production, early 1920s.)

Sakamoto Ryōma (1928) by Mayama Seika

An activist and free spirit in the events leading up to the Meiji Restoration in 1868, Sakamoto finds his thoughts on Japan's future evolving faster than his comrades can handle. Espousing, in spite of himself, different solutions to Japan's internal problems, he makes many enemies and is assassinated. Mayama, a playwright who wrote for shingeki, shimpa, and kabuki, greatly admired Shinkokugeki's Sawada Shōjirō as an actor, and challenged him by writing characters of highly complex psychology. With *Ryōma*, Sawada scored a great success.

References and further reading

Ihara Toshio. *Meiji engekishi* (History of Meiji theatre) (Tokyo: Hōshutsusha, 1955)

Kano, Ayako. *Acting Like a Woman in Modern Japan: Theater, Gender, and Nationalism* (New York: Palgrave, 2001)

Komiya, Toyotaka (ed.). *Japanese Music and Drama in the Meiji Era*, trans. Edward Seidensticker (Tokyo: Ōbunsha, 1956)

Kubo Sakae. *Osanai Kaoru: shingekishi no tame ni* (Osanai Kaoru: for the history of shingeki) (Tokyo: Kadokawashinsho, 1955)

Ōyama Isao. *Kindai Nihon gikyokushi, Taishōhen* (History of Japan's modern drama, Taishō period) (Yamagata: Kindai Nihon Gikyokushi Kankō-kai, 1969)

Powell, Brian. *Kabuki in Modern Japan: Mayama Seika and His Plays* (London: Macmillan, 1990)

FOCUS 6.1 SADAYAKKO: FIRST MODERN ACTRESS

Anderson, Joseph L. *Enter a Samurai: Kawakami Otojirō and Japanese Theater in the West,* vols. I and II (Tucson, AZ: Wheatmark, 2011)

Downer, Lesley. *Madame Sadayakko: The Geisha Who Seduced the West* (London: Review, 2003)

Kawakami Otojirō. *Jiden Otojirō, Sadayakko* (The autobiography of Otojirō and Sadayakko) (Tokyo: San'ichi shobō, 1984)

Salz, Jonah. "Intercultural pioneers: Otojirō Kawakami and Sada Yakko," *Journal of Intercultural Studies* 20 (1993), 25–73

FOCUS 6.2 TSUBOUCHI SHŌYŌ: ROMANTIC VISIONARY

Morton, Leith. "Translating the alien: Tsubouchi Shōyō and Shakespeare," in Leith Morton, *The Alien Within: Representations of the Exotic in Twentieth Century Japanese Literature* (Honolulu: University of Hawai'i Press, 2009), 10–42

FOCUS 6.3 *TABI-SHIBAI*: BARNSTORMING TROUPES

Ichikawa Hiroyoshi *et al.* (eds.). *Taishū bunka jiten* (Dictionary of popular culture) (Tokyo: Kōbundō, 1994), 451–6

Ivy, Marilyn. *Discourses of the Vanishing: Modernity Phantasm Japan* (Chicago, IL: University of Chicago, 1997)

Nygren, Christina, "Tabi shibai: popular theatre in context," in Stanca Scholz-Cionca and Samuel L. Lciter (eds.), *Japanese Theatre and the International Stage*, Brill's Japanese Studies Library 12 (Leiden: Brill, 2000), 231–40

Powell, Brian. "'Taishū engeki and the dwindling masses," *Japan Forum* 3:1 (1991), 107–13

Uchigawa Hideharu. *Waga ichiban taiko: tabi yakusha Kataoka Chōjirō* (My curtain call: Kataoka Chōjirō the travelling actor) (Tokyo: Tsukushisha, 1986)

Ukai Masaki. *Taishū engeki e no tabi* (Journey towards popular culture) (Tokyo: Shōraisha, 1994)

Interlude: Modern comedies and early musicals

NAKANO MASAAKI

One Western custom that quickly took hold in Tokyo and other urban centers among working- and middle-class audiences early in the twentieth century was a night out for vaudeville-style light comedy or musical entertainments.

Light comedy in major Osaka kabuki productions

Soganoya Gorō (1877–1948) and Soganoya Jūrō (1869–1925) were originally actors of minor roles in major Osaka kabuki productions. In 1904 they founded the first Japanese troupe specializing in "comedies" (*kigeki*, 喜劇), which came to enjoy nationwide fame as Soganoya Comedy. Their early performances were updated versions of traditional *niwaka shibai*, impromptu farce performed mainly by non-professionals at parties and in the street.

Soganoya Comedy employed stage properties, sound effects, music, and costumes, but its contents reflected the spirit of the new age, as in their masterpiece, *Muhitsu no gōgai* (Newspaper extra for the illiterates, 1904). Premiering three days after the Russo-Japanese War began, it was a farce about illiterate people who mistake the advertising bills of a Western-style restaurant for a newspaper extra reporting on the declaration of war. Soganoya Comedy established the basis for Japanese modern comedy, incorporating the customs and spirit of the new era. Both Gorō and Jūrō wrote and directed the scripts, and performed the principal roles. Their work, especially Gorō's, was popular for its sentimental human touches, mingling common people's delights and sorrows with laughter.

In 1911, the Teikoku Gekijō (Imperial Theatre) opened in Tokyo as Japan's first full-scale Western-style theatre: it had a steel-framed, reinforced concrete structure, chair seating, and European-style facilities such as restaurants, smoking rooms, and cloakrooms. European-educated industrialist Masuda Tarō (1875–1953), one of its executive directors, also wrote light, sophisticated comedies and musicals. While Soganoya Comedy's audiences

Fig 33 Takagi Tokuko (right) and Asakusa Opera revue, 1918.

were mostly working-class townspeople, those attending Masuda's works were middle class. Masuda's comedies were far more modern, played and sung by actresses educated at the Imperial Theatre Academy, modeled on European operettas and music hall repertoire.

Musicals for the masses: Asakusa Opera

Regular commercial performances of Japanese operas, the archetypal synthesis of European arts, were intended as a sure means to make the Western world recognize the extent of Japanese modernization. The training program for opera and ballet performers at the Imperial's Music and Drama Department, however, had to be canceled after five years through a failure to attract audiences. Furthermore, managers of privately operated theatre had little financial success in presenting new forms for upper- and middle-class audiences, including comedies, Shakespeare, Ibsen, operas, and ballets, or with dramas featuring actresses in female roles. The most stable source of theatrical income remained kabuki.

Ironically, it was the Asakusa entertainment district – regarded by both the intelligentsia and the well-to-do as a place for low-brow shows – that managed to develop spectators with real enthusiasm for opera and ballet. Takagi Tokuko (1891–1919), after several years' experience at American vaudeville theatres, established the Variety Company (1916) and the Kabugeki Kyōkai

(Association for Song-and-Dance Dramas, 1917), then began producing at Asakusa's Tokiwa-za. These productions proved successful in attracting spectators through American-style musicals and operettas such as *Jogun shussei* (A female army goes to war, 1917), a satire on World War I by Iba Takashi (1887–1937). Many similar musical theatres were soon established, including Takarazuka; the new genre known as "Asakusa Opera" was born.

The core repertoire of Asakusa Opera was original musical comedies or translated operas and operettas, adapted to be more comprehensible to audiences unfamiliar with such works: straight plays and dances, including ethnic dances from Spain and Hungary; modern dance by German Expressionist-influenced Ishii Baku (1886–1962), the founder of modern dance in Japan; and the 1919 production of Maxim Gorky's *The Lower Depths* by Tokiwa-za, led by Dadaist novelist Tsuji Jun (1884–1944). Western music and musical dramas, even if amateurishly performed, were made accessible through adaptation and editing. Offered at inexpensive ticket prices, they gained great popularity with young spectators. As many as half of all Tokyo residents attended Asakusa Opera.[14] However, when the theatre district burned down after the Great Kantō Earthquake (1923), Asakusa Opera fell into rapid decline.

Mass entertainment moves from stage to film

Soganoya Comedy, Masuda's comedy, and the works of Teikoku Gekijō were the foundation of modern theatre entertainment in Japan. Soganoya Comedy successors, such as Fujiyama Kanbi (1929–90), with light human comedy, were succeeded by the popular, long-running film series *Tora-san* (*Otoko wa Tsurai yo*, 1969–97), produced by Shōchiku, long-time sponsor of Soganoya Comedy.

Masuda's comedy and Asakusa Opera performers later became active in revues, musicals, and, most importantly, light dramas (*kei-engeki*) – a general term for a Western-style vaudeville entertainment format combining musicals, light comedy, slapstick, and sketch comedy. This variety format was popular among a wide range of people, extensively employed on stage, screen, and television from the 1930s to 1960s, producing such top entertainers as "the king of Japanese comedy" Enomoto Ken'ichi (aka "Enoken," 1904–70), Furukawa Roppa (1903–61), and comedy troupes such as the Moulin Rouge Shinjuku-za (1931–51), Hana Hajime and the Crazy Cats (1955–2006), and the Drifters (1956–). Many involved in these earlier musicals contributed to the postwar boom in American-style musicals and commercial comedy (see p. 285).

---

14 Masui Keiji, *Asakusa opera monogatari* (All about Asakusa opera) (Tokyo: Geijutsu Gendaisha, 1989), 192.

References and further reading

Hata Ippei. *Kigekijin mawari butai – utau stā gojū nenshi* (Comedian on stage – fifty years of a singing star) (Tokyo: Gakufushoin, 1958)

Masui Keiji and Shōwa Ongaku and Daigaku Opera Kenkyūsho (eds.). (Opera Institute of Showa University of Music) *Nihon opera shi~1952* (History of opera in Japan to 1952) (Tokyo: Suiyōsha, 1958)

Nakano Masaaki. *Moulin rouge Shinjuku-za – Shōwa kei-engeki shōshi* (Moulin Rouge Shinjuku Troupe: a history of light dramas in the Shōwa era) (Tokyo: Shinwasha, 2011)

Interlude: Takarazuka: all-girls' revue and musicals

YAMANASHI MAKIKO

The Takarazuka Revue Company is an all-female theatre that began as the Takarazuka Shōjo Kageki (Takarazuka Girls' Opera) in 1914 at a spa town near Kobe in western Japan. A cultural venture of Kobayashi Ichizō (1873–1957), the Hankyū Railroad industrialist, the town was planned as a leisure destination for affordable family entertainment; it also featured a botanical garden, zoo, and amusement park. The Takarazuka Gekijō (Takarazuka Theatre) grew into its most popular feature, the only attraction remaining today.

Takarazuka's first performance was *Don-Burako*, based on the folktale *Momotarō* (Peach boy), staged in modified kabuki style, one of the first successful operettas employing Western music sung in Japanese. Kobayashi's goals were to establish a modern Japanese musical theatre as well as to change conventional assumptions that the only professional female performers were geisha.

Student professionals

The Takarazuka Music School was established in 1919, with artistic and moral instruction based on Kobayashi's maxim, "Purity, Honesty, Beauty" (*Kiyoku, Tadashiku, Utsukushiku*). Takarazuka recruited educated, middle-class girls, and trained them as respectable "students" (*seito*). Today, only girls, from 15 to 18 are allowed to audition for the school; successful candidates must remain unmarried. The school provides two years of training in Western and Japanese performing arts – singing, dancing, and acting. All Takarazuka performers are graduates, performing as "students" and maintaining a strict senior–junior hierarchy throughout their careers.

Each troupe features a top star, usually a male-role performer (*otokoyaku*) paired with a female lead (*musumeyaku*). Takarazuka has in-house playwright-directors, composers, and orchestras that include both men and women. The company consists of five troupes of about eighty professional performers each: Flower (1921–), Moon (1921–), Snow (1924–), Star (1933–), and Cosmos (1998–).

Fig 34 Takarazuka Grand Revue: greeting fans at curtain call finale.

Foreign adaptations

Takarazuka has been responsible for introducing many forms of foreign culture to the Japanese public. The 1924 Daigekijō (Grand Theatre, 3,500 seats) featured advanced stage technology (see p. 428). The first Japanese revue, *Mon Pari* (*My Paris*, 1927), was followed by the more spectacular *Parizetto* (*Parisette*, 1930), which established the Takarazuka revue style. The company produced original scenarios as well as adaptations of foreign works, creating multicultural hybrid spectacles. Music and choreography, derived from flamboyant European revues and American shows, included fast tempos and geometrical choreographic formations. Popular French chansons were indigenized, as were jazz sections and visual extravaganzas in the manner of the Ziegfeld Follies. It was socially accepted for Japanese women to break taboos; these high-kicking line dances by respectable girls were enjoyed by middle-class family audiences.

In the 1930s, Western-style productions starring otokoyaku gained popularity among Japanese female audiences, who continue to comprise the large majority of Takarazuka audiences. The use of otokoyaku accentuates gender differences by requiring female performers to create idealized males. Takarazuka fans are devoted to their stars – leading otokoyaku have the biggest fan base, who wait outside the theatre, give them presents, and correspond with them by letter or Internet. Their role is like that of an encouraging mother or sister.

In 1934, the company acquired its own theatre in Hibiya, the Tōkyō Takarazuka Gekijō (Tokyo Takarazuka Theatre), and gained nationwide recognition. Microphones and amplified sound were introduced, further enabling grand spectacle and song. In Japan's period of colonial expansion, Takarazuka toured Manchuria and other overseas locations, performing for troops and the Japanese emigrant population. Except during World War II, when such extravagances were banned by government policy, Takarazuka has continually presented its revues. During the American Occupation, the Tokyo Takarazuka Theatre was taken over for the recreation of American ser-vicemen (renamed the Ernie Pyle Theatre after the late American war cor-respondent), but it returned to Japanese ownership and its old name in 1955.

Today the company's various troupes perform simultaneously in the Ta-karazuka Grand Theatre and Bow Hall (a 500-seat theatre annex), and Tōkyō Takarazuka Gekijō, as well as other regional theatres, and occasionally on tours abroad. A typical program consists of a musical play followed by a revue-like show with a grand finale in which major stars descend the "grand staircase," with headliners wearing elaborate costumes decorated with ostrich feathers. Representative classic works are frequently revived, including *Genji monogatari* (The tale of Genji, 1919) and *Romeo and Juliet* (1933). The Broad-way musicals *Oklahoma!* (1967) and *West Side Story* (1968) were premiered in Japanese by Takarazuka. Another popular play is *Kaze to tomo ni sarinu* (Gone with the wind), first performed in 1977 and staged more than 1,200 times.

From manga to musical

In the 1970s, when many foreign companies toured Japan, bringing their own casts, Takarazuka had to look for new material in order to compete. Their adaptation from a *shōjo manga* (girls' comic book), *Berusaiyu no bara* (The rose of Versailles, 1974), both renewed and reinvented the image of Takarazuka. The romance, exotic locales, and dramatic encounters of the teenage manga phenomenon proved easily adaptable to Takarazuka's artistic style. Staged more than 1,500 times, it is considered the most successful Ta-karazuka work to date. Since this happy marriage, Takarazuka has adapted a number of manga, anime (animated film/television), and game plots into musicals, including Tezuka Osamu's *Black Jack* (1994) and *Gyakuten Saiban* (Phoenix Wright, 2008). Another hit is the adaptation of the Viennese musi-cal *Elisabeth*, first staged in 1996.

Takarazuka has always been an important institution to train and pre-sent distinguished singers, film stars, and stage actresses, including Koshiji Fubuki, Otori Ran, Asami Rei, Amami Yuki, Maya Miki, and Dan Rei, to name a few.

References and further reading

Brau, Lori. "The Women's Theatre of Takarazuka," *TDR* 34:4 (1990), 79–95

Kobayashi Ichizō. *Takarazuka manpitsu* (Notes on Takarazuka) (Osaka: Hankyū Dentetsu, 1980)

Robertson, Jennifer. *Takarazuka: Sexual Politics and Popular Culture in Modern Japan* (Berkeley: University of California Press, 1998)

Stickland, Leonie Rae. *Gender Gymnastics: Performing and Consuming Japan's Takarazuka Revue* (Melbourne: Trans Pacific Press, 2008)

Yamanashi, Makiko. *A History of the Takarazuka Revue since 1914: Modernity, Girls' Culture, Japan Pop* (Leiden: Brill-Global Oriental, 2012)

7 ✎ Rise of *shingeki*: Western-style theatre

GUOHE ZHENG

Shingeki had its heyday from around 1929 to the end of World War II. By 1929, the spotlight of modern Japanese theatre had already shifted from pioneering artistic expressions of Tsukiji Shōgekijō to proletarian theatre. Inspired by Marxist ideals to fight for the working majority instead of entertaining only the intellectual few, proletarian theatre artists produced pieces that strongly influenced the audience, turning shingeki into a school about capitalism. This provoked government suppressions, which led to political apostasy by shingeki leaders, while a separate group of artists pursued apolitical shingeki.

The split of Tsukiji Shōgekijō

As Powell notes in the preceding chapter, the pioneering Tsukiji Shōgekijō company split into two troupes in March 1929. Several factors can be identified as immediate causes. Co-founders Osanai Kaoru and Hijikata Yoshi had conflicting artistic visions for the company, with Osanai aiming at pre-Revolution Stanislavski-style realism, while Hijikata targeted more innovative approaches to theatre including Expressionism and those of Meyerhold. Meanwhile, financially, the company faced difficulties for most of its existence. Each time a deficit was incurred, Hijikata would cover the loss personally. Hijikata's position as co-founder and his constant financial sacrifice made sympathetic company members find it unfair of the majority to try to expel him.

Politics had played a decisive role in the shingeki movement's orientation, from before the split to the postwar period. As early as January 1926, actor Senda Koreya (1904–94) resigned from the company because he could not bear its art for art's sake orientation, a clear sign of Marxist influence. His political consciousness was awakened in the aftermath of the Great Kantō Earthquake in September 1923, which killed over 100,000 in fires, tsunami, and landslides. In the wake of this devastation, anti-Korean sentiment and rumors fueled violent mobs and police to attack Koreans as saboteurs. Senda was taken to be a Korean provocateur near Sendagaya Station in Tokyo, and almost killed. This incident prompted him to take a lifelong critical stance against authoritarianism and assume his professional name, homonymous to "Sendagaya Korean."

Other members, including Kubo Sakae (1900–58) and Susukida Kenji (1898–1972), were also attracted to Marxism. They formed the Young Tsukiji School (Seinen Tsukiji-ha), a secret study group, and even tried to stage a play of their own selection. Moreover, at lengthy all-member meetings in early 1928, it was proposed that the company change its slogan from the noncommittal "experimental theatre lab," with its art for art's sake nuance, to one that actively sought a social role. Yet Osanai and Hijikata were divided on this issue, with Hijikata moving toward the left and Osanai less sensitive to the social forces shaping shingeki. The final unanimous decision was for the company to be an academic theatre. But before that, Tsukiji Shōgekijō had already staged Marcel Martinet's *Evening* (*Yoru*) in 1926, its first production of a proletarian piece, and witnessed angry shouts from the deeply engaged audience. To many members, political engagement was a tide shingeki should not – and could no longer – ignore or escape.

In March 1929, less than two weeks after announcing their resignation from Tsukiji Shōgekijō, six former members, including Maruyama Sadao (1901–45), Yamamoto Yasue (1902–93), and Susukida Kenji, launched the Shin Tsukiji Gekidan (New Tsukiji Company), with Hijikata as director. The remaining thirty-five members renamed the company Gekidan Tsukiji Shōgekijō (Theatre Tsukiji Little Theatre). Both companies still shared the building and, confusingly, also the word "Tsukiji" in their names. For the sake of clarity, the former will be referred to hereafter as New Tsukiji, the latter as Theatre Tsukiji.

From the beginning, New Tsukiji took a direction different both from the art for art's sake tendency of Tsukiji Shōgekijō and from the revolutionary agenda of Sayoku Gekijō (Left-wing Theatre), the mainstream proletarian theatre formed the year before, evident in its opening manifesto, drafted by Kubo Sakae:

> Great efforts will be made to create a close union between theatre and the spirit of the times. We believe that such a union is the only means to ensure that theatre will not be turned into a tool for reactionary propaganda, nor monopolized by the minority intellectual class, but become the most entertaining and fulfilling gathering place for the newly emerging general masses – all within the limits of the current social system.[1]

1 Ōzasa Yoshio, *Nihon gendai engekishi shōwa senchū hen I* (A history of modern Japanese theatre: Showa wartime 1) (Tokyo: Hakusuisha, 1993), 53–4; Sugai Yukio, *Tsukiji shōgekijō* (Tsukiji Little Theatre) (Tokyo: Miraisha, 1971), 80 (translations by author unless otherwise noted).

The reason behind New Tsukiji's new direction is evident. Avoidance of political radicalism was seen as the only way any company could survive, a lesson taught to shingeki practitioners through hard experience with the authorities; the desire to expand its audience beyond intellectuals and students derived from the need to avoid the financial problems that had plagued Tsukiji Shōgekijō. It turns out that shingeki leaders would find themselves grappling with the very same issues at critical junctures throughout shingeki history.

New Tsukiji's debut plays in May 1929 demonstrate both their softened social activism and populist tendencies. *Tobu uta* (Flying songs) by Kaneko Yōbun (1893–1985) depicts an early Meiji masterless samurai who criticizes the government by adapting folk songs and ballads. *Ikeru ningyō* (A doll to be manipulated), an adaptation by Takada Tamotsu (1895–1952) of Kataoka Teppei's novel, is a modern satire showing how an ambitious young man attempts to climb the social ladder only to be cheated. The production was successful in attracting the working class, with an average daily attendance of over 400 to the 468-seat theatre.

The momentum of proletarian theatre

The split of Tsukiji Shōgekijō took place when the proletarian theatre movement was gaining momentum. With its origins around 1900, when the Japanese labor movement started, accompanying the development of Japanese capitalism, the movement regained strength in the Taishō period (1912–26) after setbacks following the High Treason Incident in 1910–11.[2] Inspired by the success of the 1917 Russian Revolution, it became even more active in the late 1910s. An amateur Workers' Theatre was formed in 1920 to promote the labor movement. The performance by Workers' Theatre impressed future shingeki leaders Osanai, Hijikata, and Akita Ujaku (1883–1962), leaving Hijikata with a permanent predilection for theatre with a social theme, inspiring him to study in Europe. Workers' Theatre activities, however, were brought to a sudden end on 3 September 1923 when Hirasawa Keishichi (1889–1923), the most talented worker-playwright and actor, was killed by police for alleged arson and poisoning of well-water following the Great Kantō Earthquake.

Yet the proletarian theatre movement continued unabated. An intellectual shingeki group, Senku-za (Pioneer Theatre), had been formed in early 1923 out of a drama-reading salon created by Akita Ujaku. Members of Senku-za

---

2 In May 1910, police charged twenty-six leftists with attempting to assassinate the Emperor. Even though only five were arguably involved in the plot, twelve were hanged in 1911, including Kōtoku Shūsui (1871–1911), Japan's best-known socialist. The case was used by the authorities as pretext to silence dissidents leading to heightened repression of ideologies deemed subversive.

joined the Drama Section of the Japan League for Proletarian Arts and Literature (Puroren) *en masse* when it was founded in December 1925. Before the Drama Section was dispatched to perform in support of workers of a printing company on strike in February 1926, it acquired the name of Trunk Theatre (Toranku Gekijō), the idea being that if all props were packed into a trunk, theatre could be performed anywhere – in reality they could not afford even a trunk, making do with *furoshiki* wrapping cloths. Trunk Theatre marked the beginning of professional proletarian theatre. Its members included Senda, who had recently left Tsukiji. In 1927, Trunk Theatre was renamed Proletarian Theatre. In 1926, Zen'ei-za (Vanguard Company) was created as "a serious proletarian theatre to counter bourgeois theatres." Zen'ei-za's Anatoly Lunacharsky's *The Liberated Don Quixote* was debuted at Tsukiji Shōgekijō the day after Tsukiji's production of its own first proletarian play on 5 December 1926, evidence of their close ties. Zen'ei-za became Zen'ei Gekijō (Vanguard Theatre) in 1927 and in April 1928 it merged with Proletarian Theatre to become the influential Tōkyō Sayoku Gekijō (Tokyo Left-wing Theatre), commonly known as Sayoku Gekijō, ending a series of reorganizations in the proletarian theatre movement.[3] (See Table 7.1.)

The influence of proletarian theatre grew stronger following the tremendous success of *Bōryokudan ki* (An account of a gang of thugs, 1929) by Murayama Tomoyoshi (1901–77), acclaimed "a masterpiece of proletarian literature." Based on the famous "7 February 1923 Strike" in China,[4] the play portrays the railway workers' struggle to form a union to protect their rights even when one of their leaders is killed by ruffians hired by police and warlords.

From December 1928 through May 1931, organizations were created or merged to guide the surging proletarian cultural movement. These include the new NAPF (All Japan Federation of Proletarian Art Organizations), reorganized in 1928, PROT (The Japan Proletarian Theatre League), created in 1929 as a member of NAPF with Sayoku Gekijō at its core, and the Coordinate Association of New Theatre Companies (Shinkō Gekidan Kyōgikai) created in 1929. When Tsukiji Shōgekijō split, PROT issued a statement denying any involvement. It refers to both of the newly created companies as part of the progressive theatre movement and calls on both to join hands in the fight for the proletariat. Indeed, both produced plays of serious social criticism. Plays produced from May to October 1929 by Theatre Tsukiji, for example, include Aleksei Faiko's *Mr. Bubus*, Fujimori Seikichi's *Haritsuke Monzaemon*

---

3 Ozasa Yoshio, *Nihon gendai engekishi shōwa senzen hen* (A history of modern Japanese theatre: Showa prewar) (Tokyo: Hakusuisha, 1990), 461, 463, 473.

4 Workers on strike along the Beijing–Hankou rail line attempting to launch a general union were attacked by Warlord Wu Peifu, with fifty-two killed. Though the attempt failed, this was the first national-scale strike led by the Chinese Communist Party. It demonstrated the power of the emerging working class and helped increase the influence of CCP, founded less than two years earlier.

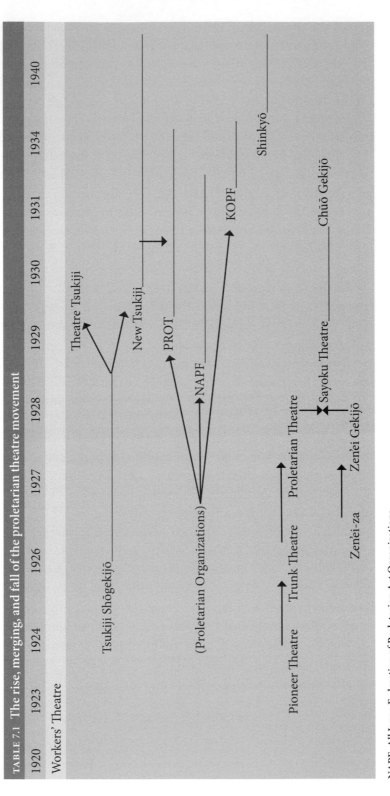

TABLE 7.1 The rise, merging, and fall of the proletarian theatre movement

NAPF: All Japan Federation of Proletarian Art Organizations
PROT: Japan Proletarian Theatre League
KOPF: Japanese Federation of Proletarian Cultural Organizations

(Monzaemon crucified), Maxim Gorky's *Mother*, Sergei Tretyakov's *Roar, China!* and *Ahen sensō* (The Opium Wars) by Ema Shū (1889–1975). Similarly, those by New Tsukiji following its above-mentioned first production include Fujimori Seikichi's *Nani ga kanojo o sō saseta ka* (What caused her to do it?), Gorky's *Mother, To the North of 50° North Latitude*, adapted from Kobayashi Takiji's novel *Kanikōsen* (The cannery boat), and *Rasupūchin no shi* (Grigorii Rasputin's death) by Maedakō Hiroichirō (1888–1957). Despite the lingering mutual grudges, the two troupes collaborated in promoting left-wing theatre, as seen in their rival productions of Gorky's *Mother* and Erich Maria Remarque's anti-war *All Quiet on the Western Front*.

While these activities were going on, however, external and internal factors resulted in multiple crises for Theatre Tsukiji. In July 1929, Shōchiku offered them the use of its Hongō-za Theatre, a business decision which, given the prosperity of proletarian theatre, Theatre Tsukiji accepted out of financial need. Theatre Tsukiji's association with a bourgeois commercial company was criticized by Sayoku Gekijō. However, such criticism alienated some of Theatre Tsukiji's right-wing members. Seven members resigned in December 1929. Later, when Shōchiku took its offer back, the troupe resorted to staging "reactionary" works in the name of "camouflage" or "temporary retreat." For this reason, Theatre Tsukiji was expelled from the Coordinate Association of New Theatre Companies in May 1930. Then Takizawa Osamu (1906–2000), a left-wing actor, resigned from what he called the "reactionary Theatre Tsukiji" and joined Sayoku Gekijō. Others followed suit, leading to Theatre Tsukiji's disbandment in the winter of 1930.

In contrast, New Tsukiji, with more unified membership, remained committed to left-wing theatre. In March 1930, it collaborated with Sayoku Gekijō in the production of *Taiyō no nai machi* (The street without sun), another monumental piece of the proletarian theatre. Adapted from a novel by Tokunaga Sunao (1899–1958), it depicts the 1926 struggle of Kyōdō Printing workers against cuts in wages and working hours, which the Trunk Theatre was dispatched to support. In March 1931, New Tsukiji joined PROT, forming a tighter relationship with Sayoku Gekijō.

The shingeki movement had been monopolized by Tsukiji Shōgekijō from its birth to around 1928. By the end of 1928, however, the spotlight shifted to the activities of the politically more committed troupes. With the success of proletarian theatre and its increased influence, Kurahara Korehito (1902–91), theoretician of the proletarian literary movement, published articles that charted the course of the proletarian theatre movement for the next few years, as reflected in resolutions of PROT assemblies. At the second and third PROT assemblies in 1930 and 1931, it was decided that the theatre movement should be bolshevized, to help overthrow capitalism in Japan and establish a country modeled on Soviet Russia. In June 1931 Kurahara explained the rationale for the new guidelines, making a distinction between the roles of theatre movement leadership and of the participating working-class masses. His proposal, however, led to a heated debate on the direction of the movement which, in turn, led to the dissolution of NAPF and creation of the KOPF (Japanese Federation of Proletarian Cultural Organizations) in October 1931. The fourth assembly of PROT, held at the Tsukiji Theatre the same month, called for the creation of the nation's first theatre fan club to counter the cultural influences from bourgeoisie and fascists.

To implement these guidelines, new styles of theatre were performed in various factories and villages. An imitation of *Sprechchor* (speaking chorus), popular then in the German proletarian theatre movement, was introduced by Senda upon his returning to Japan in 1931 from Germany, where he had participated in proletarian theatre for nearly five years. *Ikita shimbun* (Living newspapers), the Japanese *Sprechchor*, was produced four times from 1931 to 1932. With its mobility, plain language, and easy-to-follow stories, but above all its close ties with current affairs, *Living Newspapers* proved effective in awakening the political consciousness of the working class. A further implementation of the new guidelines was the joint production by Sayoku Gekijō and New Tsukiji in 1931 of *Kaze no machi* (The windy town) by Vladimir Mikhailovich Kirshon. Thanks to productions of these plays, Tsukiji Shōgekijō came to be regarded as a school for the working class about themselves and global capitalism.

Government suppression of proletarian theatre

The wide influence of proletarian theatre could not escape the attention of the authorities. In fact, government suppression of proletarian theatre had never stopped, all in the name of the Chian iji hō (Peace Preservation Law). Enacted in 1925, this law was designed to suppress anything deemed subversive to the emperor system or the socio-economic system under it. For example, shingeki found itself the target of suppression multiple times in 1927 alone. In early April, when Tsukiji Shōgekijō was to stage Kitamura Komatsu's *Saru kara moratta kaki no tane* (The persimmon seeds from the monkey), a masque adapted from a folktale depicting exploitation by capitalists and the fighting of the working class against it, over 1,000 words were cut and the title was shortened to *The Persimmon Seeds*. Later that month, Fujimori Seikichi's *What Caused Her to Do It?* found itself in trouble. It is the story of orphan Sumiko who is sold off by her uncle, abused by a circus owner, and then made to suffer as a maid. Surviving a double suicide, she turns to the church for solace but finds only hypocrisy and corruption there. In total despair and desperate, she sets fire to it. The title question, projected onto a screen at the end of the play, was shortened to only *Her* to minimize the effects of its explicit criticism. In the notorious Hokkaido Incident, in August that year, the Proletarian Theatre was to tour Hokkaido with *Who Is the Biggest Fool?* by German Communist playwright Karl August Wittfogel. However, the production was banned at the last minute for its biting social critique, a deliberate action to deliver the maximum blow, leaving the troupe stranded without even return tickets to Tokyo. The suppression continued after 1927, forcing the change of Murayama's masterpiece from *An Account of a Gang of Thugs* to *Zensen* (Frontline), when premiered in 1929 and subsequent productions.

Shingeki fought against such suppression. At Tsukiji Shōgekijō, for example, censored lines were displayed by the entrance, or printed in the programs, for audiences to have a fuller view of the play as well as the extent of the suppression. Sometimes actors pantomimed the censored lines to convey the intended message.

But as Japan continued its imperialistic ambitions in China, as seen in the Manchurian Incident in 1931, the Shanghai Incident and the setup of the Manchukuo puppet regime, both in 1932, government control became even tighter, not just on proletarian theatre, but on all theatres. From March through May 1932, many KOPF and PROT leaders were arrested, including Murayama and Ozawa Eitarō. Moreover, the authorities started intimidating spectators as well. They would search them and, if illegal documents were found, put them in jail. Censorship and sudden, last-minute cancellations of productions by the state dealt devastating blows to practitioners' livelihoods. In February 1933, proletarian writer Kobayashi Takiji (1903–33) was arrested and tortured to death. In 1934, it was no longer possible to stage any play in the name of PROT or Sayoku Gekijō. Under these circumstances, KOPF disbanded itself in April, as did Sayoku Gekijō in June, even after adopting the neutral named Chūō Gekijō (Central Theatre), followed by PROT in July. The once flourishing proletarian theatre movement came to an end.

The grand union of shingeki artists in the era of Shinkyō and New Tsukiji

How to overcome the unprecedented crisis of theatre suppression became a vital question for all shingeki practitioners. At the height of the crisis in September 1934, Murayama, who had been released from prison toward the end of 1933, published an article calling for a grand union of all practitioners into one company to carry on shingeki activities. Murayama's call was quite a departure from the proletarian theatre guidelines mentioned above. Politically, for example, it called for "progressive and artistically conscientious" theatre, instead of the revolutionary theatre prescribed by PROT a few years earlier; artistically, it called for the pursuit of professional shingeki "not

limited to a certain style ... as long as it is not reactionary."[5] The realization
of the above two goals hinged on the solid financial independence of the
proposed grand company. Shinkyō Gekidan (New Cooperative Theatre) was
thus launched in September 1934, starting an era of Shinkyō-New Tsukiji,
the latter being the only surviving left-wing shingeki troupe.

The first production of Shinkyō, in November 1934, was *Yoake mae* (Before the dawn), an adaptation of Shimazaki Tōson's novel concerning the
dazzling changes in Japan from the arrival of Commodore Perry's Black
Ships in 1853 through the early Meiji period (1868–1912), and how these
changes betrayed the expectations of the protagonist as a student of the National Learning. This was followed, in the next three years, by a series of
historical plays produced by Shinkyō and New Tsukiji. These include *Ishida
Mitsunari* by Kishi Yamaji (1899–1973), portraying the warrior-lord during
the tumultuous period leading to Japan's unification under the Tokugawa
shogunate, Fujimori Seikichi's *Tenten Chōei* (Takano Chōei the wanderer),
depicting a late Edo period Dutch medicine doctor, and Yamamoto Yūzō's
Nyonin aishi (The sad story of a woman), portraying the impact of the opening of Japan on the life of a Meiji woman. Critics have pointed out that the
choice of historical topics during this period was to avoid trouble with the
authorities. Even when portraying past events, however, these authors still
tried to convey a sense of historical inevitability.

Nevertheless, a shift can be seen in the contemporary lives staged around
this period. Veteran proletarian playwright Hisaita Eijirō (1898–1976) exemplified this shift. His *Dansō* (Fault line) but particularly *Hokutō no kaze*
(Northeast wind), produced in November 1935 and March 1937 respectively, incorporated psychological portrayal of characters, a method suggested
to him by Kishida Kunio, which he would have associated with apolitical
playwrights and dismissed as bourgeois a few years earlier.

Proletarian ideology was not entirely absent in this period, of course, but
presented indirectly, best illustrated in Kubo Sakae's *Land of Volcanic Ash*
(1938), regarded as the best of left-wing works (see pp. 390–3). David G.
Goodman notes,

> Kubo had set out to write a play that would make a scientific case for the
> necessity of [Marxist] revolution in Japan, but circumstances forced him to
> conceal this message. What emerged instead as the play's principal theme
> was [protagonist] Amamiya's struggle to maintain his integrity and his grad-
> ual acceptance on purely empirical grounds of the validity of socialist ideas.[6]

5 Sugai Yukio, *Tsukiji shōgekijō* (Tsukiji little theatre) (Tokyo: Miraisha, 1971), 123–4.
6 Kubo Sakae, *Land of Volcanic Ash: A Play in Two Parts*, trans. David G. Goodman (Ithaca, NY:
   Cornell University Press, 1986), 9.

Such were some of the ways whereby Shinkyō and New Tsukiji artists tried to overcome the crisis of theatre suppression.

Massive crackdown on shingeki and political apostasy

Throughout 1940, the military government sponsored a series of events to celebrate the 2,600th anniversary of the enthronement of Japan's first emperor, the mythological Emperor Jimmu, and to boost the sagging morale of the population as the war with China dragged on. Shinkyō participated in the celebration with *Daibutsu kaigen* (The dedication of the Great Buddha) by Nagata Hideo (1885–1949) while New Tsukiji offered *Daini no jinsei* (Second life) by Satomura Kinzō (1902–45). Scholars take such participation to be gestures of collaboration with the authorities by the only two remaining left-wing shingeki troupes – the latter is unmistakably a pro-war piece. These tokens, however, did not stop the tide of the times from moving against them.

As Japan intensified its imperialist expansion following the Marco Polo Bridge Incident in July 1937, the military authorities took decisive actions against the left-wing shingeki movement. On August 19, 1940, Shinkyō and New Tsukiji, the two remaining left-wing troupes, were forced to disband, with more than a hundred members arrested. A particularly dark period began.

One vital consequence of the round-up was *tenkō*, political apostasy under state pressure, by numerous shingeki artists. Many shingeki detainees committed the so-called "pretended" (*gisō*) tenkō to be released from prison. Among them were Senda Koreya and Murayama Tomoyoshi. Kubo also committed pretended apostasy. Yet while Senda and Murayama continued shingeki activities upon release – under other people's names as their own licenses were suspended – Kubo stopped all public activities, concentrating instead on writing a biography of Osanai Kaoru and retranslating Goethe's *Faust*.

The impact of such pretended betrayal of beliefs was enormous. That generation of shingeki practitioners came of age after the Russian Revolution and under the influence of new European artistic trends such as Expressionism following World War I. As children of their times, they shared the big dream to make the world a better place through art, one that empowered them with a strong sense of righteousness and mission. Suddenly, confronted with long incarceration, torture, and even death, however, they chose false renouncement of their ideals. Pretended or not, tenkō was a traumatic experience, as captured by Murayama in his 1934 short story *Byakuya* (White night), written after his release. Known as Japan's first piece of tenkō literature, it tells of the joy of the newly acquired freedom of the protagonist, at the price of the contempt of all around him, and his sense of unfathomable emptiness. The title is metaphoric: the world after tenkō is a white night with nowhere to hide.

Tenkō is also defined broadly to refer to apostasy in contents seen in works of playwrights who may or may not have been arrested. Miyoshi Jūrō (1902–58), whose *Kubi o kiru no wa dare da* (Who fires him, 1928) had established him as an important proletarian playwright, is an example. His later works *Kirare no Senta* (Stabbed Senta, 1934) and *Bui* (Buoy, 1940), however, reflect his skepticism toward the proletarian movement and his eventual embrace of state ideology. Broadly defined, tenkō can also be seen in works by Murayama, Hisaita, and Mafune Yutaka (1902–77).

The artistic school attempts neutrality

As left-wing theatre practitioners were going through their triumphs and struggles, shingeki activities of a different nature were carried out by a separate group of practitioners sharing neither the political zeal nor the artistic principles of the former. The artistic school (*geijutsu ha*) was led by Kishida Kunio (1890–1954). Returning to Japan in 1922 after studying theatre in France for two years, Kishida established himself outside the proletarian theatre movement. As a playwright, he wrote fifty plays between 1924 and 1935; as a theorist, he is known for his 1930 dictum "One does not write a play in order 'to say something'; one 'says something' in order for there to be a play."[7]

Tomoda Kyōsuke (1899–1937) and his wife Tamura Akiko (1905–83) were two members of the artistic school. Eager to pursue shingeki as art, and fed up with constant disputes, they resigned from Tsukiji Shōgekijō before its split. After a stint with Theatre Tsukiji, they founded Tsukiji-za in 1932, its members including Sugimura Haruko (1906–97) and later Higashi-yama Chieko (1890–1980). Here they could do what they had long sought to do – study acting techniques, sneered at by some as petty bourgeois during their Tsukiji Shōgekijō days. Tsukiji-za enjoyed support from novelist, playwright, and shingeki director Iwata Toyoo (1893–1969), playwright Kubota Mantarō (1889–1963), and Kishida; works by all three were among the first pieces staged by Tsukiji-za. Until its dissolution for financial reasons in February 1936, Tsukiji-za staged twenty-nine productions, introducing numerous artistically oriented young dramatists. Most of these dramatists were disciples of Kishida and contributors to *Gekisaku* (Play writing), the

---

7 In Kishida Kunio, *Five Plays by Kishida Kunio*, ed. and trans. David G. Goodman (Ithaca, NY: Cornell University Press, 1995), 9–10.

Tsukiji-za in-house magazine, including Oyama Yūshi (1906–82), Tanaka Chikao (1905–95), and Morimoto Kaoru (1912–46).

Another artistic troupe, Sōsaku-za (Creative Theatre), was created in 1934 by a group who resigned from Tsukiji-za. Its first production was *Itachi* (Weasels) by Mafune. The powerful language of this play impressed even left-wing critics despite the play's lack of political agenda.

The most important troupe of the artistic school is undoubtedly Bungaku-za (Literary Theatre), launched in September 1937 under the leadership of Kishida, Kubota, and Iwata. A continuation of Tsukiji-za, it also challenged the dominance of politically oriented Shinkyō and New Tsukiji to prove the value of the Artistic School as creators of art. Yet the on-going conflict with China and increasingly tight government control made it impossible for Bungaku-za to stay immune to the interference of war and politics. For example, in the same month that Bungaku-za was launched, its key member Tomoda Kyōsuke was drafted and soon after killed in Shanghai. After the left-wing Shinkyō and New Tsukiji were forced to disband in 1940, Bungaku-za was the only major shingeki company allowed to continue. Nonetheless, it was told to cancel *Saijitsu no basha* (The holiday carriage) by Prosper Mérimée because it ridiculed the authorities. Theatre, even of the purely artistic kind, could not escape the politics of the times.

Mobilization and martyrdom: shingeki in the Pacific War

As Japan was dragged deeper into its Fifteen-Year War, no company could stand aloof from the war efforts. In October 1940, Kishida resigned from Bungaku-za after being appointed Cultural Minister of the newly created Imperial Rule Assistance Association. Morimoto accepted a commission by the government in 1943 to write a play to boost Japanese morale to help rescue the rapidly vanishing dream of Japanese Empire. The resulting *Onna no isshō* (A woman's life) was performed in Tokyo in April 1945 (see below). On the other hand, Morimoto also negotiated with the authorities to make possible productions of *Pekin no yūrei* (The ghosts of Peking, 1943) and *Chōjū gassen* (Battles of birds and animals, 1944), rare contemporary satires by Iizawa Tadasu (1909–94), which exemplify the complicated interactions between politics and shingeki.

All troupes had to tread a fine line. Kuraku-za (Bittersweet Theatre), launched in July 1942, planned to produce *Cyrano de Bergerac*, but this was banned by the Tokyo Police Department as a piece by an enemy country. In contrast, Bunka-za (Cultural Theatre), launched in April 1942 as the most collaborative of shingeki troupes, had no trouble with the authorities in staging Miyoshi Jūrō's *Mikkakan* (Three days), *Osa no oto* (The sound of the loom) and *Shishi* (The lion dance), all glorifying Japan's "sacred war."

As the war intensified and the Wartime Emergency Measure Outlines (Kessen hijō sochi yōkō) were announced in February 1944, the only way for shingeki artists to continue their activities was to join the Japan Mobile Theatre Association (Nihon Idō Engeki Renmei), a semi-governmental agency established in 1941. Under this agency, theatre was expected to shoulder the mission to send more troops to the front and more labor forces to factories and the countryside. All shingeki troupes organized mobile theatres, sent to perform throughout Japan from April 1945. During a tour in Hiroshima, actor Maruyama Sadao, who had struck the gong to open Tsukiji Shōgekijō in 1924, was killed, along with eight other members of the Sakura Mobile Theatre, by the atomic bomb, days before Japan surrendered on 15 August 1945.

Ironically, shingeki achieved some of its goals only during wartime. Government support and encouragement via prizes and supervised tours took shingeki to remote regions of Japan, where it was seen for the first time by large and enthusiastic audiences responding to propaganda pieces by native playwrights. The theatrical energy and popularity would enable a great surge in activity after political and artistic suppressions were lifted – temporarily, as it turned out, as seen in the following chapter.

REPRESENTATIVE PLAYS

Onna no isshō (A woman's life, 1945) by Morimoto Kaoru (1912–46)[8]

When 16-year-old war orphan Kei wanders into the Tsutsumi home on New Year's Eve 1905, the sympathetic Tsutsumi matriarch lets her stay as a maid. The widowed matriarch talks the diligent Kei into marrying Shintarō, her elder son, for the sake of the Tsutsumi China trade business, oblivious of Kei's secret love for Eiji, the younger son. Kei becomes the pillar of the family, but estranged from Shintarō due to different values. When Eiji returns in 1928 from China as a communist, Kei informs on him. Kei and Shintarō show signs of reconciliation when the latter suddenly dies.

Commissioned by Japan's military government, the play was first produced in April 1945 amidst air-raids. One of the most staged pieces in postwar Japan, revisions to *A woman's life* reflect the changing political winds. The original version opens with soldiers marching to the front after Pearl Harbor; Morimoto's postwar version envisions a democratized Japan;

---

8 Trans. by Guohe Zheng in J. Thomas Rimer, Mitsuya Mori, and M. Cody Poulton (eds.), *The Columbia Anthology of Modern Japanese Drama* (New York: Columbia University Press, 2014).

Fig 35 Sugimura Haruko in *Onna no isshō* (A woman's life; Bungaku-za, 1948).

Morimoto's memorial production in late 1946 celebrates the promulgation of Japan's new constitution; on tour in 1952, the opening scene celebrates the Japan–US Peace Treaty. In 1960, when a shingeki delegation visited China, the play included an apology for Japan's aggression there – even though originally commissioned to justify Japan's invasion of that country.

References and further reading

Ibaraki Tadashi. *Zōhō nihon shingeki shōshi* (A brief history of Japanese theatre: expanded edition) (Tokyo: Miraisha, 1973)

Kishida Kunio. *Five Plays by Kishida Kunio*, ed. and trans. David G. Goodman (Ithaca, NY: Cornell University East Asia Series, 1995)

Kubo Sakae. *Land of Volcanic Ash*, trans. David G. Goodman (Ithaca, NY: Cornell University East Asia Series, 1986)

Powell, Brian. *Japan's Modern Theatre: A Century of Change and Continuity* (London: Japan Library, 2002)

Sugai Yukio. *Tsukiji shogekijō* (Tsukiji Little Theatre) (Tokyo: Miraisha, 1971)

Toita Yasuji. *Taidan: Nihon shingeki shi* (Interviews: a history of modern Japanese theatre) (Tokyo: Seiabō, 1961)

Zheng, Guohe. "Reflections *of* and *on* the Times: Morimoto Kaoru's *A Woman's Life*" in David Jortner, Keiko McDonald, and Kevin J. Wetmore Jr. (eds.), *Modern Japanese Theatre and Performance* (Lanham, MD: Lexington Books, 2006)

Interlude: *Manzai* and Yoshimoto vaudeville comedy

JOEL STOCKER

Manzai is two-person bantering comedy providing a popular, running satiric commentary on fashions and foibles of modern urban life. Beginning in the Heian period (794–1185), manzai (萬歳 or 万歳) was a magico-religious rite evoking good fortune and long life, performed by a group (for aristocrats) or duo (for commoners) of *tayū* (lead role) and *saizō* (subordinate role), who would sing or chant, dance, and play a *tsuzumi* shoulder drum in celebration of the New Year. In the spirit of the Japanese expression "good fortune comes to a merry gateway," the performances included humorous and auspicious qualities, grounded in the foolish saizō's dancing and misinterpretation of solemn words, and antagonistic reactions of the tayū. Performed throughout the medieval period by low-ranking, itinerant priest-diviner-entertainers (*shomoji*) in rural and urban Japan, manzai evolved during the late eighteenth century into an entertainment on the streets and makeshift stages at shrines and temples in urban amusement districts of Kyoto, Osaka, and Edo.

From festive rite to stage art

During the Meiji era (1868–1912), manzai developed into a minor act in the small, affordable *yose* vaudeville theatres of the burgeoning cities, appealing mainly to commoners. From the late nineteenth century to the late 1920s, it became a protean variety act (*iromono*) of two to six men and women performing various combinations of comic banter, songs and dances, acting, and physical arts, such as juggling, accompanied by Japanese or Western musical instruments. Manzai entertainers incorporated *karukuchi* light banter, *niwaka* improvisations (including parodies) of scenes from more respectable performing arts, and regional *ondo* singing. In the 1920s, yose suffered as film theatres grew in popularity; however, while *rakugo* storytelling declined, the ever-adaptable manzai (written as 万才 "many talents" by the mid-1920s) actually grew in popularity.

Yokoyama Entatsu (1896–1971) and Hanabishi Achako (1896–1974) are generally credited as the first to perform purely dialogue-based, stand-up comedy – called *shabekuri-manzai* – while working under the Yoshimoto Entertainment Company (Yoshimoto Kōgyō; hereafter "Yoshimoto"), a theatre and talent management company established in Osaka in 1912. In an era when most performers and audiences were still wearing kimono, Entatsu sported a Western suit, small mustache, and round spectacles, as he and Achako stood like a couple of pedestrians chatting on an urban street corner. Their style was influenced by Western comic film stars (and former vaudevillians) such as Charlie Chaplin, Harold Lloyd, and Laurel and Hardy. They also distilled manzai into *boke* (fool) and *tsukkomi* (wit) characters, bantering in a cleaned-up, office-worker version of the Osaka dialect. Their crisp, condensed repartee revolved around contemporary events and lifestyles. Yoshimoto introduced the modern written characters for manzai (漫才), associated with such popular phenomena as *manga* (漫画) and *rōman* (romance, 浪漫), in 1933. Yoshimoto expanded this bantering style of short-form comedy, then shaped it into a nationally recognized modern entertainment genre by utilizing its network of theatres, radio, television, film coverage, and professional scriptwriters.

From stage to mass media

Most manzai performers and audience members were rural migrants newly experiencing city life, industrial labor, crowded living conditions, and the bright lights of large amusement areas. Uncertainty prevailed amid the newness of modern, urban daily life and, by the late 1920s, economic depression and military escalation. Manzai appealed to the working and middle classes (e.g. "salarymen") by mediating these uncertainties in an accessible and amusing style of conversation that addressed contemporary clashes between rural and urban life, tradition and modernity, and the regional dialect of Osaka and standard dialect of Tokyo, as well as native Japanese and imported Western cultures. During World War II, as part of government policy and entertainment companies' projects to promote the war effort, manzai acts from Yoshimoto's "Laughter Brigades" (*Warawashitai*) entertained Japanese troops in the "Greater East Asia Co-prosperity Sphere," then provided humorous tales of their overseas adventures for civilian audiences.[9]

After Japan's defeat, manzai entertainers made a comeback in Kansai-area theatres, and then by the 1950s on local and national radio and television

---

9 Barak Kushner, "Laughter as matériel: the mobilization of comedy in Japan's fifteen-year war," *International History Review* 26:2 (2004), 300–30.

shows. The genre experienced a "boom" in the early 1970s at the time of the Osaka Expo when over 64 million amusement-seekers converged on the region, and again in the early 1980s when the fast-paced, iconoclastic style of manzai appealed to youth born into an affluent consumer society with palpable generation gaps.

Today, manzai entertainers regularly perform at Yoshimoto's seven theatres (seating over 3,100 total) in Tokyo, Osaka, and Kyoto, frequently tour throughout Japan, and appear daily on dozens of radio and TV shows as game- and talk-show hosts and music MCs. Moreover, Yoshimoto's manzai-centered comedy schools enroll over 800 students a year, while manzai banter is also a popular hobby in school and community amateur clubs, making manzai and manzai-like patter ubiquitous throughout the country.

References and further reading

Horie Seiji. *Yoshimoto Kōgyō no kenkyū* (A study of Yoshimoto Kōgyō) (Tokyo: Asahi bunko, 1994)

Maeda Isamu. *Kamigata manzai happyakunen-shi* (Kyoto-Osaka Manzai: an 800-year history) (Osaka: Sugimoto shoten, 1975)

Mita Jun'ichi. *Shōwa Kamigata shōgeishi* (A history of Kyoto-Osaka arts of humor in the Showa period) (Tokyo: Gakugei shorin, 1993)

8 ⌒ Wartime colonial and traditional theatre

SAMUEL L. LEITER

The lead-up to World War II (sometimes referred to as "the Fifteen-Year War") dates back to the "Manchurian Incident" of 1931, but Japan's aggressive expansionist activities originated much earlier. Japan abandoned its centuries-old exclusionary policies with the arrival of Commodore Perry's "Black Ships" in 1853; other ambitious European powers soon followed. Inspired by the large-scale expansionism of the West during the late nineteenth century, Japanese imperialists realized as early as 1874 – when they gained control of the Ryūkyū Islands from China – that Japan could supplement its limited natural resources and fortify its defenses by gaining control of weaker Asian entities.

Military strength allowed for Japanese territorial expansion. In 1876, Japan forced Korea to concede special trading privileges; the Sino-Japanese War (1894–5) brought about the annexation of Formosa (Taiwan) and other valuable territories from China. The need to eliminate Russia as a competitor for power in Asia led to the Russo-Japanese War (1904–5). Japan's conclusive victory allowed it to acquire Guandong (Kwantung) Leased Territory and Karafuto (South Sakhalin). The way was thus cleared for the annexation of Korea in 1910, making Japan a major world power. In 1914, the Japanese Navy seized Nan'yo (Micronesia) from Germany under the terms of the South Pacific Mandate.

Japan's presence spurred the economic development of its new colonial territories, including railways, bridges, and other infrastructure that could bring Japan precious raw materials. However, it also imposed severely repressive colonialist controls, with Japanese military administrators keeping indigenous people in strict subjugation while the authorities, emulating Western colonial policies, existed in an elite Japan-centric society. Development of the colonized territories included both agricultural improvements and investment in heavy industry; education of both Japanese settlers and the local population was also a priority, with an emphasis on Japanese curricula, including teaching of the Japanese language.

∽ FOCUS 8.1　Theatre in Taiwan under colonization

Taiwan became a colony of Japan for half a century following China's defeat in the First Sino-Japanese War (1894–5). Resistance against Japan in the early days of colonization and Taiwan's Chinese heritage meant that *shingeki* (*huaju*, "spoken drama") developed there later than in Japan and China, yet was influenced by both.

Japan's governance of Taiwan went through three periods: tolerance of native traditions (1895–1918), Japanization (1919–36), and imperial assimilation (1937–45); these were reflected also in the development of shingeki. The Taiwan Cultural Association was promulgated by the Japanese in 1921 to "enlighten" the population. Two troupes attempted shingeki in 1924. The Xingguang Yanju Yanjiu Hui (Starlight Theatre Research Society) was launched by Zhang Weixian (1905–77) and others, staging Hu Shi's *Zhongshen dashi* (Marriage), *Furong jie* (Plunder of the hibiscus, playwright unknown), and *Konjiki yasha* (The golden demon), adapted from the novel and successful Japanese play by Ozaki Kōyō (1868–1903). Dingxin She (Innovation Theatre), founded by Chen Kan, Zhou Tianqi, and others, was influenced by student movements in Amoy, China. In collaboration with the Taiwan Cultural Association, it staged plays promoting social reforms such as *Shehui jieji* (Social classes) and *Liangxin de lianai* (Love with a clear conscience), both by Li Weixiu (1887–1940). Presaging the same fissure that would destroy the Tsukiji Shōgekijō (Tsukiji Little Theatre) in Japan, it split in April 1925, plagued by controversy over whether shingeki should be an art or a tool to change society.

Numerous troupes appeared across Taiwan from the mid-1920s through the mid-1930s, including Yanfeng Qingnian Jutuan (Yanfeng Youth Theatre), Tainan Wenhua Yanyi Hui (Tainan Cultural Theatre), and Anping Jutuan (Peace Theatre). These produced plays advocating freedom, like *Fei ziyou zhi ziyou* (Freedom without freedom), or protested against Japanese exploitation of Taiwanese laborers, like *Han*

Dalao (Mr. Simple-minded), both by Huang Jinhuo. Shingeki performances were well received, particularly by young people and intellectuals. Its influence alarmed the colonial authorities, which started to restrict shingeki and enforce a censorship system.

Artistically, however, the quality of shingeki was still low. To realize his ideal of shingeki, Zhang Weixian, its most prominent pioneer in Taiwan, studied in Japan from 1928 to 1932 at the Tsukiji Little Theatre and Waseda University. Returning to Taiwan, he organized the Minfeng Jutuan (People's Balefire Theatre), which outperformed Japanese competitors in a 1934 shingeki festival.

As Japan embarked on the road to war in the late 1930s, the policy of imperial assimilation forced all Taiwanese to become Japanese, and pledge loyalty accordingly. Shingeki was endorsed but put under tight control under the Kōmin Hōkōkai (Society of Devotion of Imperial Subjects) through the Taiwan Engeki Kyōkai (Taiwanese Theatre Association) whose staff was entirely Japanese. Many National Youth Volunteer theatres were organized, which, along with the Japanese-managed Nanshin-za (Southern Advance Theatre) and Takasago Company, staged plays mobilizing the population for war. Anyone involved in anti-Japanese movements was severely punished, as happened to shingeki activist Ye Jianchuang, who was tortured to death in February 1945. Even so, plays were staged covertly denouncing the Japanese or expressing Taiwanese suffering and hopes for the future, such as Jian Guoxian's (1917–53) *Alishan* (Alishan Mountains), *Yanji* (The castrated rooster) adapted from Zhang Wenhuan's (1909–78) novel, and Russian playwright Sergei Tretyakov's *Roar, China!*, all produced in 1943.

Shingeki continued in postwar Taiwan but faced the challenge of decolonization and re-sinicization and control by the Nationalist government.

GUOHE ZHENG

After 1919, the Japanese acculturation of indigenous populations greatly accelerated. The goal was to transform them into faithful Japanese who, in theory, shared the same imperial nationalist identity. In practice, distinctions between the colonized and the colonizers were evident; anti-Japanese attitudes were never far from the surface and, before World War II, emerged in protest activities, which usually were violently suppressed. Still, the imperialist project greatly enriched the homeland, enabling Japan, only fifty years after the Meiji Restoration, to attend the Versailles Peace Conference in 1919 as a member of the "Big Five" nations of the world.

By the 1930s, Japan's population was growing so dramatically that its ability to feed its citizens from its own agricultural sources was threatened, making it essential that the nation expand its foreign export markets. However, when foreign tariffs prevented this, the nation's militarists saw renewed colonialism as the best way to gain new markets and raw materials. In 1931 the Japanese army orchestrated the Manchurian Incident as pretext for an unjustified incursion into vast, resource-rich Manchuria;[1] soon a colonized puppet-state named Manchukuo was created. Reprimanded by the League of Nations, Japan simply withdrew from the organization.

During the 1930s, Japan's ongoing expansionist policies in China were threatened by the emerging power of the Chinese Nationalist government. In 1937, Japanese militarists precipitated another incident, this one near Beijing, which provided the Japanese with a pretext for seizing large parts of North China and Inner Mongolia. The Japanese sought to eliminate Chinese resistance by taking over the capital city of Nanking (now Nanjing) in a brutal conquest known as the "Rape of Nanking," and setting up a puppet government there.

The outbreak of war in Europe, which the Japanese believed would quiet European criticism, gave Japan the impetus to invade the mainstays of European colonialism in Southeast Asia. Simultaneous to the surprise attack of Pearl Harbor were attacks on European and American bastions in Malaya, Singapore, the Philippines, Hong Kong, and Shanghai. Ultimately, Japanese expansion grew to include much of northeastern China, including Manchukuo, Beijing, and Nanjing; much of coastal China, including Hong Kong; Burma, Thailand, Malaya, Dutch Indies (Indonesia), Borneo, the Philippines, the Celebes, New Guinea, and numerous Pacific islands. In 1940, the Japanese government promulgated a policy called the "Greater East Asia Co-Prosperity Sphere" as a front to justify its wartime occupation of non-Japanese territories.

---

1 On 18 September 1931 Japanese soldiers caused an explosion at the Japanese-controlled train line near Mukden (present-day Shenyang), and used it as a ruse to justify retaliatory strikes.

Theatre in colonies and occupied countries

The nationalist Japanese government employed a carrot and stick policy both at home and abroad, encouraging and subsidizing propagandist plays (dispersed regionally) while censoring severely and punishing those not aligned with militarist sentiments.

Japanese occupiers provided troops and new imperial citizens with entertainment. Noh theatres were built in colonies by businesses and the government, establishing cultural outposts for entertaining both emigrant and native populations. The Imperial Rule Assistance Association (Taisei Yokusankai; IRAA) sponsored regional and factory performances to encourage public efforts in service to the state. German educational theatre served as a model for the mobile theatre movement (*idō engeki undō*) which toured colonies and occupied areas, seeking to seduce native audiences with displays of music and dance that incorporated regional folk dances of Asia. The Takarazuka Revue Mobile Corps toured many of the territories, and invited dancers from Thailand and French Indochina, attempting to incorporate their dances. The Tōhō Dance Corps visited Korea, Indochina, and China frequently between 1940 and 1942, performing in large theatres in Shanghai and Nanjing, including over sixty performances for troops. Their 1942 *Peking* was performed in Japanese and Mandarin, and was broadcast by radio from China to Japan. Just as the Japanese language would be the new lingua franca for a harmonious East Asia, these hybrid musical performances sought to incorporate all of Asia into a light musical Japanese genre.

The Japanese encouraged native theatrical performances wherever they seized power, but only if theatre could be used as a propaganda tool. Depending on the circumstances, productions were in Japanese as well as in indigenous languages.

Korea, as Japan's closest neighbor, had always been a buffer and conduit to Chinese civilization. Japan effectively seized control of Korea in the first Sino-Japanese War (1894–5), and fought with China primarily on Korean soil and seaways. This control gave Japan vital iron and coal resources and agricultural products. Theatre development followed a familiar pattern of mass entertainment and attempts to unify native sentiment with the Japanese homeland, with noh taught and performed for expatriates.

Mainland China's modern theatre has a long and complex connection to Japan. Many of the early twentieth-century practitioners of the hybrid traditional–modern entertainment form *wenmingxi*, similar to and influenced by Japanese shimpa and 1920s spoken-word *huaju*, were young Chinese studying the advanced, modern theatre of Japan, and included the Spring Willow Society, Shanghai natives studying in Tokyo. When Japan

∞ FOCUS 8.2   Theatre in Korea under colonization

There has been renewed scholarly interest recently in prewar Japanese-language "national language drama" (*kokugogeki*), a tool of colonial propaganda that also stimulated early Korean attempts at a modern theatrical idiom. After formal colonization in 1910, Japan's governance of Korea went through four periods: (1) oppression of Korean culture by the military colonial government (1910s); (2) cultural liberalization (1920s); (3) Japanization (1930s); and (4) imperial assimilation (1940s to 1945).

The reception of Japanese modern theatre on the Korean Peninsula from the 1900s to 1945 varied according to dynamic intersections of power. Korea encountered Western plays in *shimpa* (new school) and *shingeki* (modern theatre) in Japanese, and in Korean, at different historical points. From 1905 to 1915, during extreme colonialist cultural oppression, large modern theatres such as the Engeikan (Yunyegwan, Arts Hall, 1915) enabled the visits of Japanese modern theatre troupes. In the 1920s, Korea's own modern theatre movement was suppressed by the colonial government. In the 1930s, as in Japan, social and political themes were censored, replaced by light comedies and musicals. During the 1940s, as part of the colonial project, Korean shingeki was forced to perform in Japanese.

The earliest performances of shimpa were given in theatres for Japanese residents. By 1915 Seoul (Keijō) had more than a dozen legitimate theatres established by the Japanese. The chief repertoire was shimpa domestic tragedies, acted by troupes imported from Kansai. Obviously, the principal audience for such works had to understand Japanese. Yet these productions inspired natives to produce similar plays in Korean; for example, Im Seung-gu (1887–1921) adapted Japanese originals, including Kawakami Otojirō's *The Sino-Japanese War* (1894).

The greatest influence on Korean theatre was the eleven-day tour to Busan and Seoul by the Geijutsu-za (1915) led by Shimamura Hōgetsu and Matsui Sumako. Western dramas like Tolstoy's *Resurrection* were received more enthusiastically than new Japanese dramas such as *Kamisori* (The razor) by Nakamura Kichizō (1877–1941). Soon after the Geijutsu-za departed, an identically named Korean troupe appeared, while several troupes performed Geijutsu-za plays in Korean.

Until the 1920s, Japanese plays were exported to Korea. The next two decades demonstrated a new phase: Koreans such as Hyun Chul (1891–1965) and Hong Hae-seung (1894–1957), who had studied shingeki in Japan, returned to Korea as modern theatre leaders, producing mainly naturalistic, social problem plays and Korean translations of Japanese translations of Western dramas. However, Hong, who had acted at the Tsukiji Little Theatre, Tokyo's main shingeki venue, produced popular shimpa-style sentimental plays rather than serious problem plays, mainly at the Tōyō Gekijō (in Korean: Dongyang; Asian Theatre, 1935). Unlike Japan, where shingeki effectively superseded shimpa in the 1920s, in Korea both shimpa and shingeki were still in vogue.

Japanese playwright Murayama Tomoyoshi (1901–77) had a great influence on post-1930s shingeki not only in Japan but also in Korea, stemming from his blending of shingeki with Korean traditions through his adaptation of *Shunko-den* (*Chunhyanjeon,* The story of Chunhyang, 1938) based on the most famous Korean *pansori* music-drama concerning a young woman's devotion to her husband, and her efforts to repel a government official's inappropriate advances. Although performances were highly acclaimed in Japan, Murayama's adaptation was severely criticized in Seoul for lack of understanding of Korean history and culture.

Just as Japan forced the Korean populace to speak Japanese as part of the assimilation process throughout the war, Korean shingeki was forced to produce its plays in Japanese. With Japan's defeat in 1945, Korean language shingeki was revived with such productions as *Hojeob* (Butterfly, by Kim Saryang), and the dismal period of colonization was forgotten in theatre circles.

HONG SEUNYONG

pushed aggressively for rights and representatives in China in 1915 with the "21 Demands," nationalist sentiment was aroused, with theatre practitioners becoming more politically conscious in resisting what they feared as creeping colonialism. Some early plays featured heroes of Korea's resistance movement, while Shakespeare and new plays expressed the importance of resisting tyranny, racism, and colonization.

As Japan continued its aggression in the 1930s, proletarian and nationalist modern theatre practitioners from all over, supporting both Nationalist and Communist sides, gathered in non-occupied China to stage living newspaper and realistic drama in opposition to the Japanese invasion. Nationalist and Communist propaganda united in their resentment toward the Japanese invaders. This precipitated a surge in patriotic theatre of all kinds: street theatre and tours to peasant villages by leading actors, the nurturing of amateur troupes employing local folk-dance styles within their dramatic expressions, and adapting historical plays expressing resistance. Thus the tools of dramatic and proletarian theatrical expression, many learned in Japan, were turned against the mentors' aggressive nation in subsequent decades. Despite the influx of Japanese performance forms and wartime austerity, Chinese theatre continued to grow in popularity and serve as a site of resistance to the invaders, in both urban and village settings. While some artists famously refused to perform for the Japanese (most notably Mei Lanfang, who grew a moustache to avoid performing female roles), other companies produced anti-Japanese plays, in both the *xiqu* and the huaju styles.

Taiwan became a colony of Japan for half a century following China's defeat in the First Sino-Japanese War. Japan's tolerance for native traditions soon gave way to acculturation policies, paralleling developments in Taiwan's modern theatre. Resistance against Japan in the early days of colonization, and Taiwan's reliance on mainland China for inspiration on new trends in cultural movements – some leaders were mainland-educated students – meant that modern theatre developed there later than in Japan and China, yet was influenced by both.

Throughout their occupation of China, Japan undertook a variety of means in order to "Japanicize" the conquered population; these ranged from the construction of Shinto temples and the introduction of Japanese dress and language to the redistribution of land. Theatre was also used as a propaganda tool, with performances being held both for expatriate Japanese and for the conquered Chinese populace. Noh performance styles were taught to expatriates in Shanghai and monthly amateur recitals were held. Similarly, other forms of Japanese performance, such as shamisen music and nihon-buyo dance were sought out by expatriate Japanese.

Tours, however, were the largest component of Japanese theatre in China during the war. Kabuki performers had been on tour in Japanese acquired territory before the war and continued this tradition, with tours to Manchuria in 1938 and to military bases in 1939. Shōchiku split their company into two groups in order to better cover occupied China in 1941. Touring companies also interacted with the Chinese counterparts; kabuki actor Onoe Kikugorō VI visited the Ron Chung Chinese Opera School and met with noted performer Ma Lianliang. In fact, the Japanese were very invested in the use of Beijing opera (*jingu*) in order to further their wartime aims; the puppet emperor Puyi endorsed this as well.

The Dutch Indies (present-day Indonesia) fell to Japan in a series of campaigns from February to April 1942. Initially welcomed by anti-Dutch nationalists enticed into the Asian Co-Prosperity Scheme under "big brother" Japan, Indonesians quickly learned the hardships of arbitrary arrests, executions, and forced labor (often overseas). Unlike the colonial assimilation policies of Taiwan, Korea, and mainland China, Indonesia was invaded and occupied, with various nationalist organizations encouraged to combat the Dutch and their Western allies. Japan maintained overall control by ceding authority to sympathetic regional leaders.

As in Japan, theatre in occupied territories received government subsidies and support as never before in its history – as long as it served the imperial mission of self-sacrifice, Asian unity, and the image of Japan as benevolent older brother.

Theatre in Japan during the Pacific War

In Japan itself, the government encouraged both traditional and modern forms of theatre to produce plays on patriotic themes, to emphasize nationalist goals, to elicit sympathy for victims of the military effort, or to demean the enemy. There were contests for plays supporting Japan's mission. Tours by professional companies were conducted to offer morale boosts to those at the front as well as throughout Japan. Non-Japanese playwrights and directors studying in Tokyo returned to their homelands to produce suitable modern dramas there. Professional actors participated actively in fundraising efforts on behalf of the war. Classic plays were revised to incorporate patriotic messages. Amateur and professional theatricals were produced in order to educate the home front audiences on wartime events, illustrate defensive preparedness, and promote labor peace. As homeland conditions deteriorated, theatregoing underwent numerous hardships and restrictions, performances were reduced, numerous theatres were destroyed by American bombs, and the ranks of theatre artists were depleted by conscription.

This section examines the wartime situation of Japanese traditional theatre domestically; modern theatre developments are covered in the preceding chapter.

1941

During the late 1930s, Japan's traditional theatres were under pressure to be used for propaganda purposes; this soon became vital to the wartime effort. Also, Japan's foreign activities created economic conditions that would seriously affect wartime productions. Such anxieties forced kabuki to replace the all-day, nine- or ten-hour system of a single program with two programs a day, which are still prevalent, even as ticket prices and taxes were hiked. News of Japan's early war victories temporarily boosted sagging attendance, but productions soon began suffering shortages of materials for stage properties, scenery, and costumes. More threatening were restrictions imposed on what people could wear, eat, say, and think. Even classics faced extinction if considered somehow unpatriotic. In April 1942, the government dissolved the Nihon Bungeika Kyōkai (Association of Japanese Writers), thereby silencing the literary world until the war's conclusion.

Actors made continuous efforts to ensure they were seen as enabling rather than critiquing the nascent powers, even raising funds to purchase fighter planes. Kabuki-za programs carried large war-bond advertisements and propaganda slogans, like "Onward! 100 million fireballs!" When news of Pearl Harbor was broadcast to the Kabuki-za audience, it stood for the national anthem and reading of the declaration of war.

The newly created League of Touring Theatres eventually offered "condolence" performances (*ian* or *imon*) of traditional and modern genres to 15 million farmers, fishermen, miners, and factory workers. At first, mainstream kabuki touring companies were headed by leading stars. But issues technical, financial, and content-related made touring problematic, and kabuki gradually decreased its involvement. Modern theatre proved easiest to organize; traditional theatres other than kabuki were not even included.

The government used cash prizes to sponsor new patriotic plays ("Citizen Dramas" [*kokumin engeki*]); only nine were produced in kabuki, eight set in the past. Several new works were inspired by the revenge classic *Chūshingura* (The treasury of loyal retainers), a model of feudal values, including Mayama Seika's *Genroku chūshingura* (Loyal retainers of the Genroku era), produced by the independent Zenshin-za company, which shifted at war's outset from prewar progressivism to rightist ideology.

In 1940 noh had voluntarily begun revising eighteen plays. Those showing an imperial family member unfavorably went unperformed. Past history inspired the nationalistic *Wake no Kiyomaro*, about the eponymous eighth-century priest, while *Chūrei* (Loyal souls of the dead) celebrated those who already had died on the emperor's behalf (kabuki and bunraku versions later appeared). Just before Pearl Harbor, an offertory production of the classic *Kokaji* (The swordsmith) was given; its plot, concerning a new sword being forged for the emperor, was viewed as symbolic of the coming war.

1942

Traditional theatre toured throughout Japan and Asia to propagandize on behalf of the new colonial rulers, with performances tailored to local needs by the Propaganda Corps. Despite overwhelming constraints on daily life, attendance jumped; theatre was one of the few pleasures available. Interest in traditional arts also increased because of top-down emphasis on nationalism, inspiring pride in premodern cultural achievements and traditional morality. After the Americans began bombing Tokyo on 18 April, theatres began closing earlier.

Kabuki was especially active in performing benefits to raise money for wartime needs. "Condolence" tours continued, while kabuki, noh, and kyogen began visiting the Asian mainland. Trips by noh were primarily to dedicate Shinto shrines in newly captured territory; having become part of Japan, these areas required the installation of a Shinto deity. The Kabuki-za was among seven theatres of different genres asked by police to present free monthly performances for troops.

Tokyo's Teikoku Gekijō (Imperial Theatre) was used in March for a series of Theatre for the Masses (Taishū-za) programs including traditional theatre. Noh master Umewaka Rokurō gave three days of performances, and in May even performed with Takarazuka actresses.

Various kabuki classics were condemned because of their emphasis on hedonism, personal feelings over family responsibility, and criminal behavior. Spurred by Japan's military successes, kabuki staged twenty new patriotic plays this year, some based on recent events, performed in contemporary clothes and settings.

In celebration of the 500th anniversary of Zeami's death, there were two anti-Western new kyogen plays, *Takara no shima* (Treasure island), about greedy British and American "devils," and *Arawashi* (Fierce eagle), concerning Japanese flyers. Among new chauvinistic noh plays published was *Yamada Nagamasa* (a seventeenth-century adventurer), inspired by the fall of Rangoon; ultimately, seventy-two such plays, mostly unproduced, were published. One performed in 1942 was *Yoshitsune*, in which the twelfth-century general is revealed as Genghis Khan. Meanwhile, Shanghai and large Mongolian cities hosted amateur noh overseen by professionals, who trained officers and expatriates.

∾ FOCUS 8.3　Theatre in Indonesia under occupation

The Dutch Indies (present-day Indonesia) fell to Japan in a series of campaigns from February to April 1942. With the invading troops came propaganda officers – military men and also civilian *bunkajin* (men of culture) – including playwrights, composers, and film directors tasked with stimulating the morale of the Imperial Forces and sympathy among the local populace for both the war effort and pan-Asian values. This required collaboration with Indonesian artists and intellectuals who typically communicated with their Japanese counterparts in English. Theatre, minimally supported by the Dutch, assumed sudden political importance under the Japanese. Through censorship and selective support, advisers and institutions, Japan worked with Indonesian artists to create various potent genres, and stoked a sense of nationalism that outlived the colonization.

Dutch, the language of the former colonizers, was forbidden; instead, schoolchildren memorized Japanese songs, danced in kimono, and enacted Japanese-language plays. The tale of Momotarō the Peach-boy, about a small boy and his animal friends fighting fierce, foreign ogres, was a favorite on stage and radio, and frequent subject of propaganda plays in Japan as well. Articles about traditional Japanese theatre appeared in newspapers and magazines. Indonesian storytellers were trained to perform propagandistic *kami-shibai* (street theatre using paper illustrations), traveling the countryside on bicycle or performing on the back of trucks in mobile propaganda units.

Sandiwara, a new coinage for spoken-language drama, replacing the Dutch-derived term *tonil*, was supported to an unprecedented degree. Public transport charges were waived for government-backed itinerant troupes that inserted propaganda messages into plays. Censorship laws introduced in January 1943 required scripts to be approved before performances, challenging actors accustomed to improvising. Propaganda offices sponsored script contests and published winning entries in magazines and newspapers, thereby creating a stock of plays for companies lacking playwrights.

The training academy Engeki Shidōsho (Theatre Guidance Center) was formed in June 1942 to train theatre performers, produce propaganda dramas, and create variety shows to entertain military personnel. The first play the academy produced was *Seorang pro Nippon* (Someone pro-Japanese) by novice bunkajin playwright Sakuma Masaru, premiered in Jakarta in June 1942. A string of other propaganda plays – *Pendekar Asia* (Asian warrior), *Iboe Berdosa* (Sinful mother), and *Ratoe Asia* (Queen of Asia) – toured Java. Personnel from the academy transferred to Jakarta's cultural center Keimin Bunka Shidōsho (Center for the People's Enlightenment and Cultural Guidance) when it formed in April 1943. The theatre and dance division, headed by Yasuda Kiyō, often collaborated with the center's other divisions (music and visual arts). This was succeeded by the sandiwara association Djawa Engeki Kyōkai (Java Theatre Association) in September 1944, incorporating all major spoken drama companies, directed by Korean filmmaker and playwright Hinatsu Eitarō (aka Heo Yeong and Dr. Huyung). Plays and musical revues written by Hinatsu and a team of Indonesian playwrights were premiered simultaneously in different cities. Practitioners from the central office insured that standards were maintained.

After independence was declared in August 1945, the union was quickly disbanded and Japanese-introduced cultural forms likewise disappeared. The connections between artists and politicization of art engendered by the union and other Japanese-founded cultural institutions, however, were critical in the revolution against the Dutch that followed. Art collectives such as Seniman Merdeka (Artists for Freedom) fielded mobile arts units. After the war Hinatsu co-founded an internationally oriented theatre and film academy in Yogyakarta. Artists from diverse backgrounds collaborated in revolutionary plays, songs, posters, and other media to raise political consciousness among the Indonesian masses.

MATTHEW ISAAC COHEN

By the war's end, bunraku would provide ten new war-inspired plays, including *Mizuku kabane* (A water-soaked corpse, 1942), about sailors who died fighting for the emperor. New puppets were carved to provide a contemporary look for their faces; fresh music and lyrics were written to match their present-day movements.

1943

As Japanese losses mounted, programs distributed at kabuki theatres included air raid instructions. Most new war plays avoided the ongoing battles themselves and, like *Umi yukuba* (If to the sea) – focusing on a mother's sacrifice of her sailor son – sought to raise spirits by highlighting self-sacrifice or other home front issues. Plays set in battle zones, though, had technical difficulties in representing combat action. Kabuki plays with uplifting war messages declined in number; despite official urging to write additional dramas, the results were negligible. Still censors criticized any play that did not promote nationalism.

Young traditional actors were drafted or went to work in factories; bunraku lost a third of its performers. Many died in combat. In kabuki this sometimes meant actress replacements for male actors. Perhaps because it was feared that kabuki would disappear, the classic *Kanjinchō* (The subscription list) was filmed. Theatres began closing two days a month to save power. Theatre taxes rose. Kabuki's China tours ended. Paper shortages ended the six major theatre magazines, with several consolidated into a new one, the kabuki-centered *Engekikai* (Theatre world), which continues to this day.

Miikusabune (Imperial warship) was the third new wartime drama performed by the Kanze school; none outlasted the war. These war-related noh plays honored ancient personages to express the nation's stability and culture.

1944

By mid-year, American bombers were plaguing Japan from Kyushu to Tokyo. Official restrictions on theatre deepened; censorship intensified; taxes skyrocketed; theatre restaurants closed; supplies dwindled; companies mixed genders because of manpower shortages; attendance plummeted; and mainstream kabuki, considered an improper luxury, nearly expired. Early in March, nineteen first-class theatres, including all major kabuki theatres in Tokyo, Osaka, Kyoto, Kobe, and Nagoya, were ordered to be shuttered for a year, although condolence performances were allowed at the Kabuki-za. First-class actors were forced to tour or play in second-class venues with rude, inexperienced audiences. Kabuki's great stars, Onoe Kikugorō VI and Nakamura Kichiemon I, left Tokyo for half a year, replaced by inferior talents. Overseas touring became too dangerous.

Kabuki productions were limited to two and a half hours, and the two separate daily programs became a single program repeated twice. In April, four first-class kabuki theatres were allowed to reopen as long as they offered "morale plays" for workers. Closed theatres were used for non-theatrical purposes, including the manufacture of balloon bombs. On the other hand, small troupes with little-known actors found new favor. Plays fostering the war spirit, especially those picturing contemporary events, practically dried up. Bunraku's training school was closed down; noh's several magazines were consolidated into one, *Nōgaku* (Noh and kyogen).

1945

Japan's imminent collapse was echoed in the traditional theatre. Once the US Marines landed on Iwo Jima, on 19 February, kabuki stopped entirely for over a month, and subsequent performances were sporadic. Some theatre in Kyoto, however, which was not bombed in acknowledgement of the fact that to do so would be psychologically counterproductive to postwar diplomacy, remained active theatrically. Bunraku survived through March.

By the end of March, half the nation's theatre buildings and most leading kabuki venues were destroyed. The Bunraku-za burned down in March, the Kabuki-za in May. Tokyo's only remaining noh stage, at Yasukuni Shrine, was the scene of noh's last performance, meant as a prayer for victory. On 15 August, the war ended and all theatre stopped – but only for a week.

References and further reading

Brandon, James R. *Kabuki's Forgotten War 1931–1945* (Honolulu: University of Hawai'i Press, 2009)

Leiter, Samuel L. (ed.). *Rising from the Flames: The Rebirth of Theater in Occupied Japan, 1945–1952* (Lanham, MD: Lexington Books: 2009)

Liu, Siyuan. *Performing Hybridity in Colonial-Modern China* (London: Palgrave, 2013)

Mackerras, Colin (ed.). *Chinese Theater: From its Origins to the Present Day* (Honolulu: Hawai'i University Press, 1983)

Okamoto Shiro. *The Man who Saved Kabuki: Faubion Bowers and Theatre Censorship in Occupied Japan*, trans. and adapted by Samuel L. Leiter (Honolulu: University of Hawai'i Press, 2001)

Omote Akira and Amano Fumio. *Nōgaku no rekishi* (History of noh and kyogen) (Tokyo: Iwanami shoten, 1987)

Park, Sang Mi. "Wartime Japan's theater movement," *WIAS Research Bulletin* 1 (2009), 61–78 www.waseda.jp/wias/achievement/bulletin/data/sang_mi_park.pdf

Shōchiku Kabushiki Gaisha (ed.). *Shōchiku nanajūnen shi* (Seventy-year history of Shōchiku) (Tokyo: Shōchiku Kabushik Gaisha, 1964)

Smethurst, Mae J., and Richard J. Smethurst. "Two new nō plays written during World War II," in Stanca Scholz-Cionca and Christopher Balme (eds.), *Noh Theatre Transversal* (Munich: Ludicium, 2008), 31–7

FOCUS 8.1   THEATRE IN TAIWAN UNDER COLONIZATION

Hamada Hidesaburō. *Taiwan engeki no genjō* (Current state of Taiwanese theatre) (Tokyo: Tansei shobō, 1943)

Lu Sushang. *A History of Cinema and Drama in Taiwan (Zaiban)* (Taibei: Yinhua, 1991)

Qiu Kunliang. *Jiuju yu xinju: rizhi shiqi Taiwan xiju zhi yanjiu, 1895–1945* (Traditional theatre and new theatre: studies on Taiwan theatre under Japanese rule) (Taibei: Ziliwanbaoshe wenhuabu, 1992)

Yang Du. *Riju shiqi Taiwan xinju yundong (1923–1936)* (Taiwan theatre movements during Japanese colonization) (Taibei: Shibaowenhuachubanshe, 1994)

FOCUS 8.2   THEATRE IN KOREA UNDER COLONIZATION

Lee Jai-Myung. *Haebang-jeun sangyoun hikyok-gwa sangyong sinario-e ihae* (Understanding pre-liberation performed drama and screening scenarios 1940–1945) (Seoul: Pyongminsa, 2005)

Suh Yonho. *Hanguk younguksa* (History of theatre in Korea) (Seoul: Yongukkwainkan, 2003)

Yoo Min-young. *Hanguk gundae younguksa* (Korean modern theatre history) (Gyeonggi-do: Dankook University Press, 1997)

FOCUS 8.3   THEATRE IN INDONESIA UNDER OCCUPATION

Kurasawa, Aiko. "Propaganda media on Java under the Japanese, 1942–1945," *Indonesia* 44 (1987), 59–116

Interlude: *Kami-shibai*: picture-card storytelling

WASHITANI HANA

Kami-shibai (紙芝居, "paper theatre") is popular visual storytelling theatre. Especially popular from 1930 to 1950, it became a potent, multipurpose media for moral education, propaganda during the war (both nationalist and socialist), useful work for the unemployed, and entertainment for the masses. Today its pretty, elaborate panels, fair-barker promotional style, and avuncular storytelling at nursery schools and kindergartens is a far cry from the risky, street-corner vendors of horror, action, and war tales that flourished before the advent of television.

A former *rakugo* storyteller invented a sideshow attraction, narrating short dramas using paper dolls of kabuki characters called *tachi-e* (立絵 "standing pictures") with miniature stage settings. From the early 1900s to 1920s, various performers, selling sweets, visited children's playgrounds in Tokyo with portable stages and tachi-e doll shows, the genre eventually coming to be known as kami-shibai.

Around 1930, a new type of kami-shibai called *hira-e* (flat pictures) was invented which employed several illustrated cardboard panels, allowing for quick and smooth progression of scenes, multiple viewpoints, and magnification of details through cinematic "close-ups." The show could easily be constructed and performed, even by amateurs; selling sweets through hira-e kami-shibai became a ready livelihood for many unemployed people in major cities in the midst of the Shōwa Depression (1930–3).

The majority of kami-shibai stories were serial action-adventures such as *Ōgon batto* (The golden bat, 1930) or horror stories like *Hakaba Kitarō* (Kitarō from the cemetery). There were also sentimental melodramas, comedies, and variants on folktales. The daily episode of such serials always ended on a cliffhanger.

Drama delivered

Typically, kami-shibai performers rode bicycles, carrying a wooden frame equipped with a stack of storyboards and drawers holding sweets and other snacks. Visiting parks or alleys where they could attract many children, they announced their presence with wooden clappers. Those buying snacks were given better viewing positions near the front. Scenes proceeded by showing a succession of storyboards; performers not only narrated but impersonated several characters, and even added sound effects using clappers, drums, or hand bells. The *hikinuki* (pulling out) technique permitted the front storyboard to be partially removed, quickly or slowly, creating suspense or surprise.

The hira-e kami-shibai industry was based on a complicated division of labor. Bosses (*kashimoto*, the lender) ordered scenarios from writers, then contracted artists to draw appropriate pictures. Kashimoto then rented these picture-boards, with accessories like miniature stages, to performers, orally teaching them the storyline, then sold them sweets and snacks at wholesale prices.

Officials and educators became wary of kami-shibai's excessive sensationalism and sentimentality, violence, vulgar jokes, and socialistic ideas, which were strictly proscribed after the 1925 Peace Preservation Laws. Yet some officials recognized the advantages of kami-shibai as beloved local entertainment and tried to utilize them. They embarked on establishing new "educational" styles, distinguished from "street" kami-shibai. In contrast to the mostly hand-painted street kami-shibai, educational types employed print media, becoming powerful propaganda media in wartime Japan and throughout Asian territories under Japanese military occupation.

Postwar street kami-shibai prospered, reaching its peak popularity around 1948, when 2,000 titles were produced; by the 1950s, there were approximately 50,000 performers. Under the Occupation's pro-audiovisual education policies, printed educational kami-shibai first thrived as an educational tool for schools and government offices. At the end of the Occupation, these were appropriated as a publicity tool within labor and other social movements.

Hand-painted street kami-shibai, overwhelmed by television (originally nicknamed "electric kami-shibai") and other modern entertainments, began to decline in the mid-1950s. However, the narrative through segmented panels significantly influenced subsequent media like manga and anime; many famous children's picture book artists and illustrators also created excellent kami-shibai.

References and further reading

Ishiyama Yukihiro. *Shiryō de yomitoku kami-shibai no rekishi* (Understanding the history of kami-shibai by reading documents) (Tokyo: Hōbunshorin, 2008)
Kata Kōji. *Kami-shibai Shōwashi* (The history of Shōwa kami-shibai) (Tokyo: Rippū shobō, 1971)

Nash, Eric Peter. *Manga Kamishibai: The Art of Japanese Paper Theater* (New York: Harry N. Abrams, 2009)

Orbaugh, Sharalyn. *Propaganda Performed: Kamishibai in Japan's Fifteen Year War* (Leiden: Brill, 2014)

9 ∿ Maturing *shingeki* theatre

GUOHE ZHENG

With Japan's defeat in World War II, *shingeki* (modern theatre) tasted freedom from government constraint for the first time, enjoying a spectacular revival. Three companies became dominant in the 1950s, as new artists emerged while veteran artists continued their activities. Yet through failure of practitioners to reflect collectively on shingeki's wartime responsibilities, coupled with reversals of American Occupation policies and interference of the Japanese Communist Party, shingeki eventually lost direction and vitality as a movement.

Criticism of shingeki was raised from the mid-1950s from within and without, leading to the rise of *angura* (avant-garde) theatre, discussed in the following chapter. Massive resignations from major shingeki companies took place in the 1960s–1970s and experiments with Brecht and avant-garde theatre by major shingeki companies could not bridge the gap. From the mid-1970s, the surging angura showed signs of returning to shingeki, but the latter could not revitalize itself, either before or after the bursting of Japan's bubble economy and end of the Cold War. With their last founding members gone by the end of 2012, and theatre receding as a popular pastime, major shingeki companies are commissioning plays by "post-shingeki" playwrights, among other things, to engage contemporary audiences in a new age.

Revival under the Occupation, war responsibility, and the red purge

Japan's defeat brought about a dramatic change to the environment in which shingeki could operate. In October 1945, the GHQ (General Headquarters) of the Occupation authorities abolished all restrictions issued by the state on theatre, including the notorious Peace Preservation Law. Shingeki, long under strict government control, tasted freedom for the first time in its history, leading to its sudden revival. In December that year, shingeki artists in Tokyo presented a joint production of Chekhov's *The Cherry Orchard* in a symbolic demonstration of the genre's revival.

Shingeki's revival has been characterized as "sweeping," but the road to revival was by no means smooth. Such bumpiness was due to "the weighty issue of politics and art" underlying various issues in the postwar shingeki movement. War responsibilities were one vital issue. In October 1945, the Shingeki Roundtable Conference was held to discuss the specifics of the genre's revival. Kubo Sakae, one of the organizers, proposed to eliminate fellow organizers from the roster, including Kubota Mantarō. In Kubo's view, all of these organizers had collaborated with the military government during the war and should not be allowed to play a leading role in shingeki's postwar revival. Indeed, Kubota had been president of the Association of Japanese Theatre with the power to issue or suspend necessary licenses. Kubota was listed by GHQ as a war criminal, along with Iwata Toyoo and seven collaborating theatre artists; Kishida Kunio, seminal playwright and critic, was purged from public office for his role during the war.

Kubo also questioned Murayama Tomoyoshi's war responsibilities for directing plays after his release from prison, and his subsequent activities in colonial Korea. However, Murayama rejected Kubo's request for a public apology for such activities, resulting in the break between these former Shinkyō comrades. In fact, nearly everyone opposed Kubo in his pursuit of shingeki leaders' wartime responsibilities, so the proposal went no further.

Another issue concerned the nature of the postwar freedom that shingeki enjoyed under the Occupation. The Japanese Communist Party (JCP) characterized the Occupation army as liberators who would not interfere with its revolutionary agenda. It therefore declared that the goals of democratic and subsequent socialist revolutions could be achieved peacefully through the Diet under the Occupation. Moreover, it asserted that peaceful revolution under the Occupation, instead of the orthodox armed struggle as in Russia, was JCP's creative application of Marxism-Leninism to Japan's conditions. The JCP also ordered organizations under its control to implement its cultural policies based on this logic.

Kubo was diametrically opposed to this view. From the beginning, he believed that Douglas MacArthur was an occupier who would surely crack down on the JCP and shingeki. Kubo was proved correct. From the beginning of 1947, with the Cold War intensifying and the labor movement spreading, American Occupation policy showed a dramatic reversal – from democratization and demilitarization of Japan to its rearmament as an anticommunist bastion in East Asia. Shortly after the Korean War broke out in June 1950, the GHQ declared the JCP illegal and started a large-scale red purge. On 24 September 1950, as many as 110 left-wing shingeki artists were purged from the film industry. Since shingeki artists commonly contributed a portion of their income from acting in films to their companies, the purge cut off a vital source of income. Even more devastating was the way that theatre producers followed the current of the times and closed their doors to the now stigmatized shingeki companies.

The most dramatic episode of the red purge was the Zenshin-za Incident. Launched in 1931 by mostly lower-ranking actors to break away from kabuki's time-honored tradition as art and institution, Zenshin-za (Progressive Theatre) became a successful company with a repertory including kabuki, shingeki, and popular drama in the 1930s and early 1940s. The left-leaning company joined JCP *en masse* in 1949, in part to compensate for its collaboration during the war, thus making itself a target of the red purge. In May 1952, police tried to arrest Nakamura Kan'emon (1901–82), one of the founders and lead actor of a Hokkaido tour. In hide-and-seek fashion, the famous actor managed to escape from Hokkaido to communist China, where he stayed for about three and half years.

Consolidation and stabilization to 1960

Meanwhile, postwar shingeki, oblivious to the coming red purge, unfolded without collective reflections on its prewar and wartime history. Table 9.1 illustrates the development of shingeki companies. Bungaku-za's first postwar production was that of Wada Shōichi's *Kawa* (River), in March 1946. Wada was an odd choice as he had been with the politically committed New Tsukiji in prewar years, reflecting Bungaku-za's loss of direction at the time, as recollected later by Sugimura Haruko: "In the immediate postwar society where everything had to be left-wing to be politically correct, Bungaku-za's policy of neither right nor left became a target of criticism."[1] *River* was poorly received, as were Bungaku-za's subsequent pieces. Eventually, it resettled on a policy of art for art's sake as the best strategy for survival.

The image of Bungaku-za was fully restored in 1947 with a well-received production of *A Woman's Life*. For its tenth anniversary in 1948, Bungaku-za produced Kubota's *Akikusa banashi* (The tale of fall grasses) and Kishida's *Saigetsu* (The passage of time). Soon after, the hole in Bungaku-za left by the death of Morimoto Kaoru in October 1946 was filled by talented new playwrights: Katō Michio (1912–53) debuted with his *Episōdo* (Episode) in 1949, Fukuda Tsuneari (1912–94) and Mishima Yukio (1925–70) with *Kitei taifū* (Typhoon Kitty) and *Kantan* (The magic pillow) respectively, both in 1950. For its twentieth anniversary in 1956, it produced four commissioned pieces: Fukuda Tsuneari's *Meian* (Light and darkness), Iizawa Tadasu's *Yashi*

---

1 See Ibaraki Tadashi, *Zōho nihon shingeki shōshi* (A brief history of Japanese theatre: expanded edition) (Tokyo: Miraisha, 1973), 113.

to onna (The coconut and a woman), Tanaka Chikao's *Hizen fūdoki* (A topographic account of Hizen Province), and Mishima Yukio's *Rokumeikan*. (See Chapter 14) From 1947, Bungaku-za produced six experimental shows at the Mainichi Hall in the name of the Association of French Theatre Studies, including works by Molière, Beaumarchais, Sartre, and Anouilh. Bungaku-za's Atelier employed a membership system, staging not only more French plays but works by member playwrights Yashiro Seiichi (1927–98) and Yagi Shūichirō (1928–2004). Moreover, a new generation of directors emerged from this, including Kimura Kōichi (1931–) and Katō Shinkichi (1930–2005).

Haiyū-za (Actor's Theatre) was founded by Senda Koreya, Aoyama Sugisaku (1889–1956) and others in February 1944 but did not start serious activities until after the war. Its first productions, in 1946, included Gogol's *The Government Inspector* and Romain Rolland's *Le jeu de l'amour et de la mort*. In 1947, it produced Mafune Yutaka's three pieces – *Nakahashi kōkan* (The Nakahashi house), *Kiiroi heya* (The yellow room), and *Kogan* (A solitary wild goose). *The Nakahashi House* was staged at the Mitsukoshi Theatre, the first of many works produced there by different shingeki companies. At a time when few theatres survived the war, the access to this theatre was so valuable that this period has since been called shingeki's Mitsukoshi Theatre Period.

But the access was terminated in late 1952, due to reactions triggered by the political allusions of Kinoshita Junji's *Kaeru shōten* (Ascension of a frog), produced in June 1952 by Budō no Kai.[2] This experience prompted Haiyū-za to build a theatre of its own, by having its members act in films and radio shows to raise funds to help pay back the debt. The 401-seat Haiyū-za Theatre was completed in April 1954, the first theatre exclusively for shingeki since the destruction of Tsukiji Shōgekijō in March 1945. It was here that Shiina Rinzō's *Daisan no shōgen* (The third testimony, 1954), Abe Kōbō's *Doreigari* (Hunting for slaves, 1956), and Tanaka Chikao's *Maria no kubi* (The head of Mary, 1959) were produced. In 1949, Senda launched the Haiyū-za Theatre Research Institute (Haiyū-za Kenkyūjo). Its affiliated Acting School (Haiyū-za Yōseijo) not only produced hundreds of leading actors and actresses for shingeki, film, and the TV industry, but gave birth to five satellite companies, making Haiyū-za the leader in postwar shingeki (Table 9.1).

The first shingeki company created in postwar Japan was Tōgei (Tōkyō Geijutsu Gekijō, Tokyo Art Theatre) launched in December 1945 by Kubo, Takizawa Osamu, and Susukida Kenji. From the beginning, Tōgei

---

2 Ōzasa Yoshio, *Gekijō no enjita geki* (The drama played by the theatres) (Tokyo: Kyōiku shuppan, 1999), 162.

TABLE 9.1 Development of major shingeki companies, 1929–present

	Pre-war and wartime								Postwar			1959–Present
1929	1932	1934	1936	1937	1940	1944	1945	1946	1947	1949	1950	1951

Tsukiji-za ————

New Tsukiji ————

Theatre Tsukiji ————

Shinkyō I ————

Shinkyō II ———— Shinkyō II ⟶ Tōkyō Geijutsu-za

⟶ Chūō Theatre

Haiyū-za ————

Bungaku-za ————

Tōgei ————

Mingei I ———— **Mingei II**

Budō no Kai ————

*Note: The "big three companies" are in **Boldface***

declared its independence from politics, as seen in its announcement: "This company will maintain an anti-feudalist, anti-militarist and anti-fascist stance but will avoid direct connections with any political party or organization."[3] It accepted patronage from Tōhō, however, reflecting its need for financial support as well as the judgment of the commercial entertainment giant about the prospect of shingeki in postwar Japan. For its first production, Tōgei staged Ibsen's *A Doll's House* in 1946. For its second production, it staged Kubo's newly completed work *Ringoen nikki* (The apple orchard diary) in 1947. In Kubo's own words, it was a play about the war responsibilities of shingeki artists including himself. Most critics were disappointed with the piece because they had expected Kubo to create something monumental and as befitting to an era of democratic revolution as his *Land of the Volcanic Ash* had been inspiring to its audience in 1938. Such criticism reflects the influence of JCP's cultural policies. Tōgei was disbanded due to the harassment from Nichieien, an organization of film and theatre under the JCP, and the resignation of Takizawa and Susukida. Thereafter, Kubo became increasingly isolated from the shingeki movement, committing suicide on 15 March 1958 while hospitalized for manic depression.[4]

In January 1946, about three weeks after his break with Kubo, Murayama Tomoyoshi restarted Shinkyō Gekidan, attracting members of the prewar Shinkyō, New Tsukiji, and Inoue Masao, the famous *shimpa* leader. When Shinkyō had its first postwar production in February 1946 of Fyodorov's *A Happy Family*, it was announced as the company's thirty-ninth, counted from before Shinkyō's 1940 roundup. This is evidence of its commitment to politics, in contrast with the policies of Tōgei. Shinkyō's subsequent productions included Konstantin M. Simonov's *Under the Chestnut Trees Lining the Streets of Prague*, Ozawa Mikio's *Buki to jiyū* (Weapons and freedom), *The Street without Sun*, adapted from Tokunaga Sunao's novel, and Molière's *Tartuffe*. Soon, Inoue returned to shimpa and many other members also left. In 1950, when the Cominform (the Soviet-dominated communist organization of European countries) criticized the JCP for its policy regarding American occupation, the JCP split into two factions. This internal struggle continued despite the onslaught of the red purge. Shinkyō, with many JCP members, was also divided, and as a result Susukida left Shinkyō to create Chūgei (Chūō Geijutsu Gekijō, Central Art Theatre) in 1951. When the JCP managed to reunify in 1955, Shinkyō and Chūgei were reconciled

---

3 Ōzasa Yoshio, *Nihon gendai engekishi: Shōwa sengo hen 1* (History of modern theatre in Japan: postwar Showa period 1), 6 vols. (Tokyo: Hakusuisha, 1993), Vol. 0, 76.

4 Guohe Zheng, "From war responsibility to the red purge," in Leiter (ed.), *Rising from the Flames*, 279–315.

and eventually merged into a new company in February 1959, today's Tōkyō Geijutsu-za (Tokyo Art Theatre).

Shortly after the collapse of Tōgei, Takizawa, Uno Jūkichi (1914–88), Okakura Shirō (1907–59), and others created Mingei (Minshū Geijutsu Gekijō, People's Art Theatre) in July 1947. Two years later, Mingei disbanded due to JCP's interference and complaints about its leaders' negligence of their duties by acting in films, after producing Schiller's *Intrigue and Love*, Yamada Tokiko's *Joshiryō ki* (An account of a girls' dormitory) and Kinoshita Junji's *Yamanami* (Mountain ranges). In April 1950, after careful examination of what happened the year before, Mingei restarted. The success of Miyoshi Jūrō's *Honō no hito: Gohho shōden* (The person of flames: a short biography of Van Gogh, 1951) established Mingei's reputation as one of the big three postwar shingeki companies, along with Bungaku-za and Haiyū-za. In 1952, Kubo, as a guest member, directed his last work, *Nihon no kishō* (The weather of Japan). Sugawara Takashi (1903–70) directed Arthur Miller's *Death of a Salesman* in 1954 with Takizawa playing Willy Loman, another huge success. This was followed by Tennessee Williams' *The Glass Menagerie*, and Fukuda Tsuneari's *Yūrei yashiki* (The haunted house). After Kubo's suicide in 1958 and Okakura's death in 1959, Uno became a well-received director, as seen in the production of Hotta Yoshie's *Unmei* (Fate) in 1959 and Kinoshita's *Ottō to yobareru Nihonjin* (A Japanese called Otto) in 1962 (see p. 393).

Budō no Kai was formed in 1947 under actress Yamamoto Yasue and playwright Kinoshita Junji (1914–2006). Okakura, one of its directors, used the newly introduced Stanislavski system to train actors, turning the company into Japan's major Stanislavski center. In October 1949, it produced Kinoshita's *Yūzuru* (Twilight crane; see representative plays, p. 283), a piece that not only laid the financial foundation of the company, but also started a tradition of producing Kinoshita's folktale pieces including *Kitsune yamabushi* (The fox mountain monk) and *Sannen netarō* (The boy who slept three years), both in 1953. While shingeki was generally known for its progressive, Westernized outlook, Budō no Kai mined the rich vein of folktales for themes poignantly relevant to postwar issues. Due to its members' different visions on shingeki, however, Budō no Kai dissolved in 1964, having produced Miyamoto Ken's *Meiji no hitsugi* (Coffin of the Meiji period, 1962) and Kinoshita's *Okinawa* (1963).

Shingeki, traditional genres, and Western plays

Shingeki had begun with a conscious break from Japan's god-infested "irrational" traditional theatre, ambitious to create a thoroughly realistic one in the spirit of Ibsen and Chekhov. This is best seen in Osanai Kaoru's 1926 admonition that shingeki actors should "Forget kabuki. Ignore tradition. Move, don't dance. Talk, don't sing."[5] However, shingeki had not completely ignored the classical theatre around it, not least because Osanai himself, like Tsubouchi Shōyō, had dreamed of creating a national theatre. Tsukiji Shōgekijō had produced Osanai's own shingeki adaptation of Chikamatsu Monzaemon's *Kokusen'ya gassen* (The battles of Coxinga, 1928), originally written for bunraku but also performed in kabuki, telling the story of how Zheng Chenggong, born of a Chinese father and a Japanese mother, saved Ming China from the invasion by Tartary. In 1930, it produced another adaptation of the piece, this time by Kubo, presenting the protagonist as an imperialist. A further adaptation of the piece, by Yashiro Seiichi, was produced by Bungaku-za in 1958, depicting the hero as a womanizer. Bungaku-za also debuted many of Mishima Yukio's "modern noh plays."

Shingeki also collaborated with shimpa and kabuki, showing that audiences could accept three very distinct modes of realism. Shimpa actress Mizutani Yaeko I (1905–79) shared the stage with multiple shingeki artists: Sugimura Haruko in *The Moon Is a Gong* (*Tsuki wa dora nari*, 1950) by Sugahara Takashi, Takizawa Osamu in *Yang Guifei* (*Yō Kihi*, 1951) by Osaragi Jirō, and Haiyū-za's Nakadai Tatsuya (1932–) in *Everything Ends in Poetry* (*Mono mina uta de owaru*, 1963) by Hanada Kiyoteru (1909–74). Similarly, in 1957, Bungaku-za had a joint production of Fukuda Tsunenari's *Akechi Mitsuhide* with kabuki star Matsumoto Kōshirō VIII. In 1979 Sugimura Haruko again shared the stage with Mizutani Yaeko in a shimpa production of Kawaguchi Shōtarō's *The Elegant Ukiyo Tune* (*Fūryū Ukiyo Bushi*), and in 1990 with kabuki *onnagata* star Bandō Tamasaburō in *Hanaoka Seishū no tsuma* (Hanaoka Seishū's wife) by Ariyoshi Sawako (1931–84). These represent shingeki's attempts to enrich itself, continuing the vision of a national theatre seen by Tsubouchi and Osanai.

Meanwhile, shingeki's production of Western plays continued in postwar years, along with its anti-capitalist and anti-war tradition, as seen in pieces such as Gorky's *The Lower Depths* and an adaptation of Anne Frank's *The Diary of a Young Girl*. Classical and modern masterpieces were also produced, including Aristophanes' *Lysistrata*, Chekhov's plays, and Tennessee Williams' *A Streetcar Named Desire*. Theoretical writings by Stanislavski and Brecht became widely available in the 1950s, and the visit by the Moscow Art Theatre caused great excitement among the shingeki faithful. Some Western pieces were more experimental in nature, such as Haiyū-za's production of Bertolt Brecht pieces and the Bungaku-za Atelier's production of French and

5　David G. Goodman, *The Return of the Gods: Japanese Drama and Culture in the 1960s* (Ithaca, NY: Cornell University East Asia Program, 2003 [1988]), 4; Poulton, *A Beggar's Art* , 130.

ᔕ FOCUS 9.1 Mishima Yukio: provocative playwright

Fig 36 Bungaku-za's *Rokumeikan* (The deer-cry pavilion, 1956) by Mishima Yukio.

A prolific novelist, essayist, and public intellectual, Mishima Yukio (1925–70) was also Japan's leading dramatist of the 1950s and 1960s. His sixty-one works for stage and screen spanned a wide range of genres and styles, from realist *shingeki* (modern theatre) to kabuki plays in classical Japanese.

In his youth, Mishima attended kabuki every month and noh and shingeki occasionally, writing precocious critical essays about almost every play he saw. Mishima developed a love of formalism and Japan's native tradition, but he also admired classical European drama, adapting Racine's *Phèdre* to kabuki (1955). Aeschylus' *The Oresteia* and Euripides' *Heracles* inspired two of his finest modern plays, *The Tropical Tree* (1959) and *The Fall of the House of Suzaku* (1967).

Mishima's first "modern noh" play, *Kantan* (1950), was critically acclaimed at the prestigious Bungaku-za. Nine "modern noh plays" (*kindai nō*), written from 1950 to 1962, derive their plots and characters from classical noh, but are psychological dramas of love and obsession set in contemporary Japan. Thanks to early publication

in English translation, and because they are intended for presentation in a contemporary theatrical idiom, these are the Japanese plays most frequently performed abroad.

In 1956, Mishima's three-act romantic melodrama *Rokumeikan* (The deer-cry pavilion), starring the renowned Sugimura Haruko, was a huge success, touring Japan for three years. Yet his right-wing political and formalist artistic ideals ran counter to the development of postwar Japanese drama. While other dramatists were moving away from traditional constraints toward freedom of expression and eclectic borrowing from various genres, Mishima remained committed to orthodox kabuki and shingeki plays. His kabuki plays integrate poetic lyrics, music, dance, and spectacular staging reminiscent of Edo period (1603–1868) plays, but at the same time showcase his idiosyncrasies and irony. Mishima's shingeki plays preserve the "three unities" of theatre, and characters speak in the heightened discourse favored by shingeki authors of the 1950s–1960s. A notable exception is the kabuki–shingeki hybrid *Kuro tokage* (The black lizard, 1962), a detective suspense parody that explores personal obsessions of cruelty and the evil inherent in beauty, themes also found in *Sado Kōshaku fujin* (Madame de Sade, 1965), widely considered his finest play.

Mishima sought to shock, disturb, or even outrage his audiences. His 1955 *Sangenshoku* (Primary colors), which depicts bisexual men kissing, was not performed until 1963. In *The Black Lizard*, Mishima's heroine kills and preserves beautiful men and women for her museum; in *Madame de Sade*, he suggests that murder and depravity could be divine acts; in the modern noh *Yuya* (1959) he argues that deceit

makes life beautiful; in *Suzaku* he resurrects emperor-worship; in *My Friend Hitler* (1968) he presents the dictator as a moderate, rational politician whose purges were justified. These were troubling, even taboo themes, but Mishima gilded the horror and pain with gorgeous words, structural elegance, sumptuous sets and costumes, and acting by shingeki's best performers. In these plays, as in his novels, Mishima's goal was to allow, or compel, readers and audiences to enter into the psyche of disturbed or sick human beings, then recognize how alike we are to these pathetic or dangerous social misfits.

LAURENCE KOMINZ

absurdist pieces. Beckett's *Waiting for Godot* was staged by both Bungaku-za and Mingei in successful productions.

Shingeki careers, fan organizations, and amateur theatre

A word should be mentioned about how shingeki artists earned their living. For much of its history, shingeki has been under financial difficulties. Exceptions include the state-paid salary during the war for mobile theatre activities, and the Zenshin-za salary system made possible by its commercial success and communal life. Otherwise, actors had to act in films, radio shows – later in TV drama as well – to feed themselves in order to act on stage. Actors with external contracts contribute a portion of their earnings to the company. A member's income consists of a percentage of his or her contributions to the company plus the salary from the company out of stage production earnings. In the case of Haiyū-za, the ratio of company income from member contributions versus that from stage productions was 13:1 in 1960, 16:1 in 1961 and 6:1 in 1962. The company goal was to increase the ratio of the latter and reduce its reliance on the former so that the artists could concentrate more on the stage art of shingeki, their main pursuit.

Fan organizations created by and for the audience appeared after the war. FOT (Fans of Theatre), the first such organization, started in April 1946 but disbanded a year later due to rampant inflation. Inspired by Shinkyō's production of *The Broken Commandment* (*Hakai*, 1948), adapted from Shimazaki Tōson's novel portraying Burakumin, Japan's social outcasts, the Buraku Liberation League launched Rōen (Kinrōsha Engeki Kyōdō Kumiai,

❧ FOCUS 9.2   Takechi Tetsuji: traditional innovator

One of the most provocative and influential figures on the postwar theatre scene was Takechi Tetsuji (1912–88), whose career encompassed roles, in roughly chronological order, as theatre critic, producer, director, filmmaker, television host, politician, and pornographer. The son of a wealthy Osaka industrialist, Takechi began writing theatre criticism in the late 1930s. During the war he was involved in the Dangenkai (Broken String Society), which put on free productions of traditional performing arts when government restrictions had shut down most theatres.

Takechi's postwar theatre activities were attempts to find a place for Japan's traditional performance genres on the modern stage. For Takechi, kabuki as it was then being performed was neither classical nor modern theatre, but rather a haphazard collection of performance traditions and artistic styles associated with previous stars. Using his own finances and the political capital gained through his wartime largesse, Takechi mounted his own series of kabuki productions. "Takechi Kabuki" (1949–51) sought to achieve a genuinely classical art by rejecting pseudo-traditional practices and returning to original texts and historically unified performance styles. They aroused considerable interest, but also resentment toward this outsider to the insular kabuki world. His productions nonetheless succeeded in showing that it was possible to depart from received performance patterns and inject some artistic direction (*enshutsu*) into kabuki. A by-product was the training provided to Takechi's young actors, several of whom became major stars, including Bandō Tsurunosuke (later Nakamura Tomijūrō), Ichikawa Enzō (later the film actor Ichikawa Raizō), and Nakamura Senjaku (later Nakamura Ganjirō III and now Sakata Tōjūrō IV).

Takechi next turned to the even older noh and kyogen as a means of forging a link between the traditional and the modern, in productions fusing elements of noh and kyogen acting and staging with other performance traditions and texts. *Yūzuru* (Twilight crane, 1954; see representative plays, pp. 282–3), was a *shingeki* modern theatre piece performed by noh and kyogen actors with an operatic chorus; *Higashi wa higashi* (East is east, 1954), another shingeki piece (based on a traditional kyogen), was adapted into a modern kyogen that also featured a Takarazuka actress; and *Tsuki ni tsukareta Piero* (Pierrot, howling at the moon, 1955), combined a European Symbolist text, atonal music of Schoenberg, and performance by noh and kyogen actors alongside a classical soprano. While not always meeting with critical success, these productions did help break down barriers separating traditional genres, thereby opening the way for other fusion experiments.

Subsequently, Takechi continued to push the bounds of traditional arts, attaining notoriety for a *buyō* dance play set to Stockhausen's electronic music, staging the opera *Aida* in a baseball stadium, and nude noh. In the 1960s, Takechi turned to film, and it is as the filmmaker who fought and won a charge of obscenity over his tendentious *Kuro yuki* (Black snow, 1965) that he is best known today. Although many are sensational and at least three are unapologetically pornographic, Takechi's twelve feature films also include *Hakujitsumu* (Daydream, 1964) and *Kōkeimu* (Dream of the crimson chamber, 1964), two imaginative and playful adaptations of Tanizaki Jun'ichirō fiction, and a well-scripted and relatively restrained production of *Genji monogatari* (1966).

WILLIAM LEE

Workers' Theatre Cooperatives) in July 1948. With fifty-one participating units, it boasted a total membership of 8,000. Its objectives included negotiating group ticket discounts, co-sponsoring amateur theatre contests, organizing protests against ticket taxes, and coordinating productions. Due to the reversal of the American Occupation policy and the crackdown on labor movements, Rōen was renamed Tōen (Tōkyō Engeki Kyōdō Kumiai, Tokyo Theatre Cooperatives Union), becoming smaller and less active. At first, members could choose any seven shows to watch in a year for a monthly fee, which later changed into a system of recommended shows. In April 1966, its national organization, National Liaison of Workers Theatre Cooperatives (Zenkoku Rōen Renraku Kaigi), boasted 105,000 members from fifty-six participating units.

The splits of major shingeki companies, the rise of angura theatre in the 1960s–1970s, the rapid growth of Japan's economy in 1960–80 and the subsequent burst of the bubble economy deeply affected fan organizations. Membership in Osaka Rōen, for example, dropped from 212,000 in 1964 to around 2,000–3,000 in the 1980s, and to 1,400–1,500 in 1999. Deeply in debt, it was disbanded in 2007. Fan organizations nurtured by each troupe, however, still continue. It is not clear to what extent memberships of the above organizations overlap, but there is no doubt that they contributed to the creation of independent theatre lovers.

Postwar amateur theatre was a by-product of wartime mobile theatres sponsored by the government, with guidance from professional artists playing a major role in raising its standards. The most important of these amateur troupes were workers' theatres, numerous and responsive to the growing postwar labor movement. Amateur theatre contests were held annually and plays performed by workers at large corporations such as Hitachi, Toshiba, and the Japan National Railway System. Amateur playwrights emerged in the process, writing primarily one-act plays dealing with events close to their lives. But they also produced longer pieces such as Suzuki Masao's *Human Binder* (*Ningen seihon*, 1948) dealing with the 1947 general strike, one of the iconic events marking the reversal of the American Occupation policy.

This period of flourishing activity was followed by a period of retreat due to the red purge. Although workers' theatre resurged after 1955, it never reached the previous level, due to the tremendous impact of the conversion from coal to petroleum as Japan's primary source of energy. Nevertheless, amateur theatre groups, like fan organizations, constituted vital and continuing support for shingeki in the postwar years. Student amateur troupes, however, came to challenge shingeki in the 1960s as an establishment.

Problems of postwar shingeki

Postwar shingeki's conservatism had already become a target of criticism since the early 1950s. Miyoshi Jūrō condemned shingeki in articles appearing in 1951 and 1956. In 1955, Asari Keita declared a break with shingeki in an article addressed to the shingeki establishment: "There is a decisive gap between you and us … None of the plays you have produced can – or will – touch us in the least … Our goals for theatre are fundamentally different from yours."[6] Asari had by then already co-founded Gekidan Shiki, to be known later as a hugely successful producer of musicals, combining entertainment and business.

The most systematic criticism of shingeki, from a different perspective, is from Kan Takayuki. According to Kan, shingeki does not have a postwar history because all of its postwar activities amounted to nothing more than an eternal epilogue to prewar shingeki. With some exceptions, few plays have been written that deal with postwar issues. Postwar shingeki lacks elements of anti-establishment and festivity, the lifeblood of all theatre. While there was shingeki after the war, there was no shingeki movement because its leaders equated popularity with professionalism, judging success by the numbers attracted to theatre or prizes won. Consequently, shingeki became the *rearguard* instead of the vanguard of Japan's cultural movements, its role during the prewar years.

The popularity of Morimoto's *A Woman's Life* during the postwar years is perhaps symbolic of the problems of postwar shingeki.[7] The play was commissioned during the war by the government. Contrary to what one might expect of a work with such an origin, it not only survived the war but thrived thereafter, even acclaimed as "a classic of the shingeki movement … and Japan's national theatre."[8] The success of the piece, however, results from its adaptive evolution: a drama of family relationship has been adapted repeatedly to fit the changing political atmospheres of the day. Fukuda Tsuneari thus criticized the adaptation of the piece: "During the war, it was the militarist government that they catered to; after the war, it was the Occupation army. Now it is Chinese communists."[9] It is no wonder that dynamics of rebellion started simmering against shingeki.

Early efforts to overcome shingeki

Scholars have attributed the problems of shingeki to its failure to evaluate its wartime activities. Kan Takayuki digs deeper. According to him, theatre

6 Kan Takayuki, *Tatakau engekijin*, 122.
7 Guohe Zheng, "Reflections *of* and *on* the times: Morimoto Kaoru's *A Woman's Life*," in David Jortner, Keiko McDonald, and Kevin J. Wetmore, Jr. (eds.), *Modern Japanese Theatre and Performance* (Lanham, MD: Lexington Books, 2006), 189–203.
8 Koike Misako, "Nihon no kindai engeki no egaita josei" (Women as portrayed in modern Japanese theatre), *Shiatā ātsu* 6:3 (1996), 46.
9 Fukuda Tsuneari, *Fukuda Tsuneari zenshū* (Complete works of Fukuda Tsuneari), vol. IV (Tokyo: Bungei shunjū, 1987), 354.

at different times has different paradigms, a set of consensuses on theatrical imaginations. Premodern theatre, for example, was a place of religious taboos while Meiji period kabuki was a star-centered show of familiar worlds, with scripts and directing secondary considerations. In contrast, shingeki is a cultural movement in which scripts represent a new world to be presented to the audience through actors following the director's guidance. Disciples of Osanai in postwar shingeki followed this paradigm in a "Japanized" Stanislavski style, made worse by political interference. The most persistent meddling came from the JCP, which went through rollercoaster policy changes – first characterizing the Occupiers as liberators and advocating a peaceful revolution under the GHQ in 1945, then calling for armed struggles following the red purge, and finally abandoning that policy to embrace Diet democracy in 1955. It is only natural that the younger generation was disillusioned with left-wing movements, both political and shingeki, intensified after Khrushchev's 1956 revelation of Stalin's atrocities. This eventually led to efforts to overcome shingeki by creating a new paradigm for modern Japanese theatre.

Two groups made such efforts. Young hands from inside shingeki, including those of Seigei (Gekidan Seinen Geijutsu Gekijō, Youth Art Theatre) born of Mingei, were the first group. But it was the second group – a group of amateur student artists – who found themselves creators of a new paradigm for modern Japanese theatre, intended to better capture the Japanese experience in a nuclear age. These efforts, however, would not bear fruit as vanguard theatre without the baptism of the 1960 struggle against the renewal of the US–Japan Mutual Security Treaty and the worldwide 1968 student revolution, the topic of Chapter 10.

Shingeki 1960s–1980s

Meanwhile, the weighty issue of politics and art continued to haunt shingeki. In 1963, twenty-nine younger members resigned from Bungaku-za to join Fukuda Tsuneari in creating Cloud (Kumo), a new troupe, and the Modern Theatre Association (Gendai Engeki Kyōkai). The latter, in turn, split due to internal conflicts in 1975–6 into two companies, En and Subaru. Also in 1963, Mishima Yukio and thirteen others resigned in protest against the suspension of Mishima's commissioned piece *Yorokobi no koto* (The lyre of happiness) for its political contents. They soon launched NLT, the New Literary Theatre. For Haiyū-za the 1960s to 1970s were similarly eventful. Senda Koreya was criticized for losing audiences due to his academic approach. Ozawa Eitarō (1909–88), advocate of a popular approach along the lines of the JCP and Tokyo Rōen under its control, not only replaced Senda as head of Haiyū-za but, in 1964, closed Haiyū-za's Theatre Research Institute and Acting School, effectively ending Haiyū-za's status as a leading shingeki company. (Thanks to Abe Kōbō, these became the theatre program of Tōhō Gakuen College of Drama and Music in 1967.) Yet voices were later raised by Senda's disciples for Haiyū-za to resume its artistic ideals, leading to Ozawa's resignation in 1969. However, these very disciples rebelled against Senda in 1971 over the production of angura pieces, leading to the resignation of key members. In 1973, Abe Kōbō resigned from Haiyū-za due to the gap between his ideal of theatre and Senda's leftish ideology. Similarly, August 1971 through early 1972 witnessed resignation of about fifty members from Mingei including Suzuki Mizuho and Shimojō Masami, occasioned by a power struggle between Uno Jūkichi and Takizawa on the one hand and JCP-supported Shimojō on the other.

Efforts had been made to maintain the vitality of shingeki as a movement, even before the rebellions. For example, to experiment with anti-realism and other avant-garde theatre, Bungaku-za launched its Atelier in 1950 under Iwata, whose productions included Sartre's existential *The Respectful Prostitute* (1952), John Osborne's anti-establishment *Look Back in Anger* (1959), Samuel Beckett's absurdist *Waiting for Godot* (1960), and Tsuka Kōhei's angura piece *Atami satsujin jiken* (The murder case in Atami, 1973). The gap between the innovative and conservative in Bungaku-za led to the eventual resignation of progressive Kimura Kōichi in 1981 to create Chijinkai (The Down-to-Earth Theatre). Similarly, from the 1950s to the 1960s, Senda translated five volumes of plays by Brecht and directed three Brecht pieces. His introduction to, and critique of, Brecht's theory of the alienation effect not only was eye-opening to Japanese theatre artists, but enabled him to keep a distance from the JCP and its cultural defenders in postwar years. Under the influence of Brecht, for example, Senda even advocated "the knowledge and techniques to view oneself with detachment."[10] Nevertheless, Senda's avant-garde was confined to the framework of rationalism and a Marxist worldview – the reason why his open-mindedness could not bring him to accept angura theatre until very late in his life, missing an important opportunity to revitalize shingeki in postwar Japan. But it was angura theatre that commanded the spotlight of modern Japanese theatre from the 1960s through the early 1980s.

Shingeki 1990s to the present

Angura theatre itself, however, showed signs of returning to shingeki from the mid-1970s – Tsuka Kōhei, for example, produced his pieces in theatres, with the confining proscenium arch that earlier angura artists had vowed to

10 Kan Takayuki, *Tatakau engekijin*, 73–4, 80–2.

break as part of the shingeki establishment. The decline of angura became unmistakable after the death of Terayama Shūji in 1983. Shingeki, however, showed no sign of revitalization despite the easy availability of multiple new theatres built in the 1980s by large corporations at the height of Japan's bubble economy. It seems that the ideal of making the world a better place shared by shingeki and angura theatre artists – despite their differences – has been lost in Japan, making both declines inevitable.

This loss became obvious following the collapse of the Soviet Union, the subsequent end of the Cold War, and the bursting of Japan's bubble economy in the early 1990s. Playwright-director Hirata Oriza's claim testifies to this lack of ideals to make the world a better place: "Contemporary theatre should have no message to convey to the audience."[11] This loss underlines an irony about Inoue Hisashi's *Kamiya-chō Sakura Hotel* (*Kamiya-chō Sakura Hoteru*), questioning the relationship between the repressive state and shingeki by portraying Maruyama Sadao and his ill-fated mobile theatre in Hiroshima. This play was commissioned to open the first state-funded New National Theatre for modern drama in 1997. Yet Bungaku-za restored the wartime version of *A Woman's Life* the previous year "because it has drifted too far from the original."[12] Shingeki thus appeared split regarding its positions toward Japan's wartime modern state and its imperialistic legacy.

Despite such contradictions, the three major shingeki companies are still active, with professionals on the staff for Bungaku-za, Haiyū-za, and Mingei numbering respectively 217, 152, and 180. Each company stages classics, newly written plays, and translated works. All three have lost their last founding members in the last two decades – Haiyū-za's Senda (1994), Bungaku-za's Sugimura (1997) and director Inui Ichirō (2010), and Mingei's Takizawa (2000) and Ōtaki Hideji (2012). This period also witnessed commissioning of plays by major "post-shingeki" playwrights, including Betsuyaku Minoru, Makino Nozomi, and Hirata in search of ways to engage contemporary spectators.

REPRESENTATIVE PLAYS

Yūzuru (Twilight crane, 1950) by Kinoshita Junji (1914–2006)

Yohyō, a poor farmer, and his beautiful wife Tsū live a simple, happy life together. Tsū weaves a beautiful cloth for a delighted Yohyō, but friends sell

---

11 Hirata Oriza, *Toshi ni shukusai wa iranai* (Cities need no festivals) (Tokyo: Banseisha, 1997), 15–20.
12 Zheng, "Reflections," 200.

it for cash, which Yohyō now wants more than the cloth. Breaking a promise never to watch Tsū weaving, he sees a crane at the loom, which then flies away. He has lost Tsū. The most famous of Kinoshita's folktale plays, *Yūzuru* can be understood on several levels, including the warping of pure sentiment by materialism, appealing to children and adults alike. Written for shingeki, *Yūzuru*, like Kinoshita's other masterpiece *Shigosen no matsuri* (Requiem on the great meridian, 1978), has often been performed by mixed casts. Tsū was played for over forty years by shingeki actress Yamamoto Yasue (1902–93) and then by kabuki onnagata Bandō Tamasaburō; Yohyō was played over 500 times by the kyogen actor Shigeyama Sennojō.

References and further reading

Bungaku-za. *Bungaku-za gojūnen shi* (Fifty years of Bungaku-za history) (Tokyo: Bungaku-za, 1987)

Goodman, David G. *Japanese Drama and Culture in the 1960s* (Armonk, NY: M. E. Sharpe, 1986)

Iles, Timothy. *Abe Kōbō: An Exploration of his Prose, Drama and Theatre* (Fucecchio: European Press Academic Publishing, 2000)

Inoue Rie. *Kubo Sakae no sekai* (Kubo Sakae's world) (Tokyo: Shakai hyōronsha, 1989)

Kan Takayuki. *Zōho sengo engeki: shingeki wa norikoerareta ka* (Postwar theatre revised: has shingeki been superseded?) (Tokyo: Shakai hyōronsha, 2003)

Kan Takayuki. *Tatakau engekijin: sengo engeki no shisō* (Fighting theatre practitioners: postwar theatre philosophies) (Tokyo: Jiritsu shobō, 2007)

Keene, Donald (trans.). *Three Plays by kōbō Abe* (New York: Columbia University Press, 1993)

Kitami, Harukazu. *Kaisō no Bungaku-za* (Bungaku-za reminiscences) (Tokyo: Chuo kōronsha, 1987)

Matsumoto, Kappei. *Shingeki no sanmyaku* (The hills and valleys of shingeki) (Tokyo: Asahi shorin, 1991)

Miyagishi, Yasuharu. *Tenkō to doramaturugi* (Political apostasy and dramaturgy) (Tokyo: Kage shobō, 2003)

Ōzasa, Yoshio. *Nihon gendai engeki shi* (Japan's contemporary theatre history) (Tokyo: Hakusuisha), 6 vols.

Poulton, M. Cody. *A Beggar's Art* (Honolulu: University of Hawai'i Press, 2010)

Rimer, J. Thomas. *Toward a Modern Japanese Theatre: Kishida Kunio* (Princeton: Princeton University Press, 1974)

Senda Koreya. *Mō hitotsu no shingek shi: Senda Koreya jiden* (Another history of shingeki: Senda Koreya's autobiography) (Tokyo: Chikuma shobō, 1975)

Shields, Nancy K. *Fake Fish: The Theatre of Kobo Abe* (New York: Weatherhill, 1996)

Toita Yasuji. *Taidan: Nihon shingeki shi* (Tokyo: Seiabō, 1961)

Tsuzuki, Chushichi. *The Pursuit of Power in Modern Japan 1825–1995* (New York: Oxford University Press, 2000)

Zheng, Guohe. "From war responsibility to the Red Purge" in Samuel L. Leiter (ed.), *Rising from the Flames* (Lanham, MD: Lexington Books, 2009)

INTERNET RESOURCES
The Japanese Theatre Goer's Collection (16 Films) Marty Gross Films www.martygrossfilms.com/films/theatergoers/theatergoers.html

FOCUS 9.1 MISHIMA YUKIO: PROVOCATIVE PLAYWRIGHT
Dōmoto Masaki. *Gekijin Mishima Yukio (Dramatist Mishima Yukio)* (Tokyo: Gekishobō, 1994)
Kominz, Laurence (ed.). *Mishima on Stage: The Black Lizard and Other Plays* (Ann Arbor: Center for Japanese Studies, University of Michigan, 2007)
Mishima Yukio. *Five Modern Nō Plays*, trans. Donald Keene (New York: Knopf, 1957)
    "My Friend Hitler" and Other Plays of Yukio Mishima, trans. Hiroaki Sato (New York: Columbia University Press, 2002)

FOCUS 9.2 TAKECHI TETSUJI: TRADITIONAL INNOVATOR
Okamoto Akira and Yomota Inuhiko (eds.). *Takechi Tetsuji: dentō to zen'ei* (Takechi Tetsuji: tradition and avant-garde) (Tokyo: Sakuhinsha, 2012)
Takechi Tetsuji. "Artistic direction in Takechi Kabuki," trans. William Lee, *ATJ* 20:1 (2003), 12–24
    Teihon Takechi kabuki: Takechi Tetsuji zenshū (Takechi Kabuki: complete works of Takechi Tetsuji), 6 vols. (Tokyo: San'ichi shobō, 1978–81)
Tezuka, Miwako. "Experimentation and tradition: the avant-garde play Pierrot Lunaire by Jikken Kōbō and Takechi Tetsuji," *Art Journal* 70:3 (2011), 64–85

Interlude: Postwar musicals and commercial theatre

KEVIN J. WETMORE JR.

Although Takarazuka and other groups had performed Western-style musicals and musical revues in prewar years, the musical truly emerged and developed in Japan during the Occupation, from 1945 to 1952, when Hata Toyokichi (1892–1956) began staging small-scale musicals. In 1955, Kikuta Kazuo (1908–73) initiated Tōhō Musicals, a series of popular, original performances. The entertainment conglomerate Tōhō, with divisions for film and stage production, quickly seized on Western-style musicals, having both the capital and the international connections to secure rights to perform foreign hits in Japan, in Japanese, with Japanese casts. Tōhō produced *My Fair Lady* in 1963 at the Tokyo Takarazuka, Japan's first all-Japanese cast musical: proof that Japanese audiences could accept an all-Japanese cast in a musical set in a foreign land.

Within the decade, Tōhō had seven theatres for staging Western-style musicals and large-scale straight plays. Its flagship 2,000-seat Teikoku Gekijō (Tokyo Imperial Theatre) was inaugurated in 1966 with *Scaretto*, a musical adaptation of *Gone with the Wind*. Tōhō productions of *Fiddler on the Roof*, starring Morishige Hisaya in 1967, and *The King and I* (1965) and *Man of La Mancha* (1969), both starring kabuki actor Matsumoto Kōshirō IX (1942–), rapidly followed. Tōhō could offer 500 performances annually of its various musical properties at the Imperial alone. Today Tōhō, which shares a repertory with Takarazuka, continues to stage traditional American musicals alongside international hits like the Austrian *Elisabeth: The Musical*, and original musicals such as *Endless Shock* (2000), about an off-Broadway success story, directed by boy-band producer Johnny Kitagawa (1933–), that has run over 1,000 performances nationwide in revised versions.

A troupe for all seasons: Gekidan Shiki

An entirely different trajectory was taken by the world's largest producer of musicals. Gekidan Shiki (Four Seasons Theatre Company, known as

Fig 37 Kabuki star Matsumoto Kōshirō IX as Don Quixote in the musical *Man of La Mancha*.

Shiki) was founded in 1953 by Asari Keita (1933–) as a *shingeki* company staging Western dramas in translation, including Chekhov, Anouilh, and Giraudoux. Inspired by the touring American production of *West Side Story* in 1964, however, Shiki began developing native triple-thread acting-sing-ing-dancing talents, and mounting original musicals, such as *The Emperor's New Clothes* (1964). By the 1970s Shiki had grown into a massive company of over 1,000 members with nine home theatres in Tokyo, Nagoya, Osaka, Sapporo, and Fukuoka, which collectively staged over 3,000 performances a year, for an average of 800 per show of up to twelve concurrent productions. In 2014 these included *Mamma Mia!, Jesus Christ Superstar, The Sound of Music, Cats, Wicked, Beauty and the Beast*, and *The Lion King*.

Shiki is best known for Japanese-language productions of popular Western musicals including *Jesus Christ Superstar* (1973), *West Side Story* (1974), *A Chorus Line* (1979), *Evita* (1982), *Cats* (1983), *Phantom of the Opera* (1988), *Crazy for You* (1993), and *Aida* (2003). These shows attempt to replicate in every way possible their original Broadway versions, even "back translating" the book of each musical from Japanese into English to ensure consistency with American versions. Shiki also continues to produce original Japanese-language musicals, based on famous children's novels, such as *Yume kara sameta yume* (A dream within a dream, 1987) and *Yuta to fushigina nakama-tachi* (Yuta and his enchanting friends, 1989).

Returning to its original roots in provocative problem plays, its histori-cal musicals, such as the "Shōwa Trilogy," set during World War II, was composed of *Ri Koran* (1991), about the eponymous Japanese-Manchurian singer; *Ikoku no oka* (Foreign hill, 2001), about soldiers interned in Siberia; and *Minami jūjisei* (Southern Cross, 2004), about soldiers wrongly accused of war crimes.

Musical stars are born

Musicals in Japan also have launched the careers of significant performers and artists. Mao Daichi (1956–) trained with Takarazuka, and specialized in romantic male leads in musicals, including Sky Masterson in *Guys and Dolls* (1984). After retiring in 1985, Mao became a stage actress working primar-ily for Tōhō, playing Eliza in *My Fair Lady*, first in 1990, then 600 times over the next two decades. Katsuta Shigekatsu (stage name Kaga Takeshi, 1950–), best known outside Japan as "Chairman Kaga" in *Iron Chef*, joined Gekidan Shiki in 1972, originating the roles of Jesus in the 1973 *Jesus Christ Superstar*, Tony in 1974's *West Side Story*, and the dual roles of Jean Valjean and Javert in the 1987 Japanese premiere of *Les Misérables*.

Japanese musicals have grown globally in the twenty-first century, with artists such as Miyamoto Amon (1958–) who, after studying in New York and London, made his name with *I Got Merman* (1987). Miyamoto became an internationally acclaimed director of musicals, the first Japanese to direct on Broadway (*Pacific Overtures*, 2004) and in the West End (*The Fantasticks*, 2010). He has also directed numerous musicals, operas, and straight plays in Japan, and opera and musicals in Europe and the USA.

Japanese musical production differs radically from Western practice in several ways. Most productions are "*karaoke* musicals," without live orchestras. Runs are rarely extended, even for successful productions. Instead, hits are restaged, often months later, when space can be found (Shiki with its own theatres is an exception). Successful shows are remounted regularly, even for decades after the premiere. Kōshirō's *Man of La Mancha* premiered in 1969, reaching its thousandth performance in a 2002 revival, with subsequent productions in 2005, 2008–9, and 2012.

The postwar musicals paved the way for a variety of popular fusion and music-based forms. Ongaku-za (Music Company), founded by Yokoyama Yoshikazu and Ueda Seiko from 1977 to 1987, and then reestablished by others (1988–present), and Furusato Kyaravan (Hometown Caravan, est. 1983) were both created to stage original Japanese musicals, the latter with a conscious political, satiric touch about contemporary problems of farmers or regarding the Tōhoku disaster. Gekidan Shinkansen (Bullet Train Theatre Group) and Caramel Box mix pop music and multimedia live performance influenced by manga, anime, and even, in the case of Hanagumi Shibai (the Flower Troupe, founded in 1987 by Kano Yukikazu, 1960–), traditional theatre, or "Nouveau Kabuki."

Regardless of differences, and perhaps unusually, given its foreign roots, the musical is as popular in Japan as in the United States. Japanese tourists in New York and London often partake of English-language originals already enjoyed in Japan.

References and further reading

Abe Yasushi. *Gekidan Shiki Musicals: Asari Keita to Roido Webā* (Shiki Company musicals: Asari Keita and Lloyd-Webber) (Tokyo: Hinode shuppan, 1996)

Havens, Thomas R. H. *Artist and Patron in Postwar Japan* (Princeton, NJ: Princeton University Press, 1982)

Kishi Tetsuo. *Myūjikaru ga saikō de atta koro* (The greatest musicals of their times) (Tokyo: Shobunsha, 2006)

Wetmore, Jr., Kevin J. "From *Scaretto* to *Kaze to tomo ni sarinu*: musical adaptations of *Gone with the Wind* in Japan," in David Jortner, Keiko McDonald, and Kevin J. Wetmore, Jr. (eds.), *Modern Japanese Theatre and Performance* (Lanham, MD: Lexington Books, 2006), 237–49

10 ❧ Sixties Theatre

KAN TAKAYUKI

Translated and adapted by the editors

The prehistory of Sixties Theatre

Definition

"Sixties Theatre" describes a series of movements that arose in the Japanese theatre in the 1960s in opposition to existing *shingeki*, "modern theatre." Later these came to be known as the *angura* (underground) and *shōgekijō* (little theatre) movements. The main contributing social forces were local political and social upheavals that marked the turning point in postwar Japanese history, and the influence of European rebellions of the "Revolution 68." The former included large-scale activism against the renewal of the United States—Japan Mutual Security Treaty, coupled with a shift in energy policy from coal to oil despite the coalminers' determined resistance.

Before Sixties Theatre, *shingeki* (new theatre) was the preexisting modern Japanese theatre form. Originally modeled on modern European theatre, it was called "new" to distinguish it not only from traditional theatre performance but also from other genres featuring eclectic styles mixing modern Western with premodern Japanese genres, like *shimpa*. Various factions within Sixties Theatre shared a common ambivalence toward shingeki's methods and values. Mainstream shingeki after World War II was based on realism; Sixties Theatre's anti-realism pursued the censure of modernity. This paradigmatic theatrical shift consisted of three strands: challenging standard realism; searching for independence from the norms of European modernity; questioning rationalistic views of the world and humanity. This chapter will introduce the countervailing vectors leading Japan to forge its own particular experimental theatre from 1960 to 1980, as a reaction against both conservative shingeki and Western logocentricity.

Postwar modern theatre and the critical challenge of Sixties Theatre

The previous chapters showed how imported Western Stanislavskian realism, reinforced by political ideologies, encouraged a social realism that created a mainstream shingeki movement that was earnest, logocentric, and

❧ SPOTLIGHT 10.1   Rebels with many causes

Before entering the underground labyrinth of Sixties Theatre, it may help to understand some social and economic issues that briefly helped shape the environment conducive to such a dynamic, radical experiment.

RADICAL SELF-DISCOVERY

Postwar reconstruction in Japan was followed by decades of miracle growth, aided by US military spending relating to the Korean War (1950–52), capped by two milestones: the 1964 Tokyo Olympics and the 1970 Osaka Expo. Concurrent with this economic prosperity and international development Japanese society reflected, with its own particular dynamics, many of the youth culture rebellions found elsewhere.

Those active in the 1960s were likely born in the immediate postwar period, a time of great economic hardship and political confusion. With the American Occupation (1945–52) came multi-party politics, legal equality for women, agrarian land reform, and renunciation of militarism. However, these changes were soon co-opted by the resurgence of the same capitalist-military elites of prewar. This brief postwar progressive tilt was followed quickly by the cultural "recolonization" by the USA and feeling of betrayal by Marxist intellectuals.

The US–Japan Mutual Security Treaty (AMPO), signed in 1960, formalized the military-political affiliation of Japan with its recent enemy and sparked at times violent public protests. AMPO was controversial for several reasons. Many on the left wanted no part in the growing Cold War between the United States and the Soviet Union, preferring to see Japan as a strictly neutral nation. The presence of United States military bases in Japan and Okinawa were provocative, making Japan a potential nuclear target. Furthermore, many felt the government had forced the treaty upon them without time for debate.

Similar protests occurred with the 1970 treaty renewal, and 1971 "return" of Okinawa to Japanese control. Activists were also aware that the nation's rapid industrial development had been bolstered by its role as democratic bastion against Soviet aggression in Asia and as a convenient military outpost for the USA during the wars in Korea and Vietnam. The anti-Vietnam War protests throughout Europe and the USA, the 1968 Paris student revolt, and the violent, long controversy of the Narita Airport expansion project found increasing resonance among students and led to massive protests at Japanese universities.

The poster-painting, demonstrations, and agit-prop theatre "delivered" by Sixties Theatre

TABLE 10.1 Major historical developments, Sixties Theatre era

1960	Renewal of US–Japan Peace Treaty (AMPO) demonstrations; violent student protests
1963	Miike coal mine explosion
1964	Tokyo Olympics Shinkansen bullet train started, linking Tokyo with Osaka
1966	Narita airport runway expansion Student and farmer protests
1970	World Expo, Osaka Student AMPO protests Mishima Yukio's suicide
1971	Reversion of Okinawa to Japan
1972	Red Army hostage incident
1973	Oil shock

practitioners throughout the cities and suburbs were briefly in step with these radical protests. This "Golden Age" for the anti-realist, political vanguard underground movement was later frequently eulogized by Sixties practitioners. This dream cruelly dissipated with the inexorable economic surge, subsequent reinstigation of authority, and public return to apathy following the economic boom of the late seventies and early eighties.

"LITTLE THEATRES," LOFTY AMBITIONS

Sixties Theatre was known first as anti-shingeki, non-shingeki, or post-shingeki theatre for its antithesis to the rational, verbal, text-based conventions of "modern theatre." The more radical, outlaw groups accepted the name angura (underground), referring both to the culturally subterranean nature of their experiments, and "pit" and "lab" theatres in basements around Tokyo. Later the term "shōgekijō" (little theatre) was used due to the small scale of the organization, theatres, and spectators (100–300 seat, short-run productions). Confusingly, this term has continued to the present to describe non-mainstream groups, often emerging from university theatre club graduates, working on a small scale, regardless of aesthetic or political orientation. Sixties Theatre stood in opposition to institutional, orthodox shingeki (the Mingei Theatre had 600 members in 1960), the subsidized prefectural and national theatres, and also against "commercial theatre" (shōgyō engeki) – not a company of collaborators per se, but production units assembled for a particular show, usually with stellar names in the cast, aiming for profits through long runs and tours.

Sixties Theatre practitioners strove to create a new vocabulary of performance; they wanted to free the physical body in space. Connecting to indigenous Japanese performance forms, these performers privileged the body over language. They also sought new methods of company structure and organization to reflect their left-leaning political ideologies.

The scope and form of play texts also grew in radical and important ways. Many playwrights that English-speaking audiences are most familiar with came from this fertile time, the so-called "First generation" of Little Theatre playwrights (see Table 11.1). The primarily domestic, Tokyo-based phenomenon of radical theatrical experiments occurred during an isolated period of self-discovery, from 1960 to 1983. The laboratories of the Little Theatre Movement created new acting and dramaturgical methodologies, plays of great poetic and dramatic intensity, a "return of the gods" through myth, festival, and traditional forms, and new relationships between performers and spectators which continue to influence present organization and practices. Sixties Theatre in Japan, rejecting shingeki's stale "new theatre," reinvented "contemporary theatre." It was a little later and longer than the American Off-Off-Broadway movement or British fringe, resulting in a vast web of troupes, factionalism, recombinations, and new quasi-theatrical activities. The Contemporary Theatre chapter that follows describes the multifaceted splintering after this protean time.

LEGACY OF RADICALISM

Sixties practitioners confronted the hardened authorities, apathetic public, and their own diminished capabilities of recapturing the radical moment. Many Sixties directors and playwrights, including Betsuyaku, Suzuki and Kara, were eventually co-opted into the system, becoming university teachers and public theatre artistic directors. Satoh Makoto noted ironically that the negotiations with bureaucrats over permission to construct tents and temporary theatres in public parks and other open areas in the sixties gave him and others the skill set that served them well into the 1980s, when many became artistic directors of municipal halls: Satoh at Sendagaya Public Theatre and then Za Koenji, Suzuki at Iwanami Hall, Ninagawa at Saitama Arts Theatre, Kushida at Bunkamura's Theatre Cocoon, and Betsuyaku at the Piccolo Theatre near Kobe. In addition, some Sixties' directors like Suzuki, Ninagawa, and later Noda have risen from the Little Theatre Movement to become top directors at the commercial and international levels. Through the expansion of regional venues and community theatre education, and infiltration of practitioners into these spaces as teachers and producers, perhaps Sixties Theatre experimental populism has been kept alive in different forms.

DAVID JORTNER AND JONAH SALZ

straightforward in its proscenium productions. Sixties Theatre posed multi-front challenges to these existing forms. Rather than faithful depiction of everyday life, it aimed to liberate theatre from imitation.

We can summarize the new dramatic movements' claim for "artistic freedom": There is no reason why time in drama corresponds to everyday time, nor space in drama to everyday space. Drama is a fiction or construct independent of the everyday world. There is no reason why actors' physical movements or styles of speaking have to be faithful imitations of everyday life. Actors live fictions with their own styles, independent from the everyday and routine. Their bodies in this fictive world are never subservient to the script. Actors make the performance possible. The function of the script is to mediate the fiction on stage that actors produce; performance, and the direction that facilitates it, are of greater importance.

Postwar Western theatre divergence

A key distinction between the Sixties Theatre practitioners and the European avant-garde was the latter's disbelief in rationalistic views of the world and human nature. Although both followed world wars, in Europe the horrors experienced in World War II and the Holocaust gave the lie to Enlightenment ideals of rationality, human reason, and historical progress. Theatre artists such as Samuel Beckett, Tadeusz Kantor, Jerzy Grotowski, and Antonin Artaud became influential in Europe as their work explored these major modernist themes.

In Japan, however, it took more than a decade to formulate responses to the war experience in terms of theatrical expression. Distrust in rationalistic views of the world and human nature did not become a major characteristic until Sixties Theatre, although there had been premonitions. One notable force for anti-realism in the 1950s was Gekidan Shiki (Four Seasons Company), established by Asari Keita (1933–) in 1954. The company criticized postwar Japanese realist drama and sought to produce a style of recitation in performance (*rōdoku geki*) derivative of French classical theatre. Basing itself on Existentialism, it also challenged the Marxist interpretation of society and history predominant in mainstream shingeki. Though Shiki's critique had some impact, it was not enough to subvert the dominance of postwar shingeki immediately. Playwrights began to experiment with these new forms as well; although premiered at the Bungaku-za, one of the largest mainstream shingeki troupes, *Zō* (The elephant, 1962) by Betsuyaku Minoru (1937–) demonstrated key differences between shingeki and Sixties Theatre.[1] For audiences and readers accustomed to dialogue in quotidian situations,

---

1 Trans. David G. Goodman (ed.), *After Apocalypse: Four Japanese Plays of Hiroshima and Nagasaki* (Ithaca, NY: Cornell East Asia Series, 1994).

Betsuyaku's world of endless monologues delivered in abstract space argued for a new type of drama where time and space followed a distinct logic.

The ideological bases of Sixties Theatre

Power and art

To a degree perhaps not found in many other world theatres of this time, youthful theatre vanguardists were influenced greatly by European philosophical and political writings, especially the French. Sixties Theatre was composed of three theoretical pillars, namely Bertolt Brecht, Jean-Paul Sartre, and Samuel Beckett. Theorist Takeuchi Yoshimi claimed art should be conceptualized as an intellectual construct produced out of a struggle with power structures.[2] Artists in postwar Japan faced big questions of their relationships with power and politics. The first issue considered was artists' wartime "conversion" (*tenkō*) and cooperation with the militarist regime. The second was artists' postwar moral responsibility to accept their role in Japan's colonialism and wartime activities, and finally their relationship to the postwar regime. These were the questions of true democratization, of artists' reformulation of their stance toward the emperor system, and (to borrow Takeuchi's phrase), fear that the Japanese had been "re-enslaved" under the postwar regime.[3]

The generation that instituted the new theatre in the 1960s shared a common irritation with the perceived historical apathy and artistic insensitivity of the older generation. Even the shingeki movement in the decade following the war had, according to these artists, never objectively analyzed its own political and artistic responsibility during and after the war – although some playwrights wrote about it, it was as personal reflection. For Sixties dramatists, this resulted in factional in-fighting and aesthetic dead ends, so that shingeki became as hardened in its conventions as other traditional theatres.

Critical theatre

For Sixties Theatre artists, theories of artistic creation were to be based on objective self-analysis, leading to interest in the theory and practice of Brecht. Brecht criticized the core principle of Aristotle's aesthetics – empathy through catharsis – as dissolving critical distances, and saw the Stanislavski method as a theatre of assimilation derived from Aristotle's aesthetics.

---

2 "Kenryoku to geijutsu" (Power and art), in *Takeuchi Yoshimi hyōronshū dainikan* (Collected criticism of Takeuchi Yoshimi) (Tokyo: Chikuma shobō, 1966), vol. II, 136.
3 Takeuchi Yoshimi, "Chūgoku no kindai to Nihon no kindai" (Modernity in China and Japan), in *ibid.* vol. III, 47–8.

Brecht's "alienation effect" involved seeing and showing "the self-evident" as being "not self-evident" in order to maintain critical distance.

Brecht, a communist who swore allegiance to the German Democratic Republic, was nonetheless deeply critical of Stanislavski's "authoritarian" methods as canonized in Moscow, leading the Japanese Communist Party to regard Brecht as a heretic. Senda Koreya (1904–94), one of the central figures of the shingeki movement for four decades, actively introduced Brecht's theories to Japan after a formative sojourn in Germany. Yet he was repelled by the excessive rules of socialist realism in Japan and corresponding dogmatism that condemned artistic experiments as mere formalism. Senda's intention when he introduced Brecht's theory to Japan was to attack the Japanized form of the Stanislavski method. Through Senda, Brecht's theory came to have two aspects: a new practical application of socialist dramatic theory, and a critique of orthodox realism.

Brecht influenced playwriting as well. Fukuda Yoshiyuki (1931–) wrote scripts in a Brechtian style on the theme of contemporary political struggles and experimented with Brechtian methods by writing chants for political gatherings. Fukuda attempted to incorporate Brechtian methods in works such as *Tōku made ikun da* (A journey so far, 1961) and *Sanada fūunroku* (The heroic exploits of Sanada, 1963). Satoh Makoto (1943–) bore the most evident marks of Brecht's influence.[4]

Holocaust / Hiroshima

This generation owed a spiritual debt to Sartre's ideas and drama. Remarkably, virtually all theatre practitioners of the 1960s with student backgrounds performed plays by Sartre. His questioning of art's function resonated with their own search for self-identity, as he asked rhetorically, "What is literature to a starving child?" Like Sartre, Sixties dramatists believed their efforts in literature and art must be in collaboration with political activists in their shared commitment to overcome suffering.

Young Japanese socialists supported Sartre for his insights into human despair post-Auschwitz and Hiroshima, and for his radical challenges to the stubborn self-justifying conservatism of the orthodox left. They admired Sartre for his willingness to speak out and participate as a non-Marxist left-wing activist during the Algerian war, and the Czech and Hungarian uprisings, particularly because they held strong dissident feelings of their own regarding the Japanese Communist Party. Many of these actors and directors would lead the Sixties Theatre movement over the next decades.

---

4 A list of translated works by many playwrights mentioned here is in Kevin J. Wetmore, "Modern Japanese drama in English," *ATJ* 23:1 (2006), 179–205.

Beckett and the contingency of history

Sixties Theatre also bears the unmistakable influence of Beckett.[5] Both Betsuyaku's *Zō* and the dramatic rhetoric of Kara Jūrō (1940–) display the influence of Beckett's writing. Director Suzuki Tadashi (1939–), with his insistent view of "the world as a hospital" and constant awareness that human existence hangs by a thread, is perhaps the most Beckettian.

Senda, on the other hand, remained negative about the theatre of the absurd, a natural consequence of his belief in historical progress and human rationality. From Senda's point of view, the idea that human existence lacks foundation in the world seemed no more than the angst of spoiled youth or else a façade for anti-communism. This is of course why Senda, the embodiment of the avant-garde spirit of shingeki for decades, was unable to play a major role in Sixties Theatre.

The rise of the new drama in the era of political activism

The ratification of the US–Japan Mutual Security Treaty (AMPO) in 1960 led to immense controversy and factionalism within anti-establishment movements in Japan. The year 1960 also marked the great shift in national energy policy from coal to oil. This transition led to significant changes in manufacturing and agriculture, while the declining importance of the rural economy coincided with rapid economic growth in major cities.[6] As in many parts of the world, student activism on Japanese university campuses and popular struggles for social change were intense and extensive. Domestic activism included the anti-Vietnam War movement, opposition to renewal of the US–Japan Security Treaty in 1970, and struggles over Okinawa in 1972.

Student theatre and the New Drama

This great shift from rural agriculture to urban white-collar jobs gave fledgling artists in urban areas the chance to turn professional, as greater opportunities for employment in large cities provided a livelihood and economic basis for theatrical activities for aspiring youth. Their experiences in 1960s political activism gave theatre practitioners and slightly younger generations the motivation to form a new theatrical movement.

---

5 Mariko Hori Tanaka, "Special features of Beckett performances in Japan," in Lois Oppenheim and Martin Buning (eds.), *Beckett On and On …* (Cranbury, NJ: Associated University Presses, 1996), 226–39.

6 From 1951 to 1970 the rural population of Japan went from approximately 44 percent of the population to 17 percent as job opportunities opened in the urban parts of the country. See Marius Jansen, *The Making of Modern Japan* (Cambridge, MA: Belknap Press, 2000), 738.

Most leaders of Sixties Theatre had a background in student activism and college theatrics. Betsuyaku, Suzuki, founder of the Suzuki Company of Toga (SCOT), Suzuki's producer Saitō Ikuko (1943–2012), and actor Tsutamori Kōsuke (1942–2012) were all members of the Jiyū Butai (Free Stage), a Waseda University theatre circle. Waseda also spawned other theatre companies, as well as influential playwrights and directors. Kusama Teruo (1937–62) belonged to Waseda Daigaku Engeki Kenkyūkai (Waseda University Theatre Research Group), and later established the Dokuritsu Gekijō (Independent Theatre) for which he wrote and directed *Zangyaku rippō* (Cruel laws, 1963). Written in an abstract style, it took as its theme the politics of the modern state. Close associates were Tsuno Kaitarō (1938–), ideologue of the Rokugatsu Gekijō (June Theatre) and Kuro Tento (Black Tent), Fujimoto Kazuko (1939–), translator and editor of the English magazine *Concerned Theatre Japan*, published by Black Tent, and Muramatsu Katsumi (1939–2001), lead actor of Black Tent. Yamamoto Kiyokazu (1939–2010) belonged to the Tokyo Daigaku Engeki Kenkyūkai, an inter-collegiate organization, who played alongside Saeki Ryūkō (1941–) of Gakushūin University. Saeki became a producer/director of Black Tent and major theatre theorist of the 1960s. The director/scriptwriter of the Gakushūin group was Ohta Shōgo (1939–2007), who later headed the Tenkei Gekijō (Transformation Theatre), while a group at Meiji University had Kara, who later led the Jōkyō Gekijō (Situation Theatre).

Thus student theatre troupes nurtured leaders of the Sixties Theatre movement rebelling against the shingeki movements' monopoly on contemporary theatre.

Conflicts between the old shingeki hierarchy and the Communist Party

Before abandoning the fight for vanguard supremacy, shingeki did experiment with forms outside traditional realism, staging works influenced by Brecht. Senda collaborated with the playwright Abe Kōbō (1924–93) to form a postrealist shingeki movement with works such as *Dorei-gari* (Slave trader, 1955), *Yūrei wa koko ni iru* (The ghost is here, 1958),[7] and *Omae nimo tsumi ga aru* (You too are guilty, 1965).[8] During that time, Senda also directed Fukuda's *Sanada fūunroku* (The heroic exploits of Sanada, 1963) in collaboration with the Haiyū-za Studio, Yamazaki Masakazu's *Zeami* (Haiyū-za, 1963),[9] and Hanada Kiyoteru's *Mono mina uta de owaru* (Everything ends with a song, Nissei Productions, 1963). Emulating Brecht, Senda encouraged

---

7 Trans. Donald Keene in *Three Plays by Kōbō Abe* (New York: Columbia University Press, 1993).
8 Trans. Ted T. Takaya in *Modern Japanese Drama: An Anthology* (New York: Columbia University Press, 1979).
9 Trans. J. Thomas Rimer in *Mask and Sword: Two Plays for the Contemporary Japanese Theatre* (New York: Columbia University Press, 1980).

shingeki's connection with political activism, staging the choral drama *Saigo no buki* (The final weapon, 1958), a protest against nuclear weapons, as well as reportage dramas *Miike tankō* (Miike coal) and *Okinawa, AMPO soshi no tatakai no kiroku* (Chronicle of the resistance movement against renewal of the Security Treaty, 1960).

The Seinen Geijutsu Gekijō (Seigei, Youth Art Theatre), founded predominantly by research students of the Gekidan Mingei, one of the largest shingeki troupes to emerge after the war, offered an alternative view of theatre distinct from postwar shingeki through its participation in anti-AMPO activism. It spearheaded a critique-from-within of realism in existing shingeki. Its debut 1960 productions included Fukuda's *Kiroku no. 1* (Record no. 1, dir. by noh actor Kanze Hisao), Kinoshita Mokutarō's *Izumiya somemono mise* (The Izumiya dyer's shop, dir. Iwashita Hiroshi), and J. M. Synge's *Riders to the Sea* (adapted by Kikuchi Kan). By the time the company dissolved in 1966, it had produced important anti-realist parables such as Fukuda's *Tōku made ikun da* (A journey so far), Miyamoto Ken's *Mekanizumu sakusen* (Mechanism strategy), and three plays by Fukuda, *Nagai bohyō no retsu* (The row of grave markers), *Hakamadare wa doko da* (Find Hakamadare!),[10] and *Mikazuki no kage* (Reflection of the crescent moon), as well as Betsuyaku's *The Elephant*.

The Jiyū Gekijō (Free Theatre), led by Hodoshima Takeo (1903–83), produced *Burūsu o Utae* (Sing the Blues!, 1969) by Fukuda and Kan Takayuki (b. 1939), which dramatized the anti-AMPO struggles and feuds; it also staged works by the British New Left writers Arnold Wesker and John Arden. Engeki-za (Theatre Company), founded in 1960, produced *Sukurappu* (Scrap, 1962) by Inoue Mitsuharu (1926–92), directed by Takayama Tonao (1927–2003), dramatizing scars left by a Communist Party political struggle in 1950 resulting in murder. Later, this troupe produced early works of Akimoto Matsuyo (1911–2001), *Hītachībō Kaison* (Kaison, the priest of Hitachi, 1967)[11] and *Kasabuta shikibu kō* (Thoughts on our lady of scabs, 1969), thoroughly critiquing the corruption and malaise at the heart of postwar Japanese society.

The Communist Party came under increasing attack during the political struggles in 1960. Feeling that their support for artistic activities was under threat of censure as well, the party ideologues initiated a vehement counteroffensive. In his essay "Riarizumu ni okeru handō" (Backlash against realism), Sugai Yukio (1927–2001), the party's leading cultural theorist, singled out a number of works for transgressing lines of the party-dictated realism.[12] He cautioned that these works could not be contained within boundaries of

10 Trans. in David G. Goodman in *The Return of the Gods: Japanese Drama and Culture in the 1960s* (Ithaca, NY: Cornell University East Asia Program, 2003 [1988]).
11 *Ibid.*   12 *Teatoro* 231 (1963), 2–8.

party-sanctioned diversity in realist drama because they were "erasing the distinctions between the [communist] world-view and modes of expression," in some cases largely ignoring it for stylistic reasons.

Senda fought back against Sugai, stating that his "high-handed censure [was] akin to the methods of Soviet-patronized scholars in the age of Stalin, who drove political antagonists such as Meyerhold and Tairov to destruction by branding them formalists."[13] Such disagreements were one of the driving factors behind Sixties Theatre's move away from Communist orthodoxy.

The departure from mainstream shingeki

In 1964, two established shingeki performers, Uriu Ryōsuke (1935–) and Tsuki Machiko, established the Hakken no Kai (Discovery Society), staging *Shimpan Yotsuya kaidan* (New Yotsuya ghost story), written by Hirosue Tamotsu (1919–93), and directed by Uriu. In the same year, the Budō no Kai (Grape Society) broke up, with members Takeuchi Toshiharu (1925–2009), Izumi Jirō (1931–), Sakamoto Nagatoshi (1929–), and Itō Sōichi establishing the Gekidan Henshin (Transformation Company), debuting with *Tobe! Koko ga Sadojima da* (Fly! This is Sado island, 1965), by Miyamoto, directed by Takayama. Later, with figures from the younger generation such as Terada Masaki taking the leading roles, the troupe performed European and American avant-garde plays, including Kenneth Brown's *The Brig* and Jean Genet's *The Screens*. After the dissolution of Free Theatre (Jiyū Butai), Hodoshima established the Transformation Theatre (Tenkei Gekijō) with Ohta in 1968.

In 1966, Gekidan Seigei, shingeki's leading troupe in the 1960s, was disbanded. It had included several key figures of the era's theatre, such as Kara, Satoh, Murakami Katsumi (1939–2001), and Furubayashi Itsurō. In the same year, a number of new groups emerged to take its place. With his fellows at Haiyū-za, Saitō Ren (1940–2011), Yoshida Hideko (1944–), and Kushida Kazuyoshi (1942–), Satoh reformed the old Jiyū Gekijō, inviting Kanze Hideo (1927–2007) to join as a special member. Their eighty-seat performance space was located in the basement of a building in Azabu, Tokyo. Here the company premiered Satoh's *Ismene* (1966), *Chikatetsu* (The subway, 1966)[14] and *Onna goroshi abura no jigoku* (The oil hell murder, 1969), Saitō's *Akame* (Red eye, 1961),[15] and an adaptation of Ehrenburg's *Torasuto DE* (Trust DE, 1969). They were assisted by staff from Seigei, which later merged to form Engeki Center 68/71.

---

13 "Engeki techō X" ("Drama notes X"), *Teatoro* 233 (1963), 1–13.
14 In Robert T. Rolf and John K. Gillespie (eds.), *Alternative Japanese Drama: Ten Plays* (Honolulu: University of Hawai'i Press, 1992).
15 Trans. in *CTJ* 2:1 & 2 (1971).

Fig 38 Shiraishi Kayoko (left) stars in Betsuyaku Minoru's *Macchi uri no shōjo* (The little match-girl, 1967).

New theatre companies: tents and underground spaces

At this time, new theatre companies began to proliferate. Jiyū Butai (Free Stage), established at the end of 1961, had a background in student theatre, unrelated to shingeki; its first production was of Betsuyaku's *Zō* (The elephant), directed by Suzuki. In 1966, Betsuyaku and Suzuki renamed the group the Waseda Shōgekijō (Waseda Little Theatre), debuting with Betsuyaku's *Macchi uri no shōjo* (The little match-girl, 1966).[16] When Betsuyaku left, the troupe came increasingly under Suzuki's influence. Beginning with Satoh's *Atashi no Bītoruzu* (My Beatles, 1967)[17] and Kara's *Shōjo kamen* (A virgin's mask, 1970),[18] and culminating in Suzuki's *Gekiteki naru mono o megutte II* (On the dramatic passions II, 1970), the company sent shockwaves throughout the theatrical world with innovative staging, non-linear storytelling, and powerful images.

After quitting Seigei in 1962, Kara, with colleagues from Meiji University, established the Jōkyō Gekijō (Situation Theatre). Their first production was of Sartre's *The Respectful Prostitute*, and Kara's *Nijūyon-ji gojūsan-pun 'tō no shita' yuki wa Takebayamachi no dagashiya no mae de matte iru* (The 24:53 train

16 Trans. Robert N. Lawson in *Alternative Japanese Drama*.
17 Trans. Goodman in *The Return of the Gods*.
18 Trans. John K. Gillespie and Paul H. Krieger in *Alternative Japanese Drama*.

bound for the tower is waiting in front of the candy store in Takebaya, 1966)[19] directed by Sasahara Moshu (1938–).

Jōkyō Gekijō quickly became known for its exotic contents and stage locations. They performed the street play *Mishin to kōmorigasa no betsuri* (The separation of a sewing machine and an umbrella) at Sukiyabashi Park in 1965, *Koshimaki osen* (Loincloth hermit) at the outdoor Haikagura Theatre series in Toyama Heights in 1966, and *John Silver* at the Pit Inn jazz café in 1967, and the same year staged the *Giri Ninjō irohanihoheto* ("Classically" Japanese) version of *Koshimaki osen* in a red tent at the Shinjuku Hanazono Shrine. These experimental productions caused a sensation among Japanese audiences, who were fascinated by eccentric actors like Maro Akaji (1943–) and alluring actresses like Fujiwara Maki (1941–99), who took the starring role in *Koshimaki osen*, and "heroine" Li Yeoseon (1942–). Later, at Hanazono Shrine they produced *Kugutsuban Tsubosaka reigenki* (The miracle of the Tsubosaka Kannon, 1966), *Ali Baba*, and *Yui Shōsetsu* (Yui Shōsetsu, the famed martial arts trainer, 1968). When on 3 January 1969, the troupe pitched its red tent outside the west entrance of Shinjuku Station without an official permit, Kara and two others were arrested. It was the high point of the era of social unrest, when people were eager for any reason to protest; Kara had intentionally violated the law for that purpose.

Alone among playwright-directors, Terayama Shūji (1935–83) started his theatrical career without any ties to the existing theatrical world or student theatre movements. He established Tenjō Sajiki (Peanut Gallery) in January 1967, immediately achieving great acclaim with a series of high-quality productions.

Terayama, Kara, Satoh, and others took theatre out of the mainstream through both the physical removal of actors from traditional performance spaces and their willingness to work outside orthodox shingeki company structures. These student theatre circles and non-shingeki trained actors formed a range of new troupes, riding the wave of 1960s anti-authoritarian political activism, restoring physicality in performance to offer audiences new thrills.

The banquet of Sixties Theatre

Privileging the body

The movement arising from social activism of the 1960s was an encompassing artistic movement whose participants shared the radical avant-garde

---

19 Trans. Poulton in J. Thomas Rimer, Mitsuya Mori, and M. Cody Poulton (eds.), *The Columbia Anthology of Modern Japanese Drama* (New York: Columbia University Press, 2014).

∾ FOCUS 10.1   Terayama Shūji: talented trickster

Terayama Shūji (1935–83) was the *enfant maudit* of the *angura* movement. Like other innovators of the late 1960s–1980s, Terayama embraced often eccentric alternatives to *shingeki* and to Japanese social/political norms by fusing traditional Japanese performance (noh, kabuki, and popular entertainments) with Euro-American avant-garde theatre. However, unlike many others in the angura movement, Terayama was a trickster whose politics were difficult to decipher. Rather than joining protests against terrorism after the massacre of Israeli athletes at the 1972 Munich Olympics, his troupe protested the protests by singing nonsense songs and burning their props and costumes. When ultra-nationalist Mishima Yukio (1925–70) committed suicide, Terayama complained that he should have done so at cherry blossom time. Although supportive of rebellion against authority, he advocated revolutionary imagination rather than political or social revolution.

Terayama created in many media: theatre, film, radio, poetry, photography, songwriting, novels, autobiography, social criticism, dramatic theory, and even sports essays. He was born in the northeastern prefecture of Aomori, where aspects of premodern Japanese superstition, social organization, and performance traditions still thrive. Memories of his rural childhood (and/or conflicted relationship with his widowed mother) infused his work, often clashing with sophisticated, urbanized Japanese and Euro-American pop, surrealist, or avant-garde styles. Key themes include paradoxical love–hate relationships with women (mothers, whores, and virgins), traditional Japan, modernization/Americanization, and social outcasts. Controversy defined his career. At 18, he won a prestigious *tanka* poetry award, but was condemned for self-plagiarism. Later, he encouraged teenagers to run away from home, but welcomed them into his theatrical family. Critics lionized him as innovative artistic genius and demonized him as pornographic madman.

His theatre company Tenjō Sajiki (Peanut Gallery) was founded in 1967 as a "laboratory of play" to explore the limits of theatrical experience. Experiments included *Mōjin shokan* (Blind man's letter), plunging audiences into total darkness; *Nuhikun* (Directions to servants), moving audiences around in hovercraft; *Garigari hakase no hanzai* (The crime of Dr. Galigari) featuring simultaneous, seemingly random actions in different parts of a building and, in *Jinriki hikōki Soromon* (Man-powered plane Solomon), throughout a city; *Nokku* (Knock) thrust an unsuspecting (or unwilling) person into the role of actor or audience. All succeeded in upsetting the boundary of fiction and reality.

Performances incorporated circus acts, side-show freaks, dwarves, transvestites, teenage runaways, poetry, silence, magic, music, chant, fire, psychedelic lighting, actors transformed into puppets, nudity, outdoor "city plays," real and simulated violence, elaborate scaffolding for actors and/or audience, children in pornographic situations, and live actors interacting with filmed sequences in innovative, sometimes surreal ways. Tenjō Sajiki performed in Tokyo and abroad at significant arts festivals (Olympics, Shiraz, Cannes, Nancy, Spoleto) and major cities (Berlin, New York, Amsterdam), winning prestigious awards and creating occasional havoc, riots, and bloodshed. Artistic collaborators with significant independent careers include designer Yokoo Tadanori, playwright Kishida Rio, and musician J. A. Seazer.

CAROL FISHER SORGENFREI

belief in the egalitarianism of imaginative expression summarized in Joseph Beuys' slogan that everybody is an artist. In the 1960s, new liminal art forms challenging the authority of the traditional avant-garde were born all over the world, having close affinities and ties with dissident social movements.

A wide range of arts – including theatre, rock and folk music, jazz, poetry, films, and photography – collaborated in their struggles against authority.

At the same time that it looked overseas and to other artistic genres for methodology, Sixties Theatre, in its critique of modernity and authority, often referenced the spirit, philosophy, methods, forms, and strategies of premodern noh, kabuki, and itinerant minstrels to discover new methods for creating drama. Neither physical expression in the arts, collective work, nor theatrical space was an end in itself; rather, these had to be counter-strategies to overcome the modernity typified by shingeki. New methods of physicality, collectivity, and theatre-making would enable stage expression to engage in deconstruction and activism. This form of aesthetic and political engagement inevitably resulted in a perception among the general public that Sixties Theatre was an unusual, even outrageous new subculture. However, although provocative as protest against shingeki, it was never meant to be scandalous.

Kara argued in his "theory for privileging the body" that the actor's body had priority over texts and stage direction, believing the body constituted the fundamental language of the stage. "If literature has its own unique logic of time, the drama produced through the actor's body demands a similar privilege."[20] The term he uses, *tokkenteki* ("privileged"), was obviously a paradoxical one. Though the new theatres' actors were bizarrely provocative, they were – under the leadership of their director – simply untrained "no-bodies." What was paradoxical, therefore, was that their bodies had, in Kara's formulation, a special prerogative precisely because of their exoticism. Likewise, Niitaka Keiko (1934–) and Ran Yōko (1943–) of Terayama's Tenjō Sajiki were not actresses the audience could idolize, but possessed an uncanny quality which gave them a powerful bodily stage presence to express the drama's central message.

The rediscovery of collectivity and performance space

Two major differences between shingeki and Sixties Theatre were management of theatre companies and forms of performance space. The management style of shingeki troupes was similar to that of labor organizations and social activist groups. If the leader had the necessary character, the troupe was managed in a centralized democratic style modeled on communism; where the gathering of consensus was given priority, action would require a majority rule modeled on parliamentary democracy. Sixties Theatre participants, including Kara and Suzuki, held two typical critiques of these management styles. Democratic centralism was seen as a form of hierarchical

---

20 "'Bunkateki sukyandarisuto' e" ("For 'cultural scandalmongers'"), in *Koshimaki osen* (Loincloth hermit) (Tokyo: Gendai shichōsha, 1983), 34.

totalitarianism concealed beneath the coercive mask of democracy. Majority rule was also dismissed because it hindered the centralization of power necessary for creative collectives. The latter view emerged from the idealistic anti-authoritarianism of 1968.

Numerous short-lived small theatre groups, despite imaginative stagings by talented actors and directors, tended to fail due to idealistic communist beliefs that were unsuited to the persistent and sustained efforts necessary to develop a collective sense of artistic identity among group members through their close and continuous interaction over time. In the period between the late 1960s and 1973, these groups include Tokyo Kid Brothers (founded by Higashi Yutaka), Ningen-za (Human Theatre, Gōda Kazuo), Suma Kei to Sono Nakama (the actor Suma Kei and his associates), Akai Hana (Red Flower, Boku Takeshi), Engeki-dan (The Theatre Company, Ryūzanji Shō), Maka Maka (Okamato Shūzō and Ikuta Yorozu), Kūkan Engi (Spatial Acting, Okabe Kōdai), Tsumbo Sajiki (Upper Gallery, Yamazaki Tetsu), Mei no Kai (Society of Darkness, Kanze Hisao), Tenshōgikan (Planetarium, Arato Genjirō), Renniku Kōbō (Renniku Factory, Okamoto Shō), Furenzokusen (Discontinuities, Kan Takayuki), Engekigun Sōku (Hound Dog, Sekiguchi Yō), Dairakudakan (Great Ship of the Desert, Maro Akaji), Kyokubakan (Traveling Circus, Kawasemi Ragu), and TPO Shidan (TPO Division, Kitamura Sō).

Among larger troupes, Kuro Tento 68/71 (Black Tent 68/71) opted for an open democratic management style. Collective debate and final decisions were made at meetings called *hyōgikai* (meaning "soviet" or council). They thus rejected both communist top-down and majority styles of management, so crafted a new method of collectivity that allowed for a clear sense of artistic identity.

Theatrical space was also constructed in accordance with theories of collectivity, and vice versa. Sixties Theatre dismissed the traditional proscenium arch structure because they wanted to separate themselves from the tendency of modern drama – similar to the idealization of the printed page in the modern novel – to idealize the text, the writer, and therefore the structure of the theatre building itself through such focal devices as the proscenium arch.

Both Jōkyō Gekijō (nicknamed Aka Tento, Red Tent) and Kuro Tento (Black Tent) gave performances in tents as deliberate rejections of proscenium arches of modern theatre, although differing greatly in their rationales for doing so. Kara modeled Red Tent on makeshift premodern playhouses and premodern kabuki theatres that functioned in the *akusho* (literally, "bad places" or pleasure quarters) of cities. He sensed a close affinity between his troupe and premodern *kawaramono* riverbed beggars and kabuki

performers who dwelt in such places, knowing that these groups were outcastes at the bottom of the social hierarchy. His troupe, conceptualized as
equivalents of premodern outcastes, inserted otherness (in the form of the
tent) into the everyday space of the majority of "decent" citizens. The tent
lured the social majority into its domain in order to confront their hegem-
onic ideals and aesthetic values by means of provocative performance.

Black Tent, on the other hand, employed a tent as part of their "theatrical
activism." Black Tent challenged old-style shingeki activism by seeking to
engage in leftist movements in a broader sense.[21] Black Tent claimed that
their activism constituted "performance for revolution," because it was intended to bring about a complete renewal of the imagination. Their works
were therefore strongly self-referential and self-reflective. Satoh produced
his trilogy *Kigeki Shōwa no sekai* (The farcical world of Shōwa, 1973–9), intending to anatomize and critique the culture and society of the Shōwa era.

Other companies employed non-traditional spaces as well. Tenjō Sajiki,
led by Terayama, had its base in a basement theatre in Shibuya, Tokyo too
tiny to be considered a theatre (even by mid-1960s standards). Repeated experiments in street performances were given in order to destabilize the relationship between audience and stage. In 1969, Ohta's Transformation Company staged Kenneth Brown's *The Brig* (1963) in a range of non-theatrical
spaces, including a warehouse, and produced Jean Genet's *The Screens* (1964)
at an open-air theatre. Discovery Society performed *Koko ka, kanata ka,
hatamata doko ka* (Here, there, or where?, 1968), by Uesugi Seibun (1946–)
and Uchiyama Toyoichirō at the underground car park of a Buddhist hall
in Shinjuku. Situation Theatre set up their red tent in Kichijōji at the site of
a demolished public bath. After the dissolution of the Sakurasha (Cherry
Company), Ishibashi Renji (1941–) and Midori Mako (1944–) established
their Dai Nana Byōtō (Hospital Ward Number Seven) to perform in storehouses and deserted buildings. Out of necessity or principle, non-traditional
spaces nurtured the variety of semi-professional companies that comprised
Sixties Theatre.

Theatrical activism

In Japanese, *undō* (activism) refers to collective actions intended to deconstruct preexisting norms and construct anew. It is critical about what happens outside the subject, and also self-reflective and self-referential with
regard to the internalized subject. Sixties Theatre embodied this sense of
activism.

---

21 The left wing broadly distanced itself from Soviet communism, embracing socialists and grassroots
    activists strongly opposed to the power of big business as well as philosophical Marxists, existen-
    tialists, and pragmatists.

Takei Akio, however, has criticized Sixties Theatre for not being sufficiently activist, for three main reasons.[22] One is that Sixties Theatre never tried to share common political goals concerning culture and art, and hence failed to foster mutual connections exceeding the boundaries of individuals and troupes. They therefore could not form a community with the audience, as the Rōen (Workers' Theatre Association) did with shingeki tours and workers' subscriptions.

Secondly, Sixties Theatre tended toward difficult and obscure artistic expression in the mode of absurdist drama, which provoked Takei and Senda both aesthetically and philosophically. It is also possible that the obscure language of Sixties Theatre was understood as somewhat similar to Yoshimoto Takaaki's emphasis on *jikohyōshutsu* (self-expression) and concomitant neglect of *shijihyōshutsu* (dialogue with others) in his aesthetic of language theory. Yoshimoto engaged in a fierce debate with Hanada Kiyoteru, a comrade of Takei and Senda, which covered a broad cultural context. Yoshimoto argued strongly against an essentialist view of the semantic function of language, and therefore against official pronouncements of Soviet Communism and pragmatist linguistic theory.[23] The performance of Shiraishi Kayoko (1941–) –"an actor of madness" – in Suzuki's *On the Dramatic Passions II* was regarded as a clear example of artistic expression bordering on indulgence.

Finally, it was hardly surprising that Sixties Theatre dramatists should oppose "activism." Kara, for example, had openly declared his desire "to blot it out." Since Suzuki and Terayama had taken similar positions against linking theatre with politics, it was inevitable that Takei and others, who felt activism to be inevitably political, should come to regard Sixties Theatre as anti-activism. Critic Senda Akihiko tellingly wrote, "there were no consensuses, common platforms, or declarations in this dramatic renaissance of Sixties Theatre."[24] While politically engaged, Sixties Theatre dramatists lacked the overt call for direct action contained in previous shingeki works.

Tenjō Sajiki and Jōkyō Gekijō

Revolutions, of course, were not limited to the political sphere, and many Sixties dramatists saw their work as a way of restructuring theatrical ideas and modes of thought. Terayama's goal, for example, was a revolution of the theatrical imagination, as opposed to "a theatre of revolution," aiming to deconstruct shingeki's perceived exclusive connection with a traditional

---

22 Takei Akio, *Engeki no benshōhō* (The dialectic of drama) (Tokyo: Kage shobō, 2002), 187–202.
23 See Yoshimoto Takaaki, *Gengo ni totte bi towa nani ka dainikan* (On the beauty of language, vol. II) (Tokyo: Kadokawa shoten, 1978), 573–95.
24 Senda Akihiko, "Gendai engeki no renzoku to hirenzoku" (Continuity and discontinuity in contemporary drama), in *Gekiteki runessansu – gendai engeki wa kataru* (Theatrical renaissance: contemporary drama speaks) (Tokyo: Libro, 1983), 415 .

leftist political sphere. Critic Takatori Ei described a performance of *Jashūmon* (Heretic's gate, 1972):[25]

> Performers began to shout, "There's no point in revolutionary theatre … Let's dramatize all revolutions instead." In this performance, Terayama Shūji shunned even *misemono shibai* [sideshow spectacle] as he adopted the role of a revolutionary of the theatre to set the prison house of theatre free.[26]

In an interview with Jean-Marie Domenach, editor-in-chief of *Esprit* magazine,[27] Terayama spoke repeatedly of the decline of politics and depoliticization of society in order to underline his appreciation of the May 1968 Revolution as a cultural and artistic transformation rather than a political one.

Tenjō Sajiki completed the construction of its underground mini-theatre in 1969, where it staged *Jidai wa sākasu no zō ni notte* (Our age comes riding in on a circus elephant, 1969), *Inugami* (Dog god, 1969),[28] and *Sho o sute yo machi e deyō* (Throw away your books, and hit the town!). In 1970, it produced *Kegawa no Marii* (La Marie-Vison)[29] at the La Mama Theatre in New York, *Burabura danshaku* (Baron Burabura, 1970) at the Tokyo Kōrakuen complex, and its street show *Jinriki hikōki Soromon* (Man-powered plane Solomon, 1970).

Continuing its international tours, in 1973 Tenjō Sajiki produced street shows *Chikyū kūdō setsu* (Earth is empty) and *Aru kazoku no chi no kigen* (Origin of a family bloodline) in Iran, and *Mōjin shokan* (Blind man's letters) in the Netherlands and Poland. Their thirty-hour street play *Knock* (1972), written by Maboroshi Kazuma and Kishida Rio (1946–2003), was notoriously shocking.[30] *Knock* has been described as "an artistic assault … on Tokyo's Suginami ward." Actors were given lines that could be said at random or ignored completely, and scenes were performed in thirty-three locations around the ward over a time period of thirty hours. Random people were pulled into the performance as Terayama had sent them letters telling them to arrive at specific locations and times. Police were called, as residents reacted strongly to Terayama's imposition of theatricality on their everyday lives. They also toured the Netherlands, Belgium, and Germany with their *Ekibyō ryūkōki* (Chronicles of a plague, 1975), *Nuhi Kun* (Directions to servants,

---

25 Trans. Carol Fisher Sorgenfrei in *Unspeakable Acts: The Avant-garde Theatre of Terayama Shūji and Postwar Japan* (Honolulu: University of Hawai'i Press, 2005).
26 Takatori Ei, "Terayama Shūji + Tenjō Sajiki no kiseki" (Terayama Shūji and the legacy of the Tenjō Sajiki), in *Bessatsu shimpyō: Terayama Shūji no sekai* (Special edition: the world of Terayama Shūji) (Tokyo: Shimpyōsha, 1980).
27 "Terayama Shūji kaigai taidan" (Terayama Shūji interviewed on overseas tour), in *ibid.*
28 Trans. Sorgenfrei in *ATJ* 11:2 (1994).
29 Trans. Sorgenfrei in *Half a Century of Japanese Theater*, vol. VI, ed. Japan Playwrights Association (Tokyo: Kinokuniya shoten, 2004).
30 Trans. Robert T. Rolf in *Alternative Japanese Drama*.

first performed in 1978),[31] and *Remingu* (Lemmings, first performed in 1979). Such tours were typical of Sixties Theatre troupes who found challenges in working in geographically unfamiliar places (Toga for Suzuki, tents for Kara and Satoh).

Despite Kara's opposition to "activism," both Jōkyō Gekijō and Kara were committed to it in practice, if "activism" is defined as collective discourse and action for the censure of modernity and postwar history. After his arrest for the Shinjuku West Park performance in 1969, Kara produced *Koshi-maki osen furisode kaji no maki* (Loincloth hermit – kimono afire version) at a parking lot outside Shinjuku Station west entrance, and took both this and his *Loincloth Hermit – Irohanihoheto* on tour to Okinawa. His subsequent tent productions, *Shōjo toshi* (City of virgins, 1969),[32] *Jon Shirubā – ai no kojiki hen* (John Silver – beggar of love, 1970),[33] and *Kyūketsu hime* (Vampire princess, 1971) were performed at various outdoor sites in Tokyo.

In 1972, the South Korean dissident poet Kim Ji-Ha invited the group to perform their *Nito monogatari* (A tale of two cities) at Sogang University, Seoul, when the country was still under martial law. In 1973, they performed *Bengaru no tora* (Bengal tiger) in Bangladesh. The next year, they conducted a national tour with *Kaze no Matasaburō* (Matasaburō of the wind, 1974) that began in southern Fukuoka, Kyushu and ended in Tokyo, and took the same production on tour in an Arabic version to Lebanon, Syria, and refugee camps in Palestine. These tours entailed a high level of risk, exposing the troupe to the outside world in order to enhance its potential as a collective group. In this sense, these tours were riskier than the European ones made by Terayama, Suzuki, and Ohta.

Revolutionary theatre

The Black Tent 68/71 troupe under Satoh's leadership explicitly declared its commitment to an activist theatre of revolution. Their debut performance at their signature black tent was of *Tsubasa o moyasu tenshitachi no butō* (The dance of angels who burn their own wings, 1970); based on Peter Weiss' *Marat/Sade* (1963).[34] Following that, they changed their name from Engeki Center to Black Tent 68/71, announcing in their 1969 manifesto:

> What does drama mean to us? We would like to respond to this question by initiating concrete projects in the possibilities of drama as revolutionary activism. We cannot accept the demands of bourgeois theatre and shingeki,

31 Trans. Tony Raynes and Nishiguchi Shigenobu in *Experiencing Theatre* (Englewood Cliffs, NJ: Prentice Hall, 1984).
32 Trans. Leon Ingulsrud in *Half a Century*, vol. VI.
33 Trans. Goodman in *The Return of the Gods*.
34 Trans. Goodman in *The Return of the Gods*.

even though we are conscious that we ourselves are situated inside them. We wish to tear ourselves away from their constraints ... For the purpose of revolutionizing drama and its constituent factors, we have no choice but to revive the petrified *undō* (activism), giving it new meanings and strategies ... we want to eradicate shingeki as an art and institution, and form a completely new modern drama in its ruins.[35]

The five pillars of Black Tent were its base theatre, the traveling theatre, the wall theatre, and its educational and publishing activities. While they were unsuccessful in establishing a permanent performance space, Sixties Theatre did create a traveling theatre with their nationwide tours, beginning with *Angels Who Burn Their Own Wings*. The wall theatre, which never materialized, was inspired by the slogan "Les murs ont la parole" (The walls speak) from the May 1968 Paris demonstrations, when walls were used extensively for posters, graffiti, and even newspapers. Moreover, it has to be admitted that even if Black Tent did not achieve very much in terms of education, they did achieve notable success in their theatre education and learning project, including collaborating with PETA (the Philippine Educational Theatre Association), and publication of *Dōjidai tsūshin* (Newsletter to our contemporaries). The company also published *Concerned Theatre Japan*, Japan's first English-language journal on modern theatre, under the editorial leadership of David G. Goodman (1946–2011).

The end of revolutionary theatre and return to Asia

Black Tent's first performance in the black tent in 1971 was an adventurous enterprise, but as a large number of members left the troupe it underwent constitutional change. That year the troupe staged *Renren karuta nezumi kozō Jirokichi* (Passionate card game: rat boy Jirokichi) and *Nezumi Kozō Jirokichi* (Nezumi Kozō: The Rat),[36] both written and directed by Satoh, and in 1972 *Chambara kageki Tempō Suikoden* (The tale of Suiko in the Tempō era – a samurai musical), by Yamamoto Kiyokazu and directed by Satoh. Satoh then began work on *Kigeki Shōwa no sekai* (The farcical world of Shōwa) as well as revising and reviving his other works. Among the latter were *Nigatsu to kinema* (February and cinema, 1972), *Kigeki Abe Sada: Shōwa no yokujō* (Abe Sada farce: lust in the Shōwa era, 1973), *Abe Sada no inu* (Abe Sada's dog, 1975),[37] *Kinema to tantei* (The detective and the cinema, 1975), *Buranki goroshi Shanhai no haru* (The killing of Blanqui, spring in Shanghai, 1975), and *Kinema to kaijin* (Phantom and the cinema, 1976).

---

35 Senda Akihiko, "Datsu 'shingeki' undō wa nani o nashitogeta ka" (What did the anti-shingeki movement achieve?), in *Hirakareta Gekijō* (The open theatre) (Tokyo: Shōbunsha, 1976), 127–8.
36 Trans. Goodman in *After Apocalypse*.
37 Trans. Don Kenny in *Half a Century*, vol. VI, part 1.

Following a three-year suspension of tent performances after 1976, however, the company announced a complete change in policy. After much debate, they disavowed their previous work as "formalist," arguing that their drama failed to address its true constituencies, and that they needed to create a theatrical space for activists. Their slogan was *Ajia engeki* (Asian drama), self-awareness as members of the Asian geopolitical region with its culture and arts rather than of the modern nation-state of Japan, with its strong bilateral ties to the United States. Although it did not imply any specific involvement with theatres of other Asian countries, the avant-garde artistic revolution of the past decade was rejected in favor of a new political theatre.

Two factors were behind this change. One was the practical difficulty of finding locations suitable for tent theatres, together with the futile lawsuit they had mounted against the ban on their performing in public spaces in Naha, Okinawa. The other was the mental exhaustion accrued from their collective lifestyle dynamic and a perceived alienation from the audience.

Suzuki Tadashi and Ohta Shōgo

Suzuki and Ohta came from the same revolutionary background as Kara and Satoh, but focused on transformation of the theatrical experience and actors' physicality. High praise for *On the Dramatic Passions II* led to the company being invited to perform the work in a revised version with Shiraishi at Théâtre des Nations in Paris. This in turn led Suzuki to a new career as artistic director of Iwanami Hall, where he directed Euripides' *Trojan Women* (trans. Matsudaira Chiaki, adapted by Ooka Makoto) in 1974. Noh master Kanze Hisao, shingeki actor Ichikawa Etsuko (1936–), and Shiraishi of the Waseda Shōgekijō starred, using their distinct methods, synthesized by Suzuki's direction. Immediately afterwards, Waseda Shōgekijō moved their base to Toga Village (now Nanto City) in the mountains of Toyama prefecture; in the process, the majority of its members were replaced; Suzuki compared this migration to the Red Army's Long March. In doing so, Suzuki had also invited the audience to take part in a theatrical pilgrimage.

Utage no yoru (Night of the feast) was staged at the Toga Sanbō theatre as the troupe's debut production in the summer of 1976 (Waseda Shōgekijō was renamed in 1984 as Suzuki Company of Toga [SCOT]). They performed *The Trojan Women* there in 1977; the following year Kanze appeared as Dionysus and Shiraishi as both Pentheus and Agave in *The Bacchae*. Using his trademark style, Suzuki's actors contorted and manipulated their bodies in order to evoke audience empathy.

In Tenkei Gekijō, Ohta developed a style of physical expression very different from Suzuki's. The company initially used a studio in Akasaka. Their main works in the 1970s including *Sakurahime azuma bunshō* (The scarlet

∾ SPOTLIGHT 10.2   Suzuki Tadashi: theory and practice

Fig 39 Dancing maenads and fox-priests of Asian Dionysus in Suzuki Tadashi's *Dionysus* (1990).

A seminal thinker as well as teacher and festival producer, Suzuki Tadashi (1939–) is an influential force in contemporary world theatre. His directorial *mise-en-scène* is celebrated for its stunning theatricality, energetic intensity, and refined beauty. His "Suzuki Method" actor training has gained worldwide appeal, especially in the United States. His producing has energized regional theatre and global exchanges. including recently trans-Asian training and performance collaborations.

Suzuki started his theatrical career in 1958 in a student drama club of Waseda University, Tokyo. In the 1960s his troupe Waseda Shōgekijō spearheaded the Little Theatre Movement. Suzuki made a stunning international debut at Jean-Louis Barrault's Théâtre des Nations in Paris in 1972, presenting an excerpt from the pastiche *On the Dramatic Passions II* (*Gekiteki naru mono o megutte II*), showcasing his principal actress Shiraishi Kayoko. The festival also opened up new ways for Suzuki to make theatre, including the creative revitalization of Japan's rich theatrical heritage. Suzuki aimed not simply to imitate codified acting techniques (*kata*) of noh and kabuki, but also to rearticulate essentials of

premodern performance into contemporary theatre. Suzuki attempted to create a new form of theatre that can bridge noh, kabuki, and *shingeki* modern theatre.

Suzuki's signature work, Euripides' *The Trojan Women* (*Toroia no onna*, 1974), exemplified his dramaturgy. Euripides' original play is recontextualized into a double structure (play-within-a-play) of multiple spatiotemporal dimensions, blended with additional material, including verse expressly written for this production, and a Japanese pop song. Suzuki refers to his intertextual process as *honkadori*, a classical Japanese device of allusive variation, seen in texts of both noh and kabuki; the double structure is also typical of those premodern forms.

The newly recontextualized text is staged with traditional performance devices, including full-frontal acting, long sustained stillness, and group dance. In Suzuki's intra- and intercultural rendering of *The Trojan Women*, the new and the old resonate with one another as action jumps back and forth between ancient Greece and Japan at the end of World War II, alluding to the nuclear holocaust and the ravages of war on civilians, producing familiar yet disturbing visions of the human condition.

Suzuki regularly performed a sort of "self-orientalizing," making Western classics by Greeks, Shakespeare, and Chekhov relevant to contemporary Japanese. Several productions featured multinational casts. Americans, Koreans, and other non-Japanese actors shared the stage with members of Suzuki's company, speaking their own native language but performing in Suzuki style, including *Bakkosu no shinjo* (The Bacchae, 1981) and *Erekutora* (*Electra*, 1995). Suzuki's other key productions are *Ōhi Kuritemunesutora* (Clytemnestra, 1983), an all-male *Ria ō* (King Lear, 1984), and *Duonisosu* (Dionysus, 1990).

THE SUZUKI METHOD

Suzuki believed audience experience of empathy should be induced primarily on the kinesthetic and physiological bases of performance, as in noh and kabuki. His actor training program, known as "Suzuki Method" or "Suzuki Training Method," was originally developed for his actors to build stamina and physical sensibilities to interpret stage works with a powerful theatrical presence characteristic of traditional performance (Figure 40). In Suzuki's view, the rapid dissemination of Western lifestyle and increasing reliance on technology have debilitated the actor's body ("animal energy"), which had once led to the development of noh and kabuki. To this effect, he has extracted and then rearticulated essentials of premodern acting into a systematic program.

The Suzuki Method involves an assortment of strenuous physical and vocal disciplines: foot stamping and rapid or slow walking, speech and song in challenging physical positions. Attention is paid to the lower body and feet, for Suzuki believes these earth-bound movements to be central to the danced expressions of agricultural people, and on three interrelated physical functions: energy, breathing, and center of gravity. The method does not teach acting techniques as such but rather lays building blocks for performance: suppressing and instantaneously releasing energy, maintaining stillness while retaining energy by balancing two forces (upward versus downward; forward versus backward) at the center of gravity, and deep, abdominal breathing for powerful vocal delivery.

Besides heightening the actor's abilities, the Suzuki Method establishes the "rules of physicality," a set of corporeal principles that guides actors to perform together in the same style, despite differences of nationality, culture, and language. Furthermore, undergoing the rigorous training together, actors learn how to breathe, move, and speak together in unison and develop interpersonal ties, helping build the group cohesion and tight-knit ensemble work characterizing a Suzuki performance. Through actors' heightened physicality, Suzuki attempts to unify in performance fragmented and eclectic texts employed in his stage plays.

Since 1980 Suzuki has also taught his method outside Japan. Despite a failed effort to create a licensing system, Suzuki Method instructors now teach at many academic and professional theatre academies throughout the world. The Juilliard School, Royal Shakespeare Company, and Moscow Art Theatre have incorporated Suzuki training into their programs alongside their established techniques. In 1983 JPAC (Japan Performing Arts Center) launched a month-long session in Toga for foreign actors to study the training system. From this emerged the founding members of SITI (Saratoga International Theatre Institute), an ensemble-based company that Suzuki and experimental director Anne Bogart (1951–) co-founded in New York in 1992. Although Suzuki resigned as co-director after three years, SITI continues today as a leading proponent of his method in the United States.

REGIONAL AND GLOBAL PRODUCER

Since 1976, Toga village in the mountains of Toyama prefecture has served Suzuki as worksite and spiritual home as well as springboard for international activities. His group, renamed SCOT (Suzuki Company of Toga) in 1984, clearly reflects Toga's importance to Suzuki and his members. Barrault's festival became a model for Suzuki's Toga Festival (1982–99), Japan's first international theatre festival, hosting performances and

Fig 40
International
students train
in the Suzuki
Method.

collaborations among a variety of major artists worldwide. Suzuki organized more international festivals, including the Theatre Olympics, founded in 1993, to promote theatrical performances through cultural exchange.

Suzuki was co-founder and first chair of Theatre InterAction in 1996, a network of regional theatres. He challenged Tokyo's centralization of cultural events by serving as Artistic Director for two regional public theatres: the Acting Company of Mito (ACM) in Mito City in Ibaraki prefecture (1988–95) and Shizuoka Performing Arts Center (SPAC, 1995–2007). Suzuki served as first president of the Japanese Performing Arts Foundation (JPAF), a nationwide network of theatre professionals

in Japan, founded in 2000. The JPAF-sponsored Young Theatre Artists Competition has become an important gateway for Japan's young theatre artists.

Suzuki's company has performed in eighty cities in some thirty countries since Barrault's festival in 1972. Suzuki's interculturalism since the mid-1990s has extended throughout Asia. He has taught his training method to actors of South Korea, China, Taiwan, Singapore, and Malaysia, and co-founded the BeSeTo (Beijing, Seoul, Tokyo) Theatre Festival in 1994. At the 2007 festival he presented his adaptation of Maxim Gorky's *The Lower Depths*, with a cast of Chinese, Korean, and Japanese actors.

YUKIHIRO GOTO

princess of Edo, 1970), adapted from the 1817 kabuki play by Tsuruya Namboku (see representative plays, p. 137), *Kuroageha no chibusa* (Breasts of the
black swallowtail butterfly, 1971), *Hana monogatari* (Tale of flowers) and
Akauma yakyoku (Red horse serenade, 1972), *Kanaria ryōri* (Canary cui-
sine, 1973), *Nokutān* (Nocturne, 1974), *Kigeki yakusha* (Comedian, 1975),
and *Garasu no sākasu* (Crystal circus, 1976). They performed *Kiga no matsuri* (Festival of starvation) in Poland in 1975. Their 1977 performance of
Komachi fūden (The tale of Komachi told by the wind)[38] at the Yarai Noh
Theatre was notable for the unusual venue, the actors' extremely slow movements, and largely silent staging. In the so-called Station Series that followed, starting with *Mizu no eki* (The water station, 1986),[39] Ohta further
developed his method of radically decelerating actors' physical movement
to create a potent, fictional presence: "The right tension may be found in
changing the tempo of the body, which alone might have an aesthetic impact
on contemporary people"[40] (see Figure 41).

Both Suzuki and Ohta focus on the charismatic actor's body as a medium
for the transmission of ideas.

Neo-left-wing romanticism

In contrast to Suzuki's and Ohta's physical work, Ninagawa Yukio and Shimizu Kunio focused on lyricism and theatrical imagery in their examination
of revolutionary activity. The Gendaijin Gekijō (Contemporary Persons'
Theatre), known for its dramatic elegies of the 1968 protests, was dissolved
just as it had reached its peak in 1972. It had staged noteworthy plays such
as *Shinjō afureru keihakusa* (Serious frivolity, 1969) by Shimizu, Tsuruya
Namboku's *Tōkaidō Yotsuya kaidan* (Yotsuya ghost story, 1970), and Shimizu's *Karasu yo, oretachi wa dangan o komeru* (Hey raven, we load the bul-
lets, 1971), directed by Ninagawa. Soon afterwards, Ninagawa and Shimizu
established the Sakurasha, staging Shimizu's *Bokura ga hijō no taiga o kuda-
ru toki* (When we go down that heartless river, 1972), *Mōdōken* (The guide
dog, 1973) by Kara, and Shimizu's *Nakanai no ka? Nakanai no ka? 1973 nen
no tame ni* (Won't you cry, won't you cry for 1973?, 1973).

Shimizu's unique lyricism was further inspired by his encounters with
Ninagawa. *Serious Frivolity* is about the decline of the Zenkyōtō student
protest movement, *Hey Raven* about the movement to resist the opening of
Narita International Airport in 1978, *Won't You Cry?* inspired by the far-left,
black-helmeted anarchist student groups of that time, and *Heartless River*

---

38 Trans. Mari Boyd in *ibid.*   39 Trans. Boyd in *ATJ* 7:2 (1990).
40 From an interview with Ohta Shōgo in Senda Akihiko, "Chinmoku-mono no gekisei" (Theatrical-
    ity of silence), in *Gekiteki runessansu*, 201.

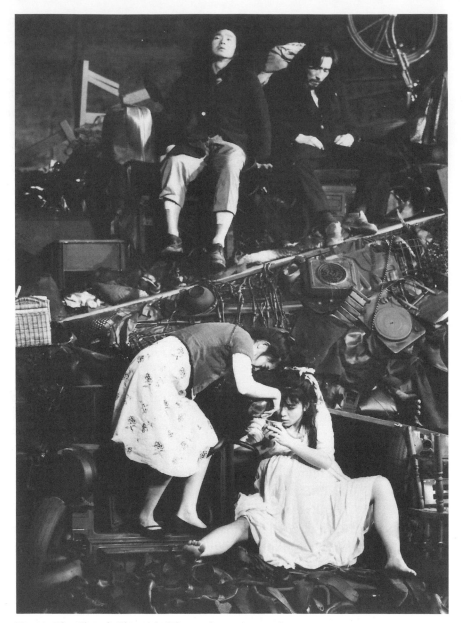

Fig 41 Ohta Shōgo's *Chi no eki* (The earth station, 1985).

reflected the United Red Army incident of February 1972, when the radical leftist group murdered fourteen of its own members. These works expressed a romantic sense of loss and passionate sympathy for young people who had been defeated in their struggle against authority and normative mainstream ideology. Yet critic Senda criticized this last play for its lack of substance, pointing out that audiences and critics were equally guilty of superficiality, and that this lack of substance was essentially a cry of despair for the defeat of ordinary people in their struggle to change the world.

Ninagawa's involvement with activism of the 1960s ended in 1974 when he directed *Romeo and Juliet* for the commercial entertainment giant Tōhō. Although it is unclear whether this was the reason behind the dissolution of Sakurasha, Ninagawa soon transformed himself into a commercial theatre brand, directing spectacular interpretations of classics for Tōhō including *Kara ban: Taki no Shiraito* (The water magician: Kara Jūrō version, 1975), *King Lear* (1975), *Oedipus* (1976), *Medea* (1978), and Akimoto's *Chikamatsu shinjū monogatari* (Chikamatsu love suicides, 1979), all to great acclaim. Ninagawa's international career began in 1983 with a tour of *Medea* to Italy and Greece. After the dissolution of Sakurasha, Shimizu set up Mokutōsha (Winter Tree Troupe), which also marked a break with Sixties Theatre as a collective movement, as Shimizu's new group centered on Matsumoto Noriko (1935–), the former principal actor of Gekidan Mingei. Having parted from Ninagawa and Shimizu, Ishibashi and other former Sakurasha members continued their angura style by establishing Dai Nana Byōtō (Hospital Ward Number Seven) to produce Kara's *Hāmerun no nezumi* (The pied piper of Hamelin), directed by Satoh.

Visionary producer and director: Kuzui Kinshirō

Another unforgettable figure of this romantic era was the director Kuzui Kinshirō (1925–). As a producer at the Nihon Arts Theatre, he had played an important role in 1960s avant-garde cinema. Kuzui started to produce plays as general manager of the Shinjuku Bunka Gekijō (Shinjuku Culture Theatre) and supported the avant-garde theatre movement at the Sasori-za (Scorpio Theatre), an underground theatre. Prior to the rise of Sixties Theatre, he promoted the performance of anti-realistic non-Japanese drama, and produced all Shinjuku performances of the Gendaijin Gekijō and Sakurasha. He introduced works of countless well-known figures from Sixties Theatre, including Suzuki, Betsuyaku, Terayama, Higashi Yutaka, Kara, Furubayashi, and Uchida Eiichi. Kuzui invited French avant-garde director Nicolas Bataille (1926–2008) to work with Sasori-za. Kuzui also had an intense sympathy for Mishima Yukio (1925–70). He produced the writer's *Kindai nōgakushū* (Modern noh plays, 1967), and, after the writer's death, produced film versions of Mishima's novels *Kinkakuji* (The Temple of the Golden Pavilion, 1976) and *Kōfukugō shuppan* (The happiness sets sail, 1980).

A plethora of drama criticism

Another remarkable aspect of Sixties Theatre is the efflorescence of intense, provocative, and intellectually stimulating critical publications. Theatre at this time was a site where radical intellectuals would develop their analyses through fierce exchanges of ideas. Someone like Terayama, who had been famous as a poet before establishing Tenjō Sajiki, naturally had a large circle of literary friends, while for Jōkyō Gekijō, Black Tent, Waseda Shōgekijō, and others, the formation of troupes and the rise of new dramatic literature provided numerous opportunities for people to come together for intellectual and social discourse. Black Tent was especially noted for the circle of artists and critics who wrote for their *Kikan Dōjidai Engeki* (Contemporary Drama Quarterly). Partly because Suzuki had been appointed artistic director of Iwanami Hall at a relatively young age, high-brow intellectuals were also drawn to Waseda Shōgekijō.

Journalists working for newspapers and news agencies also drew their readers' attention to Sixties Theatre. Mori Hideo of the *Tokyo shimbun*, Senda (1940–) of the *Asahi shimbun*, Kawamoto Yūzō (1932–2008) of the *Nihon keizai shimbun*, and other journalists devoted considerable space to contemporary theatre.

The decade saw the publication of numerous books on theatre theory and criticism. Among works by directors still considered topical are Suzuki's *Katari no chihei* (The horizons of deception, Hakusuisha, 1980), *Gekiteki naru mono o megutte* (Kōsakusha, 1977), and Ohta's *Hishō to kensui* (Flying and falling, Jiritsu shobo, 1975). Among works by those who were both practitioners and critics are *Kyokō no shintai* (The fictive body, Chūō Kōronsha, 1978) and *Gekijō no shikō* (Thoughts on the theatre, Iwanami shoten, 1984) by Watanabe Moriaki (1933–); Saeki's *Ika suru jikan* (Catabolic time, Shōbunsha, 1973); and my own *Kaitai suru engeki* (Deconstructing drama, Adin shobō, 1974). Among academic studies are David G. Goodman's *Fujisan mieta* (I could see Mount Fuji, Hakusuisha, 1983); Tsuno's *Higeki no hihan* (Criticizing tragedy, Shōbunsha, 1970), *Mon no mukō no gekijō* (Theatre beyond the gate, Hakusuisha, 1972), and *Pesuto to gekijō* (Plague and the theatre, Shōbunsha, 1980); *Hyōi no kamen* (The mask of possession, Serica shobō, 1972) and *Bara to ine* (Rose and rice, Hakusuisha, 1977) by Kogarimai Ken (1939–); and the significant contributions of Watanabe Tamotsu (1936–) as both kabuki critic and Tōhō producer, *Onnagata no unmei* (The destiny of the onnagata, Kinokuniya shoten, 1974), *Haiyū no unmei* (The destiny of the actor, Kōdansha, 1981), and *Gekihyō ni nani ga okotta ka* (What has happened to drama criticism?, Shinshindō shuppan, 1983). Among the journalists are Mori Hideo's *Gekijō e* (To the theatre, Shōbunsha, 1974); and Senda Akihiko's *Hirakareta gekijō* (The open theatre, Shōbunsha, 1976), *Gekiteki runessansu* (Theatrical renaissance, Libro, 1983), and *Gendai engeki e no kōkai* (The voyage of contemporary Japanese theatre, Libro, 1988).[41] These

---

41 Trans. J. Thomas Rimer (Honolulu: University of Hawai'i Press, 1997).

theoretical texts became the medium through which theatrical ideas were promoted, discussed, and shared between Sixties dramatists, critics, and the general public. As such, they were critical to the dissemination of philosophies, creating a fairly complete record of the theatrical ideologies of these artists and their contemporaries.

The historical fate of Sixties Theatre

Despite its influence and success, Sixties Theatre had several important limitations. It was a regional movement centered in Tokyo.[42] While keenly aware of the extreme social changes occurring in the capital, Sixties Theatre tended to ignore the growing division between Tokyo and other regions happening at that time. Shingeki had had similar problems in its early days, although it still maintained links with regional audiences and theatres, something Sixties Theatre never did.

Sixties Theatre was also monopolized by young intellectuals. While this helped to keep the movement radical and progressive, it also led to a certain self-righteous egoism, elitism, and ageism. The greatest problematic puzzle of Sixties Theatre, however, was the makeup of its audience, comprising collaborators and supporters on the one hand and those with no direct connection on the other. Critic Senda noted that, although the more activist groups tended to have their own theories about them, they could not understand their actual audience.[43]

Crucially, they failed to represent their sociopolitical Others. Sixties Theatre dramatized itself as "a monstrous alien" in its mission to subvert Japanese modernity and the trajectory of postwar Japan, but was never able to represent the relationships between Japan and its marginalized others. Sixties Theatre ultimately could not condemn male chauvinism, ethnocentrism, discrimination against physically challenged people, or the Eurocentrism and colonialism typical of developed countries. It was one thing to represent itself as an alien Other, but quite another to be able to voice the concerns of Japan's own Others.

The Sixties Theatre's residue

Problematic end of the protest movement and Sixties Theatre

The decline of the New Left followed the same logic of that of Sixties Theatre; while denouncing Japanese modernity, the postwar order, and capitalism,

---

42 Not originating in Tokyo was the revisionist wing led by Matsumoto Yūkichi's Isshinha (1970) in Osaka, and the Nagoya-based Nanatsudera Kyōdō Studio.
43 "Datsu shingeki," 135.

and while fashioning itself as "a monstrous alien," the New Left nevertheless failed to comprehend the relationship between Japan and its Others.

The protest movement faded in the 1970s as authorities reestablished order. The New Left, escalating its struggles, resorted to sectarian fighting and terrorist acts. Apart from the Sanrizuka resistance campaign against the Narita Airport construction, anti-discrimination activism was prominent within the New Left, leading to divisive internal squabbles and diminishment. The Old Left ceased to engage in class struggle, becoming no more than a popular front that ignored the issues of oppressed social minorities at the bottom of the social hierarchy, such as *burakumin*, the poor ethnic minorities, and the disabled.

Government and the police made use of festive space totally impossible. Public opinion reinforced the prohibition of tent theatres, so that theatre groups had no public spaces in which to perform. While several troupes continued their work overseas, the decline of countercultural theatre as a whole was unstoppable.

The legacy of Sixties Theatre

Text and body, three historical styles

Critic and sometime producer Watanabe offers some insight into the question of Sixties Theatre's legacy via a detailed analysis of the different "methods" of the three stars of Suzuki's *Trojan Women* in 1974: shingeki actress Ichihara Etsuko, noh actor Kanze Hideo, and Suzuki company actress par excellence Shiraishi Kayoko. Through his analysis of the different relationships between text and body adopted by the performers, Watanabe develops a historical approach toward their distinctive acting methods:

> Ichikawa speaks in order to deliver the meaning of the words ... Hers is a language of dialogue. For Kanze, words are like songs, but for Shiraishi, words come from the body ... By analyzing these differences, we can understand the differences in their "methods."[44]

Watanabe adds that "Ichikawa's lines are always wanting to be possessed by someone" and that "they beg the existence of other dramatic characters,"[45] thus being outside the body. Watanabe argues that Ichikawa's "method" is realism, the theatrical essence of "shingeki." Kanze, on the other hand, "does not seek meaning in words" but rather expresses language through "its forms": he "does not seek their meaning. Accordingly, his words are songs

---

44 "Haiyū no sugao – Kichiemon no gakuya" (The unpainted actor's face – in the dressing room of Nakamura Kichiemon), in *Haiyū no unmei* (The destiny of the actor) (Tokyo: Kōdansha, 1981), 32.
45 *Ibid.* 33.

and recitations that intoxicate the listeners, but do not make them grapple with the words' import," his words also existing "outside the body." "This stance of a singer comes precisely from distilling the methods of Japanese classical arts with their tradition of narrative singing."[46]

Shiraishi, however, differs from both these styles:

> For Shiraishi, words are not tools for communicating meaning, nor lyrics … they are complete in themselves … these words … are Shiraishi Kayoko's own, but at the same time they are impersonal, possessed by no one … Her words are autonomous … they are rooted in her humanity … She performs … her real self, hidden under everyday life.[47]

In other words, the "methods" of Sixties Theatre used language not as a vehicle for the communication of meaning, but as something based deeply within the human. These methods are thus distinct from those of Japanese traditional theatre and of shingeki and its sources in modern European drama. As Watanabe points out, the discovery of new, alternative relationships between text and body in the theatre leads to the question, "Who am I?" When the inquiry is projected onto the audience facing the stage it is shared by the whole theatre. As the self and the world reflect each other, the question "Who am I?" leads to another question, "What does it mean to be human?" That is why the discovery of a new, alternative relationship between text and body deserves to be appreciated as epoch-making history.

In my view, Sixties Theatre "ended" between 1982 and 1983. In 1982, Noda Hideki was awarded the Kishida Drama Prize for *Nokemono kitarite* (The descent of the brutes), reaching the height of his early fame. In the same year, the International Theatre Festival, hosted by the International Institute for Research in the Dramatic Arts, was held at Toga, with works by Tadeusz Kantor and Robert Wilson at Toga Art Park. Sixties Theatre could no longer be accommodated in the capital, signifying that Suzuki's "Long March" to Toga was complete. In 1983, Black Tent 68/71's production of *Akai kyabarē* (Red cabaret) also symbolized a change in their policies. The same year saw the death of Terayama. That year, Shiki set up a tent for the West End musical *Cats* in Shinjuku, thus completely transforming the significance of tent theatre.

The Sixties Theatre movement was over. Living bodies can no longer hold any concrete reality in today's global market of high-speed digitalization of information. We grapple with issues of how, and through what kind of collective, we might be able to discover a methodology of objectively viewing and galvanizing the body. We can find answers to the question of what it

---

46 *Ibid.* 37–8.   47 *Ibid.* 39–41.

means to be human as Sixties dramatists did, through raising awareness of the relationship between text and body, as well as finding organizational theories and theatrical pedagogies. Accordingly, these methods become "ways" to investigate the world and humanity through languages of the body. Above all, like Sixties dramatists, we require imagination to measure the relationship between self and the world.

References and further reading

Eckersall, Peter. *Theorizing the Angura Space: Avant-garde Performance and Politics in Japan, 1960–2000* (Leiden: Brill, 2006)

Goodman, David G. *After Apocalypse: Four Japanese Plays of Hiroshima and Nagasaki* (Ithaca, NY: Columbia University Press, 1986)

  Angura: Posters of the Japanese Avant Garde (New York: Princeton Architectural Press, 1999)

  The Return of the Gods: Japanese Drama and Culture in the 1960s (Ithaca, NY: Cornell University East Asia Program, 2003 [1988])

Rolf, Robert T., and John K. Gillespie (eds.). *Alternative Japanese Drama: Ten Plays* (Honolulu: University of Hawai'i Press, 1992)

Senda, Akihiro. *The Voyage of Contemporary Japanese Theatre*, trans. J. Thomas Rimer (Honolulu: University of Hawai'i Press, 1997)

FOCUS 10.1 TERAYAMA SHŪJI: TALENTED TRICKSTER

Ridgely, Steven C. *Japanese Counterculture: The Antiestablishment Art of Terayama Shūji* (Minneapolis: University of Minnesota Press, 2010)

Sas, Miriam. *Experimental Arts in Postwar Japan: Moments of Encounter, Engagement and Imagined Return* (Cambridge, MA: Harvard University Press, 2011)

Sorgenfrei, Carol Fisher. *Unspeakable Acts: The Avant-Garde Theatre of Terayama Shūji and Postwar Japan* (Honolulu: University of Hawai'i Press, 2005)

SPOTLIGHT 10.2 SUZUKI TADASHI: THEORY AND PRACTICE

Allain, Paul. *The Art of Stillness: The Theater Practice of Tadashi Suzuki* (New York: Palgrave Macmillan, 2002)

Carruthers, Ian, and Takahashi Yasunari. *The Theatre of Suzuki Tadashi* (Cambridge: Cambridge University Press, 2004)

Goto Yukihiro. "The theatrical fusion of Suzuki Tadashi," *ATJ* 6:2 (1989) 103–23

Suzuki Tadashi. *Engeki towa nanika* (What is theatre?) (Tokyo: Iwanami shoten, 1988)

  Naikaku no wa (The sum of interior angles) (Tokyo: Jiritsu shobō, 1973)

  The Way of Acting: The Theatre Writings of Tadashi Suzuki, trans. J. Thomas Rimer (New York: Theatre Communications Group, 1986)

  Suzuki Tadashi no sekai (The world of Suzuki Tadashi: selected works) DVD (Tokyo: Cosmo, 2011) (English subtitles)

Interlude: Butoh: dance of darkness and light

BRUCE BAIRD

Butoh is a dance or performance genre originating in Tokyo in the post-war era, primarily through the activities of Hijikata Tatsumi (1928–86; Figure 43). Butoh dances often feature near-naked dancers in white-face and body paint, with slow, precise, contorted movements either entirely improvised or highly choreographed. Butoh artists have often sought to plumb the depths of humanity or to provide a privileged aperture to timeless truths. Defining butoh must remain tentative: because of its acceptance as both theatre and contemporary dance, and rapid global expansion, butoh continues to embrace and elaborate a wide spectrum of methods and themes.

Hijikata's non-dance experiments

Founder Hijikata trained in ballet, jazz, tap, flamenco, and German Expressionist dance before breaking from those traditions. His first piece, *Kinjiki* (Forbidden colors, 1959), depicted a man having sex with a younger man, then forcing him to kill a chicken – a performance ostensibly based on the novel by Mishima Yukio (1925–70) and writings of Jean Genet (1910–86). Hijikata, however, quickly turned away from such mimetic dance. For the next decade, he led a small cohort of dancers and visual artists from the spheres of neo-Dadaism and Happenings to experiment with widening the scope of dance to include activities such as eating cake, running wind-sprints, and photographing the audience. In addition, performers staged taboo subjects and extreme states of being such as disease, madness, senility, violence, and pain.

In the late 1960s and early 1970s, Hijikata began an exhaustive and detailed examination of ways that his body-mind had been formed and socialized, at the same time an experiment in achieving a radically new generative body-mind. This experiment was based on the double assumption that he could mine his own past for new dance movements, and that such minute awareness would allow him to break free of previously unconscious physical and mental strictures. Concurrently, he turned to detailed,

Fig 42 Hijikata Tatsumi dances *Shizuka na ie* (A quiet house, 1973).

structured choreography in which dancers performed a movement or pose while visualizing various images to affect the qualities of their movements. Common visualizations included altering the character imagined to be doing the movement: an old person character's movements more stooped and slower than a young person's. Dancers also were instructed to alter the imagined context, to interpret doing movements in water or glass. Perhaps taking a hint from surrealism, Hijikata further directed dancers to imagine being eaten by insects, or jolted by electricity, assuming movements would thus be qualitatively transformed.

Expansion and diversation

Hijikata's turn from neo-Dada and Happenings to highly choreographed dances caused the small community of performers to fracture into many different kinds of dance, all claiming the term *butō* (舞踏), then a neutral term for "Western dance." Some performers such as Ishii Mitsutaka (1939–) improvised flowing movements in fields and forests. Such outwardly diverse choreographers as Maro Akaji (1943–) and Amagatsu Ushio (1949–) followed Hijikata's choreographic methods in constructing grand spectacles. Maro had also studied with Kara Juro (1940–) and performed with Jōkyō Gekidan (Situation Theatre). His Dairakudakan (Great Camel Battleship, est. 1972) included rough, humorous, and theatrical shows. Amagatsu came from a ballet background; his Sankai Juku (est. 1975) presented achingly beautiful and slowly flowing dances evoking cosmological depictions of the processes of life, death, and evolution. Suggesting butoh's roots in Rudolf Laban's (1879–1958) German Expressionist idea of cataloging a universal transcultural psychophysical vocabulary, Kasai Akira (1943–) promoted a version predicated on the idea of a one-to-one correspondence between movement and choreographic intent. Kasai studied Rudolph Steiner's anthroposophy, and viewed dance as properly expressing a unified secular mysticism spanning body, language, community, and history.

The next generation, including Tanaka Min (1945–), Goi Teru (1945–2008), and Iwana Masaki (1945–), never studied with Hijikata, yet identified with the generic term butoh. Tanaka had studied modern dance and ballet, but in the mid-1970s began experimenting with extremely slow movements, micro-movements, and improvisational dance in non-traditional spaces, primarily outdoors. In the 1980s, Tanaka worked with Hijikata and became known as a butoh performer, but now rejects that label. He continues to explore improvisation, collaboration, and minute discernment and control of all parts of the body, and the relationship between bodies and spaces, and with other bodies. New York based Eiko and Koma also disavow a connection to butoh, claiming instead to practice "delicious movement," yet reflect the philosophy and form in glacially paced movements in themes of life and death, and the natural world.

Butoh's international flowering

Practitioners today may be distinguished according to where they fall along several artistic fault lines: improvisation versus tightly structured dance; spectacle versus minimalism; and emotion and sensation versus meaning – appended quite arbitrarily to movement or emerging organically. Yet butoh's many approaches are not equally visible in Europe and America; Maro was the artist most successful in passing on his understanding to disciples, whom he encouraged to create their own companies. In the seventies, his disciples, including Carlotta Ikeda (1941–), Furukawa Anzu (1952–2001), Murobushi Kō (1947–), and Amagatsu, relocated to Europe, where they were warmly received by Europeans eager to embrace a vital new art form both strange and familiar.

At the same time, Ohno (Ōno) Kazuo (1906–2010) began performing extensively in Europe and the Americas. In the late 1960s, Ohno had parted ways with collaborator Hijikata; at age 71, he came out of quasi-retirement to appear in *Admiring La Argentina* (1977). It reprised Hijikata's dance *Forbidden Colors* (1960, revised version), to which Ohno added his own choreography, including scenes from his daily life as a janitor and homage to flamenco dancer Antonia Mercé y Luque. This dance catapulted Ohno to worldwide fame when he presented it at the Avignon Festival in 1980. Ohno shared choreographic methodology with Hijikata, but his dances and public pronouncements were oriented toward expressing a cosmological connection between himself and all humanity. Despite being just two branches from Hijikata's deep-rooted butoh trunk, soon Ohno and Maro and his lineage (particularly Paris-based Sankai Juku) were the public face of butoh in the West. There, butoh was often taken as a response to the atomic bomb. Or – perhaps due to the appearance of ethnically marked costumes in the dances of choreographers investigating their own pasts – as related to Japanese rituals or traditional folk arts such as *kagura*.

While worldwide understanding of butoh is colored by the Western filter of early touring troupes, there are now many dancers, Japanese and foreign, in Japan and around the world, either solo or in companies, either referring to themselves as butoh artists or sharing characteristics sufficient to be grouped under butoh's broad umbrella. A representative sample includes noh and Asian dance influenced Katsura Kan (1955–), American Joan Laage's Dappin' Butoh (est. 1991, disbanded 2002), Yoshioka Yumiko's experiments with technology and installation art and her production work at Schloss Broellin (Ten Pen Chii, est. 1995), SU-EN's exploration of the "Nordic Body" in Sweden, the Japanese-American Shinichi Iova-Koga's humor (Inkboat, est. 1998), and the ferociously spare work of Kaseki Yuko (cokaseki, est. 1995).

Butoh has also been influential in shaping a generation of contemporary dance performers oriented to concentration, distillation, and use of body parts in isolation to express potent and disturbing images. These dancers – including Teshigawara Saburō (1953–; Karas, est. 1985), Kurosawa Mika (1957–; Kurosawa Mika and Dancers, est. 1985), Kota Yamazaki (1959–; Rosy Co., 1996–2001, Fluid Hug-Hug, est. 2002), Tero Saarinen (1964–; Tero Saarinen Company, est. 1996), Itoh Kim (1965–; Glorious Future, est. 1995), Ohashi Kakuya (1967–; Ohashi Kakuya & Dancers, est. 1999), and Suzuki Yukio (1972–; Kingyo, est. 2000) – are sometimes termed "post-butoh," demonstrating that butoh's fire still lights the way to the future.

References and further reading

Baird, Bruce. *Hijikata Tatsumi and Butoh: Dancing in a Pool of Gray Grits* (New York: Palgrave Macmillan, 2012)

Fraleigh, Sondra Horton. *Butoh: Metamorphic Dance and Global Alchemy* (Urbana, IL: University of Illinois Press, 2010)

Fraleigh, Sondra Horton, and Tamah Nakamura. *Hijikata Tatsumi and Ohno Kazuo* (New York: Routledge, 2006)

Kurihara, Nanako. "Hijikata Tatsumi: The Words of Butoh," *TDR* 44:1 (2000), 10–28

Mikami Kayo. *Utsuwa toshite no shintai: ankoku butō gihō e no apurōchi* (Body as receptacle: an approach to the techniques of Ankoku Butoh) (Tokyo: ANZ-Do, 1993)

Ohno Kazuo, Ohno Yoshito, and Mizohata Toshio. *Kazuo Ohno's World: From Without and Within* (Middletown, CT: Wesleyan University Press, 2004)

Viala, Jean, and Nourit Masson-Sekine. *Butoh: Shades of Darkness* (Tokyo: Shufunotomo, 1988)

DVD AND ONLINE RESOURCES

Butoh: Body on the Edge of Crisis, dir. Michael Blackwood, DVD (New York: Michael Blackwood Productions, 2006)

Butoh: Piercing the Mask, dir. Richard Moore, DVD (New York: Insight Media, 1991)

Hijikata Tatsumi, *Summer Storm* DVD (San Francisco: Microcinema, 2010)

11 ∾ Contemporary theatre

M. CODY POULTON

Japanese theatre in the 1980s inherited much of its style and dramaturgy from Sixties Theatre. To some extent this was not surprising, since so many key artists from that period – including Suzuki Tadashi, Ninagawa Yukio, Kara Jūrō, Ohta Shōgo, Inoue Hisashi, and Ohno Kazuo – continued to produce challenging and fresh work. Many younger playwrights, directors, actors, and other artists trained under masters of Sixties Theatre or were inspired by them. Themes explored by *angura* (underground, vanguard) playwrights – memory and loss, quixotic quests for identity, false or dubious gods and prophets – were taken up and developed in 1980s theatre. Structurally, 1980s drama inherited angura's complex and surrealistic dramaturgy – the collage technique mastered by Kara in which several motifs and narrative strands intersect, introducing wildly disparate elements culled from Western or Japanese popular and classical culture. Typically taking their shape and themes from fantasy and dreams, they call into question the nature of reality itself, a motif sounded with frequent recourse.

Post-1980s theatre moved from fringe to mainstream culture, such that the Sixties Theatre term "little theatre" (*shōgekijō*) hardly seems appropriate any more for describing angura's legacy. Today, Ninagawa's productions are typically staged for long runs in mid- to large-sized theatres like Theatre Cocoon or Nissay Theatre in Tokyo, for 700 to over 1,000 people. The most popular playwright to emerge from the late 1970s, Noda Hideki (1955–), drew an audience of over 26,000 people on one occasion (8 June 1986, in Yoyogi Stadium) and currently stages his plays at the 834-seat Tokyo Metropolitan Theatre, where he is artistic director. Theatre of this kind, amplified by microphones and projections, has more the character of a rock concert than the intimate club-like atmosphere of "classical" angura. Unlike the devoted and eccentric amateur actors of angura, Ninagawa and Noda depend for their popularity, and even artistic survival, on casting major celebrities, singers, and actors from television and cinema.

Yet this invasion of the angura spirit into mainstream theatre was not accompanied by a similar political mobilization. By the 1980s, the Japanese public had become increasingly conservative and complacent, accustomed to the miraculous nature of Japan's postwar reconstruction. From the ashes of defeat in 1945, the country (with no little assistance from its erstwhile enemy, the United States, which needed a staging base for long wars in Korea and Vietnam) managed within a few decades to become a global economic powerhouse, second only to the United States, and overtaken by China only in 2010. Life was good, and too much money was being made by too many people to question too seriously the status quo.

Theatre also began borrowing more heavily from other media, including television, manga and anime, J-pop, and *otaku* geek video-game culture. There was accordingly a shift from counterculture to a proliferation of subcultures, each with its own community and vernacular, reflected in the theatrical style of individual theatre companies. The erosion of logocentric theatre was thus also marked by a shift from word to image, and toward increasing mediatization and mechanization of performance. Increasing privatization of Japanese life (which at its most pathological extreme is manifested in *hikikomori* youths, mostly males, who shut themselves off from society) has also been a trend countering theatre's most primal purpose: to bring people together.

Fast times

The pace of change in Japan is dizzying, even today, despite its seemingly petrified economy and political system. Theatre artists of the 1980s were already calling themselves a "third generation." The sense of vertigo has been one of the defining features of Japanese theatre and culture since the 1980s. Albert Camus' *Myth of Sisyphus* may have defined the existential experience of modern humanity: one burdened by the inertia of civilized self-awareness; life in modern Japan, on the other hand, seems more like the scene in *Raiders of the Lost Ark* in which Indiana Jones runs hell-bent down a tunnel, pursued by a giant boulder. There is a sense in contemporary Japan that, should one ever stop moving, one would either be crushed or left behind.

Two 1980s playwrights, Noda and Kōkami Shōji, exemplify the precipitous speed of contemporary Japanese life. The performances of Noda's Yume no Yūminsha (Dreaming Bohemians, est. 1976) and Kōkami's Dai San Butai (Third Stage, est. 1981) above all required youth, energy, and ferocious athleticism in their performers (including the playwright-leaders of these troupes). They ran, leapt, and flung themselves across the stage, delivering their lines at breakneck speed and often at the top of their voices. They had no regard, it seemed, for whether the register of their voices matched the meaning of the words or feelings of characters, or even whether the audience

❧ FOCUS 11.1   Five generations of contemporary playwrights

Notes:
- Some playwrights are also well-known as directors (Kushida) and novelists (Yū).
- Generations are somewhat arbitrary designations, based on playwright's age rather than public activities.
- Playwrights involved with numerous companies are listed with their major one.

1st	2nd	3rd	4th	5th
Akimoto Matsuyo 1911–2001 (Gikyoku Kenkyūkai)	**Yamazaki Tetsu** 1946– (Transposition 21)	**Ichidō Rei** (alias) (Gekidan Aoitori)	**Inoue Hidenori** 1960– (Gekidan Shinkansen)	**Aoki Go** 1967– (Gring)
Ariyoshi Sawako 1931–84	**Takeuchi Jūichirō** 1947– (Arcanum O)	**Tsutsumi Harue** 1950–	**Narui Yutaka** 1961– (Caramel Box)	**Takayama Akira** 1969– (Port B)
Inoue Hisashi 1934–2010 (Komatsu Theatre)	**Tsuka Kōhei** 1948–2010	**Nagai Ai** 1951– (Nitosha)	**Sakate Yōji** 1962– (Rinkōgun)	**Akahori Masaaki** 1971– (Shampoo Hat)
Terayama Shūji 1935–83 (Tenjō Sajiki)	**Kitamura Sō** 1953–	**Iwamatsu Ryō** 1952– (Takenaka Naoto no Kai)	**Mitani Kōki** 1961–	**Matsui Shū** 1972– (Sample)
Shimizu Kunio 1936– (Gendaijin Gekijō)	**Kisaragi Koharu** 1956–2000 (NOISE)	**Watanabe Eri** 1955– (300 Theatre Company)	**Matsuda Masataka** 1962– (Marebito no Kai)	**Okada Toshiki** 1973– (chelfitsch)
Betsuyaku Minoru 1937– (Snail Society)		**Noda Hideki** 1955– (NODA MAP)	**Suzuki Matsuo** 1962– (Otona Keikaku)	**Iwai Hideto** 1974– (Hi-Bye)
Ohta Shōgo 1939–2007 (Tenkei Theatre)		**Miyazawa Akio** 1956– (U-enchi Saisei Jigyōdan)	**Hirata Oriza** 1962– (Seinendan)	**Maekawa Tomohiro** 1974– (Ikiume)
Kara Jūrō 1940– (Jōkyō Gekijō) (Red Tent)		**Kōkami Shōji** 1958– (Daisanbutai)	**Iijima Sanae** 1963– (Jitensha Kinqureat)	**Miura Daisuke** 1975– (potudo-ru)
Saitō Ren 1940–2011 (Jiyū Gekijō)			**Suzue Toshirō** 1963– (Hachiji-han)	

1st	2nd	3rd	4th	5th
Kushida Kazuyoshi 1942– (Theatre Cocoon/ On-Theatre Jiyū Gekijō)		**Kawamura Takeshi** 1959– (Daisan erotica/ T Factory)	**Keralino Sandorovich** 1963– (Nylon 100C)	**Nagatsuka Keishi** 1975– (Asagaya spiders)
Satoh Makoto 1943– (Theatre Center 68/69) (Black Tent)		**Makino Nozomi** 1959– (MOP)	**Tsuchida Hideo** 1967– (B Kyu Practice/ MONO)	**Nozoe Seiji** 1975– (Haegiwa)
Kishida Rio 1946–2003 (Kishida Jimusho)		**Yokouchi Kensuke** 1961– (Tobiraza)	**Hitsujiya Shirotama** 1967– (YUBIWA Hotel)	**Kuro Tanino** 1976– (Niwageki Penino)
Matsumoto Yūkichi 1946– (Ishinha)			**Yū Miri** 1968– (Seishin Gogatsutō)	**Maeda Shiro** 1977– (Gotandadan)
			Mikuni Yanaihara 1970– (Nibroll)	**Motoya Yukiko** 1979– (Motoya Yukiko Theater Company)
			Kudō Kankurō 1970– (Otona Keikaku)	

DAVID JORTNER

itself could keep pace with the unfolding story. The physicality of such performances was almost as exhausting and exhilarating for spectators as it was for actors.

Both actors and audience were young, speaking to shared generational interests and concerns. People learned of performances by word of mouth or through new entertainment magazines like *Pia* (as in *Entertainment Utopia*, a weekly *Time Out*-like glossy), drawn to see their heroes act out the experience of their vertiginous times. Neither Kōkami nor Noda professed any particular interest in politics. Noda described himself as an "anarchist," but playing on the Japanese word *ana* ("hole"), suggesting a latent emptiness.

∾ FOCUS 11.2   Noda Hideki: dynamic director

Noda Hideki was born in Nagasaki in 1955. In 1976, while at the University of Tokyo, he founded Yume no Yūminsha (Dreaming Bohemians), directing and acting in high-speed, pun-driven, physical plays. *Nokemono kitarite* (Descent of the brutes, 1982) earned him the prestigious Kishida Kunio Drama Award. At the Edinburgh International Festival in 1987 it was generally well received, although critics found Noda's trademark wordplay via live commentary inherently difficult, "almost impossible given the breakneck pace of both speech and action" (*Scotsman*, 24 August 1987). Noda returned to the Edinburgh Festival with *han shin* (Half god, 1990) but disbanded his troupe shortly after, at the height of its popularity.

This sharp shift, coinciding with the end of Japan's bubble economy, was motivated by Noda's desire to explore theatre beyond the limits of the Japanese language, Japanese theatre market, and confines of the Yūminsha cast. In 1992 he obtained a year-long Ministry of Culture scholarship to study drama in London, where he attended several Théâtre de Complicité workshops, developing a key relationship with director Simon McBurney. Consequently, he was able to expand his physical techniques to include Lecoq-based expression, drawing upon commedia dell'arte and clowning. When he returned to Japan in 1993, he formed Noda Map.

Aka oni (Red demon), Noda's first major international play, was first performed in Japan and Thailand in 1999, prior to its European premiere at London's Young Vic Theatre in 2003. Three shipwrecked characters encounter a mysterious beast on an island. Facing isolation from the island's insular community, the demon is sent out to sea along with the shipwrecked trio, where it dies of starvation. While the linguistic limitations of *Descent of the Brutes* were less perceptible in *Red Demon*, the play's

approach to the refugee/immigrant theme was dismissed by critics as both heavy-handed and vague. Michael Billington claimed it lacked "cultural specificity: it seems to be about everywhere in general and nowhere in particular" (*Guardian*, 4 February 2003), while Nicholas de Jongh criticized it for "dramatizing and repeating obvious facts about bigotry" (*Evening Standard*, 4 February 2003).

Learning from these critical challenges to his first two international plays, Noda began collaborating with Irish playwright and adapter Colin Teevan. Together they co-wrote *The Bee*, Noda's first international hit, which premiered at London's Soho Theatre in 2006 (see Figure 51). Written against the backdrop of the US-led "war on terror," *The Bee* tackles the subject of violence and retaliation. Noda continued this collaboration with *The Diver*, staged in Tokyo in 2008 in Japanese and in London in English. *The Diver* is a work of intertextual adaptation that weaves together characters and stories around a central theme of revenge – the real-life story of a woman charged with murdering her lover's two children. Noda portrays the troubled nature of the woman by inventing multiple personalities that include literary vengeful spirits from the past: Lady Rokujō, from the eleventh-century *Tale of Genji*, and Ama, diver of the eponymous noh play.

In addition to these international projects, Noda continues at a prodigious pace on the Japanese stage, directing revivals of earlier work, adapting kabuki plays such as *Togitatsu no utare* (The revenge on Togitatsu, 2001) and Verdi's *Macbeth* (2004). Since 2008, Noda has worked as both artistic director of the Tōkyō Geijutsu Gekijō (Tokyo Metropolitan Theatre) and lecturer at Tama University.

MIKA EGLINTON

This playful aversion to anything ponderous or serious was also one defining feature of 1980s theatre culture in Japan. On the one hand, it reflects the development of postwar Japanese theatre out of university clubs and circles. Outside major commercial theatre companies like Takarazuka there is little opportunity today for professional actor training in Japan (see p. 481). Few universities have practical theatre schools, so most training has been haphazard; the spirit of amateur theatricals still informs much contemporary Japanese performance. Like elders Suzuki and Kara, Noda Hideki started performing as an undergraduate extracurricular activity; such university clubs remain today as incubators for tomorrow's theatre companies.

Peter Pan and pastiche

Such amateurism (sometimes inspired, sometimes just sloppy) contributed to an intensification of the youthful spirit and restless quest for novelty of so much contemporary Japanese performance. Both practitioners and audiences of 1980s theatre intentionally abstained from the more "serious" and even stultifying responsibilities of society, which expected men to be producers and women reproducers (i.e. mothers). To a certain extent, reluctance to mature reflects the protracted adolescence of the human species in all late capitalist societies, but it is one that has been intensified in Japan to an almost pathological degree. Theatre, like universities, has served in Japan as a moratorium from adult life, a place to practice socialization skills and explore burgeoning interests, fantasies, talents, and sexuality. Reflecting what cultural critic Asada Akira termed "infantile capitalism" some major features of Japanese popular culture: the "cute" (*kawaii*) and preternaturally adolescent boys and girls (*shōnen* and *shōjo*) represented not simply an escape from, but a rejection of, adulthood. Although one may discover social or political messages in some early plays of Noda and his generation, it may be equally argued that the juvenility of modern Japanese culture has been fed by distracting people with ephemeral pleasures. The Japanese equivalent of "bread and circuses" (sex and theatre) was something the Tokugawa regime particularly excelled at; some things have not changed so much.

Picking up on cultural referents in a Noda play was necessary to appreciate his work, but comprehension was not particularly the point, either for playwright or for audiences. A scattershot approach – Noda used the word *detarame* to describe it – played an important role in the dramaturgy of Noda and his contemporaries. The actor thus was paramount in bringing off the pyrotechnics and flights of fancy in Noda's texts. The remarks of shingeki playwright Kinoshita Junji (1914–2006) on the irrational and elliptical nature of kabuki dialogue are equally true of Noda's work: "It is the art of the actor which creates a theatre where such leaps can give satisfaction. And any art that finds such elements essential will naturally be filled with the unexplainable and the surprising."[1]

Resistance to meaning took on new political and social importance for those of the 1980s. Noda's grab-bag of allusions in *Suisei no shisha Jīgufrīto* (Comet Messenger Siegfried, 1985) – to Wagner and Twain, with a hint of Peter Pan – not only harks back to Kara's hallucinatory and riddling world, but also to classical kabuki dramaturgy: namely, the *naimaze*, or "weaving together" of various "worlds" (*sekai*) to create something new (*shukō*). Exemplary of the parody and pastiche of so much postmodern work, it is essentially no different from the contemporary "mash-up." Noda's *Siegfried* also rings a familiar theme: the desire not to grow up, to fly and not to land: a nostalgia for eternal boyhood.

A prolific artist with a fertile imagination, Noda continued to produce a spate of hit plays throughout the 1980s and early 1990s. Since the late 1990s, his plays like *Kiru* (Kill, 1998: a play on the word for "cut" as well as "wear") and *Egg* (2012) exhibit a new sense of historical and social conscience, rather like Murakami Haruki's mature fiction. His dramaturgy has become less complex and his messages more explicit, but losing none of his earlier playfulness.

Throughout the modern era, foreign ideas were incorporated into Japan, detached from their historical or social context; by the 1980s their ideological significance had been virtually subsumed by their potential market value. "'Imported' radical theatre practices became yet another 'brand' to be eagerly consumed by the Japanese middle class," critic Uchino Tadashi has remarked. "Under the guise of postmodern universality, contemporary Japanese theatre was able to be unselfconsciously xenophobic."[2] If Noda's work seemed Janus-faced, peering both forward into the free play of rootless signifiers and simulacra in postmodern culture, and backwards to kabuki, this was perhaps no surprise. Eighties critics like Asada and Karatani Kōjin claimed that Japan was recovering from the malaise of modernity, that its true nature – one exemplified in the culture of the Edo era – essentially anticipated postmodernism. Such dubious claims resonate with arrogance and narcissism, the least attractive qualities of that puffed-up decade in Japan, reminiscent of the "overcoming modernity" (*kindai no chōkoku*) rhetoric of 1940s ultra-nationalists. Fast times were also fat times, when it seemed the country could do no wrong, a model of everything that was new and bright.

1　J. Thomas Rimer, *Toward a Modern Japanese Theatre: Kishida Kunio* (Princeton, NJ: Princeton University Press, 1974), 9.
2　Tadashi Uchino, *Crucible Bodies: Postwar Japanese Performance from Brecht to the New Millennium* (New York: Seagull Books, 2009), 55.

If Japan could also lay claim to a tradition for what seemed so ahistorical a sensibility as postmodernism, so much the better.

1980s: dark times and false saviors

Intense physicality, gags, and rapid-fire speech were also hallmarks of Kōkami's work for Third Stage. Like Noda, Kōkami captured the light-hearted, celebratory spirit of life in Japan in the 1980s and engaged in parody and pastiche referencing television, manga, and anime. On a bare stage, lightning-quick changes of time, place, and identity reflected the experience of information overload one felt living in Tokyo during the bubble era. Mari Boyd called Kōkami's method "anti-narrative," a reaction to any serious form of social critique or message.[3] Everything was bright on the surface; yet, to a degree not seen in Noda's early work, one can detect at the heart of Kōkami's frenetic characters a loneliness and anxiety akin to the feckless heroes and heroines of Murakami Haruki's fiction. One senses that they are dancing and laughing as hard as they can for fear that, if they stop, society will abandon them. Kōkami's people are vaguely aware that, for all their sense of fun and freedom, society was not so forgiving. Kōkami's young men and women push against a "soft wall" of societal pressure. "The wall got bigger," laments a character in his play *Modan horā* (Modern horror, 1998), "from loneliness to autism, from being supervised to being brainwashed."[4] The stark contrast between dark themes and merrymaking characters living for the most part in denial reflected the willful amnesia of contemporary Japanese life, a contrast that underscored the schizoid vertigo experienced by Kōkami's characters, a sort of euphoria in dystopia.

Nami, the heroine of Kōkami's *Rarabai: mata wa hyakunen no komoriuta* (Lullaby: a hundred years of song, 2000), speaks for the 1980s generation when she cries, "I am in a passionate state of perplexity." An actor, she is forced to take over as director when her boyfriend, the theatre company's leader, runs off with another woman. Her story is the frame for another, darker tale based on an earlier work, *Hush-a-bye* (1987), in which Nami's alter-ego is haunted by a dream of another woman who she is sure exists because she has seen her in a photograph. She hires a detective to find her; the search eventually leads to a cross-dressing mental patient called Moriyama, who channels the spirit of his domineering mother to control others in a new-age cult. Sixties playwrights and directors like Betsuyaku Minoru and Suzuki often portrayed modern society as a hospital or madhouse, and the

3 Mari Boyd, Introduction to "Lullaby: a hundred years of song," in Japan Playwrights Association (ed.), *Half a Century of Japanese Theatre*, vol. III (Tokyo: Kinokuniya shoten), 239.
4 *Ibid.* 240.

sinister psychic is a typical Murakami Haruki trope; Asahara Shōkō's deadly cult Aum Shinrikyō would, of course, make such nightmares a reality for the Japanese in the coming decade. Nami slips back and forth between dream and reality, eventually extricating herself from the siren calls of madness by using theatre as therapy. The show must go on: this seems to be Nami's (and Kōkami's) solution, however dark their world.

Yet the ghosts of the past could not so easily be put to rest. Eighties Japanese theatre, much like the nation's culture at large, oscillated wildly between grand displays of self-complacent optimism and ethnic superiority and darker visions of an apocalyptic future just around the corner. In hindsight, some seem prescient; in other respects these allegories of the end time took up a tradition explored in the theatre of the 1960s, one first identified by David G. Goodman in *After Apocalypse* (1986), his seminal study of postwar Japanese drama's treatment of the experience of Hiroshima and Nagasaki. The end of the world as we know it has been a common trope running throughout postwar Japanese theatre, even during the country's economic heyday of the 1980s. Many works of that decade now seem prophetic, even though the zeitgeist then seemed far more optimistic. The meltdown of the nuclear reactor at Chernobyl in 1986 was a signal that humanity was under threat from atomic power, even when it was being used for peaceful purposes. *Asahi no yō na yūhi o tsurete* (With a sunset like the morning sun, 1981) was part of what Kōkami called his "Nuclear Warfare Trilogy." Kitamura Sō's *Hogiuta* (Ode to joy, 1979) is similarly set in the aftermath of a nuclear holocaust.

As noted earlier, the false or ambivalent prophet or savior is one of many motifs that playwrights of the 1980s would inherit from their angura mentors. It is a common thread running through much of post-1960s Japanese drama, as David G. Goodman pointed out in 1986. We encountered a charismatic villain in *Lullaby*'s Morimoto. In Daisan Erotica's (Third Erotica) *Nippon Wars* (1984), the false prophet is a disembodied brain – all that is left of a woman called Sue Ellen.[5] Kōkami's *Lullaby* and Kawamura's *Nippon Wars* both employ the motif of a tyrannical mother figure (the mad priest of Kōkami's play is male, but he wears women's clothing and is haunted, like Hitchcock's *Psycho* villain, by his mother); we see such monsters in Terayama's plays as well. No doubt this is a reflection of the dubious role women would play in the postwar period, as creators of what feminist Ueno Chizuko has called a "transvestite patriarchy" to take over for the absent father,[6] the most missing patriarch of all being the emperor, who had to renounce

---

5 Trans. Leon Ingulsrud and Shōichirō Kawai in *Half a Century*, vol. IV, 68–110.
6 Chizuko Ueno, "In the feminine guise: a trap of reverse orientalism," in Richard F. Calichman, *Contemporary Japanese Thought* (New York: Columbia University Press, 2005), 225–62.

Fig 43 Kawamura Takeshi's *Nippon Wars* (1984).

his divine status after Japan's defeat in 1945. Sinister matriarchs like these point to a lack of role models for men and a misogynistic fear of women's rising power in postwar Japanese society.

Inspired by Ridley Scott's film *Blade Runner* (1981), Kawamura Takeshi's *Nippon Wars* is set some time in a future in which androids wage almost constant battle as an antidote to the ennui of peace (Figure 43). The identity of the play's protagonist has been split into two paired androids named O and O'. O' awakes from a coma to find himself on a submarine called the Blue Whale, steaming toward the frontline of a new war. O' has no real sense of who he is or why he is there, only vague memories of having been raised in an orphanage. The play presents his training as a soldier, leading to his realization that he is in fact an android and has no control over his life.

The world that Kawamura imagines is essentially posthuman. We learn that these androids have been programmed with memories and emotions to mimic humans – "man is but a ragbag full of memories," we are told – but these memories are artificial, false; the androids belong to their mistress, Sue Ellen. Their training involves 200 lessons in socialization (e.g. Lesson 35: Orgasm; Lesson 39: Grief; Lesson 52: Controlled Anger; Lesson 70: Death), culminating in the final, and most devastating lesson of all: Revolt, in which the androids attempt to overthrow their tyrant, only to discover that this too was programmed. Free will doesn't exist. Sex is promoted but love is forbidden. The final act of disobedience for O' is an attempt to commit suicide, only to find that there is no escape: he cannot die because he is not alive. "Dear God, all men are living as the dead," he reflects. "Everything was a lie. The stars in the sky. The twilight when I wept. The hot soup in the kitchen in winter. Freshly baked biscuits …" An allegory of the regimentation of contemporary life, the play interrogates not only the accuracy of memory but also the limits of life and human agency.

1990s: sober times, and return of the Real

The fall of the Berlin Wall coincided with the death of Emperor Hirohito in 1989. Japan's superheated economy was already winding down when, in January 1995, a major earthquake and ensuing fires destroyed much of Kobe's infrastructure. Two months later, Asahara Shōkō's doomsday cult Aum Shinrikyō killed a dozen commuters and injured thousands more with Sarin nerve gas poisoning in the Tokyo subway system. Japan had seen the rise of a plethora of new religions in the aftermath of its defeat in 1945, when both state Shinto and many Buddhist sects, which had supported the war, were discredited. After the Sarin gas attack, many theatre critics drew parallels between the nihilist aesthetic of 1980s theatre culture and Asahara's cult.[7]

By the mid-1990s it was clear the economic bubble had burst. In *Toshi ni wa shukusai wa iranai* (Cities do not need festivities, 1997), playwright Hirata Oriza wrote that "most life has nothing whatever to do with what theatre in the past has enjoyed portraying, but is grounded instead in quiet and uneventful moments."[8] Hirata, who won the 1995 Kishida Kunio Drama Award for his *Tokyo Notes* (1994), became chief exponent for what critics have called "quiet theatre." The trend away from noisy, frenetic theatre had already begun by the late 1980s, with the work of Iwamatsu Ryō for Tokyo Kandenchi (Tokyo Battery Company). Iwamatsu, who wrote for two of Japan's leading male actors, Emoto Akira and Takenaka Naoto, won the 1989 Kishida Award for *Futon to Daruma* (Futon and dharma), and now writes for film and television as well. He and Hirata (who established his Seinendan theatre company in 1982 while still an undergraduate) would be joined by several other late 1980s and early 1990s playwrights, like Suzue Toshirō and Matsuda Masataka, in writing delicately crafted drama about ordinary people's lives, the so-called "quiet theatre."

This 1990s return to the "Real," a return to the mimetic as key, was however not simply a revival of shingeki mannerisms and ideological principles. The Japanese (who have borrowed much of their modern aesthetic language

---

7 Uchino, *Crucible Bodies*, 55.
8 Hirata Oriza, *Toshi ni wa shukusai wa iranai* (Cities do not need festivities) (Tokyo: Banseisha, 1997), 182.

from English and other Western languages), distinguish between the Real (*riaru*) of Hirata's style and shingeki-style Realism (*riarizumu*). For one thing, the writerly, literary quality of typical shingeki texts was something Hirata and his generation rebelled against, attempting to create a more accurate vernacular style of dialogue. Hirata thus called his own style "contemporary colloquial drama" (*gendai kōgo engeki*). One can trace his influence on the work of many younger playwrights as diverse as Okada Toshiki, Iwai Hideto, Maeda Shirō, and Miura Daisuke. Much of their drama focuses intensely on how to capture the way Japanese today actually speak and behave with one another, without recourse to traditional "dramatic" devices, presenting slices of contemporary life without creative or editorial comment. So natural does so much of their work seem that audiences who see it could easily be fooled into thinking many performances were unscripted and ad-libbed. Yet so precise is Hirata's timing that plays vary by no more than a few score seconds from performance to performance, thus virtually contradicting one of the seemingly essential characteristics of live theatre: its one-off nature.

Structurally, Hirata's plays seem anti-dramatic; they avoid or studiously downplay scenes of conflict, crisis, climax and denouement – typical arcs of conventional realist theatre. Moreover, his directing style owes nothing to Stanislavski, or to any prior actors' training methods. His closest model is arguably Ozu Yasujirō, director of the film *Tokyo monogatari* (Tokyo story, 1953), the inspiration for *Tokyo Notes*. Hirata's directorial style is resolutely behaviorist: actors are not told to seek a personal correlative (psychological "motivation") for the character's state of mind, but are drilled in correct physical posture and vocal tone, and made to repeat lines until Hirata is satisfied. He downplays subjectivity as determinant to what characters say or do, stressing instead the physical and social environment as key conditions for human behavior and interpersonal dynamics.

Hirata and many contemporaries shared with "third generation" 1980s artists an allergy to ideology, a skepticism regarding whether it is truly possible to make grand statements about life and the world. Some critics claim that such restraint reflects a conservatism characteristic of much contemporary theatre in Japan, a choice instead merely to stand on the sidelines, observe, and record. Hirata's claim to have no interest in themes or messages sounds rather like Kishida's comment that he did not "write a play in order to 'say something.' Rather, I find 'something to say' in order to write a play."[9] His drama reflects a unique and mordant attitude toward Japanese society, its relation to the world and contemporary events, and the ways in which its

9 Rimer, *Toward a Modern Japanese Theatre*, 145.

people fail to communicate or understand one another, and attempt to evade responsibility for their actions.

Playwrights Nagai Ai and Sakate Yōji, while also writing in a realist mode, nonetheless are more overtly issue-oriented. Nagai's well-made, shingeki-style plays have tackled such subjects as the status of women: *Hagi-ke no san shimai* (The three Hagi sisters, 2000); the family: *Toki no mono'oki* (Time's storeroom, 1994) and *Ani kaeru* (Brother returns, 1999); and the debate revolving around the official status of Japan's national anthem: *Utawase-tai otoko-tachi* (Gotta make 'em sing, 2005). A student of Yamazaki Tetsu, Sakate has not been afraid to treat sensitive issues like Emperor Hirohito's war responsibility, *Tennō to seppun* (The Emperor and the kiss, 2001); the major social problem of shut-ins (*hikikomori*) in his best-known play, *Yaneura* (The attic, 2002); or the continuing presence of US troops in Okinawa, *Hoshi no musuko* (Star son, 2012).

Similarly, the long and prolific career of Inoue Hisashi (1934–2010) as both novelist and playwright marked an interest not only in well-crafted texts but also in politics. Many works were satirical treatments of notable personages from Japanese history: *Dōgen no bōken* (The adventures of Dōgen, 1972), *Yabuhara kengyō* (The great Doctor Yabuhara, 1973), about an unscrupulous blind minstrel in the Edo era, *Shimijimi Nippon Nogi Taishō* (Earnest Japan: General Nogi, 1979) and *Zutsū katakori Higuchi Ichiyō* (Headache, stiff neck, Higuchi Ichiyō, 1984). His last complete work was based on the police murder of leftist writer Kobayashi Takiji, *Kumikyoku gyakusatsu* (Massacre rhapsody, 2009). *Chichi to kuraseba* (Living with father, 1994),[10] a two-hander about a survivor of Hiroshima's atomic bomb and her father, was made into a successful film in 2006. Inoue could turn dark subjects into brilliant entertainment, often sustained by a genius for wordplay comparable to Noda's.

Mitani Kōki (1961–) may have assumed Inoue's crown as most-produced playwright in mainstream Japanese theatre, but his light comedies (his company Tokyo Sunshine Boys is a nod to his idol Neil Simon) are neither as intricate nor as politically charged. Much of Mitani's work has been written or adapted for television and film, including such plays at *Jūnin no yasashii Nihonjin* (Twelve gentle Japanese, 1991), a spin on the American classic *Twelve Angry Men*, and *Warai no daigaku* (University of laughs, 2004), about comedians and censorship in prewar Japan. Inoue and Mitani proved that the Japanese theatre public still seeks to be entertained and amused, not just challenged or instructed.

---

10 Trans. Zeljko Cipris in J. Thomas Rimer, Mitsuya Mori, and M. Cody Poulton (eds.), *The Columbia Anthology of Modern Japanese Drama* (New York: Columbia University Press, 2014).

Body, soul, and text

Yet the new logocentrism in Japanese theatre went against another significant trend since the 1960s: "postdramatic" (non-verbal, non-linear narrative, multimedia) performance. Since the 1980s many troupes have attempted experiments in which the verbal is downplayed, undermined, or non-existent. Ohta Shōgo's *Mizu no eki* (The water station, 1981) and *Chi no eki* (Earth station, 1985) are silent, meditative, and deliberate works, a kind of Grotowskian "poor theatre."

Since the 1960s the physicality of the performer has been a central concern, not only in distinguishing what makes live theatre a unique art form, but also in reappraising of Japanese identity. The body in Japanese theatre presents a Foucauldian history of the country's modernization: alienation from its native roots; the experience of Western cultural hegemony and its own imperialist experiments, war, devastation, and defeat. It has been regarded as the site of the unconscious, unmediated experience, and of *eros* and *pathos* over *logos*, presenting a counter-discourse to the rationalism of modernity. Words deceive, but the body does not lie. The discourse of modern performance studies in Japan has to a great extent been a nativist one, suggesting that the Japanese physique and movement possessed distinctive qualities, determined by centuries of hard agricultural – notably wet rice paddy – labor. The significant changes to the proportions, sizes, and shapes of Japanese bodies due to diet and lifestyle in the half century call such ideas into question. More convincing perhaps is the argument that modernity has created a split personality in the Japanese people, manifested in severing thought and verbal expression from corporeal experience. Even then, such a theory presupposes a kind of golden age, before the onslaught of Western culture, when Japanese people existed in a state of psychic and physical wholeness.

Miyagi Satoshi (1959–), artistic director of the Shizuoka Performing Arts Center (SPAC), created a performance style for his Ku Na'uka Theatre Company (est. 1990) indebted to bunraku puppet theatre. Dialogue is delivered by chanters accompanying mute, puppet-like actors; a percussion orchestra provides further rhythmic shape and tension. Miyagi explains:

> Within the complex system of Japanese modernism, it became very hard to imagine a language to express an authentic emotional experience. If I touch something and it's hot, it generates something in my body. It used to be the same with language. Language came from physical experience. But modernization separated the word from the body. "I love you" no longer means anything because the physical sensation of love is no longer part of the body. Language needs the body and the body needs language. We must

Fig 44 The Ku Na'uka *Medea* features Mikari as a colonized Korean shamaness rebelling against Japanese militarists (Miyagi Satoshi director, 1999).

be able to remember that love is the place where one can forgive and one feels celebrated.[11]

Miyagi's signature work Euripides' *Medea* (1999) is set in a Meiji-era teahouse, most likely in Korea, where *kisaeng* and servants are requested to perform by a party of men in black judicial robes (Figure 44). As the men speak their lines from the story of Medea, women mime. The woman chosen to play the title role is dressed in *chima jeogori*, traditional national dress for Korean women, alluding to Japan's annexation of Korea in 1910. The frame in which Miyagi sets Euripides' play is thus an allegory of the patriarchal and imperialist nature of the modern Japanese state. The work ends in a bloody crescendo as the women slaughter their male guests.

Violence and codes

The body in Ku Na'uka's performances is still beautiful, but butoh's focus on the violent and the grotesque is more typical of postmodern dance's rejection of aestheticizing the human physique. Unlike ballet or other traditional forms of dance, postmodern performance presents the body not in order to

---

11 Carol Martin, "*Tenshu monogatari* and *Bye Bye: The New Primitive*," in David Jortner, Keiko McDonald, and Kevin J. Wetmore, Jr. (eds.), *Modern Japanese Theatre and Performance* (Lanham, MD: Lexington Books, 2006), 226.

act out a story, nor even to incarnate a piece of music, but to divest it of other semiotic systems so as to return us to something approaching an elemental experience of our physical existence. "The only reality, the only remaining document with the ability to tell the truth, is the body," says Shimizu Shinjin.[12] Shimizu regards the twentieth century as an era of unprecedented violence, one in which language has been a most lethal weapon. Marking the end of the century, his Gekidan Kaitaisha (Theatre of Deconstruction, est. 1979) created the *Bye-Bye* series, which scandalized audiences in the former Yugoslavia (no stranger to violence) and New York in the immediate aftermath of 9/11. At the Japan Society in New York, as a man whipped a woman on stage, she shrieked out the names of Japanese emperors, empires in Asia and Europe, and words in English, as if expectorating the history of violence, a history of language. Inasmuch as it is possible to do so in any artistic work, Shimizu's performances are a direct and unmediated presentation of a physical reality painful even to watch.

With his company Potudo-ru (est. 1996) director and playwright Miura Daisuke presents raw portraits, what he calls "semi-documentary theatre," of Japan's disaffected youth. Miura expresses a deep distrust in language. His signature work, *Yume no shiro* (Castle of dreams, 2006) is entirely without dialogue. Eight denizens (five men and three women) of a filthy Shibuya apartment fight, fuck, and spill a variety of bodily and other fluids. A dark portrait of the most carnal and animalistic side of modern life, the spectacle is difficult to watch (literally, as the transparent fourth-wall grows increasingly smeared and smudged). Yet it ends with redeeming glimpses of humanity: a woman weeping, the ludicrous dance of a man in underwear to the strains of the Japanese national anthem signing off the night's broadcast on NHK, Japan's national network.

In contrast, companies like Mezurashii Kinoko Buyōdan (Strange Kinoko Dance Company, est. 1990), Yubiwa Hoteru (Finger Hotel, est. 1994), and Nibroll (est. 1997), which have women directors, present a different and less overtly eroticized image, especially of the female body. Commentators have remarked that the human physique in their performances is typically childish, the movements inelegant and amateurish. As already noted, one feature of much fringe theatre since the 1960s has been a studied sloppiness and unprofessionalism. Uchino remarks that the child's or "junk body" enacted in performances of such groups is a way to portray the lack of subjectivity of modern Japanese, especially its young women. Much postmodern Japanese performance thus short-circuits the attempt in more traditional dance to tell a story and turn the lived body into an aesthetic metaphor.[13]

---

12 Quoted by Martin in *ibid*. 228.   13 Uchino, *Crucible Bodies*, 138–9.

Okada Toshiki (chelfitsch, 1997–) is a playwright of highly colloquial and elliptical monologues about the ordinary lives of young members of Japan's "lost generation": slackers and hipsters who have failed to find regular livelihoods with the demise of the country's lifetime employment system. His Kishida Kunio Drama Award-winning *Sangatsu no itsukakan* (Five days in March, 2004) depicts a couple engaged in marathon sex during demonstrations against the American invasion of Iraq in 2003. On one level, the work is a commentary on the chasm between politics and private life in Japan. Okada's colloquial style is reminiscent of contemporaries like Hirata, but the spasmodic movements of his actors, repetitive phrases, and absurd interactions continually undermine the realism of his language, acting as a sort of visual noise. Inspired by Brecht's alienation effect, Okada asks his actors to disengage their awareness from the words they are speaking when they move so that his audiences can engage critically with what they are watching on stage rather than be seduced by the mimetic illusionism of his language. His actors step in and out of character, alternately telling or enacting the tale, their continual jerky movements bearing no diegetic relationship to the story told. The Japanese body is broken, no longer able to tell its story in anything other than fragments of a lost whole. "Something beyond being dysfunctional has arrived, and, at least in Japan, bodies are behaving very strangely in the streets … And I would call these bodies 'bodies of dementia,'" noted playwright Miyazawa Akio.[14]

Nature and technology: theatre and other media

Since before the time of Wagner it has been the dream in theatre to create total art comprising various means (music, text, dance, scenery, lighting, etc.). Artists since early in the twentieth century have sought to create a synesthetic experience that may compensate for the lack of wholeness elsewhere in daily life. *Shimpa* (new school theatre) had experimented in multimedia performances like *rensageki*, which combined film with live theatre, as early as 1908. Because of the role that technology increasingly plays in the arts, perhaps more than at any other time, the lines between live theatre and other expressive media are being crossed. As earlier noted, the precision of Hirata's directing undermines one of the assumptions of live theatre: its resistance to mechanical replication. Since 2007 Hirata has been writing plays featuring robots and androids developed by Ishiguro Hiroshi, a colleague at Osaka University. Hirata claims that there is no essential difference between programming an android or robot and directing human actors, only that one can be more accurate with the former (Figure 45).

14 Cited in *ibid*. 169.

Fig 45 Hirata Oriza's *Three Sisters, Android Version*, presented by the Seinendan Theatre Company and Osaka University Robot Theatre Project (2012).

Suzuki Tadashi had relocated his troupe in 1975 to the mountainous countryside of Toyama prefecture in order to restore to theatre a sense of the natural and immediate, but many other contemporary Japanese artists see no reason not to exploit the full resources of the modern world, especially its digital technology. Today such performances demand a redefinition of live performance and pose intriguing questions regarding the relationship between the body and technology.

Dumb type, a collective founded by Kyoto University of Arts students, was a leader in Japanese multimedia performance in the 1990s and straddled the fields of performance and conceptual art, employing dance, electronic music, and digital media. *pH* (1990) employed machines, video projection, and live performance. Visually demonstrating the mechanization of contemporary humanity, a metal bridge emitting light like a barcode reader slid back and forth over the stage as dancers dove to evade it. Its artistic director Furuhashi Teiji (1960–95) died of AIDs; his final work for dumb type, *S/N* (1994), challenged contemporary attitudes toward straight and gay sexuality and the place of minorities in Japanese society. Two of dumb type's other core members, Takatani Shiro (1963–) and Ikeda Ryōji (1966–), work as independent artists on the international scene. Takatani creates video installations, and was visual director for the Sakamoto Ryūichi opera, *Life* (1999). Ikeda uses computers to create intricate light and soundscapes with sine waves, white noise, data, and video projections. Similar work is being done by the contemporary artist Umeda Hiroaki (1977–) who, like Yanagi Miwa (1967–), began as a photographer before moving increasingly into mixed-media performance.

Other conceptual artists use digital media for theatrical productions and art installations. *Mind Time Machine* (2010) by Ikegami Takashi (1961–) used cameras and computers to record the sounds and movements of dancers in a space, creating a digital feedback loop, which was then broken down, reassembled, and projected onto large screens. Like Hirata's work for androids, Ikegami's is both theatre and science, an experiment in the creation of artificial life. Nibroll, jointly led by visual director Takahashi Keisuke and choreographer Yanaihara Mikuni, is a collective of interdisciplinary artists. Onishi Keita, a member of the synthesizer band Crystal, supervised visual design for productions at the New National Theatre of Monteverdi's *L'incoronazione di Poppea* (2009) and Saegusa Shigeaki's opera *Chūshingura gaiden* (The tale of the forty-seven loyal retainers, 2010).

Although such technologies threaten to alienate spectators, Takayama Akira's Port B employs the internet and social media like Twitter and Facebook to chart new patterns of urban space and community. An heir to Terayama's radical interrogation of the relationships among performer, audience, and performance space, Takayama makes us look with fresh eyes at the world, using the city as his stage in magical mystery tours in which the audience and ordinary members of the public essentially become performers. Representative works include *The Complete Manual of Evacuation: Tokyo* (2010), sending participants, after filling out an online questionnaire, to twenty-nine "evacuation sites" around Tokyo (a maid café in Akihabara, a mosque in Otsuka, among others), and *Referendum Project* (2011), in which members of the public engaged in a referendum on the future of nuclear power after the Fukushima disaster.

Another type of urban community is created by the Osaka-based Ishinha (Reform Group), founded by artist Matsumoto Yūkichi in 1970, which creates immense, operatic, outdoor spectacles employing large casts, electronic music by Uchihashi Kazuhisa, and massive, architectural stage sets designed by Hayashida Yūji. Truly postdramatic in nature, language in Matsumoto's productions is frequently deconstructed for rhythmic and melodic effects, the Osaka dialect chanted mechanically by actors wearing clip-on microphones. Carefully choreographed movement is closer to marching than dance. The impact of Ishinha's productions, which have explored the Japanese diaspora in Brazil (*Nostalgia*, 2007) and war in Poland (*Kokyū kikai*, Artificial respirator, 2008), is both epic and cinematic.

The mechanization and mediatization of live performance has, to borrow Marshall McLuhan's terms, transformed much Japanese contemporary experimental theatre from the "hot" (intimate, carnal, ideologically charged) angura experience into something "cool" (objective and intellectual). It has changed the dynamics of the actor–audience relationship: technology and digital media have arguably created a new "fourth wall" between performer and spectator. Yet new technologies are also being used by artists like Port B and Ishinha to create a new sense of community, one which may inspire new forms of social activism.

Regionalism and compartmentalization

Though attempts have been made to promote regional theatre (for example, Suzuki's move to Toga, or establishment of public theatres in Shizuoka, Mito, and Saitama), and while many artists are themselves from the provinces, Japanese theatre today is essentially Tokyo theatre. The city is a magnet sucking everything into its nexus, yet theatregoing is intensely compartmentalized. There is great demographic stratification of Japanese theatre audiences, with those attending performances of shingeki, whether by Haiyū-za (Actors' Theatre) or at the New National Theatre, mostly over the age of 60, while those going to productions of emerging theatre are all (save for a few critics) under the age of 30. The chief inhibiting factor for going to see new theatre in Japan, as in other countries lacking public support for the arts, is economic: tickets for the cheapest productions are twice the price of those for a new movie, while those for major artists like Noda or Ninagawa may easily fetch over five times that. Word of mouth, and mountains of flyers distributed at the theatres, are still the chief means of disseminating information about new productions, especially since the demise in the Internet age of weekly magazines like *Pia*. Contemporary theatre still remains very much a niche industry, speaking to a small coterie of cognoscenti. Increasing efforts, however, have been made to internationalize theatre in Japan. A number of playwrights like Noda and Kōkami have spent extended periods of study in London, New York, and other cities abroad, often under the aegis of public institutions like the Agency for Cultural Affairs. Since Suzuki's Toga festival, established in the 1970s, annual international theatre festivals have sprung up in Shizuoka, Yokohama, Kyoto, and Tokyo. Greater links with Asian theatre artists is another trend, with the establishment of international festivals like BeSeTo (Beijing/Seoul/Tokyo), which rotates among these three cities with representative productions from each capital.

One other notable trend over the past few decades has been the demise of the ensemble system, comprised of tribe-like theatre companies organized around charismatic leaders like Terayama and Kara, and the rise of something more like the Western production system, with auditions.

Actors, playwrights, and other artists are increasingly becoming free agents. This may reflect the post-Aum sense of individualism and distrust of the "participation mystique" traditionally underlying so many social organizations in Japan. Noda and Ninagawa, two of the most successful artists, have taken this route; yet many still establish themselves, and their style, within the context of tight-knit communities that also sustain groups financially. Government support for theatre has improved, but largely during the echo of the economic bubble in the building of lavish theatres, concert and recital halls, and other public buildings, often in remote places. As the public purse becomes even more strapped, it will be even harder to sustain many of these theatres, when even some in Tokyo are already struggling to survive.

The proliferation of countercultures and subcultures that has occurred since the 1960s has given voice to members of society hitherto stifled in the dominant discourse: women, minorities, and even the disabled. Yet their impact on society remains marginal, and the club-like atmosphere of many of these groups tends to create hermetic, ingrown cultures, which can all too soon die off, replaced by the next fad, like the latest teen girl band. Novelty has ever been a hallmark of contemporary and popular Japanese culture, which ceaselessly attempts to reinvent itself even as it recycles old patterns. "Yesterday was long ago for today, today once upon a time for tomorrow," goes a popular song from the Middle Ages, and the sentiment is even stronger now. A work like Miura Daisuke's *Castle of Dreams* (2006) has already acquired something of an archival value with its now somehow quaint fashions and mannerisms. Despite the economic, political, and environmental challenges facing the country, the speed at which Japanese theatre continues to reinvent itself seems faster than ever before.

Theatre after 3/11

One problem with such constant change is a tendency to forget. "An inability to address the past in meaningful ways contributes to the current sense of malaise that many critics see as a new Japanese crisis," writes Peter Eckersall.[15] The failure to acknowledge Japan's wartime responsibility has been one characteristic that has particularly distinguished its postwar culture from Germany's, but in the wake of more recent disasters, the sense of amnesia and resignation that afflicts the Japanese populace bodes ill for the country's spiritual health, to say nothing of its economic reconstruction.

15 Takeshi Kawamura, in *Nippon Wars and Other Plays*, ed. Peter Eckersall (London and New York: Seagull Books, 2011), ix.

Nonetheless, the Japanese have access to a deep tradition of symbols and narrative motifs to interpret cataclysmic events, one dating back at least to Kamo no Chōmei's *Hōjōki* (An account of my hut, 1212), which describes how earthquakes, fire, and typhoons ravaged the capital, driving the author to seek refuge in a simple life led alone in the mountains. Since earliest times, seismic insecurity has been a barometer of the Japanese sensibility, informing its response to the evanescence and fragility of life. Natural disasters have, moreover, been turning points for social and political change. The Great Kantō Earthquake of 1923 was a violent catalyst for Tokyo's modernization and had a profound impact on the artistic and ideological course that Japanese theatre would take over the following decades. The fire and nuclear bombs that turned practically every major city into a wasteland in the final months of the Pacific War in 1945 also inscribed on the Japanese imagination a deep sense of loss – of identity, home, past, shared values and beliefs – from which arguably it has yet to recover. Although a feeling of collective victimhood has obscured the nation's own responsibility for the war, words like "holocaust" and "apocalypse," with all their theological trappings, are typically applied to describe the nature of this experience of Japan's defeat. What Susan Napier has called the "imagination of disaster" has been a defining trope of postwar Japanese popular culture, everything from *Godzilla* (1954), about a prehistoric monster awakened by US nuclear testing in the South Pacific, to dystopian manga and anime like Ōtomo Katsuhiro's *Akira* (1988).[16]

More recently, the triple disaster – earthquake, tsunami, and release of radioactive waste from the Dai-ichi Fukushima nuclear power plant – that occurred on 11 March 2011, in Japan's Northeastern (Tōhoku) region was a cruel reminder to the Japanese that they are no strangers to calamity, both natural and man-made. Memory and forgetting is the mordant theme of Miyazawa Akio's *Tōtaru ribingu 1986–2011* (Total living 1986–2011, 2011). Citizens of the present, accompanied by characters called "lighthouse keeper of forgetting" and "girl of absence," gaze back to the year of Chernobyl, 1986, while the Japanese (as if taking a leaf from *Last Days of Pompeii*) blithely distract themselves with ephemeral amusements and media gossip.

Contemporary theatre has thus been attempting to make a real contribution to the national memory and imaginary after 3/11. Port B's *Complete Manual of Evacuation* (2010) and *Referendum Project* (2011) both addressed the fragility of life in the Japanese capital, and in the company's 2012 production of Nobel Prize winning playwright Elfriede Jelinek's *Epilog? (Kein Licht II)*, Takayama led his audience on a tour of a Tokyo district transformed into a

---

16 Susan Napier, "Panic sites: the Japanese imagination of disaster from Godzilla to Akira," *Journal of Japanese Studies* 19:2 (1993), 327–51.

post-apocalyptic Fukushima. Okada Toshiki similarly addressed the disaster in his 2011 work *Genzaichi* (Current location), no longer considering Tokyo a safe place to raise a family. The need to remember and record is the first instinct of artists in the face of catastrophe, and the Japanese have over the course of centuries developed ways of expressing the unthinkable.

References and further reading

Anan, Nobuko, *Contemporary Japanese Women's Theatre and Visual Arts: Performing Girls' Aesthetics* (New York: Palgrave MacMillan, 2016)

Eckersall, Peter. *Performativity and Event in 1960s Japan: City, Body, Memory* (New York: Palgrave Macmillan, 2013)

Performing Japan: Contemporary Expressions of Cultural Identity (Folkestone: Global Oriental, 2008)

Hirata Oriza. *Engeki nyūmon* (Introduction to theatre) (Tokyo: Kōdansha gendai shinsho, 1998)

Iwaki, Kyoko. *Tokyo Theatre Today: Conversations with Eight Emerging Theatre Artists* (London: Hublet, 2011)

Kakiuchi, Emiko, Miyako Sumi, and Kiyoshi Takeuchi. "New systems for theater management in Japan: problems and prospects," *Theatre Management Japan* (National Graduate Institute for Policy Studies, Japan) 2:2 (2012), www.encatc. org/pages/fileadmin/user_upload/Journal/ENCATC_Journal_03_

Kawamura Takeshi. *Nippon Wars and Other Plays*, ed. Peter Eckersall (London and New York: Seagull Books, 2011)

Nishidō Kōjin. *Gendai engeki no jōken* (The state of modern theatre) (Tokyo: Bansei shobō, 2006)

Uchino, Tadashi. *Crucible Bodies: Postwar Japanese Performance from Brecht to the New Millennium* (London and New York: Seagull Books, 2009)

INTERNET RESOURCES

Performing Arts Network Japan http://performingarts.jp

Pia Institute for the Arts, ed. *Theater Japan,* second edition (Tokyo: The Japan Foundation, 1993)

Pia Institute for the Arts, ed. *Theater in Japan* (Tokyo: The Japan Foundation, 2008)

Theatre_Mgmt_Japan_VOL_2_ISSUE_2.pdf

Tokyo Stages: Japanese Contemporary Theatre http://tokyostages.wordpress.com

Stories of the Mirror: Glimpses of Japanese Performing Arts http:// storiesofthemirror.wordpress.com

"The Water Station" Japanese Performing Arts Research Center www.glopad.org/ jparc/?q=en/waterst/intro

FOCUS 11.2 NODA HIDEKI, DYNAMIC DIRECTOR

Eureka, special issue on Noda Hideki (Tokyo: Seidosha, 2001)

Fukushima Yoshiko. *Manga Discourse in Japanese Theatre: The Location of Noda Hideki's* Yume no Yuminsha (London: Kegan Paul, 2003)

Higeki Kigeki, special issue on Noda Hideki (Tokyo: Hayakawa shobō, 2012)

Interlude: Tokyo: world theatre capital

IWAKI KYOKO

London, New York, Paris, and Berlin are generally considered the great theatrical capitals in terms of history, diversity, scale, and quality. However, when the field of vision is expanded to the East, it is said that Tokyo has more plays in more genres spanning more centuries of tradition than arguably anywhere else in the world. To validate this hypothesis, a survey was conducted with actual documentation of performances occurring on a random day, 24 November 2012, a typical Saturday in the busy autumn culture season during a three-day Labor Thanksgiving holiday weekend.

Included in the survey were national, public, and private theatres, as well as theatre/dance festivals spread across the Tokyo metropolis. Also included were the theatres and festivals in the Greater Metropolitan area with a population of 35,000,000 people (13,000,000 in Tokyo itself), who could easily access in an hour from Tokyo on public transportation lines. We covered theatre performance, dance performances, operas, musicals, circus spectacles, traditional theatres (kabuki, noh, kyogen), and storytelling (*rakugo*), but not music concerts and *manzai* comedy (Japanese vaudeville).

Performance information was gathered from the following sources:

- *Theatre Guide*, the monthly theatre listings (all performances)
- *Pia* cultural magazine's Data Analysis Department (all performances)
- *CoRich Butaigeijutsu!* website (fringe and small venue performances)
- Real Tokyo website (interdisciplinary art performances)
- Shochiku official website (kabuki)
- *Nōgaku Taimuzu* monthly magazine, November 2012, listings (noh, kyogen)
- Nippon Engeki Kyōkai (Japanese Association of Theatre) Annual Report (primarily national and public theatre performances)

The productions were categorized according to:

- Venue type: national, public, or private
- Size: large (800 plus), medium (400 plus), or small (under 400)

Fig 46 Chiten's 2012 interpretation of Elfriede Jelinek's *Kein Licht* (No light) premiered at Tokyo/Festival.

- Genre: traditional or contemporary
- Subgenres: original plays, revivals, operas and musicals, dance, and other.

Traditional and folk festival performances, typically held annually at local shrines and temples, were not catalogued. We chose not to list, or could not gather information concerning, the myriad amateur, community, and closed performances known only by word-of-mouth or micro-promotions: flyers, posters, and personal websites. These hundreds of amateur shows, attended by eager, bouquet-bearing friends, families, and alumni, include high school and university club performances, amateur recitals in ballet and modern dance, and noh dance or *nagauta* singing. However, in terms of contemporary Japanese theatre, since there are no clear boundaries between amateurs and professionals, and since most small companies (*gekidan*) emerge by hiring a space to present their shows, these performances were included.

A wide spectrum of genres and scale

There were a remarkable 187 productions that day, spanning an extraordinarily wide spectrum of venues, plays, and prices. On 24 November 2012, one could choose among three kabuki productions, six noh performances, twenty-eight operas and musicals, ninety-three original plays, and sixteen play revivals, ranging from Shakespeare and Racine to Bernard Slade and

Japanese avant-gardists Terayama Shūji and Inoue Hisashi. International visitors were primarily dance troupes; on 24 November, a wide spectrum was available, including the Russian Mariinsky Ballet and Israeli Batsheva Dance Company. Traditional performances of all well-known genres were given – kabuki, noh, kyogen, rakugo, and kōdan – excluding bunraku, whose single professional troupe presented only in Osaka that month. The result demonstrates that Tokyo is indeed a vibrant capital of world theatre in terms of historical and geographical diversity.

One difficulty for theatre lovers seeking noteworthy performances among this creative cornucopia lies in the nebulous functional distinction among national, public, and private theatres. In Japan, even public and national theatres lease their space to private organizations to cover their fixed operating costs, with little consideration of content. For instance, *Satomi Hakkenden*, presented at the 1,841-seat Opera Stage of the Shin Kokuritsu Gekijō (New National Theatre), was a star-studded commercial production conceived and produced by Nippon Television Network Corporation. Such major corporations are the only institutions capable of paying the immense rental fee of 1.7 million yen (approximately US $14,000) on weekdays and 2 million yen per day (approximately US $16,000) at weekends.[17] On the other hand, highly respected kabuki performances are produced and presented every month at Shōchiku's privately owned venue, the 1,964-seat Kabuki-za; on this day, however, kabuki was being performed at another privately owned theatre, the Shinbashi Embujō, since the landmark Kabuki-za was in the process of reconstruction prior to reopening in March 2013.

As for mid- to large-scale straight plays, most productions cast either a pop idol or a musical star to increase their box office sales. Musicals are highly popular, with Gekidan Shiki (Four Seasons Theatre Company) importing the most successful Broadway and West End productions, such as *The Phantom of the Opera*, while the all-female Takarazuka Revue Company continues to present original musical productions. Most small-scale musicals are semi-professional fringe productions, combining manga culture and digital game-like stories. Attending one of these fringe performances, you might find a bag on your seat or a packet stuffing your program with thirty to fifty appealingly designed flyers for upcoming shows, a customary form of advertising adopted by many troupes in this insular world. Original plays are far more prevalent than revivals for all non-traditional genres.

On the same day there was also great variety in production scale. The largest hall operating was the Tokyo Takarazuka Gekijō at 2,069; the smallest, at thirty-five seats, was Raft, an alternative space in Nakano. In addition to

17 Interview with sales department staff of New National Theatre, 19 April 2013.

productions in purpose-built spaces, such as the national theatres, and commercial venues like Kinokuniya Hall (within a bookstore) and Parco Theatre (within a department store complex), performances also took place at multipurpose civic halls, underground bars, makeshift tents, and warehouses, as well as at shrines and temples: perennial sites in Japan for fringe performance.

Tickets ranged from 22,000 yen (US $222) for prime seats at the Mariinsky Ballet to 500 yen (US $5) for Shinjuku Midnight Rakugo. Although some productions were one-off events – noh plays and rakugo performances are typically held only once – most played from a few days to a week. Kabuki plays run twenty-five days of the month; Shiki's *The Lion King* has been playing to full houses at the same 1,255-seat theatre since 1998. In terms of international diversity, most productions came from homegrown Tokyo groups. Some exceptions were the Takarazuka company from Kobe, Company Greenpig from Korea, and Against Again Troupe from Taiwan, and a work from Austrian author Elfriede Jelinek directed by Kyoto-based company Chiten (see Figure 46) – the latter three all presented at the Festival/Tokyo.

Although the situation is gradually changing in Japan, most cultural activities concentrate in Tokyo. Consequently, the density of artists and productions in Japan's capital city is far more significant compared to other theatrical capitals with greater public financial support. More than 79 percent of all performances in Japan are produced in Tokyo.[18] Nevertheless, only 132 theatre buildings or halls hosting theatre regularly exist in the metropolis; this number represents a mere 18.9 percent of the total number of multipurpose halls or purpose-built theatre venues in Japan.[19] Unsurprisingly, demand for central theatre spaces is significantly high: the Honda Gekijō presented sixty-seven theatre productions in 298 days in 2011.[20]

20,000,000 visitors per year

While it is impossible to know how many spectators actually attended the 188 performances on 24 November, referencing the annual statistics of Tokyo theatregoers may provide a general picture. According to the information compiled by *Pia*,[21] in 2011 the number of theatregoers in the Tokyo Greater Metropolitan Area reached 20,810,000, despite the 11 March triple

18 Nippon Engeki Kyōkai (Japanese Association of Theatre) (ed.), *Engeki nenkan bessatsu* (Annual report appendix) (Tokyo: Nihon Engeki Kyōkai, 2013), 177–87.
19 Ministry of Economy, Trade and Industry, "II The overview of theatre (including rent halls)," *Yearbook of the Current Survey of Commerce 2004* (2005), www.meti.go.jp/statistics/tyo/tokusabizi/result-2/h16/pdf/h16-t-24.pdf (accessed 5 May 2013).
20 Honda Theatre Group, "Honda Gekijō jōen kiroku 2011" (Honda Gekijō Group Website, 2011), www.honda-geki.com/honda.kiroku2.html#Anchor-41073 (accessed 5 May 2013).
21 Pia Co. Ltd, Data Analysis Department, *Audience Statistics for Tokyo Greater Metropolitan Area in 2011*, unpublished (2012).

disaster (earthquake, tsunami, nuclear meltdown) in the Tohoku region. This number is, in fact, around 50 percent higher than the 13,915,185 audience members who attended theatre performances in London during the same year.[22] Tokyo truly is one of the most significant world theatrical capitals in terms of both diversity and volume.

Playwright Kishida Kunio (1890–1954), who worked mainly in Tokyo throughout his life, commented that "the contemporary Japanese theatre today is remarkably abundant and miscellaneous in terms of genres. This is presumably true in comparison to any country in the world. This diversity in genres could be regarded as the essence of contemporary Japanese theatre."[23] At least on 24 November 2012, Kishida's statement, after more than seven decades, rings true.

References and further reading

www.theaterguide.co.jp
http://stage.corich.jp
www.realtokyo.co.jp/stage/
www.shochiku.co.jp/play/

---

22 The Society of London Theatre, "Society of London Theatre announced eight consecutive record year of sales," The Society of London Theatre website, www.solt.co.uk/downloads/pdfs/pressroom/london_box_office_figures_2011.pdf (accessed 5 May 2013).
23 Kishida Kunio, "Nihon engeki no tokushitsu" (The essence of Japanese theatre), in *Kishida Kunio zenshū* 24 (Tokyo: Iwanami shoten, 1991 [1939]), www.aozora.gr.jp/cards/001154/files/44616_37238.html.

Interlude: Charting Tokyo theatre today: 24 November 2012

IWAKI KYOKO

Venue type	Size	Genre	Subgenre	No.	Representative productions
National	Large	Traditional		1	Kabuki, *Ukiyozuka hiyoku no inazuma* (The floating world's pattern and matching lightning bolts), Tsuruya Namboku IV
		Contemporary		1	*Satomi Hakkenden,* Takizawa Bakin, dir. Fukasaku Kenta
	Medium	Traditional		1	Noh and kyogen, *Genji monogatari yumemamoboroshi*
		Contemporary		1	Company 30-Delux, *Yellow,* written and dir. Mōri Tsunehiro
	Small	Traditional		2	Rakugo
		Contemporary		0	n/a
			Total	**6**	
Public	Large	Traditional		0	n/a
		Contemporary	Original Plays	0	n/a
			Revivals	0	n/a
			Operas and Musicals	0	n/a
			Dance and others	1	Mariinsky Ballet (Russia), *La Bayadere*
	Medium	Traditional		0	n/a
		Contemporary	Original Plays	0	n/a
			Revivals	0	n/a
			Operas and Musicals	1	Terayama Misemono Musical, *Chikyū kudosetsu* (Theory of vacant earth), dir. Ryuzanji Sho

Venue type	Size	Genre	Subgenre	No.	Representative productions
			Dance and others	3	Batsheva Dance Company (Israel), *Sadeh 21; DAH-DAH-SKO-DAH-DAH*, Teshigawara Saburō
	Small	Traditional		0	n/a
		Contemporary	Original Plays	8	*Four*, Kawamura Takeshi, dir. Shirai Akira; *Hoshi no musuko* (Son of a planet), text and dir. Sakate Yōji
			Revivals	2	*Castle of Dreams*, text and dir. Miura Daisuke; *Four Plays by Tennessee Williams*, dir. Ninagawa Yukio, Fujita Shuntarō and Inoue Sonsho
			Operas and Musicals	0	n/a
			Dance and others	3	*Kein Licht II: Epilogue?*, Elfriede Jelinek (Austria), dir. Takayama Akira; Company Natya Manjari Japan, *The Indian God of Planets Navagraha and the Dance of Praying*, choreog. Udupi Laxminarayan and Mayuri Emi
			Total	**18**	
Private	Large	Traditional		3	Monthly kabuki at Shinbashi Embujō – *Hanagata* (young actors) *Kabuki* at Meiji-za
		Contemporary	Original Plays	1	*Bokuni hono-o no sensha o* (Biting my chariot of fire), text and dir. Chong Wishing
			Revivals	0	n/a

Venue type	Size	Genre	Subgenre	No.	Representative productions
			Operas and Musicals	14	Shiki Theatre Company, *The Phantom of the Opera*, Andrew Lloyd Webber (UK); Takarazuka Revue Company – Snow Troupe, *Jin*, text and dir. Saitō Yoshimasa; *Gold Spark!*, text and dir. Nakamura Satoru
			Dance and others	3	*Johnny's World* dir. Johnny Kitagawa; *Intensio: The World of Danile Simkin* choreog. Marius Petipa, John Neumeier, and James Kudelka
	Medium	Traditional		2	Tokyo Kanze Society, noh *Nonomiya*
		Contemporary	Original Plays	3	*Hello Goodbye*, text and dir. Takeshige Yōhei; *Tono to issho* (Together with the master), based on manga of Ohba Kai, text and dir. by Naruse Yusei
			Revivals	2	*Hinoura-hime monogatari* (The story of Princess Hinoura), text Inoue Hisashi, dir. Ninagawa Yukio
			Operas and Musicals	2	*Rent*, Jonathan Larson (USA)
			Dance and other performances	1	*Le Noir, The Dark Side of Cirque*, prod. Avex Live Creative, CEO Katsumi Kuroiwa
	Small	Traditional		19	Enmanikai Teirei Noh Society, noh *Kiyotsune*, *Yōkihi*, *Akogi*; Monthly rakugo at Shinjuku Suehiro-tei

Venue type	Size	Genre	Subgenre	No.	Representative productions
		Contemporary	Original Plays	79	Company Shudan hokōkunren, *Permanent Value,* concept and dir. Tani Ryuichi; Company Nonoue, *Tokyo Allergy,* text and dir. Yamada Momoji
			Revivals	12	*Same Time Next Year,* text Bernard Slade, dir. Sasaura Nobuhiro; *Les Plaideurs,* text Jean Racine, dir. Tokyo Kandenchi Company
			Operas and Musicals	11	Pan Planning Company, *Don Juan,* dir. Koreeda Masahiko; Theatre Creative Project, *Pink Drunk, Chocolat ni Majoca*
			Dance and other performances	11	Japan Performance Art Institute, *Ce Qui Arrive? 2012,* seven short performances by Japanese avant garde artists; *Exposing Me,* choreog. Masaoka Yuiko
			Total	**163**	
Total				**187**	

Interlude: Modern theatre tomorrow: interview with Oriza Hirata

IWAKI KYOKO

Oriza Hirata (1962–) is playwright, director, owner of Komaba Agora Theatre, and leader of the Seinendan (Youth Group) Theatre Company based in Tokyo. With *Sōru Shimin* (Citizens of Seoul, 1989), he established "Contemporary Colloquial Theatre Theory" which, in contrast to Western-influenced *shingeki*, bases its grammatical structure on everyday Japanese: pronouns omitted, verbs repeated, and stress accents discarded; long pauses and simultaneous chitchat. His *Tokyo nōto* (Tokyo notes, 1994; Figure 47) received the Kishida Kunio Drama Award, and was consequently produced in Brest, France (directed by Frédérick Fisbach). His productions have regularly been invited to theatres around the globe, most recently with his "android theatre."

Hirata has published highly debated theoretical books such as *Gendai kōgo engeki no tame ni* (Approaching contemporary colloquial theatre, 1995) and *Toshi ni shukusai wa iranai* (Cities need no festivals, 1997) strenuously arguing about the development of the ever-contentious modern Japanese theatre scene from historical, aesthetic, and above all linguistic perspectives. In this interview, held on 9 December 2012, Hirata was asked to discuss Japanese contemporary theatre in the context of wider international markets, describing how creative shifts by the younger generation may lead to a "theatrical evolution from the periphery."

Native theatrical language

Hirata foresees the future by casting his eye over the past. His initial argument is that the struggle of Japanese drama to create a modern, native, theatrical language per se began during the anomalous and arbitrary development of shingeki. At the beginning of the twentieth century, Japan imported Shakespeare, Ibsen, Chekhov, and Maeterlinck almost simultaneously, eliding cultural specificities in favor of importing texts and staging from Western masterpieces. Thus, when Japanese playwrights and directors attempted to develop their own dramaturgical equivalents in Japanese settings, they inevitably achieved perplexing results: attempting to match

Fig 47 During World War III, museum patrons chat in Hirata Oriza's *Tokyo Notes* (1995).

European language locutions, dialogue often became stilted and remote. This was anathema to Hirata; from early in his career, he criticized the "unnatural" language of shingeki.

Hirata asserts that compared to Japan's successful integration of Western modern music, Japanese theatre, to which the modernization movement came late, never had time to fully digest Western dramaturgical traditions. By the 1930s Japan had entered its fascist era and arguably any cultural evolution was neglected except those directly accommodating the military and colonial project. A generation after the end of the war, the *angura* (underground) theatre movement started developing a physical language derived from Asian-rooted embodiment, yet progress evolving an idiosyncratic written language was largely omitted from this quest. Japanese theatre, specifically in the form of written texts, never had the chance to fully develop a mature style.

Whether the Japanese theatre has developed its own "contemporary" style has been debated for more than three decades. Hirata claims that this is true not only in contemporary theatre (*gendaigeki*) but also in modern theatre (*kindaigeki*). The preconditions for Japanese "contemporary theatrical style" are also debatable, since, if prewar modern theatre never bore fruit, a contemporary style cannot be cultivated from that arid soil. From this standpoint, he contends that, "I am *the* modern theatre [in Japan]."[24] By defining

24 Kitajima Takashi and Mizuushi Kentarō, "#10 Hirata Oriza: Seinendan, Agora Gekijō," *Wonderlands: A Review Magazine for Fringe Theatre* (14 September 2010), www.wonderlands.jp/interview/010hirata/ (accessed 4 February 2013).

himself as the apex of "modern theatre" and by also initiating the Contemporary Colloquial Theatre Theory, he has established himself as both exponent of non-shingeki modern theatre and chief theorist of contemporary theatre. "From the post-Hirata generation, [Japanese] contemporary theatre begins."[25]

A decade after these seemingly audacious pronouncements, Hirata is proving prescient. Many younger theatre practitioners such as Okada Toshiki of chelfitsch, Miura Daisuke of potsudo-ru, and Shu Matsui of Sample – labeled "Hirata's children" due to their articulation of a hyper-colloquial theatre language – are being introduced in the West as "not only contemporary, but also completely universal."[26] Has this single generation's success in developing its own theatrical language confirmed its transformation beyond the thorny issues of modern history to contemporary cosmopolitanism? Hirata's answer is a qualified "no." "Although the seed of modern theatre, in opposition to classical shingeki, has now finally been implanted, full modernization of Japanese theatre has yet to be achieved; another twenty years is required for it to become the de facto standard."

Outgrowing childishness

Within the next two decades, Hirata claims that improvements in three distinct areas are necessary: thematic content addressed, autonomy of theatrical language, and a form of dialogue distinct from the West.

Regarding the thematic content addressed, Karatani Kojin suggests in *Origins of Modern Japanese Literature* that the Japanese "I-novel" may have come to fruition hand-in-hand with "the confessional literary form." His main argument is that the initial establishment of the "confession as a system … produced the interiority that confessed, the 'true self': the exterior system forced the interiority to emerge." However, Karatani argues that subsequently modern literature ended in "conflating the author's 'I' and the 'I' of the work," thus failing "to create a world distinct and autonomous from that of the author's 'I.'"[27] For Hirata, this subjective tradition of the "I-novel" reflects analogous issues that Japanese theatre practitioners have also struggled against.

> Japanese theatre-makers several years senior to me may have failed in the international market because, in the West, to thematically express self-searching

---

25 *Ibid.*
26 Rémi Fort and Margherita Mantero, *Festival d'automne à Paris 2008: Dossier de presse théâtre* (Paris: Service de presse festival d'automne, 2008), 45.
27 Karatani Kōjin, *Origins of Modern Japanese Literature*, trans. and ed. Brett de Barry (Durham, NC: Duke University Press, 1998), 76–80.

is considered "childish." One reason why I have succeeded in the West is because, in form and content, I did not possess this childishness.

Yet younger artists like Okada are deliberately applying this childish Japanese "I-novel" tradition – the company's name itself is a word implying a child attempting to say the English word "selfish" – but by deftly polishing the aesthetics he has achieved a unique style, which has an eccentric appeal in the wider world.

Hirata's appraisal of the younger generation of theatre-makers is however rather negative. They will not influence the international market unless they start to speak beyond their particular, self-conscious contemplations. "Whatever it may be, they need to develop a solid theoretical basis which affirms their creative standpoint."

Japanese autonomy

The second required shift is the establishment of an autonomous Japanese "theatrical grammatical language" per se. In Hirata's opinion, most theatre-makers who have thrived in the global circuit until now, like Suzuki Tadashi and Ninagawa Yukio, have achieved their success with little choice but to "align themselves to the rhetoric of the Western theatrical canon, such as Chekhov and Shakespeare. 'Even iconoclastic Mishima, although Asian in content, had to deliver his stories in a highly logical, Western theatrical grammar.'" Hirata believes that he has in contrast continuously written "culturally Westernized stories in contemporary Japanese grammar," eventually blossoming into the aforementioned Contemporary Colloquial Theatre Theory. Consequently, Hirata shows justifiable pride in the fact that his theory has arguably materialized as the bedrock of the much-anticipated modern Japanese theatrical language.

> By the time my theory pervaded Japan in the late 1990s, ensuing playwrights could feel comfortable to write in ordinary colloquial language differing from the shingeki vocabulary. Naturally, this locally cultivated rhetorical structure led to a different content, which could not have been nurtured in a European cultural context.

Writer-directors like Okada and Miura are now regarded highly in the West precisely because they speak freely in a locally cultivated theatrical language.

Lastly, Hirata contends that Japanese contemporary theatre needs to change not only individual rhetorical elements noted above, but also inter-individual communicative forms, reflecting the idiosyncratic Japanese conversational style. Since Japan is a place where "people with virtually homogeneous values gather to create a mass, the society becomes like a *mura* [closed village]."[28] Innately discordant confrontations with racial, political, or religious polarities are less apparent than in other parts of the world; Japanese society could thus still be described as one form of *Gemeinschaft*, one which Edward T. Hall proposed as the apex of a "high-context system."[29]

When, arguably, mutual understanding is tacit rather than set as a goal, the form of communication does not materialize as a dialectic discourse, a *tai-wa* (対話): the kanji character *tai* implying the word *tai-ritsu* (confrontation). Rather, Hirata argues this is merely a conversation, a *kai-wa* (会話, group talk), in which members gather to reaffirm their aggregated values in what Hirata calls an insular, "pampered, child-like communication."

> Clearly, in the West, dialogue is the basis of modern plays. Japanese, conversely, do not share this tradition; and if reasoned by syllogism, the conclusion is that we cannot make modern theatre. However, in art, things are not that simple. Since dialogues in plays are unnatural for us, we can confront, analyze, and unravel the structure. Then hopefully, a form of dialogue distinct from the West will emerge.

Hirata praises playwrights like Yamazaki Tetsu (1946–) and Iwamatsu Ryo (1952–) as forerunners attempting to create a distinctive dialogic style. "The uniqueness of these writers is that individuals speak less autonomously [than in the West]. The characters speak proactively, yet are simultaneously induced by their context to temper their speech." In his mind, this is a subtle invention: a novel form of dialogue.

> Japanese theatre makers have always struggled with frictions between exterior style and interior content. However, because of this struggle, since they had to consciously analyze and overcome such obstacles, today a new form of international theatre has emerged. And why not? Theatre has always evolved from the periphery, as Chekhov, Stanislavski, and Ibsen emerged from Moscow and Norway in the late nineteenth century.

From this standpoint, Hirata tentatively concludes that contemporary Japanese theatre could innovate the theatre in ways less possible in the West. Pointing to the 11 March 2011 earthquake, tsunami and nuclear catastrophe, Hirata predicts that, due to these disasters, what was previously seen as a homogenized mass was disrupted, thereby requiring *tai-wa*: a dialogue in and about life.

---

28 Hirata Oriza, "Kōen: gekisakka kara mita Nihongo" (A lecture: Japanese seen from a playwright's perspective), in *Ningenbunka*, vol. XI (Inter-University Research Institute Corporation, National Institutes for the Humanities, 2010), 19–29.

29 Edward T. Hall, *Beyond Culture* (New York: Anchor Books, 1976), 127.

In *Chūshingura*, one of the most popular stories in Japan (see representative plays), when a crucial misjudgment by the daimyo of Akō ends in the confiscation of his domain, the forty-seven now masterless *rōnin* warriors are challenged to stand up against the clan's catastrophe. The members, however, are no longer a single mass. Confronted by the crucial task, they begin to tackle their fates individually, and from there, a dialogue naturally flows.

Hirata feels that Japan is now facing a national scale *Chūshingura*. What were once considered inherent bonds are now being tested by this catastrophe. Indeed, this is a tragic event, yet in terms of the evolution of theatre it may prove a catalyst to an aesthetic breakthrough. Since disaster forces the disbandment of the homogenized clan, a schism arises; in order to reestablish mutual understanding, a groping forward based on continuous discourse is required.

Some explication may be needed to clarify Hirata's rather contradictory statements. In the global circuit, Japan's cultural marginality may be advantageous in developing an idiosyncratic theatrical language lacking in the West. Yet at the same time, Hirata affirms that in the aftermath of the Fukushima disaster, through the dissolution of the harmonized mass, the theatrical dialogue in Japan may spontaneously mature to emulate the West. However, whether assailing from the periphery or aligning to the center, Hirata foresees that most theatrical innovations cannot be achieved independently. To encourage individual talents, Hirata has been keenly advocating the necessity of establishing Japan's first state-run theatre department at Tokyo National University of the Arts.

References and further reading

Hirata Oriza. *Engeki 1.2* (DVD) Kinokuniya, 2013
    Tokyo Notes (Six Language Edition DVD), Kinokuniya, 2007
    "Tokyo Notes," trans. M. Cody Poulton, *ATJ* 19:1 (2002), 1–120

PART III
Arcs and patterns

12 ∾ Premodern playwriting practices

LAURENCE KOMINZ

Plays are literary servants to non-literary masters

In Japan's premodern era (1300–1868) written texts were produced to serve specific theatrical events – multimedia, multi-participant, collaborative ventures. The authority and autonomy of play texts as literary works were immaterial. What mattered were effective performances. Some theatrical texts later acquired the status of recognized, stand-alone literary products, but neither this status nor artistic quality indicate the plays' intrinsic worth as facilitators of performance. Authors were heavily constrained by, dependent on, and subservient to conditions, requirements, and priorities that were decidedly non-literary, and often even non-verbal. Play texts in premodern Japan can be understood as literary servants used and abused by non-literary masters, including: formal codes and structural systems of performance; skills of the lead performer(s) and hierarchical requirements of the performance company; spectators, ranging from aristocratic warlord patrons to admission-paying commoners.

Service to conventions of music, dance, and spectacle

Non-literary performance systems in traditional Japanese theatre center on dance and music. Noh and bunraku (*ningyō jōruri*) are musical drama, as are most kabuki plays. When we consider opera, the West's great musical dramatic form, libretti for even the finest works are third-rate literature, never included in literary anthologies. The libretti are masterpieces nevertheless – brilliantly fulfilling their supporting roles. Japanese texts play similar roles. Zeami, the greatest dramatist of the noh theatre, was the first Japanese writer to explain the correct process for playwriting. In *Sandō* (The three elements in composing a play) he wrote:

> There are three elements required for the composition of a noh play – the seed (literary sources), the construction, and the composition. The seed should be appropriate for theatrical expression and especially effective in terms of

the Two Arts of dance and chant. If the subject concerns a character who cannot be manifested using these Two Arts, then even if the character to be portrayed is a famous person in the past or a person of prodigious gifts, no theatrical effect appropriate to the *nō* is possible.[1]

Zeami thus defines a proper subject exclusively as that which can be expressed in music and dance. "Creating a character whose very essence is involved in the art of song and dance can be termed choosing the proper seed (*tane*, 種)."[2]

Zeami then called on his playwright to "construct" (*saku*, 作) the play. This was in accordance with the principles of "*jo, ha,* and *kyū*" (序破急). Zeami borrowed these principles from musical composition for *gagaku*: jo – introductory slow tempo; ha – development of major themes in increasing, complex tempos; kyū – high tempo conclusion. The play should be divided into five movements (one jo, three ha, one kyū),[3] with an increase in impressiveness from jo, through ha and kyū. Impressiveness was tied to both performative and literary characteristics dichotomized as unimpressive versus impressive: i.e. walking versus dancing: prose dialogue versus sung poetry. Impressiveness should be understood as a continuum rather than a binary – each play segment includes a particular mix and degree of impressiveness. These rules constrain the freedom of the writer, making it impossible, for example, to end a noh play with long prose dialogue, or begin it with an up-tempo, rhythmically intense sung text. Yet Zeami considered these rules not as constraints, but rather as recipes for success that he himself had discovered, and prescriptive formulae for further success. He considered subservience of written text to formal musical and performance codes to be both rational and effective.

Next, the playwright had to consider the "composition" (*sho*) – the actual words written. The noh playwright fashioned a collage of poetry and prose, part original composition, part strategically excerpted from literary sources. Zeami maintained that well-written and well-known songs and poems were essential to success. Dialogue was for explanatory and plot purposes only and should be kept to a minimum. Plot is of minor concern – the audience knows it already because of the famous seed source. Music, poetry, and dance express the central emotions.

Creative borrowing facilitated audience recognition and intimacy, lending dignity and authority to a newly composed play. This anchoring of plays to sources, more than any other aspect of noh playwriting, situates noh texts among the great works of Japanese literature, despite the fact that literary

1 J. Thomas Rimer (trans.) and Yamazaki Masakasu (ed.), *On the Art of the Nō Drama: The Major treatises of Zeami* (Princeton, NJ: Princeton University Press, 1984), 148
2 *Ibid.* 149.   3 *Ibid.*

"composition" is tertiary to the performance-based constraints of "seed" character and music-based play structure.

Requiring a text to serve dance is potentially onerous. Before Zeami's time almost every noh dance was a felicitous or formal entertainment at a banquet or festival. Such dance was both essential and highly limited, placing major constraints on playwrights' choice of subject matter, and creation of a story or through-line. Fortunately, in the mature noh of Zeami's day, noh dance developed a wide and abstract vocabulary of stylized gestures using fans and small properties. Almost any phenomenon that could be sung about could also be expressed in dance. Through this codified combination of sung text and evocative dance, noh could readily depict battles among samurai, wizards exorcising demons, and women grieving for either lost children or betrayal in love.

In other genres, puppeteers and set designers dominated the stage with special effects, demoting dramatic texts to mere excuses for displaying visual spectacle. In *kinpira jōruri* (popular from the 1650s to 1680s), puppeteers and property technicians displayed their remarkable skills, forcing playwrights to write scenes featuring supernatural feats and amazing phenomena – real fire and fireworks, flying beasts and sorcerers.

Serving lead performers and troupe hierarchies

The actors' theatres of premodern Japan, noh and kabuki, required brilliant lead performers standing out from the rank and file, bringing success to the company as performer, artistic director, and sometimes producer.

In noh plays by Zeami, the *shite* lead characters are the only important ones, usually played by performers of high stature in their respective troupes. Zeami's term "flower" expressed the fascination of the main actor,[4] hardly mentioning the "leaves" or "shrubbery" essential for this flower to stand out. In noh the greenery would be the chorus, *waki* supporting actor, musicians, and other supporting performers. In *Sandō* Zeami focuses on how the writer creates a play that will enable the shite to blossom. There was no conflict between author and lead actor because they were one and the same – the writer used his literary skills to ensure that he "bloomed" on stage. Or he might appropriately modify a play from the existing repertory to suit his abilities.

Leading bunraku troupe performers were not puppeteers but *tayū*, chief chanters. Until Chikamatsu Monzaemon (1653–1725) emerged as bunraku's first dedicated playwright, bunraku author-chanters wrote texts playing to

4 Zeami, "Teachings on style and the flower" and "A mirror held to the flower," *passim* 3–110.

their own vocal strengths. Inoue Harima-jō (active in the 1670s) had a beautiful voice for romantic songs, and so wrote romantic plays filled with love songs, even publishing them commercially in independent volumes. Several decades later, Chikamatsu, staff playwright for Osaka's Takemoto-za, found that he had to write quite different plays for chanter Masadayū than he had for his predecessor, Gidayū. The former excelled at sung expressions of emotion, the latter at dialogue; it was Chikamatsu's charge to make each triumph.

Perhaps the most accommodating Japanese authors wrote for kabuki, which emerged as a fully commercialized star system in the late 1600s. The transition from actor-playwrights to playwright specialists took place roughly from the 1680s to 1710. The greatest actor-playwright of this era, Edo-based Ichikawa Danjūrō I (1660–1704), created a bravura form of acting called *aragoto*, featuring superhuman feats similar to those of Kinpira puppet heroes: "drinking sake out of huge cups, trampling tigers to death, throwing enemy soldiers around like stones."[5]

Actor and character merged in superheroic performance. Deities that Danjūrō himself worshiped gave superpowers to the heroes he created in his plays; Danjūrō even crossed his eyes when performing a *mie* pose, imitating the famous Fudō statue, a violent manifestation of the Buddha. When Danjūrō's plays featured heroes from preexisting literature, i.e. the young avenger Soga Gorō, their depictions had to be considerably more exaggerated than the more human-like portrayals in noh plays and the epic *Tale of the Soga Brothers*. In Danjūrō's new plays, the younger brother was depicted as a worshiper of the wild deity Fudō, and also became a red-skinned, muscle-rippling, physical specimen who uproots large bamboo with his bare hands.

This dramatic reinforcement of connections among the god Fudō, superhero characters, and actor himself enhanced Danjūrō's stature as a celebrity hero. Throngs followed him on pilgrimage to worship at Narita's Fudō temple. This symbiosis of character and actor identity underlay kabuki's star system, and its astounding financial success. Kabuki required texts that conflated star actors with fictional male characters who epitomized romantic or martial appeal, and female characters (played by men) who exuded feminine beauty, grace, and charm.

Such were the duties of the kabuki playwright when crafting characters and dialogue for leading personages in a play. But the author was faced with another, more onerous constraint – the hierarchical demands of a company of thirty or more actors. Each had to be given a certain number of lines and

5 From two different *hyōbanki* (actors' evaluation books) in *Kabuki nenpyō: yakusha dangōzuku* (1700), vol. II, 420, and *Yakusha mangokubune* (1701), vol. III, 145. See Chapter 19 for more explanation of these early works of stage criticism.

standout scenes appropriate to his stature in the company. Since plays had to be written in a matter of days by a team of playwrights, this situation led to loose, meandering stories, with numerous, often poorly integrated subplots, or fantastical leaps in location and era. Kabuki playwrights were servants to the hierarchy of their troupes.

To add insult to injury, the kabuki playwright was paid less than all but the bottom few actors in his troupe. He enjoyed no respect whatsoever as a writer of literature. The playwright's masters did not consider literary originality or quality to be essential, nor were play texts considered worthy of protection. No writer in any genre of Edo and pre-Edo literature had his work protected by copyright law, but at least aristocratic poets were denigrated or dishonored for stealing the work of other poets. Kabuki playwrights were so low in stature that stealing others' work was deemed essential and appropriate.

How did lowly playwrights regard the grandmasters of the theatre game, their all-powerful patrons? In Zeami's day the great patrons were fighting warlords, men living by the political imperative of "kill or be killed." They held immeasurable wealth and power, and could reward a performer sumptuously or punish him with banishment or death. Not surprisingly, Zeami devotes much attention in his treatises to the art of pleasing his audiences, most specifically rich, influential performance sponsors. Many different sorts of plays had to be written to entertain audiences varying greatly in literacy, according to the mood of the performance occasion.

Indeed, in premodern Japan, creating written texts was only part of a playwright's duties as a jack-of-all-trades. Playwrights were not so much "writers" as "crafters." Depending on the genre, play-crafters were responsible for musical composition, choreography, acting and singing on stage, creation of large and small stage properties, and working in teams overseeing rehearsals, as well as production duties such as casting, scheduling, accommodations to seasonal and emergency repertory, and deciding program composition. Versatility and flexibility were professional necessities.

Articulation of best practices – noh plays

Zeami was the first Japanese to articulate "best practices" in writing for the stage. For a noh play to succeed in its task of fascinating an audience through the aesthetic exploration of a human soul,[6] it is essential to create an effective, sympathetic character for the shite to portray. Zeami wrote in considerable detail about the creation and onstage depiction of diverse characters.

---

6 Kenneth K. Yasuda, *Masterworks of the Nō Theater* (Bloomington: Indiana University Press, 1989), 1.

Zeami's patrons were sophisticated, well versed in classical literature, with high expectations of artistic balance and harmony, and aesthetic beauty. It was not enough merely to write for three distinct "role types" (old man/ woman/warrior). These were like primary colors, to be mixed to create personalities of many hues. Among women characters, different sorts required different kinds of musical accompaniment, poetry, song, and dialogue. Zeami spelled out in detail the different writing styles necessary to express aristocratic court ladies, professional dancers and singers, deranged women who have lost their children, female nature spirits (dangerous and benign), and goddesses.[7] Moreover, each shite character is an individual not just a type – a well-known personage from history, religion, or the literary canon. The individuality of the shite character is developed from the "seed" source, and then honed through personal interpretation of the playwright in service to his patrons. As noh aligned itself with the ascendant religious philosophy, typically the playwright added a Buddhist consciousness to a secular story, framing the play in Buddhist concepts. Because plays succeeded in repeated performances over centuries, with only minor changes in music and staging, texts were carefully preserved even by early noh troupes.

Early in the Edo period noh texts were printed as literature, for practice by singing hobbyists and for reading, and have been part of Japan's literary canon ever since.

Plays in the age of printing, publication, and commercial theatre

In the Edo period, professional playwrights remained subordinate to higher authorities in the theatre business. Their in-house masters included theatre financiers, company leaders, and leading performers. Bunraku and kabuki were so popular that there was a demand for retail availability of published play texts. Sales might be enhanced if the claim was made that they were authentic performance texts (i.e. *jōruri shōhon*) by famous author-chanters. Other texts were sold as adaptations from the stage, with illustrations and storytelling fiction added to elements of theatrical presentation. Illustrations in *e-iri kyōgen bon* (kabuki plays with illustrations) feature characters who are specific actors wearing stage costumes, but they inhabit a world of forests, towns, and castles, not the bare kabuki stage of 1680–1710, when the books were published.

Where did the acknowledged playwright stand vis-à-vis a text sold, or a play staged with his name on the marquee outside the theatre? The playwright was

7 Zeami, 152–5.

associated with the work, and was paid (poorly) to write it, but did not have ownership of the work in any sense. Texts were routinely stolen, wholesale or piecemeal. Responsibility for texts was collective, not individual. Proof can be seen in the punishments meted out for texts violating censorship restrictions: the theatre, publisher (if it was a published text), leading actors and chanters, financiers, authors – *all* were punished.

Articulation of best practices – how to write for bunraku puppet theatre

In early puppet theatre (*ko-jōruri*, 1600–1680s) the top chanter was simultaneously troupe leader, artistic director, chief playwright, and onstage star. Over 350 plays by these chanters were published as *jōruri shōhon*, "true versions" of stage plays – literature meant to be read, with added illustrations. These ko-jōruri playwrights learned to craft plays longer than any plays yet performed. To entertain paying commoner audiences, they had to contain plot variety and visual and musical appeal. The sequential juxtaposition of two essentially different sorts of scenes was vital to their appeal. *Jigoto* scenes with dialogue and action that furthered the plot alternated with *fushigoto* scenes that entertained through music and dance. This is, of course, essentially the same structure employed by modern American musical plays.

Chikamatsu Monzaemon's teacher, the leading chanter Uji Kaganojō (1635–1711), was first to write about "best practices" in composing puppet plays. A trained noh singer, Kaganojō thought noh "the parent of jōruri," introducing the jo-ha-kyū structure, five-act plays, and noh-based musical notation, and danced *michiyuki* traveling scenes as both a virtual tour of famous places and a symbolic life-journey.

Chikamatsu's "best practices" for creating dramatic puppet plays were recorded in conversations with a colleague, Hozumi Ikan (1692–1769). Chikamatsu maintained that entertainment (*nagusami*) required the right balance between reality (*jitsu*) and artifice (*uso*). Reality and artifice should flow back and forth, as through a permeable membrane. The playwright should create women characters who forthrightly express their emotions more than most women do in daily life. If women in plays are reserved (realistic behavior), the audience will not know how they feel, and cannot empathize, becoming confused instead of entertained. Despite (and via) the constraints Chikamatsu faced as playwright, he was able to create characters who resonated with audiences, while expressing his personal feelings about human nature and social injustice.

In the generation after Chikamatsu, three-playwright teams worked collectively to create the greatest history plays of the Edo period, including

Chūshingura (The treasury of loyal retainers). Yet the development of the three-man puppet necessitated changes in playwriting. When simply costumed and rigid ko-jōruri dolls gave way to larger, more delicately articulated puppets, dialogue replaced narration for character creation, facilitating minutely detailed puppet movements. These plays were more easily adapted to the kabuki stage than were Chikamatsu's.

Articulation of best practices – how to write kabuki plays

In the 1670s–80s, as audiences began to value performance skill as much as erotic appeal, complex and sophisticated kabuki plays became necessary. Actors such as Danjūrō I wrote them to enhance their success in performances. In Kansai, Chikamatsu apprenticed first as a kabuki playwright, then as author of puppet plays, finally serving as leading playwright for both kabuki and puppet theatres.

Danjūrō I, Chikamatsu, and other playwrights of the late seventeenth century used a juxtaposition of *sekai* (世界, worlds) and *shukō* (趣向, plot devices) to craft intricate, entertaining plots in their long history plays. "Worlds" refers to well-known historical or literary realms (i.e. the Genji–Heike wars, 1160–90), complete with known characters and stories, in which a playwright situated a new play. For a Westerner, Britain during the time of King Arthur might be a sekai rich with potential for new plays. Edo period sekai clearly related to, and possibly derived from, Zeami's "seed." But Edo period plays were not created simply by presenting old worlds via new media. New stories had to be created and situated in old worlds. Shukō were new devices, including plot twists, characters, values, and motivations interwoven into the old worlds. Contemporary domestic plays did not initially use such worlds and devices. They were short, fictionalized, dramatized representations of actual recent scandals, crimes, and suicides among the commoner class. Of course, the populace was just as fascinated by scandals in the ruling samurai class, but this subject matter was almost always protected by government censorship; violators faced potentially devastating punishment.

The most exciting tales of commoner crimes were reenacted again and again, with shukō twists making each version fresh. Eventually popular, tragic, or heroic contemporary figures could become the center of new theatre "worlds," as with the heroine of *Yaoya Oshichi* (Oshichi the greengrocer's daughter), an actual girl who set fire to the city of Edo to be with her beloved.

Additionally, original juxtapositions were created by *naimaze* (内混ぜ), combining two or more worlds in a single play. The result was anachronistic fantasy, beloved by kabuki audiences who reveled in familiar characters in original, exotic situations. A similar American *naimaze* "masterwork" combining Arthurian and 1930s worlds and twists would be *Indiana Jones and the Holy Grail*. The combination of domestic and historical elements in a single play became the hallmark of Edo playwriting, from 1709 enshrined in the New Year's play tradition of combining contemporary holiday customs with the medieval world of the Soga brothers' revenge.

Uirō uri (The medicine peddler, 1718) interweaves Edo period medicinal commerce with the twelfth-century Soga brothers' samurai vendetta. To this brew, Ichikawa Danjūrō II added his own spice: a fantastic, four-minute-long, tongue-twisting peddler's spiel that he wrote himself and sold in multiple editions for readers to buy and recite out loud for fun. It was the most popular in a whole new genre of partial play texts on sale at bookstores. They were *serifu bon* – great speeches from great plays – with their authority proclaimed on book covers by star actors, not playwrights. Celebrity publishing developed early in Japan – by the 1720s.

Kezairoku (Valuable notes on playwriting) articulated best practices in kabuki writing, explaining the responsibilities of each member of a troupe's hierarchical playwriting team. These range from the chief playwright, who composes play titles, decides *sekai* and *shukō*, writes the most important scenes, and reads the play aloud to the whole company, down to the youngest apprentices responsible for properties and copying parts. These tasks are delineated, with instructions on how to do them well.

Kezairoku dealt at length with the difficulties of writing to serve multiple masters, but one of its purposes was to elevate the stature of playwrights – likening them to master strategists. It honored Chikamatsu, "god of playwrights," praising especially his sense of inner purpose, intending to teach the masses. The authors of *Kezairoku* continued Chikamatsu's discussion of "reality" and "artifice," writing in most detail about crafting "overnight pickles" (*ichiya zuke*), plays about actual scandals and crimes within days of the incidents. It was essential to combine true, factual accounts with rumors that authors knew to be false. As scandalmongers the world over have known for centuries, such partial truths are more interesting (and harder to disprove) than police records.

The authors of *Kezairoku* wrote that paying audiences should be thought of as "the enemy" – a striking break from the tradition of authors' and performers' respect for patrons. In an extended military metaphor, the financial leaders of kabuki were generals, playwrights were master strategists in the generals' employ, and actors were soldiers. Playwrights' machinations might trick or lure audiences, "the enemy," into attending kabuki, hopefully in such numbers that great riches flowed from "enemies" to "allies." Audiences were still the ultimate arbiters of theatrical success, and given the respect accorded a dangerous foe, but writers did not see them as partners. This was in direct contrast to the attitude of kabuki actors, who sought to create intimate, or at least pseudo-intimate, ties with their fans.

Some traditional plays have found their way into Japan's literary canon, probing deeply into the souls of their characters, and employing some of the finest poetic language ever created. Chief among them are noh plays by Zeami and tragedies that Chikamatsu wrote to be performed by bunraku puppets. These are Japan's finest traditional plays on the page, but on the popular stage other plays take canonical status: great, sprawling historical and revenge sagas such as *Chūshingura*, bombastic aragoto spectacles, and beautiful dance dramas.

References and further reading

Kominz, Laurence. *Avatars of Vengeance: Japanese Drama and the Soga Literary Tradition* (Ann Arbor: University of Michigan Center for Japanese Studies, 1995)

Saltzman-Li, Katherine. *Creating Kabuki Plays: Context for Kezairoku, "Valuable Notes on Playwriting"* (Leiden: Brill, 2010)

13 ❧ Traditional meta-patterns

JONAH SALZ

Creative constraints on Japanese traditional genres have produced performances of tremendous theatrical potency. Troupes have adroitly exploited their strengths, negotiating the desires and demands of spectators and patrons, and evolving conventions and customs. Genres are classified according to a great specificity of repertoire, styles, and physical stages. These developed as a result of a proclivity of performance venues throughout the medieval era, then strict enforcement of building and sumptuary regulations by the Tokugawa shogunate (1603–1868), followed by standardization through teaching under the *iemoto* (headmaster) system. While differing greatly in content, acting style, *mise-en-scène*, and spectatorship, the traditional dramatic and dance forms share a remarkable number of meta-patterns – enduring expressions of this isolated island nation's character, common historical circumstances, and artistic tendencies. This chapter explores meta-patterns of staging (role and space specialization; distinction of visual/aural channels; transformations) and spectatorship (actors' theatre; connoisseurship; local and seasonal accommodations), and their synthesis in iconic poses and imagery.

Role specialization and spatial framing

Specialization is key to the organization and aesthetics of Japanese super-elaborate performance genres. Once this was founded as a professional genre, troupe members quickly created systems of specialized roles. This occurred in noh (*shite* lead, *waki* side man, shoulder, hip, or stick drum and flute musicians, or kyogen comedian), in bunraku (chanter or puppeteer [body, left arm, leg]), and in kabuki (swashbuckling *aragoto* hero, *onnagata femme fatale* and so on). Moreover, among all traditional arts, only *katari* traditions such as bunraku and *rakugo* have required their respective chanters and raconteurs to possess broad vocal artistry, narrating in addition to portraying all characters in any play. While in some genres, such as kabuki, performers can advance to progressively more complex roles, in others an actor spends decades or even a lifetime confined to specific roles. A Shakespearian spear-carrier might later play Laertes and succeed to Hamlet, but the career trajectory of a noh accompanying waki player will never raise him to stardom. Instead he learns waki roles for each of the 200 or so plays in the repertoire, including diverse stylistic school versions and *kogaki* variants, playing this supporting role throughout his life.

As each genre developed increasingly specialist roles, playwrights were better able to utilize role types for more complex plots, which in turn created greater specificity of role type articulation and sophistication. Kabuki has a wide range of male characters, including romantic and martial heroes, clowns, villains, and so on. Bunraku characters are fixed by their wooden features, which in turn determine costuming and movement. In noh, each performer – the shite, waki, kyogen, and each of four musicians – practices independently, with typically only one partial dress rehearsal (*mōshiawase*) held a few days before a performance. This creates a dynamic tension of slippage and recovery in performance that enlivens even the most oft-repeated repertoire. Instead of a mixed stew, simmered in rehearsal, performers place distinct ingredients in the theatrical *bentō* lunchbox, garnished with their particular family and individual flavors (*geifū*, 芸風).

The lunchbox itself is highly standardized: performance specialization is made possible by spatial segmentation of fixed architectural types. One might imagine that in order to maintain popularity and presence through the centuries, traditional arts would have accommodated a wide range of performance venues. However, whereas Shakespeare is staged today in a black-box studio or The Globe, proscenium or thrust, noh actors performed for centuries almost exclusively on purpose-built noh stages with relatively fixed dimensions.[1] Similarly, orthodox conventions and practical necessity have restricted *bugaku*, kabuki, bunraku, and *yose* to custom-made theatre structures, which vary little today from their original layout and dimensions. Even when noh or kabuki troupes tour civic halls or commercial theatres, or set up open-air stages, the dance-floor, with walkway, and even side-curtain, will be erected according to traditional form and dimensions. The detailed codes of performance are acted confidently within these fixed settings; every new site becomes transformed into a "home theatre."

Separation of visual and audio channels

In most genres, specialization of role types and spatial distinctions were a product and stimulus of visual/vocal disjunctures. Early in Japanese theatre,

---

1 Most major temples and daimyo mansions maintained a practice of indoor noh-stages, complete with bridgeway and wooden floors.

audio and visual communication channels became distinguished as the domain of distinct specialists. Chinese bugaku's originally verbal dramatic content transformed to mute dance to orchestral accompaniment. Although the
noh shite (protagonist) still sings, the chorus has replaced his long speeches,
as well as descriptive passages, while the waki (accompanying actor) and
kyogen interlude narrator provide necessary framing, back-stories, and plot
complications. The shite was thus freed to concentrate on subtleties of dance
expression: projection while performing circling, masked dance would have
proved impossible on outdoor stages before large audiences. Only in kyogen,
primarily dialogue-driven drama, do actors speak or sing for themselves,
even while dancing.

Bunraku puppet theatre chanters and shamisen players accompany each
other with admirable teamwork, embellishing on a *gidayū* chanting tradition that remains an independent storytelling art. Meanwhile the three
manipulators responsible for each puppet's movements (respectively head
and right arm; left arm and properties; legs) respond to each other and
the music, breathing, grunting, and even bumping against each other to
facilitate the dolls' exquisitely graceful movements. However, the chanters
do not follow the puppets as commentators (they face the audience, and can
see the puppets only peripherally), and the puppets do not merely illustrate
the narrative. Instead, words and movements are staggered, and described
actions omitted, creating delightful and emotionally powerful disjunctures.
Audiences receive the simultaneous, multi-channel performances by storytellers, musicians, puppets, and manipulators, comprehending the visual
and aural codes according to their own proclivities and competencies.[2]
Rather than sensory overload, the combination of contrasting elements
creates a dynamic synergy surpassing, many say, that of exclusively human
performers.

Kabuki, which adapted many plots from noh and bunraku, often main-
tains the choral accompaniment and onstage musicians. However, more
than other genres, it features super-actors capable of simultaneous vocalization, dance, and acting (though kabuki actors never sing, as kyogen actors
do). Multiple expressive modes by a single actor, however, are often sequential. In the tour-de-force *Kanjinchō* (The subscription list) Benkei recites a
passionate, tongue-twisting Buddhist sutra, then immediately shows his true
colors, apologizing for having struck his master to protect his disguise. He
concludes the play with an energetic, comic, drunken dance, a ruse to cover

---

2 National Theatre performances of bunraku create a multimedia viewing experience of competing
  channels: super-titles project above stage; inexpensive, thick programs are provided with full texts,
  summaries, and research notes; rentable earphone guides provide avuncular play-by-play commentary in Japanese or English.

his fleeing compatriots. Vocal pyrotechnics, superb acting, and enthusiastic dance follow in turn in this virtuoso display.

This separation of visual and audio channels is found in narrative arts as well. *Etoki* traveling priests and nuns would point to paintings or scrolls while describing them, an early example of "moving pictures." *Misemono* (sideshow) barkers and *kamishibai* paper-theatre storytellers extended these traditions. Just as peripatetic etoki storytellers disseminated splendid artworks before the advent of publishing, and esoteric Buddhist religious doctrines before widespread literacy, *katsudō benshi* film narrators flourished during a more recent technological lag. Motion pictures in Japan were never silent, but accompanied by these *benshi*, who were often originally rakugo or other verbal art veterans. Accompanied by live music, they provided running commentary, explained foreign customs, and assumed voices for the actors, even clueing spectators in appropriate emotions. Choruses, *ai-kyōgen* interludes, and the popularity of *utaibon* libretti at noh plays, earphone guides at kabuki and bunraku, and the ongoing boom in sequential art (manga)[3] all attest to the Japanese tolerance for and enjoyment of parallel, separate expressions through aural/visual channels.

Transformation and disguise

Traditional theatre spectacle relies on the magician's *modus operandi*. While seeming to display all transparently, it surprises through feats of visual wizardry. Many plots in all genres depend on concealment and revelation. Noh interludes by *ai-kyōgen* narrators facilitate changes of masks and costumes, enabling lead actors to employ disguise and dazzling revelations in plays such as priest to spider in *Tsuchigumo* (The earth spider; Figure 48), priest to fox-spirit in *Sesshōseki* (The killing rock), and shrine maiden to titulary god in *Kamo* (The Kamo Shrine). Some transformations in noh seem to be a natural disclosure of true self – the elderly caretaker reveals himself as shrine guardian in *Takasago* (The old pine); in *Koi no omoni* (The burden of love) a gardener who dies of a broken heart returns as a vengeful ghost. Others, however, utilize seemingly arbitrary transformations, an excuse for the actor to display virtuosity. The grieving mother of *Fujito* demands a Buddhist service from the general who killed her son; in the second act, the son's resentful ghost appears, reenacting his death; mother and ghost are played

---

3 Visual storytelling leading to the *emaki* scroll and woodblock print may have originated in the "fracture of meaning" when Chinese characters were imported to represent Japanese phonemes in the eighth century. Most written characters (*kanji*) have at least two readings, demanding visual/aural synthesis. Tze-Yue G. Hu, *Frames of Anime: Culture and Image-Building* (Hong Kong: HKU Press, 2012).

Fig 48 In the noh *Tsuchigumo*, the Warrior (Umewaka Shinya) confronts the giant Earth Spider (Katayama Kiyoshi), transformed from a mysterious monk.

by the same actor. In *Funa Benkei* (Benkei in a boat), Yoshitsune parts from his lover, beautiful *shirabyōshi* dancer Shizuka Gozen, then puts out to sea, where he is attacked by the horrifying ghost of the enemy general Tomomori. The same actor portrays Shizuka's mournful farewell and Tomomori's wrath, a display of acting bravado rather than dramatic necessity.

The more down-to-earth kyogen plays derive humor from failed or partial disguises: a mountain priest as snail (*Kagyū*, Snails), nephew as demon (*Obagasake*, Stealing auntie's sake), thief as monkey (*Kakiyamabushi*, The persimmon thief), or banished servant as ghost (*Buaku*, Buaku the bold). The mean-drunk villain in *Akubō* (Bad priest) wakes to find he has been shaved and dressed in priestly robes while in a drunken stupor. Deciding to atone for his prior misdeeds, he goes off to beg for alms.

Even more malleable are bunraku's "stars"; puppet heads are removable, some including mechanisms enabling a pretty girl to sprout demonhorns, or a soldier's face to split open. Kabuki's great actors played as many as twelve roles in a single *hengemono* transformation dance play. Onstage *kurogo* assistants assist in the most dramatic transformations, as when a costume is altered (*bukkaeri*) or removed (*hikinuki*) to instantaneously reveal a completely different pattern beneath – a feat of legerdemain earning gasps and applause. The fluid movements of the dance-fan can easily express hundreds of objects and emotions, and just as readily melt into another.

Beside the obvious delight in such total, astonishing, and complicated transformations, there may be a deeper philosophical underpinning to their enduring allure. Mysterious characters revealed in the midst of a play as ghosts, spirits, or demons operate in a magico-religious world that exists outside the theatre as well, one that includes Shinto-shamanistic incarnations of gods and Buddhist beliefs in reincarnation and doubled existence. Disguised and revealed identity, often involving caste fluidity, must have amused spectators during the Edo period, as they challenged the shogunate's rigid social structure.

Connoisseurship and codes

The cultivation of appreciative, knowledgeable audiences is vital to Japanese traditional theatre's historical refinement.

Such grassroots support suggests the oft-overlooked ambitious and creative aspects of the headmaster system. Credit for diversifying and expanding market share appears largely due to this pyramid of power with a single top, thus dependent on wide support from disciples below. While appearing highly authoritative and conservative, this pyramid also promotes creativity by necessity. If one is not on top, or is directly below, one needs to seek out new audiences and disciples: new venues, new regions of Japan, new experimental plays and training workshops. In the past, a daimyo would guarantee a particular noh troupe's annual salary; patrons of today pay monthly fees or subscribe to fan clubs and buy tickets, for themselves and friends. Nurturing these deep roots enables the flower above to bloom.

Once gained, fanship is expected to last forever. Charismatic performers still draw audiences through technical mastery and fan-oriented activities (and today, blogs and YouTube clips). The Shigeyama kyogen family sponsors photo contests, dinner-cruise packages, tour packages to Bali, and "request kyogen" where spectators vote on plays to be performed that day. In a nation known for the intensity of its *otaku* geeks, traditional arts have always cultivated loyalty from fans, discriminating tastes in connoisseurs, and experiential empathy in disciples.[4] Indeed, when historically master–disciple (often father–son) feuds have threatened the stability of these family-based arts, frequently loyal amateurs have supported both sides, providing continuity until the rift is healed, perhaps in the next generation.

The limited repertory of the standard canon and school rivalries produce a loud and finely shaded forum for connoisseurs. Critics and general

4 William Kelly (ed.), *Fanning the Flames: Fans and Consumer Culture in Contemporary Japan* (Albany, NY: SUNY, 2004).

audiences delight in comparing nuances of style, whether distinguished into officially recognized schools (*ryūgi*, 流儀) or family flavors (*geifū*, 芸風), or merely accepted as individual idiosyncrasy (*kosei*, 個性). These delicate discourses surrounding Japanese arts provide it with a critical framework, nurturing yet severe.

Palimpsest of performer and role

Audiences appreciate performers both in their role in the play and as pedigreed actors. Such personal engagement of fans is apparent not only off stage but also during performances. Stairs connecting stage to auditorium, pathways through the audience, and spectators sitting on two or more sides are spatially expressing this intimacy. The conventional stage assistant proffers properties and straightens costumes, thereby permitting actors to concentrate on frontal displays of elegance and power. Actors thus do not need to turn around or even bend down to retrieve swords or fans, or worry about a wrinkled kimono sleeve. This permits traditional theatre's *shōmen engi* (frontal acting) – a practical and aesthetically powerful convention on (originally) outdoor stages. Actors generally face forward toward front and center, whether to best display the mask (noh) or makeup (kabuki), or permit clear declamation that reaches the back rows. This eschews a Western "cheating" angled approach to staging, instead creating a direct, ironically doubled persona: "I am the actor facing you / I am the character being impersonated."

This also enables ready recognition of favorite actors. Despite masks, makeup, and body expression aimed at convincing impersonation of females, demons, and ghosts, theatrical conventions make actors intentionally discernible. Noh masks do not cover the entire face, nor are attempts made to disguise the voice. Faithful connoisseur audiences appreciate family relationships among actors that can parallel or reverse roles on stage – in kyogen, a son plays the Master to the father, whose seniority earns him the main role of Servant (see Figure 11). One kabuki crowd-pleaser is *Renjishi* (The lion dance), where it is often father-and-son players who flick their long manes alongside each other, displaying the full power of the family traditions. Nihonbuyo dancers receive stage names that include both teacher's and school's Chinese characters, a pedigreed professional identity.

Most genres depend on readily identifiable famous families, a sort of territorial branding. In the star-power fueled kabuki world, performers' names are written in special, brash characters outside theatres, arranged by seniority and acting family; inside, the claque shouts out encouragement with the actors' *yagō* family names, or compares them to their ancestors. Occasionally programs are interrupted by popular *kōjō* name-taking ceremonies where fellow performers welcome the newest link in the family lineage with warm reminiscences spanning many generations. Other genres make more subtle ancestral connections. Puppet-manipulators, chanters, and shamisen players are announced by clacks and resonant declamation. Bunraku puppet masters appear unhooded, displaying a lack of emotion that makes the wooden dolls even more lifelike, but also allows a gentle smile or sorrowful gaze to seep through their famous faces. In noh, the stern-faced senior stage assistant at the back wall is often the lead actor's teacher, surreptitiously scrutinizing the son's or student's debut. The easygoing "pillow" (*makura*) that begins a rakugo performance puts the storyteller on an equal footing with listeners through deliberately relaxed topical ad libs, creating audience rapport before subtly moving on to the traditional story, the transition expressed physically by taking off a *haori* jacket.

Through such seemingly spontaneous but carefully calculated intimacies, traditional performers build rapport with spectators over generations.

Local, seasonal specialties and shared intimacies

Spectators support conservative traditional arts, examining contemporary themes via genres that maintain an invitingly familiar, intimate atmosphere. With growing popularity and regional dispersion, market niches are sought through precise local knowledge, encouraging a great sense of person, place, ritual, and seasonal accommodation. The annual diary published by leading noh bookseller Hinoki shoten assists producers planning play programs by listing the 250 plays in the repertoire by appropriate season, determined by the appearance of fitting flowers, scenery, festivals, or other poetic markers.

The kabuki calendar began at the end of the calendrical year with *kaomise* ("face showing") plays introducing newly contracted actors in a "top of the pops" format. First Month New Year's plays in Edo featured variations on the Soga brothers' revenge tragedy. Spring plays presented tragic romance, and plays during the *o-bon* festival of the dead featured ghosts and monsters, sending chills through the heat of midsummer. Seasonal flowers would echo in plum, cherry blossom, and maple scenery. However, there was flexibility within these constraints: popular characters or whole acts could be inserted in entirely distinct plays, and plays could be extended (or shortened) based on popularity; sequels and spinoffs proliferated. Certain conventions permitted accommodation to particular locales depending on where the performance was given. *Michiyuki* travel songs and kyogen *tsukushi* (compilation) sections of *kouta* short-songs consist of descriptions of famous landmarks, delightful song-and-dance travelogues. The inclusion of popular songs and their parodies into otherwise traditional plays enlivened kyogen and kabuki, showing them to be both *au courant* and influential fashion brokers.

Edo era urban consumer businesses and proprietary spectators created another layer of local and regional flavor to kabuki. Kimono or sake merchants would provide product placement through brand-name advertisements inserted (for a fee) into speeches or onstage properties; they could also publicly offer favored actors their goods, along with a small speech. Kabuki audiences had many forums to encourage their avid patronage: lookalike fashions and hand-clapping fan clubs, onstage seating popular with connoisseurs, noisy back-row claques, woodblock prints, poetry sessions, and teahouse parties with invited actors.

The practice of placing 10,000 yen notes in *obi* belts of favored actors in *taishū engeki* today is only a naked example of this intense fan–actor intimacy that fuels the seemingly staid traditional arts. Appreciative noblemen and daimyo proffered elegant kimono mid-show to favored noh actors, who would then be obliged to wear them in subsequent plays. The kabuki kaomise face-showing productions starring recently signed talents, coupled with fierce regional rivalries, gave playhouses less the feel of a Western opera than of a sporting event being cheered on by knowledgeable, stake-holding locals. At after-show teahouses catering to wealthy patrons, actors mingled freely, even providing salon versions of dances they would later be performing on stage. Today, family loyalty by amateur students of traditional arts is expected. They give twice-yearly monetary gifts to their teachers, attend teachers' performances, and even offer birthday gifts, pay New Year's greetings, and attend wedding receptions (with appropriate monetary gifts). Such activities are all part of their membership in this extended artistic family.

Well before blogs, tweets, and official websites, traditional performers were utilizing modes of personal interaction that made theatregoing both extraordinary and essential everyday activities for the urban public.

Frozen tableau: capturing the indelible moment

The above meta-patterns – dual channels, framing, fandom, frontality, and familiarity – can be seen coalescing in the flash of the temporal/spatial moment that in noh Zeami called *me-hiraki* or *mimi-hiraki* (eye-opening or ear-opening places), developed as *mie* in kabuki. *Kyōgen e-iri* (Illustrated kyogen texts, 1660), popular script collections with illustrations drawn by seemingly knowledgeable spectators,[5] display a similar connoisseur's eye. They focus on a single climactic moment, featuring actual costume and

5 http://digital.library.pitt.edu/k/kogyo/.

property accessories. Noh prints by Kōgyo Tsukioka (1869–1927) and kabuki prints similarly capture moments of high tension, efficacious for both promotional and archival functions. Later performers studied and reproduced these famous images in their *mise-en-scène*. Through this wealth of illustrations and prints, famous kabuki and bunraku scenes, and whole noh and kyogen plays, can be recognized instantly – through specifics of costume, masked or painted facial expression, dynamic stance, and properties – in a single iconic image. Posters featuring these images encourage audiences to anticipate the various plot twists to converge in an exact replication of these epiphanic moments.

Such quintessential images are reproduced onstage, climactic build-up rather than spoiler to the dramatic tension. In noh, the onstage (but conventionally "invisible") assistants smoothing and folding costumes in full view of audiences serve to display the actor to best effect. Their ministrations help the actor create dynamically still, indelible images, framed by pillar and roof: in *Tsuchigumo* the earth spider's webs unfurl and cascade over attacking warriors; in *Izutsu* (Wooden well-curb), an abandoned wife, wearing her husband's robe and hat, peers into her own doubled reflection in the well where they played as children.

Kabuki and, to a lesser extent, bunraku emphasize these "frozen moments" with clacks of *tsuke* (by onstage stage assistants), while the actor/puppet faces forward, stepping out of the temporal flow of the play to present a still yet dynamic image. Such moments are punctuated by drum and shamisen, providing an aural equivalent of zoom and spotlight. Coupled with dynamic stasis and projection of potent presence, these powerful "frozen moments" burn themselves into the imagination.[6] Traditionally, inexpensive prints, and photographs today, can be purchased: memories of a favorite actor in an iconic pose, but also a continuing standard for the next generation. These expressive iconic images, like the arts they express in condensed form, are conventionalized yet highly anticipated evidence of dynamic, living heritage, predictable yet still fascinating and emotionally moving.

6 See Samuel L. Leiter (ed.), *Frozen Moments: Writings on Kabuki, 1966–2001* (Ithaca, NY: Cornell East Asia Series, 2002).

14 ✒ Modern plays as literature

J. THOMAS RIMER

During the rise and ascendancy of *shingeki*, "new theatre," dramas created by several generations of Japanese playwrights came closest to models of Western theatre. From roughly 1910 to 1970, the playwright became central, and stage speech the most powerful tool available to the dramatist. Both prior traditional and later avant-garde Japanese theatre show far less commitment to the ascendancy of words or emphasis on (relatively) realistic dialogue. The Japanese plays of this "classic shingeki" period are thus much closer to our received ideas of theatre than those created during any other period before or since.

Cultural framework

Nevertheless, there are dangers in trying to understand and interpret these plays too quickly in terms of any purely Western model. A rich and nuanced reading of these play texts first requires a sociopolitical framework to help situate the plays in their cultural matrix. In terms of the development of shingeki, at least two fresh opportunities borrowed from Europe allowed dramatists to attempt extraordinary innovations: to write convincing, realistic spoken dialogue; and, an imperative felt particularly in left-wing circles, to introduce politics as subject matter – a topic virtually impossible to imagine in earlier theatrical periods.

One issue might be defined as the question of national patrimony. For most of this period, playwrights tended to reject the abstraction and overt theatricality of traditional theatre forms – noh, bunraku, and kabuki. During the period of shingeki's development, the strong preference for Western models persisted, notably Ibsen, Chekhov, and later Brecht, while Shakespeare remained a central locus of reference. During this period, only Izumi Kyōka (1873–1939), whose plays were generally first produced by somewhat more traditional *shimpa* troupes, and Mishima Yukio (1925–70) consistently made use of traditional Japanese theatre's aesthetic strategies.

The most highly respected literary figures of these years – Natsume Sōseki and Shiga Naoya – never wrote for the theatre. Others such as Tanizaki Jun'ichirō and Shimazaki Tōson made a few brief and youthful attempts at composing for the theatre, yet their plays never became central. In terms of national (and international) stature, Japan produced no culturally dominating theatrical figures, popular among intellectuals as well as the public, such as George Bernard Shaw, Jean-Paul Sartre, Arthur Miller, or Tennessee Williams.

In the European and American theatre of this period, plays were generally written to be performed, although many were later published. Given the limited opportunities for staging, and vicissitudes of performance opportunities in Japan at this time, however, many plays, particularly in the prewar period, were written only to be read. Without chances to see their works performed, aspiring playwrights had few opportunities to learn how to increase their skills at writing effectively stageworthy texts.

Moreover, in comparison with the Western practice, there was no general custom of reviving shingeki plays during the prewar and early postwar years. This kind of rich mixture of new plays and revivals, so important for the education and development of sophisticated theatre audiences in Europe and the United States, was largely missing in prewar and early postwar shingeki circles. Only kabuki continued to nourish its connoisseurs during this period. From our contemporary perspective, a convincing sign of the real maturity of the shingeki movement and its acceptance as a significant form of theatre in larger circles of Japanese culture can be seen by the fact that skillful revivals of important plays by Izumi, Kishida Kunio, Kinoshita Junji, and Mishima can now be seen in Tokyo and elsewhere on a regular basis.

What follows is an examination of four of the most admired plays in the shingeki tradition. They earned their reputations both as dramas of literary merit and as effective theatre. All are available in English-language translations. To Japanese readers, this particular choice of plays may seem eclectic, even eccentric; Japanese historians and critics would be far more likely to group them in terms of genre, political positioning of authors, theatre troupes which commissioned and performed them, or significance of particular performers for whom they were sometimes composed. Such a means of analysis, embedding plays in complications of the times in which they were written, makes effective cultural history but invariably downplays their dramatic and literary efficacy. To this end, while indicating something of the circumstances of the composition and presentation of each play, I hope to persuade readers of the sophistication and power of these plays.

Mori Ōgai and the intellectual underpinnings of shingeki

One of the first writers and intellectuals to live in Europe and observe theatrical activities there first hand was Mori Ōgai (1862–1922). Ōgai left Tokyo to study medicine in Germany for five years (1884–8), then returned to Japan as a brilliant European-style intellectual. He pursued a dual career, as medical doctor and writer of essays, plays, novels, and short stories.

When Ōgai returned to Tokyo, he soon became involved in efforts to reform the Japanese theatre:

> We all know that the word "play" means a theatrical performance, actors performing a drama on the stage. First the drama, then the performance. The drama is primary, the performance secondary. (What could be more natural, more obvious?)[1]

Ōgai published translations of dramas by Ibsen, Hauptmann, Strindberg, and Wedekind, culminating in 1913 with Goethe's *Faust*, still a classic.

Playwriting was only a small element in Ōgai's literary career, and all his dramas were one-act plays. *Masks* (*Kamen*), which included long and earnest conversations about Nietzschean philosophy, was performed by a small professional company in 1909, two years before Osanai Kaoru (1881–1928) founded the Jiyū Gekijō (Free Theatre), the first professional company dedicated to staging authentic performances of European drama in Japan. Ōgai translated Ibsen's *John Gabriel Borkman* for Osanai's opening production; Ōgai's *The Ikuta River* (*Ikutagawa*) was staged for the second. It was possibly the first modern Japanese play based on an ancient historical tale in which performers spoke eloquently in a new and effective colloquial stage Japanese, developed by Ōgai himself.

Ōgai's command of a refined and rich colloquial language, ability to write introspective and lyrical speech, and transposition of the historical past into the psychological present owe much to his reading of Ibsen and other European dramatists. His dramatic experiments were, in his eyes, nothing more than that, but his plays opened up new parameters for a fresh type of drama for succeeding generations.

European alienation, Japanese style: Kishida Kunio's *Mr. Sawa's Two Daughters*

In the earlier years of the twentieth century, the accomplishments of European drama and performance remained a distant ideal, to be admired even

---

1 Mori Ogai, "Surprised by the prejudice of theater reformers," in J. Thomas Rimer (ed.), *Not a Song Like Any Other: An Anthology of Writings by Mori Ōgai* (Honolulu: University of Hawai'i Press, 2004), 143.

if any direct imitation was not possible. After World War I, however, an increasing number of Japanese who entered the theatre world as performers, directors, stage designers, and playwrights began visiting Europe. They returned with an array of often competing theories and strategies for the creation of a truly contemporary theatre in Tokyo.

Among these playwrights, perhaps the most consistently gifted was Kishida Kunio (1890–1954). He had found work as a translator for the Japanese Embassy in Paris after World War I, using the French learned at the University of Tokyo. He then attached himself to the celebrated theatre Vieux Colombier, run by director Jacques Copeau (1879–1949) before returning to Japan in 1923, where he began working as both a playwright and a critic. Many early plays such as *Buranko* (The swing) and *Kami fūsen* (Paper balloon, 1925) feature small casts, balancing lyrical dialogue with great psychological realism. By the 1930s, however, Kishida, now more mature as person and dramatist, began to write full-length plays.

Perhaps the most successful of these was his *Mr. Sawa's Two Daughters* (*Sawa-shi no futari musume*, 1935). On one level a comedy of manners, by implication the play provides a strong critique of contemporary Japanese society. Kishida wrote of the play and his *Saigetsu* (A space of time, 1935) that "both are confessions, records of a mutiny against feudalistic attitudes and of a yearning for freedom … If the plays have a somewhat nihilistic flavor about them, then I must admit I meant them as caricatures, even if rather solemn ones, of contemporary Japan."[2]

The plays of Ōgai sometimes contained characters familiar with European culture, but in *Mr. Sawa's Two Daughters* Mr. Sawa, the father and the play's erstwhile protagonist, has actually lived in Europe, working for the Japanese Foreign Office. He thus represents a type of cosmopolitan Japanese that scarcely existed earlier. He is caught between two worlds, this ambiguity ultimately rendering him ineffectual, both as a father and as a member of society. As a result, his relationships with his two daughters, Etsuko and Aiko, have never been strong; now these bonds begin to deteriorate. By the end of the play, the family has effectively dissolved.

In each of the three acts, crucial family secrets are revealed one after the other, helping to destroy the tenuous relationships among the three main characters. In Act I, the daughters learn that their father has taken their housekeeper as a common-law wife. He tells his daughters that "Raku's spent half her life unhappy. And I was weak. It must have been meant to happen. Don't say anything, just act as if nothing has changed." Of course the daughters find this difficult

---

2 J. Thomas Rimer, *Toward a Modern Japanese Theatre: Kishida Kunio* (Princeton, NJ: Princeton University Press, 1974), 223.

to do. In Act II, older sister Aiko reveals that her brother's friend had seduced her at an inn; she wants nothing more to do with him and feels betrayed by her sister's lack of sympathy and father's inability to understand. In Act III, Etsuko reveals that she has fallen in love with a teacher at her school, while simultaneously encouraging another man/suitor/lover, causing a scandal. Aiko, now married to a wealthy French merchant, refuses to feel any pity for her.

> AIKO: Etsuko, remember what happened that time? I have never been so mortified in my life, and even though you comforted me with your words, in your heart you were gloating. I looked foolish to you, didn't I? It made you happy to see me dragged through the mud, didn't it? So it's not that I'm not sympathetic – I am. It's just our way of being sympathetic.[3]

Etsuko, deeply angered, now prepares to leave.

> ETSUKO: (to AIKO) Then our accounts are cancelled. Since we've come this far, let's go all the way. From now on we'll be complete strangers. I felt lonely at the prospect of being alone because I knew I had a sister. From now on, I'll have no more reason to see you.[4]

Sawa, now completely alone (his daughters' disapproval has forced him to leave Raku), paces around his sordid apartment, chewing on a piece of bread and cheese.

The play is rich in ironic and sometimes moving interchanges between Kishida's characters, as well as a number of long and effective speeches for all three main characters. Today, the play serves as an example of the kind of universal anomie characteristic of all urbanized societies at the time, Kishida evoking emotional situations familiar to any modern or contemporary reader. The author's grasp of the social conditions that bring about this sense of estrangement allows for trenchant social criticism, couched here in personal terms. Although not highly regarded by contemporaries for his lack of Marxist concern for social conditions, Kishida proves himself a dramatist of great skill and empathy. The top annual playwriting award so eagerly sought after by aspiring dramatists is aptly named the Kishida Kunio Drama Award.

Marxism and humanism: Kubo Sakae's *Land of Volcanic Ash*

The plays of Kubo Sakae (1900–58) set out to examine society on a far vaster canvas than Kishida's. Kubo was one of the most gifted dramatists in the

---

3 *Five Plays by Kishida Kunio*, ed. and trans. David G. Goodman (Ithaca, NY: Cornell University Press, 1995), 146.
4 *Ibid.* 147.

Fig 49 Kubo Sakae's *Land of Volcanic Ash* (*Kazanbaichi*, 1937). The stage, like the local economy, is dominated by flax.

history of shingeki, and his Marxist convictions helped him locate and perfect the intellectual tools needed to express his dismay at the situation of interwar Japanese society. His work and his life reveal the vicissitudes of the difficult period in the 1930s before the final closure of the left-wing theatre movement in 1940, symbolized by Kubo's house arrest by the authorities that year.

Kubo was born in Sapporo, Hokkaido, Japan's northernmost island: memories of eking out a life in that cold climate never left him. After studying German literature at Tokyo Imperial University, with a particular interest in Kaiser, Hauptmann, and Wedekind, Kubo soon joined the staff of Osanai's Tsukiji Little Theatre. *Kazanbaichi* (Land of volcanic ash, 1937), his major work, is dedicated to Osanai, although the production was presented by Shinkyō (New Co-operative), one of the troupes emerging after the period's artistic/political struggles (Figure 49). Kubo's manifesto on inaugurating the troupe makes clear the group's left-leaning attitudes.

> Our realism captures the innermost truths of man and society and, cutting through all facades, shows how – while antagonistic, contradictory, and interacting in complex ways – they develop toward a higher stage of unity.
>
> Without reducing them to stereotypes and without vulgarization, we clarify them in terms of the typical form of [class] conflict and formulate them with artistry and style.[5]

---

5 Kubo Sakae, *Land of Volcanic Ash*, trans. David G. Goodman (Ithaca, NY: Cornell East Asian Studies Program, 1986), 8.

This statement serves as summary of the dramaturgical principles undergirding *Land of Volcanic Ash*, published in 1937–8. Revived on several occasions during the postwar period, the play is still regarded as a central monument, for some *the* central monument, for the entire shingeki movement.

The scope of the play is remarkable. Divided into seven long acts, this extensive stage time is utilized by Kubo in a heroic attempt to portray all levels of society, stressing their connections and contradictions. Experiencing the play in written form can be somewhat confusing, as there are dozens of major characters as well as countless minor ones. Yet in performance the effect is compelling, thanks to Kubo's vividly realized characterizations. Scenes alternate between outdoor (a New Year's market, charcoal kilns, a flax mill, etc.) and interior ones, mostly in the home of the scientist protagonist. This structure is a highly effective means of moving the drama's many themes and characters forward. In this process, the spectator (or reader) comes to learn more and more about the plight of farmers, who attempt to raise crops in a cold climate with inferior soil, and how they are taken advantage of by local landlords and the government itself. Farmers and local merchants are strikingly characterized, their salty language strongly contrasting with the demure linguistic speech patterns of more bourgeois characters. It is clear that Kubo has truly inhabited this geographical and cultural space, feeling a genuine sympathy for almost all his characters.

Kubo doubtless had to make efforts to avoid possible cuts by censors, increasingly active during the ever-darkening interwar period. His intentions are clear, even if his stage language is surely more muted than he might have wished. Although the play concerns the inevitable social corruption brought about by capitalistic greed, his treatment of the theme is sophisticated. Rather than portraying Marxist stereotypes (good workers, evil landowners, etc.), Kubo shows how farmers, managers, and workers are themselves corrupted and demeaned financially, socially, even sexually. Kubo never preaches. There is no Marxist jargon.

The crux of the plot revolves around the government's encouragement of a certain fertilizer, one with important subsidiary military uses, but not necessarily the most effective one for crops. The one true hero of the play, Amamiya Akira, head of the Hokkaido Agricultural Station, is attempting to do the best he can for the farmers, refusing to compromise either his ideals or his scientific understanding of the problems. Kubo was not the first modern Japanese writer to create a noble figure who refuses to bow to social pressure, but by describing his protagonist in terms of his response to social and economic issues Kubo presented a strong indictment of contemporary Japanese society, then bending toward militaristic/colonialist goals. In particular, false bourgeois pieties are ruthlessly examined in the relationship between Amamiya's wife Teruko and her father, also a scientist, patron of her husband. By the end of the play, Amamiya has mustered his courage to attend an important conference, despite his wife's warnings, to defend his views and do the best he can for the future of the farmers, with whom he feels a shared destiny.

Released from house arrest following the war, Kubo got caught up in the turmoil of postwar politics; left-wing shingeki practitioners rejected his newest work. Kubo, ill and exhausted, committed suicide in 1958. His legacy remains strong, however, and his work, much like early plays of Arthur Miller in the United States, retain social and intellectual relevance.

War, politics, and memory: Kinoshita Junji's *A Japanese Called Otto*

Like Kubo, Kinoshita Junji (1914–2006) employed dramatic strategies in order to examine the parlous state of Japanese society before and during the Pacific War. He worked in the relatively liberal period during and after the American Occupation (1946–52). Kinoshita remains well known and admired for a number of his dramas, notably his early play based on a folk legend, *Yūzuru* (Twilight crane, 1949; see representative plays, p. 283), revealing his abiding humanistic and social concerns. *Otto to yobareru Nihonjin* (A Japanese called Otto, 1962) is Kinoshita's most esteemed work.

On one level, the play is a historical account of the political situation in Japan and China in the 1920s and 1930s, chronicling efforts made by Richard Sorge (1895–1944), the famous Soviet spy, to obtain information about Japan's war plans. Kinoshita focuses on the development of Sorge's relationship with Ozaki Hotsumi (1901–44), brilliant journalist, expert on China, and member of an elite group advising the government. Ozaki, because of his own worries over the development of fascism in Japan, decided to help Sorge obtain the information. Sorge and Ozaki were captured, imprisoned, and executed by the Japanese government just before the end of the Pacific War.

Sorge's activities and relationship with Ozaki remain controversial. There have been several films and books on the subject and feelings ran high for several decades concerning the political and moral significance of the incident. Kinoshita moves behind the bones of historical fact to spin a fable about the ambiguities of allegiance and the meaning of true patriotism.

Kinoshita has included foreign characters, portraying them with skill and imagination. In Kishida's *Mr. Sawa's Two Daughters*, foreigners are mentioned but do not appear on stage; in *Land of Volcanic Ash*, there is a walk-on part for a Russian refugee; but in *Otto*, two of the major characters are foreign. Mrs. Sung, cover name for Agnes Smedley (1892–1950), a famous American left-wing journalist who chronicled the early phases of the Chinese Communist revolution, as well as some minor Chinese characters, are deftly portrayed. Both Fritz, the cryptographer, and Sorge are German, although Sorge's unswerving allegiance is to the Soviet Union and international Communism. The skill and naturalness of Kinoshita's text reveal that he is comfortable writing for all these characters. *Otto* indicates a new level of sophistication in the shingeki movement, functioning comfortably on the world stage.

Otto discusses the rise of Japanese fascism and the role of the Japanese military in China with Mrs. Sung in Act I, set in Shanghai, where he meets Johnson for the first time. In Act II, Otto is back in Tokyo, attempting to lead a normal life with his wife and daughter, while watching uneasily the darkening political landscape in both countries. When Johnson approaches Otto for help in obtaining secret information, he becomes concerned that Otto "carries Japan within himself too much."

The play draws quickly to its conclusion as both men are arrested and thrown into prison. The Epilogue consists largely of a heated dialogue between Otto and the Public Prosecutor (who turns out to be Otto's childhood friend). When accused of being a Comintern spy, Otto replies in lines that close the play:

> MAN: Regarding my activities up to this point, I can say only one thing. That is, I had the foreign name of Otto, but I was a true Japanese, and acting as such, I was most certainly not in error.[6]

With the appeal and exoticism of its shifting locales, strong dialogue, and compelling characterization, *Otto* is an excellent example of the kind of postwar shingeki that reveals both political commitment and humanistic values.

History as nostalgia: Mishima Yukio's *Rokumeikan*

Like Kubo and Kinoshita, Mishima Yukio (1925–70) chose to recreate theatrically an earlier historical moment. In *Rokumeikan* (1956) this moment is when Japan opened itself to the West after the beginning of the Meiji period in 1868. Mishima's approach to this complex subject was to create not an earnest drama but a striking theatrical entertainment. Within a purposively artificial framework, the play was a genuine artistic success and possibly Mishima's most enduring dramatic work (see Figure 36).

6 Kinoshita Junji, *A Japanese Called Otto*, trans. Lawrence Rogers, in J. Thomas Rimer (ed.), *Patriots and Scholars: Sorge and Ozaki, a Japanese Cultural Casebook* (Portland, ME: Merwin Asia, 2009), 195.

Mishima remains one of the most translated of modern Japanese writers, and his novels, flamboyant lifestyle, and dramatic suicide are known throughout the world. Less appreciated abroad, however, are his plays, which for many Japanese are representative of his best work. He was one of the few shingeki playwrights who also wrote kabuki and bunraku puppet plays. In the case of *Rokumeikan*, there are also heavy traces of shimpa melodrama.

Mishima stated that, while kabuki and other forms of traditional Japanese theatre depend on *kata*, or fixed patterns, to which the audience responds with pleasurable recognition, shingeki must find new forms of stimulus and artifice, in the case of *Rokumeikan* through a special style of language:

> The audience of shingeki comes to see a drama not to seek familiarity in acting patterns, but to be awakened from sleep … A play without style can only engender the familiarity of existing quotidian emotions between audience and stage. Style as a pattern becomes necessary to eliminate that familiarity.[7]

Rokumeikan is a perfect example of a play constructed on the basis of such artifice. The title refers to the Deer-Cry Pavilion, a British-designed Renaissance-style social center built by the Japanese government in 1883 for the explicit purpose of encouraging social intercourse between foreign dignitaries and members of the Japanese aristocracy. As an unabashed instrument of Westernization, it became the greatest tangible symbol of the Meiji slogan *bunmei kaika*, "civilization and enlightenment."[8] While the structure was sold and renamed in 1890, the word *Rokumeikan* still suggests for Japanese today the complications and exoticism of that period. Mishima's choice of this unusual locale is altogether appropriate as a fullblown and highly enjoyable melodrama, complete with elegant sets and costumes.

Mishima admired Oscar Wilde's work, and there are strong parallels, particularly with Wilde's 1892 *Lady Windermere's Fan*. In terms of plot devices, both explore the dramatic possibilities inherent in the situation of a child ignorant of his or her mother's identity. Many of the plot devices driving both dramas concern the need to reveal and conceal such truths.

A second parallel concerns a linguistic strategy employed by both writers in which the characterization of a particular situation can be transformed into an abstract principle, one that can sometimes be cast as an aphorism. Asako, wife of the Baron, learns that the daughter of her good friend is in love with the young radical Kiyohara Hisao.

---

7 See Mishima Yukio, "A small scar on the left kneecap," in *My Friend Hitler and Other Plays of Yukio Mishima*, trans. Hiroaki Sato (New York: Columbia University Press, 2002), 59.
8 *Ibid.* 1.

> SUEKO: Both her parents are from aristocratic families, but like her an-
> cestors who did not know what to do with their long sleeves, she loves
> radical things. True aristocratic blood is radical blood. Just as only the
> rich can despise money, so can we with a warehouse of conventions de-
> spise conventions. An irresolute man like my husband can't be called an
> aristocrat.[9]

This device permits the kind of verbal exchanges that can quickly highlight the emotional entanglements needed to push forward the plot.

Most of the play's significant events revolve around Asako herself. While she is now at the apex of the social ladder, she had been a geisha when young; at that time, she gave birth to a boy whom she never saw again. By the end of the play, she has paid doubly for this transgression; because of a trick by her wily husband, Count Kageyama, both her son and his father die. The power struggle between Asako and her husband moves the drama forward. In order to combat his political power, she has only her wit and her love. And formidable as these forces may be, they ultimately prove unequal to the task. The image of a good woman struggling against, but losing to, a greedy, proud man who possesses her has made the play, particularly for women viewers, a perennial favorite.[10]

In the midst of the shingeki theatrical movement, so often marked by a high seriousness of social and political purpose, Mishima's emphasis on the arti-ficial nature of the theatrical experience was unusual, matched only perhaps by the fanciful and poetic plays of shimpa playwright Izumi Kyōka. In that regard, Mishima might be regarded (leaving aside his notorious right-wing politics) as predecessor to the next generation of post-shingeki playwrights, who abandoned the Ibsen/Chekhov model so much admired for several gen-erations, allowing fantasy, allegory, and subversive wit back on stage.

Reference and further reading

Brian Powell, *Japan's Modern Theatre: A Century of Continuity and Change* (London: Routledge Curzon, 2002).

---

9 *Ibid.* 9.
10 Harano Mami, *Anatomy of Mishima's Most Successful Play "Rokumeikan"* (Saarbrucken: Lap Lambert Academic Publishing, 2012), 55–6.

15 ❧ Modern meta-patterns

MARI BOYD

Stepping far enough away from Japanese theatre as a cultural phenomenon, three interrelated theatrical meta-patterns can be discerned: the Realistic, the Quiet, and the Frenetic.[1] The modern *Realistic* meta-pattern descended from premodern *sewamono* (plays of everyday life best found in *shingeki* realism). *Quietude* refers to minimalist dramaturgy drawn from Zen aesthetics and its manifestation in noh – silence, stillness, and fluidity of time-space. Two kinds of theatrical quietude are evident today: one is inspired by and adapts aspects of noh: the second is based on more modern conceptualizations of subjectivity. *Frenetic* dramaturgy employs an extroverted theatricality descended from kabuki in its use of multiple plotlines, heightened acting, elaborate costumes, and special effects.

These three meta-patterns enable us to view theatrical phenomena broadly, borderlessly, and in a transhistorical perspective. The modern period has seen two major meta-pattern shifts in theatre: the Realistic mode developed and matured into realism in the first half of the twentieth century while the Frenetic enjoyed a magnificent resurgence in the 1960s. Quietude has resurfaced periodically – in the 1920s, the late 1970s, and the 1990s. In twenty-first-century Japanese theatre, the Frenetic meta-pattern is dominant, but Quietude is also highly developed (see list of playwrights, Focus 11.1).

Modern Japanese playwrights usually write for their own theatre company and devise action and characterization to match their actors' qualities.[2] Since playwrights are frequently directors as well, their scripts may provide only basic dialogue and structure of plays, assuming much may develop during rehearsals. A playwright, as the English suffix "wright" better suggests, *crafts* a play; discussion here goes beyond the play as a piece of finished writing to attend to dramaturgy and staging as well.

---

1 This discussion extends my prefatory comments in "Quietude in intercultural performance: Phillip Zarrilli's *Told by the Wind* and Yōjirō Okamura's *Aminadab*," *Comparative Theatre Review* 11:1 (2012), 43–51, www.jstage.jst.go.jp/article/ctr/11/1/11_1_43/_pdf.
2 Workshops that serve as *de facto* auditions have become more common since the mid-1990s with the rise of production "units" hiring performers for one-off productions.

The Realistic meta-pattern

Focused on social interactions, the Realistic meta-pattern is dialogue-centered and requires verisimilitude. Verisimilitude calls forth objective reality for the reader/viewer through factual accuracy, naturalistic characterization, life-sized (*tōshindai*) action, and most importantly a sense of plausibility. Various iterations include melodramatic and comic, as well as serious dramas.

Several kinds of realistic drama flourished during Japan's attempt to move away from premodern kabuki. These included *katsureki* living-history kabuki plays, melodramatic *shimpa*, and Sawada Shōjirō's *shinkokugeki*, a genre of patriotic swordfighting plays. Shingeki realism surpassed other experimental forms in creating a fully constructed sense of reality that precluded the sensational and supernatural.

Playwrights' attraction to Western realism at the beginning of the twentieth century lay in its rational approach to social problems when creating a modern national identity was imperative. It provided them with a means to discuss ideas analytically and in an artistically compelling manner, thus raising the status of playwrights from generally disrespected scriptwriters-for-hire to serious artists. Shingeki realism had become a major theatrical form by the 1930s. A slew of Japanese neologisms for realistic drama were formulated, such as proletariat realism, socialist theatre (*riarizumu engeki*), the "developmental (*hattenteki*) realism" of Murayama Tomoyoshi (1901–77), Kishida Kunio's (1890–1954) modern realistic drama, and realism of manners (*setaiteki*), coined by Kubo Sakae (1901–58) to critique Stanislavskian and prior psychological approaches. In recent years, further terms have been proposed, like "photographic realism" and "sectional realism." These terms suggest varying perspectives taken on the nature of social reality – political, psychological, and aesthetic.

Kubo Sakae's ideology-driven realism painstakingly exposes the detrimental effect of capitalism through a panoramic view of Japanese society buttressed by an understanding of its production base as manifested in his major work, *Kazanbaichi* (Land of volcanic ash, 1937) (Figure 49). His specific objectives were to portray the unique state of agriculture in Hokkaido and to combine scientific theory with artistic form.[3] Realistic dialogue reflects the themes of scientific knowledge versus national policy, and labor exploitation by the capitalist system. Verisimilitude of staging is consistently upheld, except in poetic interludes.

Verisimilitude in the more complex sense of plausibility leading to a sense of conviction is also developed in the changing views of the scientist

3 Kubo Sakae, *Land of Volcanic Ash*, trans. David C. Goodman (Ithaca, NY: Cornell East Asian Studies, 1988), 9.

protagonist. His new theory on the superiority of potassium fertilizer over the nitrogen fertilizer already distributed to the farmers gets him embroiled in conflicts with his family, his colleagues, the farmers he is trying to save, and ultimately the government as it prepares for war. Since a switch to potassium-based fertilizer would hinder the production of ammonium sulfate, a key component not only in nitrogen fertilizer but also in explosives, the authorities object. Almost despite himself, he begins to sound like a socialist, alerting the reader/viewer to his imminent conversion to socialism as the "inevitable" solution.

Kishida Kunio, noted for his psychological realism, focused on the emotional life of his characters by using suggestion to make the invisible visible. The colloquial dialogue is appropriately character-specific, but more evocative than informative or argumentative. Two recurring themes are the loss of patriarchy and the transformation of Japanese expatriates into bohemians or vagabonds rather than cosmopolitans.

Kishida's *Ochiba nikki* (A diary of fallen leaves, 1927)[4] brings these linguistic and thematic concerns together in an in-depth portrayal of a dowager who suffers repeatedly the death, real or metaphoric, of male relatives. The unwilling matriarch's vacillation between taking and evading responsibility for younger family members is conveyed subtly through incident and language. Finally, her fanatical attachment to the granddaughter left in her care and her guilt over not having prevented her nephew's death are brought to a head when her "lost" bohemian son suddenly returns to claim his daughter after a ten-year absence in France. Both her body and her spirit fail as she sinks into rambling delirium.

Kishida uses a larger canvas in *Ushiyama Hoteru* (Ushiyama Hotel, 1928) to portray expatriate life, set in Indochina at a boarding house catering to Japanese, where social values decay and slovenliness rules. In *Sawa-shi no futari musume* (Mr. Sawa's two daughters, 1935),[5] Kishida returns to the family unit, which in its self-destructiveness now symbolizes the unfortunate past, present, and future of Japan.

The realistic drama of the latter half of the twentieth century moves away from overt ideology. High seriousness is modified by melodrama and comedy to entertain audiences who, as self-conscious consumers, desire pleasure in conjunction with meaning. Tsutsumi Harue reintroduced kabuki elements in her prize-winning plays *Rokumeikan ibun–kasō* (Strange tales of the Rokumeikan masquerade, 1988) and *Kanadehon Hamuretto* (Kanadehon

---

4 *Five Plays by Kishida Kunio*, ed. and trans. David G. Goodman (Ithaca, NY: Cornell University Press, 1995).
5 *Ibid.*

Fig 50 Nagai Ai's *Utawasetai otokotachi* (Got to make 'em sing), 2005.

Hamlet, 1992);[6] nonetheless, she provides entirely rational and credible denouements for both plays. Nagai Ai and Mitani Kōki have both won critical acclaim for the comic spirit that infuses their realistic plays.

Nagai (1983–), multiple award-winning director of the Nitosha Theatre Company, casts a satirical eye on ordinary people with minor political agendas:

> I am fascinated by the transformation of people who are not at odds with their society. Heedless of social developments, they nevertheless internalize the thinking of opinion leaders and so change unawares. Moreover, the fact that practically everyone drifts in this way is what I find intriguing, terrifying, and amazing.[7]

Nagai's comedy is intended to raise social awareness, not to register protest. She illustrates how seemingly personal problems ultimately connect with larger systems or forces in society.

In Nagai's writing process, her main coordinates are social issues, major perspectives on that topic, and setting. Once these are determined, with pictures of the cast pinned up, she elaborates on characterizations, speech patterns, and plausibility of action.

Nagai's much admired *Utawasetai otokotachi* (Got to make 'em sing, 2005; Figure 50) addresses the ominous growth of neo-nationalism, written in

---

6 Trans. Faubion Bowers, David W. Griffith, and Hori Mariko in *ATJ* 15:2 (1998), 181–229.
7 Senda Akihiko, *Gekidan: gendai engeki no chōryū* (Talks on drama: modern day theatre trends) (Tokyo: Shōgakukan, 2001), 234.

response to a 1999 law mandating that the Rising Sun flag (*hi-no-maru*) become the national flag and that "Kimigayo" be made the national anthem, despite their longstanding militaristic connotations. When some teachers refused to honor these regulations at school ceremonies, they were strictly reprimanded, and the issue became one of wide concern.

Set in the office of a high school health education teacher on the morning of commencement, the play features five characters representing three viewpoints: the principal, together with the health and English teachers, are advocates of national policy; the social studies teacher represents the opposition; and the new music teacher-cum-pianist is apolitical. The principal, it turns out, was formerly anti-establishment, even writing an article for a trade magazine defending people's right to the "freedom of spirit"; the social studies teacher longs to renege on his position; the health teacher is more dedicated to her makeup than to political issues; the music teacher is desperate to retain her new post. Only the young English teacher is a true hardliner. The play concludes with the social studies teacher lending his glasses to the pianist, who has lost her contacts, so that she can read the music score, play the anthem accurately, and retain her job. Human kindness is emphasized in lieu of political idealism, left or right.

Thus, together with a concern for social issues and verisimilitude, the comic and the melodramatic are enlisted in the contemporary articulation of the realistic meta-pattern.

The Quiet

The Quiet meta-pattern of today has been inspired either by the noh and its Zen aesthetics, as represented by the minimalistic theatre of divestiture (*ragyō no engeki*) of Ohta Shōgo, Okamura Yōjirō (1948–), and Okamoto Akira (1949–), or by other approaches to what it means to be human. These are seen in the short plays by Kishida, the absurdist drama by Betsuyaku Minoru, and "contemporary colloquial dialogue" plays (*gendai kōgo engeki*) by Hirata Oriza and others, often referred to as "quiet theatre" (*shizukana engeki*).

In discussing noh-derived Quietude, one must remember that not all noh is quiet. In its *jo-ha-kyū* structure, the *jo* and the *jo-ha* of the *ha* section are generally subdued, while the *kyū* sections are often frenetic. The focus will be on the "quiet" aspects of noh that have informed contemporary Japanese theatre. This quiescence is dependent on noh founder Zeami Motokiyo's principle of "doing nothing," and on the concept of *ma*. Literally meaning "an interval," this is a time-space term in architecture which also has an aural sense of silence broken. The deployment of ma can contribute to the mutability of time-space, deceleration of movement, and intermittent or elongated quality of vocal delivery.

Zeami's "doing nothing" is more specifically an acting method based on the concept of ma. In *A Mirror to the Flower* (1424) he explains why doing nothing can be attractive:

> [T]his is because of an underlying disposition by which the mind bridges the gap. It is a frame in which you maintain your intent and do not loosen your concentration in the gaps where you have stopped dancing the dance … This internal excitement diffuses outward and creates interest.[8]

Inner energy connects separated actions so that the ma becomes a moment of palpable intensity that captivates the audience. A heightened liveliness within the seeming static quality of performance gives actors a fuller stage presence than their actual physical actions may suggest. When this *via negativa* principle is extended to the whole play,[9] a sense of indeterminacy or multiplicity of meaning may prevail, enlisting the audience into "doing more" by exercising their own imagination and aesthetic judgment in order to gain meaning.

Ohta Shōgo, playwright, director, and head of Tenkei Gekijō (Transformation Theatre Company, 1968–88), was the most radical in his appropriation of such principles. What he called the "power of passivity" is in fact his application of ma and "doing nothing." He is best known for his completely wordless *Mizu no eki* (The water station, 1981)[10] and *Komachi fūden* (The tale of Komachi told by the wind, 1977), which premiered at the Yarai Noh Theatre in Tokyo.[11]

In *Chi no eki* (The earth station, 1985), the second of Ohta's wordless Station series (1981–98), fourteen travelers, at a greatly slowed-down pace, walk up a mountain of debris (see Figure 41).[12] Midway they rest or interact with each other mainly in silence before resuming their journey. Although the *mise-en-scène* is filled with people and decaying remnants of civilization, nothing happens. Stripped are language, speed, character, plot, climax, and denouement, Ota puts the audience into a state akin to sensory deprivation whereby they are compelled to attend to the slow movements and gestures of passing figures. As Hans-Thies Lehmann points out, "the

---

8 *Zeami Performance Notes*, trans. Thomas Hare (New York: Columbia University Press, 2008), 115.

9 Jerzy Grotowski's acting principle of stripping away pretense or theatricality to enable genuine and vulnerable engagement.

10 Trans. Mari Boyd, *The Aesthetics of Quietude: Ota Shōgo and the Theatre of Divestiture* (Tokyo: Sophia University Press, 2006).

11 Trans. Mari Boyd, *Half a Century*, vol. VI.

12 Trans. Mari Boyd, in J. Thomas Rimer, Mitsuya Mori, and M. Cody Poulton (eds.), *The Columbia Anthology of Modern Japanese Drama* (New York: Columbia University Press, 2014).

reduction to the greatest simplicity ... can be an essential prerequisite of the intensification of new modes of perception."[13] Ohta hopes the audience will gain a "perspective of death," i.e. a view from beyond life, from which humans can be observed as a species rather than as social beings, so that a merely human-centered viewpoint can be transcended.

With *The Earth Station*, Ohta's *modus operandi* was to provide actors with an outline of actions and concepts, together with literary excerpts suggesting emotions and atmosphere for specific scenes. The original script is divided into three columns: two provide the main and minor actions in free verse, the last the lighting and sound cues. Much is left to director and actors to flesh out. Ohta's method is one of divesting, i.e. the eradication of conventional elements of drama, especially those associated with shingeki, leading to prioritizing silence, slow tempo, and bare space. Ota's work is what Lyotard refers to as "energetic theatre," a "theatre not of meaning, but of forces, intensities, present affects."[14] While motifs of sterility, alienation, and dissolution of civilization are generally evident in *The Earth Station*, particular signification is suspended. The sheer indeterminacy of the situation and relations forces viewers to scrutinize the figures in the moment and to heuristically engage in a variety of readings.

Okamura, who studied with noh master Kanze Hideo, also employs ma to construct highly intense performances. His contemporary verse and mask plays, such as *Aminadab*[15] (A · mi · na · da · bu, 1997) and *Shizukuna keisha* (The quiet incline, 2009), aim to "stir the audience's unconscious so that a dynamic and primordial drama may flower in its imaginary."[16] Okamoto and Sakate Yōji exploit noh-like quietude in their respective "contemporary noh collections." In particular, Okamoto's deconstruction of noh *kata* (forms) and style challenges noh actors to sustain energy in unmoored, improvisational expressivity; he believes that such unlearning of norms enables them to access the collective unconscious. His 1998 *Mu* (Nothingness), a fusion of the abandoned old woman (*obasute*) tale and Beckett's *Rockaby*, brought together Kanze Hideo and butoh dancer Ohno Kazuo in a rich, fluid quietude.

A dialogue-based Quietude arose in the 1980s, gaining critical recognition in the 1990s when six playwrights won the prestigious Kishida Kunio Drama Prize for their Quiet plays (*shizukana geki*): Iwamatsu Ryō for *Futon to daruma* (Futon and dharma, 1989);[17] Miyazawa Akio (1956–) for *Hinemi*

---

13 Hans-Thies Lehmann, *Postdramatic Theatre*, trans. Karen Juis-Munby (London: Taylor and Francis, 2006), 101.
14 Quoted in *ibid.* 37.
15 Trans. Mari Boyd, *Sophia International Review* 33 (2011), 1–22.
16 Ami Theatre Company website, www.h7.dion.ne.jp/~babylon/a_profile.htm.
17 Trans. Yuasa Masako and Christopher Jowett, *Futon to Daruma* (Futon and Daruma) (Leeds: Alumnus, 1992).

(1993);[18] Hirata Oriza for *Tōkyō nōto* (Tokyo notes, 1995);[19] Matsuda Masataka and Suzue Toshirō jointly for their respective works *Umi to higasa* (The sea and a parasol, 1996) and *Kami o kakiageru* (Fireflies, 1996);[20] and Fukatsu Shigefumi (1967–) for *Uchiya matsuri* (Uchiya Festival, 1998).[21] Their Quietude seems a response to the bursting of Japan's economic bubble in 1990 as well as to sociopolitical upheavals and natural disasters of subsequent decades.

In stark contrast to the fantastical entertainment of the 1980s, as discussed in the Frenetic meta-pattern below, theatre began to reflect a more sober attitude to life, foregrounding sociocultural concerns and eschewing the sensational. Is there anything valuable that money cannot buy? Hirata's reply is "movement of the heart (*kokoro*)." Calling this the "real," he explained that "theatre gives form to the minute oscillations within the individual who does not, or does not want to, notice what is happening around him."[22] Thus much of the interest of these subdued plays lies in the gradual revelation of complex human relations and larger post-human issues.

Significant characteristics of dialogue-based Quietude are privileging the quotidian; difference-in-sameness in human relations; discourse of the said, unsaid, and unsayable; and conjoining of private with public.

"Privileging the quotidian" refers mainly to foregrounding everyday life as opposed to events that challenge or revolutionize society. In Hirata's *Tokyo Notes*, an international agreement to protect cultural assets from war damage has enabled Vermeer's paintings to be brought to and exhibited in Tokyo. Revealed is the extent to which a European war is affecting Japanese lives. Nonetheless a sense of unexceptional daily life predominates:

> Keeping the [war] background as only background, I put much effort into painting it into the scenery. I wanted to evoke not the "extra-daily arising suddenly from the daily" [as in *angura* theatre], but the sense of this background sticking to the air in as flat a way as possible.[23]

In "subjectivity construction," developing a sense of sameness and difference with the human environment is a fundamental process. An infant needs to gain a sense of difference to develop a separate identity from its primary caretaker; and the adult benefits from nurturing sameness and proximity in

---

18 Trans. John Swain, *Half a Century*, vol. II (2000).
19 Trans. M. Cody Poulton, *Columbia Anthology* (2014).
20 Trans. David G. Goodman, *Half a Century*, vol. I (1999).
21 Trans. Alan Gleason, *Half a Century*, vol. IX (2007).
22 Oriza Hirata, *Engeki nyūmon* (Introduction to theatre) (Tokyo: Kōdansha gendai shinsho, 1998), 44.
23 Oriza Hirata, *Tōkyō nōto/S kōgen kara gikyoku* 1 (Tokyo notes/From S. Highlands: Drama Collection 1) (Tokyo: Banseisha, 1994), 172.

significant relationships. In dialogue-based Quiet theatre, the emphasis tends to fall on revealing difference-in-sameness when the human context shifts, and alterity is revealed in those who we thought resembled ourselves.

Concerning speech, the "said" stays on the mundane conversational level and the "unsaid" refers mainly to what is already shared and implicit among characters. The "unsayable" points to taboos, secrets, and the uncanny. What ensues is a finely calculated increase of unfinished sentences, pronouns lacking antecedents, overlapping speeches, dialects and foreign languages, preverbal sound, and silence. Japan's well-known high cultural valuation of silence promotes a sensibility of "shared silence conveying more than words" (and consequent increase of the unsaid).

Collapsing binaries of public and private often take the form of private engagement in public settings, allowing outsiders and intermediaries to bring private information naturally out into the open. Easily overheard conversations of disparate visitors at the art gallery lobby in *Tokyo Notes* or among condominium inhabitants in *Uchiya matsuri* exemplify this. Material staging of this kind of Quiet theatre closely resembles that of conventional realism. However, these plays are not categorized in the Realistic meta-pattern, because silence (the unsaid and unsayable), not verisimilitude per se, is crucial in their evoking the real.

Matsuda Masataka's award-winning *Tsuki no misaki* (Cape moon, 1997),[24] performed by the Jikū Gekijo (Time-Space Theatre Company, 1990–7), is a striking example of how the four Quiet characteristics delineated above work to express emotional undercurrents of people living on a small island in Nagasaki prefecture. The quotidian is evident in how the schoolteacher and his sister have comfortably shared the old family house after their parents' decease, becoming like a couple. When he marries, she continues to live in the same house with the newlyweds. Threatened by the difference-in-sameness arising from the new dynamics of the "threesome," she is eventually driven to suicide by drowning.

Matsuda's expert handling of the said, the unsaid, and the unsayable leads to delicate ambiences. The brother's reluctantly taking a towel to his sister, changing clothes in an adjacent room, is paralleled later by his voluntarily crossing to the same but unlit room where his wife is changing. The eroticism of the latter action is accomplished with just a few monosyllables. The uncanny is evoked when the wife downs glass after glass of water, to her husband's consternation. Her garbled speech about drowning and being saved suggests that her spirit has momentarily fused with that of the drowning sister.

24 Trans. Boyd, *Half a Century*, vol. II.

Thus the Quiet meta-pattern can lead to extremes in silence, stillness, and mutability to transcend social existence and foster a perspective of death through the suspension of signification. Quietude can also inform dialogue plays about urban living through the precise control of speech flow and timing, pacing, and spatial relations among actors/characters so that a sense of the real becomes palpable.

The Frenetic

The word frenetic etymologically derives from the Greek *phren*, "seat of passion, mind, or will." The frenetic indicates delirium, insanity, and revelry; the Frenetic meta-pattern in theatre indicates excess. Frenetic celebrates life, energy, and change.

In modern Japanese theatre, seven Frenetic characteristics pertaining to dramaturgy and performance can be located. Not all may be apparent in any particular work, but their clusters are prominent in Frenetic plays.

- the collaborative creation of a performance text: a flexible script born of collective engagement of theatre practitioners
- "larger-than-life" (*hi-tōshindai*): fantasy, myths, large scale, excess, extroversion, Dionysian chaos, and carnivalesque
- actor-centeredness: physicality, multiple role-playing, cross-gendered acting, and improvisation
- eclecticism: intertextuality, meta-theatricality, mixed media, and cross-culture
- non-linearity: time–space transcendence, remembrance, dream, and simultaneity
- alogicality: deconstruction, decenteredness, accidentality, and nonsense
- ludic spirit: playfulness on both linguistic and physical levels, comic/satiric orientation, and manga/anime style.

The countercultural theatre movement, exemplified by Terayama Shūji and Kara Jūrō's dark, passionate works, favored this mode of expression, as did Tsuka Kōhei and early Inoue Hisashi with their wildly satirical plays. Following in their footsteps, but treading more lightly, came Noda Hideki, Kōkami Shōji, Watanabe Eri, and Keralino Sandrovich, who dazzled audiences with fast-paced, comic-frenetic plays. Darkness returned to the comedic in works of Matsuo Suzuki (1962–) and Nagatsuka Keishi (1975–).

Inoue Hisashi enjoys exceptionally high critical and popular regard today. A virulent critic of "shitty (*kuso*) shingeki," Inoue's plays do not fit neatly into predetermined theatrical genres. His Asakusa roots in light entertainment have sometimes been employed to dismiss his work as mindless skits. However, the application of meta-patterns shows that his plays are firmly ensconced in the Frenetic.

Inoue's early drama exhibits six of the seven Frenetic characteristics, enriched with venom and vulgarity; missing is the collective making of the performance text. Instead, he wrote his plays with detailed stage directions before or during rehearsals. If unable to finish a play, he would cancel his theatre company (1983–) production without attempting to complete the piece through workshops. Later works are more restrained in satire and playfulness; their sentimentality tends to undermine their inherent social criticism.

Written during his early Theatre Echo period (1969–75), his prize-winning *Dōgen no bōken* (The adventures of Zen master Dōgen, 1971) is a rollicking satire of religious hypocrisy past and present. No one is exempt from his barbs: even famous Zen masters Rújìng (1163–1228) and Eisai (1141–1215) are ridiculed mercilessly.[25]

Dōgen is set in the thirteenth century at Sōtō sect founder Dōgen's Kōshō-Hōrinji temple on the seventh anniversary of its establishment. In celebration, his Zen monks mount a "Life of Dōgen" skit, while uninvited but socially powerful visitors periodically disrupt its execution. Dōgen himself catnaps and dreams of a modern-day doppelgänger cultist who rapes women to purify his blood. The epilogue reveals that almost all characters are mental hospital patients suffering from "Dōgen syndrome."

This play exhibits all the hallmark features of Inoue's "let-it-all-hangout" portraits of famous cultural figures. Musicality, levity, multiple role playing, time–space disjuncture, play-within-a-play structure, and surprise reversals demonstrate the Frenetic mode. Believing sound or musicality to be more important than rationality, Inoue includes thirty-one songs in *Dōgen* and, drawing from the *gesaku* (frivolous) tradition, makes the work a *tour de force* of wordplay — such as puns, neologisms, onomatopoeia, palindromes, parody, and zeugma.[26] An endearing example of parody is the cultist's rendition of his upbringing that lampoons famous titles from modern Japanese literature. Twelve actors perform a dizzying fifty-eight roles as the narrative travels freely through time and space in the play-within-the-play as well as between the Kamakura period (1185–1333) and the 1970s, with the cultist dream-traveling to the temple in an attempt to murder Dōgen. These factors all contributed to the play's labyrinthine structure, with the final multiplication of doppelgängers functioning as a surprise ending.

---

25 Partial trans. by Mari Boyd in Nihon Kindai Engekishi Kenkyūkai (ed.), *Inoue Hisashi no engeki* (Inoue Hisashi's Theatre) (Tokyo: Kanrin shobō, 2012).

26 Zeugma is a figure of speech in which a word yokes two or more parts of a sentence, often for comic effect, e.g. "She wore a red dress and a smile."

Noda Hideki, one of the most versatile *shōgekijō* (Little Theatre) artists of the present day, has headed two companies: the Yume no Yūminsha (Dreaming Bohemians) (1976–92) and Noda Map (1993–). The Yume no Yūminsha phase was characterized by performative collaboration, ludic spirit, and exploded narrativity, resulting in complex intertextuality. According to Yoshiko Fukushima, the early Noda playmaking method was deconstructive. After meandering imaginatively for a fortnight, he would draw up a draft in twenty days. Numerous revisions through workshops turned the draft into a script. As a director who valued speed, hyperbole, and gender ambiguity, he deconstructed the script; and as an actor valuing lightness, presence, and speed, he then deconstructed his own *mise-en-scène*.[27]

Noda is as fascinated with wordplay as Inoue was, but he also has a penchant for manga-like use of words and pictures as a gestalt. He physicalizes speech as it is delivered and exploits homonyms to change scenes quickly.

Positive critical response to his international productions between 1986 and 1990 whetted Noda's appetite for a stronger global presence. He decided to navigate the language and cultural barriers more skillfully by working directly with non-Japanese artists. His Noda Map period is characterized by the shifting balance between playfulness and seriousness, local and global. Noda's plays gradually swung to the overtly serious. In both mainstage shows and "off-the-map" (*bangai*) productions, excess, linguistic play, and structural complexity gave way to social criticism with thematic depth.

Noda's award-winning *The Bee* (2006) exemplifies recent Frenetic plays[28] (see Figure 51). An adaptation of Tsutsui Yasutaka's (1934–) short story, "Plucking at each other," *The Bee* is about "becoming the other." A mild-mannered businessman transforms into a bloody-minded aggressor when an escaped convict takes his wife and son hostage. Rejecting victimhood, the businessman infiltrates the criminal's home and sends the man the severed fingers of his family, thus setting the violence spiraling out of control.

Considerable differences can be noted from Noda's earlier plays: *The Bee* is about half the length and smaller in scale, with only four actors handling eleven or more roles. The tone is much darker. Frenetic characteristics are collaborative playmaking, actor-centeredness, eclecticism, and excess, all revolving around the concept of doubling.

To circumvent the problems of translation, Noda enlisted British playwright Colin Teevan to write an English script. Taking three years, the playmaking process was highly collaborative and actor-centered: themes

27 Yoshiko Fukushima. *Manga Discourse in Japanese Theatre: The Location of Noda Hideki's* Yume no Yuminsha (London: Kegan Paul, 2003), 229.
28 Colin Teevan and Noda Hideki, *The Bee* (London: Oberon Modern Plays, 2007).

Fig 51 *The Bee* World Tour 2012 featured an international cast led by Kathryn Hunter and director Noda Hideki, who co-wrote the English version with Colin Teevan.

and scenes were developed through workshops and then the two play-wrights wrote English and Japanese scripts respectively. The English one was revised in further workshops until all collaborators were satisfied. (Noda's Japanese script had less input from his Japanese actors.)

Noda admits noh and kabuki as influential to his dramaturgy. Despite the cosmopolitan quality of the *mise-en-scène*, a closer look reveals kabuki aesthetics in the revenge theme,[29] the multiple and cross-gender role-playing that heightens the motif of doubling, the use of (microphone) cords to entrap the victim, and whirling confetti. Noh aspects are discerned in the mutating square space and characters functioning as *shite* (protagonist), *waki* (secondary character), *kokata* (child role), and chorus.

Excess, fundamental to the Frenetic, is fueled by multiplying images of mutilation. Presumably up to sixteen fingers are detached and delivered between the two households, leaving both wives and sons dead. In my view, this suggests not so much yakuza (gangster) rituals of penitence, but bunraku love suicides. Initially used by the husband, as a simple threat, finger severance becomes a fetishized bond between the two men. Fingers take on the traditional value of *shinjū-datte* (keeping a promise), in this case to keep on chopping. An alternative homosocial world is created, in which the

29 Noda has adapted kabuki plays and collaborated with the kabuki actor Nakamura Kanzaburō XVIII (2005–12).

husband can both identify with and surpass the convict as he kills his family first. With no return possible to normative society, he adds his own fingers to the pile, believing that his double, the convict, will likewise follow him to certain death.

Noda and Inoue demonstrate the playwrights' development of meta-pattern modes through time. Both eventually moved away from linguistic playfulness to more overtly serious themes while continuing to challenge audience perception and comprehension. Noda remains in a Frenetic vein, while Inoue's later plays lean heavily toward the Realistic.

Conclusion

The value of surveying plays in terms of meta-patterns is to identify shifting tendencies both intra- and interculturally. Three points become clear. First, Realism, with its serious, intellectual approach to social issues, commanded the attention of major Japanese dramatists in the early twentieth century, but lost its hold on the imagination in only sixty years, a brief period considering the total span of the nation's theatre. While its contribution to the development of dramaturgy driven rationally and persuasively toward social messages – and to humans toward social progress – is undeniable, its lack of staying power suggests that, unlike in the West, verisimilitude may not in itself be what entices people to theatre. Second, the Frenetic meta-pattern since the 1990s has proved itself a conveyer of weighty themes as well as entertainment. Lastly the Quiet meta-pattern is noticeably more developed and prevalent in Japan, where the audience has tacit knowledge through cultural exposure to other subdued art forms. In the West, quiescence still tends to be considered anti-theatrical, so that symbolist drama, Samuel Beckett's stark poetics, Harold Pinter's comedies of menace, and Jon Fosse's haunting aesthetics are the exception rather than the rule.

Finally, how may this variety of Japanese playmaking contribute to theatre in a globalized world? The physicality and dynamic inclusiveness of Frenetic plays seem to make them relatively accessible on various levels to global audiences and practitioners, and Japanese Quietude also has much to offer theatrical expressivity through its practiced use of silence, stillness, and manipulation of time–space continuities.

Interlude: Dōjōji: The lady and the bell

LAURENCE KOMINZ

Meta-patterns of transformation, inter-textuality, and enduring visual symbolism are evident in the twistings of the Dōjōji tale – a woman's jealousy transforming her into an avenging serpent – through nearly all traditional and contemporary dramatic genres (Figure 53). The snake-lady shed her skin time and again, emerging in varying forms, responding to different performers' needs and inspirations, and to widely disparate genre conventions. Originally a simple, anecdotal tale, "Dōjōji" was embellished, expanded, and situated in long, inventive multi-character, multi-plot stories to suit large-cast kabuki plays, and day-long puppet plays. Opposite to this elaboration was its distillation by creators of dance-drama such as noh or nihonbuyo. Their original poetry and choreography reframed the prose source story, extracting the essence from long heterogeneous plays: the emotional state of a single important character, the woman betrayed in love.

Hell hath no fury …

It all began innocently enough – just one of a thousand short tales in the twelfth-century *Konjaku monogatari* (Tales of times now past).[30] Two monks, one old and one young and handsome, set out on a pilgrimage to Kumano Shrine. They stop at an inn where the proprietress, a young widow, falls in love with the young monk. She climbs into bed with him, but he is adamant in his vow of celibacy, saying he will be her lover after praying at Kumano. Yet he returns home via another route to avoid her; learning of his deceit, she shuts herself in her room and dies. Transformed into a 40-foot serpent, she slithers out in pursuit. The two priests take refuge in nearby Dōjōji Temple – the large temple bell is lowered over the young priest to conceal him. The serpent then "encircled the bell and tears of blood flowed from her eyes. The great bell of the temple blazed and was burned in the poisonous hot breath of the serpent. All that remained of the

---

30 Its first broad exposure was in these assorted tales (*c.* 1150), although it first appeared in the Buddhist miracle collection *Honchō hokke reigenki* (*c.* 1040).

Fig 52 This variant Dōjōji tale, *Kane kuyō* (Dedication service for the bell; Kabukiza, 1939), features *shirabyōshi* dancer Hanako (Onoe Kikugorō VI) in demon form and *aragoto* style hero Nakamura Kichiemon I.

priest was a heap of ash."[31] Later, a senior monk organized a grand ritual reading of the Lotus Sutra, bringing salvation to the spirits of both woman and victim.

The famous tale becomes the back-story for a sequel set some years later in the noh *Dōjōji* (*c.* 1450, anonymous), the most dramatic play in the repertory, and one of the most popular (see Figure 56). A new bell is being dedicated at the temple and women are prohibited. A lady dancer appears, informing the acolytes that she has been engaged to dance at the ceremony – the ban does not apply to her, as she is a *shirabyōshi* (dressed in a male *eboshi* lacquered hat). The servants, charmed, allow her inside. Poetic lyrics (sung by the chorus) tell how the lady's spirit loathes the bell for concealing her beloved. Her dance becomes progressively wilder and more deranged; obsession is expressed through dance. Intense, arhythmic *ranbyōshi* (lit. confused steps) continue for 20 minutes, the hypnotic rhythms putting the monks to sleep. The lady, once the victim of deception, has deceived all in the temple: she leaps inside the bell, which crashes to the ground, growing hot. The head priest chants exorcism prayers as his acolytes raise the bell. A serpent-demon emerges, wearing a fanged, horned *hannya* mask and wielding an iron rod. She battles the priest, who eventually drives her away.

31 Marian Ury (trans), *Konjaku monogatari* (Tales of times now past) (Berkeley, CA: University of California Press, 1979), 95.

The original legend is told rather straightforwardly during the interlude by the Dōjōji abbot, adding psychological depth and supernatural horror to the story. The heroine was an innocent young girl, attracted to a handsome priest during his yearly visit to Kumano. Her father lightheartedly told her she could marry him some day, but when she approached the priest he fled across the Hidaka River, then into the Dōjōji Temple. Pursuing him, she confronted the flooding river, but in fury transformed into a serpent and swam across, entering the temple. An unusually dynamic plot for noh, *Dōjōji* distills the original story to three main foci: the shirabyōshi's mesmerizing dedicatory dance, leap inside the bell, and battling demoness.

Puppet and dance versions

The first puppet play about Dōjōji dates from the 1640s. In 1719 Okinawan *kumi odori* dramatists reset the play in their homeland, combining noh staging with an original love affair between a courtier and a Ryukyuan lady (see Figure 23). From the 1730s to the 1790s, so many new plays were created for the kabuki and puppet theatres on this theme that "Dōjōji pieces" became a thematic category.

Two puppet plays, written in 1742 and 1759, typify Edo playwrights' elaboration of earlier sources. The Dōjōji tale and the noh play were both too short and simple to stand alone as history plays, so playwrights situated the story within long, complex, fictional tales of imperial succession disputes in the Nara or Heian periods. Inventive subplots with many new characters, disguises, and dual identities were added to create plays more convoluted than Shakespearean comedy. The handsome priest was actually a young prince, imperial heir-apparent Anchin, who must disguise himself to escape villainous usurpers. Separated from his beloved fiancée on his incognito journey, the prince-priest captured the heart of Kiyohime, daughter of a local landholder. When he is reunited with his fiancée, Kiyohime's jealousy is multiplied by her recognition not only that Anchin has rejected her, but that he has left her to be with another woman. In one variant ending, the bell-burning scene turns out to be a dream, so terrifying that Kiyohime sacrifices her life in a successful stratagem to rescue the prince. Plays used puppetry special effects to enact the most spectacular scenes from the original tale: the lady transforming into a serpent to cross the Hidaka River, the falling bell, and dramatic emergence from the bell of a serpent-demon, or surprise redeemer.

Kabuki actor Nakamura Tomijūrō's 1753 dance-drama approach to Dōjōji was different – a distillation of popular, multi-act puppet and kabuki plays. He returned to a short sequel scene focusing solely on one character – the spirit of the girl – now named Kiyohime. *Kyōganoko musume Dōjōji* (A maiden at Dōjōji) begins similarly to the noh drama with an attractive woman entering a forbidden ceremony. A huge bell hangs over the main stage, and the *nagauta* lyrics cite reasons why a woman might dislike bells:

> I remember being parted from my love at daybreak, parted by the hateful tolling of the bell at dawn. The bell tolls at the beginning of the night, telling of the impermanence of all things; the bell tolls in the middle of the night, telling that all that lives must die.[32]

The music pays homage to noh, and the dance includes some noh-like turns and ranbyōshi steps, but now the protagonist is not just one girl who loved a specific priest but the spirit of every girl who ever loved – and in love, betrayal is inevitable. The dance concludes with Kiyohime posing malevolently atop the bell, wielding a demon's rod, wearing a kimono that reveals noh's snake-scale pattern. Female jealousy is unquenchable. Buddhist comfort is nowhere to be found (in an alternative ending she transforms into a serpent-demon defeated by an *aragoto* superhero). With its multiple changes in mood, music, and hand properties and instant costume-changes (*hikinuki*), both technically and visually *Musume Dōjōji* is a tour-de-force – the foremost masterpiece in kabuki dance and *buyō* repertories.

Numerous other variant dances and plays were created – with two jealous dancers instead of one, dramatizing the serpent transformation in mid-river, a spirit fusion of a girl/male courtier, and the ghost of a murdered nun transforming into a snake demon. *Kane ga [no] misaki* (Cape of the bell, 1759) interprets the tale in typical *kamigata mai* (Osaka-Kyoto) quieter fashion, the woman's resentment calmed. She gazes at the moon, her rancor changing to sorrowful resignation. On the premodern Japanese stage the mere mention of "bell" or image of its curve was sufficiently iconic for audiences to understand that the piece would be fueled by burning female jealousy.

Westerners encountered the Dōjōji lady at the turn of the twentieth century, though ignorant of who she was. In 1900 Kawakami Otojirō combined an aragoto play with *Musume Dōjōji* for his wife, Sada Yakko to dance – but without the bell – which would have been too unwieldy for world touring. *The Geisha and the Samurai* enthralled audiences throughout America and Europe. The girl dies of a broken heart – more suited to melodramatic Western tastes than serpent transformations. Mishima Yukio's bell (*Dōjōji*, 1957) was an oversized wardrobe with a psychopathic dancer hiding inside, threatening to disfigure herself with sulfuric acid. Choreographers in every

---

32 Karen Brazell, *Traditional Japanese Theater: An Anthology of Plays* (New York: Columbia University Press, 1998), 510. Texts of noh play *Dōjōji* and kabuki dance drama *Musume Dōjōji* included.

genre have devised their own adaptations or parodies. During butoh dancer Kasai Akira's *Shiroi kakumei* (White makeup revolution, 2003), he threw off his kimono and intentionally flipped his Kiyohime wig, dancing in naked frenzy. Nihonbuyo master Nishikawa Senrei created the bell with a cone of light (2001); in *The Bell* (2013), contemporary New York dancer Yokoshi Yasuko juxtaposed Kiyohime with *Giselle*, and ballet with buyō.[33] Elaboration and distillation, parody and essentialization of this timeless story, within and between genres, and even across the East–West cultural divide, continue to excite dramatists and dancers, and to delight audiences today.

33 www.nytimes.com/2013/03/19/arts/dance/yasuko-yokoshis-bell-at-new-york-live-arts.html?_r=0.

Theatre architecture

PREFACE TO PART IV
EVOLUTION OF JAPANESE THEATRE
ARCHITECTURE
JONAH SALZ

Japanese performance genres share the tendency to develop their own playing space. These stages remain one of the least flexible of the many components comprising a performance; for example, indoor civic halls and commercial theatres replicate "noh stages" and "kabuki stages" to the exact dimensions of their conventional models. Some stages have developed as extensions and adaptations of the rectangular or square temple and shrine sites of their origins, while others suit the specific needs of concealing and/or displaying performers and stage technologies to their best advantage, while at the same time maintaining distinctions of spectator hierarchies through spatial differentiation. When touring domestically or overseas, traditional genres bring their own temporary structures with them in the form of backdrops or side-curtains, decorative pillars, or even a raised walkway that runs through the first-floor seats.

As part of reforms begun in the early twentieth century, new Western-style theatres were constructed, doing away with aspects of earlier theatres such as bridgeways, onstage spectators, and partitioned floor-seating. Modern straight plays and musical spectaculars were produced in purpose-built theatres based on European models. The postwar reconstruction of Japanese urban areas included integration of theatres with urban shopping and cultural centers. *Angura* (lit. "underground") theatre companies adopted spaces (factories, schools, as well as sometimes literally "underground") and temporary tents outside conventional theatres as both political and aesthetic statements. Multipurpose halls gave way to specialized theatrical spaces, a few with resident professional companies. Six distinct national theatres, some housing several halls, have been constructed in the past half-century, capable of hosting the variety of theatrical activity performed today. The following three chapters by practicing architect-scholars trace salient aspects of the trajectory of Japan's physical theatre's continuous evolution.

16 ∾ Premodern patterns of spectatorship and space

SHIMIZU HIROYUKI

Although traditional Japanese theatre genres (*bugaku*, *kagura*, noh-kyogen, kabuki, bunraku) have their own unique stages, certain commonalities are here discussed concerning the particular interactive relationship of actor and audience.

Fluctuating frontality, mutual frontality, and a lateral perspective

A useful reference for understanding theatrical performance historically is the late twelfth-century work *Nenchū gyōji emaki* (Annual events scroll).[1] Three different types of cockfight are portrayed: that of commoners,[2] one in the garden of a wealthy family,[3] and another at the imperial court.[4] The commoners' cockfight, held in the grounds of a shrine, depicts commoners encircling the cocks. This ring can be divided into two groups facing each other. The cockfight held in a wealthy family's garden portrays the higher-class spectators gazing from the balcony of a mansion, bisecting the axis of vision drawn by two groups of commoners observing from the side. In the cockfight held in the imperial court, tents have been placed where the commoners were, thereby preventing that spectatorial perspective, with only the axis of the nobles' gaze remaining. Thus the performance "front" fluctuates according to participants' gaze.

In the same scroll, the scene in which a *miko* (Shinto priestess) dedicates a performance of *kagura* (sacred Shinto music and dance) to the gods in order to heal illness at the Imamiya festivals is particularly significant.[5] The main

1 *Nenchū gyōji emaki*, http://edb.kulib.kyoto-u.ac.jp/exhibit/b35/b35cont.html.
2 Commoner's cockfight: http://edb.kulib.kyoto-u.ac.jp/exhibit/b35/image/13/b35s0206.html and http://edb.kulib.kyoto-u.ac.jp/exhibit/b35/image/13/b35s0207.html.
3 Cockfight in a wealthy family garden: http://edb.kulib.kyoto-u.ac.jp/exhibit/b35/image/13/b35s0212.html and http://edb.kulib.kyoto-u.ac.jp/exhibit/b35/image/13/b35s0213.html.
4 Cockfight at the imperial court: http://edb.kulib.kyoto-u.ac.jp/exhibit/b35/image/13/b35s0210.html and http://edb.kulib.kyoto-u.ac.jp/exhibit/b35/image/13/b35s0211.html.
5 Imamiya festival: http://edb.kulib.kyoto-u.ac.jp/exhibit/b35/image/12/b35s0195.html and http://edb.kulib.kyoto-u.ac.jp/exhibit/b35/image/12/b35s0196.html.

Fig 53 Kabuki audiences are partitioned, gazing from all sides, watching *Shibaraku* (Wait a Moment!) at the Ichimura-za Theatre (Utagawa Toyokuni III, 1858).

audience for the event is the gods, while the hosts are the human Shinto priests. The dance centers on gods and humans facing each other directly: in other words, a "double frontality" as host and guest face each other. Also noteworthy is the gaze of the audience viewing the performance from the small hut to the left of the shrine, which bisects the gazes of gods and priests. In this ritual environment, the "side" is the closest and most effective place from which to observe without obstructing. Spatially, for uninvited onlookers gazing through gaps between trees, the side would probably be the best place. Thus, a lateral view becomes an extremely effective perspective according to the structure of medieval performance spaces. In fact, this side-view appears frequently in Japanese performing art spaces, such as the *waki-za* side area of noh theatres, or seats straddling the *hanamichi* walkway in kabuki (see Figure 15).

Triangular axes of vision

Normally in theatres a group called the audience views the stage. In the small kabuki theatres of the Edo period, there were two-floor galleries flanking the main audience seating. On the far left of the stage, as seen from the audience, there was a two-storey gallery set up facing the main audience (the *rakandai* and *yoshino*),[6] from where the play was viewed from behind. While

---

6 Spectators seated in the rear seemed to resemble the nirvana-seeking *rakan* surrounding the Buddha, while seating above looked like the raised viewing stands of the famous cherry blossoms of Yoshino, Nara prefecture.

this perspective might be seen as an inferior one, it was here, in fact, that the so-called connoisseurs sat. In this seating configuration, the audience could view the stage while simultaneously viewing each other's faces. If we take the fundamental arrangement of staged arts as comprising a large number of people observing a stage, rather than a dualistic spatial relationship between performer and audience, then there is also a distinct spectator who senses the relationship between performer and audience.

This spatial configuration suggests a certain empathy with the performer's consciousness in relation to the two audiences. More than a simple relationship of "seeing and being seen," the triangular axes of vision construct a relation of "seeing others who are seeing and being seen." Spatial configurations in the kabuki theatre, which allow a wealth of these assorted triangular axes of vision, were adopted from traditional Japanese theatrical spaces such as side-view seats for the Imamiya festival, or from the relationship between spectators at the front and sides of the main noh stage.

Heterogeneous segmentation

Distinctive restriction of roles, reflected in clear segmentation of space, is a common feature of traditional Japanese theatre genres. Noh actors, such as *shite* (lead actor), *waki* (side actor), and musicians, are differentiated into distinct schools with independent training systems. Members of these schools meet in the moment of performance to collaborate with and "compete against" each other. The real thrills in noh are moments of evident competition among musicians, and with actors and chorus, on stage.

Spatially as well, positions held by shite, waki, and accompanying performers are specified as the "lead actor area," "side actor area," "musicians' area," "chorus area," and so on. The noh stage space is thus heterogeneously segmented; kabuki and bunraku theatres are much the same. Players are provided with particular spaces according to their roles.

Path-like performing space

Another prominent and potent feature of Japanese theatre is the linear space such as the noh *hashigakari* (bridgeway) and kabuki hanamichi (lit. "flower-path" walkway). Such space is often seen in processions during festivals. Kyoto's Gion Festival, a medieval exorcism rite that continues to this day, features a gorgeous procession of giant, decorated wagons and palanquins which parade through town, while spectators line both sides of the streets. For audiences in this position, they see the parade performers proceed in a straight line from afar, approach, then depart. The actual performance space is physically narrow, while the audience perceives it as a temporal "coming" and "going."

In contrast to theatre's three-dimensional stage which stresses spatiality, linear performances emphasize spatial distance and temporal length. This distinction offers a better understanding of the bridgeway in noh and walkway in kabuki. In many noh plays, resentful ghosts appear to confess to traveling priests; their hearts enlightened, they then disappear. The protagonist is not of this world but of the "other world," but by passing over the bridge (hashigakari) they are able to appear in the living world, the main stage. In kabuki, as well, the hanamichi represents spatial and temporal distance, with an additional slow-motion function that elongates time, and frames the *mie* poses that accompany dramatic self-introductions and punctuate exits.

Alienation and assimilation

Ningyō jōruri puppet theatres, as with kabuki theatres, have a unique spatial construction. Puppets, puppeteers, the narrator (*tayū*), and shamisen players face the audience, displaying themselves while at the same time performing. Each compositional element is segmented, juxtaposed, and autonomous. "Estrangement" is the aspect of performance in which each theatrical element is segmented, and seen to be competing with others through their respective strategies, while "assimilation" is the fusion of those elements as they appear in integrated structures to the audience.

Estrangement is a powerful characteristic of Japan's traditional performing arts. From the performer's perspective, through the segmentation of artistic elements and introduction of a segmented theatrical space, the stage becomes diversified and stratified due to this powerful alienation. This differs from the socially stratified frontal perspective of the audience, a function of ticket prices and access. At the same time, the bridges and "flower paths" (hanamichi) disrupt the process of alienation to allow spectatorial empathy for characters and actors. Japanese performance traditions achieve potency from such oscillations of distance and proximity.

Since the Meiji period, with the introduction of Western theatrical forms and spaces, these traditional characteristics have evolved into more homogeneous and neutral theatre spaces, as discussed in the following chapters.

17 ❧ Modernization of theatrical space, 1868–1940

SAMUEL L. LEITER AND NAGAI SATOKO

At the beginning of the twentieth century, a number of privately operated theatres appeared that modernized the kabuki theatre through the introduction of new forms and technologies. This section discusses the changing face of Japanese theatre design during the first three decades of the twentieth century through theatres such as the Yūraku-za (Yūraku Theatre, 1908), Teikoku-za (Imperial Theatre, 1911), Teikoku Gekijō (Imperial Theatre, 1911), Tsukiji Shōgekijō (Tsukiji Little Theatre, 1924), and Takarazuka Daigekijō (Takarazuka Grand Theatre, 1924) and its sister, the Tōkyō Takarazuka Gekijō (Tokyo Takarazuka Theatre, 1934). These significant innovations altered the relationship of audience to stage, thereby establishing Japan's modern theatre age.

Kabuki theatre architecture reformed

In keeping with various reforms to kabuki acting and theatre management proposed by the Theatre Reform Association established in 1886, Suematsu Kenchō (1885–1920) expounded the value of Western architectural methods in the design of new Japanese theatres. He believed that innovation began with the initial design, and argued for three-storey brick structures with Western chairs rather than straw-matted floors for seating. He also wanted to abolish the system of selling tickets at adjacent teahouses, to permit audiences to wear shoes, to modernize toilet facilities,[1] and to do away with the *hanamichi* walkway,[2] while retaining the revolving stage (*mawari butai*). Suematsu's new theatre reached the planning stage, with English architect Joseph Conder (1852–1920) commissioned as designer, but the plan was finally dropped; such a theatre would not be fully realized until the Imperial Theatre (1911).

---

1 Komiya Toyotaka (comp. and ed.), *Japanese Music and Drama in the Meiji Era*, trans. and adapted Edward G. Seidensticker and Donald Keene (Tokyo: Ōbunsha, 1956), 218.
2 *Ibid.* 219. Other reformers, such as Toyama Shōichi, argued for the retention of the hanamichi.

Until the Meiji era (1868–1912), kabuki theatres seamlessly merged audience and stage through such elements as the hanamichi, *rakandai* (onstage seating), the *yuka* platform situated downstage left for chanters, and partitioned tatami-mat seating spaces (*masu*) throughout the house. Unlike much Western practice since the Renaissance, sets (except in rare cases) were not constructed on the principle of perspective with a privileged ideal spectator. However, as theatres began to modernize along with the play content, a proscenium arch was added (the earliest version at the new Shintomi-za in 1878) and the walkway and onstage seating were removed, thereby creating a clear separation between stage and audience. Audiences were now forced to view the stage from a single perspective, even in multi-storey auditoria, rather than the multiple axes possible in Edo theatres. The hierarchy of distinctions of privilege and proximity gave way to homogeneous stage and spectator spaces.

Assimilating the West: Yūraku-za, Teikoku-za, and Teikoku Gekijō

Although many sources cite the Imperial Theatre as Japan's first truly Western theatre, it actually was preceded by the Yūraku-za, near the Sukiyabashi Bridge in Ginza, which opened in 1908 as a center for high-class entertainments.[3] The 900-seat venue had Western-style chair seating, each seat numbered and equipped with a hat rack; there were two balconies as well as a proscenium arch and a drop curtain (replacing the kabuki draw curtain). The Yūraku-za abandoned the old kabuki *chaya* (teahouse) system for selling tickets and refreshments, and instituted modern, Westernized practices, including a box office and on-site restaurants. It also contained smoking rooms and lounges. The stage was 7.25 meters deep, and the proscenium was 10.8 meters wide and 5.5 meters high. The theatre was first used for musical concerts and children's theatre (*otogibanashi*), but was also where the Jiyū Gekijō (Free Theatre) gave its groundbreaking performance of Ibsen's *John Gabriel Borkman* in 1911, considered the first true *shingeki* production. Many other shingeki groups worked here subsequently, until it was destroyed in the Great Kantō Earthquake of 1923.

Upstart impresario Kawakami Otojirō, who toured the West to gain first-hand experience of theatres in major European and American cities, opened his Teikoku-za (Imperial Theatre, 1910) in Osaka with Westernized

---

3 Earle Ernst, *The Kabuki Theatre* (New York: Oxford University Press, 1974), 1st edn. 1956, 62. A theatre of the same name, built near Hibiya in 1935, is still in use today.

stage and lighting facilities. Yet it retained certain traditional features; thus a proscenium was added but the theatre still had a hanamichi and a revolving stage. This elaborate venue was dedicated to *shimpa*, seated 1,200, and containing Japan's first modern theatre lobby. Foreign-style box seating lined the sides of the auditorium, while the general seating on the orchestra floor was a combination of partitioned tatami seating and seats reserved for foreigners. The upper two storeys contained only tatami seating.

Larger and more elaborate than either the Yūraku-za or the Teikoku-za, and more consistently Westernized, was Tokyo's widely publicized Teikoku Gekijō (Imperial Theatre, 1911) designed by architect Yokokawa Tamisuke (1864–1945) in a French Renaissance style inspired by European and American opera houses. This five-storey venue (with basement) was intended as a new home for kabuki, shimpa, and Japanese dance (nihonbuyo), but could also serve for shingeki and opera. Although some contemporary theatres had included these features, none was on this scale.

The downstage pillars (*daijin bashira*) of old-time kabuki theatres were incorporated into an ornate proscenium arch, 14.5 meters wide. The electrically powered revolving stage was 14.5 meters in diameter. A truncated, removable hanamichi (which proved problematic) was placed on a diagonal at stage right, while the orchestra pit (which could be covered) and surrounding box seats created a blend of Western and Japanese styles. The three-balconied, 1,700-seat, steel-framed, reinforced concrete Imperial had a white exterior and generous amount of marble in its interior decor. The replacement of tatami floor seating with chairs and benches, also seen at the Yūraku-za, became standard.[4] This meant that spectators were much more restricted in their ability to view the action on the hanamichi than they had been on the old floormats, where they could freely shift their viewpoint to the side and rear. The Teikoku also introduced Western-style smoking rooms, powder rooms, restaurants, souvenir shops, and other amenities. Audiences accustomed to the old theatres with their adjacent teahouses and straw-mat seating were astonished by these and other modern comforts, including male receptionists and young female ushers.

In 1923 the Imperial was destroyed by fire in the Great Kantō Earthquake, which left only its walls standing. Soon rebuilt, it avoided destruction during World War II, but eventually became a movie house. After a thorough renovation, it reopened for live theatre again in 1966, and has continued

---

4 A limited number of chairs had been introduced at the first Shintomi-za in 1872, and again at the new Shintomi-za in 1878.

since then to host both traditional kabuki and Western-style modern theatre and opera.

A completely Western theatrical space: the Tsukiji Theatre

Despite the presence of the Yūraku-za and Imperial Theatre, Japan had no dedicated shingeki venue until 1924, when the Tsukiji Shōgekijō opened in Tokyo's Tsukiji neighborhood, not far from the Kabuki-za (Figure 54). This was the brainchild of shingeki pioneer Hijikata Yoshi (1898–1959) and his chief associate Osanai Kaoru (1881–1928), both of whom had studied theatre in the West and wished to create an up-to-date European-style playhouse and company capable of producing the new spoken drama. Although Hijikata desired a 250-seat "chamber theatre," Osanai's wish for a theatre twice this size won out, but average attendance was closer to what Hijikata envisioned. Post-earthquake building restrictions forced the playhouse to be built as a "barracks"-type structure, meaning it was temporary and could last only five years; building materials were thus less substantial and cheaper than would have been required by a permanent structure.

The architectural style was "Gothic-Romanesque," with both exterior and interior colored gray; interior decoration was sparse, placing the focus on the plays, not the playhouse. The seriousness of tone led some to compare it to an examination hall. Rows of seating, all on one level, were no wider than the stage itself; each seat had an equally good view of the stage. But the cheap construction led to poor heating, and audiences would often leave their seats to huddle at the radiators alongside the walls. Research on European innovations inspired a stage that employed a *Kuppelhorizont*, a permanent cyclorama that enclosed the back of the stage, curving at the top into a dome. Employed for a variety of atmospheric lighting effects, it was one of the theatre's most admired features.

The stage, with its unadorned proscenium arch 10.9 meters in width, had a number of advanced technical features, such as a four-section system that could alter the stage depth as required, a set of removable stairs that ran along the entire front of the stage down to the auditorium floor, and capacity for a forestage. There was no traditional hanamichi, although on each side of the stage there were short extensions that led to openings in the sidewalls. With the steps and potential forestage, the theatre was in tune with contemporary European efforts to escape from the boundaries imposed by the proscenium arch.

Fig 54 Barracks-type construction of the Tsukiji Theatre, a purpose-built theatre for Western-style modern theatre. Note the remnant of kabuki's *hanamichi* runway, stage right.

With its lighting booth at the rear of the house to control the floodlights and spots that illuminated the footlight-less stage, the theatre was technically comparable to similar venues in Europe. This allowed it to stage a wide variety of experimental productions in such modes as Expressionism and Constructivism, while also offering more realistic approaches.[5] After its original company bifurcated in 1926, the Tsukiji was occupied by both splinters and other shingeki groups. In March 1945, it was destroyed in an air raid by American bombers. As a bold forerunner of Western-style theatres, it provided the physical space to nurture serious dramatic work, first by translated European authors and then by native playwrights.

Grand revue: Takarazuka Daigekijō (Takarazuka Grand Theatre)

Founded in 1914 by railroad and department store magnate Kobayashi Ichizō (1873–1957), the all-female Takarazuka Kageki (Takarazuka Revue)

---

5 Gennifer Weisenfeld, *MAVO: Japanese Artists and the Avant-Garde, 1905–1931* (Berkeley: University of California Press, 2001), 220ff.

soon attracted a considerable following at its base in the hot springs resort Kobayashi also founded in the city of Takarazuka, near Osaka. In 1924, the huge Takarazuka Daigekijō (the Takarazuka Grand Theatre), seating 3,000 spectators, was constructed, replacing smaller preceding theatres. Its capacity was greater than that of any other theatre in Japan. The design was based on a range of theatres investigated by Kobayashi's team in Europe and America. A similar but smaller (2,477 seat) theatre, also known as the Tōhō Gekijō, went up in Tokyo's Yūraku-chō district in 1934 as part of an amusement center conceived by Kobayashi, used not only for Takarazuka Revue productions but for other shows sponsored by the Tōhō organization. These two theatres, which were rebuilt over the years due to fires, continue to produce spectacular musical entertainments for an audience composed mainly of female fans.

The Takarazuka Daigekijō stage was around 20 meters wide and 25 meters deep, requiring elaborate scenery to fill its space. Its technical features made it the best-equipped theatre in Asia. Advanced flying machinery was employed to help shift sets, and an enormous revolving stage, fitted with multiple elevator stages of varying sizes, was also a vital feature. Other elevator stages were located on the stage floor proper, and a German system of floorboards on pulleys helped shift scenery. Lacking sound amplification, the theatre's size required broad gestures and simple plotlines. Hanamichi-like walkways were employed along the side walls as was the "silver bridge" (*ginkyō*), a kind of forestage connecting the runways and thus enclosing the orchestra pit, with small lifts fitted into either end of the bridge. This ginkyō, inspired by France's Casino de Paris and Folies Bergère, allowed star performers to get closer to audiences while the chorus remained on the main stage behind them. Later, similar technologies were installed in the Tokyo theatre as well.

The Imperial Theatre, Tsukiji Shōgekijō, and Takarazuka theatres facilitated new expressive techniques through the development of stage technology and lighting. These theatres and others influenced by them were capable of producing multiple genres, establishing the basis for the multipurpose halls found in many modern public theatres, as discussed in the following chapter.

References and further reading

Nagai Satoko. *Gekijō no kindaika* (Theatre modernization) (Kyoto: Shibunkaku, 2014)

Otani Hachinosuke. *Gendai no gekijō kūkan* (Modern theatrical space) (Tokyo: Shinkenchiku gijutsu sōsho, 1975)

Reference

Powell, Brian. "Japan's first modern theater: the Tsukiji Shogekijo and its company, 1924–26," *MN* 30:1 (1975), 69–85

18 ❧ Postwar theatres
Development and diversification

OTSUKI ATSUSHI

Theatre construction restarted with the needs of existing theatre activities shortly after the end of World War II, then expanded with postwar revival and economic growth. Highly diverse theatres were established, reflecting varied backgrounds: client, purpose, and technological innovation. The continuing pursuit of Western-style theatre that began in the Meiji period (1868–1912) can be observed in the process.

The revival of theatre by Shōchiku and Tōhō

With the war over, Japan's theatrical arts, chiefly kabuki, needed to recover their lost performance spaces. American bombs had destroyed or heavily damaged most of the big city theatres; postwar activities were limited to the few surviving theatres, such as Shōchiku's Tōkyō Gekijō (Tokyo Theatre, 1930), and Tōhō's Teikoku Gekijō (Imperial Theatre, 1911) and Nihon Gekijō (Japan Theatre, 1933), which raised their curtains soon after the end of the war.

War-damaged theatres either belonging to or affiliated with Shōchiku included Tokyo's Shinbashi Embujō (restored in 1948), Meiji-za (1950), and Kabuki-za (1951), Nagoya's Misono-za (1947), and Osaka's Naka-za (1948). Most Shōchiku and Tōhō theatres were relatively large due to their commercial use, independent buildings unattached to larger office or shopping complexes. Even the smallest could seat approximately 1,000 people, while the larger ones held over 3,000.

Theatres constructed by new private agents

From the 1950s onwards, a new kind of private theatre developed. These were constructed in urban centres by large enterprises with no direct connection to show business. Relatively early examples are Osaka's Sankei Hall (1952), constructed by a newspaper company, Tokyo's Daiichi Seimei Hall (1952), created by an insurance company, and Tokyo's Tōyoko Hall (1954), built by a department store.

These new theatres, created in accordance with modern administrative systems, differed somewhat from the commercial and artistic goals of Shōchiku and Tōhō venues. Often, they were not free-standing buildings but comprised a portion of their client's corporate office complex or department store, enhancing the companies' images. When placed on an upper floor of a department store, as with the Tōyoko Hall, it was also presumed that a so-called "shower effect" would generate a trickle-down of customers to boost sales across the whole store. However, such theatres had limitations, being constructed according to the needs of the stores, which resulted in a lack of clear separation between audience and performers, narrow backstage areas, and technical difficulties in transporting stage sets. Moreover, these theatres were fundamentally incapable of advertising themselves at the street level, since this valuable space was utilized for stores' main sales activities.

Since these theatres had no resident company or artistic producer, they were administered as rental halls for an assortment of events, including not just plays but also speeches, concerts, and movies, which provided a stable income. This inspired the development of "multipurpose (*tamokuteki*) halls" built as proscenium theatres equipped with stage machinery appropriate for plays, as well as with movable acoustic reflectors for concerts. Thus, many early examples of such venues for dramatic presentation were called "halls" rather than "theatres." Most of these were relatively small in comparison to those of Shōchiku and Tōhō, with the largest only seating 1,000 spectators.

Around 1980, technological developments and societal changes stemming from the economic boom that led to the so-called "bubble economy" inspired the creation of "specialized theatres" in which owners often participated actively in their theatres' management; arts foundation support also surged. These venues were designed to accommodate specific genres, with seating capacity and facilities being dependent on the genre. Representative of these was Tokyo's 772-seat Ginza Saison Theatre (1987) by the Saison Group centered on the Seibu Department Store. To coincide with the theatre's inauguration, the private Saison Foundation was established to support contemporary Japanese theatres and arts.

Theatres based on urban strategies of private railway companies

Tōyoko Hall, mentioned above, was established by the Tōyoko (later Tōkyū) Department Store associated with a private railway company, the Tokyo-Yokohama Electric (Tōyoko) Railway. There are many other such examples affiliated with Nagoya's Meitetsu and Osaka's Kintetsu and Hankyū railways.

These were built with more complex urban strategies than merely attempting to create a trickle-down consumer effect within a department store. Kobayashi Ichizō, founder of the Hankyū Corporation and the Takarazuka troupe with the Takarazuka Theatre (1924), gave rise to a business model used by later private railway companies. He developed residential areas and amusement facilities along railway lines as well as department stores at the railway terminals to create a synergistic effect on railway projects. In-store theatres, as well as other facilities such as art galleries, enhanced the role of department stores. Such strategies were flexible enough to work even when theatres were not established in tandem with department stores. This allowed for such alternatives as Tokyo's Cerulean Tower Noh Theatre (2001), built by the Tōkyū Group in Shibuya as a hotel-based complex.

Theatres related to the Little Theatre Movement

The private sector also included producers unaffiliated with large corporations who developed theatres in original ways. Many had deep connections to the Tokyo-centered "little theatres" (*shōgekijō*) or underground theatre (*angura*) movements of the 1960s to 1980s. Most of these theatres seated fewer than 400 spectators.

During the early shōgekijō period, which began as a reaction to shingeki, young troupes, in accordance with their ideology, sought performance spaces outside existing venues. They appropriated spaces including the basement of a glass shop and a café second floor as their permanent theatres, and built tent theatres in public squares and parks for aesthetic, economic, and political reasons. These included the "underground" Jiyū Gekijō (Free Theatre), established in 1966, the Red Tent set up by Jōkyō Gekijō (Situational Theatre) in 1967, and the Black Tent erected by Kuro Tento (Black Tent) in 1970.

The Karagumi troupe's Shitamachi Kara-za (1988) was built as an independent theatre. After architect Andō Tadao (1941–) designed it as the Seibu Saison Group's pavilion at a regional expo, it was moved to Asakusa in Tokyo, where public performances were given for a limited time. This theatre, realized with corporate support during the bubble economy, symbolized the shōgekijō movement's loss of its radical edge.

Meanwhile, private investors built several small-scale theatres to serve the needs of different young troupes. Representative were those built by Honda Kazuo, a would-be actor turned successful restaurateur. Starting with the Suzunari (1981), the Honda Gekijō (1982), and the Ekimae Gekijō (1983), he opened a succession of theatres in the 1990s in Tokyo's Shimo-Kitazawa area.

Haiyū-za Theatre and the Shiki Theatre Company's theatres

The Tsukiji Shōgekijō had been shingeki's main theatre before being destroyed in a 1945 air raid. The large shingeki troupe Haiyū-za (Actors' Theatre), led by director Senda Koreya (1904–94), struggled to find suitable performance spaces after the war. In 1954, they built the 400-seat Haiyū-za Theatre in Tokyo's Roppongi district, the only theatre established by a genuine postwar shingeki troupe, not a commercial producer. Yet because of the need to raise funds for construction, it was built for public use rather than exclusively for the troupe.

Although Gekidan Shiki (Four Seasons Troupe) originated in 1953 as a shingeki troupe, it built many theatres exclusively for its own use after a string of successful stagings of Western musicals. The success of the big tent set up in Tokyo's Nishi-Shinjuku for Shiki's production of the British musical *Cats* (1983) marked the beginning of subsequent developments. Later, specialized permanent theatres as well as tent theatres, seating approximately 1,000, were built in big cities such as Fukuoka (1996), Osaka (2005), and Sapporo (2011) in cooperation with large corporations. In a sense, these were built on earlier successes, as Asari Keita (1933–), Shiki's producing director, had participated in Japan Life Insurance's creation of the Nissei Gekijō (1964), which had the strong backing of politics and industry.

Trends in public theatres

New public sector theatres arrived slightly later than those in the private sector, but then expanded widely. As clients were mainly local governments, the movement was not confined to big cities but flourished nationwide. These new theatres were descendants of prewar town halls (*kōkaidō*), used mainly for public meetings or speeches, and sometimes to boost national and regional prestige. Gradually, such facilities evolved into venues suitable for the performing arts. The first were multipurpose halls, similar to privately built examples. These facilities were positioned as "public facilities" aimed, as per the Local Autonomy Law, at increasing citizens' welfare. Each one was required to be fair and open in its activities, making it capable, for example, of accommodating the coming-of-age ceremony for all of the 20-year-olds in its municipality, as well as touring Tokyo hit shows, and thus many had seating for over 1,000.

Two particular issues arose relating to the public halls. One was architectural, summed up by the quip, "A multipurpose hall has no purpose at all." The desire to serve all genres highlighted the very different spatial and technical requirements of each. The other objection concerned the essentialist aspect of a "public theatre." Western-style public theatres for exclusive use by

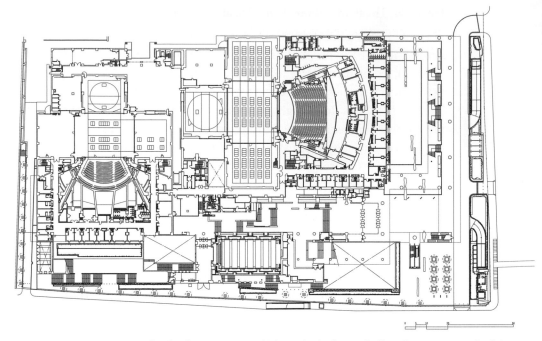

Fig 55 Stage-plan for the New National Theatre's Playhouse (left) and Opera House (right)

professional troupes to rehearse and perform high-quality works, as under-stood in Japan at that time, were thought to be necessary. These concerns, connected to the construction project of national theatres, brought about new developments in public theatres from the latter half of the 1970s.

The New National Theatre

After three decades of planning and construction, and despite numerous obstacles, Tokyo's Shin Kokuritsu Gekijō (New National Theatre, 1997) was opened for the performance of "contemporary performing arts," such as op-era, ballet, and plays, as opposed to the use of the other national theatres for Japanese traditional performing arts (Figure 55). The goal of establishing an exclusive professional troupe, following the concept of Western-style public theatres, was eventually abandoned.

The New National Theatre still achieved a number of organizational and technological goals. It demonstrated the culmination of the post-Meiji pursuit of Western-style theatres as architecture, and the creation of an influential model for subsequent construction. One prominent result was the introduction of the *tamen butai* (multiple stage), at both Opera House and Playhouse. Multiple sub-stages at the side and rear of the main stage, the same size as the main stage with interrelated stage machinery, allowed for advanced stagings and a repertoire system that can run a series of productions on alternate evenings. Nagoya's Aichi Ken Geijutsu Gekijō (Aichi Prefectural Arts Theatre, 1992) and the Saitama Geijutsu Gekijō (Saitama Arts Theatre, 1994) follow the same model, although both were realized prior to the New National Theatre during its long delay in planning and construction.

Diversification of public theatres

As private sector theatres shared the inadequacies of multipurpose public halls, two solutions were pursued. First, technological innovations solved problems brought about by the effort to be multipurpose. Various space control systems, including advanced movable acoustic reflectors for music, resolved troubles arising from the multipurpose setup. Secondly, specialized theatres that rejected the model of one integrated space for all genres were also developed. The allocation of technical resources and seating capacity was rationalized, although sometimes it was necessary to build more than one theatre in order to cope with multiple genres. Thus, complexes combining different specialized theatres began to be built. The Kumamoto Kenritsu Gekijō (Kumamoto Prefectural Theatre, 1983) in Kyūshū, which had both a concert hall and a theatre, is one of the earliest examples, as are the Aichi and Saitama theatres described above.

Apart from such new projects, spaces for the arts (including performing arts) were created by converting existing buildings made obsolete in areas of industrial and population change. Representative are the Kanazawa Shimin Geijutsu Mura (Kanazawa Citizens' Art Center, 1996), converted from a former spinning factory, and the Kyōto Geijutsu Sentā (Kyoto Art Center, 2000), converted from a former elementary school.

Corresponding to the diversification of architecture, some public theatres began setting up artistic organizations through which to originate their own productions. Specialists in the private sector, many of whom had been involved in the Little Theatre Movement, further diversified the scope of public theatre. Especially significant were the Hyōgo Kenritsu Amagasaki Seishōnen Sōzō Gekijō (Amagasaki Youth Creative Theatre of Hyogo prefecture, nicknamed the Piccolo Theatre, 1978) and the Setagaya Public Theatre (1997). The former broke away from the practices of multipurpose rental halls, establishing a theatre academy (1983), stage technology school (1992), and theatre company (1994). The latter was the first to identify itself as a "public theatre," which derived from the continuous participation in the project by Satoh Makoto (1943–), a former leader of the Little Theatre Movement. Satoh's involvement in this theatre began at the planning stage;

he later became the first artistic director, then played a similar role at the Za Koenji (Koenji Public Theatre, 2009).

Also noteworthy are the series of theatres created by Suzuki Tadashi (1939–) in collaboration with architect Isozaki Arata (1931–). Suzuki, also a leader in the Little Theatre Movement, argued against the over-concentration of theatres in Tokyo, moving the base of his troupe's activities to Toga, a small mountain village in Tōyama, and refurbishing a traditional house as the Toga Theatre (1976). His success there, where he earned the local government's trust, led to his subsequent opening of such unique theatres as the Mito Geijutsu Kan (Art Tower Mito ACM Theatre, 1990) and a cluster of theatres for the Shizuoka Performing Arts Centre; Suzuki served as artistic director at all these theatres. The latter was the first in Japan to consummate the long-awaited marriage of a Western-style public theatre with an artistic director, and an exclusive professional troupe.

Twenty-first century prospect

In 2012, the Law of Enhancing Theatres, Concert Halls and Other Facilities (Act No. 49) was established as the first contemporary law aimed directly at general theatre. Various attempts related to public theatres described above were accompanied by an additional awareness of the concept of "public theatre," questioning anew the notion of "public." This new law followed on this tide, describing desirable theatres as *atarashii hiroba* (new commons). Future theatres will certainly be affected by this law. Architecturally, the recent trend to develop spaces for different activities, not exclusively theatrical, set at the front rather than at the back of the facility, will be advanced.

References and further reading

Itō Masaji and Theatre Workshop. *Engeki no tameno kūkan* (Space for theatrical performance) (Tokyo: Kajima Institute, 1995)

Ozasa Yoshio. *Gekijō ga enjita geki* (Plays performed by theatres) (Tokyo: Kyōiku shuppan, 1999)

Shimizu Hiroyuki. *21 Seiki no chiiki-gekijō* (Regional theatres in the twenty-first century) (Tokyo: Kajima Institute, 1999)

Shimizu Hiroyuki, Otsuki Atsushi, *et al. Nihon no gendai-gekijō* (Contemporary theatres in Japan) (Tokyo: Shokokusha, 1997)

Interlude: National theatres and funding

BARBARA E. THORNBURY

The architecturally striking, even monumental, national theatre buildings in Tokyo, Osaka, and Okinawa manifest Japan's highly developed, government-administered infrastructure of support and promotion of the arts. The principal manager of that infrastructure is the Agency for Cultural Affairs (Bunkachō), established in 1968 within what is now called the Ministry of Education, Culture, Sports, Science and Technology. One of the Agency's responsibilities is to carry out the Law for the Protection of Cultural Properties. It also oversees several independent administrative institutions, the semi-autonomous, publicly funded units that carry out the operational functions of the Japanese government. One is the Japan Arts Council, the executive body for the national theatres. The Japan Foundation, with which the Agency sometimes vies in sponsoring cultural exchange tours abroad, is an independent administrative institution under the Ministry of Foreign Affairs.

Six national theatres

Japan's first National Theatre, with its sweeping view of the Imperial Palace grounds at the center of Tokyo, opened in 1966. A burgeoning economy and a growing sense of national pride found expression in public affirmations of Japanese culture; over time, five more national theatres have been constructed – three in Tokyo and one each in Osaka and Okinawa. Collectively, they aim "to preserve and promote traditional performing arts, and to promote and popularize modern performing arts in Japan."[1]

They provide wide public access to the performing arts: ticket prices can be more than 50 percent lower than at commercial theatres. It is possible to see kabuki at the National Theatre for only 1,500 yen (US $15), while the best seat in the house usually costs no more than 12,000 yen (US $120). In contrast, at Shōchiku's newly reopened Kabuki-za theatre, also in Tokyo, the range for kabuki is generally between 4,000 and 20,000 yen.

---

1 "Japan Arts Council" www.ntj.jac.go.jp/english/outline/activities.html.

To ensure a reliable pool of new, professionally qualified performers and production specialists, the national theatres offer training programs to young adults (only males in the traditional arts) selected through a public application process. Graduates of traditional performing arts courses then typically apprentice within the *iemoto* system, although such institutional training has been criticized as arbitrary and incomplete (see Interlude, p. 99).

Considerable energy goes into cultivating new audiences. "Appreciation classrooms" aimed mainly at schoolchildren include lively lecture-demonstrations and a sampling of professionally staged dramas. The theatres have also made a sizeable investment in Japanese/English earphone translation and commentary systems (for kabuki and bunraku), a seat-back titling system for noh and kyogen, and supertitles for opera and other forms of drama.

The national theatres offer research materials in a variety of media, lectures, and museum-style exhibits. The freestanding Traditional Performing Arts Information Center and its Cultural Digital Library opened in 2003.[2]

The theatres: specialization and outsourcing

The five theatres are showcases for particular genres, but also rent their facilities to fill their calendars. The original Kokuritsu Gekijō (National Theatre) is mainly a showcase for kabuki (1,610 seats) and bunraku (in the 590-seat small theatre), but also presents folk performing art and other traditional dance and musical events. Less constrained by the exigencies of profit-making faced by commercial kabuki theatres, the National Theatre regularly stages plays in their historically complete form and occasionally introduces newly written plays. Although bunraku is associated geographically with Osaka, the National Theatre productions have vastly increased interest in the art in the Tokyo area.

The 300-seat Kokuritsu Engeijō (National Engei Hall, 1979) is the smallest of the national theatres, opened within the same complex as the original National Theatre. *Engei* is a blanket term for a variety of "vaudeville"-style arts – storytelling, such as *rakugo* and *manzai*, and even small-scale acrobatics and feats of dexterity. Giving nostalgically low-brow engei a dedicated space points to a policy of non-elitism within the taxpayer-funded national theatre system.

The 591-seat Kokuritsu Nōgakudō (National Noh Theatre, 1983) sponsors productions by performers drawn from across the spectrum of schools of noh and kyogen. Regional players are given a Tokyo venue, with frequent productions of rare and revived plays, while the hall is rented as a neutral

2 See "Bunka Dejitaru Raiburarī" (Digital Culture Library), www2.ntj.jac.go.jp/dglib/.

ground for new works such as Umehara Takeshi's "Super-kyogen" or mixed-genre productions of Shakespeare and Yeats.

The Kokuritsu Bunraku Gekijō (National Bunraku Theatre, 1984) is in the Nipponbashi neighborhood of Osaka, near the bustling Dōtombori entertainment district of its origins. Bunraku headlines the 753-seat main hall, along with other types of traditional performing arts. Films of classic productions and performances of engei are features of the 159-seat smaller hall.

The Shin Kokuritsu Gekijō (New National Theatre, 1997) is part of a cutting-edge arts, retail, and office complex in Tokyo's Shibuya ward. It encompasses the 1,810-seat Opera House, 1,000-seat Playhouse, and 440-seat flexible Pit. Programming is resolutely global in scope, a blend of the institution's own new and reprised productions of operas, ballets, musicals, and works of modern and contemporary theatre and dance originally written, composed, and choreographed in Japan and around the world.

The newest of the national theatres, the Kokuritsu Gekijō Okinawa (National Theatre Okinawa, 2004), opened in Urasoe City, outside Naha, Okinawa. Programming in its two performance spaces – 632 and 255 seats – focuses mainly on *kumiodori* and other performing arts of Okinawa. The controversy and ambiguity often clouding relations between Okinawa prefecture and the Japanese central government is reflected in local complaints that this national theatre facility is too little, too late – despite upbeat official pronouncements that it is "the point of exchange for promoting tradition and culture in the Asia-Pacific region."[3]

"Living National Treasures"

"Cultural properties are indispensable to our understanding of our history. They symbolize Japanese culture, and we must protect them at all costs."[4] Originally enacted in 1950, Japan's Law for the Protection of Cultural Properties recognizes and supports a range of cultural properties, from historically significant paintings, sculptures, and buildings to theatre, music, the applied arts, and folk-cultural practices. Even natural sites, plants, and animals are included. The Ministry of Education, Culture, Sports, Science and Technology, working through the Agency for Cultural Affairs, confers national designation based on recommendations of scholars and specialists. "Important Intangible Cultural Properties" include *gagaku*, noh, bunraku,

3 "National Theatre Okinawa," www.nt-okinawa.or.jp/en/.
4 Sasaki Jōhei, President, "Goaisatsu" (Greeting), National Institutes for Cultural Heritage, accessed 28 June 2012, www.nich.go.jp/english/past.html.

kabuki, kumiodori, and engei.[5] A 1975 revision of the law created the category "Important Intangible Folk Cultural Properties" – like Iwate prefecture's Hayachine Kagura, Yamagata prefecture's Kurokawa Noh, and Hyōgo prefecture's Awaji Ningyō-jōruri. The so-called Living National Treasures are one type of Important Intangible Cultural Property, designating individuals as the embodiment of a particular art or skill. Small honorary stipends are intended to promote teaching and transmission to the next generation of performers. Current designees include Nomura Man and Mansaku II (kyogen), Nakamura Kichiemon II (kabuki), and Miyagi Nōhō (kumiodori).[6]

The Law for the Protection of Cultural Properties proclaimed the status of the performing arts as a fundamental element of cultural heritage in postwar Japan. The opening of national theatres starting in 1966 and the formation soon after of the Agency for Cultural Affairs and Japan Foundation grew out of an era of rapidly increasing prosperity and the concomitant desire to shape national identity and build international prestige through new cultural institutions at home and exchange-tour initiatives abroad. The New National Theatre asserts Japan's contributions to "Western"-style performance and confirms her place in transnational conversations on contemporary performing arts. Political pressure on the Japanese central government to show more respect toward Okinawa, one of the country's least prosperous prefectures and a major site of American military bases, contributed to the decision to build a national theatre there. The most pressing issues now are how to continue developing a corps of talented performers and to sustain audience support for the performing arts. As budgets for education and arts shrink throughout the post-bubble economy, government support for non-hardware elements of the national theatre complexes remains remarkably underfunded by international standards, as Japan does not have the custom of (or tax breaks for) private donations.

Reference and further reading

Havens, Thomas R. H. *Artist and Patron in Postwar Japan: Dance, Music, Theater, and the Visual Arts, 1955–1980* (Princeton, NJ: Princeton University Press, 1982)

5 Following Japan's example, UNESCO starting in 2001 enacted a worldwide system of cultural property designations, the Intangible Cultural Heritage of Humanity, which includes noh-kyogen, bunraku, kabuki, gagaku, and Okinawan kumiodori.
6 There is also a secondary, more widely inclusive tier of "Living National Treasures" – artists who are selected for the "Important Intangible Cultural Property general designation."

PART V
Theatre criticism

19 ❧ Premodern practitioner principles: Zeami to Chikamatsu

WILLIAM LEE

Unlike in the West, where ever since Aristotle's *Poetics* drama has been central to discussions of literary history and theory, for most of their history Japan's theatrical arts were treated first and foremost as performance. Only in the Meiji period (1868–1912), when Japanese scholars began adopting Western typologies, did plays come to be considered examples of literature. Unsurprisingly, much premodern writing on theatre focuses on the context and features of stage presentation rather than texts. This discourse, moreover, was at first produced almost exclusively by performers themselves. Not until the Edo period (1603–1868) did there emerge a genre of theatre criticism by outsiders.

Noh: maintaining the flower and mystery

Critical and theoretical writing on the theatre can be said to begin with Zeami Motokiyo (1363?–1443?), often considered the founder of noh. Zeami did not so much found noh (then called *sarugaku*) as seek to ensure his own troupe's continuing advantage in a competitive performance world by codifying its successful practices. These had been developed under his father's (Kan'ami, 1333–84) and then Zeami's leadership, winning for their troupe, the Kanze-za, the patronage of shogun Yoshimitsu (1358–1408) and members of his court.

Zeami's thoughts on noh are found in a series of some twenty surviving texts. *Fūshikaden* (Teachings on style and the flower) was written in fragments between 1400 and 1418. Other texts followed in more regular succession, most produced while Zeami was in his late fifties or sixties. Often labeled "treatises" in English, these texts were not intended for the general public or even members of the profession as a whole, but rather written in the tradition of *hiden* (secret transmissions) established by religious or poetic lineages. Such confidences were intended only for chosen disciples or a particular son or relative succeeding as family head.

For Zeami, an important part of his family's legacy was the notion of *hana* (華 / 花 "flower" or "blossom"). This may be taken as a metaphor for the display of supreme artistry. The performer's ability to achieve such excellence was for Zeami the best guarantee of professional success. Attaining this level of accomplishment required mastery of fundamental skills, and for this reason *Fūshikaden* and many subsequent texts take up the issue of training. In *Shikadō* (The way to the attainment of the flower, 1420), the basic elements of noh are broken down into the "two arts" (*nikyoku*) of song and dance and "three role types" (*santai*): old person, woman, and warrior. In Zeami's training regimen, the child starts with the two arts and only later takes up the study of the three roles. All aspects of noh "acting," including the portrayal of complex characters, are achieved through subtle combinations of these primary arts and forms.

In addition to mastery of fundamentals, hana requires a sympathetic awareness of the occasion of performance and the spectator's mood, and "[I]f an actor masters the various elements of *nō* that he has learned to remember, he can show his art, basing it on the taste of the moment and the kind of plays that his audiences appreciate."[1] The real secret of hana lies not only in knowing the audience's tastes, but in then drawing on one's store of skill and experience to offer them something unexpected or "novel" (*mezurashiki*). Spectators should not be aware of the performer's intentions; otherwise they will come to expect such innovation and be less impressed when they encounter it. Hence the need for concealment: "When there are secrets, the Flower exists; but without secrets, the Flower does not exist."[2]

In *Kakyō* (The mirror of the flower, 1424), we have Zeami's most extended discussion of the concept of *yūgen* (幽玄). While sometimes rendered into English as "mystery and depth," the term is here given a class-based reference: "Grace [*yūgen*] is best represented in the character of the nobility, whose deportment is of such a high quality and who receive the attention and respect not given to others in society."[3] Yet the creation of yūgen does not necessarily depend on the nobility of characters portrayed; as a "beautiful and gentle style," yūgen can be the ideal of any performance. Thus Zeami exhorts his descendants: "Do not depart from yūgen, no matter what the object of your imitation."[4] This statement is all the more significant given that "imitation" (*monomane*) had been a specialty of the troupe Zeami inherited from his father. In several of his writings Zeami praises certain *dengaku* masters and performers of the rival Ōmi sarugaku who, as he put it in *Sandō* (Three courses, 1423), "made *yūgen* in dance and singing the basis of

---

1 *Fushikaden*, in J. Thomas Rimer (trans.) and Yamazaki Masakazu (ed.), *On the Art of the No Drama: The Major Treatises of Zeami* (Princeton, NJ: Princeton University Press, 1984), 52–3.
2 *Ibid*. 60.   3 *Ibid*. 93.
4 Thomas Hare (trans.), *Zeami Performance Notes* (New York: Columbia University Press, 2008), 113.

their style."[5] Zeami clearly saw the benefit in adding more of the beauty and grace of musical and dance performance to sarugaku. This willingness to subordinate imitation to stylization ensured subsequent Japanese performing arts would follow a course that eschewed realism in favor of mannerism.

Kakyō also introduces the term *myō* (妙), denoting for Zeami the highest manifestation of hana, the artistry of an actor who "has transcended all stages of his art to the point where he performs everything with ease and exhibits every skill without care, thus achieving a selfless art that rises above any artifice."[6] Myō is also a Buddhist term, one frequently found in the compound *myōhō*, denoting the "wondrous law" or teachings of the Buddha. The concept of myō figures prominently in a number of Zeami's later works.

One also finds in the later writings instances of the use of Zen concepts and language. In *Kyūi*, Zeami employs the term *kyakurai* (doubling back) to characterize the situation of the artist who, after having achieved the highest level of hana, returns to play in the more rudimentary styles associated with the lowest levels. The term forms part of the Zen trope *kōko kyakurai*. Meaning literally "leaving the beyond and coming back," its Zen sense is that of a return to the phenomenal world after having achieved enlightenment. The term appears again in the late work *Kyakuraika* (The flower of returning, 1433). Here Zeami discusses a secret technique called "the effect of doubling back" (*kyakuraifû*). This technique was not to be transmitted to anyone under the age of 40, and not to be used before the age of 50. The exact content of the secret of kyakuraifū is not made clear in this brief text, but it is apparently related to the realization that, "Once you are truly enlightened, you don't do things that are unnecessary."[7] The term translated here as "enlightenment" is *tokuhō*, literally "getting the *dharma*."

The frequency of such language in the later writings makes it tempting to read them as an example of Zen aesthetics. Yet Zeami's predilection for Buddhist (including Zen) concepts and terminology, not to mention his allusions to the *Analects* and other Chinese classics, can also be more simply interpreted as the author's effort to further articulate his teachings by drawing on other available intellectual traditions. Indeed, some of Zeami's most Zen-sounding assertions are revealed to be restatements of earlier ideas. The secret of kyakurai, for example, is prefigured in *Kakyō*: "When the actor passes fifty, then he can begin to use the technique of 'doing nothing.'"[8] While this technique may in part be mandated by the older actor's declining physical strength, it also follows naturally from the remark made earlier in

5 *Ibid.* 163.   6 Rimer and Yamazaki, *On the Art of the No Drama*, 99.
7 Hare, *Zeami Performance Notes*, 428.
8 Rimer and Yamazaki, *On the Art of the No Drama*, 106.

the same text that audiences often find an actor effective even when he is doing nothing, such as in the interval between different musical or dance seg-
ments of a play. Despite the Zen overtones, what we would today recognize
as the concept of the "empty moment" (*ma*) is important to Zeami precisely
because of its effect in performance, not as a spiritual concept.

Theory after Zeami

Although the headship of the Kanze-za officially passed to Zeami's nephew
On'ami, his son-in-law Zenchiku (1405–68?) of the rival Komparu-za troupe
is often considered his legitimate artistic heir. Zenchiku received authorized
transmission of some of Zeami's texts. One can, moreover, point to numerous examples of the use of Zeami's terminology and typologies in Zenchiku's
writings. Yet in almost every case what is taken is only a starting point, only
one textual source which, along with other artistic, religious, and philosophical traditions, is used to construct a theory of sarugaku contrasting sharply
with the legacy of Zeami.

Most striking about Zenchiku's writings is that most contain little practical information about sarugaku *performance*. Instead a series of attempts is
made at interpreting the art as an intellectual or spiritual activity by exploring its supposed affinities with other, more prestigious, intellectual systems.
This is certainly the case with Zenchiku's *rokurin ichiro* works, a series of
texts inspired by a set of diagrams depicting six circles of varying complexity
and a sword. The earliest extant text, *Rokurin ichiro no ki* (Record of the six
circles and one dewdrop, 1655), contains not only the diagrams and Zenchiku's brief description of them, but also commentaries by two leading
contemporary intellectuals, the priest Shigyoku (1383–1463) and the court
official and scholar Ichijō Kanera (1402–81). The first points to parallels with
certain aspects of Kegon Buddhist philosophy, while the second references
terms and concepts from the *Book of Changes* and other Chinese classics and
neo-Confucian works.

In the next text in the series (1456), Zenchiku adds a new level of commentary of his own, this one drawing on medieval Shinto discourses seeking
to establish correspondences between myths of native *kami* and the great
continental traditions. While later sections of the work attempt to relate
this to the Way of Sarugaku, the cosmological perspective derived from
various sources remains. The implication is that the spiritual progress of the
sarugaku performer mirrors and reflects the same cosmological states and
processes.

As Zeami's "artistic successor," Zenchiku certainly takes his mentor's
vision of the Way in a more literal direction. Zeami had noted parallels

between the artistic path he was trying to articulate and other (especially Buddhist) paths, but remained focused on the goal of effective performance. In contrast, Zenchiku takes such parallels as indications of some deeper cosmic unity, which the Way of Sarugaku, precisely because of this unity, must surely provide access to. If for Zeami the profession of the sarugaku performer was *like* a spiritual path, for Zenchiku it *was* a spiritual path.[9]

Given the tradition of secret transmission, it is doubtful whether either of these visions of the Way had much impact on later generations of noh performers. Portions of Zeami's *Fūshikaden* and one of his texts on singing did find their way into the work now commonly referred to as the *Hachijō kadensho*, which dates from the late sixteenth century and went through several printed editions during the following centuries. Most of Zeami's writings, however, remained largely unknown until discovered in the Meiji period and published as *Zeami jūroku bushū* (Sixteen texts by Zeami, 1909). Zenchiku's works also languished in obscurity until the twentieth century.

In contrast, *Hachijō kadensho*, compiled by some unknown performer or performers championing the cause of the Yamato noh troupes, was the most widely disseminated guide to noh practice from the late sixteenth to the late nineteenth century.[10] In addition to the pieces by Zeami, it incorporated writings by later generations of performers. Much of the work deals with specific aspects of noh, such as drum-playing and flute music. Moreover, many discussions of style and technique are related to specific plays or contexts, giving the collection great practical value for the working noh performer.

Kyogen: restrained hilarity

Theoretical writing on kyogen arises later than that on noh, reflecting the fact that kyogen was slower to become formalized and organized into schools. By the Edo period, however, kyogen had joined noh in being both recognized and regulated by the shogunal government. This new-found status demanded a suitable textual foundation, which was provided by Ōkura Tora'akira (1597–1662) in *Waranbegusa* (Leaves for children, 1651). Like Zeami's writings, this lays down the principles of the art and the traditions of its author's own (Ōkura) school. *Waranbegusa* also follows the *hiden* convention of insisting on the need for secrecy: "This book is not to be shown to outsiders.

---

9 Noel J. Pinnington, *Traces in the Way: Michi and the Writings of Komparu Zenchiku* (Ithaca, NY: Cornell University East Asian Program, 2006), 252.
10 Eric C. Rath, *The Ethos of Noh: Actors and their Art* (Cambridge, MA: Harvard University Asia Center, 2004).

It contains the words of the ancients only in order to allow our descendants and pupils to maintain the old rules and not to commit errors."[11]

Despite this continuity, the mention of "pupils" (*deshi*) hints at the new social context. Both noh and kyogen had considerable amateur followings, providing new economic opportunities. It also made it important to distinguish among the official schools (Ōkura, Sagi, and Izumi) and between these and other, illegitimate, examples of kyogen. For Tora'akira, an important source of legitimacy was the close connection with noh:

> *Kyōgen* is a derivative of *nō*, related like block to cursive script. If *nō* can be likened to linked poetry [*renga*], *kyōgen* is like light verse [*haikai*] … The *kyōgen* popular today have no substance and are performed in haste and roughly. Rambling remarks are made, the actor twists his face, opens wide his eyes and mouth, makes meaningless gestures, and laughs. This pleases those of low station but embarrasses those with discernment. Such *kyōgen* pieces are like comic pieces in the *kabuki* so popular today; they are not the *kyōgen* of the *nō* and cannot even be called the *kyōgen* of *kyōgen*.[12]

The mention of kabuki reminds us that many of the performers in the early history of that new performance art were drawn from the ranks of professional and amateur kyogen troupes. The immediate target of Tora'akira's remarks, however, was the rival Sagi school's less restrained approach to comedy. Tora'akira's teachings of the *Waranbegusa*, together with his compilation of playscripts around the same time, helped elevate and codify what had previously been a largely improvisational theatre.

Ningyō jōruri (bunraku): imitation and stylization

While by the early Edo period, both noh and kyogen enjoyed a privileged status, *ningyō jōruri* (bunraku) and kabuki were only just beginning. The practitioners of these new itinerant arts naturally turned to noh for models and sources of legitimacy. Thus the *jōruri* chanter Uji Kaganojō (1635–1711), in the preface to *Takenokoshū* (A collection of bamboo shoots, 1678), a collection of scenes from his most popular plays, insists that jōruri, while a new art, is really an offspring of noh. As evidence, he provides an account of a jōruri performance of the noh-derived ceremonial piece *Okina*, describing noh-like music and costumes. He then explicates the musical structure of jōruri, borrowing heavily from noh's model of the "five voices" as found in the *Hachijō kadensho*. Finally, Kaganojō argues that jōruri can acquire some

---

11 Steven Addiss, Gerald Groemer, and J. Thomas Rimer (eds.), *Traditional Japanese Arts and Culture: An Illustrated Source Book* (Honolulu: University of Hawai'i Press, 2006), 208.
12 *Ibid.*

of the dignity and recognition accorded noh by maintaining similarly high standards of professionalism and decorum.

Kaganojō's attitude toward noh is reverential throughout; he is aware his attempt to ascribe similar artistic principles to the humble art of jōruri is audacious. He also claims to regret divulging secrets of the tradition. Yet not only was *Bamboo Shoots* printed, it was intended as practice material for amateur chanters. The preface, for example, contains an explanation of musical notation used in the excerpts, and for this reason alone can be regarded as an important codification of the art. Its availability to the public through the publishing business reflects both the popularity of the new art of jōruri and the emergence in the Edo period of the commercial mode of cultural production.

In the preface to his own collection, *Jōkyō yonen Gidayū danmonoshū* (Gidayū collection of jōruri scenes, 1687), chanter Takemoto Gidayū (1651–1714) similarly offers advice to would-be performers. Unlike rival Kaganojō, Gidayū is much more willing to accept the newness of jōruri. For him, noh is at best the foster-parent of his art, which does not stem directly from any one older tradition but rather draws on many to create something new and unique. Gidayū is aware that his preface constitutes yet another example in the genre of secret transmission, but his point is that any useful teachings on jōruri cannot rely on authorities of the past but must be focused on the particular technical performance features of the new art. We can perhaps recognize a jab at Kaganojō in what Gidayū has to say about those who set too much stock in the old secret teachings:

> [T]o use quotations from the Kadensho in order to brandish pompously one's authority is distasteful. Those who skip their practice sessions and try to learn solely from secret teachings will never learn to perform well …To gain proficiency in Jōruri or any other art, one must practice and study day and night to master the essential principles.[13]

According to Gidayū, any useful teachings on jōruri cannot, therefore, rely on authorities of the past but must focus on particular technical features of the new art.

Although Gidayū is thus able to maintain a healthy skepticism toward secret transmissions, in many ways his preface has much in common with the foundational writings of Zeami. Gidayū too is aware that he is not merely transmitting but also defining a way of art. Accordingly, he too puts great stress on what makes a performance art successful, namely technical

13 C. Andrew Gerstle, *Circles of Fantasy: Convention in Chikamatsu's Plays* (Cambridge, MA: Harvard University Press, 1986), 190–1.

proficiency, mastery of a stylistic range, and sensitivity to spectator moods and tastes. "The ability to entertain without boring one's audience," he declares, "should be considered the secret tradition of the art of jōruri."[14] Gidayū is also concerned with structure. In *Bamboo Shoots*, Kaganojō had focused primarily on musical structure, which he took mostly from the noh model of the "five voices." Gidayū instead discusses musical styles in the context of the five-part structure of a daily jōruri program. This structure may owe much to noh, but for Gidayū it is less a derivative of noh than what by that time had become an established jōruri convention.

Universally regarded as the greatest writer for jōruri, Chikamatsu Monzaemon (1653–1724) unfortunately did not leave behind any writings of his own on his craft. The Confucian scholar Hozumi Ikan (1692–1769), however, recorded some of the playwright's thoughts on the subject in *Naniwa miyage* (Souvenirs of Naniwa, 1738). Like Gidayū, Chikamatsu emphasizes the need to master particular technical requirements. For the puppet theatre playwright, this meant fitting words to the musical rhythm of jōruri and imbuing them with the emotion necessary to animate the wooden puppets. Such stylization, moreover, applies not just to a play's language but also to its storytelling and character portrayal. Despite a trend toward realism in both the contemporary jōruri and kabuki, Chikamatsu famously rejected the faithful depiction of reality as an artistic principle: "Art is something which lies in the slender margin between the real and the unreal ... It is unreal, and yet it is not unreal. Entertainment lies between the two."[15] While this passage is often taken as an important statement of Japanese aesthetics, "art" (*gei* 芸) is used here not as an abstract concept or ideal but as a synonym for "entertainment" (*nagusami* 慰). Chikamatsu, in other words, shared with Zeami and Gidayū the conviction that the true test of a performance genre lies in its ability to move audiences.

Kabuki: insider and external critiques

Chikamatsu also wrote for kabuki theatre during the Genroku era (1688–1704), commonly considered the period of its first flowering, when the first great actors appeared. An actors' theatre, kabuki has also been from the beginning a commercial enterprise. Dispensing with traditional forms of patronage, it appealed directly to the market, with actors its greatest commodities. Stars responded by creating distinctive styles and founding lineages, but the market logic of kabuki ensured that lineage would be treated

14 *Ibid.* 192.
15 Donald Keene (trans.), *Anthology of Japanese Literature: Earliest Era to Mid-nineteenth Century* (New York: Grove Press, 1955).

differently from before. A system of yearly contracts meant that actors could move among theatres, forming different companies each year. This severely weakened the troupe or school identity found in noh and kyogen, resulting instead in a focus on individual stars.

This new arrangement is reflected in the growth and diversification of writing on theatre. Modern scholars use the term *gekisho* (劇書, "theatre writings") to describe a portion of this large body of kabuki-related material. In its narrowest sense, this refers to writings by kabuki professionals about their craft. These include *Yakusha rongo* (Actors' analects, 1776), a collection of anecdotes by and about actors of Kamigata (Kyoto-Osaka); a similar Edo version, *Kokon yakusha rongo sakigake* (Pioneering analects of past and present actors, 1772); and *Kezairoku* (Notes on playwriting, 1801), a work, probably by the Osaka playwright Namiki Shōzō II (?–1807), which combines theatre lore on playwrights with a discussion of practical matters in an effort to codify the "way" of the playwright.[16] All attempt to maintain the aura of secret transmission, coming closest to following in the tradition begun by Zeami.

Although the complete printed edition of *Yakusha rongo* is dated 1776, most individual parts were written much earlier. Three focus on famous actors of the Genroku stage. *Ayamegusa* (The words of Ayame) praises the art and dedication of *onnagata* (player of women's roles) Yoshizawa Ayame (1673–1729), who declared, "if he [i.e. an onnagata] does not live his normal life as if he was a woman, it will not be possible for him to be called a skillful *onnagata*."[17] Both *Nijinshū* (Dust in the ears) by Kaneko Kichizaemon, a Kyoto actor who co-wrote many of the kabuki plays attributed to Chikamatsu, and *Kengaishū* (Kengai collection) focus largely on Sakata Tōjūrō (1647–1709), star *tachiyaku* (player of leading male roles) and *zamoto* (troupe leader). Tōjūrō is commended for his attention to detail, commitment to creating characters realistic in appearance and action, and respect shown to the profession and fellow professionals. This consideration extends to playwrights, evidence of the greater importance attached to play-creation following the development of the multi-act play (*tsuzuki kyōgen*).

The *Actors' Analects* also succeeds in conveying useful advice for the practicing actor, including the need to be diligent in rehearsal, refrain from playing to the audience, and temper realism with decorum. Such sentiments have

---

16 *Yakusha rongo* is discussed below; the other two works are in Nishiyama Matsunosuke et al. (eds.), *Kinsei geidōron* (Premodern art theories) and *Nihon shisō taikei* 24 (Encylopedia of Japanese thought) (Tokyo: Iwanami shoten, 1972); translation of *Kezairoku* in Katherine Saltzman-Li, *Creating Kabuki Plays: Context for Kezairoku, 'Valuable Notes on Playwriting'* (Leiden: Brill, 2010), 168–226.

17 Charles Dunn and Torigoe Bunzo (trans.), *The Actors' Analects* (New York: Columbia University Press, 1969), 53.

been previously encountered, but such continuity does not conceal the fact that the *Actors' Analects* is a work very different from its predecessors. As a collection of random and at times contradictory statements and observations, it lacks the proprietary and authoritative voice one finds in Zeami's writings. This is not merely the result of a lack of editing; it is a reflection of a very different socio-economic context of performance. Zeami had embraced the tradition of secret transmission not only to protect his best insights from his rivals, but also as economic strategy, a means of creating cultural capital which could be exchanged for patronage. In the Edo period, kabuki actors and playwrights continued to pay lip service to the convention, but since the economic basis of the new theatrical form lay in attracting a large market of consumers, there was less need to keep professional matters secret. Indeed, from the economic point of view, raising fans' interest by providing more information, including access to supposed secret traditions, could only be beneficial.

This perhaps explains the symbiotic relationship that developed between kabuki and the publishing industry. The *Actors' Analects* was published by the Hachimonjiya, a Kyoto house which had long been printing and selling materials related to the theatre, including texts of jōruri plays, kabuki *e-iri kyōgenbon* (illustrated play books), and actor critiques. This material for amateur and fan markets constituted a whole other category of geki-sho, one largely driven by the publishing business and sharing features with genres of popular writing (*gesaku*). Depending on how far the boundaries are stretched, this category of kabuki-related texts could also include visual materials (e.g. actor prints) and fan-based productions.[18]

The most important of the commercial publications for fan readership were the *yakusha hyōbanki* (records of the evaluations of actors), later known as *kabuki hyōbanki*. Originally modeled on *yūjo hyōbanki* (evaluations of courtesans), which commented on and ranked prostitutes of the licensed districts, the first yakusha hyōbanki (beginning about 1660) focused more on actors' appearances and charms rather than on acting. An important turning point was the publication of *Yarō tachiyaku butai ōkagami* (Great mirror of lead male stage roles, 1687), which not only classified actors according to their role type (*yakugara*), but also gave pride of place to adult actors playing leading roles. Hachimonjiya's *Yakusha kuchi samisen* (Actors' oral shamisen, 1699) set the standard for years to come. This was published in a three-volume set, one each for the actors of Kyoto, Osaka, and Edo.[19] Hyōbanki usually came out twice a year, one evaluating

18 See C. Andrew Gerstle, Timothy Clark, and Akiko Yano, *Kabuki Heroes on the Osaka Stage, 1780–1830* (London: British Museum Press and University of Hawai'i Press, 2005).

19 *Yakusha kuchi samisen*, in Kabuki hyōbanki kenkyūkai (ed.), *Kabuki hyōbanki shūsei* (Kabuki hyōbanki collection), vol. II (Tokyo: Iwanami shoten, 1973), 173–289.

the season-opening *kaomise* performances in the eleventh month, the other the New Year and spring performances. Typically, a hyōbanki would list actors, classified according to role type and ranked by grades, followed by a prologue or preface, critical comments and gossip on individual actors, and an epilogue. They were also often illustrated.

Hyōbanki were written by professional writers, often those who also wrote in popular fiction genres, and some of the wit and style of those genres can also be found in the kabuki commentary. *Actors' Oral Shamisen* is the work of the *ukiyozōshi* (floating-world fiction) author Ejima Kiseki (1667–1736). The prologue to his Kyoto volume brings together a wealthy, pleasure-loving merchant and a cynical Buddhist priest from the provinces. This device is maintained in the body of the critique as well, with commentary on individual actors taking the form of a conversation between these fictional observers. In the section on Tōjūrō, the priest questions the actor's preeminent position, pointing out that his dancing skills were limited and that he always played the same *keiseigai* (prostitute buying) roles. The merchant argues that it was precisely due to Tōjūrō's skill in such roles that plays involving scenes with courtesans became the convention for the season's second production. He then praises Tōjūrō's fresh reinterpretation of the role in the recent play *Keisei hotoke no hara*. Tōjūrō's ability to give new life to conventional roles can perhaps be likened to Zeami's concept of hana as novelty.

Authored by writers outside the profession and produced for a wide readership, hyōbanki were essentially different from earlier examples of writing on theatre. Rather than codifications of an artistic tradition by and for those in the profession, these are appreciations of the art from the theatregoer's perspective. To be sure, the opinions of the writers do not necessarily represent the views of the audience in general, but they are nonetheless expressions of judgment and taste. Thus they come closer to our modern notion of theatre criticism than any "secret transmission."

References and further reading

Addiss, Steven, Gerald Groemer, and J. Thomas Rimer (trans.). *Traditional Japanese Arts and Culture: An Illustrated Source Book* (Honolulu: University of Hawai'i Press, 2006)

Hare, Thomas (trans.). *Zeami Performance Notes* (New York: Columbia University Press, 2008)

  Zeami's Style: The Noh Plays of Zeami Motokiyo (Stanford, CA: Stanford University Press, 1986)

Keene, Donald (trans.). *Anthology of Japanese Literature: Earliest Era to Mid-nineteenth Century* (New York: Grove Press, 1955)

Pinnington, Noel J. *Traces in the Way: Michi and the Writings of Komparu Zenchiku* (Ithaca, NY: Cornell University East Asian Program, 2006)

Rimer, J. Thomas (trans.) and Yamazaki Masakazu (ed.), *On the Art of the Nō Drama: The Major Treatises of Zeami* (Princeton, NJ: Princeton University Press, 1984)

Thornhill, Arthur H. III. *Six Circles, One Dewdrop: The Religio-Aesthetic World of Komparu Zenchiku* (Princeton, NJ: Princeton University Press, 1993)

20 ⮆ Modern criticism: wrestling with Western realism

NAKANO MASAAKI

Translated by DANIEL GALLIMORE

Starting with journalists and interested amateurs, the twentieth century saw the emergence of a new "industry" of documenting, analyzing, and speculating upon the rapidly changing theatre scene. Japan has also been fortunate to have nurtured many playwright-directors who have written on their own work and that of others, as well as on more general issues of importance to theatre practitioners. While theatre was late to gain recognition as a subject worthy of academic study, there are a number of university programs, especially in Tokyo, which train stage professionals and academics, the latter contributing to scholarly debate in domestic research groups as well as international critical discussions on contemporary Japanese theatre.

The early reception of modern Japanese drama

The first fifty years of theatre criticism following the Meiji Restoration in 1868 were devoted to Westernization and rationalization of existing practices and conventions, thus largely centered on kabuki, the dominant theatrical genre. The actual movement toward theatrical reform began in 1886 with the Theatre Reform Society established by diplomat Suematsu Kenchō, who had studied literature at Cambridge. Members came from the political, business, and academic elites. Sociologist Toyama Masakazu produced what was the first treatise on theatre reform in modern Japan, *Engeki kairyōron shikō* (A personal view of theatre reform, 1886), followed the same year by a similar work by Suematsu.[1] Both argued for the greater amenability of kabuki to upper-class audiences, for example by replacing female role specialists (*onnagata*) with female actors, the abolition of the *hanamichi* walkway and raised *chobo* platform of *jōruri* narrators and shamisen players, a review of the system for selling tickets through teahouses attached to theatres, the radical improvement of playscripts, and the construction of Western-style

---

1 This chapter breaks from the reference precedent in noting only the year when significant Japanese critical works were published. In this way, we hope to describe the broad trajectory of modern Japanese drama criticism, yet make Japanese references readily accessible to those reading Japanese.

theatres, of which the principal model at that time was the opera house. Yet such proposals were summarily rejected as superficial by theatre aficionados and literati such as Tsubouchi Shōyō, the pseudonymous Muichian Muni and Nihontei Shōfū, and Mori Ōgai.

Alternative views of the development of a modern theatre also emerged from Ishibashi Ningetsu, who called for a Western-style dramaturgy based on Aristotle and Lessing (1890), while Nagai Tetsu (1884) and Taniguchi Masanori (1887) adopted chronological Western styles of historiography to explain Japanese drama. Newspaper critics, such as Aeba Kōson, Sugi Ganami, Matsui Shōyō, Oka Onitarō, Morita Shiken, and Okamoto Kidō, campaigned for better plays less subject to the preferences of theatre owners. Miki Takeji established the journal *Kabuki* (1900–14), combining scholarly inquiry and insight. Thus modern theatre criticism in Japan was born.

One genre that emerged unrelated to kabuki reform was *shimpa*. Originating in the Freedom and Popular Rights Movement of the 1880s, shimpa was gradually established as a realist genre reflecting Japanese social mores. Although employing kabuki-like stylization, it has retained broad popular appeal to this day, with important critical studies including those of shimpa actor Yanagi Eijirō (1937, 1948, 1966, 1977). Comprehensive studies of this fertile and controversial premodern era include works by Matsumoto Shinko (1974 and 1980) and Kobitsu Matsuo (1998 and 2001).

Mori Ōgai and Tsubouchi Shōyō

During the Meiji era, "drama" came to be called *engeki* (演劇) as distinct from *shibai* (芝居) referring mostly to kabuki plays. The two leading figures who sought to define this new engeki were Mori Ōgai and Tsubouchi Shōyō; their respective theories were to have a huge influence on later criticism, playwriting, and dramatic movements. Although they were equally opposed to the Theatre Reform Society, and both recognized the importance of dramatic texts, their viewpoints diverged in other respects. An army doctor who had studied in Germany and introduced the works of Goethe into Japan, Ōgai drew from Goethe in *Engekijō ura no shijin* (The poet behind the theatre, 1890) in arguing that drama was "a display of poetic sentiment." He maintained that drama possessed the power to transcend historical differences between two cultures as distinct as Japan and Germany.

Theatre for Ōgai had aesthetic significance, whereas for Shōyō drama was primarily valuable for its realism; he was to apply this belief to a range of genres, including historical and musical drama. Shōyō was basically conservative in outlook; his view of realism was founded on his love of traditional drama. In their anti-idealism debate (*botsuri ronsō*, 1891–2), begun as a debate on the significance of Shakespeare translation, Shōyō took an inductive approach that denied the subject, while Ōgai argued deductively, drawing on the aesthetic theories of Karl von Hartmann to emphasize the role of ideology. In terms of their influence, Shōyō's successors were the scholars Shimamura Hōgetsu and Kawatake Shigetoshi, and Ōgai's were directors Osanai Kaoru and Hijikata Yoshi.

If Shōyō was "English" in inspiration and Ōgai north European, then a younger leader of the new drama was the south European-inspired Kishida Kunio. Having studied in France under Jacques Copeau, his first collection of essays, *Warera no gekijō* (Our theatre, 1926), championed established plays of high literary quality performed with a new manner of speech delivery appropriate for modern Japanese drama. The journals he founded, *Higeki kigeki* (1928–9) and *Gekisaku* (1932–40), presented work by a series of talented young dramatists, contributing hugely to experiments in dramatic style and criticism. Significantly, the literary critic Kobayashi Hideo basically accepted Kishida's ideas, while recognizing the limits of literary drama in engaging audience sympathies (1936).

Modern drama

The two decades between 1906 and 1929 were some of the most productive in the history of Japanese theatre criticism, charting the remarkable rise of *shingeki* ("new drama") following the death of Ibsen in 1906; both Ibsen's dramaturgy and his social realism were vital influences. The appearance of new plays and organizations to produce them fostered a criticism based on an understanding of Western trends. Watsuji Tetsurō (1909) discussed the Bungei Kyōkai (established by Shōyō and Hōgetsu in 1906), and Mayama Seika the Jiyū Gekijō (established by Osanai Kaoru and kabuki actor Ichikawa Sadanji II in 1908). As one might expect, the accumulation of social capital through industrialization, together with shifting tastes of the times, influenced the theatrical world. When Hōgetsu launched his Geijutsu-za in 1913, he was thinking equally of dramatic art and of entertainment. This "dual path" garnered much support among his audiences, although his associates were fiercely critical of what they saw as a retreat from principles. Yamamoto's critique (1914) is typical of the antagonism between idealists and realists in the contemporary shingeki.

The main forums for writing about and criticism of new plays in the early period were journals such as *Shigarami sōshi, Waseda bungaku, Geijutsuden, Shinshichō, Subaru, Mita bungaku,* and *Shirakaba,* and journals for cognoscenti such as *Engei gahō* and *Shin engei,* on genres ranging from kabuki, shimpa, and shingeki, to *kigeki* (comedy). Representative of the new criticism are collections by Nakamura Kichizō (1913) and Komiya Toyotaka (1914). Miyake Shūtarō's essay "Shimbun engekihyō ni tadasu" (An inquiry into newspaper theatre reviews, 1917) represented a declaration of war on the older drama critics by younger ones with a clearer awareness of the issues, suggesting that a generational shift had already occurred. Although the basic form of modern drama was prose rather than verse, poetic dramas and criticism by Kitamura Tōkoku (1893) and Iwano Hōmei (1905 and 1906) also made significant contributions.

Osanai's rejection of the current Japanese theatre when he founded the Tsukiji Little Theatre in 1924 with Hijikata Yoshi had led to a fierce exchange of opinions among playwrights, notably Yamamoto Yūzō (1924), concerning differences over the meaning of "directing." As the "father" of shingeki, Osanai had been inspired by European directors such as Craig, Reinhardt, Stanislavski, and Meyerhold, and in essays such as "Nihon engeki no shōrai" ('The future of Japanese drama, 1928) he clarifies his own understanding of East–West theatre. Since a majority of shingeki companies active today trace their lineage to the Tsukiji Little Theatre it has been the object of many academic studies, including those by Osanai (1928) and Hijikata (1969) themselves, and testimonies of people directly associated with the company, such as assistant director Mizushina Haruki (1931), special effects artist Yokokura Tatsuji (1976), stage designer Yoshida Kenkichi (1971), and spectator Asano Tokiichirō (1970).

Criticism of traditional drama also developed markedly in the 1920s. Artist Kishida Ryūsei noted the picturesque qualities of kabuki in *Engeki biron* (Theatre aesthetics, 1930), Ishiwari Matsutarō (1930) and Miyake Shūtarō (1930) wrote on bunraku, while Sakamoto Setchō's reviews established the conventions of noh criticism.

Proletarian drama, the commercial theatre, and the Asia-Pacific War

The proletarian drama movement in Japan was to a large extent underpinned by anarchist ideology. Prosperity resulting from World War I promoted the growth of the working class in new cities and the rise of mass culture. This in turn raised critical interest in the popularization of the arts, or rather in artistic activities by ordinary people. Figures central to the debate were literary scholar Honma Hisao (1916), anarchist Ōsugi Sakae, who translated Romain Rolland's essays (1917), and sociologist Gonda Yasunosuke in "Minshū goraku mondai" (Issues of popular entertainment, 1921). However, with the formation of NAPF (All Japan Federation of Proletarian Arts) in 1928 and its affiliate, PROT (Japanese Proletarian Theatre Federation), and especially an article by one of PROT's leaders, Kurahara Korehito (1928), the movement took a more uniformly Bolshevik line.

On the critical side, figures such as Murayama Tomoyoshi, Sano Seki, and Hijikata Yoshi, and on the theoretical side Kubo Sakae, Sugimoto Ryōkichi, and Senda Koreya, contributed actively to the movement's journals, *Puratto* and *Engeki shimbun*. Yet the two main leaders, Murayama and Kubo, disagreed about everything, and after PROT was dissolved in 1934 and replaced by the leftist Shinkyō Gekidan (an association of modern theatre companies), the familiar battles over social realism were fought again, with Murayama standing for "developmental realism" (1934) and Kubo for "anti-capitalist realism" (1935). Murayama was the organizer and Kubo the writer, although both of them tended to emphasize the voice of their members above their personal opinions. Miyoshi Jūrō (1952) questioned this dogmatism and left the organization, promoting the individual's private resistance to authority in postwar years.

Between the 1930s and the 1940s, the literary Kishida faction stood out prominently against the proletarian movement that had engulfed the theatre world, but it was the commercial theatre that represented the greater challenge. In the marketing of both productions and performance methods, the contribution of businessman Kobayashi Ichizō in founding the Takarazuka Revue (1913) and Tōhō production company (1932) are paramount. Shōyō had himself been a keen advocate of popular drama (1918), and his ideas on a "new national theatre" were to some extent fulfilled by the success of the Takarazuka Revue. Moreover, the periodicals Kobayashi founded, *Kageki* (since 1918) and *Tōhō* (1934–74), were not simply promotional outlets for his companies but critical forums for reviews of popular theatre the critics had previously ignored. Indeed, contributions to a special issue of *Tōhō* on *Gendai taishū engekiron* (Theories of popular drama in the present age, 1937) by Kubo and others reveal significant splits of opinion on the purpose of "mass drama."

The organization of an arts festival by the government's propaganda bureau in 1940 to celebrate 2,500 years of imperial rule, together with voluntary dissolution of the Shinkyō and New Tsukiji theatre groups, was symbolic of the subordination of Japanese theatre to the new military order, from this time through 1945 entirely subject to militarist control. "National (*kokumin*) theatre" became the new keyword of drama criticism, albeit in a somewhat distorted fashion due to pressure imposed by the regime. Representative of this movement are Ōyama Isao's collection *Kokumin engekiron* (National theatre theory, 1943), with limited opposition from playwright and critic Iizawa Tadasu and critic Hanamori Yasuji.

Politics versus art in the postwar era

The end of the war in 1945 and the ensuing Allied Occupation had a complex effect on those theatre groups who had been politicized in the prewar shingeki movement. To start with, the Allied authorities (GHQ) allowed left-wing and shingeki groups and popular entertainers to work freely, as "they had been suppressed under the wartime system," while traditional theatre such as kabuki was restricted for its feudal contents. Murayama's article "Shingeki no susumu michi" (A way forward for shingeki, 1946) and Niizeki Ryōzō's "Nihon engeki no dentō" (Japan's theatrical tradition, 1945) are historically significant statements for the restoration of the Japanese theatre.

At the same time, the "policy of liberation" confused the issue of wartime responsibility. Criticism of those who had colluded with the militarist regime was prominent from the popular theatre, for example comedian Furukawa Roppa's "Sensō riyōshatachi" (Quislings of Japanese theatre, 1945). A nude cabaret that opened at the Teito-za theatre in January 1947 and portrayal of a prostitute as lead in *Nikutai no mon* (Gates of flesh) at the Kūki-za that August – at a time when prostitution was all too evident in the early postwar society – were both critical sensations. The smarter critics and their publications did not take these productions seriously, but they were covered by tabloids such as the *Tokyo Times* and *Nikkan Sports*, as well as idol fanzines such as *Art Weekly* and *Screen Stage*.

The "red purge" of the 1950s took the shingeki anti-establishment wing once again into the kind of struggle that they had endured during the fifteen-year war. As the political associations of theatre came under scrutiny, the main voice of resistance came – not surprisingly – from Kishida, who sought to strengthen ties between literature and drama. His movement and the Kumo no Kai (Cloud Society) attracted wide support, including from such playwright and director luminaries as Mishima Yukio, Fukuda Tsuneari, Tanaka Chikao, Kinoshita Junji, and Senda Koreya, and created new opportunities for novelists to write plays (Kishida, 1950 and Miyamoto, 1951). Kishida's efforts enabled prewar experiments in dramatic style to be passed on to the postwar generation, achieving remarkable results, for example Tanaka's manifesto on the assimilation of metaphysical themes with dramaturgy in *Gekiteki buntai josetsu* (Introduction to dramatic style, 1977–8) and Kinoshita's revival of folktales as materials for contemporary drama in *Engeki no dentō to minwa* (Folk tales and theatrical tradition, 1956). Mishima's contribution is perhaps less easily explained. His short story *Onnagata* (The female role specialist, 1957)[2]

2 Donald Keene (trans.), *Death in Midsummer and Other Stories* (New York: New Directions, 1966); "Backstage essays," in Hiroaki Satō (trans.), *My Friend Hitler and Other Plays by Yukio Mishima* (New York: Columbia University Press, 2002).

and study of kabuki (1959), while written in a highly literary style, locate the onnagata, which had long been regarded as a theatrical oddity, in a new framework that transcended modern aesthetics.

Academic involvement in theatrical activities spurred an objective reexamination of the fifty years of shingeki activity that had passed since the Bungei Kyōkai and Jiyū Gekijō. Fukuda's essay "Engekiteki bunkaron" (A theory of theatrical culture, 1965) indicated basic faults in the historical direction of shingeki that were common to all of Japanese modernity, while Abe Kōbō (1959) sought to release modern Japanese drama from the spell of realism; both writers took a multifaceted approach to the issue of theatricality.

Senda instigated the initial postwar revolution in acting and actor training. He published the first practical theory of acting in Japan, *Kindai haiyūron* (The modern actor, 1949), and instituted the first practical courses in acting at the Haiyū-za company and later at Tōhō Gakuen College. Moreover, from the late 1950s Senda pioneered Brechtian drama and theory in the Japanese theatre. When introduced through translations of essays and plays, Brechtian anti-realism was readily absorbed by the experimental avant-garde, notably by *angura*, the underground theatre movement of the 1960s.

Critical repositioning since the 1960s

Japanese drama of all genres has experienced phenomenal growth and diversity since the 1960s, due in no small part to the groundwork laid by pioneers such as Osanai and Kishida. Yet while shingeki had been largely defined in modernist terms such as realism, the angura theatre of the mid-1960s and *ankoku butō* ("dance of darkness") sought to overcome the limitations of modernism by incorporating traditional Japanese performing arts and popular entertainments with Western performing arts. The positive reception of these innovative and unconventional theatre practices was due partly to the new critical approach grounded in the anthropology, folklore, and semiotics of Yamaguchi Masao, Nakamura Yūjirō, and Amino Yoshihiko, and to the reassessment of popular entertainments by Ōzawa Shōichi, Ei Rokusuke, and Takenaka Rō.

Much of the best post-1960s criticism was written by insiders, leaders of the theatre movement at that time: Terayama, Satoh, Kara, Suzuki, Hijikata, and Ohta.[3] Japan remains a country of public intellectuals

---

3 English translations of many sixties' theatre critics are found in David G. Goodman (ed.), *Contemporary Theatre Japan*, vols. I.1–II.4 (1969–73).

often independent of academe. Important criticism was and remains written by journalists for newspapers as well as magazines like *Shingeki* (Modern theatre), *Engekikai* (Theatre world), *Higeki kigeki* (Tragedy and comedy), *Teatoro* (Teatro), *Serifu no jidai* (Age of dialogue), and *Shiatā ātsu* (Theatre arts). Senda Akihiko, former theatre critic for the *Asahi shimbun*, covered the angura movement from its inception in the mid-1960s and his reviews are invaluable records of avant-garde theatre from the 1960s and 70s. Other important independent critics include Watanabe Tamotsu and Dōmoto Masaki, who write on both traditional and modern theatre. Ōzasa Yoshio's massive eight-volume history of modern Japanese theatre is a standard resource; worthwhile too are his collections of more occasional criticism. Some theatres also engage in publishing informative journals on contemporary performance, such as the Setagaya Public Theatre's *SEPT* and SCOT's *Engekijin* (Theatre people).

Essays and books on post-angura theatre criticism have been regularly published by critics including Nishidō Kōjin, Ōtori Hidenaga, Senda Akihiko, Uchino Tadashi, and Shichiji Eisuke. In academe, the Kindaigeki Kenkyūkai (Modern Drama Research Circle) of the Japan Society for Theatre Research has published several invaluable collections of essays and anthologies, ranging from early shingeki works to studies of individual playwrights including Kishida, Kubo Sakae, and Inoue Hisashi. The doyenne of modern drama studies in Japan, Inoue Yoshie has been an indefatigable editor and trenchant critic and scholar of twentieth-century and contemporary Japanese theatre and television drama, especially work written and performed by women. Such work has laid the groundwork for new revisionist studies of post-1960s culture and theatre in Japan. Uchino Tadashi and Iwaki Kyoko are two notable critics who write in both Japanese and English on the contemporary Tokyo theatre scene.

Academics who have spent time researching overseas have also helped introduce Euro-American playwrights and theoretical works to Japan, and contributed to international journals and books. These include Takahashi Yasunari (Beckett and Shakespeare), Kishi Tetsuo (Pinter and Shakespeare), Uchino Tadashi (Little Theatre), Mōri Mitsuya (Scandinavian and theory), and Takahashi Yūichirō (performance studies).

References and further reading

Hirata Oriza. *Engi to enshutsu* (Acting and directing) (Tokyo: Kōdansha, 2004)
Matsumoto Kappei. *Nihon shakaishugi engeki shi* (History of Japanese socialist theatre) (Tokyo: Chikuma, 1975)

Matsumoto Shinko. *Meiji engeki-ron shi* (History of Meiji theatre theory) (Tokyo: Engeki shuppansha, 1980)

Nomura Takashi (ed.). *Kindai bungaku hyōron taikei 9, engeki ron* (Modern literary criticism survey, theatre theory) (Tokyo: Kadokawa shoten, 1972)

Senda Akihiko. *Nihon no gendai engeki* (Japanese modern theatre) (Tokyo: Iwanami shinsho, 1995)

Sugai Yukio. *Kindai Nihon engeki-ronsō shi* (History of modern Japanese theatre debates) (Tokyo: Miraisha, 1979)

21 ∾ English language scholarship
A critical overview

DAVID JORTNER

Since the European "discovery" of Japan in the sixteenth century, diplomats, scholars, intellectuals, and artists have been fascinated by theatrical arts witnessed or read in translation. Many undertook the task of teaching and writing about Japanese theatre for Western readers, thus creating a genealogy (of sorts) of Western scholarship on Japanese theatre. This chapter on the English-language historiography of Japanese theatre will explore how narratives, translations, and studies of Japanese theatre have intersected with larger perceptions and geopolitical positionings of Japan and the West.

Any study of such a diverse field forces scholars to impose some order. In this study, works are divided into five major eras:

1 pre-Meiji era (–1868): amateur observation
2 Meiji to World War II (1868–1945): scholarly (primarily literary) recognition
3 Cold War (1946–66): overviews of theatrical performance and text
4 postmodern revolution to bubble economy burst (1967–91): global recognition and participant-observation
5 globalization to today (1991–2013): generational conversation and an end to exceptionalism.

As with any study of this sort, these are arbitrary delineations. Not all scholarly work can be mentioned; thus this chapter will merely suggest prevailing trends and attitudes. Areas of scholarship may overlap and boundaries may blur. Despite these limitations, it is hoped that this will serve as both overview of Japanese theatre scholarship in English and guide to current trends.[1]

---

1 For partial accounts or wider artistic influences see Ury Eppstein, "The stage observed: Western attitudes towards Japanese theatre," *MN* 48:2 (1993), 147–66 (early and Meiji), Hazel Durnell, *Japanese Cultural Influences on American Poetry and Drama* (Tokyo: Hokuseido 1983) (American literature), and Earle Ernst, "The influence of Japanese theatrical style on Western theatre," *Educational Theatre Journal* 21 (1969), 127–38 (postwar theatre).

Amateur description until 1868

The first Western observers of Japanese theatre were amateurs writing about performance in the context of their diplomatic or commercial visits. Under the Tokugawa shogunate's closed nation (*sakoku*) policy, foreigners were limited to treaty ports in Nagasaki and Yokohama; however, they occasionally saw theatre in cities such as Osaka and Edo as a part of specially arranged visits. Visitors included government officials, merchants, and/or scientists who went to the theatre as a part of their leisure time in Japan. Their diaries, letters home, and travel journals focus more on sociological description of theatre than aesthetic analysis.

The first English-language record of Japanese performance comes from the *Diary of Richard Cocks*. Cocks lived in Hirado, Nagasaki, from 1613 to 1623, serving as head of the British East India Company trading post. Cocks notes the presence of "cabuques" (kabuki) entertainers and performers at feast occasions.[2] Lord Rutherford Alcock's *The Capital of the Tycoon: A Narrative of Three Years' Residence in Japan* (1863) also mentions kabuki. He gave the first English-language description of this theatre, describing a kabuki performance, including details of seating and spectators. He also mentioned staging features more advanced than anticipated, including the *mawari butai* (revolving stage) and *hanamichi* walkway.

Much of Alcock's narrative concerns observations about the audience, "altogether bewildering when we try to judge them by our canons of morality or taste."[3] What seems to offend him most is the audience's lack of shame when witnessing sexual advances of a serving girl toward a loyal retainer. Many early observers experienced a similar cultural disdain for the morality espoused in Japanese entertainments, art forms not to be admired but rather a showcase for decadent, bizarre, and mysterious behavior.

Recognition as literature, 1868–1945

The second era of scholarship saw an enormous increase in the popularity and availability of Japanese texts. As Japan "opened" to the West, the world was exposed to Japanese culture. Scholars and travelers were essential to this endeavor. The Japanese also were active in promoting their culture abroad through exhibitions, scholarship, translation, and program guides. Translation was the primary means of transmission as Western scholars, with the

2 Richard Cocks, *Diary of Richard Cocks, Cape-merchant in the English Factory in Japan, 1615–1622: with correspondence* (London: Hakluyt Society, 1883).
3 Lord Rutherford Alcock, *The Capital of the Tycoon: A Narrative of Three Years' Residence in Japan*, vol. II (New York: Harper and Brothers, 1863), 112.

assistance of Japanese colleagues, attempted to describe a canon of drama corresponding to their own ideas about the roles, aesthetics, and purposes of literature.

At the same time that the Japanese government was transforming the nation's social and economic principles along Western models during the Meiji Restoration, Western artists and intellectuals became fascinated with traditional, "unimproved" Japanese culture. There followed an enormous growth of interest in all things Japanese, especially in its arts and literature. Many Western scholars and artists began to see Japan's appealing clarity and simplicity, proximity to nature and sensitivity to passing of seasons, asymmetric harmony, and decorative elaborations as a possible antithesis to the West. Artists and intellectuals were influenced by Japanese ideas and aesthetics; dealers and collectors sought the originals, while the *Japonisme* artistic movement embraced this culture for inspiration and source material.[4] Poets (Conrad Aiken, Amy Lowell, and Stéphane Mallarmé) and artists (Vincent Van Gogh, Claude Monet, and Paul Gauguin) were influenced by the Japonisme movement, spreading its influence throughout the West. Japanese expatriates and cultural ambassadors also popularized Japanese culture through writings such as Okakura Kakuzō's (1862–1913) *Ideals of the East* (1903) and *The Book of Tea* (1906), and Noguchi Yone's (1875–1947) *The Spirit of Japanese Art* (1915).

This era saw a resultant growth in availability of translations of Japanese plays, especially noh and kyogen drama. Scholarship showed a marked preference for translation, and subsequent comparison to Western texts, as opposed to an attempt to understand the written plays as texts for staged performance; publication (especially in journals, books and periodicals) was the norm.

Scholars fell into three camps. Some were invited by the Japanese government to lecture in the new university system (Edward Morse, Ernest Fenollosa, Robert Nichols, and Frank Lombard). Others were transient observers who wrote or lectured about their experiences on their return, such as Hermann Rosse. Finally, others were Japanese scholars or performers who had spent significant time abroad, fluent in English. These cultural mediators, including Okakura, Michio Itō (1892–1961), Noguchi, and Sakanishi Shio (1896–1976), provided translations in periodicals and produced anthologies of plays.

They were assisted by an increased awareness and eagerness for information about Japan in the West. This was seen in the growth of professional

4 Christopher Benfey, *The Great Wave: Gilded Age Misfits, Japanese Eccentrics, and the Opening of Old Japan* (New York: Random House, 2003); Victoria Westin, *Japanese Painting and National Identity: Okakura Tenshin and his Circle* (Ann Arbor: Center For Japanese Studies, University of Michigan, 2003).

journals and magazines, and the establishment of academic societies and foundations with a Japanese or Asian focus: *The Far East* (1870), *The Oriental Review* (1911), and *Monumenta Nipponica* (1938). All three published articles on Japanese theatre. The Japanese government also produced materials on their culture for Western audiences, especially as nationalist discourses fanned a groundswell of national pride in the 1930s. The Board of Tourist Industry published booklet-length introductions to noh by leading literature scholar Nōgami Tōyochirō (1934), an overview of *Japanese Drama* (noh, kabuki, and bunraku, 1935) and kabuki (1938). In addition, groups such as the Japan Society, London (1891) and of New York (1907) sponsored talks, lectures, and scholarship. These were all venues for the promotion of Japanese theatre and promulgation of knowledge to Western audiences.

Theatrical tours and exhibitions also promoted awareness of Japanese theatre. Theatre artists such as Hanako (Ōta Hisa) and Kawakami Otojirō and his wife Sadayakko went on theatrical tours of the United States and Europe. Morse and Fenollosa helped museums facilitate the purchase and exhibit of masks, costumes, and other performance artifacts (some newly available out of necessity when noh actors lost their shogunal patronage). Finally, the Meiji government sponsored a series of industrial expositions, drawing visitors from across the globe, where they saw a variety of Japanese performance forms.

Some Western scholars were increasingly concerned about the loss of traditions through Meiji Japan's policy of *bunmei kaika* (civilization and enlightenment). For the Japanese, this program of Westernization was necessary in order to "catch up" with the West in terms of science, technology, and public policy. Yet many Western scholars, having only recently been granted access to the country, felt Japan was losing its heritage. Ironically, even as they contributed to its demise, they saw their mission as historians, museum curators, and collectors to preserve "Old Japan."[5]

Scholarship during this period often saw theatre as an open window to understand Japanese culture, society, and psychology. Asataro Miyamori's foreword to *Tales from Old Japanese Dramas* (1915) declared:

> People in England and America probably do not realize what a large part is played by the Theatre in the life of the Japanese people. This volume will give them some idea of it; and, as a nation, like an individual, reveals perhaps more of its true self in its amusements than in the serious business of life, a perusal of these pages … may help towards a wider understanding of the Japanese national character.[6]

---

5 See Benfey, *The Great Wave*, 65.
6 Asataro Miyamori, rev. Stanley Hughes, *Tales from Old Japanese Dramas* (New York: G. P. Putnam, 1915).

These scholars connected theatre with nation, providing foreigners with an accessible perspective on its "exotic" culture and beliefs.

The reader's sense of Japan as unfamiliar territory also explains the preponderance of translations in this period, providing neophytes a base of information and awareness. Kyogen scholarship from this era is almost exclusively based upon translations; there are over twenty translated plays in magazines or journals from this era. In order to frame the alien art, the connection between kyogen and Western comedy was emphasized in explanatory notes. Several translated works contained passages explicitly linking the plays with classical theatrical tropes familiar to Western audiences. Michio Itō [Itow] and Louis Ledoux's translation of *She Who Was Fished* (*Tsuri onna*), used in recent stage performances and published in *The Outlook* magazine (1923), declares that kyogen "have the same use as the satiric dramas played by the Greeks at the end of their great trilogies, but are in some ways more closely akin to those rough comedies which preceded the development of Greek tragedy."[7] Arthur Sadler compares noh favorably to Western musical-drama, saying it is "somewhat equivalent of opera, though it avoids the artistic defect of this form of entertainment, the attempt to combine first-class singing with acting of the same grade and at the same time fitness for the part."[8] The ability to connect noh with Greek theatre, Italian commedia dell'arte, or opera may also explain the reasons for its popularity at a time when Jacques Copeau was rediscovering the classical tradition in French comedy using strict training methods somewhat modeled on Japan.

Shio Sakanishi's *A List of Translations of Japanese Drama* (1935) confirms the preponderance of noh and kyogen: there were approximately twice as many kyogen translated into English as there were kabuki, and twice as many noh texts as kyogen. This may reflect the length of the respective texts (noh and kyogen were shorter and thus more appropriate for journals or magazines) as well as their relative accessibility as texts. Western audiences may have had difficulty understanding the intricate neo-Confucian relationships in kabuki, but could more readily enjoy kyogen earthy farces or noh's ghostly tales.

The scholarly literature also illustrated a bias against popular or "degenerate" kabuki, echoing a similar one in Japanese scholarship toward homegrown vaudeville, music hall, and light opera. Basil Hall Chamberlain, for example, declaims, "From the Noh theatres of the high born and learned to the Shibai or Kabuki theatres of the common people is a great descent, so far as taste and poetry are concerned, though the interest of the more

7 Michio Itō and Louis Ledoux V, "She Who Was Fished (*Tsuri Onna*)," *The Outlook* (31 January 1923), 218–19.
8 Arthur Sadler, *Japanese Plays* (Sydney: Angus and Robertson, 1934), ix.

vulgar exhibitions, viewed as pictures of manners ... will be of greater interest to most foreign spectators."[9] Stories from kabuki were often summarized, but the scripts themselves untranslated. Arthur Sadler's *Japanese
Plays* and Zoë Kincaid's *Kabuki: The Popular Stage of Japan* (1925) were
rare exceptions. Reflecting native prejudices, noh and kyogen were still the
primary texts translated.

Many translations mentioned here would not hold up to contemporary
critical standards. Arthur Waley, for example, published *Nō Plays of Japan* in
1921, providing nineteen new translations. However, Waley's interest in the
noh was primarily literary, accordingly seeing it as "ammunition for modernism in its battle against realism."[10] As such, Waley's work inaccurately
highlights the triumph of poetic lyricism over pedantic authority. In most of
his noh translations, Waley cut the *aikyōgen* interlude speech to maintain the
"mood." (There is some question as to how much Waley knew about the role
of the aikyōgen, as they were in all likelihood not part of his source texts.)
While current scholars may take issue with Waley's decisions, his work succeeded in making noh relevant to his popular audience and provided new
models for the theatre (as evidenced by his explaining noh dramaturgy via
a noh version of *The Duchess of Malfi*): Copeau and Brecht knew of noh
through Waley's translations.

Many scholars shared a similar disdain for Western drama and believed a
greater understanding of Japanese theatre could lead to theatrical revitalization. Sheldon Cheney and Hermann Rosse wrote a series for *Theatre Arts*
magazine,[11] the latter describing the noh approvingly:

> whatever success the other types of theatre may attain, the ultra-stylistic,
> rhythmic-symbolical will always have its strong appeal ... How much more
> satisfactory artistically is it to have some splendidly trained, gorgeously
> dressed individual slowly emerge from the green-room, turn his masked
> head and mount his imaginary horse ... than the spectacular Western man-
> ager's ex-cavalry horses lumbering through some Tudor tilting match![12]

Like Waley, Cheney and Rosse saw Japanese theatre as a possible force for
revitalization of the Western art form.

Perhaps no figures espoused this more forcefully than Ezra Pound (1885–
1972) and Ernest Fenollosa (1853–1908). Fenollosa collected a great deal

---

9 Basil Hall Chamberlain, *Japanese Things* (London: John Murray, 1905), 463–4.
10 John W. DeGruchy, *Orienting Arthur Waley: Japonism, Orientalism, and the Creation of Japanese
Literature in English* (Honolulu: University of Hawai'i Press, 2003), 12.
11 Samuel L. Leiter, "When Theatre Arts looked eastward," in Stanca Scholz-Cionca and Samuel L.
Leiter (eds.), *Japanese Theatre and the International Stage*, Brill's Japanese Studies Library 12 (Leiden: Brill, 2000), 59–80.
12 Hermann Rosse, "Sketches of oriental theatres I," *Theatre Arts* 2 (Summer 1918), 142.

of material on noh through notes on lessons and translations (done largely by the uncredited Hirata Kiichi [pen-name Tokuboku, 1873–1943]). After his sudden death in 1908, his widow gave Fenollosa's translations and notes to Pound; with the assistance of Arthur Waley, he published *Noh, or Accomplishment* in 1916. The book, with its introductory notes and preface by W. B. Yeats, had a tremendous impact, influencing poet-playwrights Yeats, Wallace Stevens, T. S. Eliot, and Tennessee Williams, who saw it as a new theatrical manifesto. The integrity of these translations is questionable, as Pound admitted that he was more interested in the lyric quality of the work than in strict accuracy. Yet the book remains in print, testament to Pound's success in conveying noh through brilliant poetic license.

Postwar academic and popular interest, 1945–1966

The third era was defined by increased geopolitical awareness of Japan and subsequent investment in its culture by both Western scholars and nations. An unintended legacy of World War II, the Occupation, and Cold War was exposure of thousands of Westerners to Japanese culture. This era also saw an increase in universities and their scholarly presses, and academic appointments, all of which increased opportunities for theatrical scholarship. While translations remained popular, they tended to focus more on a single genre or performance type; kabuki and bunraku came to greater scholarly awareness. Finally, Japanese theatre tended to be analyzed more as unique performing arts, moving away from comparative studies with Western drama.

Fewer events have had a greater impact upon Western scholarship of Japanese theatre than the Second World War. Scholars naturally published little about Japanese performance at this time.[13] Yet the aftermath of the war, especially the Occupation of Japan (1945–52), the Cold War, and the ethos of military preparedness (including conscription in the United States and Great Britain) exposed many budding scholars to the field. Faubion Bowers, Earle Ernst, and Donald Keene were either introduced to Japanese language and literature or gained further education due to their wartime and reconstruction activities. Service in the Occupation forces resulted in lengthy stays in Japan for some; Bowers and Ernst oversaw and censored theatre.[14] Ironically through their work as censors for film and theatre, these scholars grew to appreciate kabuki and bunraku; in several cases they acted as advocates for

13 There were several translations of noh plays as well as an article on Zeami's treatises in *MN* 3:2, 3:4, and 4:1 (1940–1). *Life* magazine published an essay on *Chūshingura*, claiming the play "reveals the bloodthirsty character of our enemy." "The 47 Rōnin," *Life* (1 November 1943), 52.
14 Samuel L. Leiter (ed.), *Rising from the Flames: The Rebirth of Theater in Occupied Japan, 1945–1952* (Lanham, MD: Lexington Books, 2009).

the art form. In addition, the United States maintained (and continues to maintain) military bases in Japan that opened up Japanese culture and theatre to scholars throughout the Cold War.

The Cold War and resultant positioning of Japan substantially increased awareness and scholarship of Japanese theatre as the United States government (along with Western allies) shifted perceptions of Japan as defeated enemy to valued partner. This was partially accomplished through cultural histories that reconstructed Japanese identity in the West. "[A]s part of a national project to cultivate friendly relations during the cold war... kabuki was energetically promoted as a way for Americans to learn about and develop appreciation for Japanese culture – and thus replace negative wartime images."[15] Awareness of Japanese classical theatre was enhanced further through goodwill/promotional tours undertaken by kabuki troupes. These included the 1954 Azuma Kabuki troupe tour and 1960 Grand Kabuki tour, both to the USA.[16] They were preceded by a flurry of scholarly and popular articles explicating kabuki to American audiences, including multiple essays in popular media by Bowers[17] and scholarly work by Scott.[18]

The postwar era planted seeds that bore fruit in the tremendous growth in the American and British university systems beginning in the 1960s. Before, specialist scholars were affiliated with schools in Japan, but now many found work within emergent Asian studies, Japanese language, or theatre departments of domestic universities such as the School of Oriental and African Studies, University of London (P. G. O'Neill and later C. Andrew Gerstle), University of Hawai'i (Earle Ernst and James R. Brandon), University of Wisconsin (A. C. Scott), Pomona College (Leonard Pronko), Columbia University (Donald Keene), and Brooklyn College (Samuel L. Leiter and Benito Ortolani).

This expansion of Asian theatre scholarship within Western higher education had numerous repercussions. The creation of Japanese language/ literature and theatre programs gave many scholars a supportive base; in many instances, these institutions strenuously encouraged their research, practice, publication, and travels. Asianists integrated Japanese theatre history and practice into undergraduate and specialist graduate classes,

---

15 Barbara Thornbury, "Negotiating the foreign: language, American audiences, and theatre from Japan," *Theatre Journal* 6:2 (2009), 256.

16 Technically, the Azuma troupe tour was a combination of kabuki and *nihon buyō* dances, acrobatic performances, and musicians, nonetheless promoted in the United States as "kabuki." Kevin Wetmore, "1954: selling kabuki to the west," *ATJ* 26:1 (2009), 78–93 and Barbara Thornbury, "America's kabuki-Japan 1952–1960: image building, myth making and cultural exchange," *ATJ* 25:2 (2008), 193–230.

17 Faubion Bowers, "Kabuki is Broadway bound ..." *Theatre Arts* 37 (September 1953), 66–8; "Concerning kabuki," *Saturday Review* (27 February 1954), 22–5.

18 A. C. Scott, *The Kabuki Theatre of Japan* (London: George Allen and Unwin, 1955).

cultivating the next generation of scholars. The growth in Japanese theatre activities at universities also paralleled a growth in university presses such as Hawai'i, Michigan, Cornell, and Columbia publishing translations and other scholarly works on Japanese theatre by this new generation of specialists. Finally, these schools actually staged plays and even created programs (both undergraduate and graduate) that emphasized Asian theatre; some, supported by the Japan Foundation or Culture Ministry eager to put a cultured, human face on the economic machine, were able to bring in masteractors for long-term workshops and directing. The University of Hawai'i, for example, created the first Asian theatre program in the United States in 1950; Scott at Wisconsin created the Asian Experimental Theatre Program in 1963.

There was also a push to introduce readers to Japanese theatre as a performing art, and to provide cultural context. Bowers' *The Japanese Theatre* was aimed at a general audience and served as a good introductory text. Other introductory books were also generated for visitors going to Japan (Figure 56); for example, *The Kabuki Handbook* by Aubrey and Giovanna Halford is "not a history of Kabuki nor an aesthetic appreciation, but a playgoer's manual, a guide" with synopses for over a hundred kabuki plays. Similarly, noh summaries were published by O'Neill and Murakami Upton, and kyogen by Don Kenny.[19]

This era also saw the publication of works geared toward scholars and artists. Earle Ernst's *The Kabuki Theatre* (1956) was representative of books placing Japanese performance into cultural and historical contexts. This era also saw the beginnings of specialized scholarship on music, audience, dance, and design. These not only explored more specific elements of the Japanese theatre, but helped move scholarly dialogue away from theatre as literary pursuit toward performance.[20]

Interest in kabuki and bunraku rose. The scholarly move of kabuki from popular theatre to "classical" theatre spurred a dramatic increase in research and publication. While until 1945 there were only four scholarly works on kabuki, the period 1946–68 saw over thirty. Previously only one article had been written solely about bunraku;[21] in the 1960s both A. C. Scott[22] and

19 Faubion Bowers, *The Japanese Theatre* (New York: Hermitage House, 1952); Aubrey and Giovanna Halford, *The Kabuki Handbook* (Rutland, VT: Tuttle, 1956), xv; P. G. O'Neill, *A Guide to Nō* (Tokyo: Hinoki shoten, 1955); Murakami Upton, *A Spectator's Handbook of Noh* (Tokyo: Wanya shoten, 1963), and kyogen by Don Kenny, *A Guide to Kyogen* (Tokyo: Hinoki shoten, 1968).

20 Earle Ernst, *The Kabuki Theatre* (Oxford: Oxford University Press, 1956); William Malm, *Traditional Japanese Music and Musical Instruments* (Tokyo: Tuttle, 1959), and John Lovel, "Theatre audiences of Japan," *Theatre Survey* 5 (November 1964), 99–106. These works often included photographs of stage productions in order to clarify performative ideas.

21 See Zoë Kincaid, "The puppet in Japan," *Theater Arts* 13 (March 1929), 207–9.

22 A. C. Scott, *The Puppet Theatre of Japan* (Rutland, VT: Tuttle, 1963).

Fig 56 From Francis Haar, *Highlights of Japanese Theatre* (Tokyo: Tuttle, 1952). The jealous woman ascends the stairs to the Dōjōji Temple bell, watched by priests. Stage assistants prepare to drop the bell.

Donald Keene[23] published book-length studies, the latter a copiously illustrated large-format book.

Theatre as a performed (and experienced) art, 1967–1991

The fourth scholarly era continued analytical study of Japanese theatre as performing art. A growth in graduate programs and linguistically proficient scholars was matched by a theatrical community that embraced Japanese theatre and performance theories. There was a distinct increase in available translations, not only of plays but also of important theoretical manifestos. The participant-observer also now emerged: artist-scholars training either in Japan or with Japanese theatre companies as a part of their scholarly work.

23 Donald Keene, *Bunraku: The Art of the Japanese Puppet Theatre* (New York: Kodansha, 1965).

One reason for this growth in Western scholarship was the expansion of masters and doctoral programs, both in Japanese language and literature and in theatre arts. These programs produced a generation of scholars and practitioners who were linguistically capable and interested in participating in performance training as well as writing about it. The establishment of the field of performance studies as a disciplinary area in the 1980s also shifted scholarship from textual-based criticism toward anthropological contextualization and performance; this allowed greater integration of Asian performance forms into mainstream curricula. Japanese theatre as seen through the refractory lens of director-theorists Craig, Copeau, Artaud, Brecht, Grotowski, Brook, Schechner, and Barba led Western avant-garde historians back to Asia. These graduate programs also trained the next generation of faculty, thus increasing the number of scholars employed in the study of Japanese theatre. This led naturally to a corresponding increase in scholarship; articles about Japanese theatre began to appear in non-specialist journals such as *Theatre Journal* and *TDR*.

The implementation of context and seeing the theatre as performance is embodied in works such as Peter Arnott's *The Theatres of Japan*, which includes chapters on early dance performance, noh theatre, kabuki, and the modern stage, and informatively discusses dramatic literature from a European comparative perspective. Japanese influences abroad are documented by kabuki specialist Earle Ernst.[24] Leonard Pronko's *Theater East and West* (1967, revised 1974) similarly combined a spectator's passion with a scholarly eye for telling detail, an inspiring and influential work of scholarship that examines Asian theatre forms as tools for the reinvigoration of the Western stage. Unlike previous eras, which viewed such work in an "orientalizing" spirit, Pronko sees that "Asian theater can offer us a rich repertoire of techniques on which we may draw, seeking out Occidental parallels to oriental classical forms. Not imitation, but re-creation."[25] Pronko includes not only detailed descriptions and analysis of both noh and kabuki but also their potential for adaptation for Western stage productions and audiences. The continuing potency of this manifesto is evidenced by the spectrum of essays by scholars and artists in many fields contributing to *Theatre East and West Revisited* (*Mime Journal*, 2006), where Barba declared it "a book with legs."

---

24 Peter Arnott, *The Theatres of Japan* (St. Lucia: University of Queensland Press, 1967); Earle Ernst, "The influence of Japanese theatrical style on Western theatre," *Educational Theatre Journal* 2:1 (1969), 127–38.
25 Leonard Pronko, *Theater East and West: Perspectives toward a Total Theater* (Berkeley: University of California Press, 1967), 5.

This era saw the rise of the participant-observer: scholars either trained in and performing with Japanese theatre traditions, or observing those companies first hand. While such activities had occurred previously, growing accessibility and ease of travel gave scholars a plethora of performance, training, and observation opportunities. Richard Emmert and Karen Brazell trained in noh; Donald Keene, Don Kenny, Laurence Kominz, and Jonah Salz in kyogen. Pronko, Brandon, and Andrew Tsubaki attended the National Kabuki Theatre's training program, distilling its teachings for transmission to their own university students and workshops to actors, and informing their publications. David G. Goodman, Tsuno Kaitarō, and Fujimoto Kazuko, members of avant-garde Theatre Center 68/69, published Japan's first English-language theatre journal *Concerned Theatre Japan* (1969–73).[26] As Brandon wrote of this "third wave": "They learn the intrinsic values of the performing system by assimilation, directly and without the intermediacy of a Western interpreter … they enter that cultural world, not solely as scholars or observers as in the past, but as 'doers'."[27] This idea of scholars as "doers" was being reenacted throughout Western universities; however, there is some irony in the idea of vanguard theatre practitioners "discovering" classical Japanese forms.

For contemporary theatre artists, the Saratoga International Theatre Institute and Suzuki Company of Toga offered workshops in director Suzuki Tadashi's (1939–) acting methods. Others took workshops in butoh dance or martial arts. The University of Michigan under William Malm practiced various Japanese musical instruments. Many scholars took advantage of these programs; they learned experientially as well as from texts, then shared that information with the academic community.

Scholars during this period tended to be linguistically sophisticated. Many were fluent in Japanese and/or had lived in Japan for a substantial amount of time; thus they were familiar with idiomatic and contemporary expressions. Translations they produced were significantly more accurate than those of previous years. Moreover, there was an astounding amount of material, often extremely specific, translated and published, on specific genres (Keene (ed.), *Twenty Plays of the Nō Theatre*, 1970) or eras (Goodman, *Return of the Gods: Japanese Drama and Culture in the 1960s*, 1988), some with copious stage directions and photographs facilitating understanding of performance. Rimer and Yamazaki's elegant translation of Zeami's treatises (1984), and Rimer's translation of Suzuki (1986) exposed Westerners to historic and

26 Despite *Concerned Theatre Japan*'s limited impact upon its initial run, it provided a basis for much of later scholarship on 1960s *angura* (underground) theatre.
27 James R. Brandon, "A New World: Asian theatre in the West today," *TDR* 33:2 (1989), 36.

current aesthetic ideas which were embraced by both scholars and Western theatre artists who saw possibilities inherent in incorporating Japanese theory with Western (often) avant-garde theatre.

Shingeki (modern theatre) also received scholarly attention. While there had been a significant number of shingeki translations previously, scholarship on shingeki as well as the avant-garde *angura* and *shōgekijō* (little theatres) only began to develop in the 1970s. Publications began placing individual shingeki playwrights in their theatrical contexts, for example Rimer's Kishida Kunio (1974), as well as multiple biographies of Mishima. Translations of shingeki often included significant notes detailing sociopolitical contexts.

One way in which information on recent scholarship and touring companies was shared was through the Association for Asian Performance (AAP) and its journal, the *Asian Theatre Journal* (*ATJ*). Originally formed as the Afro-Asian Theatre Project in 1965, AAP serves the scholarly community as a locus and clearinghouse for information through conferences, its website, and the *ATJ*, published biannually. As the primary Western journal solely dedicated to the scholarly study of the performing arts of Asia, *ATJ* has been at the forefront of Japanese theatre scholarship, with over 150 scholar and artist members across the globe. Since 1983 it has published over twenty Japanese plays in translation as well as articles ranging from noh to contemporary political performance.

An end to Japanese exceptionalism, 1991–present

The current era, from the collapse of the Japanese bubble economy in 1991 to the present, has seen a wide variety of scholarship, of both traditional and new genres. The sheer amount of scholarly material available in English has reached a critical mass where scholars are now able to build upon earlier English-language works. This period has seen a greater specificity in scholarship, with works being produced on specific companies, playwrights, or eras. There is an awareness of groups outside the theatrical mainstream as well as increasing availability of English-language materials written by Japanese scholars. This has facilitated an end to the idea of Japanese exceptionalism and placement of Japanese theatre within a global theatrical context.

The earlier proliferation of university positions led to scholars of Japanese theatre becoming established in programs with graduate students, thus generating a second and third generation of Western scholars with strong interest in Japanese theatre. These scholars built upon the work initiated by their mentors/colleagues, creating a scholarly "conversation" about

Japanese theatre. Shelley Fenno Quinn's *Developing Zeami* (2005) builds off the work of Rimer (1933–), Hare (1952–), and Ortolani (1928–), among others.

Many publications also have a specific focus from a historical and/or a performative point of view, including the four-volume *Kabuki Plays on Stage* (edited by Brandon and Leiter, 2002–3) and ten-volume *Half a Century of Japanese Theater* produced by the Japan Playwrights' Association (2000–6). Both contribute new translations but also include substantial prefaces placing the plays and authors within their cultural and historical contexts. Copious stage directions, photographs, and/or floor-patterns helped novices imagine the actual performance.

Notable historical records of Japanese theatre have been published, including broad overviews (Ortolani's *The Japanese Theatre*, 1990) and more specific time frames (Brian Powell's *Japan's Modern Theatre*, 2002). Still others have been even more specific, covering a relatively narrow period and genre (such as Brandon, *Kabuki's Forgotten War 1931–1945* [2009] or Leiter's *Kabuki at the Crossroads: Years of Crisis 1952–1965* [2013]), or individual genres in socio-perspective (Robertson, *Takarazuka*, 1998). Scholarly examinations have been written of theatre by marginalized cultures/identities in Japan. Scholarship on women in Japanese theatre has been a popular topic and focus of special editions of journals *Women in Performance* and *TDR*. Works such as Edelson's *Danjūrō's Girls* (2009) and Ayako Kano's *Acting Like a Woman* (2001) have led to reassessing the role of women in Japanese theatre history. Finally, Japanese scholarly materials have become available in English, such as Kawatake Toshio (traditional theatre), Takahashi Yasunari (Beckett, Yeats), Senda Akihiko (play criticism), Kishi Tetsuo (Shakespeare), Mitsuya Mōri (comparative theatre), and Uchino Tadashi (contemporary theatre). Many of these scholars spent time at Euro-American academic institutions, bringing comparative theoretical perspective to their work.

The spread of technologies such as video recording and the Internet have made the world of Japanese theatre that much more accessible to both scholar and neophyte. Video recordings of Japanese performance forms have increased in both popularity and availability in the West, some with English subtitles. Japanese theatre now has a significant presence on the Web; sites exist for the genre as a whole as well as for specific performance forms. Likewise, numerous Internet sites (many bilingual) exist for individual playwrights, companies, and/or performance venues. The Japanese government's informative sites include ones devoted to UNESCO-designated noh-kyogen, bunraku, and kabuki, and, through the Japan Foundation, interviews with contemporary artists on the Performance Art Network. The newly bilingual online Comparative Theatre Review (www.jstage.jst.go.jp/browse/ctr) introduces contemporary Japanese theatre scholarship.

The sense of "Japanese exceptionalism," itself a holdover from both the end of Meiji and the Cold War eras, has dissipated in the past decade. "Japan" is no longer seen as extraordinary and, as a result, Japanese theatre forms such as bunraku are viewed not only in a Japanese context but also in the global context of puppet performance. Partially this is a result of moving into a postnationalist discourse. While previous theatre history textbooks included separate chapters on Japanese, Chinese, or "Oriental Theatre," thus excluding them from mainstream (i.e. Western) theatre history,[28] the recent *Theatre Histories* replaces the standard Western narrative of theatre history texts (which often only had a single chapter on Asia/Africa) with "a global perspective that allows the performances of many cultures to be considered, not in the margins of western theatre but in and of themselves, and as they illuminate each other and our understanding of human expressiveness at large."[29] For example, kabuki theatre is not seen as unique or "othered" but contrasted with seventeenth-century French theatre in a chapter on "Theatre and the state."

Japan, as a nation, has also established a world presence through the export of popular culture, again disrupting its sense of the country as "exotic." "Cool Japan" films, martial arts, food, television, and manga have penetrated Western markets; these are familiar gateways through which a new generation of scholars may discover performative roots. On the more elite level, sponsored exhibitions of masks, costumes, fans, and photographs are often accompanied by well-illustrated catalogues with scholarly comment (Leiter, *Japanese Theater in the World*, 1997). Internationally minded directors like Suzuki, Ninagawa Yukio, Noda Hideki, and Hirata Oriza are regular presences at international theatre festivals and European touring circuits – inspiring translators and scholars to integrate their global Japanese sensibilities into Western academic discourse (Thornbury 2013).

This period also saw historiographical analyses of Western views on Japanese theatre, including Ury Eppstein's "The stage observed: Western attitudes towards Japanese theatre."[30] Kevin Wetmore's extensive taxonomy of "Modern Japanese drama in English"[31] and Iezzi's "Kyōgen in English: a bibliography"[32] have compiled an exhaustive list of resources in English. Such works demonstrate the increased awareness of and resources on Japanese

---

28 See Carol Fisher Sorgenfrei, "Desperately seeking Asia: a survey of theatre history textbooks," *ATJ* 14:2 (1997), 223–58.

29 Phillip Zarrilli, Bruce McConachie, Gary Jay Williams, and Carol Fisher Sorgenfrei, *Theatre Histories: An Introduction* (New York: Routledge, 2006), xvii.

30 *MN* 48:2 (1993), 147–66.   31 *ATJ* 23:1 (2006), 179–205.   32 *ATJ* 24:1 (2007), 211–34.

theatre in English, as well as a sufficient corpus to examine them as historical documents.

Still, one wonders if Japan will continue to draw Western scholars as it has in the past century. As demonstrated above, geopolitical events of the twentieth century helped to put Japan at the forefront of the Western imagination; such events both figuratively and literally moved Westerners onto the Japanese islands and promoted the study of Japanese culture. In 2014, East Asian awareness is centered more on China than Japan; it is not surprising that more money and resources and students are flowing now to the study of Chinese language and culture. This has resulted in an increase in Chinese theatre scholarship (as language programs shift from Japanese to Chinese), presaging a potential decline in funding for and Western interest in Japanese theatre scholarship. Nonetheless, new technologies and innovations, such as the spread of multilingual websites, video, reference systems, and image catalogues (e.g. GLOPAD, www.glopad.org/jparc/ and that of the Waseda Theatre Museum) allow scholars even greater access to Japanese performing arts archives than ever before.

Among non-Western theatres, the Japanese stage is the most researched and studied by Western scholars. It is not coincidental that the first Asian book in this Cambridge series written by numerous experts is *A History of Japanese Theatre*. English-language scholarship has a significant history of its own, illustrating the conflicts, confusions, and misunderstandings present at the intersection of Western scholarship and Japanese theatre. From the earliest amateur recordings of performances, where it was regarded with suspicion, through the growth of the *Japonisme* movement and resultant explosion, writings on Japanese theatre reveal as much about Western orientalist attitudes as they do about their subject. Scholars throughout the Cold War era saw this as well, but also had an awareness of Japanese theatre as a performance form with a rich history outside a Western context. The postmodern revolution and emergence of participant-observers brought a new generation of scholars who saw possibilities for greater education and artistic creation; these scholars were also often able to navigate the difficult issues involved in cross-cultural study.

Japanese theatre has now become firmly canonized as one of the great forms of world theatre; the study of its classical, modern, and contemporary genres is now firmly ensconced as part of Western theatre history and theory curricula. It continues to influence Western artists and scholars; further study will continue to develop new comparative works or explore lesser-known playwrights, dramatic works, and theatres.

References and further reading

Cody, Gabrielle H., and Evert Sprinchorn (eds.). *The Columbia Anthology of Modern Drama* (New York: Columbia University Press, 2007)

Thornbury, Barbara. *America's Japan and Japan's Performing Arts: Mobility and Exchange in New York 1952–2011* (Ann Arbor: University of Michigan Press, 2013)

Interlude: University scholarship and training

NAKANO MASAAKI

Translated by JONAH SALZ

The state of Japanese academic research may be understood somewhat through examining the major scholarly societies and journals related to Japanese theatre. All established scholarly groups ceased during World War II; present organizations were reestablished in the postwar years.

The all-encompassing Japanese Society for Theatre Research (Nihon Engeki Gakkai, 1949–, www.jstor.org) covers not just Japanese but all the world's stages, in all periods. As of 2014, there were over 630 members. The annual conference solicits papers on a given theme, such as "Takarazuka" (2013) or "Theatre and media" (2011). *Theatre Studies: Journal of JSTR* is published biannually; there are today also four sub-divisions of the Society. The focus of the Modern Japanese Theatre History Working Group (1975–) is on modern dramatic texts; although they do not publish a journal, they have produced several monographs on Kishida Kunio, Inoue Hisashi, and other prominent figures. The Theatre and Drama in Education Working Group (1985–) examines theatre education from a practical perspective, publishing *Research in Drama and Theatre Education* annually. The Comparative Theatre Working Group (1988–) explores foreign theatre and inter-culturalism, publishing the *Comparative Theatre Review*, in both English and Japanese; it has been available online (www.jstage.jst.go.jp/browse/ctr) since 2012. These groups are based in Tokyo, while the Modern Theatre Working Group (1990–), renamed the Modern and Contemporary Theatre Working Group in 1998, publishes *Modern Theatre Studies*.

There are individual societies for a number of playwrights, including Yeats, Wilde, Beckett, and Miller, as well as large, active IASIL (Anglo-Irish Literary Society) and Shakespeare associations.

Traditional folk and classical performance genres have several general and genre-based research societies. The Japanese Society for History of Performing Arts Research (1963–) publishes the journal *Geinōshi kenkyū* (History of the performing arts), and holds annual meetings for both scholars and practitioners. The 2013 meeting featured "Visual documentation of traditional arts," with contributions from scholars, archivists, and documentary film-makers.

There are separate societies for the study of noh, kyogen, and bunraku. The Association for Kabuki (1987–) publishes *Kabuki Studies*, and the Association for Noh and Kyogen Studies (2002–) publishes *Noh and Kyogen*. The Japanese branch of the AICT (Association Internationale des Critiques de Théatre)/ IATC (International Association of Theatre Critics–Japan, 1981–) publishes *Theatre Arts* and Kansai region's *Act*. An annual report, in both Japanese and English versions, is published by the International Theatre Institute/Japan branch *Theatre Yearbook: Theatre in Japan* (ITI, iti-japan.or.jp).

University and academy theatre programs

While it is evident that the study of theatre history and theory has been recognized as appropriate for research, in comparison with Euro-American countries Japan has a paucity of theoretical or practical theatre courses offered for academic credit. Theory and history are taught at Waseda University (1946–), Meiji University (1938–), Kyōritsu Women's University, and, in Kansai, Osaka University. Under the leadership of Tsubouchi Shōyō, Shimamura Hōgestu, and Kawakate Shigetoshi, the Theatre Museum at Waseda University (1928–) was developed into a research center with a vast collection of materials in Euro-American theatre, kabuki, and bunraku, many available in the searchable database (www.waseda.jp/enpaku). Kishida Kunio established a theatre program at Meiji University, specializing in Japanese and European modern and contemporary theatre. Kyōritsu hosts the only women's college theatre program, with valuable archive materials on European theatre. In Kansai, Osaka University's graduate program in theatre studies (1975–), which produces the bulletins *Studies in Theatre* and *Intermission,* continues to lead research in theatre outside of Tokyo (www.let.osaka-u.ac.jp/theatre).

Academic training in theatre

Actor training has traditionally been done through apprenticeship, whether under a master within an established school in traditional forms, or in a young actors' academy within one of the large shingeki companies like Bungaku-za or Mingei. Most actors learn on the job; university drama clubs have served as incubators for many *angura* and contemporary theatre troupes. Yet gradually, physical training in dance and theatre has become accepted within academic curricula nationwide. Practical training programs are offered in Tokyo at Nihon University (1921–), Obirin University (2000–), Tamagawa University (2003–), Tama Art University (1999), and Tōhō Gakuen College of Art and Music (1966–). The private Nihon University has a long history of nurturing students in a wide variety of arts courses in addition to theatre, including film, broadcasting, photography, and the fine arts. The Tōhō program succeeded the Haiyū-za training program, developing actors for a range of productions from straight plays to musicals. These five programs collaborated to form the League of Tokyo Theatrical Arts Universities in 2013.

In Kansai (Kyoto-Osaka), programs in theatre are offered at Osaka Arts University (1974), Kinki University (1988–), and Kyoto University for Arts and Crafts (1991–). The latter boasts the Shunju-za, Japan's first university-sponsored theatre, capable of hosting straight plays as well as grand musicals (with an orchestra pit but also with a rotating stage, lifts, and *hanamichi* for kabuki). Their Performing Arts Center publishes the stimulating, theme-based journal *Butai geijutsu* (Performing arts). Recently, students wishing to become stage, film, television, and animation voiceover artists have been trained there, and indeed nationally there has been a growing demand for practical theatre courses.

The vitality of modern Japanese drama is clear enough from the number of productions. However, the repeated closures of traditional companies, decline of newspaper drama review columns, changing commercial context, and diversifying audience base have led to increased uncertainty. As forces of digitalization and globalization continue apace in the twenty-first century, both Japanese theatre criticism and academic theatrical education have had to reconsider not only what they do and say, but also their relevance as institutions.

Reference and further reading

Tomita Hiroyuki. *Nihon engeki kyōiku shi* (History of Japanese theatre education) (Tokyo: Kokudosha, 1998)

PART VI
Intercultural influences

22 ✺ Seven stages of Shakespeare reception

DANIEL GALLIMORE AND MINAMI RYUTA

Japan has seen a variety of Shakespearean productions, adaptations as well as literal and less literal translations, since the first kabuki adaptation of *The Merchant of Venice* in 1885. Styles and conventions adopted in producing Shakespeare's plays reflect not only the development of modern Japanese theatre but also the country's shifting relationships with the imagined West. Shakespeare has been the most influential Western dramatist since the Meiji Restoration in 1868, still one of the most widely performed of all playwrights in Japan. This section offers a brief overview of how Japanese Shakespeareans have continually sought to create original styles of interpretation.

Patrice Pavis remarks that in intercultural theatre, the target culture preserves "only a few elements of the source culture selected according to very precise norms ... Every relationship with a foreign culture is determined by the purpose of the artists and cultural mediators who undertake its adaptation and its transmission."[1] The introduction of Shakespeare in Japan was similarly mediated. When *The Merchant of Venice* was produced in Japan in 1885, it was adapted into kabuki, then popular mainstream theatre, to reduce its foreignness. *Sakuradoki zeni no yo no naka* (Mercenary affairs under the cherry blossoms), contributed to "the construction of the modern Japanese nation ... through partial and often mutually contradictory identification with and differentiation from the West, as represented by Shakespeare."[2] Shakespeare thus served as a stalking horse for transforming Japanese theatre, but also, during the early stages of Shakespeare's reception in Japan, Western realistic or mimetic drama became the standard regarded as suitable for the development of a modern Japanese drama. Shakespearean plays staged in translation by *shingeki* companies in the 1950s and 60s indicate that Western, particularly English, productions enjoyed the canonical position of models to be imitated. By contrast, reflecting Japan's ascendancy to the status of

---

1 Patrice Pavis (ed.), *The Intercultural Performance Reader* (London: Routledge, 1996), 16.
2 Yukari Yoshihara, "Japan as 'half-civilized': an early Japanese adaptation of Shakespeare's *The Merchant of Venice* and Japan's construction of its national image in the late nineteenth century," in Minami Ryuta, Ian Carruthers, and John Gillies (eds.), *Performing Shakespeare in Japan* (Cambridge: Cambridge University Press, 2001), 21.

economic superpower in the 1980s, Ninagawa Yukio's (1935–) productions of *Macbeth* (1980) and *The Tempest* (1987) show how practitioners such as Ninagawa have finally been able to transcend their Western models.

The significant position that Shakespeare has occupied in Japan is also illustrated by English literary scholar Takemura Satoru, made during the period of militarism: "With the publication of Dr Tsubouchi's translation of Shakespeare's complete works, Japan is … now on equal terms with the Great Powers of the world."[3]

Referring to the pioneering translation of *The Complete Works* completed by Tsubouchi Shōyō (1859–1935) in 1927, Takemura clearly regarded reception of Shakespeare as a measure of a nation's culture and civilization, and means to differentiate Japan from so-called "inferior" Asian nations. This desire to absorb world civilization without forsaking national pride is asserted even more bluntly by a jingoistic slogan from a wartime English literature textbook: "Down with the Yanks and the Brits! They are our enemies … Seize Shakespeare! He is ours as well."[4] In the postwar era, Shakespeare has been a significant contributor to the development of Japan's cultural capital, with jingoism being replaced by economic nationalism and an enduring belief in Shakespeare's universality.

Seven stages of adaptation and interpretation

The history of Shakespeare's reception in Japan can be divided into seven stages along this intercultural continuum:[5]

1 "prehistory"
2 kabuki adaptations

---

3 Takemura Satoru, *Nihon eigaku hattatsu shi* (The development of English studies in Japan) (Tokyo: Kenkyūsha, 1933), 210.

4 Yamato Yasuo, *Eibungaku no hanashi* (Tales of English literature) (Tokyo: Kenbunsha, 1942), 1. It is also discussed in Minami Ryuta, "Shakespeare as an icon of the enemy culture in wartime Japan, 1937–45" in Irene R. Makaryk and Melissa McHugh (eds.), *Shakespeare and the Second World War: Memory, Culture, Identity* (Toronto: University of Toronto Press, 2012), 163–79.

5 Anzai Tetsuo suggests four stages: (1) adaptation in the Meiji era; (2) the shingeki movement in which Shakespeare was more read than staged; (3) revision of the shingeki movement by Fukuda Tsuneari between 1955 and 1970; (4) the Little Theatre Movement from the late 1960s, followed by Shakespeare productions in Odashima Yūshi's translations. See Anzai Tetsuo (ed.), *Nihon no Sheikusupia hyakunen* (A hundred years of Shakespeare in Japan) (Tokyo: Aratake shuppan, 1989), 3–15. Later, Anzai revised this division with a fifth stage, which begins with the opening of the Tokyo Globe in 1989. See Anzai, *Kanata kara no koe* (Voices from the other side) (Tokyo: Chikuma shobō, 2004), 297–328. Murakami Takeshi, who takes performance scripts performance as his main criterion, divides the reception history into seven periods: (1) adaptations, 1885–1905; (2) adaptations and Tsubouchi Shōyō's translations, 1906–*c*. 1920; (3) Tsubouchi Shōyō's translations, 1920s–*c*. 1960; (4) Fukuda Tsuneari's translations, 1960s; (5) rival translations I, *c*. 1970–4; (6) Odashima Yūshi's translations, 1975–85; (7) rival translations II, *c*. 1985–. See Murakami Takeshi, "Shakespeare and *Hamlet* in Japan: a chronological overview," in Ueno Yoshiko (ed.), *Hamlet in Japan* (New York: AMS Press, 1995), 239–308.

3 *shimpa* adaptations
4 early shingeki translations
5 mature shingeki replication of British productions
6 Little Theatre adaptations in contemporary style
7 reinvention.

Although the stages are in roughly chronological order, there are inevitable overlaps, as traditional genres such as kabuki continued adapting Shakespeare in the early twentieth century even as shimpa and shingeki troupes were beginning to do the same, while a hundred years later different genres stage Shakespeare in a spirit of coexistence, sometimes even collaboration.

Coincidence and appropriation

The first stage presents a kind of "prehistory" of Shakespeare performance in Japan. A couple of pre-Meiji kabuki plays contain striking albeit wholly coincidental similarities with *Romeo and Juliet*, although it is likely that Shakespeare's name did not become widely known in Japan until Nakamura Keiu's translation of Samuel Smiles' *Self-Help* (1859), which quotes a few of Polonius' lines from *Hamlet*. Touring productions by the Miln Company (1891) and Allan Wilkie Company (1912) provided Japanese audiences with rare opportunities to see Shakespeare performed in his original language.

The second phase covers 1885 to the early 1900s, when Western books and plays, including Shakespeare, were adapted for the kabuki theatre as it sought to modernize or Westernize itself. Numerous adaptations and free translations appeared in print, although it was only Udagawa Bunkai's adaptation of *The Merchant of Venice* (1885, mentioned above) that can be considered part of the actual reform movement. Toward the end of the 1890s, kabuki reverted to strictly Japanese materials, bowing to the more progressive shimpa companies who were also staging contemporary docudrama, Sino-Japanese war front "reportage," and stage versions of newspaper serials and novels.

The third phase centers on shimpa adaptations of Shakespeare, which started in 1901 with the Ii Yōhō Company's staging of *Julius Caesar*, followed by Kawakami Otojirō's (1864–1911) landmark productions of *Othello, The Merchant of Venice*, and *Hamlet* in 1903, with his wife Kawakami Sadayakko (1871–1946) in the lead female roles. These shocked purists with their use of modern dress, not to mention Hamlet's initial appearance down the *hanamichi* walkway riding a bicycle. Sadayakko's sensual Desdemona and Ophelia were also novelties for audiences accustomed to all-male kabuki.

The fourth stage, in which Shakespeare plays became available in una-dapted versions both in print and on stage, began with the Bungei Kyōkai (Literary Arts Association) productions of *Hamlet* in 1907 and 1911. These used new translations by Tsubouchi, which remained in general use through the 1960s, and also mark the beginnings of shingeki theatre: actresses played female roles for the first time. Shingeki practitioners began to establish a modern drama distinct from traditional theatre by endeav-oring to stage contemporary naturalistic or expressionistic plays exactly as they were produced in Europe. During this fourth phase, Shakespeare became a subject read and studied rather than staged, since most shingeki companies preferred to perform politically progressive modern Euro-pean plays. Professional Shakespeare production ceased in 1938 with the worsening international situation, but quickly resumed after 1945, at the initiative of Japanese actors rather than the Allied occupiers. *A Mid-summer Night's Dream* was staged under Hijikata Yoshi's direction at the Teikoku Gekijō (Imperial Theatre) in 1946, while Zenshin-za's 1947 *The Merchant of Venice* toured nationally to local factories and community centers.

Yet Shakespeare was still not considered as important as living Japanese and Western playwrights until the rise of Fukuda Tsuneari (1912–94) and the Bungaku-za (Literary Theatre) in the 1950s, leading to the fifth phase. Fukuda's production of his own translation of *Hamlet* for the Bungaku-za in 1955 is considered especially important, revising shingeki notions of natu-ralism through an impeccable imitation of the London Old Vic 1953 pro-duction Fukuda had personally witnessed starring Richard Burton. Thus, Fukuda's influential production was still a replica of a Western model, as were other typical shingeki Shakespeare productions, inevitably raising con-cerns about originality.

Traditional theatre reentered the Shakespearean arena at this time as well. In 1960, Fukuda directed kabuki actors Matsumoto Kōshirō VIII (1910–82) as a noted Othello and Nakamura Kanzaburō XVII (1909–88) as Richard III, exploiting their theatrical presence rather than actual kabuki acting techniques. More recently, Ninagawa cast the kabuki actor Arashi Tokusaburō (1933–2000) as one of the witches in *Macbeth* (1980), perform-ing the play's famous opening scene in kabuki style; over the past decade Ninagawa has cast kabuki *onnagata* as Shakespearean heroines, for example Ichikawa Ennosuke IV (1975–) as Katharina in *The Taming of the Shrew* (2010), although again for their distinctive presence rather than use of spe-cific techniques.

The sixth phase dawned with the Royal Shakespeare Company's three visits to Japan in 1970, 1972, and 1973, together with the Bungaku-za's

∾ SPOTLIGHT 22.1   Colonial *Othello* in Taiwan

The 1903 adaptation of *Othello* was meant as a first step toward achieving what Kawakami Otojirō referred to as *seigeki* ("legitimate theatre," or dialogue-based straight plays without singing and dance, as opposed to kabuki).[6] The setting and casting were modified to suit the Japanese context, with Muro Washirō, Kawakami's Othello, being dispatched as governor-general of the post-First Sino-Japanese War (1894–5) colony of Taiwan to pacify the natives and *dohi* (insurgents) (Figure 57). This production was significant both as an expression of existing gender hierarchies through Shakespeare's early modern mixed-gender play, and as colonialist spectacle. Robert Tierney further sees it as an opportunity for Kawakami to improve actors' status from outcastes to respected members of imperial Japanese society.

REPRODUCING GENDER HIERARCHIES

Kawakami and Sadayakko had recently returned from their extensive and pioneering tour of Europe and the United States, with the anticipation that Sadayakko would fulfill her mission of becoming the leading modern stage actress of imperial Japan. As Kano Ayako has documented, Sadayakko's achievement was significant in the formation of gender categories in modernizing Japan:

> She performed the role of an exotic geisha-girl while abroad, thereby confirming the schema of an Orientalized and feminized Japan objectified by the West, and then returned to Japan to perform the role of a modern girl supporting the modern masculine Japanese national subject, thereby contributing to the reproduction of imperialism.[7]

The first heroine she played on her return was the submissive and virtuous Desdemona, murdered by her jealous husband Othello.

Kawakami apparently decided that Desdemona, the most virtuous and submissive of Shakespeare's heroines, required no modification for the Japanese stage. Kawakami tellingly gave as reason for choosing *Othello* the fact that it has few strong female parts in comparison with Shakespeare's other plays, many of which include important active roles for women.[8]

Leading roles in Kawakami's version are filled, predictably, by Japanese officers who governed colonial Taiwan, and who also dictate the direction of the play. In contrast, women have few stage appearances and few lines when they do appear on stage, and are very much secondary to the drama's exposition. Both Desdemona (Tomone) and Emilia (Omiya) the wife of Iago (Iya Gōzō), performed by kabuki actress Ichikawa Kumehachi, are merely victims whose fate is to be murdered. Likewise, the prostitute Bianca (Biwaka), who chases after Cassio (Katsu Yoshio), vanishes with hardly a word spoken, having received off-hand treatment from Cassio and being driven away.

In the Kawakami adaptation, Sadayakko contributed to the reinforcement and partial redefinition of gender roles then underway in the modern nation-state of Japan. Moreover, the provocative impact of tabooed sexuality between Othello and Desdemona, performatively all the more visible on stage due to the miscegenation in the original, is completely absent from the Japanized version, although Washirō is referred to as *burakumin* (a traditional outcaste group in Japanese society) and the couple's wedding is Christian, when Christian activities were severely curtailed in 1890s Japan.

COLONIALIST IMAGININGS –
REPRESENTATIONS OF INDIGENOUS
TAIWANESE

Immediately prior to the opening performances, Kawakami risked a field expedition to Taiwan, where he made two discoveries: natives living on the so-called "Island of Pirates" (the Penghu, or Pescadores) and indigenous people,

---

6 This chapter is translated and adapted from the author's book *Joyū no tanjō to shūen* (2008).
7 Ayako Kano, *Acting like a Woman in Modern Japan: Theater, Gender and Nationalism* (London: Palgrave Macmillan, 2001).
8 Otojirō Kawakami, "'Osero' o totta riyū (Why I chose *Othello*)," *Kabuki* 34 (1903), 21.

Fig 57 Kawakami Otojirō (center) in *Othello* (1911) transferring Shakespeare's Cyprus to Taiwan, a recently colonized territory.

disparagingly referred to in imperial Japan as *seiban*, literally "uncultivated barbarians," if opposing Japanese rule, or otherwise *dojin* (native brigands). The verbal exchange that takes place between native and mountain indigenous manservants in novelist Emi Suiin's (1869–1934) script speaks clearly of the stereotypical racial class structure in the colony segregating Japanese, *Shinajin* (Han Taiwanese of Chinese descent), and seiban.

The resistance of the indigenous and Han Taiwanese proved a headache for imperial Japan in the governance of Taiwan, the colonial authorities seeking to control and suppress the two groups under separate policies. In the Kawakami adaptation, the Han Taiwanese are depicted as cunning people who exploit the aboriginals for financial gain, and their way of speaking is caricatured as broken Japanese. Of course, Kawakami did not bring any actual seiban back with him from Taiwan for performances. Thus what took place on stage was "a strangely perverse imitation"[9] in which "we Japanese" performed "those natives" exclusively for an audience consisting of Japanese, without any thought given to the returned gazes or discourses of the aborigines.

Apart from being made to sing folk songs, the "seiban" represented by the Kawakami troupe had no lines to speak, but simply "hopped and leapt about screaming some sort of incantation."

Although representations of seiban in the 1903 *Othello* adaptation at the Meiji-za were limited to the opening scenes of Act IV, these being inserted casually to impart a little comic relief, Kawakami did not neglect to service the desires of the imperial subject, then riding high on the mounting wave of nationalism between successful campaigns against China and Russia. The Kawakami troupe, having played at being typically "Japanese" in response to the exotic gaze of audiences in the Western empires, now, back in Japan, played at being "Western" colonial masters who subject indigenous peoples in colonies to their rule. This *Othello* was about colonial power and pride, not about the perils of interracial relations. Its hierarchies were clearly evident: Japanese imperial officers, including the burakumin Washirō, Japanese females, Taiwanese of Chinese origin, loyal natives, and finally the rebellious and barbarian aboriginals.

IKEUCHI YASUKO

9 Sakai Naoki, "Kyōkan no kyōdōtai to hinin sareta teikokushugiteki kokuminshugi 2" (The community of sympathy and disavowal of imperialistic nationalism 2), *Gendai shisō* (Contemporary thought) (May 1995), 25

Shakespeare Festival in 1972. The Shakespeare productions of this period reflect shingeki's response to the Sixties' *shōgekijō undō* (Little Theatre Movement) or *angura engeki* (underground theatre). Some companies turned for inspiration to traditional or indigenous theatrical arts and dance, and some to circuses and side shows given at festivals in shrine precincts, and some young shōgekijō companies staged adaptations of Shakespeare plays reflecting contemporary political unrest. Some shingeki companies tried to present Shakespeare as immediate and relevant to contemporary audiences, these attempts culminating in Deguchi Norio (1940–) and his Shakespeare Theatre's remarkable staging of the complete Shakespeare canon and Ninagawa's large-scale commercial Shakespeares of the 1980s, both continuing today. The sixth phase, therefore, shows how theatre practitioners were influenced by Jan Kott's view of Shakespeare as their "contemporary," moving away from strict imitations of English language productions toward developing their own native styles.[10]

Demythologizing Shakespeare

The Japanese Shakespeare "boom" of the 1970s and 80s owed much to accessible published Shakespeare translations by Odashima Yūshi (1930–), popularized in performance by Deguchi's Shakespeare Theatre between 1975 and 1981. Ninagawa also used Odashima's version for his legendary samurai *Macbeth*, and continued to use the Odashima translations until he initiated his staging of the complete Shakespeare canon (the Sai-no-Kuni Shakespeare Series) in 1998, since when he has employed instead the female translator Matsuoka Kazuko (1942–). Odashima's translations are sometimes mistakenly called "colloquial"; his style remains poetic and non-realistic, but sounds crisper and less dignified than precursors like Fukuda, and enjoys wordplay. Crucially, his phrasing was much easier to handle for young actors who had started their careers with Little Theatre troupes rather than shingeki companies such as Bungaku-za, which generally emphasized literary values over physicality.

The trend of the seventh phase has been toward experimental, even radical, interpretation and internationalization of "Japanese" Shakespeare, both legacies of the shōgekijō movement. The maturity of Shakespeare in Japan was signified by the opening of the Tokyo Globe in 1988, an indoor replica of London's Globe Theatre with state of the art facilities. The Tokyo Globe not only staged a string of Shakespeare productions but also offered young actors opportunities to work with noted Japanese and foreign directors. One

10 Kott's *Shakespeare Our Contemporary* was published in Japanese in translation in 1968.

who developed there was Yamazaki Seisuke (1957–), who launched a pioneering "Shakespeare for Children" project with *Romeo and Juliet* in 1995. Yamazaki's innovative, physical, minimalist productions have turned out to be successful in training young actors as well as popularizing Shakespeare. When the Tokyo Globe was closed in 2002, Yamazaki took over "Shakespeare for Children," staging seventeen Shakespeare plays in characteristically reduced and physical format.

To those working in the shōgekijō movement, Shakespeare was no longer sacred. Freed from shingeki's conventional staging methods and bardolatry, shōgekijō practitioners successfully produced Shakespeare's plays in their own way, often drastically rewriting them. Directors such as Ninagawa, Suzuki Tadashi (1939–), and Kurita Yoshihiro (1957–) have taken their productions overseas, and Suzuki has gained particular renown for his deconstructive interpretations, including *Don Hamlet* (1972), *Lear* (1984), *Macbeth* (*Sekai no hate kara konnichiwa*: Greetings from the end of the world, 1991) and *Juliet* (1993). He has also directed *Lear* with American actors, *Macbeth* for the Playbox Theatre in Melbourne, Australia (1992), and *King Lear* for the Moscow Art Theatre (2004). Practitioners of the younger, post-shōgekijō generation such as the playwright, actor, and director Noda Hideki (1955–) also became popular in the late 1980s. Noda's productions of *Twelfth Night* (1986), *Much Ado about Nothing* (1990), *Richard III* (1990), and *Midsummer Night's Dream* (1992) were characteristically frothy and postmodern in style. A more recent example of the radical approach is Gekidan Shinkansen's *Metal Macbeth* (2006), a sci-fi/heavy metal rock musical. Under its director Inoue Hidenori (b. 1960), the company recreates Shakespeare plays, including *Richard III* (2009) and *Othello* (2011), as contemporary pop theatrical events, referring broadly to trending culture, music, and manga.

Tradition and reinvention

This final phase of Shakespeare's reception (so far!), which may be called the age of reinvention, is one that has continued into the early twenty-first century, not only of Shakespeare but of traditional Japanese theatre. Ueda Kuniyoshi (1934–), who has worked on noh adaptations of Shakespeare's plays since the 1980s, has created *Othello* (2000), *Hamlet* (2004), *King Lear* (2007), and *Romeo and Juliet* (2015) with professional noh masters according to the aesthetics of noh drama.[11] Odashima's former colleague at Tokyo University, Takahashi Yasunari (1932–2002), a Lewis Carroll and

---

11 See also Minami Ryuta, "Is no Shakespeare in Noh Shakespeare?" in Be Bi-qi Beatrice Lei and Ching-Hsi Perng (eds.), *Shakespeare in Culture* (Taipei: Taiwan National University Press, 2012), 181–201.

❧ SPOTLIGHT 22.2 Ninagawa's *Macbeth*

Ninagawa Macbeth was not only a landmark production in the career of director Ninagawa Yukio (1935–) but also epoch-making in terms of the maturity of Shakespeare production in Japan and international recognition of Japanese culture. Premiering in Tokyo in 1980, when presented at the Edinburgh International Festival in 1985, it brought Ninagawa instant acclaim, leading eventually to an annual series of touring productions to London that continues today (Figure 58).

The concept of a Japanese *Macbeth* was already well known through the popular film adaptation *Kumonosujō* (Throne of blood, 1957) by Kurosawa Akira (1910–98) using noh masks to universalize characters as specific types. Like Kurosawa, Ninagawa set his production in premodern Japan, albeit in the late sixteenth rather than the fifteenth century, but, unlike the wandering cinematic eye, Ninagawa's audience was focused squarely on a massive proscenium arch in the shape of a *butsudan* (Buddhist altar). The transition from medieval Scotland to Japanese medieval feudal society, with its supernatural belief systems, was straightforward.

Ninagawa was inspired by the family altar where he would offer prayers of consolation. One day, as he was conversing with the souls of his dead father and elder brother, it occurred to him that atrocities as terrible as those in *Macbeth* could have been committed by his ancestors, or even by himself had he been born into different circumstances. Ninagawa had also expressed shock at the Japanese Red Army lynching of fourteen of its own members in 1972 in the mountains near Tokyo, believing that the universality of Shakespeare's play lay in this common history of human carnage. Although the Red Army incident marked Ninagawa's personal break with 1960s radical politics, he was still influenced by the participatory style of 1960s *angura* (underground) theatre, seeking to break down any barriers to empathy imposed by *Macbeth*'s supernatural elements. When Macbeth

was cornered at the end of the play, a noise similar to teargas used by Japanese riot police could be heard. Although Ninagawa had shifted in the 1970s from overtly political to commercial theatre, his *Macbeth* seemed to synthesize these two aspects, undoubtedly a political statement against excesses on both sides.

EVANESCENCE AND POWER

The performance begins with two old crones (who could represent mothers of lynched Red Army victims) moving slowly down the aisle onto the stage to the tolling of a Japanese temple bell. Offering prayers to the dead, they join the audience as witnesses to Ninagawa's vision of fallen warriors, thus framing the performance of Shakespeare's *Macbeth*. The universality of this vision is heightened by the gradual replacement of the temple bell with the dreamy Sanctus from Fauré's *Requiem* and Samuel Barber's elegiac *Adagio for Strings*. The traditional Japanese cultural trope of the continual descent of cherry blossoms throughout the performance connotes the transience of warriors' lives. Macbeth was deluded into believing that these blossoms represented fragile impermanence when they actually became Malcolm's unstoppable army in disguise.

The aesthetic beauty of the *mise-en-scène* appealed to British audiences at a time of admiration for Japan's economic success. *Guardian* critic Michael Billington thought he had never seen "a production as achingly beautiful" (19 September 1987), while Japanese response to the spectacle was also positive:

> This stage picture speaks to a basic sense of beauty in Japanese culture, an image that always shows a double meaning: extravagance and unease, life and death, triumph and corruption, eternity and the moment, flourishing and silence, the sublime and the coarse.[12]

These lyrical effects served to support mannered and histrionic performances by Hira Mikijirō as

---

12 Senda Akihiko, *The Voyage of Contemporary Japanese Theatre*, trans. J. Thomas Rimer (Honolulu: University of Hawaiʻi Press, 1997), 126–7

Fig 58 Ninagawa Yukio's samurai *Ninagawa Macbeth* (1980).

Macbeth and Kurihara Komaki as Lady Macbeth. Despite praise for their kabuki-like acting, both came from the modern Japanese theatre. Indeed, the production's success as a whole may be seen as representative of the achievements of modern theatre over the preceding eighty years in terms of its bold direction, articulate acting, sophisticated design, and, above all, original Shakespeare interpretation. Moreover, since Ninagawa had not originally intended to take the production overseas, and his so-called "Japanesque" concept was initially for the benefit of ordinary Japanese theatregoers unfamiliar with Shakespeare or radical Japanese drama, *Ninagawa Macbeth* should be considered not a showcase for Japanese culture, but rather a significant step in the director's journey to interpret Shakespeare afresh for Japanese audiences in a theatrical language they could understand.

DANIEL GALLIMORE

Beckett scholar, also scripted a couple of lively kyogen adaptations of Shakespeare comedies for Nomura Mansaku (1931–) and his son Nomura Mansai (1966–): *Horazamurai* (The braggart samurai, based on *The Merry Wives of Windsor*), and *Machigai no kyōgen* (The kyogen of errors, based on *The Comedy of Errors*, staged at the London Globe in 2001). Takahashi's son-in-law Kawai Shōichirō (1960–) has continued the tradition in less kyogenized but no less experimental formats, with Mansai contributing his distinctive skills to the roles of Richard III (*Kuni nusubito*: The country stealer, 2007), and *Macbeth* (2009). Kurita Yoshihiro's (1957–) Ryūtopia company also makes much of the signification of the noh stage, albeit in a somewhat eclectic style that employs kabuki actors and modern translations. They have so far staged *Macbeth* (2004), *King Lear* (2004), *The Winter's Tale* (2005), *Othello* (2006), *Hamlet* (2007), *The Tempest* (2009), and *Pericles* (2011), with *The Winter's*

Tale and *Hamlet* touring Europe in 2008 and 2010 respectively. Ryūtopia is highly representative of local Shakespeare productions that have cropped up over the last couple of decades. Based in northwestern Niigata (a traditional noh centre), it has always cast local amateurs in supporting roles alongside established professionals.

The nativization of Shakespeare in Japan has been inseparable from its internationalization, stretching back to early amateur productions by foreign residents in Yokohama in the 1860s. The last five decades have seen numerous exchanges with foreign companies such as Kenneth Branagh's Renaissance Theatre and directors like Terence Knapp and John Caird; directors such as Ninagawa, Suzuki, and Kurita have also "exported" their Shakespeare productions on foreign tours. Yet internationalization means more than the plain import and export of Shakespearean drama. In 1997, the Japan Foundation Asia Center produced their intercultural *LEAR*, written by Kishida Rio (1946–2003), a former Terayama Shūji collaborator, and directed by Singaporean director Ong Kang Sen (1963–). Artists from Japan, China, Thailand, and Indonesia collaborated on this inter-Asian production, a pioneering example of how theatre festivals and networks of Asian theatre artists have now made Japan a site where artists from different cultural backgrounds may encounter each other through Shakespeare.

Such reinventions owe much to the availability of multiple translations, notably those of Matsuoka and Kawai. Matsuoka started her project of translating the Complete Works with *Hamlet* in 1995, while Kawai began with the same play in 2003. Both work with leading directors, their translations primarily for specific productions, but also published for general readers. This unprecedented availability of translations has highlighted the instability of Shakespeare's texts in Japanese, encouraging some practitioners to stage their own versions. Writer-director Nakayashiki Norihito's (1984–) *Nyotai* ("female body") Shakespeare series, which started with *Nōsatsu* [*Seductive*] *Hamlet* (2011) followed by *Zecchō* [*Climax*] *Macbeth* (2012). Nakayashiki follows the plot faithfully, but draws on the casual idiolect current among young Japanese people.

It would clearly be mistaken, therefore, to assume that in its seventh stage or "age" Shakespeare performance in Japan has sunk into the state of "mere oblivion." Even if the volume of new productions has shrunk from the height of the Shakespeare boom (when, for example, there were no fewer than nine new productions of *A Midsummer Night's Dream* playing in Tokyo in 1989), the quality and diversity of production has surely grown, reflecting the drive toward creativity observed throughout this chapter, as well as contingencies such as the development of better theatres and technologies. Since Shakespeare is not a native playwright, there is no "national" Shakespeare theatre in Japan, although there are some theatre companies dedicated to Shakespeare performance with "Shakespeare" in their names, and Ninagawa's Sai-no-Kuni Saitama Arts Theatre in the suburbs of greater Tokyo comes quite close to fulfilling that role, at least in terms of popularity.

There can be no doubting Shakespeare's significance to the Japanese theatre. The playwright Inoue Hisashi, whose five-hour long *Tempō 12-nen no Shakespeare* (Shakespeare in the 12th year of the Tempō era, 1974) is a theatrical celebration of Japan's Shakespeare culture, claims the Bard is "a rice chest," a staple from which Japanese audiences continue to feed.

References and further reading

Kennedy, Dennis, and Yong Li Lan (eds.). *Shakespeare in Asia: Contemporary Performance* (Cambridge: Cambridge University Press, 2010)

Kishi, Tetsuo, and Graham Bradshaw. *Shakespeare in Japan* (London: Continuum, 2005)

Minami, Ryūta, Ian Carruthers, and John Gillies (eds.). *Performing Shakespeare in Japan* (Cambridge: Cambridge University Press, 2001)

Niki, Hisae. *Shakespeare Translation in Japanese Culture* (Tokyo: Kenseisha, 1984)

Sasayama, Takashi, J. R. Mulryne, and Margaret Shewring (eds.). *Shakespeare and the Japanese Stage* (Cambridge: Cambridge University Press, 1998)

Trivedi, Poonam, and Minami Ryuta (eds.). *Re-playing Shakespeare in Asia* (London: Routledge, 2010)

SPOTLIGHT 22.1 COLONIAL *OTHELLO* IN OKINAWA

Emi Suiin. "Hon'an Osero [1903]" (An adaptation of Othello), in *Sheikusupia honyaku bungakusho zenshū* (Anthology of translated works of Shakespeare) (Tokyo: Ohzorosha, 2000)

Ikeuchi Yasuko. *Joyū no tanjō to shūen: pafōmansu to jendā* (Birth and demise of the actress: performance and gender) (Tokyo: Heibonsha, 2008)

Tierney, Robert. "Othello in Tokyo: performing race and empire in early twentieth century Japan," *Shakespeare Quarterly* 62:4 (2011), 514–41

SPOTLIGHT 22.2 NINAGAWA'S *MACBETH*

Gallimore, Daniel. "Yukio Ninagawa," in J. E. Hoare (ed.), *Britain and Japan Biographical Portraits*, vol. III (Richmond, Surrey: Routledge, Japan Library, 1999), 324–37

Im, Yeeyon. "The pitfalls of intercultural discourse: the case of Yukio Ninagawa," *Shakespeare Bulletin* 22:4 (2004), 7–30

Kishi, Tetsuo. "Japanese Shakespeare and English reviewers," in Sasayama Takashi, J. R. Mulryne, and Margaret Shewring (eds.), *Shakespeare and the Japanese Stage* (Cambridge: Cambridge University Press, 1998), 110–23

Ninagawa Yukio, and Hasebe Hiroshi. *Enshutsujutsu* (The art of directing) (Tokyo: Kinokuniya shoten, 2002)

Senda, Akihiko. *Ninagawa Yukio no geki sekai* (The theatrical world of Ninagawa Yukio) (Tokyo: Asahi shimbun, 2010)

Yong, Li Lan. "Shakespeare and the fiction of the intercultural," in Barbara Hodgdon and W. B. Worthen (eds), *A Companion to Shakespeare and Performance* (Oxford: Blackwell, 2005), 527–49

INTERNET SOURCES

Global Shakespeares http://globalshakespeares.mit.edu/#

Shakespeare in Asia http://sia.stanford.edu/

23 ❧ Traditional training internationally

JONAH SALZ

Knowledge of Japanese traditional theatre outside Japan took many forms: from travel accounts by visitors, tours abroad, translations, and lecture-demonstrations (see Chapter 21, p. 463). For nearly a century, intensive, custom-made training programs by Japanese masters have existed, flourishing today in domestic and international courses and collaborations.

Fascination, imitation, acquisition, adaptation

As with so much else in twentieth-century intercultural performance, such experimental experiential learning began with Denishawn, the dance company of Ruth St. Denis and Ted Shawn. While on an extended tour of Asia in 1925 with a fifty-person troupe, they were particularly fascinated with kabuki, taking personal lessons from star actor Matsumoto Kōshirō VII (1870–1949) and his Fujima dance school. While in Tokyo, members trained four hours a day for thirty-six days at Imperial Theatre rehearsal rooms or rooftop, accompanied by shamisen. Film excerpts of young Denishawn dancers show a high-spirited but serious group absorbing the choreography of *Momijigari* (A maple-leaf viewing party).[1]

While recognizing the value of their experiences, the two company heads deviated on how best to appropriate the acquired techniques. Shawn, who had succeeded with his pseudo-Japanese *Spear Dance* (1919), learned how to apply authentic kabuki makeup, then purchased a wig, fans, and expensive costumes. He performed both Princess and Demon roles in a condensed version of *Momijigari* on Denishawn's triumphal return tour 1926–7 throughout the USA; however, it was not revived.[2]

---

1 From the Jacob's Pillow Dance Festival archive, MA. Dancers included future dance scholar Jane Sherman and dancer-choreographers Doris Humphrey and Charles Weidman, who write of the rigors and precision of the training. See Jane Sherman, *The Drama of Denishawn Dance* (Middletown, CT: Wesleyan University Press, 1979); Andrew Mark Wentink, "'From the Orient ... oceans of love, Doris': the Denishawn tour of the Orient as seen through the letters of Doris Humphrey," *Dance Chronicle* 1:1 (1977), 22–45; Ted Shawn, *One Thousand and One Night Stands* (Garden City, NY: Doubleday, 1960).
2 Japanese dance troupes in turn staged replications of Denishawn dances within a year of the troupe's departure. See *Denishawn: The Birth of Modern Dance* (West Longbranch, NJ: Kultur Films, 1992).

St. Denis had long been fascinated by Japan, studying dance with a "former geisha" in Los Angeles for six weeks prior to her acclaimed 1913 *O-Mika*. This employed remarkably authentic backdrops and costume; photographs displaying a stillness and frenzy perhaps influenced by Sadayakko, whom St. Denis had seen at Loie Fuller's Exposition in Paris. When actually visiting Japan, however, she contented herself merely observing; a promotional film catching her posing in kimono holding a shamisen. Like Shawn, she respected the forms and spirit she witnessed: "If you will master to any degree the Japanese art of dance, anything else you do will be better done. For … I know nothing, not even the ballet at its strictest, which can exceed the precision and discipline of Japanese technique,"[3] which, if mastered, "everything else you do will be better done."[4] Later in life, however, she advised objective observation rather than infatuated imitation, even going so far as to urge those smitten with Asian arts *not* to study there:

> [I]f you have creative qualities in your own spirit capable of being roused, capable of bearing a child by Japan … Japan is your husband. You go to Japan and you start imitating. You're not creating anymore; you're observing. You're giving a very good imitation … and you come back after maybe two years of study with some very excellent things, but they are not of the quality of your original ecstasy.[5]

St. Denis continued performing popular "oriental dances" on her return to the USA. However, despite their exotic external appeal, these were not replications but rather inspired adaptations of Javanese, Chinese, and Japanese dances. Her most successful solo dance was *White Jade* (1926), a Chinese-themed dance projecting the stillness and grace of Japanese and other Asian dance forms seen on tour.[6]

Disciplehood and diversity

The divergent Denishawn responses – authentic imitation versus creative adaptation – have continued as the opposing beacons by which artists have sought to steer via lessons in Japanese theatre, in Japan or in their home countries. While few performers could afford to spend significant time studying in Japan, some could nevertheless extend invitations to guest masters. Japanese

3 Agnes de Mille, *Martha: The Life and Work of Martha Graham, a Biography* (New York: Random House, 1956 [1991]), 44.
4 Jane Sherman, *The Drama of Denishawn Dance* (Middletown, CT: Wesleyan University Press, 1979), 151.
5 "Ruth St. Denis interview, oral history project" transcription (Berkeley: University of California Bancroft Library, 1985), 47–8.
6 Denishawn, *The Birth of Modern Dance*.

traditional theatre has been taught at overseas universities, professional academies, and theatre companies for half a century, and, more recently, offered as intensive workshops in Japan as well.

Table 23.1 lists the history of such programs in Japan or overseas that have been offered continuously or regularly.[7] There are literally thousands of one-day workshops, lecture-demonstrations, or semester-long residencies given all over the world by performers who, since the 1980s, include "workshop" in their vocabulary and pedagogy, even domestically. The majority of intensive programs are in the USA, whether because of the relative wealth of American funding organizations and universities, the lack of established training programs like those at European institutions, or the "pioneer spirit" of teacher-organizers. Training in traditional Japanese forms, along with Suzuki Method and butoh, has become a regular option in dance and theatre programs and other artistic institutions in the USA and Europe. Kabuki is taught, especially via its nihonbuyo dance forms, but the genre most inimical to workshops is perhaps bunraku. Because the remaining professional troupe is heavily subsidized and organized by the National Bunraku Theatre, plans for extended or domestic overseas workshops are hampered by performers' hectic schedules and caution for the precious puppets.[8]

Beginning in the 1960s, many non-Japanese began studying in Japan with Japanese masters in "disciplehoods" similar or identical to those of Japanese natives. Compared to the armchair Western critics who observed Japanese theatre in translation or on occasional tours, or scholars documenting performances in Japan, a distinct "third wave" arose from:

> the training which young Western actors, musicians, singers, puppeteers, and maskers are now receiving while living in China, Japan, India, Korea, Thailand, Indonesia, and elsewhere in Asia. They are enrolled in Asian theatre schools; they are the pupils of Asian master artists; they are learning to perform specific genres of Asian theatre. In such master–pupil relationships the centuries-old idea of Western political and cultural dominance of Asia is shattered, displaced, rendered obsolete.[9]

This third wave of participant-scholars has created new developments, both in Japan and in their home countries.

---

7 Not included here are nihonbuyo classes by resident teachers, such as Sachiyo Itō in New York or Kansuna Fujima in Los Angeles, who primarily teach to Japanese-American female hobbyists, seeking the same "beauty, grace, and elegance" of *buyō* training that many young women undertake in Japan, and a return to their roots. Hawaiʻi and the West Coast of the USA are particularly blessed with devoted licensed masters who develop their practice in ways similar to that in Japan, with regular costumed recitals and appearances at cherry blossom and summer festivals.

8 Martin Holman conducted intensive summer workshops with regional, community-based amateur troupes; the Tonda Bunraku Troupe in Shiga prefecture train foreign students in summer.

9 James R. Brandon, "A new world: Asian theatre in the West today," *TDR* 33:2 (1989), 36.

TABLE 23.1 Charting international training

Host Institute	Start	Organizer	Teacher	Noh	Kyogen	Kabuki
University of Hawaiʻi[i]	1951[ii]	Earle Ernst	Onoe Kikunobu, Kuroemon II			•
	1969	James R. Brandon	Nakamura Matagorō V, Ganjirō III (Sakata Tōjūrō IV);			•
	2004	Julie Iezzi	Nomura Shirō, Mansaku, Matsui Akira, Oshima Kimie. Shigeyama Akira, Shigeyama Dōji, Maruishi Yasushi	•	•	•
IASTA[iii]	1960	John D. Mitchell	Matsumoto Kōshirō			•
	1964		Kita Sadayo, Tomoeda Akiyo	•		
Pomona College, CA[iv]	1965	Leonard Pronko	Pronko			•
University of Illinois[v]	1969	Shozo Sato	Sato			•
Towson State, MD	1975					•
University of Kansas[vi]	1970	Andrew Tsubaki	Tsubaki	•	•	•
Canadian Academy, Kobe[vii]	1971	Mitsuko Unno	Fujima Kansome			•
University of Wisconsin[viii]	1972	A.C. Scott	Onoe Kuroemon II			•
	1981	Royall Tyler	Matsui Akira	•		
	2000	David Furumoto	Furumoto			•
ISTA[ix]	1980	Eugenio Barba	Sawamura Sōjūrō, Azuma Katsuko, Hanayagi Kankichi, Nomura Kosuke, Matsui Akira	•	•	•
Theatre of Yugen[x]	1981	Yuriko Doi	Nomura Mansaku, Nomura Shiro	•	•	
	1999	Jubilith Moore				
	2014	Tanroh Ishida				

Institution	Year	Organizer / Location	Artists	
Traditional Theatre Training[xi]	1984	Jonah Salz Kyoto Art Center	Udaka Michishige, Urata Yasuchika, Takabayashi Shinji, Katayama Shingo, Shigeyama Akira, Fujima Kansome, Nishikawa Senrei, Wakayagi Yayoi	•
International Noh Institute (INI)	1984	Rebecca Ogamo	Udaka Michishige	•
INI-Milan[xii]	1994	Monique Arnaud	Monique Arnaud	
International Theatre Institute (ITI), Japan Centre	1988	Odagiri Yoko	Nakamura Matagorō V, Sawamura Tanosuke VI, Kanze Tetsunojō, Nomura Man	•
SOAS "In the Noh"	1990	David Hughes	Matsui Akira	•
Theatre du Soleil	1991	Ariane Mnouchkine	Nomura Mannojō, Nakamura Matagorō,	•
ARTA[xiii]			Shigeyama Shime, Umewaka Norinaga, Fujima Kanjurō VIII	•
Portland International Performance Festival; Japan in Motion	1991–2002	Michael Griggs	Matsui Akira, Shigeyama Akira, Maruishi Yasushi, James R. Brandon	•
	2002–2012	Laurence Kominz	Laurence Kominz	•
NTP-Tokyo	1991	Richard Emmert	Emmert, Matsui, Oshima Kimie,	•
Bloomsburg, PA	1998	Betsy Dowd	David Crandall	•
Reading	2011	Ashley Thorpe	Emmert, Matsui	
Royal Holloway[xiv]	2014			•

TABLE 23.1 (continued)

Host Institute	Start	Organizer	Teacher	Noh	Kyogen	Kabuki
TTRP Singapore[xv]	2000	Kuo Pao Kun	Kanze school actors	•		
ITI	2012		Kuwada Takashi			
Nagomi no kai[xvi]	2010	Hybrl Ondrej	Shigeyama Shime, Motohiko		•	
Ryokurankai	2009	Jakob Karpoluk	Matsui Akira	•		

i James R. Brandon, "Kabuki in English: toward authenticity," in *International Conference Journal: Japanese Tradition: Search and Research* (Los Angeles: University of California Press, 1981); "Bridging cultures: 101 years of kabuki in Hawaii," in *Performing Arts of Asia: The Performer as (Inter)Cultural Transmitter, Working Papers Series 4* (Leiden: International Institute for Asian Studies, University of Leiden, 1996).

ii First kabuki in 1924; but regular performances with Japanese advisers since 1951.

iii Samuel L. Leiter, "Authentic kabuki: American style," in *Frozen Moments: Writings on Kabuki, 1966–2001* (Ithaca, NY: Cornell East Asia Series, 2002), 183–92; John D. Mitchell and Miyoko Watanabe, *Staging Japanese Theatre: Noh and Kabuki* (Key West: Florida Keys Educational Foundation, 1994).

iv Carol Sorgenfrei, "Leonard Cabell Pronko," ATJ 28:2 (2011), 375–91.

v Sato Shozo, *Soul of Japan: Introducing Traditional Japanese Arts to New Generations* (Tokyo: Keio 2004).

vi Andrew T. Tsubaki, "Obei ni okeru nogaku kenkyū no jittai to watakushi nokyogen o chūshin toshita enshutsu katsudo: 1960 nen kara 20 seiki no owari made" (The state of nohkyogen scholarship in the U.S. and my own directorial activities – 1950–present), *Sōgō geijustu toshite no nō* (Noh as total theatre) vols. VII–XIV (2001–9); John D. Swain, "Andrew T. Tsubaki," ATJ 28:2 (2011), 368–74.

vii Mitsuko Unno, *The Challenge of Kabuki: Canadian Academy on Stage*, trans. Ann B. Gary (Tokyo: Japan Times, 1979).

viii Siyuan Li, "A. C. Scott," ATJ 28:2 (2011), 414–25.

ix Eugenio Barba, *A Dictionary of Theatre Anthropology* (London: Routledge, 2005).

x Erik Ehn (ed.), *Theatre of Yugen 25 Years: A Retrospective* (San Francisco, CA: Theatre of Yugen, 2004).

xi Jonah Salz, "Traditional theatre training," *Kanze*, November, 1992 (in Japanese): 75–7; "Traditional Theatre Training@30: disciplehood in Kyoto," *T.T.T. 30th Anniversary Publication* (Kyoto: Kyoto Art Center, 2016).

xii Diego Pellecchia, "The International Noh Institute of Milan: transmission of ethics and ethics of transmission in a transnational context," in Stanca Scholz-Cionca and Andreas Regelsberger (eds.), *Japanese Theatre Transcultural: German and Italian Intertwining*, 32–50.

xiii Ariane Mnouchkine, www.theatre-du-soleil.fr/thsol/sources-orientales/les-sources-orientales/japon/?lang = fr.

xiv Ashley Thorpe, www.theatrenohgaku.org: "How can Westerners study Japanese Noh? An interview with Richard Emmert, Director of the Noh Training Project and Theatre Nohgaku," *Theatre, Dance and Performance Training* 5:3 (2014), 321–33.

xv Theatre Training & Research Programme; Intercultural Theatre Institute http://iti.edu.sg.

xvi http://eu-japanfest.org/n-english/n-program/2010/12/the-little-kyogen-theatre-nagomi-kyogenkai-czech-shigeyama-motohiko-hybl-ondrej.html.

∾ SPOTLIGHT 23.1   Matsui and Emmert: pedagogic noh pioneers

Two names emerging repeatedly from training non-Japanese in noh are Akira Matsui (1946–) and Richard Emmert (1949–). Beginning with a year-long residency at Smith College in the USA in 1978, Matsui has been a frequent teacher and performer at overseas institutions, including Michigan State University, University of Wisconsin, and University of California, Berkeley. He has taught in London's SOAS and Eugenio Barba's ISTA in Germany, Spain, and Poland. He established the noh study group Ryokurankai in Warsaw in 2011, and continues to visit regularly. Many former students later contributed as teachers, directors, composers, and playwrights for subsequent generations of students.

Matsui is a peerless pioneer of intercultural experiments, often teaching traditional noh to performers who then collaborate with him in fusion productions. He has worked with Axel Tangerding of the Meta Theatre Company in Germany on adaptations of Lafcadio Hearn stories, and starred in the Noho Theatre Group's *At the Hawk's Well* (1986), *Ophelia* (1992),[10] and Beckett's *Rockaby* (1986),[11] which he has performed in six countries with local actors. He performed in a multicultural dance-play *Dragon Bond Rite* (1997), *Forgiveness,* a Chinese-Korean-Japanese-American production directed by Chen Shi-Zheng (2000), and *Siddhartha* by Teater Cahaya (2003), and with a multinational hundred-person cast in Eugenio Barba's *Ur-Hamlet* at Konigsburg Castle in Denmark (2005). Overseas workshops and performances are integral to his professional identity.

Richard Emmert is Matsui's frequent co-teacher and co-director, a dynamic producer of diverse noh activities, contributing to noh's expansion as both a traditional form and a potential base for chamber-opera overseas. As a student performer in Earlham College, he starred in Arthur Little's noh-style *St. Francis* (1970), then directed the music for it in Tokyo in 1975. At the graduate program at Tokyo University of Arts, he studied noh theory under scholar and playwright Yokomichi Mario while training in dance, chant, and *hayashi* instruments. Emmert composed music for his first English-language noh, Noho's Yeats' *At the Hawk's Well* (Kyoto, 1981) (see Figure 1), then re-directed it in Tokyo (1982) and Australia (1984). He has taught noh dance and music overseas, including projects with Matsui at Earlham College (1988), University of Sydney (1984 and 1989), and University of Hawai'i (2009). He also composed for and directed numerous English noh, including *Drifting Fires*,[12] *Eliza*,[13] and *The Gull*.[14] His annotated translations (with Monica Bethe) of noh plays, and summaries of noh plays, make noh's complex musical and verbal structures accessible for initiate audiences.

Emmert continues to spread the gospel of noh as dramaturgical lodestone. His Noh Training Project (NTP) offers regular intensive workshops in Tokyo, Bloomsburg, PA, and Reading (and since 2014, Royal Holloway, University of London) in the UK. Remarkably, veterans of two decades of NTP's activities in Bloomsburg since 1995 have continued to gather from far-flung regions to champion

---

10 Jonah Salz, "East meets west meets Hamlet: get thee to a noh master," in Judy Lee Oliva (ed.), *New Theatre Vistas* (New York: Garland, 1996), 149–63.

11 Jonah Salz, "Leonard's bastard son: the Noho Theatre Group's first two decades," in *Theatre East and West Revisited. Mime Journal*, ed. Carol Davis (2003), 135–53.

12 Janine Beichman, "*Drifting Fires*: an American nō," *ATJ* 3:2 (1986), 233–60.

13 Kerrie Schaefer, "Reality and fantasy: the performing body in an Australian noh play," *TDR* 35:4 (1991), 92–106.

14 Daphne Marlatt, *The Gull* (Vancouver: Talonbooks, 2009).

English noh as Theatre Nohgaku (2000–).[15] They rehearse, offer residencies, and produce new works, including a revival of *Hawk's Well* (2002), David Crandall's *Crazy Jane* (1983), Greg Giovanni's *Pine Barrens* (2006), a well-received European and Asian tour of British-Chinese playwright Jannette Cheong's *Pagoda* (2009 and 2011) and Deborah Brevoort's *Blue Moon over Memphis* (2014). Theatre Nohgaku also produces regular specialist workshops in noh costuming (by Monica Bethe in Kyoto), playwriting, and music.

Matsui and Emmert have helped create appreciation of traditional noh, and have also stimulated intercultural appropriations. Time will tell what effect their experiments on noh's outer edges will have on the orthodox noh world.

JONAH SALZ

Domestic accommodations: learning to bow

Gradually, Japan has become increasingly receptive to short-term intensive workshops, rather than the standard "lifetime training" trajectory of traditional *keiko* (practice). While scholars like Fenollosa (1890s) and Donald Keene (1950s) initially studied as amateurs one-on-one with teachers for several years, other foreign scholars have received tailor-made, intensive, and group programs. In response to the increased interest among overseas scholars and practitioners in studying performance in Japan, and support from the Japan Foundation and Asian Cultural Council, since the 1980s a number of immersive programs for non-Japanese have been initiated in Japan.

From 1984, Traditional Theatre Training (TTT) has offered noh, kyogen, and nihonbuyo to foreign actors, students, and teachers (and to Japanese since 1990) for six weeks (later three) during the summer in Kyoto (Figure 59). Normally, Japanese students practice two or three times per month at their teacher's home studio or community education center. TTT could hire professional performers at reasonable cost to offer intensive, group lessons culminating with a recital by offering classes in summer, when actors and students from Europe and the USA are most free, subsidized by foundations and, from 1994, Kyoto City. Over 350 students from twenty countries have participated in TTT over the past thirty years. Since 1988, the International Theatre Institute Japan branch has sponsored annual ten-day workshops in rotating genres, most conducted at national theatres. These included noh and kyogen, *bugaku* and folk-dance, as well as the rare opportunity to study kabuki.

Some intensive program graduates continue their studies in Japan, or on return visits. The majority return to their home countries; scholars integrate their newfound knowledge into lectures on Japanese literature or world theatre and dance, while dancers, directors, and playwrights bring

15 www.theatrenohgaku.org.

Fig 59 Participants on Kyoto's summer intensive Traditional Theatre Training program learn buyō from Wakayagi Yayoi.

lessons of stillness, timing, grace, and energy to new fusion works of dance and theatre.[16]

Meanwhile, exposure to Westerners' learning processes – memorizing dialogue as melody, asking many questions – influences Japanese masters' teaching methods. Traditional pedagogy fosters an approach of unquestioning imitation. Disciples are expected to "steal the secrets" through constant attention, rather than try to understand through explanations. TTT noh and kyogen masters developed exercises for regular or short-term workshops to group warm-up with basic stance and movements independent of the fixed repertoire. Although such short cuts are perhaps necessary for short-term artists and scholars, they are unusual in the trajectory of rote repetition and lifetime training for native amateurs and professionals. Contact with foreigners can bend traditional career trajectories. Udaka Michishige, a noh performer, teacher, and mask-carver, has trained non-Japanese for over three decades, including the first three years of TTT. His long-term disciple Rebecca Teele Ogamo achieved the rank of licensed teacher (*shihan*) and became the first foreigner admitted into the professional Noh Theatre Association (1997).[17] Udaka continues to teach non-Japanese students, tours

16 Jonah Salz, "Pidgin–creole performance experiment and the emerging entre-garde," in James Brandon (ed.), *Noh and Kyogen in the Contemporary World* (Honolulu: University of Hawai'i Press, 1997), 210–42.

17 Ogamo places her own apprenticeship in context in "Women in noh today," in Carol Davis (ed.), *Theatre East and West Revisited,* Special issue of *Mime Journal* 17 (2002–23), 67–80.

overseas, has published in English on masks,[18] and has experimented with a new noh, concerning nuclear devastation.[19]

Disciplehood delivered

While few can afford the time and overcome the considerable linguistic obstacles to study in Japan, since the 1960s Japanese masters have frequently been invited abroad for short-term courses or to co-direct plays. Tokyo-based translator Don Kenny has not only performed English kyogen since 1975, but also taught foreign and Japanese students in his own *dōjō*, and toured frequently overseas, proselytizing the joys of the stylized comedy.[20]

Nomura Manzō's workshop at the University of Washington for six months in 1968, and subsequent US tour, was pioneering in this regard. Yet the flagship of such immersive programs is the kabuki program at the University of Hawai'i.[21] Unique to Hawai'i are regular kabuki performances, in English, in traditional wigs and costumes, accompanied by live orchestras, for multi-week runs to paying audiences. Among Hawai'i's emigrant community are Japanese masters of dance and musical instruments, wig styling, and makeup. The enviable location also makes it an attractive place for Japanese masters to spend weeks or months offering intensive training, the daily six- to ten-hour rehearsals at a single theatre a respite from their normal grueling performance and teaching schedules. Japanese-American students performed fully costumed, large-scale kabuki plays (mainly *shin-kabuki*) for many years prior to World War II. Since 1951, when kabuki actor Onoe Kikunobu assisted Earle Ernst, Hawai'i has invited primarily kabuki but also noh, kyogen, bunraku, and modern theatre actors and musicians to oversee a semester or year in training student actors for performances (in English), in rotation with Chinese, and Indonesian genres. The program prospers with a unique combination of ingredients: a base community of emigrant spectators eager to embrace their native genres translated to English, professors with long experiential training in Asian genres (indeed, many trained at the University of Hawai'i graduate school), and an international graduate

---

18 *The Secrets of Noh Masks* (Tokyo and New York: Kodansha, 2010).
19 Diego Pellecchia and Udaka Michishige, "Conservative adaptation in Japanese noh theatre: an interview with Udaka Michishige," in *Theatre and Adaptation: Return, Rewrite, Repeat* (London: Bloomsbury Methuen, 2014), 77–90.
20 Lisa Kuly, "Translation, hybridity, and 'the real thing': Don Kenny's English kyōgen," *Performance Paradigm* 2 (March 2006).
21 James R. Brandon, "Bridging cultures: 100 years of kabuki in Hawaii" in International Institute for Asian studies working papers, in Clara Brakel-Papenhuijzen (ed.), *Performing Arts of Asia: The Performer as (Inter)cultural Transmitter*, IIAS working papers series 4 (Leiden: International Institute for Asian Studies, 1996).

student body willing to immerse themselves in foreign languages and forms. Kyogen, noh, and kabuki are first taught in Japanese, then translated to syllable-synchronized English, in an effort to maintain the same vocal tension and melody as the originals.[22]

Two Midwestern American experiences demonstrate the scope of intentions and practice. Shozo Sato at the University of Illinois, Champaign-Urbana brought another immersive cultural experience to a very different climate for four decades, beginning in 1968. In addition to teaching kabuki in English in Fine Arts and, later, Dance departments, he also instructed tea ceremony, flower arranging, and calligraphy. A. C. Scott, a scholar of both Chinese and Japanese theatre, staged some productions by noh and kabuki actors at the University of Wisconsin, but eventually realized that teaching their essential dynamics through martial arts and t'ai ch'i was more effective than trying to replicate traditional forms directly. The Asian/Experimental Theatre Program continues to help performers achieve a "state of directness, simplicity, and intensity,"[23] continued by Phillip Zarilli,[24] and now David Furumoto, who occasionally teaches and directs kabuki, but more frequently creates fusion productions of Western classics using his own methods, informed by kabuki and other Japanese dramatic genres.

Tradition tensions

There is an inherent tension to such training in traditional arts: students cannot hope to become proficient enough to turn professional in Japan. Although such training's worth is unequivocal, a surprising but typical critique of such experiments is by Ernst, who believes attempts to *replicate* Japanese forms are sterile one-off experiments, lacking permanent influence:

> We have nothing to gain, as some would claim, by a mere imitation of the noh or any other ancient form of drama, of its masks, its symbolism, its conventions, its costumes: it is rather in tracing the spirit of which these outward forms and accessories were the expression that we may find something of value.[25]

Yet many dance and theatre programs teach such techniques, finding in them useful dynamics of stage presence, breathing, and form. Others

22 James R. Brandon, "Performance training in Japanese nō and kyōgen at the University of Hawai'i," *Theatre Topics* 3:2 (September 1993), 101–20.
23 Siyuan Liu, "A. C. Scott," *Asian Theatre Journal* 28:2 (2011), 414–25.
24 Phillip Zarilli, *Psychophysical Acting: An Intercultural Approach after Stanislavski* (London: Routledge, 2009).
25 Earle Ernst, "The influence of Japanese theatrical style on western theatre," *Educational Theatre Journal* 2:1 (1969), 127–38, at 137, 138.

promote them as stepping-stones to intercultural productions. Sato also directed acclaimed fusion productions of *Kabuki Medea, Kabuki Faust*, and *Kabuki Macbeth*, first at the University of Illinois and later produced by professional companies in Chicago and abroad. Portland State University offered production courses in noh, kyogen, kabuki, Suzuki, and butoh during its summer-long Portland International Performance Festival (PIPFest) (1992–2001), and in Japan in Motion Festivals (2002–12), but also comparative workshops in Shakespeare, noh, butoh, and commedia dell'arte.

Some programs outside academe provided stimuli to intercultural experiment. In Japan, TTT students training in the mornings then rehearsed plays in the afternoon and evenings with the Noho Theatre Group's Nohow (Noho workshop), including noh-kyogen influenced playwrights Synge, Yeats, and Mishima, short plays by Beckett, and bilingual kyogen.[26] Other students have discovered, especially in noh and kyogen, dramaturgical lessons that aid their playwriting and directing. Some fortunate to have observed or trained in bunraku[27] have applied these techniques to new puppets used in opera (*Madame Butterfly*), mainstage theatre (*War Horse*), and experimental works (Mabou Mines' *Shaggy Dog Animation*, dir. Lee Breuer, 1978; Paula Vogel, *The Long Christmas Ride Home*, 2003; London's Blind Summit Theatre). Traditional techniques and spirit are thus freely appropriated, then added to tools in the actor's "bag of tricks."

Intercultural research and experiment: IASTA, Yūgen, ISTA

Workshops for professional performers have been offered overseas by Japanese and non-Japanese teachers. Given that many Japanese modern theatre companies in the 1960s began offering classes in traditional theatre as part of their lessons in vocalization and presence, it is perhaps unsurprising that some overseas professionals have applied Japanese traditions to their own experimental works. Although academic institutions have facilities, finance, and students to support long-term training by guest Japanese masters, a few professional theatre institutions have also managed to make Japanese tradition available as actor training. Théâtre du Soleil's affiliated organization ARTA (Research and Traditions in Acting) offers workshops by invited Japanese masters, embraced by director Ariane Mnouchkine for their "gestural precision, clarity of line, bringing an extreme truth and

---

26 Timothy Medlock and Jonah Salz, "Chasing contagious comedy: new kyogen *Henpecked Husband* in rhymed, bilingual version," *Ryukoku University Intercultural Studies* 17 (2012), 41–75.

27 Nancy Staub (ed.), "American bunraku" (theme issue), *Puppetry Journal* 41:3 (1990).

an extreme artifice together."[28] These workshops provided discipline and technical skills that enrich her highly intercultural productions, including a kabuki version of *Richard II* and bunraku-style tragedy *Tambours sur la digue* (Drums on the dike).

John D. Mitchell's IASTA program offered short-term immersions, providing professionals with techniques and spirit of Japanese forms. Noh master Kita Sadayo (1926–2003) with Tomoeda Akiyo (1940–, now Living National Treasure) and leading kabuki actor Onoe Baikō VII (1915–95) were invited for months of intensive practice of plays by theatre professionals in New York City. Scripts, translated syllable for syllable, allowed participants to absorb the discipline, grace, and energy of the traditional forms.[29] Japanese traditional noh-kyogen is the basis for San Francisco's Theatre of Yūgen's name (*yūgen* meaning the noh ideal of "mysterious beauty"), black-box theatre (Noh Space), and ethos. Founded by Nomura Mansaku's disciple Yuriko Doi in 1978, Yūgen trains its members in kyogen and noh as a basis for interpreting Shakespeare and Molière, English kyogen,[30] and new noh by contemporary playwrights.[31] Carol Fisher Sorgenfrei's kabuki/flamenco interpretation of *Blood Wedding* and Erik Ehn's five-play fusion noh cycle were particularly ambitious. In 2014, innovative kyogen actor Nomura Mansaku's disciple's son, Ishida Tanroh, became artistic director, moving the troupe in yet another new direction.

Taking a more scientific approach, Eugenio Barba invited nihonbuyo, kyogen, and noh actors to his long-running, peripatetic ISTA programs based in Denmark (see Figure 60). Lecture-demonstrations exploring specific themes such as Subscore, Performer's Bios, Improvisation, and Flow often extracted practical techniques and evocative metaphors easily grasped by participant scholars and performers.[32] Japanese guest artists also appeared as actors in Barba's "theatrum mundum" productions of *Ego Faust* (2000) and *Ur-Hamlet* (2006) (see Figure 63) where, rather than attempt to meld distinct traditions, Barba welded them into a complex construction of confluences and interferences, allowing guest masters the comfort of their own traditions while bending them toward a highly structured whole. Barba's analysis of the lessons of breath, form, presence, and improvisation in his classic

---

28 Quoted from *Richard II* (1981) Program Note in David Williams (ed.), *Theatre of Collaboration: Le Théâtre du Soleil* (London: Routledge, 1997), 90.

29 Samuel L. Leiter, "Authentic kabuki, American style," in *Frozen Moments: Writings on Kabuki 1966–2001* (Ithaca, NY: East Asia Program, Cornell University Press, 2002), 183–92.

30 Yuriko Doi, "Theatre of Yugen's direction of kyōgen in English and kyōgen fusion plays," *ATJ* (Spring 2007), 247–61.

31 Erik Ehn (ed.), *Theatre of Yugen 25 Years: A Retrospective* (San Francisco, CA: Theatre of Yugen, 2004).

32 www.odinteatret.dk/research/ista.aspx.

Dictionary of Theatre Anthropology (2005) and *Burning the House: On Dramaturgy and Directing* (2010) drew heavily on his encounters with Japanese artists for inspiration. Moreover, many of the Japanese actors involved – Kanze Hideo, Nomura Kōsuke, and Matsui Akira – were inspired by this excavation of layers of their arts that they themselves had taken for granted, spurring their own further intercultural research and collaborations.

The fourth wave: creative mastery

Brandon's third wave of practitioner-scholars studied directly from Asian masters, but one can now see the rise of a fourth wave: students studying under these non-Japanese disciples who have returned as masters to teach on their own. Normally, invited Japanese masters train non-Japanese students aided by interpreters, but the gradual increase in foreign expertise has permitted workshops taught entirely without Japanese input. When the National Theatre in Tokyo began its training program for young kabuki actors,[33] Leonard Pronko participated in this program, while Andrew Tsubaki and James Brandon took private lessons in noh, kyogen, and kabuki during the late sixties and early seventies. Each subsequently returned to his home institution and employed the newly acquired techniques in his teaching and directing: Tsubaki at University of Kansas, Pronko at Pomona College in California, and Brandon at Michigan State and University of Hawai'i.[34]

Along with Laurence Kominz at Portland State University (kyogen, kabuki),[35] and Monique Arnaud (noh) in Milan,[36] they developed pedagogical styles that enable American and European students to learn the forms quickly and effectively. Pronko's workshop technique, adapted from his teacher Hanayagi Chiyo,[37] involves enthusiastically demonstrating female and male walks, poses, and dance-forms in a methodical manner easy to understand and imitate.[38] These teachers, as well as Kenny, Richard Emmert, Salz (kyogen), and Iezzi (kabuki), have also been in demand for short-term intensive programs

33 "Training course for safeguarding of intangible cultural heritage," *Asia-Pacific Database on Intangible Cultural Heritage (ICH)* by Asia-Pacific Cultural Centre for UNESCO (ACCU), www.accu. or.jp/ich/en/training/curriculum/pdf/word/lecture5_word.pdf (accessed 22 November 2014).

34 Unfortunately, this "unlicensed" use of kabuki was, perhaps, the reason the National Theatre afterwards banned foreign academics from the program.

35 "Authenticity and accessibility: two decades of translating and adapting kyōgen plays for English and bilingual student performances," *ATJ* 24:1 (2007), 235–46.

36 Diego Pellecchia, "The International Noh Institute of Milan: transmission of ethics and ethics of transmission in a transcultural context," in Stanca Scholz-Cionca and Andreas Regelsberger (eds.), *Japanese Theatre Transcultural: German and Italian Intertwinings* (Munich: Iudicium, 2011), 32–50.

37 Leonard C. Pronko and Tamono Takayo (trans.), *The Fundamentals of Japanese Dance: Kabuki Dance* (Tokyo: Kodansha, 2008).

38 Jack Coogan and Leonard C. Pronko, *Kabuki for the West*, Insight Media, distributors (2009).

at other academic and dramatic arts institutions in the USA and overseas. Just as Japanese universities and government institutions by the end of the Meiji period (1868–1912) found that they no longer needed their "foreign advisers," Western theatres and universities may one day find sufficiently masterful native purveyors of Japanese traditional theatre. Trained and even licensed in Japan, these intercultural entrepreneurs may develop flexible pedagogies more marketable and suited to the Western classroom or rehearsal room than their Japanese masters, as is already the case with the Suzuki Method (both music and actor training), taiko drumming, and butoh.

Beyond such teaching, however, can foreign students of noh and kyogen ever be accepted as world-class performers, on a par with Japanese colleagues? Critic Gondo Yoshikazu remarked on Theatre Nohgaku's Kyoto English noh tour that "they were so proficient, it was almost boring" – authentically noh-like. Assessing the future of foreigners in noh, he compared it to Japanese studying ballet: "It took a century to overcome the ridicule of their short legs and assumed lack of Western musical understanding before Japanese began winning the top prizes in Lausanne."[39] Or, as Brandon puts it, if we can accept Seiji Ozawa as a top conductor of classical Western music, why not appreciate a talented non-Japanese kabuki actor in the future?[40]

Nonetheless, there are few opportunities for foreign students of noh or kabuki to devote the years of training essential to master classical disciplines, as there would be for ballet and classical music students. Makeup and masks cannot disguise telling accents and unfamiliar body types difficult for Japanese traditionalists to accept. Yet as students of the fourth wave surface as disciples of non-Japanese who brought knowledge back from the source, the disciples' approach Japanese traditional theatre at several steps removed from the forms' origins. They may never have visited Japan, or even felt the need to. Like global variants of Zen Buddhism, judo, manga, and sushi, a new international version of Japanese classical forms may emerge.

References and further reading

Brandon, James. "A new world: Asian theatre in the West today," *TDR* 33 (1989), 261–9

Preston, Carrie J. *Learing to Kneel: Noh, Modernism, and Journeys in Teaching* (New York: Columbia University Press, 2016)

SPOTLIGHT 23.1 MATSUI AND EMMERT: PEDAGOGIC NOH PIONEERS

Anno, Mariko, and Judy Halebsky. "Innovation in nō: Matsui Akira continues a tradition of change," *ATJ* 31:1 (2014), 126–52

39 Personal interview, November 2012.　　40 Brandon, "A new world," 37.

Bethe, Monica, and Richard Emmert. *Noh Performance Guides.* Tokyo (Aoinoue, Ema, Atsumori, Tenko, Miidera, Matsukaze, Fujito) (1992–97)

Emmert, Richard. *The Guide to Noh of the National Noh Theatre*, 7 vols. (Tokyo: National Noh Theatre, 2012–)

"Classical noh in English translation: a performer's perspective," *Waseda Journal of Asian Studies* 15 (1993), 18–33

Noh in English CD with booklet (Tokyo: Teichiku Records, 1990)

24 ✎ Intercultural theatre: fortuitous encounters

JONAH SALZ

Japan's somewhat reluctant "opening" to the West during the Meiji Restoration (1868–1912) coincided with Western fascination for Japan generated through international expositions, touring troupes, and travelers' diaries. These helped to establish Japanese dance and theatre in the Western imagination as "original," "authentic," "ancient," and "exotic." Western artists also discovered that they could effectively incorporate these aspects into their own works, whether through emulation of physical techniques, appropriation of staging techniques, adaptation of stories and structures, or inspired meldings. This chapter examines the influence of Japanese theatre overseas in milestone intercultural performances.

Intercultural performance: fruitful misunderstandings

Postcolonialism and global artistic cross-pollination through international performance festivals and online forums have made appropriations between Western and non-Western cultures increasingly the norm of vanguard experiments. However, the problematic term "intercultural theatre" has recently become more ubiquitous and mutually influential than previously described. Adaptation of plots, techniques, and structures, and the variable Western interpretations of Japanese traditional theatre's "essence," have all depended on willing and able partners in Japan. Often these advisers and collaborators are in turn changed by their encounter with Western artists and their methods, resulting in similar attempts to change the substance or structures of their own arts, solving problems from a continuously fertile state of "in-betweenness."[1]

The path to significant intercultural performance is not necessarily straight or predictable, as evidenced by the confusion of language used to describe it. Cross-cultural theatrical interactions have been described variously as hybrids and creoles, melting pots and stews, fissions and fusions, an

---

1 Erika Fischer-Lichte, "Interweaving cultures in performance: different states of being in-between," *New Theatre Quarterly* 25 (2009), 391–401.

hour-glass of sifting between Source and Target cultures, and a crossroads.[2] In the early decades of the twentieth century, Japanese theatre practitioners assimilated Western naturalism and problem plays into their nascent modern theatre, but neither consistently nor thoroughly. Brecht's influence came much later than initial contact, while Beckett's was almost immediate; kabuki male *onnagata* (female role specialists) played alongside actresses in new plays for many decades. Luck of timing and receptive circumstance, and the accidental careers of a few pioneering artists, created modern theatre's variegated textures.

Simultaneously, Western scholars' and artists' interest in postimpressionism and art for art's sake, symbolism, futurism, montage, and transcendental philosophies discovered in Asia in general, and in Japan in particular, a living museum of endless inspiration. There was a renewed fascination with Greek and medieval performance traditions including poetry and song, masks, dance-drama, ritual, and total theatre, which redirected attention to Asian dance-theatre traditions. This interest was met eagerly by native hosts, producers, and essayists, who situated Japanese arts as both deserving of Western study and distinct within Asia. Euro-American painters, composers, and dancers early on discovered both surface and structural aspects to emulate; somewhat later, theatre practitioners found inspiration for their own experiments.

Numerous vanguard twentieth-century directors and theorists have studied and adapted Japanese traditional theatre, including Craig, Copeau, Meyerhold, Eisenstein, Brecht, Brook, Wilson, Mnouchkine, Barba, Suzuki, Lepage, and Sellars. Since many have been extensively covered elsewhere, this chapter confines itself to a few especially illustrative examples of serendipitous encounters and misinformed adventures, and their far-reaching repercussions: the dance-play *At the Hawk's Well*, the opera *Curlew River*, and the musical *Pacific Overtures*.

Gyrating *Hawk*: Fenollosa to Pound to Yeats to Itō

William Butler Yeats' noh-influenced *At the Hawk's Well* (1916), although performed only a few times for an elite audience, resonated with many of the pioneers of twentieth-century dance and theatre.[3]

Yeats' encounter with noh depended on many chance events. American philosopher Ernest Fenollosa studied under preeminent noh actor Umewaka

---

2 Patrice Pavis, *Theatre at the Crossroads of Culture* (London: Routledge, 1992).
3 Richard Taylor, *The Drama of W. B. Yeats: Irish Drama and the Japanese No* (New Haven, CT: Yale, 1976); Masaru Sekine and Christopher Murray, *Yeats and the Noh: A Comparative Study* (Gerrards Cross: Colyn Smythe, 1990), 121–7.

∿ SPOTLIGHT 24.1   Early twentieth-century influence in Europe: Craig, Copeau, Brecht

At the turn of the twentieth century, Western practitioners who were dissatisfied with the naturalist tradition looked eastwards seeking new inspiration. Avant-garde practitioners discovered Japanese drama through tours by Kawakami Otojirō and Sadayakko, and later by Hanako,[4] and through translations by Basil Hall Chamberlain or Noël Péri. They found in Japan

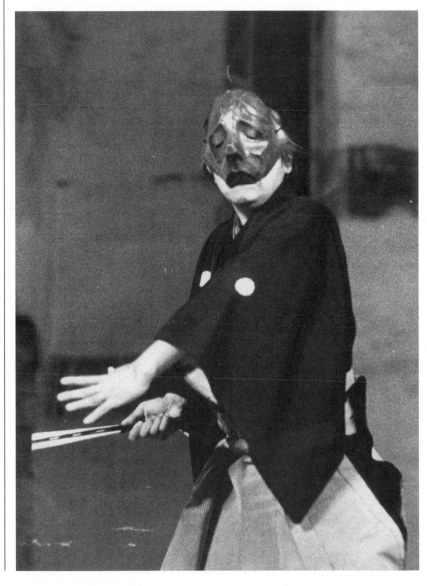

Fig 60 At Eugenio Barba's Bergamo 1977 workshop, noh master Kanze Hideo improvises with a mask made by Donato Sartori.

4 See James R. Brandon, "On Little Hanako," *ATJ* 5:1 (1988), 92–100.

a "total theatre,"[5] neither easily divided by genre (dance/song/drama) nor dominated by the primacy of the written text. Perhaps most importantly, Japanese theatre made no attempt to imitate "real life," resonating with vanguard artists' aversion for the aesthetics of realism, which reflected a wider social and political revulsion for the bourgeois individualism that naturalist drama represented.[6]

CRAIG'S MASKS, COPEAU'S REGIMEN

Ezra Pound and W. B. Yeats were crucial in disseminating noh among European theatre practitioners. Pound's edition of Ernest Fenollosa's 1915 translations of noh plays, and detailed preface, drew parallels with European morality plays and Greek tragedy. Yeats' sometime scenic collaborator Edward Gordon Craig (1872–1966) was more cautious in his approach to Asian theatre, too often superficially embraced by others.

> We have nothing to gain by a mere imitation of this or any other ancient form of drama …
> It is rather in tracing the spirit of which these outward forms and accessories were the expression that we may find something of value … to aid us in shaping the masks, the symbols, and the laws of our theatre which is to be.[7]

His face hidden by a mask, his body concealed beneath layers of costumes, the noh actor was a fitting model for the *Übermarionette*, Craig's ideal of the dehumanized actor. This quest for the selfless actor drew Craig to appreciate the Japanese ethics of devotion, exemplified in articles published in his journal.[8]

Similar ethics of selflessness and dedication to the art as a "way of life" inspired the practice of actor/director Jacques Copeau (1879–1949) who, after condemning the *cabotinage* (quackery) of bourgeois realism,[9] moved his company from Paris' Vieux Colombier theatre to the countryside. Under the direction of actress Suzanne Bing, they rehearsed the noh *Kantan* (The Kantan pillow), although it was never performed.[10] Bing stated that their *Kantan* was not an attempt to approximate noh, but an adaptation in the troupe style, whose principles they thought to be strikingly similar. More than aesthetics, Copeau valued noh "because it was the strictest theatrical form that he knew."[11]

One can trace noh's influence through Copeau, the fountainhead of the French corporeal mime school later developed by Étienne Decroux, Jean and Marie-Hélène Dasté, Jacques Lecoq, and Jean-Louis Barrault. Decroux (1889–1991) codified a method of corporeal mime that resonated with the noh notion of "body" as empty vessel for "character."[12] Lecoq (1921–99) developed his technique around the "neutral mask," initiated by Copeau, who drew inspiration from the noh *ko-omote* mask, which forced the actor to act without using facial expressions (Figure 60).[13]

5 "Total theatre" refers to the fusion of literary, visual, and musical elements, stemming from Richard Wagner's notion of *Gesamtkunstwerk*, later pursued by the modernists. Contemporary exemplars Robert Lepage, Robert Wilson, and Ariane Mnouchkine have all employed Japanese theatrical techniques and collaborators.

6 Erika Fischer-Lichte, "The reception of Japanese theatre by the European avant-garde (1900–1930)," in Stanca Scholz-Cionca and Samuel L. Leiter (eds.), *Japanese Theatre and the International Stage* (Leiden: Brill, 2001), 27–42.

7 Edward Gordon Craig (ed.), *The Mask: A Journal of the Art of the Theatre* 6 (Florence: Arena Goldoni, 1913), 265.

8 Craig describes the devotion of Lafcadio Hearn's assistant in "A Japanese pupil," *The Mask* 4 (1908), 203–13.

9 Jacques Copeau, "An essay of dramatic renovation: the Théâtre du Vieux-Colombier," trans. Richard Hiatt, *Educational Theatre Journal* 19:4 (1967), 447–54.

10 Jacques Copeau, *Registres V: Les registres du Vieux Colombier, troisième partie 1919 à 1924*, ed. Norman Paul (Paris: Gallimard, 1993), 392.

11 Jacques Copeau, *Journal: 1901–1948*, ed. Claude Sicard (Paris: Paulhan, 1999), 211.

12 Thomas Leabhart, "Jacques Copeau, Étienne Decroux, and the 'Flower of Noh'," *New Theatre Quarterly* 20:80 (2004), 315–30.

13 Donato Sartori, "Masks, East and West confronted," trans. Diego Pellecchia in Scholz-Cionca and Regelsberger (eds.), *Japanese Theatre Transcultural*, 168–72.

BRECHT'S PARABLES AND CLAUDEL'S DRAMATURGY

If the French were inspired by acting and masks, the Germans drew upon the dramaturgical structures of noh. Bertolt Brecht's "learning piece" *He Who Said Yes* (*Der Jasager*, 1929) was based on the noh *Tanikō* (The valley rite), in which a boy following monks on pilgrimage falls ill and, following a rule prescribing purity within the congregation, is hurled into a valley. Brecht transformed the noh into a socialist parable: the boy gives his life for the greater good. In response to criticism, Brecht wrote an alternative version, *He Who Said No* (*Der Neinsager*, 1930), where the boy refuses to submit to the rule, and a second version of *He Who Said Yes*, in an attempt to provide a stronger justification for the boy's sacrifice.[14] Though inspired by Chinese theatre acting techniques in the formulation of the notion of "alienation" (*Verfremdung*), Brecht was interested not in noh performance aesthetics but in its ethical content, which helped him shape his theory of the didactic play, where "the theatre becomes a place for philosophers."[15]

Practitioners such as Copeau and Brecht knew noh only in translation or as described by others,[16] a form of *ignorance bénéfique* (blissful ignorance)[17] which allowed a certain freedom of interpretation. Paul Claudel (1868–1955), who served as French ambassador to Japan between 1921 and 1927, was among the first practitioners to see Japanese theatre in performance. *Blackbird in the Rising Sun* (*L'oiseau noir dans le soleil levant*, 1927) collects his lyric appreciations of noh, kabuki, and bunraku. His adoption of noh dramaturgy, between dream and reality, can be traced in *The Satin Slipper* (*Le soulier de satin*, 1925) and *The Book of Christopher Columbus* (*Le livre de Christophe Colomb*, 1930).[18]

Claudel's first-hand knowledge was an excellent exception; the first Western understanding of Japanese theatre was through the literary text in translation. This is particularly true in the case of noh: while kabuki first toured Europe in 1928, not until the 1950s could Western audiences see a live performance without travelling to Japan. Among spectators for a noh-kyogen company in Dijon in 1957 was French actor/director Jean-Louis Barrault, who had already absorbed noh principles such as dramatic use of silence and of stylized gesture accompanying verse while training with Dullin, and collaborating with Claudel when staging *Satin Slipper* (1943) and *Columbus* (1953). Despite this background, the actual performance in Dijon left Barrault unmoved. He staged *Columbus* in Japan in 1960 under the influence of noh principles such as internalized acting and minimalism of stage design.[19] He attended Kanze Hisao's performance of the noh *Hashitomi*, and this time was greatly impressed. When Hisao was selected as Japan's representative in an exchange program to Paris in 1962, Barrault himself hosted him for several months.

Noh has profoundly influenced many leading early twentieth-century practitioners. Whether inspired by its ethics (Craig and Brecht), rigorous training methods (Copeau and descendants), or expressive means (Barrault), European practitioners were ready for the exotic yet precise tropes of the noh dance, chant, and stories.

DIEGO PELLECCHIA

---

14 Anthony Tatlow, *The Mask of Evil: Brecht's Response to the Poetry, Theatre and Thought of China and Japan* (Berne: Peter Lang, 1977), 186–7.

15 Brecht, *The Measures Taken and Other Lehrstücke* (London: Methuen, 1990), 6.

16 Even Waley's influential translations relied on a letter from Oswald Sickert describing noh in performance – the renowned translator famously never visited Japan.

17 Georges Banu, *L'acteur qui ne revient pas: journées de théâtre au Japon* (Paris: Gallimard, 1993), 109.

18 Nishino Ayako, "L'adaptation claudelienne du no: dans l'histoire de la reception occidentale du no," *Cahiers d'études françaises Université Keio* 13 (2008), 48–63. Claudel's dance piece *The Woman and her Shadow* (*La femme et son ombre*, 1922) was adapted to noh by Kimura Tarō and Izumi Yoshio in 1968.

19 John K. Gillespie, "Interior action: the impact of noh on Jean-Louis Barrault," *Comparative Drama* 16:4 (1982), 325–44.

Minoru V (1858–1911) and, when frequenting the theatre, taking assiduous notes and attempting translations, he was assisted by Hirata Kiichi (1873–1943). In 1913 their unpublished papers were entrusted to American poet and editor Ezra Pound (1885–1971), who published the revised plays and notes as *Certain Noble Plays of Japan* (1916).[20] Yeats, who had been inspired when hearing drafts read, wrote an introduction in which he claimed to be attempting to invent an "aristocratic form … of drama – distinguished, indirect and symbolic."[21]

Yeats, already a famous poet and playwright, had given up on drama, frustrated by the challenges of working with actors, and the tipsy bourgeois audiences he needed in order to pay for productions, as well as the political dynamics inherent in play selection. Poet and essayist Noguchi Yonejirō had visited Pound and Yeats at Stone Cottage in 1913, perhaps persuading them that noh was performed for an elite few, with few properties or sets besides masks and fan, by aristocratic amateurs with little rehearsal in a private house with partitions removed.[22] Yeats discovered that his "must be the ancient theatre that can be made by unrolling a carpet or marking out a place with a stick, or setting a screen against the wall."[23]

As Pound polished and published the translated noh plays, he and Yeats grew curious as to how their dramaturgy might be applied to Irish legends. In 1916, Yeats wrote *Hawk's Well*, depicting an Old Man visited by a Young Warrior, awaiting a miraculous flow of water, bewitched by a Guardian Hawk. Pound and Yeats struggled to produce the play, hampered by their limited knowledge of noh performance practice. Edward Gordon Craig had earlier introduced Yeats to the imaginative use of screens; illustrator Edward Dulac created masks. Pound then met a young Japanese dancer performing animal-influenced Japanesque impromptus to Chopin and Debussy at society parties. Michio Itō (1892–1961) was a recent refugee from eurhythmics at the Dalcroze School. He had taken nihonbuyo classical dance lessons in Tokyo, but noh bored him. Still, Itō and artist friends demonstrated noh-style dance and chant for Yeats and Pound. Eventually, Itō devised a climactic *Hawk's Dance* blending Japanese delicacy with sweeping flight for performance of

---

20 Akiko Miyake, Sanehide Kodama, and Nicholas Teele (eds.), *A Guide to Ezra Pound and Ernest Fenollosa's* Classic Noh Theatre of Japan (Orono, ME: National Poetry Foundation, 1994).

21 Ezra Pound and Ernest Fenollosa, *The Classic Noh Theatre of Japan* (New York: New Directions, 1959), 201.

22 *Ten Kiogen* (1907) and *The Spirit of Japanese Art* (1915).

23 W. B. Yeats, *The Variorum Edition of the Plays of William Butler Yeats* (London: Macmillan, 1966), 416.

At the Hawk's Well in March 1916 at Lady Cunard's salon, repeated only once.

This inspired, if misinformed, adaptation proved an influential success, resonating deeply with its collaborating artists. Pound reaffirmed his faith in Imagism, employed noh tropes in his *Cantos*, and extolled noh's virtues for another half century. He too attempted a series of new kyogen and noh plays, including a lyric ghost-play based on Wagner's *Tristan and Isolde*.[24] Yeats the playwright was reinvigorated by the potential for a few performers to produce aesthetically powerful expressions from minimal sets, properties, and even rehearsal. He published three more "plays for dancers" and a kyogen; later plays employ noh dramaturgy. These bare-stage meldings of poetry, movement, and myth, framed by the return of unquiet spirits, inspired plays by T. S. Eliot, Thornton Wilder, and Samuel Beckett,[25] among many others. Despite its long and varied journey from Umewaka to Fenollosa to Pound to Yeats, noh had somehow survived as a model of ancient, potent dramaturgic strategies.

Michio Itō and modernism

Young Itō, who had gone to Europe to study dance, found himself ineluctably pulled back by commercial patronage and spectator expectations to his homeland's traditions. With the success of his *Hawk* dance, Itō was invited to New York, restaging the play in 1917 with Japanese performers and music by Yamada Kósçak (Kōsaku, 1886–1965), who later became a leading Japanese composer-conductor. Encouraged by Neighborhood Playhouse owner Irene Lewisohn (who had studied Kongō school noh for six months), he directed and performed in noh in English: *Tamura and Hagoromo*, in the Fenollosa/Pound translation, and the kyogen *Busu* and *Kitsunezuka* (1918). These pioneering English-language noh featured masked dancers to the chorus singing the entire text. Itō found success in choreographing for Broadway musicals then Hollywood films, opened up a dance studio, and gave large-scale recitals.

He returned to Japan in 1939 to play the Old Man and direct *Hawk's Well* with his talented brothers and sister-in-law acting the major roles

---

24 Nobuko Tsukui, *Ezra Pound and Japanese Noh Plays* (Baltimore, MD: University Press of America, 1983).

25 Jonah Salz, "Convergences and resonances in the dramaturgy and mise-en-scène of noh and Samuel Beckett", in Kevin Wetmore (ed.), *Irish Dramas in Japanese Theatre: Studies in Comparative Theatrical Performance* (Lewiston, NY: Mellen, 2014), 69–117.

Fig 61 Michio Itō directed and played the Old Man in Yeats' *At the Hawk's Well* to younger brother Senda Koreya's Cuchulain, here attempting to drink from the well, guarded by the Hawk-Princess played by sister-in-law Itō Teiko (1939).

and designing lighting, sets, and costumes; his younger brother, *shingeki* stalwart Senda Koreya, played the Young Man. Itō, pioneer of harmonized East–West art dance, was forcibly repatriated after Pearl Harbor, ultimately directing musical extravaganzas for Occupation GIs at Tokyo's cavernous Ernie Pyle (Takarazuka) Theatre. *At the Hawk's Well* was repeated several times, including a 1962 memorial performance to Itō, with music by Yamada.[26]

Other waters were drawn from Yeats' deep *Well*. Itō commissioned a mask for a revival of the *Hawk's* dance in 1926 from young Japanese-American sculptor Isamu Noguchi, son of Yonejirō. Isamu's mask was his first of many stage commissions, famously for dancer-choreographer Martha Graham (who had quit Denishawn before its 1925 tour to the Orient, and taught dance at the Neighborhood Playhouse, choreographed occasionally by Itō). Noguchi's noh-influenced (he saw them in Japan for the first time in 1931), minimalist, exposed, and integral stage and property designs became signature elements of Graham's myth-laden works from 1935 to

26 Taro Oshima, *W. B. Yeats and Japan* (Tokyo: Hokuseido Press, 1965), 37–60.

1960s.[27] Graham's notebooks testify to the deep impact of her reading and observation of noh performances in New York, which fed her own views on physical expression, breath, and spirit.[28] Thus a single play helped forge the connections that reverberated through many Euro-American modernist movements.

The *Hawk* returns

Yeats' *Hawk* eventually returned to its nest. *At the Hawk's Well* was adapted and performed in 1949 by Umewaka Minoru (1900–86), grandson of Fenollosa's teacher, in noh musical style composed by Yokomichi Mario (1916–2012). However, unhappy with the incongruities of Yeats' plot with authentic noh, Yokomichi rewrote it as *Takahime* (Hawk princess, 1967). Here the Hawk Guardian became a Mountain Spirit, and focus shifted to the Old Man as the *shite* (main actor) who, having waited a whole lifetime for the miraculous well's flow, returns after the *waki* (support actor) Cuchulain's fight with the Hawk, his mask changed into a bitter Ghost trapped in the mountain. The play enjoyed many revivals, considered a successful attempt at "new noh" under many directors. Freed from orthodox noh constraints, collaborators conceived innovative techniques: Kanze Hisao wrote music that included two-part canon singing and unusually lengthy soft repetitions (*jitori*). Unusually also, masks were employed for all three characters, and half-masks for the Chorus of Rocks, who danced while singing, before being replaced by a more conventional eight-person, seated chorus. Lighting effects were also employed.[29]

As an aspiring director in Kyoto, I, too, was drawn to Yeats, directing the Noho Theatre Group's 1981 performance of *Hawk's Well* on a noh stage, in English, featuring professional noh musicians (see Figure 1). Richard Emmert composed the music for this, the first of his many "English noh." However, our intercultural visions inevitably diverged. Dissatisfied with the lyric enunciation and choral power, Emmert redirected the play in Tokyo with the same cast (1982), then in subsequent years revived it with his own noh-trained, English-speaking chorus, while I redirected it twice in Kyoto.[30] The *Hawk* continues its spiral flight.

27 Martin Friedman, "Noguchi's imaginary landscapes," *Design Quarterly* 106/7 (1978), 1 + 3–99; Dore Ashton, *Noguchi East and West* (Berkeley: University of California, 1994).
28 Agnes de Mille, *Martha: The Life and Work of Martha Graham, a Biography* (New York: Random House, 1956), 44.
29 Mariko Anno, "Isso-ryu nohkan (noh flute): tradition and continuity in the music of noh drama," DMA dissertation, University of Illinois at Urbana-Champaign, 2008.
30 Rebecca Teele (ed.), "Noh/kyogen masks and performance," *Mime Journal* (Pomona, CA: Pomona College Theater Department, 1984).

Channeling Japan: *Curlew River* and *Pacific Overtures*

As most Japanese theatre is musical-drama comprised of dance, chant, and songs, it naturally influenced European and American composers and choreographers, as well as playwrights and directors.

Japanese customs (kimono, fans, hairstyles) and theatrical spectacle (kabuki white-face and flamboyance, men-in-black stage assistants) lend themselves to parody and Broadway exaggeration. Performances of Gilbert and Sullivan's light opera *The Mikado* (1885), whose premiere coincided with the Japanese Village exhibition vividly described in Mike Leigh's *Topsy-Turvy* (1989), often featured yellow-faced *japonaiserie* of exaggerated billowing kimono and giant fan dances. Revivals of Belasco's play and Puccini's opera *Madame Butterfly* frequently employed native maids as deportment advisers, designers, and choreographers for correct presentation of interiors, kimono, and *hara-kiri*, and made stars of white European performers impersonating Butterfly as coquettish *musume* maid with steel resolve.[31] Asian singers have often been given international opera opportunities as Cio-cio-san, beginning with Miura Tamaki (1885–1946), whose 1915 London debut as Butterfly led to a lifetime of orientalist opera divadom.[32]

Staging Asian-themed plays outside Asia often encourages borrowing from kabuki and other Japanese traditional genres, thereby stimulating further intercultural experimentation, which themselves become part of Western performance history. Jerome Robbins employed an eclectic pan-Asian approach when choreographing the "Uncle Tom's Cabin" scene in Broadway's *The King and I* (1952), mixing Cambodian dance elements elegantly with aspects of kabuki and bunraku: symbolic properties, black-clad stage assistants, percussive entrance music, and frontal self-introductions.[33] The Japanese stage itself has inspired Western *mise-en-scène*. Kabuki enthusiast director John Dexter employed noh's bare-square frontality in *Equus* (1973, John Napier, designer), and then a spiral *hanamichi* (walkway to main stage) in David Henry Huang's gender-bending *M. Butterfly* (1988, Eiko Ishioka, designer), framing the *Madame Butterfly* opera as critical take on the male gaze of Asia. In just a century, the Western musical shifted from *The Mikado*'s lampooning of barbaric Japan as British light opera to a postmodern fracturing of the *Butterfly* story, while effortlessly accepting "exotic" Japanese conventions as creative options.

---

31 Mari Yoshihara, "The flight of the Japanese butterfly: orientalism, nationalism, and performances of Japanese womanhood," *American Quarterly* 56:4 (2004), 975–1001.
32 Messager's *Madame Chrysanthemum*, Jones's *The Geisha*, Mascagni's *Iris*, Franchett's *Namiko-san*.
33 Dancer Michiko, the "oriental dance consultant," and Yuriko (Eliza) had both studied with Michio Itō's sister-in-law Itō Teiko; Yuriko was Martha Graham's leading dancer for four decades.

Chance encounters, crammed knowledge, and willful ignorance produced two gems of modern intercultural musical-theatre: Benjamin Britten's
chamber opera *Curlew River* and Stephen Sondheim's *Pacific Overtures*.

Going with the flow of noh

A planned encounter took an unexpected turn resulting in an entirely new
direction for one of Britain's greatest modern composers. When Britten
toured Asia in 1955–6 concerting and lecturing, he immersed himself in
musical performances; in Japan he attended *gagaku*, noh, kabuki, and geisha dances.[34] Although he had read the Fenollosa–Pound translations, he
was unprepared for an epiphany when watching *Sumidagawa* (The Sumida
River; see representative plays, p. 35), "among the greatest theatrical experiences of my life."[35] Japanese hosts and noh actors, eager for foreign recognition, had learned to shorten and sweeten programs for visiting dignitaries
like Tagore, Chaplin, and Einstein (who preferred kyogen). Britten needed
no special treatment, immediately requesting to see another performance of
the same play, and even requesting an audio recording.

Stimulated by noh's staging potential, Britten set about finding an equivalent musical and dramatic context:

> The solemn dedication and skill of the performers were a lesson to any sing-
> er or actor of any country and any language. Was it not possible to use just
> such a story – the simple one of a demented mother seeking her lost child –
> with an English background (for there was no question in any case of a pas-
> tiche from the ancient Japanese)? Surely the Medieval Religious Drama in
> England would have had a comparable setting – an all-male cast of ecclesi-
> astics – a simple austere staging in a church – a very limited instrumental
> accompaniment – a moral story?[36]

The problem of how to adapt these ascetic Japanese musical and staging
conventions to Western music-theatre gestated for six years. The "parable
for church performance" was reset in the English Fens, enacted by all-male
acolytes at a monastic service, with Buddhist philosophy transposed to
Christian sentiments. William Plomer's libretto borrowed liberally from a
translation of the play.[37] Britten was influenced by English plainsong and

---

34 Peter F. Alexander, "A study of the origins of Britten's *Curlew River*," *Music & Letters* 69 (1988),
    229–43.
35 Quoted in Eric Walter White, *Benjamin Britten: His Life and Operas* (London: Faber and Faber,
    1970), 420.
36 Quoted from libretto cover in *ibid.* 248.
37 Compare http://atravelingyeshivasideshow.com/pdfs/Sumidagawa.pdf with William Plomer,
    Curlew River: A Parable for Church Performance (London: Faber and Faber, 1964).

nagauta shamisen singing, but also noh's choral dynamism and *portamento* gliding between notes.[38] Gagaku-like heterophony was emulated in instrumentation: five untuned drums, bells, a gong, and solo flute to paint his bleak landscape: "this minimum suffices to render river, marsh and circling birds with startling vividness."[39]

The production premiered as "a parable for church performance" in 1964. Director Colin Graham (1931–2007), working with Plomer, devised a staging that would reproduce noh's ceremony. However, Britten specifically warned Graham not to see noh, lest he be overly influenced.[40] Nevertheless, Graham's staging, recorded in extensive production notes published with the orchestral score, demonstrated his understanding of the power of Japanese simple clarity; the Madwoman, Ferryman, and Traveler wore masks. Graham warns:

> The action of the story itself should be as formalized as a ritual: unlike naturalistic acting, emotion should never be expressed with the face or eyes but always by a rehearsed ritualistic movement of the hands, head, or body.[41]

After a processional and robing ceremony, the Abbot and monks climbed to a "raised and raked circle … approached from two directions by a spiraling ramp following the curve of the circle."[42]

A vital musical discovery was that the setting, masks, and formal movements isolated singers, precluding the services of the conductor:

> Each of the vocal parts must be given a measure of freedom that might include an element of rhapsody, and that some way would have to be found in the score of specifying which part (whether vocal or instrumental) had precedence at any moment, and (accordingly) who should lead and who should follow in the different episodes of this new musical democracy.[43]

Graham resolved this problem through ensemble performance:

> There is no conductor, but at every point in the score an instrument or voice leads the rest of the ensemble in a straightforward musical fashion, sometimes from a particular movement or gesture from the stage. This of course requires intensive rehearsal before a true integration of performance can be achieved either musically or dramatically.[44]

---

38 Mervyn Cooke, "Distant horizons: from Pagodaland to the Church parables," in Cooke (ed.), *Cambridge Companion to Benjamin Britten* (Cambridge: Cambridge University Press, 1999), 165–87.
39 Robin Holloway, "The Church Parables (II)," in Christopher Palmer (ed.), *The Britten Companion* (Cambridge: Cambridge University Press, 1984), 219.
40 Cooke, "Distant horizons," 181.   41 *Curlew River* (Decca, 1989), CD booklet, 5.
42 *Ibid.*   43 Holloway, "The Church Parables," 209.   44 CD booklet, 5.

Such interdependence also necessitated a new musical symbol, dubbed "the curlew," indicating that "the performer must listen and wait till the other performers have reached the next bar line, or meeting-point – i.e. the note or rest can be longer or shorter than its written value."[45] Britten had discovered *ma* (間), the intuited sense of timing so essential to (conductorless) Japanese traditional music.

As with Yeats' *Hawk's Well*, *Curlew River* pulled those already leaning toward new directions. Rather than "influence," Cooke feels *Curlew* drew upon Britten's "inherent stylistic affinity" to Asian music via Debussy.[46] Britten's ballet music for *The Prince of the Pagodas* (1957), based on Balinese gamelan rhythms, referenced Colin McPhee, Poulenc, and Debussy. Britten completed the trio of Church Parables; *The Fiery Furnace* (1966) and *The Prodigal Son* (1968) employed similar framing devices, chamber orchestra, masks, and staging. Graham directed both, then continued collaborating on contemporary operas including *An Actor's Revenge* (1979) and *Jōruri* (1985) by Miki Minoru (1930–2011), featuring Western orchestration with koto and shamisen, and Japanese-style narration. Their final collaboration was *Sumida River* (1995), a chamber opera premiering at a noh theatre; a Britten tributary returned to source.

Pacific Overtures: American kabuki

Colonialist expansion is the theme, and intercultural appropriation the means, of Harold Prince/Stephen Sondheim's ambitious *Pacific Overtures* (1976) (Figure 62). The risk of mounting an expensive Broadway musical usually precludes experimenting with Japanese theatre techniques, yet producer-director Harold Prince had the power and vision to direct this fusion of kabuki and Broadway musical on an unprecedented scale. Prince asked John Weidman to rewrite a draft play about Japanese reaction to the 1854 invasion by Perry's "Black Ships" as "American kabuki." However, having optioned and publicized it, Prince realized it would work better as a musical, calling in long-term collaborator Stephen Sondheim. He describes the framing conceit as creating "a mythical Japanese playwright in our heads, who has come to New York, seen a couple of Broadway shows, and then goes back home and writes a musical about Commodore Perry's visit to Japan."[47] Prince and Sondheim went on a ten-day fact-finding trip to Japan, contrary

45 Britten and Plomer, with Graham notes, *Production Notes and Remarks on the Style of Performing* Curlew River (London: Faber and Faber, 1965), 210.
46 Mervyn Cooke, *Britten and the Far East: Asian Influences in the Music of Benjamin Britten* (Martlesham: Boydell and Brewer, 1998), 226.
47 Craig Zadan, *Sondheim and Co.*, 2nd edn. (New York: Da Capo Press, 1994), 210.

Fig 62 Al Hirschfield's playful rendition of the original Broadway production of the ambitious Japanese cultural pastiche *Pacific Overtures* (1976).

to their host's expectations, were "enthralled" by a six-hour noh program. Prince praised "the rhythm of Kabuki theatre … there's such incredible energy all harnessed in this dignified way – [which] probably made me reconsider energy in Western terms for the rest of my life."[48]

The play was a fantasy built on American images of Japan, yet incorporating numerous stage conventions of kabuki and bunraku. An all-male, mostly Asian-American cast portrayed caricatures of geisha, sumo wrestlers, maidens, daimyo, and soldiers. The play included a bunraku-style narrator and wooden clappers for punctuation: actors wore kimono with whitened faces, caricatures against stark, cartoonish sets (designer Boris Aronson collected Japanese prints). Interior scenes were played on raised platforms, while action was purposefully horizontal and flat. Black-robed stage assistants slid screens evoking woodblock prints, which would also "function as an on-stage editing device, effecting cuts, dissolves and transitions between episodes and foreshortening the width and depth of the playing area."[49] The *hikimaku* curtain was drawn to the percussive beats of traditional clacks.

48 Carol Ilson, *Harold Prince: A Director's Journey* (New York: Limelight, 1989), 230.
49 Foster Hirsch, *Harold Prince and the American Musical* (Cambridge: Cambridge University Press, 1989), 113.

Sondheim appears to have studied Japan more casually: by reading haiku and an anecdotal history. At first he found the theatre "just silly and screaming and endless and slow and boring," but gradually grew intrigued.[50] The minor-mode key he chose, influenced by the Japanese pentatonic scale and the Spanish guitar of Manuel de Falla, proved ambiguously oriental, an intentional mix of harmonies and contrapuntal singing not found in Japanese music. The unadorned, monosyllable lyrics suggested Japanese poetry. As a Japanese enactment of an American viewpoint on Japan's history, Sondheim purposefully aimed for a non-grammatical "translator-ese."[51] In "Four Black Dragons," two commentators accompany the shogun's wife's lament, one supporting her emotions, the other coolly descriptive, a duality unknown in Japanese music, yet it is a function of the chorus Sondheim attributes to the Japanese theatre's structure of "comment and internal soliloquy."[52] Sondheim's favorite song, "Someone in a tree," blends haiku-like description with a *Rashomon*-effect of multi-perspective subjectivity. Whether he misunderstood the Japanese model, or purposely avoided facile imitation, Sondheim songs seemed both ethereally Eastern and ironic.

Choreographer Patricia Birch was initially scared to dabble in foreign theatre, but finally took Prince's advice to create "our own Kabuki."[53] She credits early training with Martha Graham, and her assistant, licensed buyō dancer Fujimoto Haruki, who taught her how to use Japanese fans and folk-dance and kabuki movement. Although she immersed herself in research, Birch found striving for authenticity an impediment, telling Fujimoto, "If I'm vulgarizing anything, let me know, otherwise leave me alone."[54] Commodore Perry's blazing entrance to the stage, like the genuine man-of-war's entrance into Edo Bay, reeks of bombastic goodwill. Wearing the long white wig of the kabuki lion-dance *Renjishi*, he prances down a makeshift hanamichi, striking poses, legs and arms akimbo, and swirling his mane in a bravura demonstration of American might. Near the play's end, a stunning effect was achieved *à la* kabuki through *hikinuki* instantaneous costume-changes. As the Lords demand driving the intruding Westerners back into the sea, the Emperor, until then played by a puppet controlled by black-hooded handlers, speaks for the first time: "In the name of the Emperor – enough!" His mask and robe are suddenly stripped to reveal a Western general in full regalia.[55]

50 Zadan, *Sondheim*, 210.   51 Ilson, *Harold Prince*, 235.   52 Hirsch, *Harold Prince*, 115.
53 Zadan, *Sondheim*, 215.   54 *Ibid.*
55 Stephen Sondheim and John Weidman, *Pacific Overtures* (New York: Dodd, Mead, and Company, 1976), 132–3.

Despite such celebrated moments, and ten Tony Award nominations, *Pacific Overtures* drew mixed reviews, losing its investment. A less kabuki-fied revival (1984) and director Miyamoto Amon's Broadway debut (2004, following a triumphant National Theatre Japan production) fared much the same. Reviewers were critical of the concept itself: beneath the pageantry and sentiment was a dry historical treatise confined to a particular historical time, performed by imperfect English-speakers. Yet Prince's musicals of startling stage spectacle that followed – *Sweeney Todd* (1979), *Evita* (1979), and *The Phantom of the Opera* (1986) – demonstrated that kabuki-like grandeur and excess could succeed with more familiar contents and dramatic structures.

Vanguard milestones, detours, or dead ends?

All productions described have been revived, reinscribed, returned to Japan, and reinvented. Fortuitous timing and proximity were often instrumental, an early seed resulting in a much later, fuller flowering, sometimes only understood retroactively. Counterintuitively, the resultant fusion performances were frequently the product of misguided judgments, creative frictions, and downright studied ignorance. Moreover, as these germinal intercultural experiments continued to be performed, analyzed, and revived, they stimulated artists lacking direct experience with original sources. Their legacy can be found in mainstream, much-revived works such as Bejart's ballet/kabuki fusion *The Kabuki* (1986), Anthony Minghella's over-the-top *Madame Butterfly* featuring bunraku dolls and shifting screens (2005, English National Opera), and Britain's National Theatre/Handspring Company's puppetry wizardry in *War Horse* (2007). The intercultural well is deep, its river long, and its ocean wide.

References and further reading

Brandon, James. *Noh and Kyogen in the Contemporary World* (Honolulu: University of Hawai'i Press, 1997)

Davis, Carol (ed.). *Theatre East and West Revisited*, Special issue of *Mime Journal* 17 (2002–3)

Longman, Stanley Vincent. *Crosscurrents in the Drama: East and Southeastern Theatre Conference* (Tuscaloosa: University of Alabama Press, 1998)

Pavis, Patrice (ed.). *The Intercultural Performance Reader* (London: Routledge, 1996)

Pronko, Leonard. *Theater East and West: Perspectives toward a Total Theater* (Berkeley: University of California Press, 1967)

Sang-Kyong Lee. *East Asia and America: Encounters in Drama and Theatre* (Sydney: Wild Peony, 2000)

Interlude: Early influence from Europe

YOSHIHARA YUKARI

Intercultural experiences of progressive actors, directors, and playwrights in Europe early in the twentieth century were fundamental stimuli to their careers, as well as to the "modernization" or "improvement" of Japanese theatre. Kawakami Otojirō (1864–1911) and his wife Sadayakko (1871–1946), Shimamura Hōgetsu (1871–1918), Ichikawa Sadanji II (1880–1940), Osanai Kaoru (1881–1928), Hijikata Yoshi (1898–1959), and Kishida Kunio (1890–1954) actively sought to reinvent Japanese theatre by energetically incorporating elements from Western theatre.

In 1893, Kawakami visited France, becoming the first Japanese theatre artist to go on a fact-finding trip to Europe. Among his acquisitions was a script of Dumas fils' *La dame aux camélias*, whose leading role would be performed by Sadayakko at Osaka's Teikoku-za (Imperial Theatre) in 1911. When the Kawakami troupe toured the USA and Europe from 1899 to 1902, they saw Henry Irving and Ellen Terry in *The Merchant of Venice* in Boston, and Olga Nethersole in her scandalous production of *Sapho* in New York. Their visit to the American Academy of Dramatic Arts inspired Kawakami to establish an acting school in Japan. In 1900 Loïe Fuller (1862–1928), modern dance pioneer and lighting innovator, invited Kawakami's troupe to perform at her theatre at the Paris World Exposition, and later on tour in Europe. After returning to Japan, where they made various efforts to modernize and westernize Japanese theatre, they returned to Paris in 1907 for additional theatre research, learning not only about performance techniques but also about theatre management. This experience led to the establishment in 1908 of the Teikoku Joyū Yōseijo (Imperial Training School for Actresses).

Shimamura, a young lecturer at Waseda University, was sent to Europe by his mentor, Tsubouchi Shōyō, from 1902 to 1905. Among the 150 productions he attended in London and Berlin, he saw Terry in Ibsen's *Vikings of Helgeland*, Irving in Sardou's *Dante*, and Herbert Beerbohm Tree in Tolstoy's *Resurrection*. Shimamura's experiences contributed to his later introduction of naturalism to Japan's budding modern theatre movement.

The progressive kabuki actor Ichikawa Sadanji II (1880–1940), hoping to find ways to reinvigorate kabuki, recently eclipsed by *shimpa* activities, visited Europe in 1906–7 with critic and playwright Matsui Shōyō, seeking to learn from Western acting, training, elocution, stage management, and stage technology. In France, they interviewed Sarah Bernhardt and saw *The Hunchback of Notre Dame*; in Germany, they attended *The Merchant of Venice*, Wedekind's *Spring Awakening*, Maeterlinck's *Aglavaine and Sélysette*, Ibsen's *The Pillars of Society*, and Gorky's *The Lower Depths*; in England, they viewed Hauptmann's *The Sunken Bell*, Shaw's *The Man of Destiny*, and the "Don Juan in Hell" scene of Shaw's *Man and Superman*. They attended numerous plays at a Shakespeare Festival organized by Beerbohm Tree. They also spent three weeks studying elocution, diction, and the art of expression, along with the Delsarte system, at the Royal Academy of Dramatic Art.

Upon returning to Japan in 1908, Sadanji and Matsui staged a Western-style version of *The Merchant of Venice*. Sadanji and Osanai soon established the Jiyū Gekijō (Free Theatre, 1909–19), a subscriber-supported art theatre modeled on London's Stage Society. Sadanji also revived the long-forgotten kabuki play *Narukami* in 1910, a story about a wizard-priest seduced by a princess, possibly inspired by Frollo's infatuation with Esmeralda in *The Hunchback of Notre Dame* (see representative plays, p. 136).

In 1928 Sadanji organized the first kabuki tour outside Japan, the first visit of a major foreign theatre company to the recently established Soviet Union. He met leading directors Sergei Eisenstein, Vsevolod Meyerhold, and Konstantin Stanislavski. Sadanji's *Chūshingura* (The treasury of loyal retainers) (see representative plays, p. 160) inspired Eisenstein to create his famous cinematographic principle of montage.[56]

Directing inspiration

The intercultural experiences of Osanai and Hijikata Yoshi – two great figures in early *shingeki* – were fundamental to their choice of plays and directing style. Osanai visited Moscow in 1911–12 to see plays produced at Stanislavski's Moscow Art Theatre, which became one of the principal models emulated by the nascent shingeki movement. While Osanai was not much impressed by Reinhardt's expressionism, Hijikata, studying in Berlin in 1922–3, was greatly influenced by it. In 1924, Osanai and Hijikata cofounded the Tsukiji Shōgekijō (Tsukiji Little Theatre), whose architecture, management, and European repertoire were modeled on theatres visited abroad.

---

56 Eisenstein wrote the essays "The unexpected" (1928) and "The cinematic principle and the ideogram" (1929) after seeing Sadanji's performances. See *Film Form*, ed. and trans. Jay Leyda (London: Dennis Dobson, 1951).

Ironically, on his return from his second trip to Moscow in 1929, Osanai advocated hybridity and a return to roots:

> In order to create new arts, Japanese theatre in the future should strive not only to synthesize all oriental art traditions, such as the arts of India, China, Siam and the South Sea Islands, but also to incorporate Western theatrical traditions. The core should be the kabuki poses which have been developed in Japan for some centuries.[57]

Tsukiji subsequently adapted the kabuki *Battles of Coxinga* featuring elements influenced by Javanese shadow-puppetry and Chinese opera, as well as kabuki movement. But this intercultural thrust was curtailed by Osanai's sudden death, aged 48.

So few were the innovators in early modern Japanese theatre that those who did have the opportunity to study abroad resonated greatly on their return. Kishida Kunio apprenticed for two years from 1921 at the Théâtre du Vieux-Colombier, the playhouse founded by Jacques Copeau. He then founded the art-for-art's sake Bungaku-za in 1937 with another European returnee, Iwata Toyoo (1893–1959). Senda Koreya (1904–94) during his Berlin sojourn of 1928–32 was converted to Brecht, whose intellectual cynicism provided a dry remedy to the sentimental if passionate shingeki of the proletarian theatre movement. His translations of Brecht's essays and plays from the late 1950s was to have a profound affect on the anti-realist *angura* movement.

Thus many of the important innovators in Japanese drama in the prewar and postwar years developed their cultural identity and vision for Japan while studying abroad. Throughout the early modern period of Japan's search for style and substance, chance encounters and playgoing experiences abroad, tempered by their natural proclivities and the spirit of the times, profoundly influenced the course of modern Japanese theatre history.

References and further reading

Nihon Enshutsuka Kyōkai (Japanese Director's Association) (ed.). *Umi o koeta enshutsuka tachi* (Theatre directors who went overseas) (Tokyo: Nihon Enshutsuka Kyōkai, 2012)

Watanabe Tamotsu. *Meiji engeki-shi* (A history of Meiji theatre) (Tokyo: Kōdansha, 2012)

---

57 Nihon Enshutsuka Kyōkai (Japanese Director's Association) (ed.), *Umi o koeta enshutsuka tachi* (Theatre directors who went overseas) (Tokyo: Nihon Enshutsuka Kyōkai, 2012), 125.

Interlude: Asian energy versus European rationality: interview with Ninagawa Yukio

MIKA EGLINTON

Internationally acclaimed theatre director Ninagawa Yukio (1935–2016) has staged countless productions in Japan since the late 1960s, as well as internationally (see p. 492, Spotlight 22.2). Born in Saitama, near Tokyo, he aspired to become a painter, but gave up this ambition at the age of 20 in order to become a stage actor, later choosing to focus on directing. As a proponent of the anti-establishment Little Theatre movement (*shōgekijō undō*), he cofounded the Gendaijin Gekijō (Contemporary People's Theatre) in 1967, directing Shimizu Kunio's *Shinjō afururu keihakusa* (Sincere frivolity) in 1969. The company was disbanded in 1971, but in the following year he established the Sakura-sha (Cherry Blossom Company), which lasted until 1974, where he directed avant-garde plays by Shimizu and others. Soon after came a major turning point in his career: critical accolades for his debut in the commercial theatre with his first Shakespearean production, *Romeo and Juliet*, at the Nissay Theatre in Tokyo's business district and vast Tōhō Theatre.[58] Since then, he has been at the forefront of Japanese theatre, directing a wide range of Japanese and Western classic and contemporary plays. He has served as Artistic Director of Ninagawa Studio, the Saitama Arts Theatre, and Tokyū Bunkamura Theatre Cocoon, and as an Associate Director of Shakespeare's Globe Theatre in London.

A project to direct the entire Shakespearean canon has produced thirty-one to date, several touring overseas. In Britain he has created productions for the Royal Shakespeare Company, the National Theatre, and the Barbican Centre, and in 2006 he established the Saitama Gold Theatre, which works with actors aged 55 and older. In 2009, he established the Saitama Next Theatre, devoted to young actors. A coveted director among new playwrights, and one of the few Japanese directors whose name alone will draw

---

58 "Commercial theatre" (*shōgyō engeki*) is a distinct branch of *shingeki* (modern theatre), antithetical to the left-wing politics of most shingeki companies and all Little Theatres of the 1960s.

audiences, since the turn of the century Ninagawa has directed annually an astonishing eight plays on average.

I don't believe that there is such a thing as an epoch-making theatre event, but that there are certain changes to theatrical trends in postwar Japan. For those involved in theatre from the 1950s and 60s, Western theatre was always already the ideal model. Some Japanese directors tried to imitate or copy Western styles by going to see productions of Chekhov at the Moscow Art Theatre or productions of Shakespeare in London. When I began my acting career, the Stanislavski system was in fashion. We read *An Actor Prepares* as though it were a bible, trained to analyze texts and subtexts with great rigor, if not obsession. In this way, actors who could analyze and articulate subtext were regarded as good, and those who could not were dismissed. There were of course brilliant actors who did not fit the system, yet still had intense stage presence.

After Stanislavski's system, Pavlov's discoveries in physiological reflex behavior and Brecht's alienation techniques were introduced into Japan. So when I started directing, I wanted to take an alternative approach to Stanislavski. I also wanted to break with the shingeki convention of actors fashioning themselves as Caucasian by dying their hair and wearing fake noses. That being said, in my aversion to the Stanislavski system there is a contradiction. When you go to Europe, particularly the UK, the Stanislavski system turned out to be useful in establishing a common ground. Since British acting methods are often variations of Stanislavski, my knowledge of the system helped me to direct actors there.

Decline of the rational

The "underground theatre" managed to deconstruct premodernity and tradition, which had mostly been lost through the process of Japan's modernization and Westernization. From the 1960s to the beginning of the 1970s there were many successful attempts to create theatre in a Japanese way, with a particular focus on the body. Suzuki Tadashi and Terayama Shūji, for example, were praised overseas for such work. I believe this contributed to the decline of Japanese people's worship of European theatre.

Today is very different. Compared to the "underground" era, the scope of creative ambition has shrunk. Many practitioners and audiences prefer to create and see small stories based on everyday life. They are no longer interested in confronting the establishment, but prefer to coexist with authority in a peaceful way.

The most influential playwright of the modern era is undoubtedly Kara Jūrō. Because of him, shingeki was destroyed, and the direction of Japanese theatre changed forever. His use of space and language, totally different from European drama, was revolutionary for modern Japanese theatre. "An elder sister wearing a red negligée committed suicide and was found floating in a wooden tub in a tofu shop," or "walking on a crossing in Shibuya, I turned back to see a half-broken comb and realized it was my long-lost brother." When I read these sentences, I could picture the margins of premodernity and modernity somehow joining temporarily. Envious of Kara's linguistic power that could produce such vivid images, to compete I trained my visual representation skills. I started using large numbers of actors on stage, with outcaste, monstrous, strange faces. Of course, I was impressed by Noda Hideki, but the person I see as my rival, the one who really frustrated but also motivated me, was Kara.

Non-theatrical theatre and Asian theatricality

These days I am seldom impressed or shocked by the theatre I see overseas, and have no desire to imitate it. Like Peter Brook's works in the early 1970s, there was a lot of incredibly powerful theatre with which we wanted to compete, to draw inspiration from, but also to critique. Then in the early 1980s, Théâtre du Soleil created world theatre by exploiting the raw potential of theatricality. I think, however, that European theatre has been in decline for some time.

The technology and media that surrounds us, such as the Internet, mobile phones, and other hyper-personalized technologies, have become part of the dominant culture, but they lead to fragmentation. As a result of these influences, theatrical power derived from living beings and language, "analogical power," has been weakened and gradually replaced by pseudo-science and image-based media technologies.

I think theatre that is not recognized as such nowadays will become theatre in the future. This kind of theatre can already be seen: characters existing virtually through projections on screens, but also through more complex interfaces such as smart phone screens. In contrast, analog theatre still exists and continues to exploit fresh bodies. So theatre will divide between these two poles and coexist as a minor cultural expression.

In the near future I suspect that Asian theatres will continue to emerge, as their wild, obscene, and ritualistic power based on human physicality will gain attention in contrast to the more psychology-based theatres of Europe. Within the next five years, I really want to see the battle of the rationality of European theatre and the fecundity and physicality of Asian theatre.

However, I recognize that in the process of globalization, the differences between Japan and other Asian countries grow increasingly blurred. Differences still exist however. As I see it, one trait of Asianness is multitude, which is why I like to use more than fifty actors on stage. I now want to show the power of life, of multitude, rooted in Asian theatre, in contrast to European theatre and its obsession with psychological realism.

Personally, I am highly critical of media-controlled theatre, such as robot theatre [of Hirata Oriza, see pp. 358–64 above]. I don't see that as evolution. In my view, evolution means to find a way to support the inevitable degeneration of the body. I believe that theatre must deal with physiology in a universal sense, including the experience of individuals in old age, through sickness and decay. That is the only way for theatre to survive and why I started the Saitama Gold Theatre for people over 55. Elderly people have trouble remembering lines and stage plotting, which is why we use prompts. By including human aids, we are protecting the physiology of human life and not relying on technology.

EPILOGUE: FROZEN WORDS AND MYTHOLOGY

EUGENIO BARBA

My first contact with a Japanese theatre was in 1964: a book in French, Zeami's *The Secret Art of Nō*, translated by Réné Sieffert. It was one of those texts where words are frozen and only many years later thawed to life within me, acquiring a sense that matched my professional experience.

At the time, Japanese theatres – as well as those from other Asian countries – were totally disregarded in Europe. Almost no books or other sources of information were available about them and we came across them only as footnotes in historical books concerning legendary tours before World War II.

Only in 1972 did I have the opportunity to see the whole panoply of Japanese theatres – noh, kyogen, kabuki and *shingeki*. Odin Teatret, in a pioneering and rather monumental initiative, had invited to our Holstebro, Denmark home such masters as Kanze Hisao and brother Hideo, Nomura Mannojō, Sawamura Sōjūrō and Terayama Shūji with their ensembles – more than seventy artists. For over a week they gave performances and demonstrations on their apprenticeship and particular techniques. It was an overwhelming encounter. However, I felt I could not adapt what I had seen to my personal practice.

Encountering the spine

I don't speak Japanese and my possibility of dialogue with Japanese performers about their technique was non-existent. My knowledge of the various Japanese acting genres remained bookish and intellectual. Then I met nihonbuyo dancer Azuma Katsuko, who opened my eyes. She introduced me to her living technique, and her professional ethos. And she did this in such a way that what for me was previously abstract insight began to have a relevance to my personal practice and questioning.

During Odin Teatret's tour in Japan in 1980, professor and theatre director Watanabe Moriaki took me to watch Katsuko teaching children and shingeki actors who wanted to become familiar with her style. This close contact lasted only a few hours, but I fell irremediably in love with Katsuko's

Fig 63 Eugenio Barba directs noh actor Matsui Akira and Afro-Caribbean dancer Augusto Omulú in *Ur-Hamlet*. Jonah Salz interprets.

spine: I was enthralled by the way her torso was radiating energy in spite of stillness. She didn't speak English and I had to rely on the generous availability of Professor Watanabe. The consequence was that I invited them both to the first session of ISTA, the International School of Theatre Anthropology, which was to take place a few months later in Germany.

At ISTA, day and night, for two whole months, I was able to ask her questions, make her repeat a short sequence over and over again, a few gestures or just a transition from one movement to another, admire her in the power of a full performance with costume and orchestra, then see the same dance in jeans and a shirt with no musical accompaniment. Thus I began to discern the technique at work that was hidden from the eyes of the spectators. Most important of all was Katsuko's openness as she explained to me her working terminology and repeatedly showed me how it was applied in practice. Watanabe *sensei* was invaluable not only as translator but also as an expert in modern theatre, pointing out similar or equivalent expressions in Western theatre.

It was Katsuko who, during the three first sessions of ISTA, gave me an empirical knowledge of her technique, developing my capacity for *seeing*. In 1983, during a two-month stay in Tokyo, she took me to her kyogen lessons with Nomura Mannojō (now Man), to watch classes of martial arts, the tea ceremony, and Shinto rituals and, above all, to follow her work with her master Azuma Tokuhō. I still remember Katsuko, in spite of her age and expertise, washing the floor before dancing for her master.

Beneath the skin

I owe Katsuko and Watanabe *sensei* my first knowledge in detecting the technical scenic anatomy of a Japanese performer underneath the seductive skin of the performance. I consider Katsuko one of the founders of ISTA and one of my main sources of Theatre Anthropology. In the following years, other artists shared their experience with me and helped me sharpen this particular way of watching a performer from the perspective of recurring technical principles: Ohno Kazuo and Nakajima Natsu from butoh, Nomura Kosuke (Manzō VI) from kyogen, Hanayagi Kanichi and his fellow performers from nihonbuyo, Suzuki Tadashi and Ohta Shōgō from shingeki, and more. Noh master Matsui Akira, besides teaching at the last three ISTA sessions, was one of the protagonists in *Ur-Hamlet*, a performance I directed with more than one hundred performers and musicians from many genres and countries.

I feel I owe much to Japanese theatre in general, and particularly to those artists who shared with me their tradition and personal techniques. When I founded Odin Teatret in 1964, we were a group of amateurs longing for technical knowledge. Not only Zeami's frozen words, but also famous *onnagata* kabuki female role specialists and images from *ukiyo-e* nourished my imagination and were turned into exercises and themes for improvisations for my young inexpert actors. Personal creativity is always nourished by personal mythology. And Japan's culture and theatre have no doubt had a preponderant place in mine.

FURTHER READING

Compiled by DAVID JORTNER

Classical Japanese theatre

Addiss, Steven, Gerald Groemer, and J. Thomas Rimer (trans.). *Traditional Japanese Arts and Culture: An Illustrated Source Book* (Honolulu: University of Hawai'i Press, 2006)

Arnott, Peter D. *The Theatres of Japan* (St. Lucia: University of Queensland Press, 1967)

Brazell, Karen. *Traditional Japanese Theater: An Anthology of Plays* (New York: Columbia University Press, 1998)

Brown, Steven T. and Sara Jensen (eds.). *Performing Japanese Women*, Special edition of *Women in Performance* 12:1 (2001)

Cavaye, Ronald, Paul Griffith, and Senda Akihiko. *A Guide to the Japanese Stage: From Traditional to Cutting Edge* (Tokyo: Kodansha International, 2004)

Griffis, William. *A History of Japan, 660 BC to 1872 AD* (Berkeley, CA: Stone Bridge Press, 2010)

Hall, John Whitney (ed.). *The Cambridge History of Japan*, 6 vols. (Cambridge: Cambridge University Press, 1988–99)

Inoura, Yoshinobu, and Kawatake Toshio. *The Traditional Theatre of Japan* (Tokyo: The Japan Foundation, 1981)

Keene, Donald. *Seeds in the Heart: Japanese Literature from the Earliest Times to the Late Sixteenth Century* (New York: Henry Holt, 1984)

  World within Walls: Japanese Literature of the Pre-modern Era, 1600–1867 (New York: Holt, Rinehart and Winston, 1976)

Leiter, Samuel L. *Historical Dictionary of Japanese Theatre* (Lanham, MD: Scarecrow Press, 2014)

  (ed.). *Japanese Theatre in the World* (New York: Japan Society and the Japan Foundation, 1997)

Malm, William P. *Japanese Music and Musical Instruments* (Rutland, VT: Charles E. Tuttle, 1959)

Marra, Michele. *Representations of Power: The Literary Politics of Medieval Japan* (Honolulu: University of Hawai'i Press, 1993)

Ortolani, Benito. *The Japanese Theatre: From Shamanistic Ritual to Contemporary Pluralism* (revised edn.) (Princeton, NJ: Princeton University Press, 1990)

Parker, Helen S. E. *Progressive Traditions: An Illustrated Study of Plot Repetition in Traditional Japanese Theatre* (Leiden: Brill, 2006)

Pronko, Leonard. *Theater East and West: Perspectives toward a Total Theater* (Berkeley: University of California Press, 1967)

Provine, Robert, Yoshihiko Tokumaru, and J. Lawrence Witzleben (eds.). *The Garland Encyclopedia of World Music*, vol. VII: *East Asia: China, Japan, and Korea* (New York: Routledge, 2002)

Raz, Jacob. *Actors and Audiences: A Study of Their Interaction in the Japanese Traditional Theatre* (Leiden: Brill, 1983)

Scholz-Cionca, Stanca, and Samuel L. Leiter (eds.). *Japanese Theatre and the International Stage* (Leiden: Brill, 2001)

Thornbury, Barbara. *The Folk Performing Arts: Traditional Culture in Contemporary Japan* (New York: State University of New York Press, 1997)

Tokita, Alison, and David Hughes. *The Ashgate Research Companion to Japanese Music* (Farnham: Ashgate, 2008)

Varley, H. Paul. *Japanese Culture* (Honolulu: University of Hawai'i Press, 2000)

Modern Japanese theatre

Eckersall, Peter. *Theorizing the Angura Space: Avant-garde Performance and Politics in Japan, 1960–2000* (Leiden: Brill, 2006)

Goodman, David G. (ed.). *Concerned Theatre Japan*, vols. I.1–II.4 (1969–73)

Havens, Thomas R. H. *Artist and Patron in Postwar Japan* (Princeton, NJ: Princeton University Press, 1982)

Japan Playwrights Association (ed.). *Half a Century of Japanese Theater*, vols. I–X (Tokyo: Kinokuniya, 2000–6)

Jortner, David, Keiko McDonald, and Kevin Wetmore (eds.). *Modern Japanese Theatre and Performance* (Lanham, MD: Lexington Books, 2006)

Keene, Donald. *Dawn to the West: Japanese Literature in the Modern Era* (New York: Holt, Rinehart and Winston, 1984)

Nara, Hiroshi (ed.). *Inexorable Modernity: Japan's Grappling with Modernity in the Arts* (Lanham, MD: Lexington, 2007)

Poulton, M. Cody. *A Beggar's Art: Scripting Modernity in Japanese Drama, 1900–1930* (Honolulu:University of Hawai'i Press, 2010)

Powell, Brian. *Japan's Modern Theatre: A Century of Continuity and Change* (London: Japan Library, 2002)

Powers, Richard G., Hidetoshi Kato, and Bruce Stronach (eds.). *Handbook of Japanese Popular Culture* (New York: Greenwood Press, 1989)

Rimer, J. Thomas. *Toward a Modern Japanese Theatre: Kishida Kunio* (Princeton, NJ: Princeton University Press, 1974)

Rimer, J. Thomas, Mitsuya Mori, and M. Cody Poulton (eds.). *The Columbia Anthology of Modern Japanese Drama* (New York: Columbia University Press, 2014)

Rolf, Robert T., and John K. Gillespie (eds.). *Alternative Japanese Drama: Ten Plays* (Honolulu: University of Hawai'i Press, 1992)

Takaya, Ted T. *Modern Japanese Drama: An Anthology* (New York: Columbia University Press, 1979)

Wetmore, Kevin. "Modern Japanese drama in English," *ATJ* 23:1 (2006), 179–205

Internet and audiovisual resources

Performing Arts Network Japan http://performingarts.jp
The Japanese Theatre Goer's Collection (16 Films) Marty Gross Films www.
    martygrossfilms.com/films/theatergoers/theatergoers.html

Index

Page numbers in italics refer to figures.